Jochen Felsenheimer, Phillip Gisdakis, and Michael Zaiser

Active Credit Portfolio Management

Dr. Jochen Felsenheimer works for HVB Corporates & Markets and is currently heading the Credit & Credit Derivatives Strategy team, a department of HVB Global Markets Research. He holds a PhD in Economics from Ludwigs-Maximilians-Universität München.

Dr. Philip Gisdakis is a Quantitative Credit Strategist. He studied Mathematical Finance at the University of Oxford and holds a PhD degree in Theoretical Chemistry from Technische Universität München.

Michael Zaiser is a Credit Strategist at HVB Corporates & Markets. He studied Business Administration and Mathematics at Johann Wolfgang Goethe-Universität Frankfurt am Main.

Jochen Felsenheimer, Philip Gisdakis, and Michael Zaiser

Active Credit Portfolio Management

*A Practical Guide to
Credit Risk Management Strategies*

WILEY-VCH Verlag GmbH & Co. KGaA

All books published by Wiley-VCH are carefully produced. Nevertheless, authors, editors and publisher do not warrant the information contained in these books, including this book, to be free of errors. Readers are advised to keep in mind that statements, data, illustrations, procedural details or other items may inadvertently be inaccurate.

Library of Congress Card No.:
applied for

British Library Cataloguing-in-Publication Data:
A catalogue record for this book is available from the British Library.

Bibliographic information published by Die Deutsche Bibliothek
Die Deutsche Bibliothek lists this publication in the Deutsche Nationalbibliografie; detailed bibliographic data is available in the Internet at http://dnb.ddb.de

© 2006 WILEY-VCH Verlag GmbH & Co KGaA, Weinheim

All rights reserved (including those of translation into other languages). No part of this book may be reproduced in any form – by photocopying, microfilm, or any other means – nor transmitted or translated into a machine language without written permission from the publishers. Registered names, trademarks, etc. used in this book, even when not specifically marked as such, are not to be considered unprotected by law.

Typesetting: Steingraeber Satztechnik GmbH, Ladenburg
Printing and Binding: Ebner & Spiegel, Ulm
Cover Design: init GmbH, Bielefeld

Printed in the Federal Republic of Germany
Printed on acid-free paper

ISBN-13: 978-3-527-50198-4
ISBN-10: 3-527-50198-3

Contents

Foreword   13

Introduction and Acknowledgements   17

Part I Markets   19

1 **Market Structure**   21
- 1.1 Market Development   22
- 1.1.1 Historical Development   22
- 1.1.2 Size and Growth of the Market   27
- 1.2 Market Participants   27
- 1.2.1 Banks   28
- 1.2.2 Insurance Companies   29
- 1.2.3 Funds and Asset Managers   30
- 1.2.4 Retail Clients   30
- 1.2.5 Hedge Funds   30
- 1.3 Issuing Debt from a Company's Viewpoint   31
- 1.4 Ratings and Rating Agencies   33
- 1.4.1 Are Ratings an Efficient Source for Pricing Credits?   36
- 1.5 Credit Classes   39
- 1.5.1 High-Grade Universe   39
- 1.5.2 High-Yield and Crossover Credits   40
- 1.5.3 High-Quality Segment   41
- 1.5.4 Asset Backed Securities   42

2 **Instruments**   45
- 2.1 Straight Bonds   45
- 2.2 Bonds with Embedded Options   47
- 2.3 Exotics   48
- 2.3.1 Payment-in-Kind Notes   49

2.3.2	Hybrids or Subordinated Corporate Bonds	50
2.4	Hybrid Bank Capital	53
2.5	Single-Name Credit Derivatives	55
2.5.1	Credit Default Swaps	55
2.5.2	Digital Default Swaps	58
2.5.3	Equity Default Swaps	58
2.5.4	Recovery Default Swaps	60
2.5.5	Constant Maturity Credit Default Swaps	61
2.6	Portfolio Credit Derivatives	62
2.6.1	Basket/Index Swaps – iTraxx Europe Benchmark	62
2.6.2	Default Baskets	65
2.6.3	Standardized iTraxx Tranches	67
2.6.4	Spread Options	68
2.6.5	Future Contracts	70
2.7	Outlook on Product Development	70

3 Company and Debt Instrument Analysis 73

3.1	Sovereign Risk and Government Support	74
3.2	Business Risk	74
3.3	Financial Risk	82
3.3.1	Off-Balance-Sheet Adjustments	86
3.3.2	Adjustment of Ratios	91
3.4	The Rating Agencies' Methodology	93
3.5	Evaluation of Specific Debt Instruments	96
3.6	Recovery Rate Estimates	99

4 The Economics of Credit Spreads 103

4.1	Macro Drivers	103
4.1.1	Credits in the Business Cycle	103
4.1.2	Yields and Spreads	106
4.1.3	Credits and Exchange Rates	108
4.1.4	Credits and Commodity Prices	109
4.1.5	Credits and Inflation	111
4.1.6	Credits and External Shocks	113
4.2	Micro Drivers	115
4.3	Credit Quality	117
4.3.1	Credit Quality Trend	117

4.3.2	Default Rates 117
4.3.3	Recovery Rates: The Collins & Aikman Case 120
4.3.4	Implied Ratings 122
4.4	Equity–Debt Linkage 123
4.4.1	The Basic Merton Approach: Structural Models 123
4.4.2	Merton in Practice 128
4.4.3	Leap-Put Skewness as an Equity–Debt Indicator 131
4.4.4	Empirical Evidence for the Equity–Debt Linkage 133
4.5	Market Technicals 136
4.5.1	Is there a New Issuance Premium? 137
4.5.2	Technical Bid 138
4.5.3	The Impact of Syndicated Loans on Corporate Bonds 139

Part II Models   141

5   Fixed Income Basics   143
5.1	Basic Valuation Concepts 143
5.1.1	The Discount Function 143
5.1.2	Spot Rates and the Term Structure of Interest Rates 149
5.1.3	Forward Rates 154
5.2	Obtaining the Term Structure of Interest Rates 158
5.3	The Yield to Maturity 159
5.4	Measurement of Interest Rate Risk 162

6   Spread Measures   171
6.1	Basic Considerations 171
6.2	Yield Spreads 173
6.3	Z-Spreads 177
6.4	Asset Swap Spreads 180
6.5	Spread Measures for Floaters 184
6.6	Spreads and the Real Economy 186
6.7	Conclusion 192

7   Basics of Credit Risk Models   195
7.1	The Components of Credit Risk 196
7.2	A Single-Step, Two-Stage Model 198

7.3 A Multi-Step Model for Zero Coupon Bonds 202
7.4 The Multi-Step Model 208
7.5 Continuous-Time Approach 210
7.6 Recovery Treatment 217
7.6.1 Fitch's Recovery-Rating Methodology 228
7.7 The Term Structure of Credit Spreads 231

8 Single-Name Models 237
8.1 Reduced-Form Models 238
8.1.1 Binomial Tree Models for Default Risk 244
8.1.2 Reduced-Form Models and Illiquid Claims 249
8.2 Structural Models 250
8.3 Rating-Based Transition Matrix Models 260
8.3.1 Redefining the Default Event 265

9 Portfolio Models 271
9.1 The Loss Distribution and its Impact on Portfolio Derivatives 273
9.2 Independent Defaults 276
9.3 Default Dependency 282
9.4 Term-Structure Effects 288
9.5 Valuing First-to-Default Baskets 289
9.6 Valuing CDO Tranches with the HLPGC Model 292
9.7 Spread Dispersion 296
9.8 Price Discovery versus Model Competition 300

10 Valuation of Credit Derivatives 303
10.1 Credit Default Swaps 304
10.1.1 Discrete-Time Model 305
10.1.2 Obtaining the Survival Probability Curve 311
10.1.3 Forward CDS Valuation 314
10.1.4 CDS Sensitivities 316
10.1.5 Continuous-Time Model 318
10.1.6 Bloomberg's CDSW Function 319
10.2 Options on Credit-Risky Instruments 322
10.2.1 Single-Name Credit Default Swaptions 323
10.2.2 Index Swaptions 326
10.3 CDS Indices 327

10.4	n^{th}-to-Default Baskets	330
10.5	Collateralized Debt Obligations	337
10.5.1	Standardized iTraxx Tranches	338
10.5.2	Compound and Base Correlation	341
10.5.3	Sensitivities of iTraxx Index Tranches	346
10.6	Exotic Derivatives	357
10.6.1	Equity Default Swaps	357
10.6.2	Constant Maturity Structures	358
10.6.3	Digital Default Swaps and Recovery Swaps	360

11 Portfolio Risk Measurement 365

11.1	Risk Measures	365
11.1.1	Market Risk versus Credit Risk	365
11.1.2	Value at Risk and Conditional Value at Risk	367
11.1.3	Risk Components	372
11.2	Credit Portfolio Models	373

Part III Management 377

12 Principles of Credit Portfolio Management 379

12.1	The Role of ACPM in the Asset Allocation Process	379
12.2	Management Styles: Passive or Active	386
12.2.1	Passive Management	386
12.2.2	Active Management	388
12.3	Quantitative and Fundamental Credit Research	389
12.4	Diversification in Credit Portfolios	391
12.5	Credit Risk Management in an ALM Environment	393
12.6	Credits in the Global Asset Allocation	394
12.6.1	Increasing Importance of Credit-Risky Instruments	394
12.6.2	Credits, Government Bonds, and Equities	395
12.7	Building Blocks of Credit Portfolio Management	397
12.7.1	Step 1: Investment Targets	398
12.7.2	Step 2: Risk Factors	400
12.7.3	Step 3: Economic Variables	401
12.7.4	Step 4: Forecasting and Scenario Assessment	401
12.7.5	Step 5: Sensitivities	402
12.7.6	Step 6: Portfolio Optimization Analysis	403

12.7.7	Step 7: Portfolio Adjustments	404
12.7.8	Step 8: Performance Analysis	405
12.8	Key Portfolio Figures	406

13 Portfolio Allocation 409

13.1	Indices	410
13.1.1	The Function of Indices	410
13.1.2	The iBoxx € Index Universe	411
13.1.3	Analyzing the RDAX	413
13.2	Sector Allocation in a Markowitz Framework	418
13.3	Quality Allocation	421
13.4	Tools to Derive the Optimal Allocation	424
13.4.1	Alpha and Beta	425
13.4.2	The Shortcomings of a Beta Analysis	425
13.4.3	Aggregated Z-Scores	427
13.4.4	Equity Volatility as a Tool in the Allocation Process	428

14 Performance Measures 431

14.1	Tracking Error	432
14.2	Sharpe Ratio and Treynor Ratio	433
14.3	Information Ratio	435
14.4	Summary	436

15 Performance Analysis 437

15.1	Return Accumulation	437
15.2	Return Attribution Analysis	438

16 Hedging Credit Risk 443

16.1	Hedging on a Single-Name Level	443
16.1.1	Basic Considerations	443
16.1.2	Hedging Default Risk	445
16.1.3	Hedging Spread Risk	448
16.2	Hedging on a Portfolio Level	452
16.2.1	Basic Considerations	453
16.2.2	Hedging Systematic Spread Risk for a Single Cash Bond	453
16.2.3	Hedging Systematic Spread Risk for a Credit Portfolio	458

16.2.4   Finding the Right Hedging Instrument   462

17   Trading Strategies   469
17.1   Trading Cash Bonds   469
17.2   Trading Strategies with Single-Name CDS   472
17.2.1   Plain-Vanilla CDS Trades   474
17.2.2   Switch Ideas   474
17.2.3   Curve Trades   475
17.3   Portfolio Derivatives Trades   476
17.3.1   Single Name versus Sector or Market   476
17.3.2   Core–Satellite Strategies   477
17.3.3   Sector and Segment Trades   478
17.3.4   Trading the Skew   479
17.3.5   Basis Trades   481
17.3.6   First-to-Default Baskets   482
17.3.7   iTraxx Tranches versus Default Baskets   485
17.3.8   Playing the Steepness of the iTraxx Curve   488
17.4   Spread Options: Single and Complex Strategies   489
17.5   CPPI Strategies Including iTraxx Indices   490
17.6   Correlation Trading   492
17.7   Capital Structure Arbitrage Trades   494
17.8   Recovery Trades   495
17.9   EDS versus CDS and the Role of DDS   496
17.10   CDS–Cash–Repo Arbitrage   500
17.10.1   The Repo Market   500
17.10.2   How an Arbitrage Trade Works   501

18   Operational Issues: Accounting   503
18.1   An Introduction to IAS 39   504
18.1.1   The Scope of IAS 39   504
18.1.2   Categories of Financial Instruments   505
18.1.3   Measurement   507
18.1.4   Recognition and Derecognition   512
18.1.5   Embedded Derivatives   513
18.1.6   Hedge Accounting   515
18.2   IAS 39 Accounting for Credit Instruments   518
18.2.1   Bonds and Loans   518

  18.2.2 Credit Default Swaps 521
  18.2.3 Total Return Swaps 523
  18.2.4 Credit Linked Notes 525
  18.2.5 iTraxx Products 526
  18.2.6 Other Instruments of Interest 527

19 Operational Issues: Basel II 529
  19.1 An Introduction to Basel II 529
  19.1.1 The Basic Structure 529
  19.1.2 The Standardized Approach 533
  19.1.3 The Foundation IRB Approach 534
  19.1.4 The Advanced IRB Approach 538
  19.1.5 Securitization Transactions 540
  19.1.6 Credit Risk Mitigation 543
  19.2 Basel II for Credit Instruments 547
  19.2.1 Credit Default Swaps 547
  19.2.2 Total Return Swaps 550
  19.2.3 Credit Linked Notes 551
  19.2.4 Default Baskets 553
  19.2.5 iTraxx Products 555

Part IV Appendix 557
  A.1 Analytics with Bloomberg and Reuters 559
  A.1.1 Bloomberg 559
  A.1.2 Reuters 560
  A.2 Default and Recovery Data from Rating Agencies 563

References 569

Index 575

Foreword

> "My ventures are not in one bottom trusted, nor to one place; nor is my whole estate upon the fortune of this present year."
> Shakespeare, *The Merchant of Venice*, 1596-97

Credit Portfolio Management – an old topic? In the many centuries of bank history and even before the introduction of institutional lending activities, the basic principles of credit portfolio management remained unchanged. Careful selection of credit risks to avoid losses, and diversification ("Don't put all your eggs in one basket") were the major principles of risk management. However, until the end of the second millennium, the implementation of these principles had been a challenging task.

If the credit quality of an issuer deteriorated, possible reactions were limited to challenging negotiations with the borrower to reduce risk, for example, by reducing lending exposure or by demanding additional collateral. An early recognition of declining quality was a prerequisite to sell credit risk to other market participants. Reducing idiosyncratic risk was only possible through denying additional lending, while regional diversification required the expansion of infrastructure, for instance, enlarging the branch network.

This situation changed dramatically in the last five to ten years. It is not an exaggeration to describe this period as a revolution in capital markets. Credit risk has developed into an asset class of its own, and is well on its way to being on the same level as fixed income, foreign exchange, and equity markets. This is true with respect to turnover as well as the variety of tradable instruments.

The major impulse for this development was the creation of the market for synthetic credit risk, which awakened the credit market from the sleepy phase when syndicated loans, corporate bonds, and collateralized debt dominated. The beginning of this development was characterized by the emergence of asset backed securities (ABS), which allow the transfer of receivables from smaller-sized clients to financial markets. In addition, new investors were encouraged to participate in a market previously dominated by banks.

The most important innovation, however, for the development of credit markets in the last few years was the emergence of credit derivatives, which made credit risk tradable in a very efficient way. The structure of credit derivatives is simple and standardized: very liquid for a huge variety of names and the pricing is rather transparent.

Active Credit Portfolio Management. J. Felsenheimer, P. Gisdakis, and M. Zaiser
Copyright © 2006 WILEY-VCH Verlag GmbH & Co. KGaA, Weinheim
ISBN: 3-527-50198-3

A special feature of credit derivatives is their suitability as an underlying for more complex structures, so-called derivatives squared, such as CDOs or indices which allow investors to construct exactly the risk profile that perfectly matches their portfolio and strategy. The rapid growth of the synthetic market was accompanied by the trend towards specialized market participants, like credit hedge funds or credit asset managers, which significantly contributed to the further development of credit markets. As the valuation of credits is rather complex in comparison with other asset classes, the credit market provides an interesting platform for quantitative approaches, for example, to identify arbitrage opportunities. This is due to the asymmetrical risk profile of credits. In line with equity markets, correlation in credit markets has a significant impact on the risk and return profile of a credit portfolio. Analyzing credit correlation is far more complex than is the case for equities. It is both exciting and challenging that the credit market is far from being as efficient as equity markets, which offers interesting opportunities but, at the same time, also contains huge risks.

Last but not least, secondary markets have a massive influence on primary markets, as the pricing of credit risk is becoming more transparent, which also affects traditional lending business. This also has an impact on the efficiency of financial markets and in the end on the behavior of companies. The turnover in the synthetic credit market already exceeds corporate debt.

Where do we go from here? It is obvious that this dynamic development will continue, with volumes increasing further, as there is still a huge number of potential market participants who will enter or even increase their activities in credit markets. The variety of instruments and therefore the complexity will increase. Efficiency will rise on the back of an accelerating number of market participants. It will be interesting to see how credit markets will react to a crisis. Indeed, we have already experienced several crises (among others, the General Motors and Ford downgrades to junk status in May 2005), with the credit market demonstrating remarkable stability. However, we have yet to experience a truly major crisis, such as a more pronounced economic downturn or the surprising default of a large, well-known obligor. In such a scenario, we will see whether credit derivatives will reduce systematic risk via diversification, or if they contribute to a domino effect and aggravate the crisis.

This book comes at exactly the right point in time. It presents a broad and comprehensive description of existing instruments and strategies in the field of credit portfolio management.

It is suitable for everyone involved in trading credit-risky instruments, as well as for asset managers and credit portfolio managers in banks.

Credit Portfolio Management – an old topic? This book as well as current developments in credit markets demonstrate the opposite: Credits are currently the hottest topic in the market place!

Dr. Thomas Bretzger
Head of Active Credit Portfolio Management
HVB Group

Introduction and Acknowledgements

The basic framework for this book grew out of several papers we published within HVB's Corporates & Markets Credit Strategy Group. As is the case with our daily analysis, in this book we cover euro credit markets, focusing on corporate bonds and credit derivatives, while we largely ignore other instruments like asset backed securities (ABS) and covered bonds.

Our motivation to combine practical and theoretical topics is reflected in the structure of the book. In the part "Markets", we discuss the euro corporate bond and credit derivatives markets including their structure, participants, and available instruments. In the "Models" part, we provide the basic valuation framework for fixed income securities and discuss credit risk models in detail. In addition, we show how correlation models work and we modify the valuation framework to include hybrid instruments, like equity default swaps. Finally, we summarize our findings and show how to bring models and markets in line in the part "Management", so that we can identify efficient mechanisms to derive optimal credit portfolios.

This structure obviously causes some redundancies with respect to instruments and valuation, especially in the "Markets" and the "Models" chapters, which we think will help the reader to use this publication as a reference book without having to read it from the first to the last page.

This book would not have been possible without the support of many individuals. First of all, special credit for the design of the book and very helpful comments goes to Jürgen Schulze. We are very grateful for editorial support from David Dakshaw, Jonathan Schroer, and Edda Nee. We thank our colleagues Felix Fischer and Sven Kreitmair from the company research side, who contributed the "Company and Debt Instruments" chapter of this book. We want to thank Thorsten Weinelt, Global Head of Research at HVB, who supported this project from the very beginning, while we continuously benefited from the challenging and inspiring environment at HVB Corporates & Markets. Moreover, thanks go to Bloomberg, Reuters, and Moody's, who provided us with useful data series and analytical tools. Last but not least, we are especially grateful for the full support of our families who demonstrated patience and understanding as we spent weekends and evenings writing this book.

Active Credit Portfolio Management. J. Felsenheimer, P. Gisdakis, and M. Zaiser
Copyright © 2006 WILEY-VCH Verlag GmbH & Co. KGaA, Weinheim
ISBN: 3-527-50198-3

Part I

Markets

1
Market Structure

In this chapter, we outline the structure of the euro credit market and provide a detailed description of market participants, which is crucial for understanding the development of the market with respect to available instruments and specific spread trends. The euro-denominated credit market was established at the beginning of 1999, when the euro was introduced. Over the last few years, the market experienced significant development as a result of regulatory changes, the introduction of new products and instruments, as well as the entry of new market participants.

The following is not only a descriptive study of the beginning of the euro credit market but also includes several facts that help to understand how we ended up where we currently are. The euro credit market is still much smaller than the US$ credit market and has fewer innovative products, especially in the credit derivatives area. Nevertheless, the euro credit market is trying to catch up with its US counterpart, primarily driven by the rising importance of the euro in the international monetary system. As the euro becomes more important as a foreign exchange reserve currency, international central banks are increasing exposure to euro-denominated assets, including corporate credits.

The EU enlargement and the accompanying monetary integration process are still in progress, which is an important factor for the utilization of the euro in the international monetary system. As a result of an increasing number of participants, euro credit markets are becoming more liquid and transparent. Understanding these developments is crucial for credit portfolio managers, as markets are not solely driven by fundamentals, but also by regulatory adjustments and structural changes. Besides a description of market developments, we also highlight the impact of specific milestones in the history of euro credit markets.

Active Credit Portfolio Management. J. Felsenheimer, P. Gisdakis, and M. Zaiser
Copyright © 2006 WILEY-VCH Verlag GmbH & Co. KGaA, Weinheim
ISBN: 3-527-50198-3

1.1 Market Development

1.1.1 Historical Development

With the introduction of the euro on January 1, 1999, the euro credit market was born. The first members of the iBoxx universe were previously issued bonds, denominated in the pre-ecu currencies such as the Deutsche Mark, with euro bond issues following soon after the introduction of the euro: General Motors, Alcatel, and Repsol were among the first companies that tapped the euro corporate bond market in February 1999.

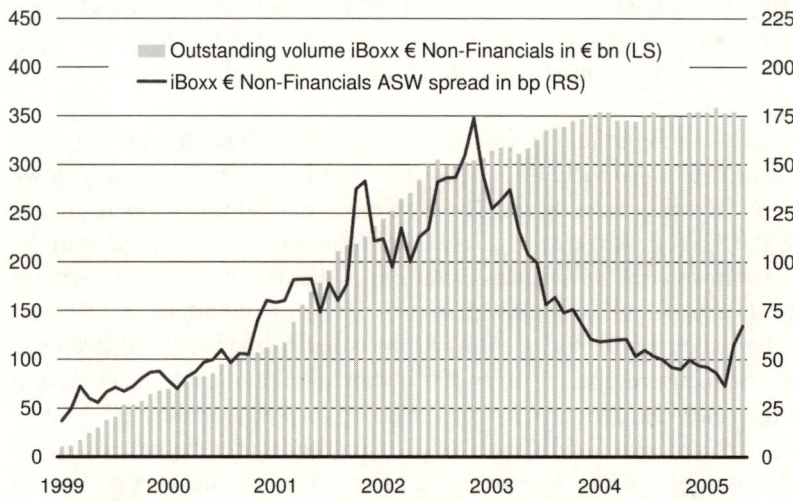

Fig. 1.1: Market growth and spread development from 1999 until 2005

In the first year of the euro credit market, secondary trading was limited, with the focus being on new issues. Any spread widening was driven by the change of the market structure (new issues from lower-rated names) rather than by a fundamental trend. In 2000, spreads started to widen as issuance quality declined, while the fundamental environment also deteriorated. Primary market activity remained strong, and credits gained in importance as a new asset class. This strength was also reflected in new market participants who wanted to benefit from the attractive risk–return profile of corporate debt. Simultaneously, credit portfolio management became more sophisticated, while liquidity in the secondary market grew rapidly and pricing became more transparent.

In 2001, the first negative company news hit the market which contributed to a deteriorating sentiment. Then 9/11 triggered a massive spread blowout, the first overshooting phenomenon the euro credit market experienced. In the aftermath of 9/11, credit spreads recovered almost completely to pre-9/11 levels. However, credit players recognized that managing alpha (the preferred strategy in the early years) might not be sufficient to properly manage credit portfolios. Beta management gained in importance in the aftermath of 9/11. The first (but certainly not the last) turmoil that hit euro markets took place in 2002, driven by rising concerns about the healthiness of companies' balance sheets (*Enronitis*). Against the backdrop of a potential credit crunch scenario, euro corporate spreads reached their historical high in October 2002. Despite the impending war in Iraq in late 2002, spreads tightened due to decelerating micro-fundamental risks as companies adopted a more bondholder-friendly policy (deleveraging and balance sheet repair).

Following the occupation of the Baghdad airport in March 2003 by US forces, which was accompanied by a sharp decline in global risk aversion, spreads knew only one direction: south. In the second half of 2004, the *technical bid* (cf. section 4.5.2) was the dominating driver for euro credits. Although credit fundamentals started to deteriorate moderately, technical-driven demand and forced-to-invest behavior kept spreads at very subdued levels. In the first half of 2005, the multiple downgrades of Ford and General Motors (GM) hit the market, accompanied by resurfacing leveraged buy-out (LBO) fears and the negative impact from correlation trades all of which combined to drive a credit spread trend reversal.

Until 2003, new issuance activity was fairly strong as more and more companies perceived corporate bonds to be an attractive funding tool. As a result of balance sheet repair via deleveraging and due to the resurrection of the syndicated loan business, primary market activity in the investment-grade universe declined by 50 percent from 2003 to 2004.

The most recent development in euro credit markets is that smaller-sized companies (e.g., German small- and medium-sized companies [SMEs]) focused increasingly on the bond market as a funding source. The rising importance of the high-yield market is also driven by *fallen angels*. Fallen angels are former investment grade-rated companies, which experienced one or multiple downgrades to junk status. Since such famous names as Fiat, Ford, and GM joined the high-yield club, there is a new depth to this sector that has contributed to the strong growth of the high-yield market. However, once *rising stars* (previously sub-investment-grade companies that have been upgraded to investment grade) will resurface and leave the high-yield segment, this trend might reverse.

The major key for the development of euro credit markets towards market completion, more transparency, and rising liquidity is the strong growth of the credit derivatives market. While we discuss single instruments in detail in chapter 2, figure 1.2 shows the time frame of the introduction of first-, second-, and third-generation credit derivatives. The basic building block for portfolio derivatives is still the single-name credit default swap (like a binary option in the equity derivatives market), launched in the mid-1990s in the US. Recently introduced instruments are constant maturity credit default swaps (CMCDSs), second-generation collateralized debt obligations (e.g., CDO squared), CDS on ABS, and credit spread options.

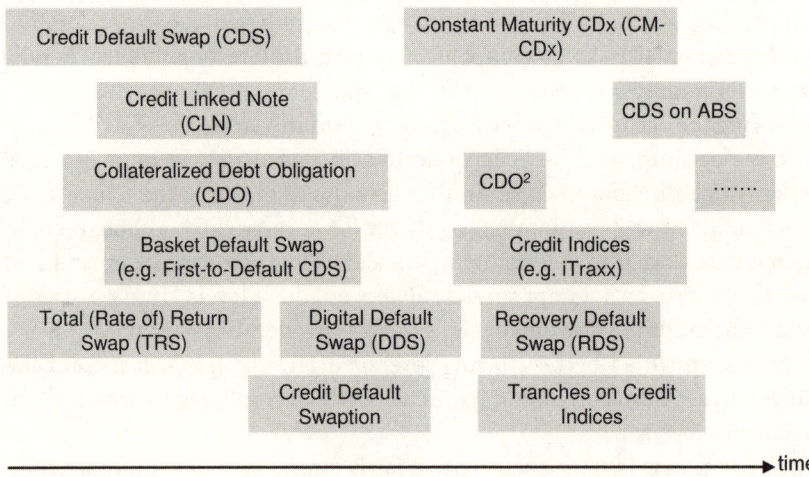

Fig. 1.2: The evolution of the credit derivatives market

While plain-vanilla derivatives experience rising liquidity, there are also tailor-made instruments which are designed to fulfill only the needs of specialized accounts (e.g., hedge funds) and hence, will experience less liquidity. A major trend is the completion of the term structure of credit risk in the most liquid instruments (which allows the introduction of forward contracts) and the rising importance of correlation as an asset class. In a future step, the introduction of options on liquid tranches would even enable investors to trade the volatility of correlation. In addition, there will be even a credit future available soon, based on the most popular and liquid instrument in the derivatives world (the iTraxx CDS indices). The contractual standard of the future will be similar to plain-vanilla fixed income futures (e.g., the Bund future) traded on the Eurex. This credit future contract will be highly appreciated by investors, as it provides a high degree of liquidity and offers a simple way to gain exposure to directional spread risk. Pricing would be rather straightforward, in line with well-known, above-mentioned future contracts and without any sophisticated modeling needs.

A milestone for credit investors was the introduction of iTraxx indices across the whole maturity curve (3Y to 10Y contracts as it is already the case for highly liquid single-name CDS). As the iTraxx is priced along the whole curve, forward contracts can be easily introduced as well. Forward CDS contracts offer the opportunity for investors to speculate on spreads for a specific time interval in the future and are crucial for portfolio management as well as for asset–liability players. As the iTraxx family also includes tranches, a term structure of correlation can be derived. Playing the correlation curve emerged to a central trading strategy for correlation desks.

From a theoretical point of view, there is a broad range of highly interesting instruments, including floating-spread products or tranche options. However, since there is, in our view, only a small portion of the credit community that is able to correctly price and trade such exotics, we do not expect the establishment of a liquid market. The focus will remain on liquid products, which serve hedging needs, trading activities, and the exploitation of arbitrage opportunities for a larger number of credit players.

Due to the close relationship between the corporate bond and the derivatives market (ongoing market integration), these markets cannot be analyzed in isolation. This is not only the case for pricing issues but also from a strategic point of view.

The ongoing demand for leveraged credit instruments, the rising importance of correlation trading, and the market entry of new investors (which implemented internal risk management systems and solved regulatory issues) will contribute to ongoing strong growth of the credit derivatives market. This trend is favorable for credit markets as a whole, but there are also potential problems accompanying the enormous growth of the credit derivatives market, while the underlying cash market stagnates. We believe that the amount outstanding of CDx (the collective term for all credit derivatives) exceeds the amount of physical debt outstanding for many companies.

While we do not share the view that risk-transfer instruments are financial weapons of mass destruction, we pay particular attention to a general problem of accelerating activity in the credit derivatives market: rising systemic risk. This problem is directly linked to the risk transfer and dispersion function of credit derivatives. While credit risk can be divided into its components (probability of default, loss given default), which can be traded separately, the incentive to build up credit exposure will increase. While credit derivatives allow an easy risk transfer among the investor base, reducing the unsystematic risk for a specific investor, the overall amount of originated systematic risk will rise. This could lead to increased vulnerability of the financial system as a whole.

Besides a pure pricing relationship, structural developments might also have a significant influence on the valuation, as the following example highlights. Without exactly quantifying the notional amount of CDS contracts, there are at least a few names having less deliverable obligations outstanding than the amount of CDS contracts. As physical settlement is the market standard, the question arises of what happens in case of a credit event. It is obvious that (depending on the ratio between the amount of CDS contracts outstanding and deliverable obligations) not all CDS contracts could be settled physically. Protection buyers, who do not carry the reference obligation on their books, might face a serious problem: They have to purchase the deliverable obligation. In case the notional amount of CDS contracts exceeds the amount of deliverable obligations, there will be several protection buyers who are not able to settle physically (as there is not enough paper around). Despite the ISDA (International Swaps and Derivatives Association) rules, there will be an agreement that fits the needs for both counterparties in such a case (e.g., cash settlement).

Protection buyers who do not own the deliverable obligation are looking for paper in secondary markets. In the dealer poll following the credit event, the recovery rate will be derived from prices for the outstanding bonds of the company in the aftermath of the credit event. Rising demand from protection buyers will trigger higher prices and, therefore, a higher recovery value. The worst case scenario for the protection buyer would be a price increase of up to 100. In this case, the protection buyer has to pay 100 in cash terms for the deliverable obligation, while he receives nothing from the protection seller because there is no loss! While those protection buyers who already carry the deliverable obligation are not directly affected, the beneficiary is the protection seller in this obviously unrealistic case. However, this mechanism could push up the recovery rate far above 40 percent, the standard assumption for pricing CDS contracts.

The fact that recovery assumptions are underestimated in case of a large CDS-to-cash bond ratio with respect to the outstanding amount means that spreads of outstanding issues trade above the theoretical fair level because the recovery value is higher in case of a credit event. From a relative value point of view, two obligors that have different CDS-to-cash bond ratios (all other pricing-relevant factors being equal) should trade at different levels. The higher this ratio, the lower the spread.

1.1.2 Size and Growth of the Market

Credits have become a more vital segment of European capital markets, which is reflected in their accelerating market share. Using the iBoxx € index universe as a reference, high-grade corporate debt (non-financials and financials) has the second largest share following sovereign debt. We will discuss indices in detail in section 13.1. In the iBoxx spectrum, the amount of corporate debt outstanding exceeds the amount of sub-sovereigns and agencies and also the amount of covered bonds.

Given the fact that credit derivatives are over-the-counter contracts (OTC), there is only very limited information about the size of the market. However, the Bank of International Settlement (BIS) released a new statistic[1] regarding the volume of (single-name and portfolio) CDS outstanding in March 2005. Banks, reporting dealers, and non-financial (but reporting) institutions carry more than US$ 4,500 bn each for protection long and protection short positions on their books. However, long positions exceed short positions by US$ 158 bn, reflecting that the majority of banks are still protection buyers.

1.2 Market Participants

Companies' increasing interest in bond financing (please refer to section 1.3) explains the supply side, while demand for spread products arises because credit-risky assets offer a very attractive risk–return profile, not only on an isolated basis, but also from a macroeconomic viewpoint.

Credit investors are broadly distributed across all industries, including funds, insurance companies, hedge funds and, naturally, banks. Besides pure carry strategies (picking up yield versus government debt) of yield hunters, credits also play an important role for balance sheet arbitrageurs (equity versus debt). A common practice is to split market participants into two groups: so-called real money accounts (like funds and insurance companies) and leveraged players (like hedge funds).

Especially in the credit derivatives universe, the positioning of market participants plays an important role when analyzing market moves. A study periodically published by Fitch, the *Global Credit Derivatives Survey*,[2] provides interesting insights into the growth of the market, the global positioning as well as the top reference entities. According to empirical market overviews from the British Bankers' Association and Fitch,[2] banks are the major protection buyer group hedging their lending business, whereas insurance companies dominate protection selling activities, actively searching for income-generating opportunities.

Moreover, the 2004 survey highlights that

- the CDx market still is the fastest growing segment in the derivatives universe, with single-name CDS experiencing the largest growth: plus 100 percent to US$ 1,900 bn. Portfolio derivatives grew by 49 percent, amounting to US$ 754 bn.
- hedge-fund activity increased significantly, which has an impact on liquidity and volatility.
- although global banks remained net buyers on average, there is a rising number of entities for which banks are selling protection. This reflects the trend towards more trading-oriented CDS exposure rather than hedging positions, which dominated in previous years.
- the market share of the global insurance sector declined, indicating that interbanking transactions gained in importance.
- the credit quality of CDx exposure declined significantly, with demand for super senior protection declining and trading flows in sub-investment-grade issues rising.
- top reference entities remain benchmark issuers in the cash market, for example, Ford, General Motors, DaimlerChrysler, France Telecom, Deutsche Telekom, and Telecom Italia.

1.2.1 Banks

Besides playing the term structure of interest rates (long-term lending financed by short-term funding), the basic business of banks is lending money to companies and receiving compensation for the potential risk that the company might not be able to fulfill its obligation (e.g., in the syndicated loan business). Consequently, banks carry credit exposure on their balance sheets from their basic business operations. As a result, banks have established a sophisticated system of credit risk management with which they carefully analyze credit risk and actively manage credit portfolios. Understanding the behavior of banks is crucial for credit portfolio management as banks are still the major intermediary in the market for credits.

Besides active credit portfolio management units, also treasury departments as well as proprietary trading desks are taking part in the market for credits. While treasury departments use corporate credits (cash or synthetic) like asset–liability managers, proprietary desks act like hedge funds.

Excursus 1: The Pro-Cyclical Nature of Banking

Naturally, banking is a pro-cyclical business, as banks tend to increase their lending activity during accelerating growth periods, which augments the risk of overheating the economy. In contrast, banks reduce lending in economic downturn scenarios, aggravating an economic downturn. This is not only a hot topic in economic theory, since it affects policy actions from the government as well as from central banks, but it also has a significant impact on internal models. *Pro-cyclicality* might also raise problems on the risk management side if probabilities of default (PD) are underestimated in cyclical upturns, leading to exaggerated risk taking by banks. In sluggish growth scenarios, default rates are overestimated, leading to a further reduction of lending activity, which triggers an aggravation of companies' financial flexibility given the lack of access to funds.

This kind of self-fulfilling prophecy is also related to risk-sensitive capital requirements of banks. If internal risk models overestimate the default probability, capital requirements will be too high in bad times and too low in good times. Banks are forced to increase lending when the economy is doing well and have to decrease lending during recessions.

Therefore, cyclical factors have to be taken into account when analyzing credits, as the behavior of institutional investors has immense effects on the market for credit risk.

1.2.2 Insurance Companies

Insurance companies search for assets that match their liability side, and consequently insurance companies are, in general, investing in the cash bond market and are protection sellers in the CDx market. Insurance companies are usually buy-and-hold investors rather than trading-oriented accounts. The market impact of insurance companies is limited compared to that of banks, but the regulatory framework (for example capital requirements) might trigger a kind of lemming-like behavior in case of tail events. For example, this was the case for German insurance companies in the aftermath of the bursting of the equity bubble in 2000.

1.2.3 Funds and Asset Managers

Besides pure credit funds (e.g., asset manager and pension funds), the share of credits in umbrella funds is steadily increasing. Fund managers are highly sophisticated players who often have their own credit research teams, although their ability to use innovative instruments is limited due to regulatory constraints.

1.2.4 Retail Clients

Although credit markets have still high entry barriers (e.g., minimum transaction volumes), credits are also gaining in importance in the retail market, with many new products being placed recently for retail clients. These retail products often use credit structures as the underlying, such as first-to-default baskets.

1.2.5 Hedge Funds

Although capital structure arbitrage desks existed long before the introduction of the euro credit market, hedge funds broadly entered the credit market in 2004, as a lack of alternatives and opportunities forced them to search for carry assets. While hedge funds still focus on lower-rated names and distressed debt, capital structure arbitrage (playing equity versus debt) and correlation trading become more and more popular for hedge funds. Capital structure arbitrage as well as correlation trades are technical- and model-driven and do not directly focus on fundamental considerations, in contrast to real money accounts (banks and insurance companies).

According to a study by Fitch[3], we highlight the major topics regarding the role of hedge funds in credit markets. The report shows that leverage rose continuously during the last few years, adding to the risk of more pronounced spread moves in case tail events happen. While markets are more transparent and liquid under normal market circumstances, they also will become more vulnerable when unexpected events occur. The key findings of the report are:

- Credit-oriented hedge funds experienced strong asset growth.
- The impact of hedge funds on credits is much higher than the market share would suggest (less than 10 percent of the outstanding notional), given the high trading volume and the leverage they use.

- Hedge funds add liquidity to credit markets, especially to the high-yield universe and to the credit derivatives world.
- The major risk is a forced deleveraging of funds (e.g., via rising margin requirements) in response to market disruption.
- This might trigger second-round effects, such as rating volatility in the high-yield segment, and third-round effects, such as declining new issuance activity.

The major question is if credit risk exposure has become more diffused, or if it has become reconcentrated within certain hedge funds? The fact is that most hedge funds continue to rely on short-term funding, leveraging their credit exposure. According to Fitch, the leverage of hedge funds in the credit derivatives business amounts to about 10. Having said this, the market share of hedge funds in the credit derivatives market is around 30 percent (and more than 80 percent in the distressed debt market) on the back of much more active trading positions compared to the major market participants (banks and insurance companies). In addition, the global amount of credit derivatives outstanding is expected to have reached US$ 8,400 bn in 2004.

Although hedge funds improved their risk management systems since the Long Term Capital Management (LTCM) crisis in 1998, this does not mean that there is no remaining risk. Major concerns (e.g., by the Fed) are related to operational risk, lemming-like behavior and regulatory restrictions.

Lemming-like behavior became obvious recently when a significant share of hedge funds started to implement the same trade, which was the case in May 2005, resulting in the first so-called correlation crisis.

Regulatory restriction includes margin requirements from banks (which act as counterparties), which, in combination with high leverage, can trigger forced selling even when the price decline of the underlying is rather subdued (see Aiyagari and Gertler[4]). Margin requirements can trigger a domino effect, leading to an overshooting of credit spreads, clearly exceeding the fundamental fair value.

1.3 Issuing Debt from a Company's Viewpoint

Above, we discussed the motivation for investors to participate in the credit markets, explaining the demand for corporate bonds. The other side of the coin, however, is the supply side. Why are companies tapping the corporate bond market? Understanding the demand–supply pattern is crucial for credit portfolio management because market technicals have a significant impact on the price-setting process in credit markets.

There are several reasons for companies to issue bonds:

- The corporate bond market might be an attractive funding source because bond issuance reduces the dependency on credit facilities of banks and hence eliminates the funding sensitivity resulting from the pro-cyclical lending behavior of banks. Against this backdrop, the availability of syndicated loans is a major driver for primary market activity of companies. A high availability of syndicated loans argues for decelerating issuance activity and vice versa.
- The company has to fulfill fewer covenants than is the case for plain-vanilla credit facilities from banks (which are often explicitly tied to balance sheet ratios). Bond issuance provides more flexibility with regard to future business operations due to the absence of such targets.
- By issuing debt, companies give an incentive for banks to provide the company with other (non-profitable) business. Bond issuance is often coupled with plain-vanilla banking services (e.g., an export facility).
- In contrast to shorter-dated credit facilities, the maturity of corporate bonds is much longer on average. Companies can exploit favorable funding levels, reflected in issuing ultra long-dated bonds, such as Telecom Italia's 50-year bond issued in March 2005.
- Optimizing the capital structure of the company using a weighted-average cost-of-capital approach (WACC). That means there is an optimal capital structure depending on the costs of equity and debt. Moreover, it might be favorable for a company to increase financial leverage in order to boost the return on equity.
- Placing corporate debt in the credit market elevates the profile of the company in the capital market, reflecting professional behavior and the ability to match the requirements that have to be fulfilled in case of a bond issue. Bond issuance is thus a preferred tool when preparing for an IPO.
- There may be only limited ability to tap the commercial paper (CP) market, which is related to the credit quality of the company. Funding through CP programs is only profitable for higher-rated companies and is too expensive for lower-rated companies in the high-yield universe.

Besides these obvious advantages, there are also limitations with a corporate bond issue: Pricing in the secondary market is rather volatile; issuance-related costs are much higher than for bank facilities; there are extra costs due to the more complex documentation; there is additional effort on the investor-relations side given a supplementary investor group with special interests; and last but not least, management's attention is necessary during the launch of the bond.

1.4 Ratings and Rating Agencies

Bond ratings are an assessment of the issuer's ability to service a specific bond in a timely manner. Issuer ratings provide basic information about the inherent credit risk of a specific issuer, while it is only a rough indication of the inherent credit risk of a specific instrument, as subordination has to be taken into consideration. While credits are senior to equity, the level of seniority varies among different types of debt securities. Rating agencies address this problem and assign different types of ratings, including long-term and short-term ratings, as well as an instrument-specific rating. In this section, we will provide a short introduction and overview of the rating methodology, without claiming completeness. We focus on the three most popular agencies (Fitch, S&P, Moody's) and try to analyze the basic ideas and similarities of the three agencies rather than describing differences among their approaches. Although the risk assessment provided by the three agencies on single issuers and instruments can diverge, differences are, in general, rather small (one or two notches), reflecting that there is obviously a strong correlation among ratings from the big three agencies. If there is a split rating (for example, if S&P assigns an A– rating and Moody's a Baa1 rating to a company), in practice, market participants prefer a conservative approach and take the worst rating into account. In the following, we highlight the crucial factors that determine the creditworthiness of an issuer, divided into qualitative and quantitative factors:[5]

- The qualitative analysis of an issuer includes industry risk, the operating environment, the market position, the management, and the accounting policy of a company. Industry risk focuses on the current status of the industry within the economic cycle. Things to watch are the cyclical character of an industry, the market structure within a sector (from competition to monopoly), entry barriers, and the demand structure. The operating environment refers to risks and opportunities of an industry regarding social, demographic, technological, and regulatory changes. The market position is crucial to determine the company's ability to react to rising competition, which depends on the size, the market share, the products, geographical diversification, and the comparative cost position. Management is a key qualitative factor for rating agencies. Most important are the corporate strategy, the risk tolerance, and the funding policy

of a firm. When analyzing the accounting policy, different accounting standards have to be taken into consideration to accurately reflect the company's financial performance.
- Quantitative rating aspects are based on ratios that measure the profitability of a company in relation to its operating strategy, leverage targets, dividend policy, potential acquisitions, and basic financial goals. In this respect, cash-flow ratios are at center stage, with the usual cash flow terminology being used (for an example, please refer to chapter 3). Earnings and cash flows are key elements to determine the financial health of an issuer. In addition, the capital structure and the financial flexibility are taken into consideration and reflected in several ratios, which are split into earnings measures (e.g., earnings before interest, taxes, depreciation, and amortization [EBITDA] and free cash flow), coverage ratios (e.g., EBITDA divided by interest expense), leverage ratios (e.g., debt/EBITDA) and profitability ratios (operating income divided by revenues). All these ratios determine the so-called credit metrics of a company.

As mentioned above, rating agencies assign a short-term and a long-term rating to a company. The short-term rating primarily has an impact on the company's ability to tap the commercial paper market, whereas the long-term rating is more relevant for bond investors.

The main rating is the so-called issuer rating, which is in line with the rating for senior unsecured debt. Consequently, subordinated instruments carry a lower rating. In table 1.1, we refer to the rating scale of S&P, ranging from AAA to D by notches. A notch is the difference between two neighbored ratings (the gradation unit).

Without going into too much detail, there are also differences among the big three rating agencies' methodologies. This becomes obvious when we look at the rating methodology for CDOs. Given the rising importance of credit derivatives, accompanied by the relative complex valuation of structured credits, investors have to take model risk into consideration.[6]

The *weighted-average rating factor* (WARF) is a methodology to derive the credit quality of a collateral pool of assets used by Moody's and Fitch. It is based on the weighted average of each rating category to generate the expected defaults.

In contrast to Moody's, S&P addresses the first dollar loss for a given rating category as opposed to mapping expected losses into a specific rating category, implemented through its proprietary model called the CDO Evaluator. The model is based on the credit rating of each asset in the collateral pool, the

Tab. 1.1: Long-term credit ratings

S&P, Fitch	Moody's	Definition by S&P
AAA	Aaa	The obligor's capacity to meet its financial commitment is extremely strong.
AA+ AA AA–	Aa1 Aa2 Aa3	Differs from the highest rating only to a small degree. The obligor's capacity to meet its financial commitment is very strong.
A+ A A–	A1 A2 A3	Somewhat more susceptible to the adverse effects of changes in circumstances and economic conditions. However, the obligor's capacity to meet its financial commitment on the obligation is still strong.
BBB+ BBB BBB–	Baa1 Baa2 Baa3	A BBB-rated obligation exhibits adequate protection parameters, while adverse economic conditions or changing circumstances are more likely to lead to a weakened capacity of the obligor to meet its financial commitment on the obligation.
BB+ BB BB–	Ba1 Ba2 Ba3	Less vulnerable to non-payment than other speculative issues. However, it faces major ongoing uncertainties or exposure to adverse business, financial, or economic conditions that could lead to the obligor's inadequate capacity to meet its financial commitment on the obligation.
B+ B B–	B1 B2 B3	More vulnerable to non-payment than BB-rated obligations, but the obligor currently has the capacity to meet its financial commitment on the obligation. Adverse business, financial, or economic conditions will impair the obligor's capacity or willingness to meet its financial commitment on the obligation.
CCC+ CCC CCC–	Caa1 Caa2 Caa3	Vulnerable to non-payment and dependent on favorable business, financial, or economic conditions for the obligor to meet its financial commitment on the obligation. In the event of adverse business, financial, or economic conditions, the obligor is not likely to have the capacity to meet its financial commitment on the obligation.
CC	Ca	Highly vulnerable to non-payment.
C	C	The C rating may be used when bankruptcy petition has been filed or similar action has been taken but payments on this obligation are being continued.
D		Default.

Source: S&P, Fitch, Moody's

number of assets in the pool, industry concentration, and default correlation and uses Monte Carlo simulations to generate a probability distribution of defaults.

At Moody's, ratings are based on an assessment of the probability that the collateral will generate sufficient cash flows to meet the obligations under each class of rated notes. The valuation is based on a statistical analysis of historical default rates with various ratings and the diversification requirements the CDO is covenanted to satisfy.

Fitch's ratings are generated by the tool VECTOR, addressing the probability of a first dollar loss (in line with S&P). The default distribution within a portfolio is calculated using Monte Carlo simulations, fed by individual default rates and correlation data. The analysis is based on historical realized defaults, while (pairwise) correlation is derived from equity markets.

1.4.1 Are Ratings an Efficient Source for Pricing Credits?

A long-lasting discussion with respect to ratings includes the question whether rating agencies are lagging behind the market. Many publications have been written on this topic using several examples. We briefly discuss the rationale of rating agencies against the background of the existence of informational inefficiencies in credit markets and identify the problem of informational asymmetries in financial markets as an important factor for the behavior of rating agencies and the market's reaction to rating decisions.

In October 2003, markets reacted very positively to better-than-expected third-quarter results for Ford on October 16, with the Ford 6.75% 01/2008 issue tightening in by about 25 bp. S&P obviously did not share the view of investors and stated concerns that the financial unit would not be able to further subsidize meager operating units. Hence, S&P put the company on Watch negative as of October 21, causing a blowout in spreads by about 100 bp. The divergence between the reaction of markets and the rating agency was directly linked to different opinions concerning the results. The question remains why thousands of investors had a different opinion than S&P's.

It is, however, not always the rating agencies that run ahead of the market. In figure 1.3, we show that markets already discounted a downgrade of Fiat to junk status in mid-2002. Moody's confirmed the market's perception by removing the company from the investment-grade universe a day before Christmas of 2002. Another example for such a front-running of markets was ABB, whose bonds already traded at junk levels in mid-2002, before both agencies (Moody's and S&P) downgraded the company to sub-investment grade in October and December 2002, respectively. This underpins market fetishists who believe in the market's function as an information intermediary: The market knows best!

From a purely theoretical standpoint, there are three parties involved: the rating agency, the rated firm, and investors. The former is a kind of intermediary, transferring information about the company to the investor. Moreover, the information from the company is converted into a rating view, which is used

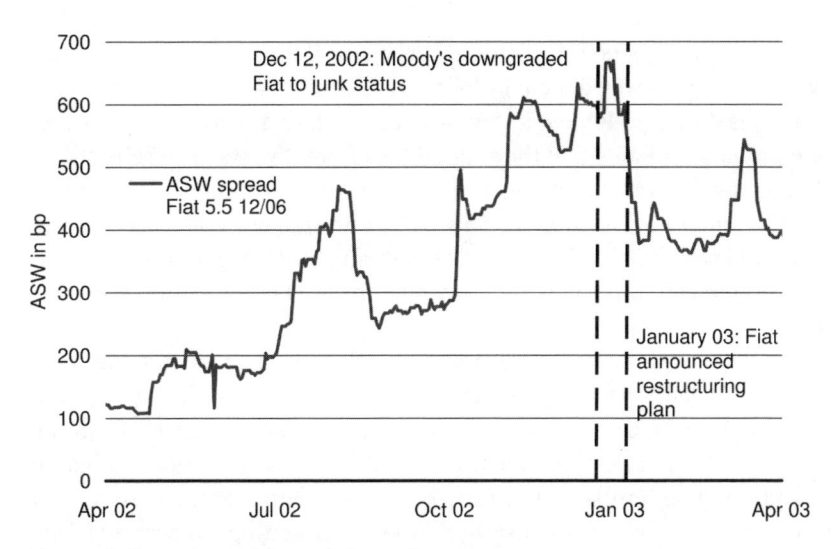

Fig. 1.3: Rating action and the market's reaction

by investors as a pricing input. In many cases, this is even the most important pricing input, for instance, if there is a downgrade to sub-investment grade and investors are forced to sell due to investment limitations. Consequently, there is a direct link between the rating agencies' view and the price of outstanding debt of the company.

Investors trust the rating agency and think that the process of converting information is efficient and leads to a correct assessment of the company. As the rating agency has inside information, the investor relies on the agency and could not (ex ante) evaluate the company on his own. Ex post, perhaps, there could be different views, as is even the case at different rating agencies, which is also reflected in the existence of split ratings.

As the rating agency has an information monopoly, the investor is dependent on the agency's ability to compile a complete and accurate report. Looking only at the agency–investor relationship and assuming the agency has the competence to efficiently process information, there is no reason for any informational asymmetries, and markets tend to be efficient. However, there remain two problems: Does the agency possess the necessary information, and does the relationship between the rated company and the rating agency have an impact on rating actions?

First, analyzing balance sheet items, especially credit protection ratios, could lead to different outcomes as there is a broad range of different opinions and not the absolute truth. If the rating terminology is publicly available and known by all participants, there is no informational problem. If the rating agency is completely transparent, investors could follow rating actions and even anticipate future actions if they evaluate relevant balance sheet items correctly. Nevertheless, the problem remains that there could be different views (also reflected in split ratings by different rating agencies) and/or the incomplete information on how the rating process works. This is, in our opinion, not a major problem and could be solved easily by simply increasing the transparency. Different views are preferable from an investor's standpoint as it helps to improve market efficiency.

We focus rather on a structural problem. The major threat for investors is linked to the institutional agreement among the company, the agency, and the investor. There are completely different demands on the agency from the company than from investors. Such problems reflect a typical case of game theory and could be compared to widely-known standard examples. Assume a car dealer has the order from a customer to sell a car, getting ten percent of the price as a commission. Hence, the car dealer has the intention to sell the car for a high price to boost his commission, while the car owner also benefits from a higher price. Assuming further that the car owner and the car dealer have better knowledge about the condition of the car (the major price determinant) than the buyer, both have the intention to make the car better than it is. In any case, the loser is (most likely) the buyer. The good news is that there is a very simple solution to this problem: the car dealer has to provide a guarantee regarding the condition of the car.

Translating this idea to our case, with the car dealer being the rating agency, the car owner being the company, and the buyer being the investor, the information inefficiency among the three parties could be solved via a guarantee. The rating agency must guarantee that it made a best effort to use a transparent rating methodology and will provide continuous updates on the condition of the company. This will help prevent negative surprises and will tend to clarify the reasons for different views of the rating agency and the investor. The guarantee of a rating agency is simply its reputation within the market place and consequently, rating agencies have the intention to assign ratings in line with the fundamental risk assessment, which is theoretically the major factor also for the pricing of instruments in debt markets. Nevertheless, it is obvious that there are differences between markets and rating agencies with respect to information flow, which is reflected in a faster reaction of markets compared to ratings. This is rather an overshooting-like character of financial markets, while credit ratings are still good indicators of a company's creditworthiness in the long term.

1.5 Credit Classes

While we focus primarily on corporate bonds and related derivative instruments, the credit universe is very heterogeneous, including several asset classes and instruments. In this section, we provide a brief summary on instruments that are closely linked to pure corporate credits. For example, there are many issuers of bonds that are owned by governments to a certain extent and hence are classified as sub-sovereigns or agencies rather than as non-financial corporates. Especially in the utilities sector, which has historically experienced strong government participation, the classification varies among different index providers. We follow the iBoxx definition, which splits up the entire high-grade non-sovereigns universe into sub-sovereigns and agencies, collateralized debt, corporates financials, and corporates non-financials, whereas many market participants refer only to the latter when talking about credits. The iBoxx € index construction subsumes financials and non-financials as subindices of the iBoxx € Corporate index, as both financials and non-financials bonds bear corporate credit risk. With respect to sectors, the financials universe includes banks, financial services, and insurance companies. The non-financials universe is separated into industries, with telecoms and utilities being the most important.

1.5.1 High-Grade Universe

Financial companies issue paper across all subordination levels, while non-financials issue primarily senior debt and in special cases also subordinated bonds (hybrids). The majority of straight bonds issued by companies are issues from the so-called EMTN program. *Euro medium-term notes* (EMTNs) are continuously offered notes with maturities ranging from nine months to fifty years. Telecom Italia, which issued a fifty-year bond in March 2005, was the first company in this maturity bracket. EMTNs are flexible in structure and market timing because of the type of issuance (based on the mechanism of the commercial paper market). EMTNs are traded in the euro market.

Besides the high-grade spectrum, sub-investment-grade issuers are gaining market share as a rising number of smaller-sized companies discover the debt market as an attractive funding source.

1.5.2 High-Yield and Crossover Credits

High-yield or speculative-grade bonds, which are sometimes colloquially referred to as junk bonds, are characterized by significantly higher credit risk than investment-grade or high-grade bonds. The designation as speculative-grade bonds becomes apparent when examining the historic default patterns of rated bonds. Empirical evidence shows that the default rate for issuers or bonds rated sub-investment grade steeply increases compared to investment-grade rated issuers or bonds. According to a Moody's study, the default rate for North American issuers rated in the broad Ba rating category (ratings of Ba1 to Ba3; S&P and Fitch equivalent: BB+ to BB–) increases to 1.4 percent compared to 0.3 percent for Baa-rated issuers (ratings from Baa1 to Baa3) over a one-year time horizon and to 12.9 percent from 2.4 percent over a five-year time horizon. As a result, sub-investment-grade bonds have a higher yield than investment-grade-rated issues to compensate investors for the higher default risk included in high-yield bonds.

Issuers and bonds are faced with a rating downgrade if their creditworthiness deteriorates in line with, for example, a general economic downturn, changing industry fundamentals, and characteristics or changes in the regulatory environment an industry operates in. If a former investment-grade rated bond becomes downgraded to sub-investment grade, it is commonly referred to as a *fallen angel*. In fact, fallen angels are nearly twice as likely to default especially in the first three years following the downgrade, compared to a control group of original high-yield bonds. On the other hand, fallen angels are also more likely than their counterparts in the control group to migrate back to investment-grade territory again, the same study discovered. Bonds formerly rated sub-investment grade that return to investment grade are commonly referred to as *rising stars*.

Although there is no clear-cut definition, sub-investment-grade issuers that have – from a business risk perspective – investment-grade characteristics and could potentially become rising stars are commonly referred to as *crossover credits*. The characteristics displayed by such crossovers may vary among different industries, jurisdictions, and stages in the economic life of the company. Broadly speaking and at the risk of overly generalizing, they typically include the ability to generate meaningful cash flows through the economic cycle, usually facilitated by a broad and diversified business and product portfolio as well as a limited concentration in terms of customers and retail markets. However, stretched financial figures as a result of aggressive acquisition or investment activity, excessive stock buy-backs, a prolonged market downturn, and so on, have impacted the credit profile, that is, the company's creditworthiness to such a degree that an investment-grade rating is no longer warranted. Once and if these financial issues are resolved and the financial profile stands on a sound footing again, an upgrade to investment-grade rating may be possible.

1.5.3 High-Quality Segment

Sub-Sovereigns, Agencies, and Supranationals

The European market for sub-sovereigns and agencies (SSA) consists of three main groups of issuers: *sub-sovereigns*, *agencies*, and *supranationals*. The group of sub-sovereigns consists of regional governments and municipalities like the State of Berlin, the Generalitat de Valencia, or the City of Rome. This subsegment, which makes up for around 30 percent of the market total, is dominated by German federal states (75 percent of all sub-sovereign issuers). In order to qualify as an agency, an entity has to fulfill one or more of the following criteria:

- It is fully or partly publicly owned, like Bank Nederlandse Gementeen (50 percent government-owned) or the Swedish Export Credit Corp (100 percent government-owned).
- It enjoys an explicit or implicit government guarantee or some other form of support, like the German KfW Bankengruppe, which benefits from a direct and unconditional government guarantee.
- It has a public policy mission, like the French CADES, which assumes current and future financial obligations from the social security system.
- It is established under public sector law and operates either under public sector law (like the Austrian ASFIN, which operates under a specific public ASFIN law), or under private law with a specific purpose. An example of the latter is Spain's CORES, which manages the strategic petroleum reserves; it operates in a strictly defined regulatory environment.

Agencies are the largest group of issuers, making up more than half of outstanding bonds. Again, they are heavily dominated by German issuers.

Supranationals are agencies per se, except that in terms of ownership and mission, they have been expanded from one national identity to several nations. Creditworthiness of supranational institutions is underpinned by three factors:

- They normally benefit from preferred creditor status, an implicit agreement between borrower and lender that such an institution will enjoy priority over other creditors.
- The quality of their shareholders and their proven commitment of support is very high, although in most cases no direct guarantee is given.

- The regulatory environment ensures financial stability and/or supportive mechanisms for their debt obligations.

Supranational issuers account for roughly one-sixth of the SSA market. The largest single issuer is the European Investment Bank (EIB), which accounts for more than 90 percent of all outstanding supra issues.

Covered Bonds

A *covered* or *mortgage bond* is an on-balance sheet obligation of the issuing institution. Typically AAA-rated, a covered bond receives the legal structure, the issuer's backing, and the pledge of quality assets. Assets that remain on the balance sheet of an issuing bank are employed as collateral in order to raise the credit profile of the debt product above the profile of the issuer and eventually reduce funding costs. Investors have a dual claim on (1) the issuer and (2) the cash flows of the underlying cover pool. The cash flows of the cover pool are protected from the insolvency of the issuer, who is obliged to respect certain rules that mainly refer to (1) the eligibility of assets, (2) the valuation of cover assets, (3) cash flow adequacy, and (4) over-collateralization.

Regular covered bonds are debt instruments secured against a pool of assets wherein asset quality, cash flow adequacy, and counterparty risk are purely determined by a legal framework such as the upcoming new legal frameworks in Belgium, Italy, Norway, and Portugal. Classical-styled covered bonds are issued by Austrian, Danish, German, Luxembourg, and Spanish institutions, while a subsidiary style dominates in France and Ireland.

Structured covered bonds are regular covered bonds that are structurally enhanced and include repackaged covered bonds and contractually enhanced covered bonds. *Replicated covered bonds* are debt instruments secured against a pool of assets wherein asset quality, cash flow adequacy, and counterparty risk are mainly determined through clauses regulated under private law (issued in the UK and the Netherlands).

1.5.4 Asset Backed Securities

Asset backed securities (ABS) are securities that are backed by a pool of receivables. Basically, banks or firms compile a portfolio of receivables, with either the underlying risk of such receivables being synthetically hedged by way of a credit default swap or guaranties or with the receivables being legally and economically sold to a third party by way of a true sale. True-sale ABS are more common than synthetic transactions and lead to the receivables being disposed of and removed from the originator's balance sheet.

Investors sell protection on such a portfolio by investing in issued notes, credit default swaps, or guaranties with all of these financial instruments referencing to the underlying pool of receivables. Hence, ABS investors only bear the risk that arises from such receivables, and are generally independent of the originator's potential default.

ABS offer a plethora of different receivables being securitized or structures being applied. The originators' main incentives to conduct an ABS transaction are:

- Risk management (the transfer of specific risks to third parties without recourse; structural modification of the risk of the overall or remaining credit portfolio).
- Balance sheet management (increase of liquidity in case of true-sale ABS; increase of the equity ratio by way of freeing up regulatory capital; increased profitability by way of investing freed-up capital in new investments offering a better risk–return profile).
- Liquidity and yield management (development of a broader investor base; access to cheaper funding as the respective notes typically have better ratings than the originator; generation of fee as opposed to interest income).

The investors' main incentives to invest in ABS are:

- From a single investment point of view: benefiting from the spread pick-up ABS historically offered when compared to corporate bonds with the same risk (in terms of rating) and maturity.
- From a portfolio perspective: benefiting from the plethora of asset classes ABS may be based on and structures that may be applied (e.g., by way of leveraging credit risk), leading to a potentially higher efficient line of the investor's overall credit portfolio triggered by increased investment alternatives.

2
Instruments

The universe of credit-risky assets emerged continuously during the last few years and now includes a broad variety of instruments that have specific risk-return characteristics as well as differentiating payoff profiles. All of these instruments form an integral part of the spectrum of credit-risky instruments.

2.1 Straight Bonds

The basic instruments are fixed rate bonds (or straight bonds), which account for the majority of issues available. In the following, we skip the basics, which involve well-known fixed income analytics of government securities. The additional credit risk will be analyzed separately later on. Besides straight bonds, floating rate notes are the most popular instruments. For a very useful and detailed analysis, please refer to Fabozzi.[7]

Although practitioners use the analytical framework of information services such as Bloomberg and Reuters, there is a key factor in implementing spread calculation in practice that is worth mentioning: the cash flow structure of an instrument. The bond structure is a set of parameters which determines the cash flow structure behind an fixed income instrument and has to be considered in the valuation framework of single bonds. Key parameters in the bond structure includes the redemption price, irregular coupon features (e.g., short first coupon, etc.), coupon frequency, the coupon calculation method, settlement conventions, and the calendar.

In table 2.1, we show the characteristics of several straight corporate bonds (including maturity, coupon, and rating), as well as key risk figures. From the cash flow structure and the clean price of the bond, we derive the yield to maturity and the modified duration of a specific bond. Based on these figures, we calculate spreads on an asset swap level (ASW spread).

Tab. 2.1: Key risk measures for straight bonds

Bond name	Rating Moody's / S&P	Mid price	Yield	Mod. Dur.	ASW spread	Spread vola	Z-score	Spread beta	Break even
BMW 5.25% 09/2006	A1/NR	103.22	2.26	1.03	4.4	2.7	-2.5	0	-0.9
DCX 3.75% 10/2006	A3/BBB	101.42	2.52	1.12	29.1	8.8	-1.7	0.7	8
DCX 5.625% 01/2007	A3/BBB	104.32	2.6	1.39	34.1	12	-1.5	0.9	8.3
TOYOTA 4.125% 01/2007	Aaa/AAA	102.65	2.28	1.41	0.9	1.1	0.7	0	1.3
PEUGOT 4.875% 01/2007	A2/A-	103.69	2.36	1.44	9.2	1.8	-2.1	0	3.3
VW 4.75% 02/2007	A3/A-	103.42	2.45	1.46	17.6	3.8	-1.4	0.1	5
DCX 6.125% 03/2007	A3/BBB	105.55	2.68	1.57	38.9	11.9	-1.5	0.9	8.5
RENAUL 6.375% 10/2007	Baa1/BBB+	108.24	2.53	2.02	14.8	2.7	-1.3	0.2	4.5

The spread volatility is the annualized sixty-day standard deviation calculated on an ASW spread basis.

The Z-score measures the difference between the current spread and the sixty-day average in units of standard deviations, making different bonds with different spread levels comparable. Normally this number is between +2 (cheap) and −2 (expensive).

Spread beta is the historical beta of an individual bond compared to the entire universe, also calculated on an ASW basis. A beta bigger (smaller) than 1 means that if the average ASW of all euro corporates increases by 1 bp, the ASW of the bond is expected to increase by more (less) than 1 bp.

Breakeven spread changes represent the number of basis points the spread of a bond can widen over a fixed period of time before the total return on the credit exceeds that of an investment in a risk-free asset (Euribor), under the assumptions of an unchanged yield curve and an unchanged spread to the swap curve during the investment horizon. For example, a three-month breakeven of 5 bp means that if the spread to the swap curve widens about 5 bp in three months, the excess return of the bond versus the risk-free investment is zero (the total return of both investments is the same).

2.2 Bonds with Embedded Options

Especially high-yield bonds often carry embedded options, with call options being the most popular. A discrete (Bermudan-style) call option embedded in fixed income securities gives the issuer the right to repurchase the bonds from the investor on dates from a detailed call schedule – e.g., on all interest payment dates after the first call date. This option favors obviously the issuer of the bond. In contrast, a put option favors the bondholder: A put option gives the bondholder the right, but not the obligation, to sell back the bonds to the issuer at the put dates. Beside such discrete options the embedded option can also be American-style (continuous) or European-style. When calculating risk measures, embedded options have to be taken into account, for example, by applying yield-to-call or spread-to-worst methods.

To provide investors with an additional compensation in case of a downgrade, telecom companies started to issue bonds including step-up features. In case of a previously-specified downgrade, the coupon payment increases by a pre-determined amount. Hence, the investor earns a higher coupon income as compensation for a deteriorating credit quality. Step-up features are often coupled with step-down features, which trigger a declining coupon if the company

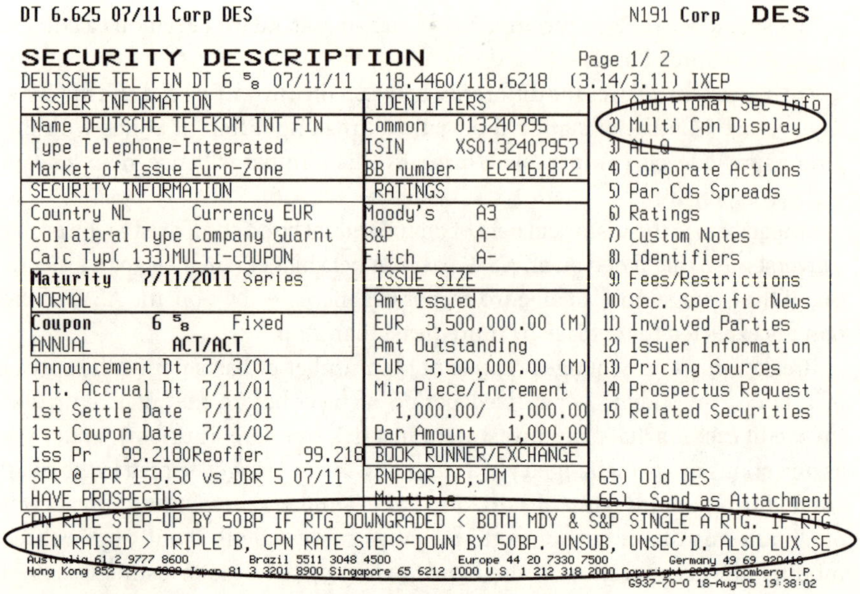

```
DT 6.625 07/11 Corp DES                                    N191 Corp   DES
SECURITY DESCRIPTION                              Page 1/ 2
DEUTSCHE TEL FIN DT 6 5/8 07/11/11   118.4460/118.6218  (3.14/3.11) IXEP
┌──────────────────────────────┬──────────────────────────┬──────────────────────────┐
│ ISSUER INFORMATION           │ IDENTIFIERS              │ 1) Additional Sec Info   │
│ Name DEUTSCHE TELEKOM INT FIN│ Common      013240795    │ 2) Multi Cpn Display     │
│ Type Telephone-Integrated    │ ISIN     XS0132407957    │ 3) ALLQ                  │
│ Market of Issue Euro-Zone    │ BB number   EC4161872    │ 4) Corporate Actions     │
│ SECURITY INFORMATION         │ RATINGS                  │ 5) Par Cds Spreads       │
│ Country NL     Currency EUR  │ Moody's       A3         │ 6) Ratings               │
│ Collateral Type Company Guarnt│ S&P          A-         │ 7) Custom Notes          │
│ Calc Typ( 133)MULTI-COUPON   │ Fitch         A-         │ 8) Identifiers           │
│ Maturity   7/11/2011 Series  │ ISSUE SIZE               │ 9) Fees/Restrictions     │
│ NORMAL                       │ Amt Issued               │ 10) Sec. Specific News   │
│ Coupon    6 5/8   Fixed      │ EUR  3,500,000.00 (M)    │ 11) Involved Parties     │
│ ANNUAL         ACT/ACT       │ Amt Outstanding          │ 12) Issuer Information   │
│ Announcement Dt   7/ 3/01    │ EUR  3,500,000.00 (M)    │ 13) Pricing Sources      │
│ Int. Accrual Dt   7/11/01    │ Min Piece/Increment      │ 14) Prospectus Request   │
│ 1st Settle Date   7/11/01    │     1,000.00/  1,000.00  │ 15) Related Securities   │
│ 1st Coupon Date   7/11/02    │ Par Amount     1,000.00  │                          │
│ Iss Pr   99.2180Reoffer  99.218│ BOOK RUNNER/EXCHANGE   │                          │
│ SPR @ FPR 159.50 vs DBR 5 07/11│ BNPPAR,DB,JPM          │ 65) Old DES              │
│ HAVE PROSPECTUS              │ Multiple                 │ 66) Send as Attachment   │
│ CPN RATE STEP-UP BY 50BP IF RTG DOWNGRADED < BOTH MDY & S&P SINGLE A RTG. IF RTG   │
│ THEN RAISED > TRIPLE B, CPN RATE STEPS-DOWN BY 50BP. UNSUB, UNSEC'D. ALSO LUX SE   │
Australia 61 2 9777 8600      Brazil 5511 3048 4500    Europe 44 20 7330 7500    Germany 49 69 920446
Hong Kong 852 2977 6000  Japan 81 3 3201 8900  Singapore 65 6212 1000  U.S. 1 212 318 2000  Copyright 2005 Bloomberg L.P.
                                                                       G937-70-0 18-Aug-05 19:38:02
```

Fig. 2.1: The multi-coupon bond function on Bloomberg

is upgraded. In figure 2.1, we show the description page in Bloomberg for the Deutsche Telekom 07/2011 issue, which includes a step-up and a step-down feature. The bond was issued in July 2001 with an initial coupon of 6.625 percent. Due to several downgrades of Deutsche Telekom by S&P and Moody's, the coupon increased to 7.125 percent in July 2002, while several upgrades of the company in 2003 and 2004 triggered a decline of the coupon back to 6.625 percent by the beginning of July 2005. In contrast to straight bonds, coupon adjustments have to be taken into account when calculating yield and spread figures, which can be done using Bloomberg's multi-coupon function.

Recently issued hybrids carry so-called interest deferral features, which we explain in the following section.

2.3 Exotics

The evolution of credit markets is also reflected in the rapid development of new structures and instruments. We include in this category payment-in-kind (PIK) notes, hybrid issues, and also subordinated financial bonds, which are exotic either in terms of the bond structure or because they represent only small market volume compared to the outstanding volume of senior debt.

2.3.1 Payment-in-Kind Notes

As a result of declining risk aversion, yield hunters moved down the credit quality curve in 2004. The introduction of PIK notes accounts for this trend. These notes are placed by holding companies of leveraged issuers and are subordinated to high-yield bonds. That said, the issuance activity for PIK notes clearly corresponds with the spread trend in high-yield markets.

At the end of 2004, private equity sponsors (PES) started to utilize PIK notes, with Kabel Deutschland being the first issuer in the new market segment. *Payment-in-kind* means that the coupon is not paid in cash but accrues until maturity (or a potential call), which means that, in economic terms, a PIK note is similar to a zero coupon bond. In contrast to many bank mezzanine loans, no equity component (e.g., a link to the dividend payments of a company) is included. Typically, a holding company above the issuer of a high-yield bond sells PIK notes, which are usually contractually subordinated to the high-yield issue.

Tab. 2.2: Examples of PIK-Notes

Issuer	Kabel Deutschland	Jefferson Smurfit	Cognis
ISIN	XS0207677740	XS0210355722	XS0209488179
Issue date	Dec 2004	Jan 2005	Jan 2005
Amount	€400 mn	€325 mn	€530 mn
Issue Price	99	100	99
Pricing	Euribor +850 bp	11.5%	Euribor +900 bp
Maturity	Dec 2014	Oct 2015	Jan 2015
Call date/price	May 2005 at 100	Jan 2007 at 102	Jul 2005 at 101
Further call features*	NC 6M 100, 102, 101	NC 2Y 102, 101	NC 6M 101, 102, 101

* e.g., NC 6M means the note is non-callable on any time before six months at the respective call price

The proceeds of the note, in general, are paid out as a special dividend to the private equity sponsor. These proceeds are often used to bridge finance his exit. Accordingly, the issuer of a PIK note has a very short first-call option, with the call price being near par. This limits the upside potential in terms of price gains.

In case of promising exit candidates, the likelihood that the note will be called within a very short period is high. Although PES have a strong interest in a good performance of the company because they will receive all excess proceeds from the exit, one can argue that their economic interest decreases as they already receive a payment via the dividend. In case of default, the expected recovery rate is close to zero, according to a recently published study from Fitch, which corresponds to a rating below existing cash-pay high-yield notes. In a default case, however, the investor may receive equity in case the company emerges from bankruptcy.

Therefore, we expect PIK notes to be more volatile in a bearish market mode, while liquidity in secondary markets is very thin (which aggravates the problem of selling the note in a spread-widening scenario).

We view PIK notes as a diversification opportunity for existing high-yield portfolios. However, in a more bearish environment, refinancing credit facilities with private offerings of senior secured notes (as announced by Cablecom at the end of March 2005) might be a more appropriate tool for companies.

2.3.2 Hybrids or Subordinated Corporate Bonds

Following the issue of a €500 mn subordinated note by Casino Guichard Perrachon, the French food retailer, in January 2005, other firms have entered the market with similar bonds: Germany-based Südzucker, Bayer, and the two Scandinavian utilities Vattenfall and Dong. All in all, subordinated bonds have a positive impact on the credit quality of the senior debt and hence on the issuer rating, while they offer attractive spread levels for carry hunters.

Whereas the Casino bond has a five-year maturity, the others are perpetual (or 1000 years in the case of Dong) with a call option for the issuer after a period of ten years. If these options are not exercised, all three bonds will provide increased remuneration for bondholders of 100 bp, providing an incentive for issuers to repurchase the bonds in cash. The size of the step-up seems to have developed as a compromise between the interests of bondholders, which prefer a high likelihood of redemption, and those of rating agencies, which treat the bonds partially as equity and which are therefore interested in a very long duration.

Principal and interest payments of these bonds are subordinated to all other debt obligations and rank senior only to common shares. Despite this deep subordination, companies' ability to defer payments on the notes is limited to certain triggers. In the case of Vattenfall, deferral of the subordinated bonds is triggered if the ratio of funds from operations (FFO) to interest costs falls below 2.5× from currently 8.1× (based on 2004 figures).

For these kind of bonds, S&P and Moody's normally assign ratings that are two notches below the rating for senior debt (three notches in the case of Vattenfall). Rating agencies consider the bonds to have an equity content of 50 percent (Vattenfall: 60 percent). Remuneration will, however, be treated as normal interest payments.

Issuers' motivation for these new debt instruments is different. In the case of Dong, a combination of senior and subordinated debt was used to refinance the acquisition of Elsam without endangering the rating. Vattenfall uses this kind of financing to increase its debt capacity for potential future acquisitions. Südzucker uses the hybrid to cement its rating, which was under pressure prior to the announcement. It should be mentioned that the effects on credit metrics of Vattenfall are ambiguous as the FFO interest coverage deteriorates due to the higher interest payments on the subordinated bond. Other ratios (e.g., total debt/total capitalization) should develop quite well with the new issue.

Possible candidates for hybrid issuance are companies whose rating is under pressure and which do not have the possibility to raise equity in the short term, as is the case with state-owned utilities.

Tab. 2.3: Overview subordinated bonds

Issuer	Maturity	Call option	Call date	Step-up	Rating SO bonds	Rating senior debt
Casino	2010	no	–	–	–/BB+n	–/BBBn
Vattenfall	perpetual	yes	2015	100 bps	Baa2p/BBB–s	A3s/A–s
Südzucker	perpetual	yes	2015	100 bps	Baa2n/BBB–s	A3n/A–s
Dong	3005	yes	2015	100 bps	Baa3s/BBB–s	Baa1s/BBB+s

Given the accelerating activity of hybrid issuance, the need for an appropriate valuation model appeared. First the bad news: Quantifying the fair spread valuation is a mission impossible as the necessary parameters are not predictable. The good news is that the additional risks of hybrids versus senior debt are well known. The name of the game from an investor's viewpoint is simply investing in the senior piece of a lower-rated company versus buying the subordinated paper of a higher-rated company at the same spread.

There is an ongoing debate concerning relative value approaches. None of these approaches adequately explains the risk premium investors demand for taking hybrid risk. And since there is no closed-form model that explains the fair spread of hybrids, the valuation is not as simple as just calibrating the model to market quotes. Finally, valuing hybrids faces a similar problem as valuing step-up/step-down features since one has to simulate future rating changes.

A simple approach tries to evaluate the isolated features included in hybrid issues. First, one can calculate the historical premium for subordinated risk in terms of expected loss, taking into account historical recovery rates for senior and subordinated debt given a rating and maturity-related default probability. Then, an implied market risk premium for taking subordinated risk has to be added. This can be done by calculating the spread difference of senior versus subordinated debt, for example, in the insurance sector.

Now one has to quantify the compensation for taking the risk of special features, such as the call feature and the interest deferral feature:

(1) *Call feature*: Despite a coupon step-up in case the company does not call the bond at the call date, the risk an investor faces is that calling the bond at the call date is not attractive from a company's perspective.

- If the company is downgraded to a certain rating category (accompanied by a corresponding spread level), calling the bond might be unprofitable from an issuer's perspective. We can use rating migration tables to derive the probability of reaching this rating level at the call date. This is the idiosyncratic risk of a call feature.
- A second risk is the possibility that the systematic risk premium increases significantly although the quality of the company remains stable. In case the average spread for investment-grade bonds increases to a certain spread level, calling the bond will be unprofitable. This can be solved by simulating a process which fits historical spread dynamics, a kind of spread forecasting model.

(2) *Interest deferral feature*: A way to quantify the deferral risk is to look at the historical dividend discipline of the company. However, in quantitative terms, an interest deferral (a delayed coupon payment) means that the discount rate increases, having a negative impact on the present value of this specific coupon payment. This effect is almost negligible compared to other risk factors.

In summary, an exact valuation is impossible. Looking at issued hybrids, investors easily absorbed the paper and spreads tightened significantly in the secondary market. We conclude that hybrids are attractive funding tools for specific companies (those with stable cash flows) in non-cyclical sectors and in a favorable market environment.

2.4 Hybrid Bank Capital

In contrast to corporate bonds, financials issuers provide the market with a full range of securities covering the whole capital structure of a financial institution, in particular banks. The motivation behind these instruments is the optimization of financing costs, which is driven by regulatory and rating considerations. The valuation of subordinated bank debt requires an understanding of the bank's capital structure, and distinguishing between the economic capital and regulatory capital is crucial.

- *Economic capital*: This is the capital a bank should have to secure against unexpected losses. It is the difference between assets and liabilities on the balance sheet (less preferred shares, trust-preferred securities, or other supplementary capital instruments) that is available to meet a bank's loss on an ongoing basis.
- *Regulatory capital*: This is the capital a bank must have. It consists of those elements of a bank's balance sheet that are eligible in the context of calculating capital ratios by the regulator. In addition to economic capital, regulatory capital also includes subordinated debt. From a regulator's standpoint, bank capital can be regarded as a safety net to absorb unexpected losses without the interest of depositors being affected. In times of financial stress, a bank can decide whether to defer dividends or interest payments to holders of hybrid capital – or even to cancel them. In liquidation, bank capital ranks behind the claim of depositors and therefore allows the bank to repay the depositors ahead of reimbursing holders of subordinated debt.

In contrast to the regulator's point of view, the rating agencies are concerned about timely repayment of interest and principal and view capital as an element to absorb losses. Rating agencies are more cautious about including the full amount of instruments (e.g., preferred shares) as capital because banks tend to maintain payments on these instruments even in times of stress. The rating agencies place more importance on a bank's ability to generate capital from its operational business, risk management, and operating environment rather than calculating pure capital ratios.

We will now review the debt instruments issued by banks. Subordinated paper can be divided into Tier 1 issues, Upper Tier 2 (UT 2), and Lower Tier 2 (LT 2) bonds, and Tier 3 paper.

The characteristics of Tier 1 issues are as follows:

- Perpetual. The issue must be perpetual, but call features are possible. A limited step-up (maximum 100 bp) is eligible with a call after ten years, or after five years without a step-up.
- Subordination. The issues are senior only to equity, but subordinated to all others.
- Non-cumulative coupons. Deferred coupons or dividends are non-cumulative. The coupons can be canceled and do not have to be repaid.
- Loss absorption. The issues must be able to absorb losses before other creditors (depending on subordination). Principal and interest may be written down to allow issuer to remain solvent.
- Non-payment of interest is not a default.

For UT 2, the following characteristics apply:

- Perpetual. Upper Tier 2 issues are perpetual in most countries (Germany, Austria: *Genussschein* has a minimum term of five years).
- Subordination. They are senior to Tier 1, preferred, and equity.
- Deferrable, but cumulative coupons. Coupons can be deferred at issuer's option, but they have to be paid in the future, including interest on interest.
- Loss absorption. They must be able to absorb losses before other creditors (depending on subordination). Principal and interest may be written down to allow issuer to remain solvent.
- Non-payment of interest is not a default.

LT 2 issues are subject to the following features:

- Dated. They have a minimum maturity of five years.
- Subordination. They are subordinated only to senior debt.
- A deferral of coupons is not allowed.
- No loss absorption. That is, no write-down of principal and interest is eligible.
- Non-payment of interest is an event of default.
- Amortization. In the last five years of an issue (UK: four years), LT 2 issues are written down on a straight-line basis. In order to avoid the amortization, many banks have issued ten-year issues with a step-up and call after five years.

Tier 3 can be characterized as follows:

- Dated. They have a minimum maturity of two years.
- Subordination. Tier 3 issues rank pari passu to LT 2.

- There is no amortization.
- There is no loss absorption. That is, no write-down of principal and interest is eligible.
- Both interest and principal can be deferred due to the regulatory lock-in clause (maturity extension and cumulative coupon deferral).
- Established to support market risk in the trading book on a regulatory basis, but does not participate in trading losses.
- This is considered a weak form of capital. Rating agencies do not include it in their analysis of capital ratios, and some regulators, such as Norway, Spain, and Denmark, refuse to recognize it.

Tab. 2.4: Overview of different subordination levels (as of August 18, 2005)

Seniority	Bond	Features	Spread
Senior	HBOS 3.375 % 06/2010		1
LT 2	HBOS 5.5 % 07/2009		9
UT 2	HBOS 6.055 % 11/2049	perpetual, callable 10/2015 at 100	47
Tier 1	HBOS 7.627 % 12/2049	perpetual, callable 12/2011 at 100	53

2.5 Single-Name Credit Derivatives

As mentioned before, the credit derivatives universe is the most rapidly evolving market segment and includes a huge variety of different instruments. The basic classification is to divide the credit derivatives world into single-name derivatives and portfolio derivatives. While the former refers to a specific obligor, portfolio derivatives have more than one underlying reference obligation. In any case, credit default swaps are the basic instrument within the credit derivatives universe.

2.5.1 Credit Default Swaps

A *credit default swap* is a bilateral, OTC-traded contract. The protection seller takes on credit risk until maturity and receives a premium from the protection buyer. In case a credit event occurs, the protection seller compensates the protection buyer for the loss. Credit events under standard market documentation are bankruptcy, failure to pay, and restructuring. Contract details are specified in the 2003 ISDA swap documentation and the 2003 ISDA Credit Derivatives Definitions.[8]

In figure 2.2, we illustrate the payment structure in a CDS transaction in the case of default and non-default for unfunded and funded transactions. The payoff structure is fairly simple if no credit event occurs. Until maturity, the protection buyer pays a protection fee (the premium payment) to the protection seller. At maturity, the contract expires without any compensation payments. Only if a credit event occurs, the protection seller has to compensate the protection buyer for the loss via physical or cash settlement.

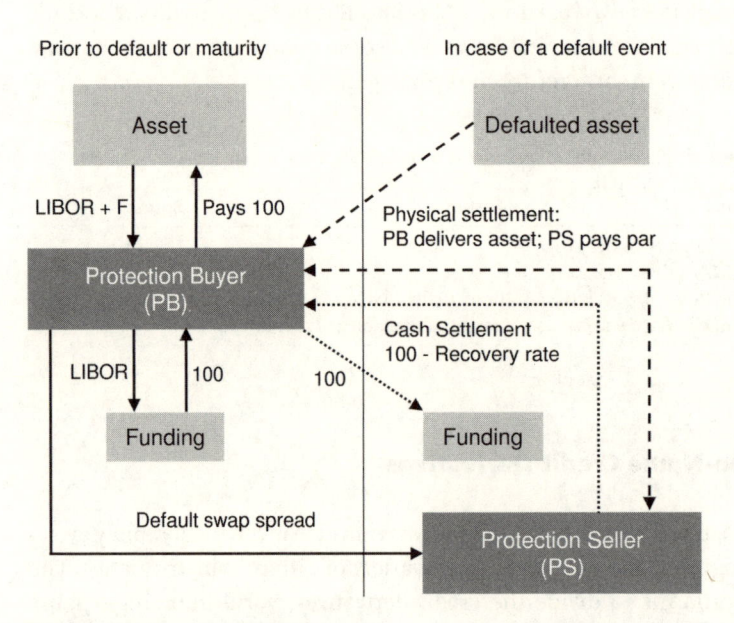

Fig. 2.2: Payoff profile of a CDS

In a standardized contract, credit events are defined as follows:

- *Bankruptcy, filing for protection*: The company becomes insolvent; that is, it is unable to pay its debts. Creditors are protected via the bankruptcy process (for non-sovereigns only).
- *Failure to pay*: This means failure of the reference entity to make payments due following a grace period to avoid accidental triggering due to an administrative mistake. Failed payments have to amount to at least US$ 1 mn.
- *Restructuring*: This event refers to changes in the debt obligations of the reference entity. Restructured liabilities or debt have to amount to at least US$ 10 mn. In the US documentation, modified restructuring is the standard practice, including the so-called modified restructuring limitation

(the maximum maturity of deliverable obligations equals thirty months). In Europe, modified-modified restructuring is the market standard. This means that deliverable obligations comprise only those that are not involved in the restructuring. (For a more detailed description please refer to the *ISDA 2003 Credit Derivatives Definitions*[8]).
- *Repudiation, moratorium*
- *Obligation default, obligation moratorium*

However, an increasing number of contracts exclude restructuring as a credit event due to legal problems and discrepancies in the exact definition.

In general, the protection premium is paid on a quarterly basis and is measured in basis points of the notional amount. Following a credit event, the default swap contract can be settled in two ways, by physical or cash settlement.

In case of physical settlement, the protection buyer delivers the defaulted asset to the protection seller and receives the par value in cash within thirty days (the settlement period). Physical settlement has become the market standard. The advantage of physical settlement is that there is no need to determine the market price (recovery value) in the case of a credit event.

In case of cash settlement, the protection buyer receives the par value minus the recovery value of the reference credit in cash. The recovery value is the result of a dealer poll two to three weeks after the credit event (so that the recovery value can stabilize), while liquidity constraints complicate the price determination.

With respect to regulation issues, many regulatory bodies play a role in the CDS market across different regions and markets. Besides regulatory mechanisms from the Basel Committee, the NAIC (National Association of Insurance Commissioners), the Financial Accounting Standards Board (FASB), and rating agencies can have an impact on the economics of a CDS. They can affect the price and also have an impact on the divergence between credit default swaps and cash bond spreads.

Based on the *ISDA 2003 Credit Derivatives Definitions*,[8] a standard documentation has been developed, which defines the legal framework of CDS contracts. This includes basic terms like the reference entity, the definition of credit events, deliverable obligations, and settlement terms. The standardization of credit default swap contracts leads to increasing transparency and tradability of contracts. Ahead of the final trade, the protection seller provides an indicative term sheet to guarantee that both counterparties use the same documentation (legal language).

Besides market risks (default risk, migration risk, and spread risk), there is counterparty risk (and settlement risk) in CDS transactions, as credit default swaps are bilateral contracts.

2.5.2 Digital Default Swaps

A *digital default swap* (DDS) is a zero-recovery CDS.[9] In case of a credit event, the protection seller has to pay 100 percent of the notional amount to the protection buyer. That means that the protection seller receives an additional premium for taking the risk of zero recovery (the recovery assumptions in CDS contracts based on non-financials typically amounts to 40 percent) in the default leg. On the other hand, the additional premium, in general, is around 50 percent above the CDS spread. DDS contracts are quite popular in the financials universe. Protection selling via a DDS based on a financial entity generates the same spread income as a CDS on a non-financials entity with a higher default probability, while the loss given default (LGD), however, might be the same. Moreover, using DDS and CDS allows us to bet on the realized recovery value versus the basic assumption of 40 percent recovery rate in plain-vanilla CDS contracts. If an investor expects the recovery value of a specific reference entity to be below 40 percent, selling protection on the CDS and buying protection on the DDS can be an attractive opportunity. If a credit event happens, the investor receives 100 percent of the notional, while he has to pay below 40 percent to the protection buyer of the CDS. This trade generates a profit in case of a credit event. If the PV of this profit exceeds the PV of the negative spread carry (as the DDS premium is above the CDS premium), the trade generates a positive P&L. For a detailed discussion please refer to section 10.6.3.

2.5.3 Equity Default Swaps

An *equity default swap* (EDS) is like a CDS contract, except for one major difference.[10] The trigger event is not a classical credit event (default, failure to pay, or restructuring) but a certain drop of the share price. Most of the contracts are standardized with the threshold levels being fixed at 30 percent (a drop of the share price of 70 percent). The standardized recovery rate is 50 percent. The major elements are:

- *Premium*: The protection buyer pays a premium on a regular basis (quarterly) until maturity if no trigger event occurs.
- *Protection amount*: The protection seller pays the protection amount if a trigger event occurs. In standardized contracts, the recovery value is fixed at 50 percent.
- *Trigger event*: Occurs when the underlying stock price falls below a certain threshold. In standardized contracts this is 30 percent.

The payoff structure of an EDS contract is closely related to that of a CDS contract. The protection seller receives the EDS premium payments until a trigger event occurs, which triggers the conditional payment – the so-called default payment – by the protection seller to the protection buyer. However, there are two differences between EDS and CDS contracts: the trigger event and the recovery payment. An EDS default is triggered if the share price hits a previously specified default barrier, which is usually 30 percent of the share price at initiation of the transaction. This is in contrast to a plain-vanilla CDS, where default is triggered on the occurrence of a credit event, such as bankruptcy, failure to pay, and restructuring. However, since the probability is quite large that the company's stock price will drop more than 70 percent following a credit event, the EDS shows a similar payoff profile to a standard CDS contract.

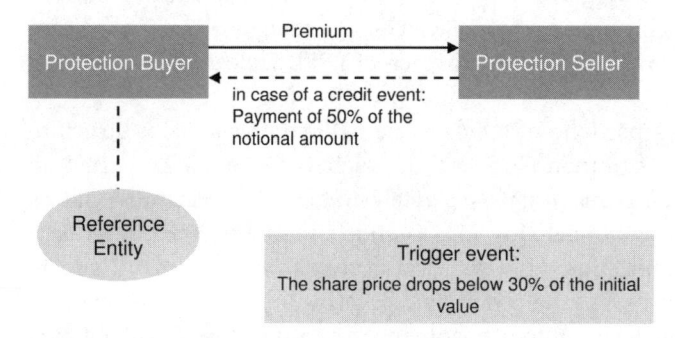

Fig. 2.3: Payoff profile of a (standardized) EDS

The EDS provides protection against a significant drop in the share price and against credit risk (through the correlation between the risk of a jump in stock prices and default events). Hence, the EDS payoff resembles an American-style far-out-of-the-money put option with swap-styled premium payments. Nevertheless, from a contractual point of view, a credit event may occur without an accompanying dip in the share price, triggering the CDS contract but leaving the EDS contract intact, although this outcome is unlikely. On the other hand, the EDS barrier can be triggered without the occurrence of a credit event. Another difference between EDS and CDS contracts is that the conditional payment in an EDS contract is fixed, usually 50 percent of the contract's notional amount, while the loss given default for a standard CDS is unknown in advance, as it is determined by the recovery value of the reference asset.

EDS contracts have already become highly standardized. The trigger event is usually calculated as a drop to 30 percent of the initial share price; the recovery rate is fixed at 50 percent. A rising number of contracts have a time to maturity of five years and the same payment dates as ISDA-based CDS contracts (i.e., March 20, June 20, September 20, and December 20). As an example, the 5Y (30 percent strike price and 50 percent recovery) EDS for DT traded in May 2005 at 85/115 bp, while the corresponding CDS quote is 36/39 bp. These levels indicate the lower liquidity (bid–ask spread) and the higher risk (higher spreads) of EDS compared to CDS contracts.

In a portfolio context, the combination of single-name EDS to portfolio EDS contracts (resembles the development of the iTraxx in CDS markets) provides attractive payoff profiles for investors. This combination comes in two different formats: an index EDS pegged to the value of an equity index, and a basket EDS having a portfolio of single-name EDS, similar to the iTraxx. With the first instrument, default is triggered if the whole index drops to the default barrier; with the second, each single-name EDS can default individually, as in the case with the iTraxx universe. For valuation aspects of an EDS, please refer to section 10.6.1.

A *basket EDS* is a portfolio of single-name EDS contracts. This structure is parallel to that of common CDS baskets, such as iTraxx indices. Instead of trading all portfolio constituents separately, this portfolio derivative allows the investor to trade all underlying EDS contracts in one contract, offering a certain level of diversification. However, default events are triggered on a single-stock basis. For each event the conditional payoff will be settled. In the case of a portfolio of equally-weighted constituents (as in the iTraxx), the notional amount will be reduced by $1/n$ (n denotes the number of constituents) and the spread is paid on the remaining notional amount. This is fully in line with the mechanism implemented in iTraxx contracts.

An *index EDS* is simply an EDS contract on a portfolio of stocks, for example, an equity index such as the DAX. In this contract type, the default event is only triggered if the index (average stock price) drops to the trigger level. Hence, a single-name event is not sufficient.

2.5.4 Recovery Default Swaps

Recovery default swaps (RDS) are contracts which fix the recovery rate at the strike level in a forward-style manner and thus eliminate the recovery risk. At initiation of the contract, the counterparties only fix the strike level and the maturity of the contract. In contrast to CDS contracts, there are no premium payments. In case of a credit event, the contract is settled via physical delivery based on the contracted strike level. If no default event occurs, they expire without any exchange of cash flows. A long position in the RDS with a strike of 40 percent results in a positive payoff if the real recovery rate is above 40 percent. As the contract is forward-styled and not option-styled, it will involve a negative payoff in case the recovery rate is below the strike level. Current market levels for RDS on the iTraxx Europe Benchmark are around 35 to 40 percent. The combination of a CDS and a RDS contract will result in a digital default swap. This structure offers credit default protection with a fixed recovery-on-default, and has thus only uncertainty about the default probability.

2.5.5 Constant Maturity Credit Default Swaps

Against the background of the tight spread valuation in 2003 and 2004, market participants are searching for new variants besides plain-vanilla CDS structures. One of these variants is the *constant maturity credit default swap*, which is a kind of CDS floater that provides insurance against default. The premium payment is reset quarterly and adjusted to the current premium of a plain-vanilla default swap with a fixed maturity (e.g., five years) at a fixed percentage, the so-called participation rate. The constant maturity concept can be easily transferred to all kinds of spread-paying instruments, like constant maturity STCDOs, with CMCDS being the most basic instrument.

A typical CMCDS trade has a 5Y term and references to the prevailing 5Y CDS premium on a quarterly basis during that five-year term. Assuming a participation rate of 65 percent, the protection seller receives 65 percent of the current premium of a 5Y CDS every quarter until the expiration date or until a credit event occurs. If the spread widens, the quarterly premium increases.

Obviously, the pricing of a CMCDS is closely linked to the valuation of a CDS. The concept of a participation rate is the crucial link between both instruments. The most intuitive way to look at CM concepts is using the analogy of the interest rate swaps universe. In equilibrium, the fair level of a fixed rate on a swap equals the present value of floating leg cash flows to the present value of fixed leg cash flows. Based on this concept, the fair participation rate is the rate that equates the present value of payments of a regular CDS to the present value of CMCDS payments.

CMCDS valuation requires determination of the expected payments, which can be derived from implied forward CDS premiums. Then, the cash flows can be projected for both a regular CDS and a CMCDS, which enables us to calculate the participation rate that matches the present value of cash flows of both instruments (for an exact calculation, a convexity adjustment has to be taken into account). If the curve shape and spread levels implied by forwards are realized during the horizon of the contract, the CMCDS and CDS have the same return at maturity. In other words, trading CMCDS versus CDS reflects the view that the forward curve will not be realized. CMCDS are less sensitive to parallel shifts of the CDS curve, but are more sensitive to a flattening or steepening of the credit curve.

2.6 Portfolio Credit Derivatives

2.6.1 Basket/Index Swaps – iTraxx Europe Benchmark

The merger between iBoxx Ltd and Trac-x LLc in 2004 created a new entity, the International Index Company (IIC). IIC includes the iBoxx cash indices and the credit derivative index business of iBoxx and Trac-x in Europe, in the US, and in Asia. The label for the bond indices is iBoxx, while the derivatives indices are known as iTraxx, which is the most liquid, transparent, and popular portfolio CDS. The iTraxx index family offers exposure to the whole euro-denominated credit universe, including investment-grade and high-yield names. Given the high liquidity of the index family, investors are able to implement several strategies. Besides taking directional market risk, the index family offers opportunities for hedging activities (on a macro level) and allows relative value plays between the overall market and single sectors, between different sectors, or between different market segments (subordinated versus senior financials, high grade versus high yield).

The so-called Master Index is the iTraxx Europe Benchmark, which includes the 125 most liquid names in the credit default swap universe. CDS volumes of single names through a dealer poll define liquidity, while the index composition is administered by the IIC. The iTraxx Europe cannot be characterized as an index due to the fact that no index level is calculated by the IIC. It is rather a basket of single names that acts as the underlying for several swap and tranche products.

Quoted prices for these products are a result of supply and demand within credit markets. However, Markit, the leading provider for credit default swap levels, provides market quotes for the underlying index constituents. All 125 names are equally weighted for simplicity reasons. This means that the iTraxx Europe Benchmark is built as a diversified credit index rather than as a tracking instrument for investors who want to replicate the cash credit market. The index is tradable unfunded (in CDS format) and funded (as a note issued by iBond Securities Plc and rated by S&P and Moody's), with standard maturities of one,

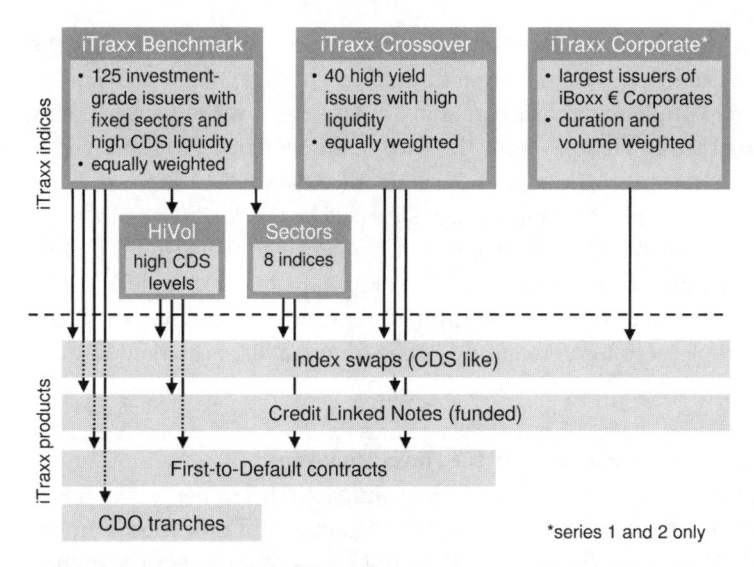

Fig. 2.4: Overview of the iTraxx universe

three, five and ten years for the swap and five years for the note. There is a new series of the index every six months. The first two series, however, have a different maturity profile to bring the iTraxx Europe Benchmark in line with its counterparts in Asia and the US.

The portfolio construction rules are based on the following criteria. Each market maker submits a list of 200 to 250 European-listed names which have had the highest CDS trading volume over the previous six months, excluding internal transactions. The volumes of names that have the same ticker on Bloomberg but trade separately in the CDS market (e.g., Arcelor and Arcelor Finance) are added together to determine the overall issuer volume. Thus, all market makers send a list ranked by issuer volume to the index provider, who excludes all names rated BBB– and Baa3 with a negative outlook. As the number of constituents per sector remains fixed across all iTraxx series (e.g., twenty telecommunication, media and technology [TMT] issuers), the most liquid names within each sector are allocated to the respective index until all subindices are full. This means that the index always contains twenty TMT issuers, even if more than twenty names with the highest trading volume stem from this sector. Regardless of the trading volumes, all constituents within the overall index and single sectors are equally weighted.

The iTraxx Europe Benchmark is the most liquid product within the index family, which provides a broad-based exposure to European credits. The index does not include non-European names, with General Electric being the most popular exclusion. Given its well-diversified character, the iTraxx Europe could be used to implement basic core–satellite strategies, with the index being the basic exposure to credits. With the help of single-name CDS and sector subindices, a strategic sector view as well as a fundamental bottom-up view could be implemented. Moreover, the index will be the leading instrument for portfolio hedges, not only for credit portfolio managers but also for trading desks and treasury activities. Since the iTraxx Europe acts as the underlying for standardized tranches, options, and futures, also correlation traders will use the index to implement trade ideas and hedge for directional (market) risk.

> **Excursus 2: Credit Linked Notes in the iTraxx Universe**
>
> On May 25, 2005, the International Index Company (IIC) issued three iTraxx notes. These credit linked notes (CLN) refer to Series 3 of the iTraxx Europe Benchmark, HiVol, and Crossover indices and have a time to maturity of five years. The notes, which are collateralized by AAA-rated *Pfandbriefe* for the Europe and the HiVol and with repo collateral for the Crossover, are issued by iBond Securities Plc, a Dublin-based special purpose vehicle (SPV). Currently, the issued amount is €500 mn per note. However, the notes are designed to be flexible and the notional amount can be increased or reduced. IIC intends to list the notes on the Irish Stock Exchange.
>
> - The CLNs for the funded iTraxx Europe Benchmark and iTraxx Europe HiVol are structured as floating rate notes with quarterly coupon payments and are both indexed to the 3M-Euribor. The EUR Benchmark bond pays a spread of 40 bp, while the HiVol pays 80 bp. However, these spreads differ slightly from the quoted deal spreads of the Series 3 of the respective iTraxx basket swaps (iTraxx Europe Benchmark is 35 bp and iTraxx Europe HiVol 60 bp). This difference stems from the fact that spreads are adjusted such that the respective contracts are issued close to par. For example, the iTraxx Europe Benchmark traded at around 35 bp on March 20, 2005 (the roll date into Series 3), which is close to the 35 bp in the unfunded swap contract, while it was around 40 bp at the end of May 2005.
> - The CLN for the iTraxx Europe Crossover is a fixed rate bond with a current coupon of 6.25 percent, which is paid semi-annually.

> While the maturity date for all three issues is June 20, 2010, the final redemption payments will be delayed until July 5, 2010, to allow for a credit observation period (see below). The IIC intends to issue a new series every six months, which parallels the periodical rolls of the underlying iTraxx swaps.

2.6.2 Default Baskets

Default baskets perfectly mirror the basic mechanism behind the whole credit derivative world and provide a good means to show the function and application of credit derivatives. A basket default swap is similar to a credit default swap in which the credit event is linked to a certain number of defaults in the underlying basket of credits. In the following section, we concentrate our analysis on the most liquid basket products such as first-to-default baskets (FTD). The more general concept of nth-to-default baskets are interesting from a theoretical point of view, while $n > 2$ is rare in practice. However, default baskets are the most popular so-called correlation instrument, as pricing depends not only on the spread level of the constituents but also on the joint default probability (default correlation) of the basket members.

Regarding the mechanism of a first-to-default basket, the legal construction as well as the trigger events are similar to a single credit default swap. In contrast to the CDS, a basket contains a limited number of single reference credits (in general between three and ten), and the protection buyer pays a regular premium to the protection seller.

There are two major underlyings in basket products, sovereign debt and corporate credits. In the following, we refer to the latter as it covers risk more comprehensively (all risk components of a sovereign basket are contained in a credit basket but not vice versa). In the case of a trigger event (failure to pay, bankruptcy, restructuring), the protection seller pays par value minus recovery value of the defaulted issue to the protection buyer, given a cash-settlement agreement (the calculation agent calculates the recovery price and the protection seller pays the protection buyer an amount equal to par minus recovery value). In the case of a physical settlement, the protection buyer hands over deliverable obligations and receives the notional amount. Following the first default, the FTD contract is terminated and the protection buyer loses any further protection for the other basket constituents. As the protection buyer is only insured against the first default, the basket spread is below the sum of the CDS levels of all basket credits.

A basket is attractive for both counterparties, as protection is cheaper compared to using CDS on single names, while the protection seller generates additional spread (leveraged exposure to a basket of credits) as it enables the investor to earn a higher yield than any of the credits in the basket. In other words, the investor is increasing his return without increasing the exposure to credit risk! A leveraged investment could also have regulatory advantages, and investors who are usually only allowed to take on investment-grade exposure could increase their risk position without moving down the credit curve to the high-yield spectrum. In any case, the protection seller has to closely monitor his delta and gamma positions (gamma is defined as the sensitivity of the delta to spread changes), as these are highly sensitive to price changes of the underlying credits and could be understood as additional risk components.

The investor of a default basket is also exposed to spread swings (as he carries a short position in credit risk), which could be hedged by selling protection via CDS. In case the spread of one or more portfolio constituents changes, the protection buyer's initial position is over or underhedged. For the implementation of optimal hedging strategies, the hedge ratio needs to be determined, and this requires knowing the spread delta of the position. Besides the problem of determining portfolio Greeks, using historical data, or modeling those stochastic processes, in case of a default of one basket constituent, negative effects on the spread of the remaining issues could cause a loss when the position is unwound. Another possibility for an investor in an FTD to hedge against default is to buy protection for a combination of nth-to-default baskets, including similar credits. The problem of this strategy is to find counterparties who are willing to sell protection on similar baskets.

Besides the difficulty of determining sensitivities for a delta hedge, hedgers via long protection also carry a long position in gamma (sensitivity of the delta in respect to spread changes). In case of spread widening of a basket credit, the delta will rise and the basket is overhedged. Hence, the hedger will try to sell protection at wider levels. In case of narrowing spreads, the basket is underhedged and the hedger will buy back protection at lower levels. Accelerating spread volatility favors the hedger and could help to compensate for the negative carry of a hedged FTD basket. The possibility of dynamic hedging, however, is overestimated, as adjustment trades to spread changes are limited because of the (at least for the time being) lack of liquidity for individually structured products and CDS on exotic names in secondary markets. In addition, because of the small deal size of baskets (single-digit million figure), dynamic hedging requires to sell or buy credit risk in very small portions (e.g., €20,000), which is not realistic. Maturity mismatch could be another problem as CDS markets lose significant liquidity in non-standardized maturities.

2.6.3 Standardized iTraxx Tranches

The evolving market for securitization of credit risk emerged in the mid-1990s and includes a broad variety of instruments. Besides the overall asset backed securities market (ABS, RMBS, CDO, CDO squared, etc.), synthetic CDOs have emerged as a major segment. The field of synthetic CDOs have gained enormous popularity, being the most fertile area of growth and innovation in the structured credit markets. Synthetic CDOs have contributed to as well as benefited from the explosive growth in the use of single-name CDS. From their initial application as a mechanism of risk transfer from bank balance sheets to manage regulatory capital requirements, they now encompass every facet of credit risk covering a wide range of assets from corporate bonds and loans, structured finance obligations, and CDO tranches themselves.

In the following, we focus on the most liquid part of the CDO universe, standardized tranches of the iTraxx universe. From the perspective of actively managing credit portfolios, liquidity and transparency are necessities for optimizing portfolios and implementing hedging strategies. Although a rising number of so-called bespoken transactions have been executed since the last few years, iTraxx tranches are by far the most liquid instrument, which is quoted by almost thirty market makers.

Based on the iTraxx Europe Benchmark, the iTraxx family even comprises a series of tradable and standardized tranches which offer leveraged exposure to the European high-grade credit market. Besides taking long positions, shorting tranches is also possible. Single-tranche CDOs (STCDOs) offer a very efficient way to hedge credit risk, while being the most appropriate instrument to reduce or eliminate correlation risks.

The tranches are split into the categories: 0–3% (Equity), 3–6% (BBB), 6–9% (AAA), 9–12% (Junior Super Senior Low), 12–22% (Junior Super Senior High) and 3–100% (Investment Grade), with the percentage related to total loss. This means that in case five names out of the index universe experience a credit event at a recovery value of 40 percent, the first loss piece is still intact since total loss is only 2.4 percent. A new series is launched every six months, while future attachment points could change in line with the risk profile of the underlying index. From a risk and return profile, iTraxx tranches equal other investment-grade CDOs. The most important difference is high liquidity in iTraxx tranche products, while synthetic CDOs are rather a buy-and-hold investment. While all

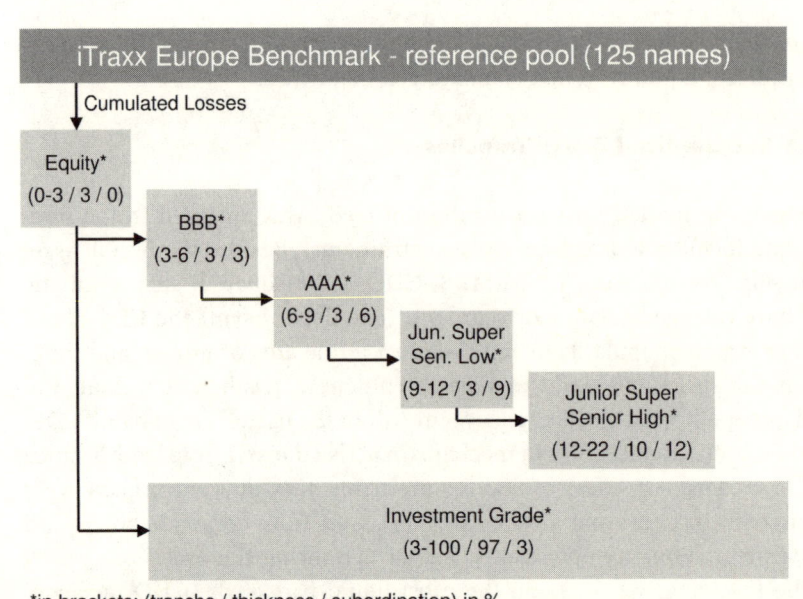

```
┌─────────────────────────────────────────────────────────┐
│  iTraxx Europe Benchmark - reference pool (125 names)   │
└─────────────────────────────────────────────────────────┘
       │ Cumulated Losses
       ▼
┌──────────┐
│ Equity*  │
│(0-3/3/0) │──┐
└──────────┘  │  ┌──────────┐
              └─▶│  BBB*    │
                 │(3-6/3/3) │──┐
                 └──────────┘  │  ┌──────────┐
                               └─▶│  AAA*    │
                                  │(6-9/3/6) │──┐
                                  └──────────┘  │  ┌───────────┐
                                                └─▶│ Jun. Super│
                                                   │ Sen. Low* │
                                                   │(9-12/3/9) │──┐
                                                   └───────────┘  │  ┌──────────────┐
                                                                  └─▶│ Junior Super │
                                                                     │ Senior High* │
                                                                     │(12-22/10/12) │
                                                                     └──────────────┘

          ┌───────────────────────────────────────────────┐
          │           Investment Grade*                    │
          │           (3-100 / 97 / 3)                     │
          └───────────────────────────────────────────────┘
```

*in brackets: (tranche / thickness / subordination) in %

Fig. 2.5: The tranche spectrum of the iTraxx

tranches above the equity piece are quoted in standard spread terms, the price quotation for the 0–3% tranche is quite different. An iTraxx equity tranche always pays a constant spread of 500 bp on the (remaining) notional amount, while market makers quote a percentage of the notional amount that has to be paid as an upfront payment when entering into such a contract as a protection buyer. As tranche pricing is highly complex and directly linked to several risk factors (directional market moves, implied correlation, recovery assumptions, spread volatility, etc.), iTraxx tranches offer an attractive opportunity for pure credit derivative players rather than for credit portfolio managers.

2.6.4 Spread Options

Standardized spread options are already traded in the market place. They offer the opportunity of more complex hedging and trading strategies which generate interesting payoff structures. A liquid option market allows investors to implement their views on credit markets in a more leveraged way and to actively trade and hedge spread volatility. The underlying for the option can either be single-name credit risk or CDS baskets, such as the iTraxx. However, an exact definition of an investor's risk positions (the Greeks: delta, gamma, vega, and theta) requires an appropriate pricing model. As this class of instruments is rather new, we include a short introduction to credit options.

The universe of credit options covers a wide range of instruments: bond options, options on single-name and portfolio CDS contracts (so-called credit default swaptions), and even options on correlation products, such as FTD baskets and CDO tranches. To better understand the structure of the instruments, it is helpful to classify the options into the following categories:

- According to the type of underlying (bond, asset swap package, single-name CDS, CDS index, FTD basket, or CDO tranche), including the definition of the strike level (price or spread-based strike for bond options)
- Whether it includes default protection or not (knock-out-on-default feature)
- The payoff profile (i.e., call or put options)
- The option style (European, Bermudan, or American)
- The settlement style (cash or physical delivery)
- The moneyness (at, in, and out of the money)
- Whether it is an outright or an embedded option (i.e., callable or putable CDS contracts).

The first two categories are specifically related to the credit market, while the latter are quite common in all option markets.

Bond options can be considered the least standardized category among the credit options universe, since there are a lot of underlyings available: fixed rate bonds, floating rate notes, asset swap packages, and so on. In addition, most bond options appear in the form of embedded options. With increasing liquidity, the market attracts arbitrageurs who isolate mispriced embedded options and sell them in the market. This resulted in a more appropriate pricing of bonds, which include option features. Moreover, these options often include the default risk in addition to the spread risk, since the option can also be executed in case of a credit event. The valuation depends on whether the strike is defined as a price or as a spread. Price-based option also includes interest rate risk, since the price of a fixed rate bond also depends on the risk-free yield curve. Spread-based options often refer to floating rate notes or asset swap packages.

Credit default swaptions on iTraxx indices are of central interest and they can be considered to be options on CDS contracts. A call (protection) credit default swaption refers to an option to buy protection at a specified CDS rate at maturity and are also called payer default swaptions, while a put (protection) option refers to selling protection (a.k.a. receiver default swaptions). The most common and therefore most liquid contracts are 3M-into-5Y European-styled swaptions, which means that the option expires in three months and will deliver a 5Y CDS contract. For liquid names, they are quoted for a string of strike rates, which allows for the valuation of out-of-the-money options.

The most important feature of standard single-name CDS options is that they offer protection against spread changes and not against default risk, as most of these CDS swaptions are so-called knock-out-on-default contracts. On the other hand, index spread options (e.g., on the iTraxx Europe Benchmark) do not have such a knock-out-on-default feature, as these contracts will survive a credit event in the underlying pool. The owner of a call option can just buy protection on the rest of the index for the previous fixed strike rate. Thus, default protection is also excluded for index options. Moreover, market participants are starting to trade options on FTD baskets and CDO tranches, which refers to correlation options.

In general, a liquid market in the underlying (bonds, CDS, or correlation products) is a prerequisite for a liquid option market, since market participants have to hedge their option exposure by trading the underlying – as is done in plain-vanilla equity option markets. This is usually done by delta hedging, using a pricing model. Analogous to the interest rate swaption market, option prices can be quoted in terms of implied Black-Scholes volatilities.

2.6.5 Future Contracts

The introduction of Future contracts based on iTraxx indices is planned in 2006. Although the final construction has not been officially announced yet, the goal is to create a highly liquid derivative instrument that offers the opportunity to build up or reduce exposure to credit risk in an efficient way. The design of the contract (expiration dates, price quotation, etc.) will be closely linked to Eurex standard futures, like Schatz, Bund, Bobl, and Buxl contracts.

2.7 Outlook on Product Development

Despite the issuance of subordinated bonds and PIK notes, the innovative power of the plain-vanilla cash market is clearly limited. While we do not exclude the development of new tailor-made hybrid issues, the lack of standardization will prevent the establishment of an important market segment with respect to the size of outstanding instruments. The product development in the cash bond market will remain driven by market trends (as was the case for hybrid issues which benefited from an overall bullish sentiment in the second half of 2004 and the first half of 2005) rather than by pent-up demand for new structures. While the underlying bond market matures, fresh ideas in the credit derivatives spectrum will continue to attract investors' attention and generate additional demand for credit risk.

As an accelerating number of market participants will enter the credit derivatives market (when they have solved their internal risk management and regulatory issues), the strong growth of credit derivatives markets will persist in the coming years. This will be accompanied by the ongoing development of new instruments. While plain-vanilla derivatives will experience rising liquidity, there are a couple of exotic derivatives that are tailor-made instruments. While these exotics will be traded by only a few investors (hedge funds, etc.), the trend towards standardization of equity default swaps, digital default swaps, recovery default swaps, and spread options will continue. The major trends in portfolio derivatives and liquid correlation products in the iTraxx spectrum will be the introduction of various maturities in line with single-name CDS contracts (1Y, 2Y, 3Y, 5Y, 7Y, 10Y). Given the establishment of correlation as an own asset class, the next step in the evolution of correlation markets might be the introduction of options on synthetic STCDOs, enabling investors to trade the volatility of correlation.

The most common instrument in the derivatives world will be introduced in the iTraxx universe, too. As mentioned above, the IIC plans a future contract on iTraxx indices, without officially having announced many details yet. We expect that an iTraxx future contract will be strongly appreciated by the investor base, as it provides a high degree of liquidity and offers a simple way to gain exposure to directional spread risk. Hedging will become much easier using a future contract, and the standardized contract will offer the opportunity to implement cross asset arbitrage trades, including equity, interest rates, and credit futures.

The enlargement of already liquid portfolio derivatives across the whole maturity curve (1Y to 10Y contracts as is the case for single-name CDS) allows investors to actively trade the overall credit curve, which is already the case in the interest rate market. While duration-neutral hedging strategies can be easily implemented if the whole credit curve can be traded, standardized forward contracts can also be introduced.

From a practical point of view, there is a broad range of highly interesting instruments. However, the focus will remain on liquid products, which serve hedging needs, trading activities, and the exploitation of arbitrage opportunities for a larger number of credit players.

Recovery swaps will significantly gain in importance, especially in a bearish market environment. Besides the probability of default, the loss given default is a key parameter in credits, defining the expected loss. Consequently, long positions in credit risk include recovery risk, which can be easily eliminated by using recovery swaps. In an environment of declining credit quality and rising default rates, recovery risk will become a major topic in case of a higher probability of default.

From a portfolio manager's point of view, hedging a credit portfolio with minimized transaction costs requires a liquid option market. As buy-and-hold investors are not bothered by limited spread moves, a more pronounced spread widening can trigger immense losses from a marked-to-market perspective. Spread options are an attractive tool to protect credit portfolios from lasting negative spread trends. From a trading perspective, credit options offer the opportunity to trade spread volatility. We think that the spread volatility market will achieve the same meaning as is the case in equity markets. However, standardization is crucial to increase liquidity and provide transparent pricing with low bid–offer spreads.

Equity default swaps and digital default swaps will gain in importance as they offer the ability to implement (capital) arbitrage strategies and an attractive risk-and-return profile from a single-instrument perspective. Real money accounts will enter the debt–equity playground, as total return strategies become more attractive in the aftermath of the bursting of the equity bubble in 2000 and 2001. DDS are attractive instruments in arbitrage strategies (CDS versus EDS versus DDS) and offer a more attractive risk–return profile than CDS for specific obligors. Especially for issuers who have a safe-haven status (governments, financials, and high-quality corporates), a DDS pays a spread pickup while the probability of default is almost zero.

Last but not least, well-known concepts from the credit derivatives side will be transfered to linked asset classes. This includes trigger baskets (a default basket based on EDS) as well as simple FTD structures on obligors from the agencies or collateralized debt spectrum.

3
Company and Debt Instrument Analysis

Dr. Felix Fischer, CFA,
and Dr. Sven Kreitmair, CFA
Co-Heads Corporate Credit Research
HVB Corporates & Markets

In this chapter, we focus on the credit analysis for non-financial companies. We first introduce the evaluation process for an issuer and close with the evaluation of a specific debt instrument. The ultimate goal of credit analysis is to attain an assessment of a debt issuer and/or a debt issue. A specific risk assessment (rating or score) should in theory indicate the same credit risk across countries, industries, sectors, and accounting regulations. Nevertheless, an assessment is in the end an opinion and can differ among agencies and analysts. In general, an issuer assessment evaluates the capacity and willingness to meet financial commitments, and an issue rating is the creditworthiness of a specific financial obligation (loan, bond) or derived instrument (CDS). First, we focus on the industry and issuer assessment process, using a methodology similar to those used by the rating agencies in their respective rating processes. Usually, the rating consists of a combination of sovereign risk, business risk, and financial risk, as indicated in table 3.1. In general, in the investment-grade category, the business risk and financial risk factors are weighted fairly evenly. This is in contrast to the sub-investment-grade category, where financial risk factors are weighted more heavily and ultimately dominate at the lower end of the spectrum.

Tab. 3.1: Corporate credit issuer rating analysis

Sovereign risk and government-related issuers	Business risk	Financial risk
Baseline default risk	Industry characteristics	Financial policy
Supporting government rating	Competitive position	Financial flexibility
Default dependence and correlation	Management	Profitability and earnings protection
Degree of support		Cash flow protection
		Capital structure

Active Credit Portfolio Management. J. Felsenheimer, P. Gisdakis, and M. Zaiser
Copyright © 2006 WILEY-VCH Verlag GmbH & Co. KGaA, Weinheim
ISBN: 3-527-50198-3

3.1 Sovereign Risk and Government Support

To start the corporate credit evaluation process, the analyst first has to know the relationship of the corporate to its sovereign. In this chapter, we want to introduce the main points to take into account when dealing with *sovereign risk* and *government support* and their relation to a corporate credit rating. There are two general rules of thumb: (1) In emerging markets, the local currency corporate rating is capped at the sovereign foreign currency rating. The reason is that in a scenario where inflation, currency devaluation, or fiscal crisis causes the government to default on its foreign currency debt, usually the corporate issuer is also unable to service its debt. (2) Without a guarantee or other form of formal support arrangement, a state-owned corporate issuer does not intrinsically carry the same level of credit risk as its sovereign owner. Nevertheless, state ownership can bolster a company's credit profile through implicit support.

In this connection, Moody's in April 2005 presented a systematic approach to this topic in its paper "Application of Joint Default Analysis to Government Related Issuers".[11] The approach comprises the following steps: (1) the assessment of the baseline default risk, which measures the likelihood that the issuer will require an extraordinary bailout; (2) the supporting government's rating is examined; (3) an estimate of default correlation between the two entities is made; (4) the degree of government support or the likelihood that the government will step in and bail out a debt issuer, is weighted. Typical attributes of state support include: percentage of state ownership, privatization status, governance and business model, political tolerance for government intervention and support, national importance of the issuer, and possible sources of delays in providing support. Prominent examples of firms with low or medium government support are EADS, Finmeccanica, Volkswagen, Deutsche Post, Deutsche Telekom, France Telecom, Electricité de France, SAS, Statoil, and Fortum.

3.2 Business Risk

The business risk assessment comprises the non-financial aspects of credit analysis. The non-financial analysis starts top-down with the industry risk assessment. The company-specific analysis focuses on the competitive position of the respective firm within the industry. Furthermore, the quality of the management has to be assessed. While, in general, a scoring model might be used to quantify the business risk, the exact weighting of the different factors is challenging, as certain factors may be more or less important for the respective firms. For example, the litigation risk of the tobacco industry is crucial when analyzing US tobacco companies and hence should have a high weighting, whereas litigation risks are of low importance for food retailers.

The industry risk assessment encompasses several factors such as cyclicality, competitive landscape, risks of technological changes, and the legal and regulatory environment.

In general, a low degree of cyclicality is favorable as companies that operate in a stable environment have more predictable cash flows. In addition, a company in a cyclical environment has to be in a stronger financial position to weather a cyclical downturn, which usually leads to weaker cash flows and a deterioration of its financials. However, also an upswing can be problematic as companies often tend to pursue exaggerated investments at high prices (multiples are usually higher). A good example is the steel industry. In addition, an upswing of the industry often leads to additional working capital requirements, as rising sales and increased capacity utilization normally lead to rising inventory levels and higher sales receivables. On the positive side, cyclical companies in an upswing often are able to rapidly improve their financial profile. To assess the degree of cyclicality, past industry sales figures and projected industry growth rates (over several years) are useful.

The Porter model[12] is a helpful tool to evaluate the competitive landscape of the industry. The analysis focuses on five industry forces: rivalry, power of suppliers, power of customers, barriers to entry or threat of new entrants, and threat of substitutes. Rivalry within the industry is determined by:

- *The number of firms within the industry*: In general, the larger the number of firms, the higher the degree of rivalry. Rivalry intensifies if the firms have similar market shares. For example, the fragmented cement industry in Germany experienced a drastic price decline until HeidelbergCement became the clear market leader following a medium-sized acquisition. Previously, no clear market leader had been established, with Dyckerhoff and HeidelbergCement both having had similar market shares.
- *Market growth*: The lower the market growth, the higher the degree of rivalry within the industry, as firms are only able to grow by increasing their market share. In industries with high growth rates, firms increase their revenues simply by industry growth. An example of an industry with a low level of growth and a very high level of rivalry is the stagnating German do-it-yourself (DIY) market.
- *Fixed cost base*: The higher the fixed cost base, the higher the rivalry. In order to attain efficient production, firms in an industry with a high fixed cost base must try to maximize their capacity utilization. Accordingly,

firms must sell a large quantity of products, which often leads to price pressure.
- *Level of product differentiation*: The lower the degree of product differentiation, the higher the rivalry as the only effective parameter is the price.
- *Switching costs*: The lower the switching costs from one product to another, the higher the degree of rivalry as customers can easily switch from one firm to another.
- *Exit barriers*: High exit barriers exist if the costs for abandoning a product are high. A common exit barrier is asset specific. Asset-specific characteristics make it difficult for the respective firm to sell assets as these are highly specialized. Also regulatory requirements can lead to high exit barriers resulting in increased rivalry.

The power of suppliers in general is determined by:
- *The number of suppliers*: In general, the fewer the suppliers in an industry the stronger their bargaining power. For example, there are only four suppliers of petroleum needle coke, which is the raw material for carbon electrodes. Having few suppliers puts additional pressure on companies in need of this raw material. However, this problem is mitigated by the fact that only two major producers for electrodes exit.
- *Threat of backward integration of customers*: If customers have the ability to pursue a backward integration strategy, it puts pressure on suppliers to keep prices at reasonable levels, as too high prices would lead to the entrance of new market participants.
- *Threat of forward integration of suppliers*: If suppliers have the capability to pursue a forward integration strategy, they tend to be strong as the customers will want to avoid new competitors coming to the market.
- *Degree of supply complexity*: If the product that is supplied tends to be complex and cannot be easily replaced suppliers tend to be more powerful as there are fewer alternatives and switching suppliers is more difficult.

The power of customers is determined by similar factors as those defining the power of suppliers. Hence, the total number of customers, the threat of backward integration, the degree of forward integration, and the costs to switch to other products are the determining factors for the power of buyers. However, the power of customers very often changes during a cycle. Hence, for cyclical industries like the chemical industry, the power of customers also is determined by the phase of the cycle.

The threat of new entrants is determined by:

- *Regulation*: To enter a specific business, governmental permission is often needed. For example, the utility industry is a highly regulated industry. Hence, the threat of new entrants is limited.
- *Technological know-how*: If a high degree of specific technological know-how is necessary to operate in a specific sector, high barriers to entry exist. In addition, the technological know-how is often protected by patents. Accordingly, it is often impossible for new entrants to enter the market. An example of a technological wonder with a successful patent is the Polaroid camera.
- *Capital intensity*: A high degree of capital intensity to enter the industry creates high barriers to entry, as new entrants often will not want to enter markets that require a lot of advance capital spending. For example, the cement industry has a high degree of capital intensity, leading to virtually no new entrants.
- *Economies of scale*: If a firm in a certain industry has to generate high sales in order to be profitable, high economies of scale exist: The higher the minimum efficient scale, the higher the barrier to entry as significant investments are necessary in order to operate profitably.

The threat of substitutes is determined by:

- *The product characteristics*: The more unique and complex the product is, the less easily it can be replaced by substitutes. The uniqueness also refers to technology. An industry that faces a significant substitution risk is the German cable sector, where the recently launched DVB-T (terrestrial transmission of TV signals with the possibility to broadcast more than 20 different channels) threatens the prospects of cable companies.
- *Switching costs*: The higher the switching costs to a substitute, the lower their threat. If it is virtually impossible to switch to another product (e.g., in the case of long-term contracts), the threat of substitution is limited.

Figure 3.1 shows an assessment of the competitive landscape of the machine-tool industry.

The faster the technological changes within an industry, the more capital expenditure requirements exist. Firms that fail to keep up with new technologies face the risk of being pushed out of the market as older technologies usually do not meet customer demands. Hence, the failure to invest can cause the exit of certain players. In industries where technologies change rapidly it is vital that the firm is very innovative, being able to offer the best and most attractive products. In addition, strong financial muscles are a success factor, as only

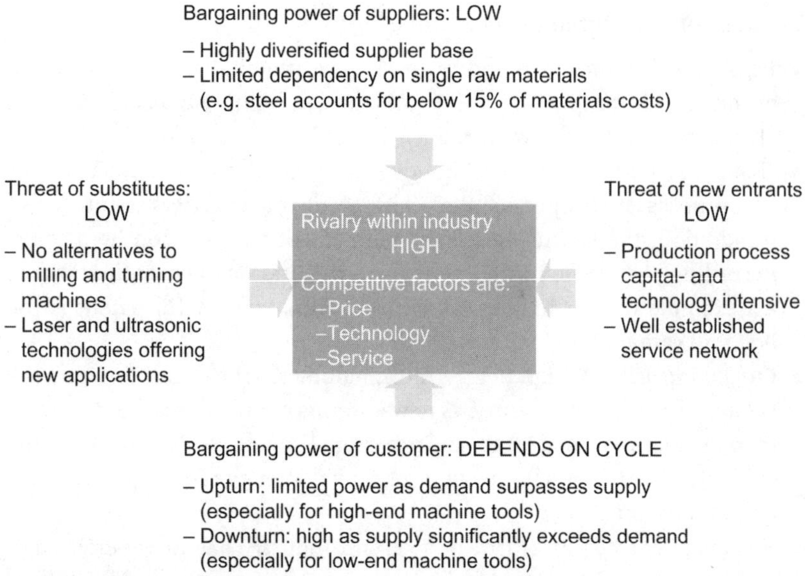

Bargaining power of suppliers: LOW

– Highly diversified supplier base
– Limited dependency on single raw materials
 (e.g. steel accounts for below 15% of materials costs)

Threat of substitutes: LOW	Rivalry within industry HIGH Competitive factors are: –Price –Technology –Service	Threat of new entrants LOW
– No alternatives to milling and turning machines – Laser and ultrasonic technologies offering new applications		– Production process capital- and technology intensive – Well established service network

Bargaining power of customer: DEPENDS ON CYCLE

– Upturn: limited power as demand surpasses supply
 (especially for high-end machine tools)
– Downturn: high as supply significantly exceeds demand
 (especially for low-end machine tools)

Fig. 3.1: Competitive forces of the machine-tool industry

financially sound firms are able to survive the possible failure of one launched new technology and have the capability to launch a heavy capital expenditure program for a new technology.

Assessing the legal and regulatory environment of an industry is also a crucial part of industry analysis. The legal and regulatory environment can be both favorable as well as unfavorable for industry players. In general, regulation that tends to keep competition low is favorable for industry players. An example is the US defense industry, which strictly limits the access of foreign competitors. However, regulation on environmental standards tends to increase risk for a specific industry (e.g., the intended emission rules by the European Community might put significant capex requirements on certain industries). Another element is governmental support for specific industries. Industries that operate in jurisdictions with a high degree of state support tend to have a more favorable risk profile. An example is the European banking industry, which in general has favorable supporting mechanisms. At least as important as the regulatory environment is the legal environment, which can significantly alter industry risk. The following factors should be considered:

- *Jurisdiction*: The jurisdiction is basically the determinant of possible legal contingencies. The amount of claims usually granted, the existence of punitive damages, the court system (particularly jury courts versus judge courts), and possible bonding requirements are to be considered. In this context, the risk of operating in the US is significantly higher than in other jurisdictions. First of all, the compensatory damage awards granted are much higher than those awarded in the rest of the world. Second, the system incorporates the element of punitive damages, which often significantly exceed the compensatory damages, and in contrast to most other jurisdictions are a claim of the damaged party, which motivates people to file claims. Third, the first court level often is made up of jury courts with little or no legal knowledge. Accordingly, decisions often do not have a sound legal background. The necessity in some states of posting a bond to appeal an unfavorable decision further increases the risk of operating in the US. Furthermore, also shareholder lawsuits generally lead to much higher claims than in other jurisdictions. Thus, jurisdiction plays a major role in assessing risk.

- *Type of production*: Depending on the products produced, environmental liabilities can arise. Industries like the chemical or the oil industry have higher risks toward environmental contingencies in comparison to industries like banking.
- *Type of product*: Products that can harm personal health pose a higher risk than products that do not cause health problems. A good example is the US tobacco industry, which faces multi billion-dollar claims due to the health risks associated with tobacco. Pharmaceutical companies and industries having some exposure to asbestos are likewise subject to significant claims. Products that can potentially injure someone, for example, firearms or even cars also carry substantial litigation risks.

After the industry risk assessment has been completed, the company analysis assesses the competitive position of the specific company within the industry as well as its management and corporate strategies.

Factors determining the competitive position within the industry are:

- *Relative size*: The larger a company is (in terms of sales) in comparison to its competitors, the better its ability to pursue a specific strategy. Companies that have the largest size also tend to have the highest pricing power, as the smaller players often tend to follow the pricing policy of the market leader. Being the market leader therefore reflects a successful strategy.
- *Degree of specialization*: If a company is not among the market leaders in terms of size, it should focus on specific niches in which it operates, such as innovative products or a specific relationship to certain customers to

gain a competitive advantage. Firms that neither have critical size nor operate in a specific niche tend to get squeezed out of the market.
- *Relative cost position*: The cost position determines what minimum prices a company has to charge in order to break even. Companies having the lowest break-even point can still operate profitably in an industry environment in which other players incur losses, which eventually can lead to the exit of some firms. Hence, being among the cost leaders determines the ability to master a cyclical downturn.
- *Product quality*: If a firm is not among the cost leaders but if the quality of its products is perceived as higher in comparison to other industry products, the company is able to charge higher prices for its products. Hence, this offsets a relative disadvantage the company may have in terms of its cost position.

To summarize, firms that are either among the market leaders or that operate in successful niches and either are the most cost-efficient or offer the highest product quality tend to have the highest credit quality. In contrast, firms that are *stuck in the middle* and do not have a specific advantage tend to have a lower credit quality. A good example is the automotive industry. The Japanese Toyota is among the world's largest manufacturers (it is the only automotive producer with major positions in Europe, Asia, and North America) and in addition among the cost leaders. Its products are perceived as solid and economical. In contrast to Toyota, Porsche operates solely in the top-end sports car and SUV niche. Its products are perceived as unique, offering market leading quality. Both firms are highly successful and their respective credit quality is high, which leads to low financing costs. In contrast to these two, Ford and General Motors, despite their large size, face both cost and quality problems. Also as a result of high health care costs, both have a significant cost disadvantage in comparison to Toyota. In addition, the products of both are not placed (with a few exceptions) in a specific niche and are not perceived as offering major advantages in comparison to Japanese cars. Hence, both Ford and GM do not offer quality or cost leadership. As a result, their credit quality is significantly below that of Toyota or Porsche.

Assessing the quality of management is among the most difficult tasks of credit analysis. The key challenge lies in differentiating good managers from managers that are just good at presenting an investment story. Managers with good presentation skills are not necessarily good business managers. However, one advantage of managers with good presentation skills is that they will more easily gain access to capital, be it equity or debt. Some items that should be looked at when assessing management capabilities are:

- *Industry expertise*: To evaluate the industry expertise, a closer look at the curriculum vitae of the board is helpful. The average amount of years spent within the industry is an important factor.
- *Track record*: The past track record of management is a good indicator of how likely it is to perform in the future. For listed companies, it is helpful to compare previous guidance given by management with the financial results achieved. Also, the fulfillment of specific promises in the past is a helpful indicator in determining the reliability of management. For example, management that states that it does not plan major acquisitions and then announces a major purchase is not very credible. Also helpful is to check whether statements submitted to equity analysts match the statements submitted to credit analysts. It is a warning signal if separate bondholder and equity conference calls are held. The credit analyst should participate in both calls.
- *Composition of management*: The different positions of management often require different skills. Hence, it is important that management has the right people in the right place. A CEO should have profound industry expertise, high communication skills, and also strong links within the business community. A CFO should be very solid in accounting; a background as an auditor may prove helpful. The COO should have a high degree of expertise in optimizing production and internal processes. Here a background gained at a consulting firm or as a restructuring advisor is helpful; also a background from another industry might be appropriate. For example, it may be suitable for a COO of an industrial company to have a background from a highly efficient automotive firm as he might be able to transfer efficient production processes (like just-in-time) to the industrial company.
- *Interaction of management*: It is also crucial that management interacts efficiently. While this aspect is hard to evaluate, a meeting with management in addition to analyzing the organizational structure of the firm may prove helpful in evaluating how well management interacts.
- *Personal involvement of management*: The higher the equity stake management holds, the higher its interest that a company performs well. A high equity participation of management is particularly supportive for equity-sponsor driven deals, as it is the intention of management to get the company in the shape for an initial public offering (IPO). An IPO normally massively improves the credit quality of the firm, particularly if, as usual, equity is injected as part of the IPO. However, a high management stake in a publicly listed company is not necessarily favorable for

debt investors as management will tend to put even more emphasis on shareholder value (like share buy-backs, special dividends, etc.) in order to improve the equity value.
- *Management compensation*: Depending on the type of compensation, management will try to steer the firm. This may be favorable or unfavorable for bondholders. Here the analyst has to look at the particular goals management has to reach in order to increase its compensation. If, for example, management has incentives to achieve specific sales targets, it is not necessarily positive for bondholders, as the company will most likely pursue an aggressive growth strategy. However, if targets like maximum working capital or an improvement of cash flow levels are used, it is in the best interest of debtholders.

The strategic direction of the firm is determined by its management. To evaluate the strategy, the following topics should be looked at:

- *Diversification*: In general, the higher the degree of diversification, the higher the ability to cope with difficulties in certain areas. A firm that has a diversified customer base from a broad range of industries is better positioned to master a cyclical downturn. Also the revenue share of the largest customers of total revenues is a helpful indicator.
- *Focus*: Does the company strategy focus on price or quality leadership? Market leadership or profitable niches? A stuck-in-the-middle position may lead to competitive pressure.
- *Growth*: Expansion determines the financing needs of a firm. If the strategy is concentrated on external growth, the analyst should look at the way the financing is planned (equity versus debt).

3.3 Financial Risk

In the financial risk analysis part, it is crucial to assess the more qualitative factors: financial policy and financial flexibility of the company. On the quantitative side, further areas to assess are the profitability, the capital structure, and the cash flow generation of the company.

The most important part of the financial policy assessment is the aggressiveness of management. Aggressiveness is, among others, determined by actions like share buy-backs, increased dividend payments, or special dividends. The way acquisitions are financed (debt versus equity) is another indicator of management's aggressiveness. Debt financing is usually detrimental for the company's credit quality. Another concern is the risk tolerance of the company, which can be defined as the maximum debt-leverage the management is willing to take, and the intention to achieve or maintain certain financial performance objectives. Another area of financial policy is the degree of aggressiveness or conservatism of the company's accounting practices. A meeting with management to discuss and assess the commitment to meet and maintain goals is crucial for credit analysis.

Another important measure in determining a corporate rating is the financial flexibility of the company. In general, the degree of the financial flexibility is defined by sustainable, organic, through-the-cycle cash flow generation plus internal sources (e.g., asset sales, reduction of capex and dividends) and external sources (e.g., credit lines, bond and stock markets). Access to capital (debt and commercial paper, equity, insurance coverage) and how it will change in a stress scenario are important. Potential sources of capital are basically the company's cash and cash equivalents position and also its bank credit facilities. With regard to the latter, it is important to consider the type of loan facility (committed or uncommitted), the undrawn amounts, the maturity, the collateral, the restrictiveness of covenants, the notification period, and the quality of the lender. Another factor of financial flexibility is the issuer's debt-maturity profile – which is important, as a heavily short-term-geared maturity profile involves high refinancing risk in a stress scenario. The ability to defer or reduce capex is also important for the company's financial flexibility. An analyst can assess this ability by identifying the necessary maintenance capex level or by comparing the ratio *capex/depreciation* (a ratio above 1 can indicate the ability to reduce capex if necessary) and/or *capex/sales* in an industry comparison or over a certain time horizon. If a company is able to dispose of assets and possesses non-core or discontinued operations or liquid marketable securities, that is a positive factor for its financial flexibility. Usually, large and therefore well-known companies have better access to capital markets and therefore greater financial flexibility. Moreover, the ownership and the affiliation of the issuer must be reviewed, as the shareholder(s) and/or intercompany arrangements can be an important source of capital.

Before we delve into the more quantitative aspects of financial risk analysis, we provide a short introduction on how to read and identify the linkages between the profit and loss statement, the cash flow statement, and the balance sheet (see figure 3.2). An important conclusion in looking at the three parts is that the income statement ends with the net income. The statement of cash flows starts again with this position. *Funds from operations* (FFO) is the result of net income plus non-cash expenses (e.g., depreciation/amortization or increase of provisions), minus non-cash income (e.g., reduction of provisions). The operating cash flow is the sum of FFO plus or minus changes of working capital. The narrow definition of working capital is: inventory plus accounts receivables minus accounts payables. A broader definition of working capital defines working capital as current assets minus current liabilities excluding financial assets and liabilities. The free cash flow, which is available for debt repayments and therefore crucial for the creditworthiness of the company, can be defined as cash flow from operating activities minus capex minus dividends.

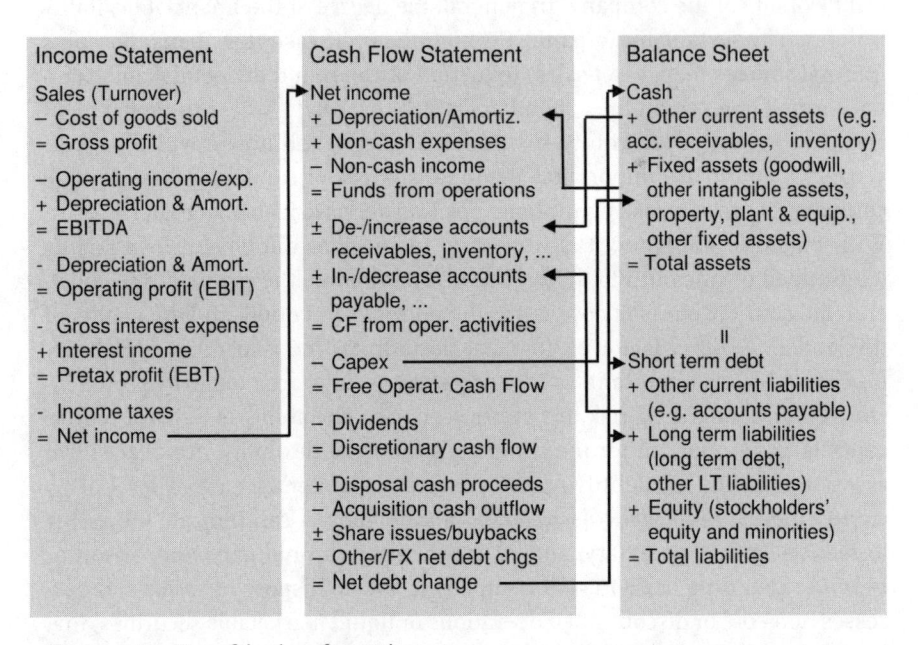

Income Statement	Cash Flow Statement	Balance Sheet
Sales (Turnover) – Cost of goods sold = Gross profit – Operating income/exp. + Depreciation & Amort. = EBITDA – Depreciation & Amort. = Operating profit (EBIT) – Gross interest expense + Interest income = Pretax profit (EBT) – Income taxes = Net income	Net income + Depreciation/Amortiz. + Non-cash expenses – Non-cash income = Funds from operations ± De-/increase accounts receivables, inventory, ... ± In-/decrease accounts payable, ... = CF from oper. activities – Capex = Free Operat. Cash Flow – Dividends = Discretionary cash flow + Disposal cash proceeds – Acquisition cash outflow ± Share issues/buybacks – Other/FX net debt chgs = Net debt change	Cash + Other current assets (e.g. acc. receivables, inventory) + Fixed assets (goodwill, other intangible assets, property, plant & equip., other fixed assets) = Total assets II Short term debt + Other current liabilities (e.g. accounts payable) + Long term liabilities (long term debt, other LT liabilities) + Equity (stockholders' equity and minorities) = Total liabilities

Fig. 3.2: Interaction of the three financial reports

Often EBITDA (earnings before interest, taxes, depreciation, and amortization) is used as a cash flow proxy. The reason for this is that the EBITDA measure is easy to use for calculations and forecasts and also in situations without a cash flow statement. It is used as a standard in capital markets (especially in equity and corporate finance evaluation), and therefore the market reacts to EBITDA-based ratios. However, in contrast to FFO or free cash flow, EBITDA does not include cash outflows for tax, net interest, working capital, capex, and dividends. Moreover, it can be manipulated with non-cash and/or nonrecurring items and can differ due to diverse accounting rules. However, by subtracting interest payments, taxes, acquisitions, capex increases in working capital, and share buy-backs and adding disposal proceeds, equity increases, and decreases of working capital to EBITDA, the change in the net debt position can be approximated (foreign exchange effects have to be considered as well).

The net debt position is calculated as short-term debt plus long-term debt minus cash and cash equivalents. With regard to the cash position, usually only cash equivalents can be counted, which means instruments with a maximum maturity of 90 days. Apart from the net debt position, the linkage between balance sheet and cash flow statement can also be seen at the working capital level. There is also linkage between the income statement and the balance sheet, because net income that is not distributed to shareholders changes the equity position.

In order to derive a rating, it is important to note that all of the following ratios should not be considered separately, but more in the context of a comparison across time (through business cycles) and in comparison with industry peers to reach an accurate conclusion.

The company's earnings power is a critical determinant of credit protection. The profitability and earnings generation indicates the ability to create internal equity capital, to attract external capital, and to withstand business risk. Moreover, the higher the earnings power of the company, the higher the value of the firm's assets and therefore its recovery prospects. Key ratios in this financial risk area are: *return on capital* (in percent), *operating income/sales* (in percent), and *EBIT interest coverage* (multiple). The first ratio measures whether capital (debt plus equity) generates value. The second ratio is used to determine whether revenues are profitable or not. The last ratio indicates whether the profit (before taxes and interest) is sufficient to make the interest payments of the company.

The second set of financial ratios relates to cash flow protection ratios. The *EBITDA interest coverage* indicates how many times EBITDA covers annual interest payments. The shortcoming of this ratio is, as mentioned previously, that EBITDA is only a cash flow proxy. It has to be noted that investment-grade companies generally have ready access to external cash to cover temporary shortfalls. Non-investment-grade companies lack, however, this degree of flexibility and generally have fewer alternatives to internally generated cash for servicing debt. Another important ratio is *FFO/total debt*. FFO is an important measure as it indicates the cash flow generation without fluctuations in working capital, which can be significant in certain heavy goods industrial sectors throughout the year. This is at the same time also the shortcoming of this ratio: It does not measure true cash flow as it ignores ongoing net working capital investment requirements. Another relevant ratio is *free operating cash flow/total debt*. This ratio examines cash flow from operations after capex and is critical to capital-intensive firms and growth companies. It does not include dividend payments, which are most of the time not really discretionary as long as the company is generating net income. It is important to know that strong free cash flow can also be caused by low growth (low working capital needs) or a declining market, in which case there is danger that this high level of cash flow generation might not be sustained. In contrast, high growth companies can have thin or negative cash flows because of high investments and working capital build-ups, which can offer prospects of enhanced protection after the high growth phase. *Total debt/EBITDA* is mostly used in the high-yield sector.

The third section of financial ratios assesses the capital structure, the debt leverage, and the asset protection of the company. The capital structure measures a company's total funding sources and the priority of claims. Moreover, the value of all corporate assets is ultimately measured by their long-term earnings power. In this context, a key ratio is *total debt/capital* (in percent). Capital here is defined as equity plus debt. Companies and equity markets frequently publish and use the *gearing ratio*, which is mostly defined as the ratio of net debt to equity (plus minority interests). In credit analysis, the *equity book value* serves as an indicator of how much of a buffer the company has before it would have to file for insolvency (assuming an insolvency filing has to occur at equity's book value of zero). The disadvantage of this measure is, however, that it is influenced by the discretionary use of different accounting rules and can either overstate or understate the true economic value of this buffer. An alternative measure would therefore be the *market capitalization* of the company, which is basically the enterprise value minus net debt.

3.3.1 Off-Balance-Sheet Adjustments

As not all financial liabilities are disclosed in the financial statement – often due to accounting regulations and discretionary financial management decisions – the analyst has to adjust his ratios for these commitments.

Operating lease adjustments often represent a significant part of the liabilities of a firm, particularly in certain industries like airlines or hotels. In contrast to financial leases, operating leases are not part of the reported liabilities but only discussed in the notes of the financial statement. The adjustments that should be made, in our view, affect the following items (please refer to figure 3.3 for an overview).

Example: ThyssenKrupp AG   FY 2003/04

2004/2005	178
2005/2006	153
2006/2007	132
2007/2008	117
2008/2009	105
thereafter	758
Sum of PV at 10% first 5 years	559
+ NPV rest	362
= NPV total (adjustment to debt)	920
× 10% implicit interest expense	
= Addition (adjustment) to interest expenses	92
Operating lease obligations year 1 (proxy for rent expense)	178
− Implicit interest expense	92
= Addition (adjustment) to depreciation	86

Fig. 3.3: Lease debt adjustment calculations

- *Debt*: As an operating lease contract is similar to a debt-financed on-balance sheet purchase, the debt figure should be adjusted accordingly. We believe that a net present value approach similar to that of S&P is the correct way to adjust financial debt. As a discount factor, it is reasonable to use the average interest rate that a company has to pay. Hence, the lease payments obligations in specific years (part of notes) have to be discounted. For lease payments exceeding five years (usually no exact maturity profile is given for lease obligations exceeding five years), the average maturity of the remaining operating leases can be determined by dividing the lease payments due after five years by the average annual lease obligation for the first five years. This leads to the expected final maturity of the last leasing payment. From this final payment, the average maturity exceeding five years is derived to determine the number of years with which the leasing obligations exceeding five years should be discounted. The following example might clarify this: A company has annual operating lease obligations of 100 in each of the first five years. In addition, the company has 500 operating lease obligations in the following five years. To calculate the average remaining maturity after five years, 500 is divided by the average annual lease obligation of the first five years (100). Then this result (5) is divided by 2 (2.5). This number is then added to 5 to get the number of years ($5 + 2.5 = 7.5$) by which to discount the 500. We do not believe that the $8\times$ leases approach of

Moody's is appropriate. If in a specific year the leasing payments are low as the company entered into a significant new operating lease contract at year's end, this approach significantly underestimates the outstanding leasing obligations. If operating leases are only short term (e.g., only three-year operating lease contracts), the adjustment is too high.
- *Interest expenses and EBIT*: Multiplying the net present value of the operating leases with the discount rate is appropriate to make the interest expense adjustment. As EBIT increases accordingly, margins on an adjusted basis increase.
- *Depreciation, EBITDA, FFO, and FOCF*: As the assets of the operating lease contracts would have to be taken on the balance sheet, they would consequently have to be depreciated. Further assuming that annual investment in these assets would equal depreciation and accordingly amortization of the outstanding principal, the annual lease payment (as a proxy operating lease obligation in year 1 can be used) that is not used for interest payments is added to depreciation. Consequently, the depreciation adjustment increases EBITDA. Also FFO increases as, according to the model, depreciation equals investments. However, as investments increase accordingly, free operating cash flow (operating cash flow minus capex) remains unchanged.

The topic of underfunded defined benefit pensions and other postretirement obligations increased in importance in 2001, 2002, and at the beginning of 2003. The reason was mainly that during this time, equity values and therefore pension plan assets lost value. This, in turn, led to an increasing underfunding status of off-balance-sheet pension plans and caused some US firms to announce plans for substantial pension contributions in order to comply with ERISA (employee retirements income security act) requirements. During this time, credit spreads for companies like General Motors and Ford suffered as investors started to increasingly factor in these liabilities as debt-like. In Europe, most companies have unfunded pensions and therefore do not have any pension plan assets. Consequently, no attention was paid to European names. Nevertheless, in February 2003, S&P reviewed the unfunded postretirement liabilities at more than 500 rated European companies and placed its long-term and some short-term credit ratings on ten European corporates on CreditWatch with negative implications (Arcelor, Michelin, Deutsche Post, GKN, Linde, Pilkington, Portugal Telecom, Rolls-Royce, ThyssenKrupp, TPG N.V.). The agency stated that it would start to view unfunded postretirement liabilities as debt-like in nature, given the future call on cash these liabilities necessarily represent, despite the difficulties of precisely valuing such liabilities and the various estimates involved. Moreover, the agency stated that it believes that the risks arising from such liabilities have increased as a result of intense public debate on stricter funding rules, a continuing rise in health-care costs, ongoing deterioration in equity values, and a weakened global economic environment. S&P adjusts key credit metrics to take into account postretirement liabilities, which effectively reduces the distortion caused by differing funding levels and shifts the focus of the issue to the nature of companies' financial policies. Certain key financial measures (including cash flow to financial liabilities, and capital structure) were adjusted in order to facilitate more accurate comparisons between the companies that faced unfunded postretirement obligations and those that did not. For companies that have material after-tax unfunded postretirement obligations, S&P will increasingly focus on adjusted credit metrics, as these better reflect the debt-like nature of the liabilities. For more details, please refer to S&P's article[13] "Adjusting Financials for Postretirement Liabilities" dated March 3, 2003. HVB Corporate Credit Research uses an approach that is similar to S&P's. As an example, we included our calculations for FY 2003/04 for ThyssenKrupp in figure 3.4. ThyssenKrupp is the most prominent example, which led to a public discussion over rating agencies after S&P's change in its rating methodology and the subsequent downgrade of ThyssenKrupp on February 21, 2003, from BBB to BB+.

In addition to the above-mentioned adjustments, other off-balance sheet liabilities exist, which should be adjusted accordingly:

Example: ThyssenKrupp AG	FY 2003/04
Pension benefit and health-care obligations (funded / unfunded)	8,862
– Plan assets (funded)	1,537
= Deficit	7,325
– Unfunded pension liabilities (= equals mostly pension liabilities on balance sheet)	7,189
= Difference	136
– Tax benefit assumption (35% of difference)	48
= Adjustment 1	88
Pension provisions included in balance sheet	7,189
+ Adjustment 1	88
= Pension liabilities adjustment for debt	7,277

Fig. 3.4: Pension debt adjustment

- *Environmental liabilities and other claims*: If certain environmental liabilities or other claims like cleanup costs exist, the net present value of the expected payments should be added to the financial debt. The cash outflow due to the environmental liabilities will lead to higher debt levels. Even if the exact amount cannot be quantified, the credit analyst should evaluate the outcome of certain scenarios (e.g., court decision or warranty payments) and look at the potential impact on the financials. This is also true for guaranteed debt of other firms where a drawing is likely.
- *Securitization*: If a firm makes use of a sales receivables program, the value of the sold receivables should be added to the debt. While it may be argued that an adjustment should not be made if the sale is non-recourse, often certain credit lines are involved for sales receivables programs. If the business fundamentals deteriorate, banks often cut these lines, as was the case for Rhodia. In addition, a comparison between two firms where one does not make use of a sales receivables program is more meaningful by adjusting these items, as the firm that does not make use of the sales receivables program has an additional source of liquidity.
- *Joint ventures and equity method investment*: Depending on the strategic importance of joint ventures, a pro-rata consolidation of the company's stake in the respective joint venture should be made.
- *Project finance debt*: Often certain projects of a company are financed with project-related debt, usually with special-purpose vehicles (SPVs), which is served by the cash flows of that specific project. This debt does not appear on the balance sheet. While project finance usually is non-recourse, firms often have a high interest in certain projects. Therefore, an adjustment should be considered based on the qualitative assessment of the importance of the project. Consequently, debt as well as cash flows should be adjusted.
- *Purchase commitments*: Purchase commitments usually do not need to be adjusted as these usually refer to purchases that occur in the normal course of business. However, in certain cases an adjustment might be considered. For example, if the company has pursued a take-or-pay contract (for example for industrial gases) and has to make a payment for goods that actually are not of value for the firm, an adjustment might be considered.

In order to calculate *FFO/net debt* (adjusted), we first take the reported FFO and then add the lease adjustment, which was mentioned earlier. We then calculate the reported net debt and add the already mentioned debt adjustments (please refer to figure 3.5). These are, in general, operating lease debt, pension

Example: ThyssenKrupp AG	FY 2003/04
Cash flow from operations	2,559
− Change in working capital	-86
= FFO reported	2,645
+ Lease adjustments (depreciation)	86
= FFO adjusted	2,731
Total debt reported	4,232
− Cash and cash equivalents	1,392
= Net debt reported	2,840
+ Pension adjustments	7,277
+ Operating leases (= NPV total)	920
+ Guarantees, take-and-pay contracts, etc.	0
+ Securitized receivables	1,070
+ Other commitments (e.g. put options)	0
= Net debt adjusted	4,944

Fig. 3.5: Adjustment of FFO and net debt

debt adjustments, and other contingencies. In this way, the analyst arrives at ratios that are adjusted both in the numerator and the denominator.

As the analyst intends to arrive at meaningful, comparable, and consistent debt-adjusted ratios, the other side of the equation also has to be adjusted in order to arrive at meaningful ratios. This is especially true for the adjustment with nonrecurring, one-off and extraordinary items. The most prominent examples are disposal gains or losses, restructuring expenses, and FX gains or losses. The occurrence of these items is largely at the discretion of the company's management and can distort the time comparison analysis as well as overstate or understate the company's sustainable operating performance presented in its profit and loss statement. Another adjustment for EBIT and EBITDA involves the lease and pension adjustments as mentioned earlier. We present an example for this adjustment in figure 3.6.

3.3.2 Adjustment of Ratios

In this part, we show the remarkable effects of the ratio adjustment. In figure 3.7 we analyze two important interest-coverage ratios. ThyssenKrupp's *EBIT net interest coverage* (EBIT/net interest) is $8.2\times$ on a reported basis. An adjusted calculation results in a somewhat weaker $7.4\times$. The same is true for the *EBITDA net interest coverage* (EBITDA/net interest), which is $15.2\times$ on a reported basis and a lower $12.6\times$ on an adjusted basis.

Example: ThyssenKrupp AG	FY 2003/04
Sales	39,342
− Operating expenses	37,553
= EBIT reported	1,789
± Other adjustments (restructuring, one-offs, etc.)	3
+ Lease adjustment (implicit interest expense)	92
+ Pension adjustment (net pension cost - service cost)	420
= EBIT adjusted	2,304
EBIT reported	1,789
+ Depreciation & amortization	1,516
= EBITDA reported	3,305
± Adjustments as above	515
+ Lease adjustment (depreciation)	86
= EBITDA adjusted	3,906

Fig. 3.6: Adjustment of EBIT and EBITDA

The comparison of the company's reported net debt/EBITDA ratio to its *adjusted net debt/EBITDA* ratio reveals the impact of the ratio adjustments. In the example shown in figure 3.8, the *net debt/EBITDA debt leverage ratio* worsens to 3.8× from 2.2× on a reported basis. This is mainly due to the significant off-balance-sheet debt of the company, which has to be taken into account. The

Example: ThyssenKrupp AG	FY 2003/04
EBIT reported	1,789
÷ Net interest reported	218
= Reported EBIT net interest coverage	8.2x
EBIT adjusted	2,304
÷ Net interest adjusted	310
(= 218 net interest reported + 92 implicit interest)	
= Adjusted EBIT net interest coverage	7.4x
EBITDA reported	3,305
÷ Net interest reported	218
= Reported EBITDA net interest coverage	15.2x
EBITDA adjusted	3,906
÷ Net interest adjusted	310
= Adjusted EBITDA net interest coverage	12.6x

Fig. 3.7: Impact of adjustments on interest-coverage ratios

Example: ThyssenKrupp AG	FY 2003/04
Net debt reported	6,209
÷ EBITDA reported	2,887
= Reported net debt to EBITDA	2.2×
Net debt adjusted	14,948
÷ EBITDA adjusted	3,977
= Adjusted net debt to EBITDA	3.8×
FFO reported	2,766
÷ Net debt reported	6,209
= FFO reported to net debt reported	44.5%
FFO adjusted	3,220
÷ Net debt adjusted	14,948
= FFO adjusted to net debt adjusted	21.5%

Fig. 3.8: Impact of adjustments on debt leverage ratios

same is true for the *FFO/net debt ratio*, which weakens to 21.5 percent from 44.5 percent on a reported basis.

3.4 The Rating Agencies' Methodology

Among the difficulties for an external analyst to understand and to reconstruct the rating of the three rating agencies is that there is a different weighting of business risk and financial risk factors. Moreover, rating agencies use different approaches to business risk assessment and have different ratios, ratio definitions, and ratio scales, as well as diverse debt and ratio adjustments. Nevertheless, in the following we provide some examples of S&P and Moody's ratings.

We use again the example of ThyssenKrupp. The analyst has to calculate and adjust relevant ratios. This is difficult to do as rating agencies also use different adjustments. In the case of S&P, the agency publishes on an annual basis its "CreditStats: Industrial Comparative Ratio Analyses". It is important to know that this is only the scale for credit ratings in the industrials sector. For the utility sector, for example, there are different scales. In tables 3.2, 3.3 and 3.4, we interpolated the 2003 median ratios. This interpolated median ratio scale table can be used to assign every ratio a certain rating. Once the analyst has calculated these kinds of ratios, he can calculate either an average or a weighted

Tab. 3.2: ThyssenKrupp's credit metrics

	2002/03	2003/04	LTM Q1 2004/05
Sales	35,327	39,342	41,029
FFO/net debt	17%	23%	24%
FFO/total debt	16%	20%	23%
FOCF/net debt	23%	8%	22%
FOCF/total debt	22%	7%	21%
Net debt/EBITDA	4.5	3.1	3.0
Total debt/EBITDA	4.7	3.5	3.2
EBIT/net interest	5.0	7.4	7.3
EBIT/gross interest	3.5	5.9	7.3
EBITDA/net interest	10.6	12.6	11.4
EBITDA/gross interest	7.5	10.0	11.4
Net debt/capital	64%	58%	59%
Total debt/capital	65%	61%	61%
Return on capital	6%	9%	12%
EBITDA margin	9%	10%	10%

Tab. 3.3: ThyssenKrupp's credit metrics transformed to ratings

	2002/03	2003/04	LTM Q1 2004/05
Sales	AAA	AAA	AAA
FFO/net debt	B+	BB	BB
FFO/total debt	B+	BB–	BB
FOCF/net debt	A–	BB–	BBB+
FOCF/total debt	BBB+	B+	BBB+
Net debt/EBITDA	B+	BB+	BB+
Total debt/EBITDA	B	BB	BB+
EBIT/net interest	BBB	A	A
EBIT/gross interest	BB+	BBB+	A
EBITDA/net interest	A	A	A
EBITDA/gross interest	BBB	A–	A
Net debt/capital	B+	BB–	BB–
Total debt/capital	B+	BB–	BB–
Return on capital	CCC	B+	BB+
EBITDA margin	CCC–	CCC–	CCC–

average. The problem is that the weighting of the single ratios is discretionary to the agency's analyst and is not disclosed. It is also crucial to know that certain ratios are considered more important than others in specific industries.

Tab. 3.4: S&P's rating transformation table

	AAA	AA+	AA	AA–	A+	A	A–	BBB+	BBB
Sales	32,109	20,026	13,984	10,675	7,367	4,058	3,589	3,121	2,652
FFO/total debt	198%	125%	89%	74%	60%	45%	42%	39%	37%
FOCF/total debt	111%	72%	53%	44%	35%	26%	23%	20%	17%
Total debt/EBITDA	0.2	0.9	1.2	1.4	1.6	1.8	2.0	2.3	2.5
EBIT/gross interest	26.6	21.1	15.6	11.4	11.3	7.1	6.2	5.3	4.4
EBITDA/gross int.	27	20.8	17.7	15.2	12.7	10.2	8.9	7.6	6.3
Total debt/capital	7%	23%	31%	33%	36%	38%	42%	40%	43%
Return on capital	28%	28%	28%	24%	20%	17%	16%	14%	13%
EBITDA margin	25%	24%	23%	22%	20%	18%	17%	16%	14%

	BBB–	BB+	BB	BB–	B+	B	B–	CCC+	CCC
Sales	2,111	1,571	1,030	819	608	398	330	263	195
FFO/total debt	32%	27%	22%	18%	14%	11%	8%	6%	3%
FOCF/total debt	15%	12%	10%	8%	5%	3%	2%	1%	0%
Total debt/EBITDA	2.9	3.2	3.6	4.1	4.6	5.1	5.5	6.0	6.4
EBIT/gross interest	3.7	3.0	2.3	1.8	1.7	1.2	0.8	0.7	0.3
EBITDA/gross int.	5.3	4.2	3.2	2.8	2.3	1.9	1.5	1.4	1
Total debt/capital	47%	52%	56%	63%	70%	78%	92%	106%	120%
Return on capital	12%	12%	11%	10%	9%	8%	7%	6%	5%
EBITDA margin	15%	15%	15%	15%	15%	14%	14%	13%	13%

By the way, there exists a remarkable correlation between the size of a company in terms of sales and assets and its rating. Usually, the larger a company is, the better rated and vice versa. This is logical, as a larger company is in general better diversified across products, customers, and regions and has a stronger name recognition ("too big to fail") and therefore stronger financial flexibility. That is obviously also the reason why smaller companies with a sales turnover below €1-2 bn rarely get an investment-grade rating, just from a business profile point of view.

Rating agencies use certain industry-specific rating methodologies to assess the business profile rating and the financial profile rating. This concept stresses the systematic approach of a peer group analysis. For example, in its rating methodology publication "Global Auto Supplier Industry" dated June 2005,[14] Moody's presents the key considerations that drive its rating of global auto supplier companies. In this industry, the key rating factors are: (1) scale, diversification, and competitive position; (2) revenue growth; (3) cost position and profitability; (4) cash flow variability; (5) financial policy and capital structure; and (6) credit metrics. Important credit metrics in the auto supplier industry are: sales, one-year adjusted EBIT margin, five-year adjusted EBIT margin, cash and cash equivalents/total assets, adjusted net debt/adjusted net capitalization, total coverage ratio, adjusted RCF (post working capital)/adjusted net debt, FCF/adjusted gross debt, adjusted gross debt/EBITDAR (R = rent), and return on average assets. In its rating methodology report "Global Telecommunications Industry" dated February 2005,[15] Moody's outlined its core rating drivers of telecommunications companies. The six core factors are: operating environment, strategy and execution, technology, financial strength, developed or emerging market and generic rating factors (corporate governance, liquidity, sovereign ceiling considerations). In the appendix of this research report, Moody's provided the average financial metrics for telecoms by rating. These metrics are: total revenues, total assets, total debt, EBITA/revenue, EBITA/average assets, RCF/total debt, FFO/total debt, FCF/total debt, (FFO + interest expense)/gross interest expense, (EBITDA − capex)/gross interest expense, capex/revenue, capex/gross PP&E, and capex/depreciation expenses.

3.5 Evaluation of Specific Debt Instruments

Once the assessment of the credit quality of the issuer is made, the different debt instruments can be evaluated. The value of different debt instruments of an issuer can vary substantially. This is mainly due to the fact that, depending on the structure of the debt instrument, recovery prospects in the case of insolvency can vary substantially. The first step to evaluate structural issues is to determine who the issuer is. Often (especially for high-yield bonds) the issuer of a debt instrument is a holding company with typically no operating assets, the operating assets often are in subsidiaries. However, the creditors of the operating companies rank ahead the creditors of the holding company. Hence, in the case of a default, the claims of the creditors of the operating subsidiaries rank more senior, which leads to substantially lower recovery prospects. Figure 3.9 shows an example of the simplified structure of a high-yield issuer including a PIK note.

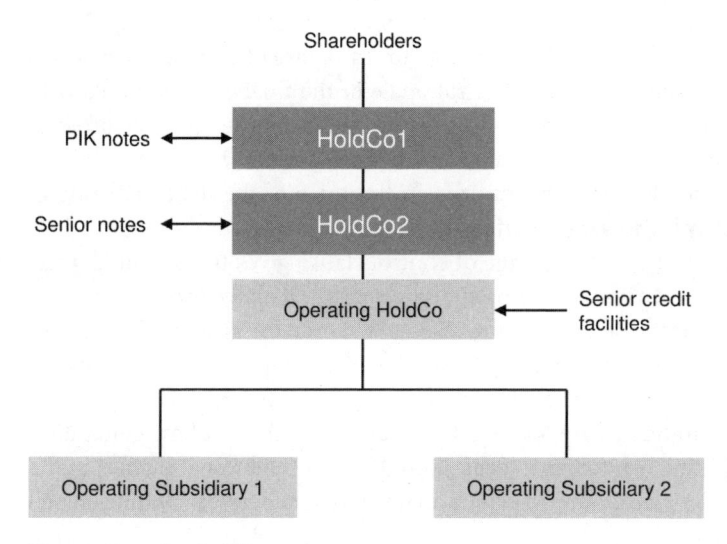

Fig. 3.9: Example of a PIK-note structure

However, mitigating the so-called structural subordination are pledges for certain assets of the operating companies as well as upstream guarantees of the operating subsidiaries. In addition, the existence of intercompany loans is favorable (from holding to operating company), as the holding company has a direct claim against the operating subsidiary. Even if the issuer is the operating company, the debt instruments and particularly high-yield bonds often contain a contractual subordination clause, which basically puts other claims (mostly bank debt) ahead of the bondholder. In addition, the analyst has to check whether the assets of the issuer are pledged to other creditors, like in the case of real estate financing, as these assets rank ahead of the debtholder.

In addition to analyzing structural questions, the analyst has to evaluate the documentation of the specific debt instrument and particularly its covenants, as these are intended to protect bondholders. However, too tight covenants are not favorable as they might limit the necessary operating flexibility of the company. A breach of covenants leads to so-called technical default and gives the debtholders the right to redeem their claims. Often negotiations between debtholders and the company prevent a technical default (e.g., consent payment). The following covenants, if they leave sensible headroom, are favorable for bondholders and are often part of the documentation of high-yield bonds:

- *Financial covenants*: These covenants require the company to meet specific financial hurdle ratios. A fixed charge coverage test, a *net debt/EBITDA* maximum and an *EBITDA/interest* minimum are often used. The levels usually tighten over time. The rationale of the financial covenants is to ensure that the company will pursue a financial strategy that protects debtholders. When financial covenants are close to being breached, it usually leads to a significant drop in the price of the debt instrument, particularly for weaker credits.
- *Change of control*: The change of control clause gives the debtholder the right to redeem the instrument at a set price, usually 100 or 101. The reasoning for a change of control clause is to protect the debtholder from a takeover that would lead to a deterioration of the credit profile. A change of control clause is particularly suitable for LBO candidates. Characteristics for LBO candidates are low equity valuations, high cash flow generation capabilities, a limited size (even though LBOs tend to get bigger) and a shareholder's structure in which major shareholders are willing to sell their stakes.
- *Negative pledge*: A negative pledge prohibits the issuer from granting a security interest that ranks ahead of the debtholder. The covenant is to protect against the above discussed subordination.
- *Cross default*: A cross default clause triggers a default of the debt instrument if there is a default of any other debt instruments of the issuer. It ensures that the debtholder will rank equally (except for priority claims) with other creditors in the case of default.
- *Restriction of payments*: Provides that the issuer is not allowed to make more than a specific amount of certain payments, like dividend payments to shareholders, payments for acquisitions, or payments for capital expenditures. The provision ensures that the cash flow of the company is at least partly used to improve the financial ratios of the company.

- *Additional indebtedness*: Limits the maximum amount of additional debt the company is allowed to incur. Protects the debtholder against an over-leveraging of the company.
- *Limitation of sale and leaseback transactions*: Ensures that only a certain amount of the company's assets can be sold and leased back. It ensures that bondholders do not become structurally subordinated and that the company does not use these off-balance-sheet arrangements to incur additional indebtedness, which might be limited due to another covenant.
- *Step-up clauses*: Provide that the coupon increases in a certain event like a downgrade below a certain level (usually coupon increases at next coupon date). The intention is to increase the compensation for bondholders if the credit quality decreases. In the case of a rating step-up clause, the coupon usually steps down if the rating increases again above the set level. However, step-up clauses can be problematic as a company that has a deteriorating credit profile will be burdened by additional interest expenses. Examples of companies that issued bonds with a step-up clause are ABB and KPN.

When looking at covenants, it is vital to read the small print of the documentation as often many exceptions exist, limiting the effectiveness of debtholder protection. To evaluate specific issues, the documentation of the other outstanding debt instruments also has to be reviewed. For example, the British pound bond of Stagecoach was among the best performing bonds in 2000, while the euro-denominated bond was among the worst performing bonds. When Stagecoach decided to sell a unit that contributed about half the company's revenues, it paid back its sterling bonds at 111.82 (bonds traded at 93 before redemption). The sterling bond contained a clause in its documentation to protect bondholders in case the company did something materially prejudicial to its lenders. After evaluating the clause, Stagecoach decided to redeem the bonds. However, the euro bonds did not have the same clause and were not repaid. Consequently, bond prices took a hit, with the yield of the bonds climbing from 6.1 to 7.8 percent.

3.6 Recovery Rate Estimates

For risky debt instruments, the analyst should estimate the recovery rates in order to evaluate the potential loss. However, estimating recovery prospects can be extremely challenging, especially if the issuer has assets in several jurisdictions as bankruptcy laws differ substantially (especially the ranking of certain claims). Hence, this makes it difficult to evaluate the position of the bondholder in the bankruptcy process. Recovery prospects also vary significantly depending on the industry. Table 3.5 shows average recovery rates by country and industry. In general, recovery prospects in Europe tend to be lower than those in the United States. In terms of industries, the utility and energy sectors have good recovery prospects, while in the telecom and technology sectors, they are low. The data provided are from a survey conducted by Moody's.[16]

Tab. 3.5: Average recovery rates per country and industry

Country/Industry	Weighted by volume	Unweighted
United States	35.4%	35.4%
Canada	27.0%	34.5%
United Kingdom	23.9%	28.9%
Other Europe	23.7%	30.2%
Utility - Gas	56.4%	51.5%
Oil and Oil Services	53.4%	44.5%
Hospitality	45.7%	42.5%
Utility - Electric	47.3%	41.4%
Miscellaneous	43.3%	39.5%
Transport - Ocean	42.3%	38.8%
Media, Broadcasting and Cable	43.5%	38.2%
Transport - Surface	35.1%	36.6%
Finance and Banking	51.6%	36.3%
Industrial	35.1%	35.4%
Retail	34.8%	34.4%
Transport - Air	33.3%	34.3%
Automotive	27.4%	33.4%
Health Care	28.2%	32.7%
Consumer Goods	26.7%	32.5%
Construction	29.5%	31.9%
Technology	25.5%	29.5%
Real Estate	24.3%	28.8%
Steel	26.0%	27.4%
Telecom	17.1%	23.2%

An approach to estimating recovery prospects includes:
- *Determining priority claims*: First priority claims should be evaluated as these have to be serviced in advance of the holder of the debt instruments. Hence, if the bankruptcy proceeds are not sufficient to satisfy the priority claims, then the holder of the debt instruments will be left with nothing.
- *Evaluating the claims that rank pari passu*: If the bankruptcy proceedings are higher than the amount of priority claims, they will be distributed on a proportional basis among the holders of the debt instruments and

claims that rank on the same level. Hence, the claims that rank on the same level have to be determined.
- *Estimating the bankruptcy proceeds*: To estimate bankruptcy proceedings, the different segments can be evaluated by an EBITDA multiple approach. Hence, the expected EBITDA is multiplied by a certain factor to derive the value of the segment. To estimate the specific multiple, it is often a good idea to use the multiples of firms in similar industries. If the firm has certain assets (like land) that are non-EBITDA generative but have a certain value, the expected proceeds should be added. Once the analyst has estimated the company's value, he can make a certain adjustment (e.g., 25 percent) to reflect the usually lower disposal proceeds in bankruptcy proceedings.
- *Estimating the recovery rate*: The expected recovery rate is simply derived by subtracting the priority claims from the estimated bankruptcy proceedings. The amount that is left over is then divided by the amount of claims that rank pari passu with the debt instruments (including the amount of the debt instrument).

However, the recovery estimation is only a very broad approximation. Hence, a sensitivity analysis (by using different EBITDA multiples) to evaluate possible ranges should be made.

4
The Economics of Credit Spreads

4.1 Macro Drivers

4.1.1 Credits in the Business Cycle

In this section, we discuss the attractiveness of corporate debt investments through the business cycle. Although it is a very simplistic approach, the market tone in credits does depend strongly on the current stage of the business cycle. Equities are the favored asset class in a strong growth and low-yield environment, and government bonds benefit from their safe-haven status in economic downturns. Credits lie somewhere in the middle, as earning the spread carry versus government bonds can be seen as the right strategy in a moderate growth environment when equity investments do not show an attractive risk–return profile.

Although there are other factors involved, this rough assignment is in line with theory and also with the historical spread development in credit markets. In a recession, earnings power and cash flow generation decline (accompanied by increasing default rates), whereas in a boom period, equities are the major beneficiaries. Credits also perform well in an economic boom, as fundamental credit drivers underpin a tight valuation, but they underperform equities in absolute terms. From a relative value perspective, credits are the preferred asset class in a moderate growth environment.

When we analyze the relationship between spreads and the business cycle, the crucial question is, who is leading whom? In figure 4.1, we depict economic growth and the long-term corporate bond spread in the US, highlighting the positive correlation between both time series. At first glance, economic growth lags behind the long-term corporate bond spread, which is consistent with academic research on this topic.[17] From a long-term perspective, the lagging character of economic growth is fairly logical if capital markets are efficient in discounting expectations about the future. Assuming the majority of investors have the right view about economic developments, growth patterns are already factored into credit spreads. Spreads are therefore leading economic growth and not vice versa. One could argue that markets might be wrong by building up expectations. But history shows that in a long-time perspective, markets

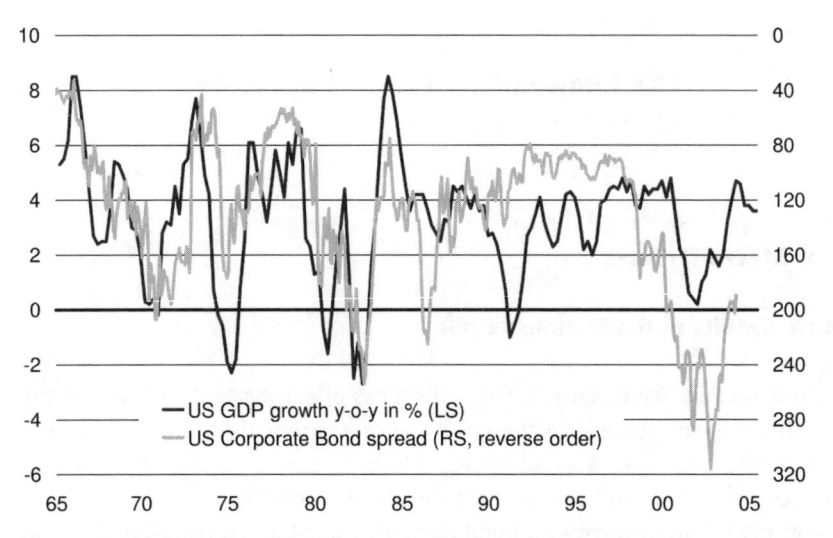

Fig. 4.1: The business cycle and credit spreads: Who is leading whom?

do a good job in anticipating future developments and lagging spreads are the exception.

Unfortunately, the macro environment is obviously not the only spread driver. But it is rather crucial also for several other spread determinants, such as company profitability, equity markets, rating actions, and so on. The good news is that, in the end, it is all about cycles.

Investing through the cycle is crucial for credit portfolio management as there is a close link between the business cycle, the default cycle, and the spread cycle. Smoothing the investment process and anti-cyclical behavior is key for long-term investors, while pro-cyclical behavior is more appropriate for short-term investors.

Which economic data serve as an indicator for credit spreads? Obviously those that best depict the business cycle. Hence, credit strategists face the same problem as economists do: the predictive power of economic indicators is not stable, and lousy correlation is one of the key problems of portfolio management.

Moreover, macro data releases have not only a direct impact on credit markets, but are also affecting credits indirectly through other markets, for example government bonds and equities. Consequently, there is not a one-dimensional interdependence between economic indicators and credit spreads but rather a highly complex relationship including several indicators that add up to an overall picture of fundamental credit drivers. The key indicators for credits are:

- *Hard economic indicators*: Economic growth is supportive for credit markets because strong global growth patterns underpin earnings growth and cash flow generation of companies, leading to improved credit protection ratios. However, equities rather than credits are the preferred asset class in a boom period. That said, in an accelerating growth scenario, there might be a rising incentive for companies to switch to a more shareholder-friendly policy (e.g., increasing dividends and share buy-backs), which, in the end, does not favor bondholders. There might then be allocation shifts out of credits into equities in a boom phase. Most important data releases include (among others) GDP data, labor market statistics, capacity utilization, retail sales, and factory orders.
- *Soft economic indicators*: Positive soft indicators point in the same direction as hard indicators, with one important difference: The spread impact from soft indicators is predominantly sector-specific. Consumer confidence readings will help companies from the consumer sector rather than utility companies. The most important data releases include consumer confidence readings, IFO indices, and the ZEW (Zentrum für Europäische Wirschaftsforschung) index in Euroland, as well as the PMI (purchasing manager index), the ISM (Institute of Supply Management) indices, and the University of Michigan confidence index in the US.
- *Inflation and commodity prices*: In general, inflation hurts credits in the same way as it does all fixed income securities. Data releases are divided into consumer price index (CPI) and producer price index (PPI) figures. From a company perspective, inflating input (commodity) prices (for example rising oil prices) are obviously negative in case the companies cannot shift higher input prices directly to their customers.

Example 1: US Labor Market Data

Basic economic theory suggests that accelerating growth goes hand-in-hand with rising employment. Consequently, there should be a positive link between positive employment data and credit spreads. In the figure below, we depict the relationship between credit spreads and US payroll data. Although both time series are negatively correlated from a medium-term perspective (which is in line with economic theory), short-term decoupling is an often-seen phenomenon.

The payroll miracle...

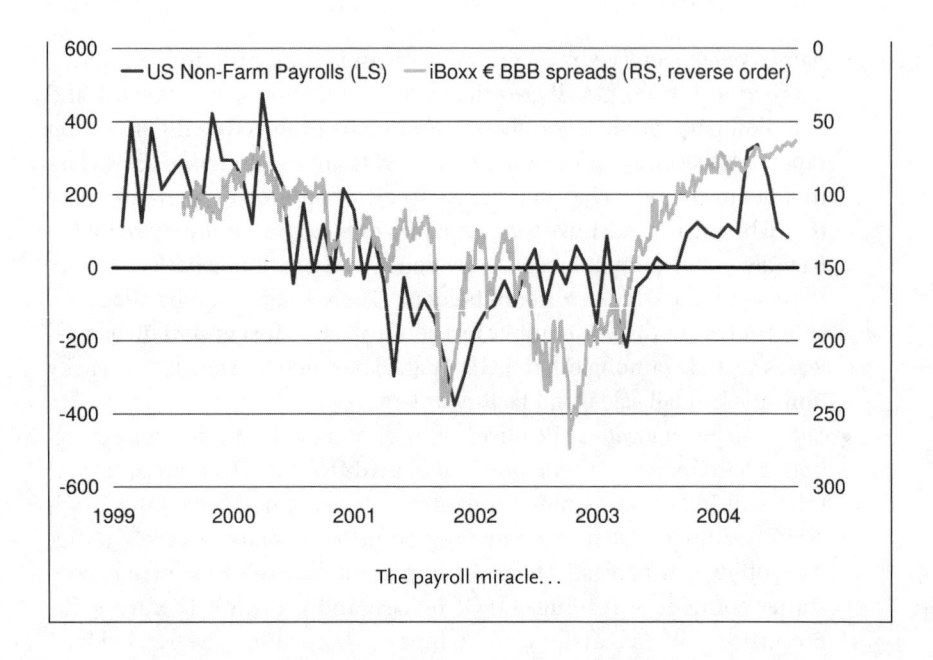

4.1.2 Yields and Spreads

Two diametrically opposed theories about the relationship between government bond yields and credit spreads divide the investment community. So-called spread–yield aficionados argue that declining government bond yields will trigger allocation shifts into credits as investors search for additional carry. This is especially true for asset–liability accounts like insurance companies, which have to generate an asset return that matches their liability side. If government yields are high enough to match the required return of those investors, they are not forced to build up credit exposure, as there is no need for additional carry. Thus, yields and spreads would be positively correlated. Yields will decline when credit spreads are tighter, while spreads widen if government yields rise.

In contrast, the fundamental theory argues that both sovereign debt and credit markets are primarily driven by macro fundamentals. A deteriorating growth scenario triggers declining interest rates and hence lower sovereign yields. In this scenario, one would expect wider credit spreads due to increasing default rates and worsening credit protection ratios given declining earnings growth. The opposite is true in case of a brightening of the macro outlook, when credit markets benefit from accelerating earnings growth potential. Consequently, spreads and yields are negatively correlated. Lower bond yields correspond with wider credit spreads and vice versa.

Unfortunately, the world is not as easy as just choosing one of these two theories. In figure 4.2, we depict the spread–yield relationship over the last seven years (1999 to 2005). The fundamental theory has been verified five times (2005, 2003, 2002, 2001, and 2000), while spread–yield aficionados proved correct only in 1999 and 2004.

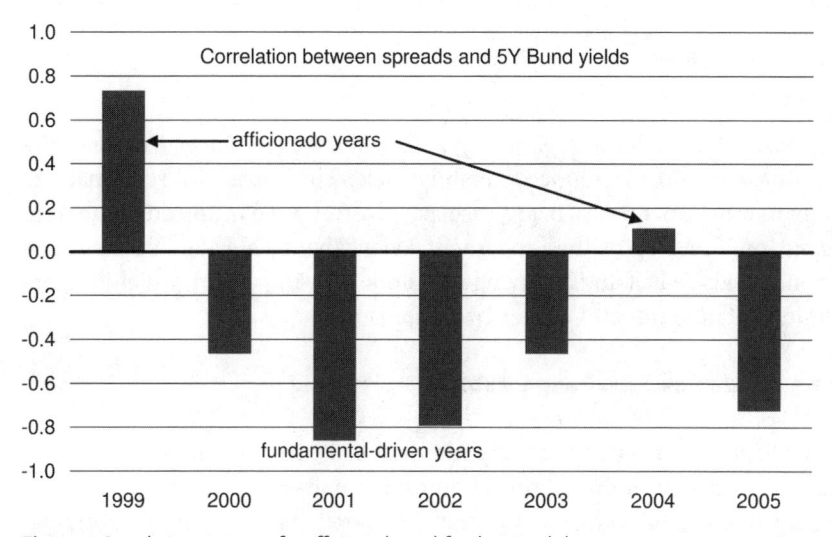

Fig. 4.2: Correlation patterns for afficionado and fundamental-driven years

Monetary policy action plays an important role for fixed income securities in general and has significant impact on credit spreads in particular. There is statistical evidence for a 50 percent translation of interest rate changes to ten-year government bond yields (the long-term impact from monetary actions of the Federal Reserve on ten-year US Treasury bonds on average).

In accordance with economic theory, expansionary monetary policy will be implemented in an economic downturn, triggering lower interest rates to boost growth. Lower interest rates generate a marked-to-market gain on outstanding debt, but declining growth prospects will trigger reduced earnings power and cash flow generation, arguing for wider spreads. On the positive side, lower interest rates mean declining refinancing costs for companies.

In general, monetary tightening would have a negative impact on bond markets in general, but that can be only temporary. According to US data, interest rate hikes went hand-in-hand with credit spread narrowing on a longer perspec-

Tab. 4.1: Rate hike cycles and spread performance in the US*

	−3M	−2M	−1M	0	1M	2M	3M	4M	5M	6M	6M cum.
1972	4	15	−22	−80	−2	2	5	−13	0	−12	−20
1976	−6	−1	0	1	15	−24	−9	−13	5	−9	−35
1986	−9	1	1	−21	−17	−5	−33	−7	26	−2	−38
1994	1	−3	−5	−6	−2	2	−3	1	−4	3	−3
1999	−2	1	2	5	2	11	1	−5	−7	−7	−5

*Change in bp of average corporate bond spread over US Treasuries.
Source: Moody's, Bloomberg

tive (please refer to table 4.1). Since 1972, the US has experienced five times the beginning of a more pronounced rate-hike cycle. The impact on credit markets on a six-month horizon was, in any case, positive, reflected in spread tightening. This outcome underpins the fundamental view about yields and spreads: rising bond yields reflect an improving economic growth pattern, which triggers declining default rates and tighter credit spreads.

4.1.3 Credits and Exchange Rates

Globalization not only affects the international exchange of goods and services, but it also has a direct impact on capital markets given the proceeding integration of capital markets. Consequently, exchange rates have several effects on international companies, which are linked through foreign markets via exports of products or imports of input factors, like raw materials. In a simple two-country model, depreciation of the local currency (i.e., appreciation of the foreign currency) will lead to a rise in the competitiveness of domestic companies in global markets and the demand for domestic goods. This is what governments try to achieve when implementing a beggar-the-neighborhood policy by depreciating their own currency at the expense of foreign countries. Besides this macroeconomic view, however, there are also two major effects on a company level:

- *Translation effect*: Translation gains and losses arise from foreign subsidiaries and are rather an accounting issue. Assume a European company with a subsidiary in the USA reporting earnings in US dollars. In case the euro declines against the dollar, the earnings of the subsidiary will rise when translated into the parent company's income statement. A

depreciation of the domestic currency has a positive effect on the company's balance sheet in line with the macroeconomic effect.
- *Transaction effect*: The transaction effect is closely related to the macroeconomic impact of exchange rate swings. A company is able to increase market share abroad when the foreign currency appreciates and vice versa.

Furthermore, the ongoing capital market integration must be considered when analyzing the impact of exchange rates on credit markets, as global demand for assets is closely related to exchange rate expectations. Without going into too much detail, expectations of a weaker euro will trigger declining interest for euro-denominated assets, which also hurts euro credit markets as foreign demand declines.

To sum up, companies particularly affected by the sharp increase of the euro against the US dollar, for example, are those who:

- generate a significant portion of their sales in the US
- have their cost base in euro (no natural hedge through production plants in the US)
- operate in a very competitive market
- and have only partially hedged their exposure.

The issuance of foreign debt is also an important factor, as companies with significant US dollar (in this case) debt experience lower interest payments and a positive translation effect. The overall impact of a higher euro–dollar exchange rate is not easy to estimate and varies from company to company.

4.1.4 Credits and Commodity Prices

Except for specific companies from the basic resources sector (gold mining, steel companies, etc.), commodities are input factors. Hence, rising commodity prices simply increase input costs of companies, and consequently negatively affect earnings and cash flow generation, if companies are not able to pass on prices to consumers. Although commodity-price sensitivity is highly company-specific, we focus on oil prices as a major source of uncertainty for credit investors.

The direct impact of higher oil prices for oil-dependent companies is rising input costs, which is definitely negative. But there are also indirect effects that might impact markets, so-called second-round effects. Higher oil prices have an impact on consumer confidence readings. In particular, declining consumption negatively affects the cyclical consumer industry. In addition, higher oil prices will have an impact on growth prospects, which is also a negative factor for credit markets. On the contrary, rising oil prices underpin inflation fears, which might trigger a more restrictive monetary policy by central banks, causing a downward shift in the yield curve, which brings us back to the spread and yield discussion above. Last but not least, exchange rates play an important role for non-US companies, as the price per barrel is denominated in US dollars. An appreciation of the euro versus the US dollar means that the oil price in euro-denominated terms reduces the rising input costs for European companies.

The absolute level of oil prices, however, is only one side of the coin. The major question is whether oil prices are driven by imbalances in demand or supply:

- *Demand driven*: If oil prices increase due to higher demand after an accelerating global growth momentum, the negative effect from higher input costs can be overcompensated for by rising demand. This was the case in 2004, when demand from China drove oil prices to record highs, without a negative impact on credit-risky assets.
- *Supply driven*: Political tensions or supply shocks have fundamentally a negative impact on corporate credits without any compensation on the macro level (e.g., via higher growth). A temporary sharp rise in the oil price will have only a negligible growth impact, while stabilization at a high level would significantly reduce growth expectations.

With respect to geopolitical tensions, oil prices are a crisis indicator, reflecting global risk aversion. In this case, credit spreads and oil prices are positively correlated. Higher oil prices coincide with wider credit spreads. In figure 4.3 we depict US corporate spreads and the oil price since 1990. There is no constant correlation pattern between both time series. However, it is obvious that external shocks (like Iraq War I) triggered a rise in the oil price and also a widening in credit spreads. At such a time, spreads and the oil price are highly positive correlated.

But this is not true for a large part of the analyzed periods. The oil price increase from 1994 to 1997 against the background of strong economic growth was accompanied by a stable trend in credit spreads. The strong increase of the oil price since the end of 2002 from US$ 23 per barrel to US$ 65 per barrel in August 2005 occurred in an accelerating growth period, driven by rising demand rather than by an increase of risk aversion. At the same time, long-term US corporate spreads tightened significantly from their all-time-high of over 300 bp to 190 bp in mid 2005.

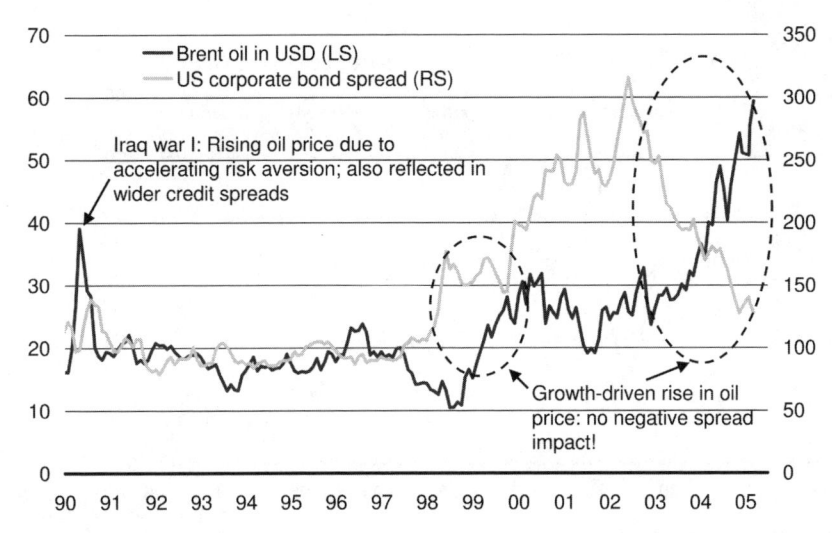

Fig. 4.3: Oil prices, GDP growth, political crisis, and credit spreads

Having said this, there are two major sectors strongly linked to the oil price: chemicals and energy.

Oil companies can benefit from a high oil price if they are mainly involved in downstream production. Integrated oil producers benefit from a high oil price in the downstream production but might suffer on declining refining margins in Europe. For integrated oil companies, there is a positive impact of rising oil prices. According to the rating methodologies of agencies, a rating is determined by the performance through the cycle. Thus, oil price peaks and consequently a stronger operating performance have only very little impact on credit quality. Even worse, the high volatility of earnings normally increases credit risks.

The chemical sector is closely linked to commodity prices, as increases in input prices cannot be easily passed on to customers. The lower the value chain, the higher the impact from rising oil prices. Oil price sensitivity is usually higher for European companies than for US and Asian-based chemicals, as the latter purchase several input factors based on natural gas.

4.1.5 Credits and Inflation

Rising inflation, in general, is negative for all (straight) fixed income securities, as it triggers rising yields which cause a marked-to-market loss. This loss is the direct impact of inflation on credits. As is the case with commodity

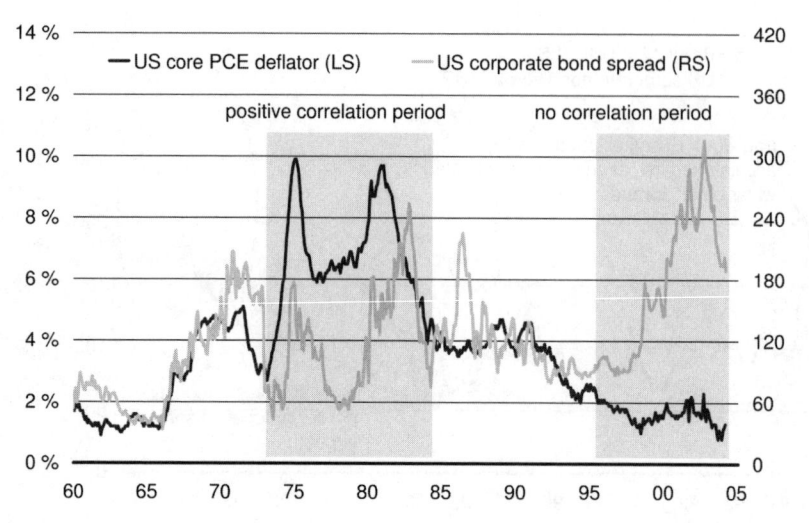

Fig. 4.4: Inflation and credit spreads

prices, there are indirect effects from inflation readings on credits, including potential action of central banks as well as the impact on exchange rates and also on different asset classes.

In figure 4.4, we show that in the high inflation periods (1973–75 and 1979–82) credit spreads widened significantly. Rising inflation, however, seems to be a sufficient condition for wider spreads, but not a necessary condition as the period from 1995 to 2002 shows, when inflation remained subdued at the same time that credit spreads widened significantly.

> **Excursus 3: Consumer Price Versus Asset Price Inflation**
>
> The resurfacing discussion about rate cuts in the US and in Euroland in mid-2005 was accompanied by expectations that inflation will remain subdued. Following this discussion, the impact of inflation on credit spreads returned to the spotlight. An additional topic regarding inflation worth mentioning is that if excess liquidity flows into assets rather than into consumer goods, this argues for low consumer price inflation but rising asset price inflation.
>
> In late 2000, the Fed and the European Central Bank (ECB) started down a monetary easing path, which was boosted by external shocks (9/11 and the Enron scandal), when central banks flooded the market with additional liquidity to avoid a credit crunch. Financial markets in general benefited from this excess liquidity as reflected in the positive performance of almost

all asset classes in 2004, which argued for overall liquidity inflows, but not for allocation shifts.

It is not only excess liquidity held by investors and companies that underpins strong performing assets in general, but also the pro-cyclical nature of banking. In a low default rate environment, lending activities accelerate, which might contribute to an overheating of the economy accompanied by rising inflation.

From a purely macroeconomic viewpoint, private households have two alternatives to allocate liquidity: consuming or saving. The former leads to rising consumer price inflation, whereas the latter to asset price inflation. The figure below shows that real goods inflation readings in 2005 in Europe (HICP) is fairly subdued. In contrast, the year-on-year performance of credits and equities based on total return figures shows a continuous price increase in risky assets since the beginning of 2004.

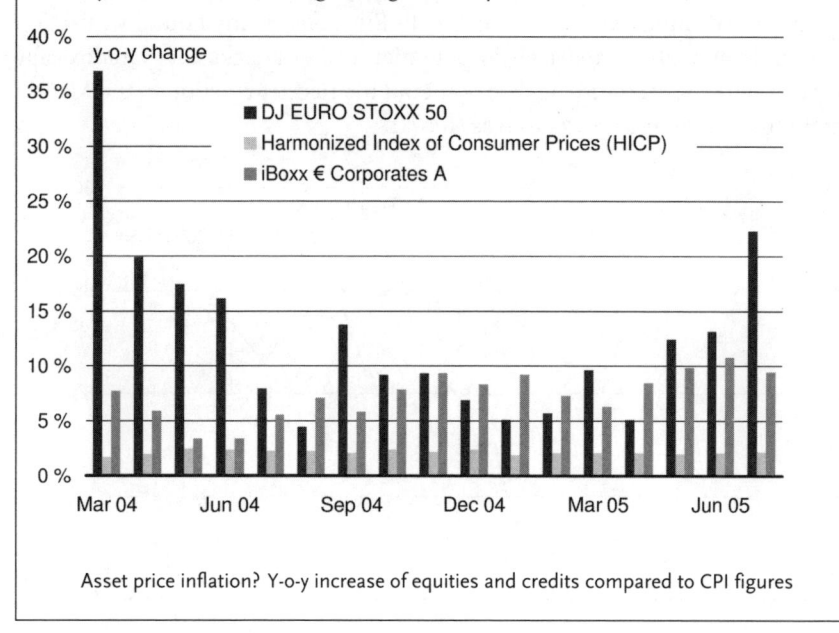

Asset price inflation? Y-o-y increase of equities and credits compared to CPI figures

4.1.6 Credits and External Shocks

Credits are vulnerable to external shocks, as is the case for all risky asset classes. Geopolitical tensions, oil price shocks, or political crises increase uncertainty among the investor base, triggering a general flight-to-quality at the cost of risky assets.

However, geopolitics is only one of many credit drivers. When looking at the evidence from the first Gulf War, increasing risk aversion, weak equity markets, and sliding consumer confidence put pressure on spreads just prior to the war. Looking at the market reaction when Iraq invaded Kuwait in August 1990, Baa credit spreads, which tightened initially, blew out as the risk of war increased and peaked as the US finally started the first air strikes on Iraq in January 1991. Similarly, equities sold off and consumer confidence plummeted. Shortly before the war was over in late February 1991, spreads started to tighten below pre-war levels.

Although the (direct) impact of terror attacks on economies is rather negligible, the London bombings brought geopolitical tensions back on the agenda. But following 9/11, Madrid, Istanbul, and London, market participants are by now used to dealing with terror attacks. In this respect, any liquidity injection by central banks that are driven by potential further attacks can paradoxically support markets. In figure 4.5, we point out the market reaction to the Madrid bombings in March 2004 as well as to 9/11.

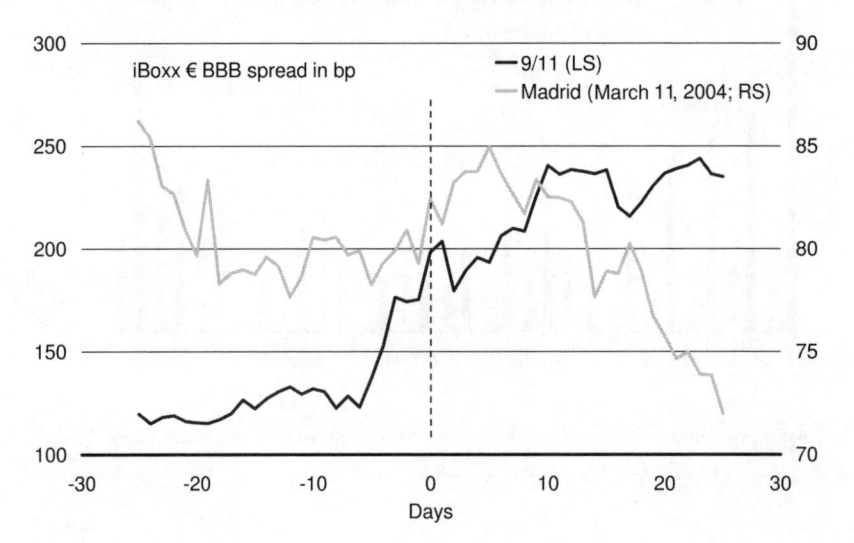

Fig. 4.5: Lines of terror: 9/11 versus Madrid bombings

The systematic impact from external shocks on credit markets is from an economic point of view probably subdued, while the impact on single names differ significantly. Rising geopolitical tension triggers an increase in idiosyncratic risk factors, and spread dispersion in the credit universe should increase. Besides aerospace-related companies, insurance companies and the tourism-related sector are strongly affected by external shocks. One can argue that the London bombings did not generate enough momentum to hurt credits, while share prices are much more sensitive. In information-efficient markets, however, the price adjustment is smoother than is the case in less efficient markets like credits. In the latter, there is a certain threshold of risk tolerance. Until risk aversion falls below this threshold, market reaction is relatively subdued. In case risk aversion exceeds the threshold, the price adjustment is rather dramatic. This reflects the negatively skewed risk–return profile of credit-risky instruments.

4.2 Micro Drivers

In chapter 3, we discussed in detail the crucial balance sheets items that determine the credit quality and consequently the rating of a company. While company analysis is a key part of active credit portfolio management, we focus on macro trends that might have an impact on the whole market although we consider these a micro driver. Against the background of the importance of leverage and the capital structure, a general trend towards deleveraging and balance sheet repair as well as the impact from rising M&A activity or surfacing LBO risks are important topics for active credit portfolio management.

The impact of merger and acquisition activities is company-specific; it does not affect the entire market. A merger between a better-rated and a worse-rated company, generally, favors bondholders of the worse-rated at the cost of bondholders of the better-rated name. Consequently, the overall market impact is hard to determine. As a rule of thumb, accelerating M&A activities support equity rather than credit markets, although the effect of an M&A deal on a single company's credit protection ratios might be positive.

The principle idea behind a leveraged buy-out (LBO) transaction is that the investor borrows money to buy a controlling interest in a company by using the company's assets as security for the loans (leveraged structure). Hence, the LBO investor purchases a company using a relatively limited amount of equity and a large amount of debt. He uses the company's cash flow to repay his loans and, at a later stage, he sells the company and uses the proceeds to pay back the rest of outstanding debt.

Companies that typically are suitable candidates for a LBO bid are firms whose equity is significantly undervalued, or firms that have a strong deleveraging capability after the LBO transaction. In case the equity is significantly undervalued, the investor's gain will come from the higher disposal price (assuming leverage stays unchanged). But even if the company cannot easily be sold for a higher price, the LBO may still be attractive if the firm is able to significantly reduce its debt. Other criteria also include a high free float, a manageable size, the willingness of banks and capital markets to finance the respective transaction, and the absence of poison pills (e.g., put options in the case of change of control).

In figure 4.6, we highlight Marks & Spencer's 5Y CDS spread following Philip Green's announcement of a takeover bid in June 2004. The market's reaction on the announcement triggered a spread widening of around 200 bp.

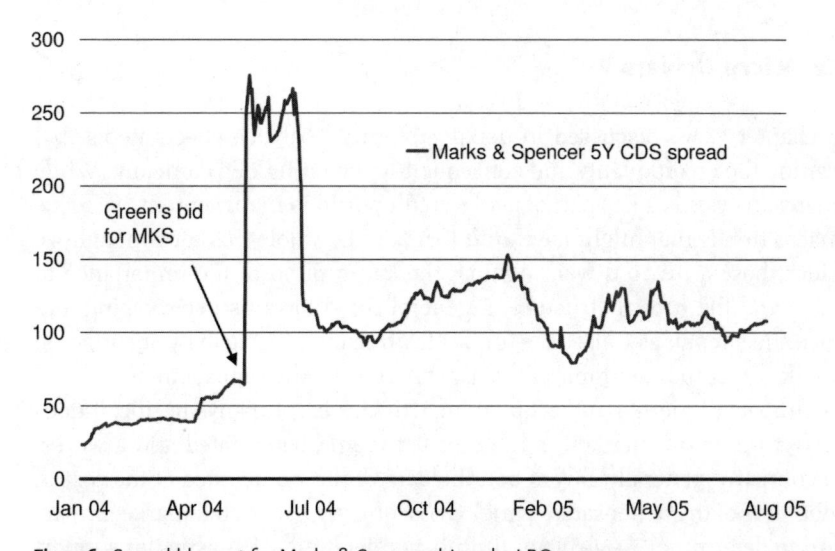

Fig. 4.6: Spread blowout for Marks & Spencer driven by LBO rumors

Besides the usual suspects (UK retailers), the universe of potential LBO candidates rose significantly during the last few years as private equity funds generated significant money inflows. This even puts names with a market cap of more than €10 bn in the LBO spotlight. As identifying LBO candidates is a tough task, how can an investor implement hedging strategies against LBO risk? A rather imperfect hedge (but the most efficient in terms of transaction costs) is buying protection on a respective CDS basket including the usual suspects. Even if no company in the basket is involved in an LBO, these names will underperform in case of resurfacing LBO fears, and could at least partially compensate investors in a specific LBO bid.

4.3 Credit Quality

4.3.1 Credit Quality Trend

Credit quality has the most obvious impact on spread valuation, as the rating of a company is the major criteria for investors. The rating of a company includes several issues discussed above and hence centralizes several spread-relevant factors. Moreover, many accounts have rating restrictions, for instance, they are only allowed to invest in high-grade names. Consequently, there is a structural demand overhang (market segmentation theory of credits), which favors higher-rated names.

The major drivers of rating quality, which also determines the default rate forecast of rating agencies are:

- The expected economic development, which in the end affects earnings growth and cash flow generation potential
- Exchange rates, which have an impact on export-oriented names
- Input prices (oil and raw materials), which could squeeze margins in many industries through rising production costs
- Consumer confidence, which especially affects cyclical industries
- The financial policy of companies, for example, a more shareholder-friendly policy (including accelerating share buy-back activities and increasing dividends)
- New issuance quality as a major input factor for expected default rates.

In figure 4.7, we show the importance of credit quality for credit spreads, reflected in the extremely high correlation between the rating drift (downgrade-upgrade ratio, which equals upgrades minus downgrades relative to the number of rated issuers) and credit spreads.

4.3.2 Default Rates

According to empirical studies, there are three major factors explaining the credit risk premium. Besides compensation for the risk of default (most important factor, determining around 85 percent of historical spread levels), spread volatility (more than 10 percent) and the liquidity premium are the main spread drivers. While the liquidity premium is losing importance given the rising liquidity and transparency of euro credit markets, spread volatility is not relevant for buy-and-hold investors who have no incentive to close their position until maturity.

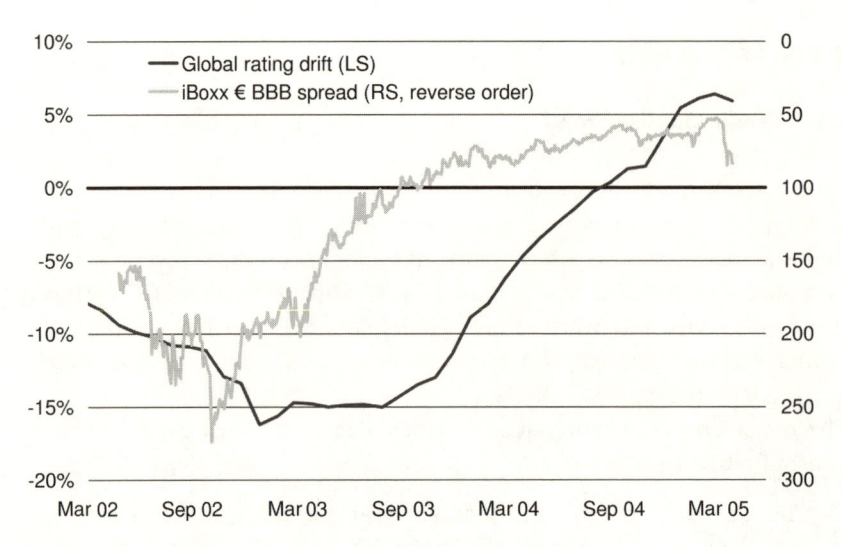

Fig. 4.7: Rating drift and credit spreads

Against this backdrop, the loss given default (according to the current spread level and expected default and recovery rates) should be the best single explanatory factor for the current spread valuation. In figure 4.8, we point out historical spreads for long-term BBB-rated US corporates and the global speculative grade default rate according to Moody's. Although there is no constant correlation between both time series back to 1970, credit spreads and default rates have moved closely together since the mid-1990s.

Consequently, buy-and-hold investors will try to estimate the default rate, which enables them to calculate the fair spread level. In case the current spread level is above the fair value, buy-and-hold investors are willing to take credit risk and vice versa (ignoring all other risk components and also technical factors).

Although Moody's possesses a spread forecast model, expected default rates can be calculated only for the next twelve months, which is not enough time given the preferred investment horizon for long-term-oriented investors. This means that historical transition matrices and default probability tables are taken into account. Hence, the best guess for the expected five-year default rate is the default rate over the last five years.

The average five-year cumulative default rate for BBB-rated names is relatively stable over time (back to the 1920s), while spreads experienced large moves in the respective time horizon. In our database, long-term BBB spreads in the US marked an all-time low of 51 bp in February 1966, while they reached a record high at 382 bp in October 2002. Why do spreads swing dramatically while the

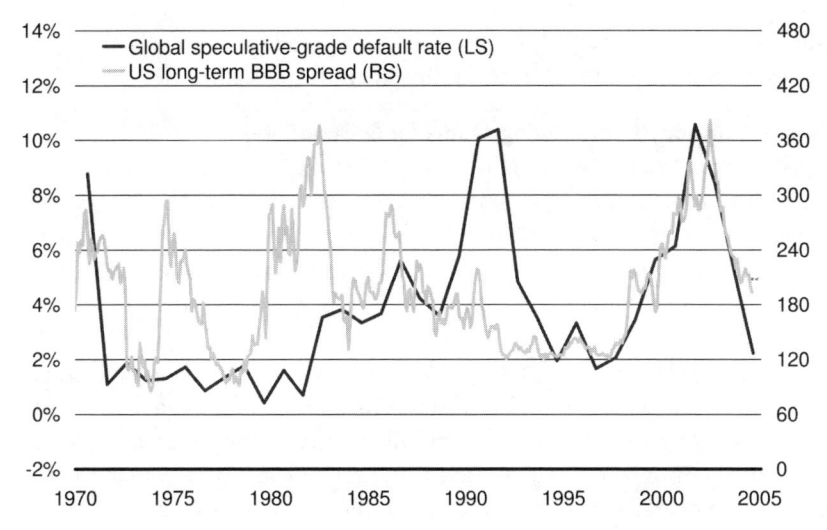

Fig. 4.8: Credit spreads and the default cycle

five-year default premium is constant? To answer this question we have to think in terms of cycles.

From this perspective, using the average five-year cumulative default rate determines the outcome of the analysis above, as it does not take into account the current stage of the business cycle, and hence the default rate as well as the spread cycle. In case the average default cycle is five years, with the average cumulative five-year default rate remaining the same on average, the specific date of a five-year buy-and-hold investment in respect to taking default risk is irrelevant in respect to the expected loss (which we determined as the crucial spread driver).

Is the average five-year cumulative default rate, however, the appropriate measure for default risk? In our view, we have to take into account the current default risk given the state of the business, default, and spread cycles. For this purpose, we use the one-year default rate as a proxy for the default cycle. In 2002, the one-year default rate for BBB-rated names reached a cyclical high of 1.21 percent, while it was zero in both 2003 and 2004. Even if the five-year default rate were to remain stable over time, an investor would prefer to step into the market at the cyclical high of the default rate. Moreover, if the required five-year default premium were to remain constant as well, credit investors should increase exposure at above average spread levels and reduce credit risk when spread carry is below average. That said, the average five-year cumulative default rate is only one part of the story. In addition, there is a cyclical default premium, which accounts for the current state in the default cycle.

> **Excursus 4: Moody's Forecasting Model for Default Rates**
>
> Moody's default rate forecasting model is primarily based on the number of defaulters over the past year using statistical techniques that cope with several problems, for instance, that the number of defaults represents only a small fraction of the number of issuers. The probability for a specific number of speculative-grade defaulters in a specific month is extracted from a Poisson distribution.
>
> The current specification of Moody's default forecasting model includes six variables plus an intercept and an interaction term. The model is based on the corporate bond universe rated speculative grade, the speculative grade universe rated Ba or below, incorporating the real industrial production trend, new speculative-grade issuers lagged count, the ten-year treasury (nominal) yield, and the treasury bond–bill spread (ten-year, ninety-day).
>
> According to Moody's, the default forecasting model also accounts for the well-known aging effect, incorporating that the hazard rate of default (forward default rate) is a function of time in the market for new issuers. Each issuer will reach a critical period when the success of the enterprise is most uncertain and hence the risk of default is at a maximum. If the issuer's business plan is successful and the company begins to generate sufficient revenues to pay down the debt, the critical period has been survived and the default probability declines. Based on historical default data, Moody's found that the hazard rate of default did start low, rising rapidly to a peak at about four years, then decreasing almost as rapidly to about ten years. Factoring in this trend, Moody's accounts for the effect of new issuance activity by considering the age of the rated universe using the historical hazard rate curve.
>
> The full detail and specification of Moody's default rate forecasting model was presented in the August 1999 special comment "Predicting Default Rates: A Forecasting Model for Moody's Issuer-Based Default Rates".[18]

4.3.3 Recovery Rates: The Collins & Aikman Case

Optimizing credit portfolios requires knowledge of the loss distribution. And the expected loss of a single company is not only determined by the probability of default but also by the loss given default (one minus the recovery rate). Moreover, the recovery rate is crucial regarding the valuation of credit derivatives. However, recovery risk is still an unknown variable, as the Collins & Aikman case showed.

Collins & Aikman, a US auto supplier, filed for Chapter 11 protection in mid-May of 2005. Until February 2005, the CKCR 10.75%12/2011 issue traded around 600 bp, in line with its B2 rating. In mid-March, Moody's downgraded the company to Caa1, which was accompanied by a significant spread widening to around 900 bp. On May 13, 2005, Moody's further downgraded the company to Ca, and four days later the company filed for Chapter 11 protection. In the course of these events, spreads exploded to about 1800 bp. Following the default event, Collins & Aikman's issues were traded at distressed debt levels, with the expected recovery rate being the major price determinant.

Shortly after the default, the bond traded at around 40 percent of its notional amount, which corresponds to the long-term average recovery value (historical average). On Friday, June 24, 2005, this market-implied recovery rate dropped to the level of about 26 percent.

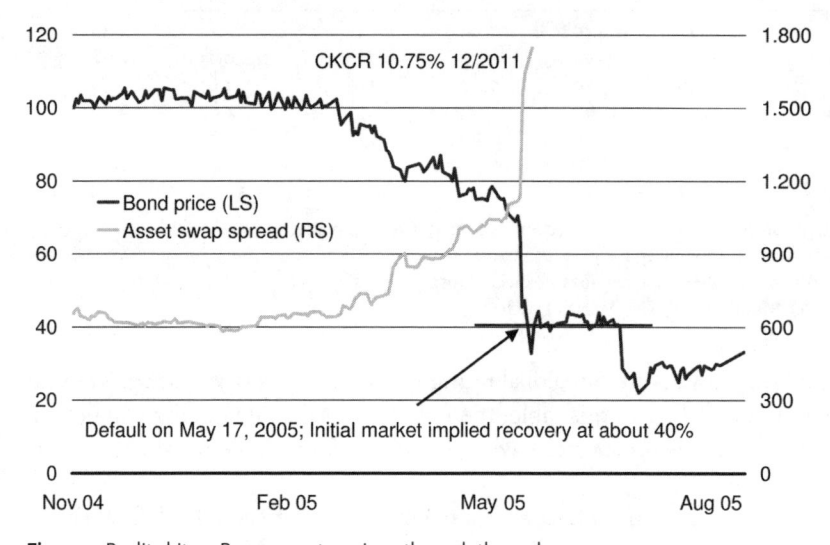

Fig. 4.9: Reality bites: Recovery-rate swings through the cycle

In a recession, recovery rates tend to be low, while in a strong growth environment recoveries are higher on average. Unfortunately, forecasting the recovery value belongs to the most difficult tasks in financial analysis, as the balance sheet of companies close to default changes significantly and very often unpredictably. Hence, the market will continue to assume an average recovery rate of

40 percent, offering attractive trading opportunities for distressed debt trading desks. The good news is that there is a simple tool to eliminate recovery risk: recovery swaps. A recovery swap allows the investor to fix the recovery rate in case of a credit event (please refer to the section 2.5.4 for details).

4.3.4 Implied Ratings

Determining the key parameters in credit portfolio management, probability of default and loss given default, is a key part of credit portfolio management. As mentioned before, both parameters can be derived by using historical data or by implied information in market quotes. Exactly the same procedure can be used in respect to ratings.

Tab. 4.2: Default-risk premium by rating classes for a 5Y horizon

	Default probability*	Recovery rate*	Expected loss	Spread	Implied expected loss	Premium
Aaa	0.12	74.10	0.03	3[†]	0.14	4.48
Aa	0.20	41.10	0.12	15[†]	0.73	6.22
A	0.50	45.20	0.27	32[†]	1.61	5.87
Baa	2.08	41.60	1.21	57[†]	2.87	2.37
Ba	10.72	44.00	6.00	277[‡]	13.85	2.31
B	30.48	37.80	18.96	435[‡]	21.75	1.15
Caa–C	59.72	12.30	52.37	620[‡]	31.00	0.59

Default probabilities, recovery rates and expected losses in percent;
Asset swap spreads in bp for June 30, 2005;
Premium = implied expected loss / expected loss (dimensionless).
Source: Moody's*, iBoxx[†], Merrill Lynch[‡]

In table 4.2, we point out global rating migration rates (1970-2003, five-year horizon). According to this table, the risk that a AAA-rated name will default within five years is 0.11 percent, while the figure for a single B issuer amounts to 20.3 percent.

While there are several factors that determine credit spreads, default risk is the dominating issue, especially for buy-and-hold investors. That raises the question whether single rating classes (accompanied by a certain spread level) offer more or less compensation for default risk than others. Against this background, we calculate the so-called default premium (implied expected loss divided by expected loss). The ratio reflects the premium an investor gets for taking the risk of default. The outcome of our analysis shows that high-grade names pay a higher default premium than high-yield credits. This underpins market segmentation theory, which states that there is lower demand for high-yield bonds due to regulatory constraints as many investors have to fulfill quality constraints and are not allowed to invest in high-yield markets.

4.4 Equity–Debt Linkage

Equity markets are still a key indicator for credits, which is theoretically verified and historically proven. The basic idea of most market participants is simple: As long as the equity share of a company is high enough to fulfill debt obligations, the risk of default is rather subdued. Consequently, strong equity markets are supportive for credit spreads.

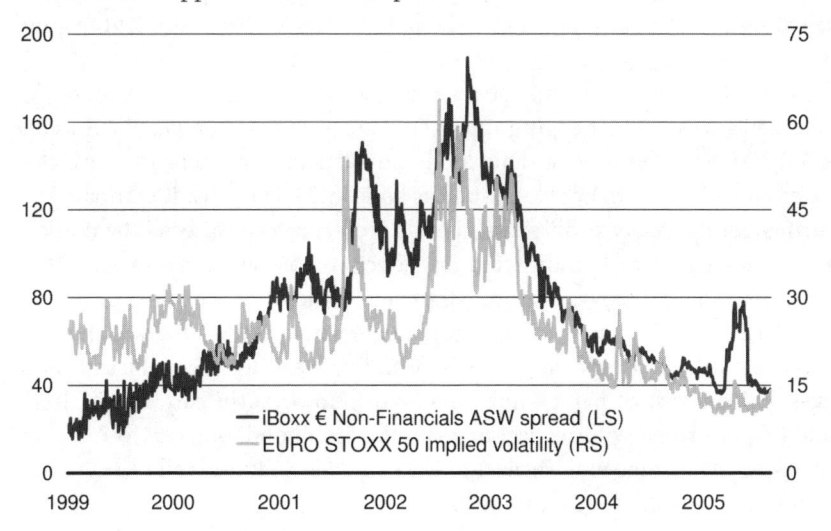

Fig. 4.10: Implied option volatility and credit spreads

4.4.1 The Basic Merton Approach: Structural Models

The name structural models is derived from the fact that balance sheet information is used to construct a measure of credit risk. These models were introduced by Merton (1974), who extended the pioneering approach by Black and Scholes (1973).

Although modeling default risk (i.e., defaultable debt) is their main task, they even aim to answer a more general question: How can the debt of the firm be linked to its share price? One can distinguish between models where default can only be triggered at the time of maturity or at coupon dates from those where default already occurs when the value of the firm hits a specific (time-dependent) barrier. Furthermore, there are models with an endogenous, in contrast to an exogenous, bankruptcy level. Most popular practical implementations include Moody's KMV or the CUSP model from Credit Suisse.

The linkage between debt and equity can in general be used in two different ways, which are based on a different view of market efficiency. One approach would be to assess the relative value of debt and equity to exploit mispricing. This approach would mean that interested investors have to look for market inefficiencies. Another approach would be to look for a stable link between the two markets that can be used for hedging purposes, in other words, to hedge a credit exposure by trading in the equity. While the first approach refers to so-called capital structure arbitrage, the latter refers to a cross-asset-hedging approach.

To model the debt–equity linkage (in a capital structure arbitrage framework, as well as in a cross-asset-hedging approach), one uses a Merton-type firm-value model (FVM, a.k.a. enterprise value models or structural models) to assess the relative value of credit-risky assets, such as bond and CDS spreads compared to the firm's equity. As spreads of cash bonds are likely to be affected by market inefficiencies (such as liquidity and tax effects), it is beneficial to use CDS spreads instead. Moreover, trading strategies, which involve short positions in credit risk, can be more easily implemented in the CDS market than in cash bond markets, as shorting a cash bond involves the rather illiquid repo market and the risk of being short-squeezed. However, in case the analysis should be performed with respect to a specific cash bond, one can first assess the debt–equity linkage with respect to CDS spreads and then refer to the cash bond by analyzing the CDS–cash basis.

The following basic input factors are needed to price the credit risk using a structural model:

- the firm's asset value,
- the corresponding asset volatility, and
- the debt–equity ratio.

Depending on the specific model, other parameters may be necessary. The most severe problem with structural models is that the parameters are not directly accessible, while, usually, the asset value and the asset volatility are unknown. Furthermore, problems arise due to potentially complex capital structures. To circumvent these difficulties, proxies for the parameters have to be used.

As the equity and equity option markets are quite liquid, those quantities can be used to approximate the asset value and asset volatility. However, problems arise here as well. One can either use balance sheet information (e.g., total debt) to derive the asset value (assets = debt + equity) or use the proxies directly as a substitute for the actually needed variables. The first approach causes problems because the equity and debt value information is available within different time frames. Stock prices can be derived from the market with high frequencies (i.e., daily), while balance sheet information is available only on a quarterly basis. This discrepancy causes discontinuities in the aggregated time series and distorted volatilities. The second approach can be viewed as a special case of the first one, with either the debt value equal to zero or a constant value. For the special case debt = 0, the default barrier needed to calculate the default probability with a structural model has to be adjusted. A suggestion regarding this point would be to trigger default if the stock price drops to a certain level (see below for a more detailed analysis).

Besides the challenges regarding parameter estimation, another aspect relative to modeling structural models has to be addressed. In the most basic approach, the contingent claim analysis is based on plain-vanilla European option techniques. The model company has a very simple liability structure. The debt is a zero coupon bond with a specific maturity date, and the equity is the payoff of a call option with the firm's assets as the underlying and the face value of the zero coupon bond as strike price K. Thus, the equity value in this model is the value of the respective call option. As the model is set up with a fixed time horizon (European option style), a default event can only be measured at maturity. The model assumes that at maturity the firm's assets are liquidated and the proceeds are used to pay off first the bond and then the shareholder (in exactly this order, as we apply the strict priority rule). In case the asset value exceeds the face value of the bond, the rest is paid to the equity sponsor. If the asset value is below the face value, the bondholder receives the asset value and the owner of the firm receives nothing, that is, the option that models the equity expires worthless. As we assume a limited liability company, the owner does not have to compensate bondholders for losses in credit risk. As a consequence, the value of the credit-risky zero bond is given as its discounted face value (using the risk-free interest rate) plus a short put option on the assets.

In this framework, only the asset value at maturity matters, with the path of the asset value during the life of the contract being irrelevant. It can drop below the strike price K of the option (i.e., the face value of the bond) without triggering a default event. From an economic point of view, this is a clear limitation of the model.

To cope with this problem, different option payoff structures are used to estimate the default probability. Instead of a plain-vanilla European call, we can use a down-and-out call option (knock-out option) to model the equity value. Models using this technique are so-called first-passage-of-time models. In addition to the strike price of the option K (the face value of the bond as well), one has to specify the down-and-out barrier of the option D. In this model framework, a company is in default if the value of its assets at maturity is below the face value of the bond, or if it hits the default barrier during the life of the bond for the first time. In the latter case, the bondholders take over the firm immediately, liquidate the assets, and use the proceeds to repay the debt. Obviously, this framework depends on the level of the default barrier D. We can distinguish between two different scenarios regarding the level of the default barrier:

- $D \geq K$: If the default barrier is above the strike price (i.e., the face value of the bond), the bondholders are fully protected and hence experience no credit risk at all (as the asset value exceeds the face value of debt). In case the asset value hits the default barrier D, the liquidation will always deliver more than the face value. Thus, a first-passage-of-time model with a default barrier above the face value of the bond is not able to capture credit risk and can be ruled out. The same argument applies to a default barrier that equals the strike.
- $D < K$: If the default barrier is below the strike price, default can be triggered in two ways. First, the asset process never hits the default barrier, but the asset value is below the strike price at maturity. This will leave the bondholders with a loss that equals the difference between the face value and the final asset value. Second, default occurs before maturity if the asset process hits the default barrier. In this case, bondholders take over the company immediately, liquidate all assets, and use the proceeds to satisfy their claim. In this case, we know the loss in advance, which is the difference between the face value of the debt and the default barrier. In any case, the loss given default is limited to an amount of face value minus default barrier.

While a Merton approach is a very elegant solution to price debt using information from equity markets, there are several shortfalls in practice. There is not one model that generates a stable relationship between debt and equity of a firm for all companies in the credit universe. While calibrating Merton-based models to market prices is a tough task because there are some non-observable input factors that have to be estimated, there is another crucial disadvantage. The assumption that only markets drive the debt–equity ratio, which is a major

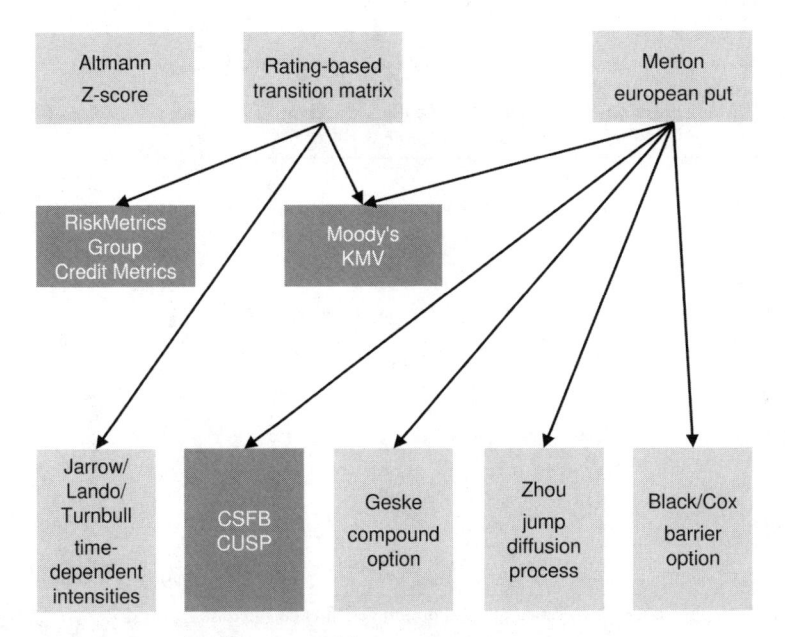

Fig. 4.11: Hierarchy of Merton models

factor in the model, is obviously misleading. If the capital structure is a target of the financial policy of a company, it is not only asset value and asset volatility that determine the debt–equity ratio.

General findings show that structural models do not accurately measure credit spreads. Although specific models generate good results for single companies, the general outcome of using Merton models is that they underestimate spreads for highly volatile companies, while they overestimate spreads for low-yield companies.

While the asset value and the outstanding notional amount of debt are input factors for all models, model-specific input factors are the recovery rate, the volatility of the recovery rate, jump frequency, and jump intensity. As some input factors are not observable in the market, estimations are necessary.

In the following, we use five models (the Merton approach, CreditGrades, Duffie/Lando, Zhou, and Black/Cox) to calculate implied CDS spreads for sixteen liquid German names and compare the outcome with market levels.

In table 4.3, we highlight that there is no key-of-wisdom model. On the contrary, an analogy between model spreads and market quotes seems to be rather accidental. The above-mentioned failure of these models, however, is affirmed: the spread of low volatility companies is underestimated. This is

Tab. 4.3: Merton models: Implied spread levels are not consistent with market quotes

	Merton	Credit Grades	Duffie Lando	Zhou	Black Cox	Market
BASF	0	0	0	0	0	13.45
Bayer	34	76	42	51	41	26.57
BMW	1	0	2	3	1	22.65
Continental	33	65	42	42	40	36.79
DaimlerChrysler	19	40	25	30	23	68.13
Deutsche Telekom	46	107	54	74	54	37.92
E.ON	2	9	3	7	2	18.50
Henkel	11	25	14	24	12	24.12
Linde	18	53	23	35	20	25.87
Lufthansa	246	420	269	220	327	66.54
Metro	54	114	64	72	65	43.96
RWE	62	164	68	121	72	20.65
Siemens	5	17	8	9	6	16.03
ThyssenKrupp	14	36	19	23	16	78.85
Tui	277	430	289	268	378	192.57
Volkswagen	133	250	147	158	169	66.93

* data from December 2004. Two times implied option volatility (at the money) is used.

even true despite the fact that two times the implied volatility is used as an input factor, which improved the fit of these models significantly. Although further modifications (adjusting the equity–debt ratio) can help to improve this result for specific companies, it does not affect the general outcome of our analysis: Merton models fail to predict market spreads accurately.

Despite these problems there is a failure of the Merton approach that makes the model inaccurate with respect to a crucial factor: the equity–debt ratio. The change in this ratio clearly affects the outcome of the model as a lower ratio argues for a wider spread (as the risk of a default increases) and vice versa. But the model only works if these changes are driven by markets! In case there is a force majeure, a basic mechanism of the model is canceled. This is exactly the case if the capital structure is a goal of the financial policy of a company.

4.4.2 Merton in Practice

How does a capital structure arbitrage trade work in practice? In simple terms, a declining share price and rising implied equity volatility should be accompanied by wider credit spreads. In case of divergent trends, arbitrage trades are implemented to benefit from the return of volatilities, prices or spreads to the fair (model-based) pricing relationship. However, the word "arbitrage" is misleading as these trades have a speculative character rather than generating "risk–free profits". This became obvious in May 2005, when capital structure arbitrageurs lost money by betting on General Motors, including a long position in credits, hedged by a short position in equities. Unfortunately, markets discounted restructuring rather than bankruptcy and the immense spread widening was accompanied by a rising share price (Kerkovian's bid), which triggered losses on both sides of the position (please see figure 4.12). In the default scenario, the investor receives the recovery value on the long credit position but the short equity position will more than offset the loss assuming a share price of zero. In the restructuring scenario, in contrast, assets might be shifted to benefit the shareholder at the expense of the bondholder, and the capital structure player realizes a double loss on the credit (losing notional amount minus recovery value) and on the equity position (due to the expected rise of the share price).

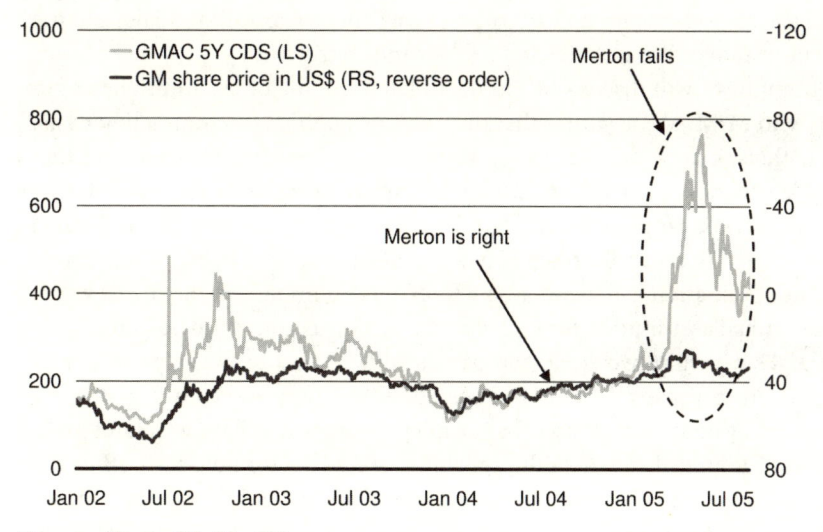

Fig. 4.12: Merton failed for GM

> **Excursus 5: Taking M to the Power of Four**
>
> Despite the accelerating development of new instruments and trading strategies during the last few years in the credit derivatives playground, the basic ideas from Merton (ME), Modigliani/Miller (M/M), and Markowitz (MA) are still being discussed. The relationship of M/M and ME is crucial for understanding capital structure arbitrage. The good news is that, under specific

assumptions (no bankruptcy costs), M/M and ME are consistent. This means the capital structure does not affect the investment value of a firm, but it affects relative investment values of debt and equity holdings.

M/M separates the financing and production decisions of a firm, stating that the value of a firm (not the stock price) is independent of its capital structure. The investment value is determined by the present worth of all future distributions to security holders. They highlight an arbitrage-free mechanism (in contrast to previous papers) that guarantees this law. This point becomes obvious if we assume that only one security is issued bearing all the risk, whether this is a bond or a stock. Similarly, if an individual owned all various types of securities, his risk would also be independent of the capital structure. Modern thinking is that the present value of the sum of two uncertain income streams equals the sum of the separate PVs. M/M assumes perfect and complete markets: there is no risk-free arbitrage opportunity, and operating income and the PV function are not affected by the capital structure. It thus assumes there are no bankruptcy costs and no tax differentials, and the discount rate is also not affected by the capital structure.

Although we will discuss ME in detail later, the major assumptions are in line with M/M. ME assumes that the market is perfect (no transaction costs, etc.), that no new debt is issued until the old debt has expired, and that the PV function is not dependent on the capital structure as there is only one (M/M's last assumption is fulfilled). That said, equity and debt can be defined as options with the strike price K (equals the face value of debt). While equity and debt valuation is dependent on K, K has no impact on the firm's value.

The crucial assumption for both approaches is that there are no bankruptcy costs. Comparing two equal companies with respect to future profit generation, with company A being financed by equity only and company B being financed by debt only, positive bankruptcy costs means that the default probability of B exceeds the default probability of A. This would clearly affect the value of the firm. The assumption that there are no bankruptcy costs makes ME and M/M compatible (ME also assumes that bankruptcy costs nothing).

The other side of the coin is that both approaches are not fully consistent with market quotes, which is also a problem in our model. In a simple ME approach (defining debt as a binary European option), we can deduce the implied default probability (also binary as there is default or not). Default probability is also a parameter in every basic CDS valuation model. Consequently, we derive a link between both models. Time-passage-barrier models that fit with their pendants on the equity front would be much more appropriate, but very difficult to calibrate to CDS valuation. New Merton approaches with incomplete information, for example Duffie and Lando[19] (2001), provide a more realistic picture of markets but are not consistent with M/M.

4.4.3 Leap-Put Skewness as an Equity–Debt Indicator

Besides implied option volatility, there is additional information in stock option markets that is useful for credit investors. Skewness as a parameter in a modified Black and Scholes framework could be used as an indicator for default probability (and hence for credit spreads) as it reflects the implied probability of a tail event in equity markets (e.g., a crash in stock markets). In our view, leap-put skewness is superior to implied option volatility in equity–debt linkage.

The leap-put skewness in figure 4.13 is derived from DAX index options. LEAPS (long-term equity anticipation securities) are index or equity options that exceed nine months, with expiration dates of up to three years. When calculating implied volatility for LEAPS, the third month applies to index options and non-US equity options. The variance-gamma (VG) model deals with distributions more general than normal (Black and Scholes) for calculating op-

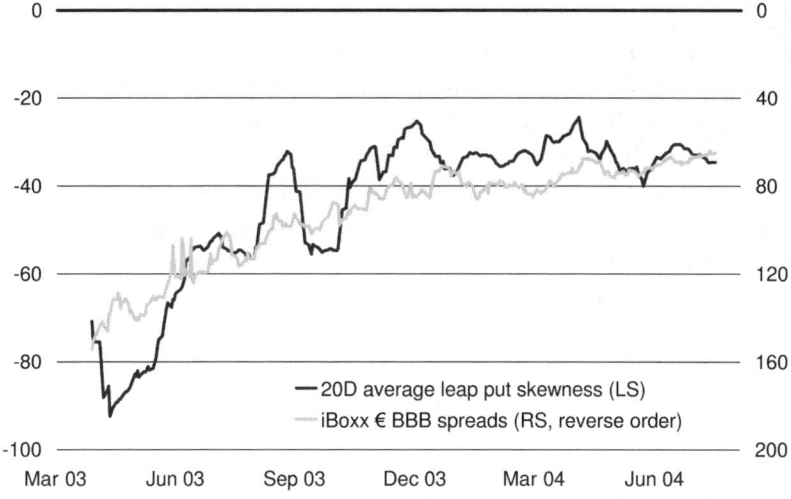

Fig. 4.13: Good bye implied option volatility. We welcome leap-put-skewness in the equity–debt linkage

tion prices. In the VG model, distribution functions are defined by skewness, kurtosis, and volatility.

Equity derivative players are very familiar with the fact that implied option volatility varies significantly for different strike prices (volatility smile), and therefore the VDAX, which is derived from at-the-money options, provides only a small portion of available information. The VDAX index represents the implied volatility of the DAX German stock index, assuming a constant 45 days remaining until expiration of the DAX index options. In practice, the volatility discounted in out-of-the-money options exceeds the implied volatility of at-the-money options. As the shape of the smile is not stable over time, there must be a driver for volatility smiles. A very intuitive interpretation is that a steeper smile signals that markets discount a higher probability of tail events (e.g., a crash in stock markets), while a flatter smile reflects declining risk aversion. The higher the expected probability of a crash, the higher is the demand for (worst-case) protection, and consequently, the higher the option premium, as reflected in an increasing implied option volatility for far-out-of-the money puts. Hence, a flattening trend in the volatility smile should go hand-in-hand with tighter credit spreads and vice versa.

Now we translate this idea into a more sophisticated framework and use a variance-gamma model, based on Baver[20] (2003). This model explains stock price dynamics instead of a Brownian motion in the original Black and Scholes model by implementing two new parameters: skewness and kurtosis to describe asymmetry and fat tails of distributions. Especially the former (skewness) is of special interest for us as it reflects the skew of the probability distribution towards tail events. In case the skewness is strongly negative, option players assign a higher probability to tail events, willing to pay a higher premium for far-out-of-the-money puts, which is reflected in a rising implied option volatility. In this case, a large portion of risk aversion is discounted in equity markets. This occurrence is also reflected in wider credit spreads, as credit investors receive the risk premium (spread) primarily for taking tail risk. In contrast, a skewness near zero means that investors do assume a low probability of tail events, paying only a small premium for tail event protection, reflected in a lower implied option volatility. This should go hand-in-hand with tighter spread levels. Figure 4.13 confirms our idea, as the (absolute) decline in skewness since March 2003 was accompanied by a significant narrowing trend in BBB spreads.

To sum up, a highly negative leap-put skewness could be interpreted as an indicator for implied probabilities of huge downward moves in stock markets. On a single-name basis in a Merton framework, such downward moves are accompanied by a rising likelihood that a company is not able to repay its debt. The skewness is, consequently, directly linked to credit spreads, which compensate investors for carrying default risk (the tail event for bondholders). That said, swings in the leap-put skewness have an impact on spreads. The advantage of using skewness in the equity–debt linkage rather than implied option volatility lies in the fact that the former directly reflects the risk for tail events. In contrast, implied option volatility is derived from at-the-money options (calls and puts) and highlights the discounted overall risk aversion rather than the probability of a worst-case-scenario.

4.4.4 Empirical Evidence for the Equity–Debt Linkage

The time has come for an empirical examination of the equity–debt linkage. In the following, we will examine whether a link between credit spreads and the equity market (stock price and volatility) exists on a single-name basis and on an index level. Second, the focus will be on the stability of the interrelationship. While the linkage works quite well on a medium to long-term basis, fair credit spreads calculated by the model can temporarily deviate from market quotes, indicating possible mispricing. Hence, a simple econometric approach may be utilized as an indicator for technical pressure within credit markets. Finally, we conclude that the stability of equity–debt linkage is significantly improved on an index level.

The major result from any Merton-type model is that the pricing of a corporate liability is linked to its asset valuation. As already outlined, stock prices are often used as a proxy due to the unobservability or limited observability of asset prices. Against this background, credit spreads should be negatively correlated with stock prices, although the relationship will regularly be a non-linear one. A basic Merton approach typically resorts to Black-Scholes assumptions, whereas the asset (stock) volatility is treated as a given parameter. However, equity derivatives markets already internalized that volatility is indeed a major risk factor that should not be taken for granted. For this reason, we perform an econometric analysis by taking stock prices and implied option volatility as exogenous variables in order to explain credit spreads.

We first start our examination of the equity–debt linkage on a single-name basis, focusing on five representative names from the DAX universe.

For each of these names, we estimated the parameters of the following regression approach (with having the usual properties of a linear regression model):

$$\ln \mathrm{CS}_t = b_0 + b_1 \cdot \ln \mathrm{SP}_t + b_2 \cdot \mathrm{SV}_t + \epsilon_t$$

with

$$CS_t = \text{CDS spread for the name at time } t$$
$$SP_t = \text{stock price for the name at time } t$$
$$SV_t = \text{implied put-option volatility for the name at time } t$$

Tab. 4.4: Five representative names from the DAX universe

Company	CDS spread	Stock price	Volatility
Commerzbank	26.5 bp	€17.50	18.80
Deutsche Telekom	24.7 bp	€15.84	14.84
Volkswagen	45.1 bp	€37.32	19.45
E.ON	16.6 bp	€68.85	17.49
ThyssenKrupp	43.0 bp	€17.13	17.19

Data as of March 8, 2005
Source: Bloomberg

As a geometric Brownian motion typically acts as a process assumption for credit spreads and stock prices, we decided to take the logarithms of these variables. In this case, both variables should follow a normal distribution, which is a desirable characteristic for linear regression approaches. It should be noted that we are aware that the chosen functional form does not reflect the characteristics of our model discussed before. However, we prefer our approach due to simplicity reasons. In addition, a linear relationship can be quite a good approximation for a limited range of values and a limited time frame for the examination. The following results are based on time series data from January 1, 2004, to March 8, 2005.

Figure 4.14 depicts the overall performance for each of the five names, measured by the coefficient of determination. An average determination coefficient of 63.34 percent states that about two thirds of the total (logarithmic) spread variance can be explained by only two variables, the (logarithmic) stock price and its implied volatility. Although this result proves a good explanatory performance of the model, there are obviously credit spread movements that are not attributable to these two variables. This may be due to the simplicity of the supposed relationship by the model, the existence of technical factors that affect the credit market but not the equity peer, and so forth.

It is no surprise that the stock volatility seems to have a stronger impact than stock price levels, particularly in a setting with little stock price changes and default barriers that are far below current levels. But only a slight change in volatility is necessary to alter the distribution of stock prices significantly, and

```
■ Coefficient of determination
```

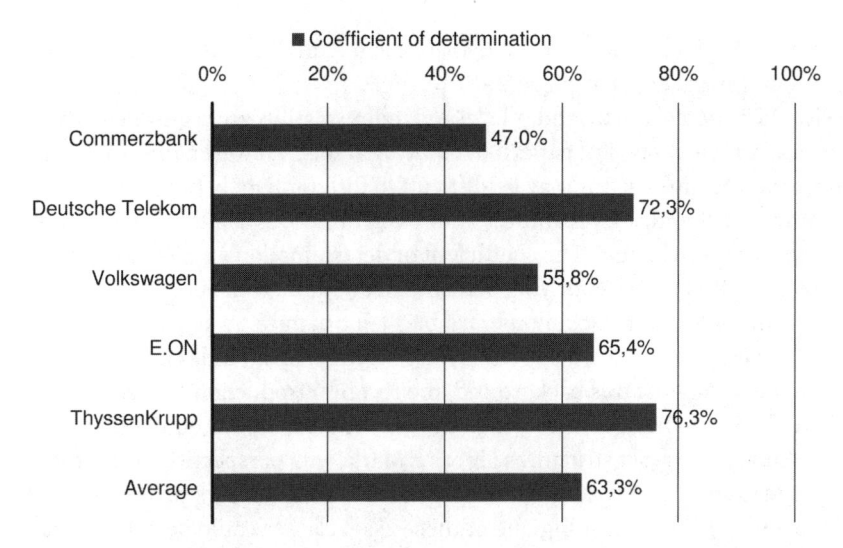

Commerzbank	47,0%
Deutsche Telekom	72,3%
Volkswagen	55,8%
E.ON	65,4%
ThyssenKrupp	76,3%
Average	63,3%

Fig. 4.14: Determination far from perfect

hence the default probability in a Merton universe is strongly affected. Anyway, the results shown above impressively make clear that a pure Merton approach on a single-name basis seems insufficient to explain credit spread movements adequately.

The previous insights raise the question of how results change on an index level. To answer this question, we defined an index comprising all five names on an equally weighted basis (20 percent each). While the calculation of an equity or credit index is straightforward, the calculation of the implied index volatility is more time-consuming. We solved this problem by resorting to a well-known formula from portfolio selection:

$$\sigma_{PF} = \sqrt{\sum_{i=1}^{n} \sum_{j=1}^{n} w_i w_j \rho_{ij} \sigma_i \sigma_j} \qquad (4.1)$$

with

w_i = 0.2 for all i (in accordance with our index weighting scheme)
σ_i = implied stock volatility of stock i

As the portfolio weightings (20 percent each) and implied stock volatilities are already known, one has to make assumptions concerning the correlation structure, that is, the correlation parameters ρ_{ij}. For this purpose, we estimated pairwise correlation figures for the five available names and assumed them to be constant for the entire time period.

It should be noted that the index level and index volatility are highly negatively correlated, which is a typical pattern in equity markets. However, this raises the issue of multicollinearity: it may be difficult to differentiate between the influence of the stock index level and the index volatility. Despite this reservation, the results are convincing. The coefficient of determination surges by about 13 percentage points to a level of 76.5 percent. In addition, t-values indicate a significant impact for both exogenous variables (−3.09 and +20.35). In short, the linkage between equity and debt seems to be stronger on an index level than for single names. Against this background, the recent introduction of credit index products like the iTraxx indices paves the way to hedge pure equity or credit portfolios via cross asset structures. From a Markowitz perspective, combining equity and credit instruments within a portfolio context offers diversification opportunities. Hence, avoiding one of these asset classes could be detrimental to the investor's risk–return profile.

In practice, using equity to hedge credit exposure will not provide a perfect hedge, as there is still around 23.5 percent of the credit spread variance left that is attributable to other market factors. The credit spread development in the medium to long term is pretty well explained by the regression model, while there are temporary deviations from this equilibrium path. In our view, these deviations are mainly attributable to technical factors in the market.

4.5 Market Technicals

In the previous sections, we primarily focused on the driving forces on the demand side, while in this section, we analyze the other side of the market. Technicals have a major market impact, especially on the cash credit market as there is only a limited supply of paper available. That said, primary market activities are also crucial for liquidity in the secondary market.

Market technicals sometimes clearly dominate credit fundamentals, which was the case in 2004 when companies reduced debt to repair balance sheets following the credit crunch scenario in 2001 and 2002. The cash richness of companies triggers declining funding needs, as (besides investment activities) refinancing is a dominating motivation for tapping the bond market. Against this background, the volume of syndicated loans increased significantly, offering companies a flexible and cheap funding source. In addition, investment and debt-financed LBO and M&A activities are key determinants for supply–demand imbalances.

4.5.1 Is there a New Issuance Premium?

In theory, one would argue that companies wanting to issue additional bonds (not to refinance redeemed issues) have to pay a new issuance premium. At least in case demand is stable, investors would enforce a spread pick-up for fresh paper compared to outstanding issues as an incentive to buy the new one. Moreover, the amount of debt is increasing, causing a deterioration of credit protection ratios, which argues for somewhat wider spreads as compensation. However, this is only one side of the coin as accelerating primary market activity underpins liquidity in credit markets, which argues for a decline of the liquidity premium, leading to somewhat tighter spreads.

A large fraction of market participants focuses on credit fundamentals, which is the appropriate focus for those with a longer investment horizon. Techies, in contrast, focus on the liquidity situation and new supply as major driving forces for credit markets.

Figure 4.15 shows that peaks in new supply have no direct impact on secondary spreads and hence do not underpin the old story that new issues could be sold only by paying a new issuance premium, which will trigger wider spreads of outstanding bonds. This argument is rather theoretical and the supply–demand

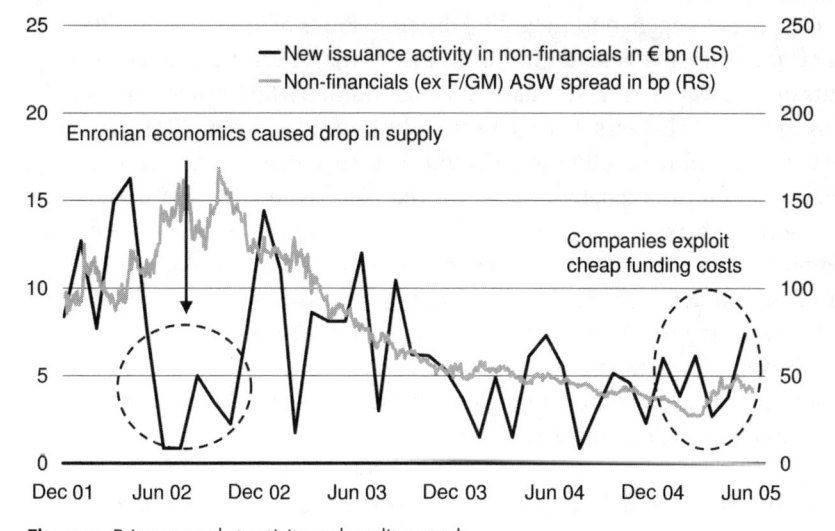

Fig. 4.15: Primary market activity and credit spreads

mechanism is more complex. In the case of an external shock or a sharp deterioration in sentiment (Enronitis, 9/11), wider spreads went hand-in-hand with declining new issuance. This result is obvious, as rising risk aversion will trigger lower demand in both primary and secondary markets. Lower demand causes spread widening in the latter and limits new supply in primary markets.

While we do not ignore structural changes on a micro level (e.g., UMTS in the telecom sector), new issuance activity as well as narrowing credit spreads are rather negatively correlated. In the first half of 2003, issuance picked up sharply as many companies used historically low all-in funding costs to satisfy their refinancing needs. Simultaneously, major credit drivers (macro and micro fundamentals, recovering stock markets, a bottoming out of the negative rating trend) underpinned a friendly market environment. Against this background, credit spreads tightened significantly.

To sum up, Say's law that supply creates its own demand fits with a bullish market environment. If spreads in the secondary market are tight, real money accounts use primary markets to increase exposure to credits. Given sufficient demand, new issues will be priced on the curve, without offering a notable new issuance premium.

4.5.2 Technical Bid

While supply is only one side of the coin, analyzing demand is much more challenging. As there is only one player on the supply side, the demand side is much more heterogeneous, including different kinds of investors. Besides real money accounts like pension funds and asset managers, innovative developments in the credit derivatives markets bring additional liquidity to plain-vanilla credit markets. This was reflected in the technical bid from CDO arrangers, which was a dominating theme for credit markets in the second half of 2004.

Following the strong deterioration in credit quality in 2001 and 2002, especially German banks reduced risk-weighted assets to cut loan-loss provisions, fighting against rating pressure. When the macro picture brightened in 2003 and 2004 and default rates declined impressively, banks lost interest income due to the strong reduction of risk-weighted assets. To generate additional interest income, investments in CDO tranches were viewed as an appropriate tool (given the lack of supply in the cash bond market on the back of ongoing deleveraging and low premiums of loans).

A plain-vanilla investment in a synthetic CDO mezzanine tranche has a gearing (leverage) of around 7.5 (dependent on the tranche size, subordination, correlation, and absolute spread level). This means that a CDO investment of

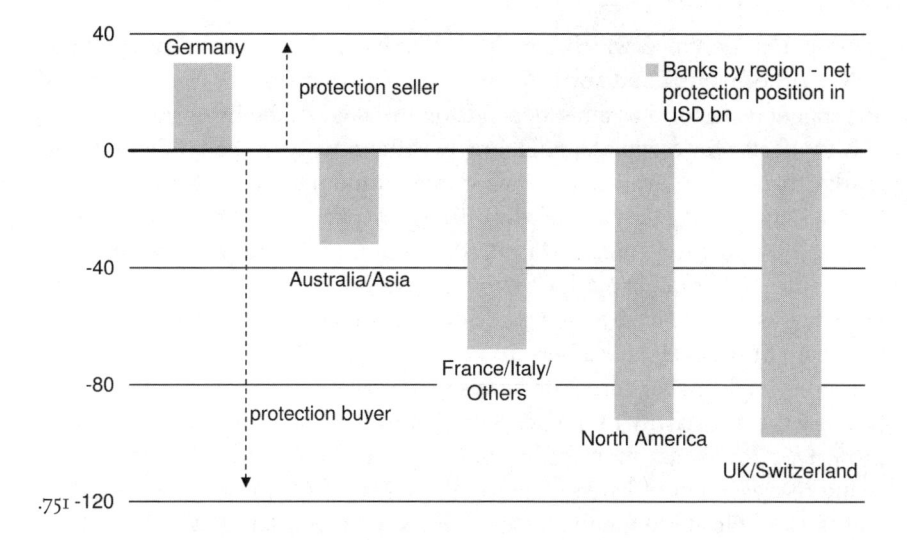

Fig. 4.16: Only German banks are protection sellers within the industry in 2003

€200 mn creates hedging needs for the CDO manager or structurer of €1.5 bn. Hedging needs will be filled by selling protection in the single-name CDS market as well as in portfolio derivatives (such as iTraxx indices). This trend triggers tight premiums in the credit default swap market. While this also pushes cash spreads in the cash bond market tighter, as the last possibility is hedging with cash bonds, the technical bid has also an impact on the basis (the spread difference between credit default swaps and cash bonds).

4.5.3 The Impact of Syndicated Loans on Corporate Bonds

In 2004 and 2005, a persisting imbalance in supply and demand clearly dominated credit fundamentals. This trend is closely linked to the pro-cyclical behavior of banks with respect to their lending business, which is also reflected in the syndicated loan market. While excess liquidity triggers forced-to-invest behavior, excess liquidity is only a temporary phenomenon, depending on the current stage of the business cycle. Excess liquidity causes both increasing demand for risky assets at the same time that asset prices are rising, as available assets are rare while liquidity is plentiful. In such a situation, a rising number of investors are forced to move down the asset quality curve to generate sufficient return to match their liability side (insurance companies) or to match their high management fees (hedge funds). In addition, leveraged credit instruments are gaining in importance, which explains the accelerating growth of the synthetic CDO market in 2004 and 2005. Nevertheless, also demand for credit risk is not an exogenous factor but rather depends on the stage of the investment cycle.

A key factor for corporate bond supply is the activity in the syndicated loan market. In the US, syndicated loans in 2004 amounted to US$ 1,285 bn, the largest figure during the past six years. In 1999, for example, the volume of syndicated loans in the US reached only US$ 677 mn. In the aftermath of the tough years 2001 and 2002, banks have continuously increased their syndicated loan exposure as they wanted to generate additional interest income following the reduction of risk-weighted assets in the crisis years. The substitutive character of syndicated loans for corporate bonds argues against a strong acceleration of primary market activity in the bond market if the syndicated loan business is growing. However, a drop in the volume of syndicated loans results from a rising risk aversion of banks. The consequence of such a scenario would be an easing of the above-mentioned demand–supply imbalance, which has obviously a negative impact on the technical situation for the corporate bond market. To sum up, the technical environment of corporate bond markets is driven by the overall liquidity situation and the existence of substitutive instruments (for example syndicated loans).

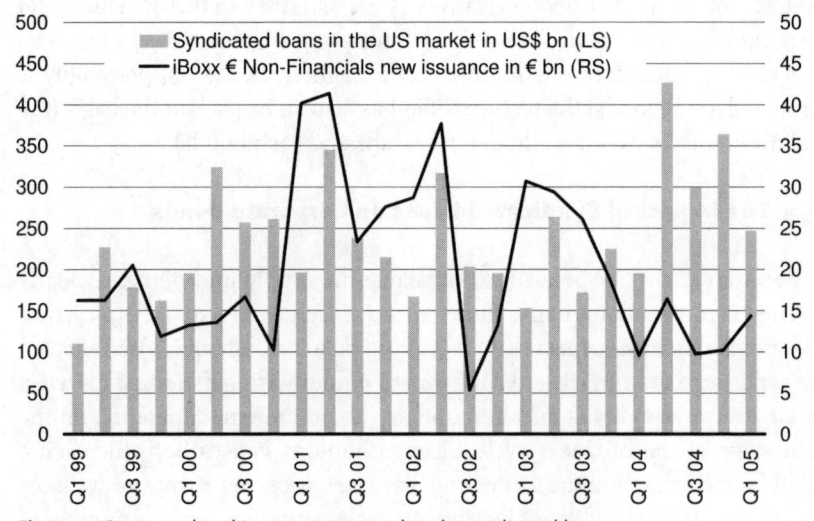

Fig. 4.17: Corporate bond issuance stagnated as the syndicated loan market increased

Part II

Models

5
Fixed Income Basics

At first glance, credit portfolio management deals with the well-defined topic of credit risk. Unfortunately, this is only part of the picture. First, many credit-risky instruments do not solely contain credit risk but are subject to other risk factors as well. This is particularly true for credit-risky bonds and loans, as these also bear interest rate risk. Managing a cash bond portfolio involves keeping an eye on both credit and interest rate risk simultaneously. Second, the concepts used in practice to manage credit risks are similar to those available for interest rate risk. This is mainly due to the fact that interest rate return and credit return are often measured on the same scale, namely as a percentage period return relative to a given notional amount. In the interest rate world, one deals with yields, spot rates, and forward rates, while credit attention is usually focused on the basis of (credit) spreads, which will be formally introduced in the subsequent chapter.

Readers familiar with fixed income theory may want to skip this chapter. However, a brief review of the chapter may be helpful in order to become familiar with the nomenclature we will use throughout the book. In any case, the chapter provides only a brief overview of the most important concepts that are required in the context of credit portfolio management. Readers who find it difficult to understand the concepts presented here are advised to refer to a textbook on fixed income theory for further details.

5.1 Basic Valuation Concepts

5.1.1 The Discount Function

In the context of borrowing or lending money, we are accustomed to thinking in terms of interest rates or yields. The reason is self-evident. An interest rate or yield relates to the return of a fixed income investment on the invested amount and for a standard time period (typically a year). At first glance, this seems to be a good basis for comparisons across different instruments and investment horizons.

Unfortunately, the concept of interest rates shares some weaknesses, which we will discuss in this section. One major disadvantage is that interest rates are not the easiest way to reflect basic valuation principles arising in fixed income markets, as will be demonstrated shortly. We postpone the issue of interest rates to a subsequent section in this chapter.

In the following, we focus on fixed income investments of any kind, assuming that all future cash flows of the respective investments are known and are not subject to default risk.

The future cash flows of a single investment are denoted by CF_i due at time T_i $(i = 1, 2, \ldots, n)$. With t being the current point in time, $\tau_i = T_i - t$ denotes the time that has to elapse until the respective cash flow CF_i becomes due.

Given this stream of cash flows, no-arbitrage considerations lead to the following pricing equation:

$$P_t = \sum_{i=1}^{n} R_t(\tau_i) \cdot CF_i \qquad (5.1)$$

The factors $R_t(\tau_i)$ are referred to as *discount factors*. The discount factor depends on the time until the respective cash flow becomes due. According to this equation, the current price of a fixed income security can simply be calculated as a linear combination of its future cash flows. In this context, the discount factors $R_t(\tau_i)$ act as weightings for this procedure. Later we will point out how to obtain these discounting factors from observable market prices.

What is the meaning of a single discounting factor? For this purpose, consider a fixed income security that has only one future cash flow at time $T > t$ amounting to one monetary unit ($CF = 1$). Such a security is often referred to as a *zero coupon bond* with a notional amount of 1 and remaining time to maturity of $\tau = T - t$. According to formula 5.1, the price at time t is given as

$$P_t = \sum_{i=1}^{n} R_t(\tau_i) \cdot CF_i = R_t(\tau) \cdot 1 = R_t(\tau)$$

Hence, the discount factor $R_t(\tau)$ $(\tau \geq 0)$ can be interpreted as the current price of a zero coupon bond with a notional amount of 1 and remaining time to maturity of τ. It reflects the current value (present value) of a single future payment.

> **Example 2: Valuing a Fixed Coupon Bond**
> An investor wants to calculate the (dirty) price of a fixed coupon bond, whose (remaining) maturity is three years and which pays a yearly coupon at the end of each year amounting to 5.0 percent. Accordingly, the cash flow stream, as

suming a notional amount of 100 (to obtain a price that is quoted in percent), can be taken from the following table:

Point in time	$\tau = 1$	$\tau = 2$	$\tau = 3$
Cash flow CF	5	5	105
Discount factor $R_t(\tau)$	0.95120	0.88695	0.82285

The last row shows the discount factors for these three points in time, which we assume to be provided by the fixed income market. According to formula 5.1, we obtain the current arbitrage-free price for the security:

$$P_t = 0.95120 \cdot 5 + 0.88695 \cdot 5 + 0.82285 \cdot 105 \approx 95.59$$

At the current point in time t, there is a discount factor for each $\tau \geq 0$. These are often combined to the *discount function* $R_t : \mathbb{R}_0^+ \to \mathbb{R}$, $\tau \mapsto R_t(\tau)$. Based on the above interpretation and on no-arbitrage considerations, the discount function should fulfill the following criteria:

1. The very first discount factor $R_t(0)$ has a value of 1, i.e., $R_t(0) = 1$.
2. All discount factors $R_t(\tau)$ are positive, i.e., $R_t(\tau) > 0$ for all $\tau \geq 0$.
3. All discount factors $R_t(\tau)$ are not greater than 1, i.e., $R_t(\tau) \leq 1$ for all $\tau \geq 0$.
4. The discount function $R_t(\tau)$ is monotonously decreasing, i.e., $R_t(\tau_1) \leq R_t(\tau_2)$ for all $\tau_1 > \tau_2 \geq 0$.

The first condition is self-evident. The expression $R_t(0)$ simply refers to a zero coupon bond which becomes due immediately. As it pays one monetary unit, it should be worth the same amount.

Positive discount factors are necessary to avoid simple arbitrage opportunities. If a discretionary discount factor $R_t(\tau)$ were zero, this would mean a free lunch in the future, because this zero coupon bond would be free of charge. A negative value would make one's day, as the free lunch is even associated with getting additional money immediately.

Discount factors above 1 have to be excluded, if we presume that keeping money in one's pocket is free of charge. If the one-year discount factor amounted to 1.2, one could exploit an arbitrage opportunity by selling the one-year zero coupon bond for a price of 1.2, keeping the money until the end of this period, and paying an amount of 1 as stipulated in the contract. This would result in an riskless profit of 0.2 monetary units.

A similar argument applies for the fourth criterion. Indeed, it makes sense that the discount factor should become smaller (more precisely: not become greater) the later we receive a payment. If this condition did not hold, that is, we presume $R_t(\tau_1) > R_t(\tau_2)$ for any $\tau_1 > \tau_2 \geq 0$, an arbitrage opportunity can be exploited by doing the following:

- Sell the zero coupon bond with time to maturity τ_1 with a notional amount of 1 at a price of $R_t(\tau_1)$.
- Use the proceeds from this sale to invest in the zero coupon bond with time to maturity τ_2. This investment has a notional amount of $R_t(\tau_1)/R_t(\tau_2)$, which exceeds 1.
- Wait until the zero coupon bond with time to maturity τ_2 becomes due. Keep the notional amount of $R_t(\tau_1)/R_t(\tau_2)$ in your pocket free of charge.
- Wait until the zero coupon bond with time to maturity τ_1 becomes due. Use the money in your pocket to repay the notional amount of 1 of this zero coupon bond. Use the remaining money in your pocket, amounting to $[R_t(\tau_1)/R_t(\tau_2)] - 1 > 0$, to have a party.

To clarify the concept of the discount function and its properties, figure 5.1 depicts an example that was observed on June 21, 2005. Please note that all four conditions are met.

Interest rate aficionados may ask, What are the advantages of using discount factors instead of interest rates to price fixed income securities? First, they are

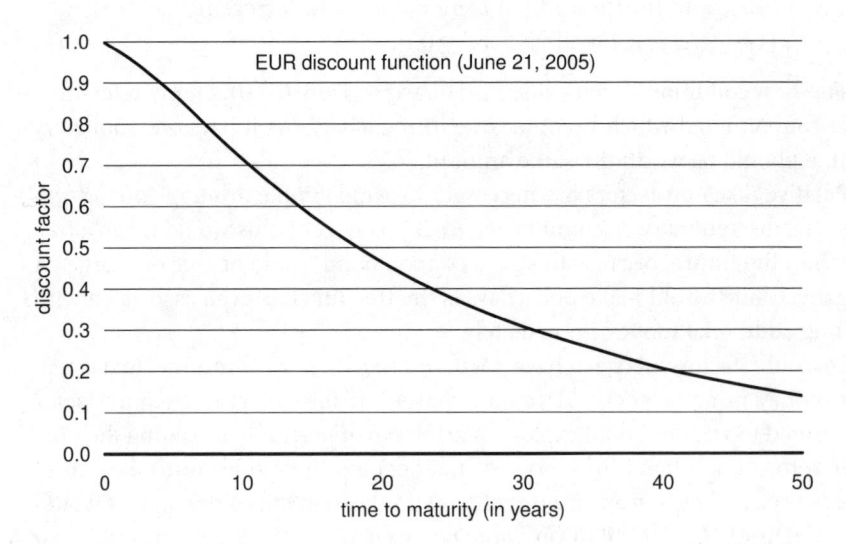

Fig. 5.1: The euro discount curve on June 21, 2005

a direct result of the no-arbitrage condition. Arbitrage-free valuation theory leads to the fundamental result shown in equation 5.1, providing an easy way to value any security with a fixed cash flow stream by means of a simple linear combination (linear pricing function). As we will see in section 5.1.2, prices of fixed income securities and interest rates are always related in a non-linear manner. But there are other issues as well that should be mentioned. Working with interest rates requires us to specify several conventions, as we will see shortly. Hence, interest rates are never unambiguously defined unless these conventions have been determined.

Dealing with discount factors does not depend on such specifications with the exception of how the variable t (time) is measured. In practice, this topic is associated with the terms *day count conventions* and *business day conventions*. From a technical perspective, these rules define how to map actual payment dates (according to the Gregorian calendar) onto the real number axis, which we use to describe time parameters mathematically. Figure 5.2 illustrates this idea.

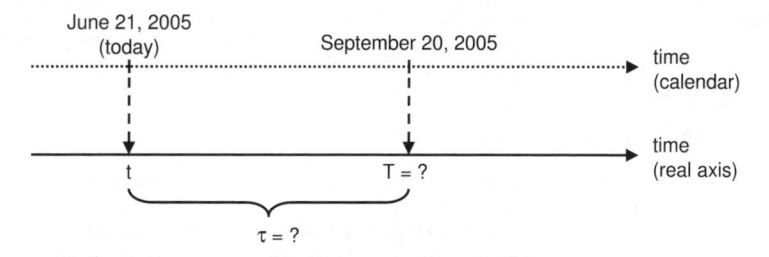

Fig. 5.2: Mapping the Gregorian calender onto a real time axis

The value of t, which refers to the current point in time (today), can be chosen arbitrarily. However, if we focus on processes over time, the variable t is consecutively increased. In this case, only the starting point of t would be subject to arbitrariness. Once t is determined, the main question is how a future date can be mapped onto this real time axis. Hence, the parameters T and $\tau = T - t$ have to be determined in accordance with some well-defined rules.

In a first step, we have to determine the value date of a respective payment. If it actually coincides with a weekend or a bank holiday, business day conventions (BDC) apply. These business day adjustments reschedule the value date of a cash flow in accordance with a specific set of rules. The following table gives an overview of possible conventions:

Tab. 5.1: Business day conventions

Convention	Treatment of non-business days
Following	Take the subsequent business day.
Modified Following	Take the subsequent business day as long as it belongs to the same month. Otherwise, take the preceding business day.
Preceding	Take the preceding business day.
Modified Preceding	Take the preceding business day as long as it belongs to the same month. Otherwise, take the subsequent business day.

Second, day count conventions (DCC) apply to map the value date onto the real number axis. In any case, measuring $\tau = T-t$ is always done by calculating a simple ratio. While the numerator reflects the number of days between two specific points in time (usually $\tau = T - t$), the denominator contains the number of days for a reference period (usually a year). The respective day count convention determines how to count the days in the numerator and the denominator of this ratio. Please refer to table 5.2 for the most important conventions.

Tab. 5.2: Day count conventions

Convention	Rule description
Act/Act	The actual number of days between two dates is used in the numerator and the denominator.
Act/365	The actual number of days between two dates is used in the numerator and the denominator, with the exception that the effect of leap years is ignored. All years are assumed to have 365 days.
Act/360	The actual number of days between two dates is used for the numerator, while a year is assumed to have 12 months of 30 days each for the denominator.
30/360	All months are assumed to have 30 days, resulting in a 360 day year. If the first date falls on the 31st, it is changed to the 30th. If the second date falls on the 31st, it is changed to the 30th, but only if the first date falls on the 30th or the 31st.
30E/360	Similar to 30/360. However, if the second date falls on the 31st, it is changed to the 30th.

All day count conventions shown above presume a year as a reference period. Hence, one year is always equivalent to one unit on our time axis.

Loans and savings accounts are typically subject to 30/360, while Act/Act usually applies for euro-denominated bonds. Act/360 often applies in the context of credit derivatives like credit default swaps or index swaps. However, there is no general rule that is applied.

Unless otherwise stated, we assume Act/Act as the basis for measuring time when using the discount function, irrespective of the actual day count convention of instruments under discussion. It avoids any distortion arising from simplifying assumptions like ignoring leap years.

5.1.2 Spot Rates and the Term Structure of Interest Rates

Although discount factors result from arbitrage-free valuation, they pose a significant problem: People are not used to thinking in terms of discount factors and prefer using interest rates or yields instead. These measures facilitate an economic comparison among different instruments and terms, as interest rates and yields provide return information on a standardized basis. They are always related to the notional amount of the investment; in other words, yields and interest rates are relative performance measures.

Therefore, the idea is to convert discount factors into such data. However, the result is significantly affected by a few decisions that have to be made in advance. The first question is whether the resulting interest rate reflects a total return for a specific investment horizon or is expressed in terms of a specific period, for example a year. It depends on the purpose of analysis which measure to take. In most cases, a period return (typically a year) is preferred to allow for intertemporal comparisons.

A second question has already been brought up, the selection of a day count convention. In the following, we adopt the day count convention that is used for the discount function (typically Act/Act). The calculation of interest rates would be complicated if we used a different day count convention than for the discount function.

A third issue relates to how compounding effects are taken into account. When dealing with fixed income products, one usually refers to a base investment. This could be a savings account that typically credits accrued interest at the end of each year. If US government bonds are the benchmark investment, one would apply a semiannual compounding, as coupons are paid twice a year. It should be noted that choosing a compounding method does not represent any real-world activity, but rather a fiction to allow comparisons across different investments that might be subject to different payout frequencies.

Simple compounding as a first alternative historically originated with commercial trading activities. The interest payment is simply calculated as the product of (1) amount invested, (2) stipulated interest rate, and (3) elapsed time, ignoring any effects from crediting for accrued interest at the end of some period. Applying this notion to a zero coupon bond investment would result in the following equality, with $r_t(\tau)$ denoting the interest rate:

$$R_t(\tau) \cdot r_t(\tau) \cdot \tau = 1 - R_t(\tau) \tag{5.2}$$

The right hand side of the equation states the interest payment as the difference between the whole repayment amount, which amounts to 1, and the initial investment. Solving the equation for $r_t(\tau_i)$ renders:

$$r_t(\tau) = \frac{1 - R_t(\tau)}{\tau \cdot R_t(\tau)} \tag{5.3}$$

Please note that for every time to maturity τ ($\tau > 0$) there is a respective interest rate $r_t(\tau)$. A rate $r_t(\tau)$ is referred to as a *spot rate*, and it depicts the yield of a zero coupon bond investment of a specified term τ. In this case, the yield calculation is done based on the simple compounding convention.

In practice, simple compounding is often used in the context of savings accounts (terms of up to one year) and interbank money market transactions (term deposits), which are based on the London Interbank Offered Rate (Libor) provided by the British Bankers' Association or the Euro Interbank Offered Rate (Euribor), which is sponsored by the European Banking Federation (FBE). They can be interpreted as the interest rates at which prime banks could borrow funds from other prime banks, in marketable size. Libors are available for several currencies (EUR, USD, GBP, JPY, CHF, CAD, AUD, DKK, NZD) and terms (1 or 2 weeks, 1 to 12 months), while the Euribor is limited to one currency, the euro. Terms for the Euribor are identical to those for the Libor, with the exception that there is also a three-week Euribor available. The Libor is based on the Act/360 day count convention (Act/365 for GBP) and mostly on the Modified Following business day convention.

Although Libor and Euribor cannot be taken as perfect risk-free interest rates, they act as good proxies. Thus, it is easy to calculate respective discount factors by solving equation 5.3 for $R_t(\tau)$:

$$R_t(\tau) = \frac{1}{1 + r_t(\tau) \cdot \tau} \tag{5.4}$$

The *linear compounding* method is very similar to simple compounding, as it does not account for crediting for accrued interest at some point in time. However, the interest rate is calculated based on the amount repayable instead of the initial amount invested. Hence, equation 5.2 needs a slight modification, replacing the initial investment amount of the zero coupon bond $R_t(\tau)$ by its notional amount on the left side:

$$1 \cdot r_t(\tau) \cdot \tau = 1 - R_t(\tau) \tag{5.5}$$

Solving for $r_t(\tau)$ renders:

$$r_t(\tau) = \frac{1 - R_t(\tau)}{\tau} \qquad (5.6)$$

Linear compounding has become popular for the US Treasury bill market, where instruments have maturities of one year or less and have a payment structure of a zero coupon bond. Similar instruments can be found in the European government bond market, for example, treasury discount paper (Bubills) and federal treasury financing paper in Germany.

Similar to the procedure shown for simple compounding, discount factors can be calculated based on available interest rates which are subject to linear compounding:

$$R_t(\tau) = 1 - r_t(\tau) \cdot \tau \qquad (5.7)$$

Simple and linear compounding suffer from the fact that crediting for accrued interest is totally ignored. This may be feasible for short-term investments, but is less realistic when turning to longer-term investments. The *discrete compounding* method presumes a specified frequency of crediting for accrued interest. In practice yearly, semiannual, and quarterly compounding is often used, but other frequencies are possible as well.

Let us start with *yearly compounded* interest rates. If we compare a zero coupon bond with time to maturity τ to a term deposit, which is compounded on a yearly basis and has the same maturity date, both investments should be equivalent. An investment of $R_t(\tau)$ should result in the same terminal value of 1. Hence, the following equation must be valid:

$$R_t(\tau) \cdot (1 + r_t(\tau))^\tau = 1 \qquad (5.8)$$

Accordingly, we obtain

$$r_t(\tau) = \sqrt[\tau]{R_t(\tau)^{-1}} - 1 \text{ and} \qquad (5.9)$$

$$R_t(\tau) = (1 + r_t(\tau))^{-\tau} \qquad (5.10)$$

Formulas for semiannual and quarterly compounding can be defined in almost the same manner. For example, when switching from yearly to semiannual compounding, one has to halve the interest rate (due to the shortened interest period), while doubling the number of interest periods. Equation 5.8 then has the following appearance:

$$R_t(\tau) \cdot \left(1 + \frac{r_t(\tau)}{2}\right)^{2 \cdot \tau} = 1 \qquad (5.11)$$

Tab. 5.3: Discrete compounding

Method	Spot rates	Discount rates
yearly	$r_t(\tau) = \sqrt[\tau]{R_t(\tau)^{-1}} - 1$	$R_t(\tau) = (1 + r_t(\tau))^{-\tau}$
semiannually	$r_t(\tau) = 2 \cdot \left[\sqrt[2\cdot\tau]{R_t(\tau)^{-1}} - 1 \right]$	$R_t(\tau) = \left(1 + \frac{r_t(\tau)}{2}\right)^{-2\cdot\tau}$
quarterly	$r_t(\tau) = 4 \cdot \left[\sqrt[4\cdot\tau]{R_t(\tau)^{-1}} - 1 \right]$	$R_t(\tau) = \left(1 + \frac{r_t(\tau)}{4}\right)^{-4\cdot\tau}$
general	$r_t(\tau) = m \cdot \left[\sqrt[m\cdot\tau]{R_t(\tau)^{-1}} - 1 \right]$	$R_t(\tau) = \left(1 + \frac{r_t(\tau)}{m}\right)^{-m\cdot\tau}$

Other compounding frequencies can be similarly used. Table 5.3 gives an overview of how to adjust the formulas.

Semiannual compounding is regarded as the market standard in the United States, as most government and corporate bonds have two coupon payment dates a year. In Europe, market participants are used to yearly coupon payments, hence supporting the concept of yearly compounding.

The general formula in the last row presumes that each year is divided into $m \in \mathbb{N}$ subperiods of equal length. In finance theory rather than in practice, another compounding convention called *continuous compounding* is often used to simplify the algebraic treatment of the interest rate phenomenon. It can be regarded as an extreme case of the general discrete compounding formula shown above, while infinitely increasing the compounding frequency per year. The limit of the discount factor expression is:

$$R_t(\tau) = \lim_{m \to \infty} \left(1 + \frac{r_t(\tau)}{m}\right)^{-m\cdot\tau}$$
$$= e^{-r_t(\tau)\cdot\tau} \qquad (5.12)$$

Or from the perspective of spot rates:

$$r_t(\tau) = -\frac{\ln R_t(\tau)}{\tau} \qquad (5.13)$$

Although working with continuous compounding often involves natural logarithms and exponential functions, the application is rather simple as we will shortly see. Most pricing models for derivatives make use of this convention. Against this background, we recommend becoming familiar with formulas 5.12 and 5.13, as we will regularly resort to this specific convention.

Example 3: Calculating Spot Rates
Based on the discount factors provided in example 2, we can calculate spot rates for various compounding conventions. The results are listed below:

Point in time	$\tau = 1$	$\tau = 2$	$\tau = 3$
Discount factor	0.95120	0.88695	0.82285
Simple compounding	5.13%	6.37%	7.18%
Linear compounding	4.88%	5.65%	5.91%
Yearly compounding	5.13%	6.18%	6.72%
Semiannually compounding	5.07%	6.09%	6.61%
Quarterly compounding	5.03%	6.04%	6.55%
Continuous compounding	5.00%	6.00%	6.50%

After having developed several compounding methodologies, it should be emphasized that the discount function is unambiguous as long as a certain day count convention has been chosen. The value of the respective spot rates, however, depends on an additional compounding convention to be stipulated. A sensible comparison between different interest rates must always be made based on an explicitly stipulated compounding convention.

As previously noted, there is a spot rate for each discount factor. In other words, each term $\tau > 0$ has its own spot rate $r_t(\tau)$, which can be derived from the respective discount factor $R_t(\tau)$. The function

$$r_t : \mathbb{R}^+ \to \mathbb{R}, \ \tau \mapsto r_t(\tau)$$

is often referred to as the *term structure of interest rates* given a specific compounding convention.

Figure 5.3 corresponds to figure 5.1, where we have shown the euro discount function on June 21, 2005. The associated spot rate curve was calculated based on continuous compounding methodology, resorting to formula 5.13.

A term structure of interest rates is referred to as *flat* if the spot rate is constant for all future maturities. In addition, it is called *normal* (*inverted*), if the spot rate curve is strictly monotonously increasing (decreasing).

In the present case, the spot rate clearly depends on the time to maturity, which should not come as a surprise. A flat term structure is rather a theoretical case. In addition, the shape of the spot rate curve can be characterized as normal on the whole, although the shape of the curve, particularly at the short end, does not comply with the definition of a normal term structure of interest rates.

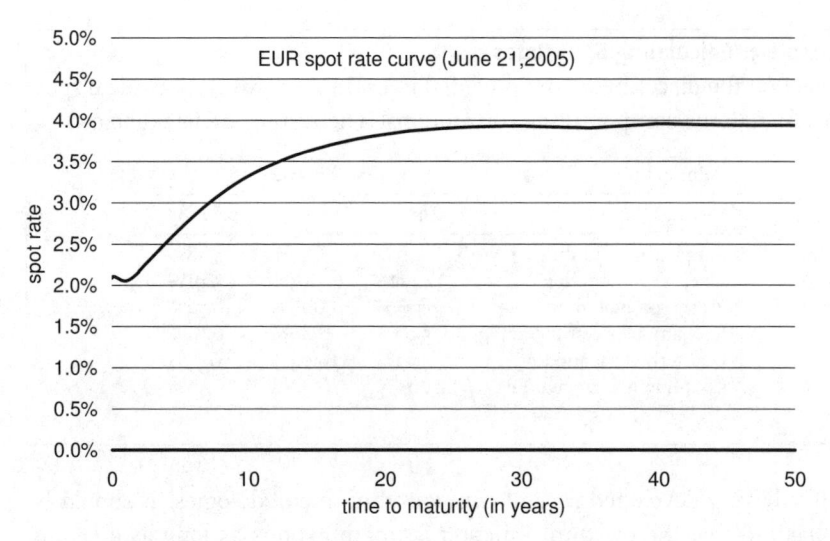

Fig. 5.3: The euro term structure of interest rates on June 21, 2005

5.1.3 Forward Rates

A spot rate always relates to an immediate zero-coupon-bond-type investment, which means a cash outflow today (at t) and a cash inflow at a later date (in case of a long position). Hence, a spot rate corresponds to a period which starts today and ends at a future date. Forward rates do the same with the exception that the starting date of the period also lies in the future. Figure 5.4 illustrates this concept.

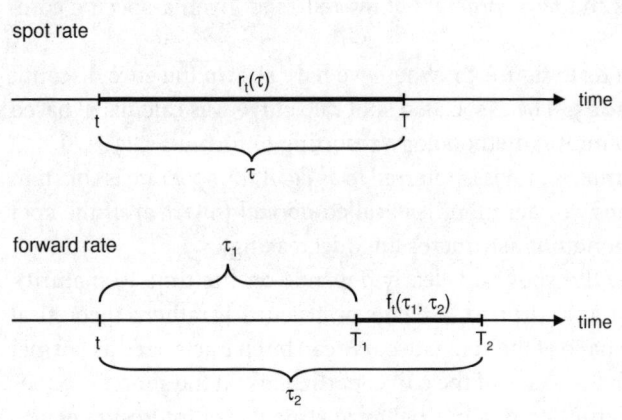

Fig. 5.4: Spot rates versus forward rates

The starting date of the period is denoted by T_1 and the end of the period by T_2. The time difference from today's perspective is denoted by τ_1 and τ_2, which is in accordance with the nomenclature we used for discount factors and spot rates. The term $f_t(\tau_1, \tau_2)$, provided $\tau_1 < \tau_2$, will serve as the corresponding mathematical description for forward rates.

It is very important to distinguish forward rates from future spot rates. A forward rate is a fixed interest rate that is stipulated today (at time t), although the first cash flow will not take place until T_1. Using a future spot rate, on the other hand, simply involves waiting until T_1 and then making an investment at the then prevailing spot rate $r_{T_1}(T_2 - T_1)$. Please note that this spot rate is unknown today, as it depends on the market conditions at this future date T_1. Technically, $r_{T_1}(T_2 - T_1)$ has to be regarded as a random variable.

Now we will turn to a discussion of how forward rates $f_t(\tau_1, \tau_2)$ can be calculated. For this purpose, we return to the notion of purchasing a zero coupon bond with a notional amount of one. However, as we focus on an interest rate that relates to a future time period, we buy the bond forward. This means that we do not perform a spot trade – meaning to deliver the bond immediately at t – but postpone the settlement of the trade (seller delivers bond, buyer pays for it) to T_1.

If no such trade is available on the market, we can generate the payout profile synthetically by means of the following procedure:

- Today, buy a zero coupon bond with a notional amount of 1 and maturity T_2. This generates the required cash inflow of one monetary unit at time T_2, but a cash outflow today which amounts to $R_t(\tau_2)$.
- In order to avoid any net cash flow today, finance the position by selling a zero coupon bond with a notional amount of $R_t(\tau_2)/R_t(\tau_1)$ and maturity T_2. This results in a net cash flow of zero today, as the product of notional amount $R_t(\tau_2)/R_t(\tau_1)$ and price $R_t(\tau_1)$ yields a cash inflow that exactly offsets the cash outflow.

In a nutshell, the forward contract has a cash outflow of $R_t(\tau_2)/R_t(\tau_1)$ at time T_1 and a cash inflow of 1 at time T_2.

Provided continuous compounding, we can define the forward rate similarly as we did for spot rates in equation 5.12:

$$\frac{R_t(\tau_2)}{R_t(\tau_1)} = e^{-f_t(\tau_1,\tau_2)\cdot(\tau_2-\tau_1)} \tag{5.14}$$

Solving for $f_t(\tau_1, \tau_2)$ renders

$$f_t(\tau_1, \tau_2) = -\frac{\ln R_t(\tau_2) - \ln R_t(\tau_1)}{\tau_2 - \tau_1} \tag{5.15}$$

Hence, each forward rate $f_t(\tau_1, \tau_2)$ ($\tau_1 < \tau_2$) can simply be calculated from the given discount function. Forward rates do not provide any new information in addition to the discount curve. Please note that formulas 5.14 and 5.15 are based on continuous compounding. Choosing another compounding convention would alter the formulas respectively.

Formula 5.15 allows an additional insight. Forward rates can be regarded as a generalization of the spot rate concept, as forward rates are not restricted to time periods that start today. On the other hand, spot rates can be interpreted as a special case of forward rates by setting $\tau_1 = 0$. Formula 5.15 then becomes the well-known formula for spot rates under continuous compounding:

$$f_t(0, \tau) = -\frac{\ln R_t(\tau) - \ln R_t(0)}{\tau - 0} = -\frac{\ln R_t(\tau)}{\tau} = r_t(\tau) \qquad (5.16)$$

> **Example 4: Calculating Forward Rates**
> We resort to our simple three-period example in order to demonstrate the calculation of forward rates (given continuous compounding):
>
> | Point in time | $\tau = 1$ | $\tau = 2$ | $\tau = 3$ |
> |---|---|---|---|
> | Discount factor | 0.95120 | 0.88695 | 0.82285 |
> | Spot rate | 5.00% | 6.00% | 6.50% |
>
> The forward rate for a one-year period starting at the end of the first year amounts to (see formula 5.15):
>
> $$f_t(1, 2) = -\frac{\ln 0.88695 - \ln 0.95120}{2 - 1} = 7.00\%$$
>
> On the other hand, the forward rate for a one-year period starting at the end of the second year amounts to:
>
> $$f_t(2, 3) = -\frac{\ln 0.82285 - \ln 0.88695}{3 - 2} = 7.50\%$$

Forward rates may provide valuable information in practice. From a theoretical point of view, the forward rate function $f_t(\tau_1, \tau_2)$ with $0 \leq \tau_1 < \tau_2$ is just an alternative description of the term structure of interest rates or the discount function; however, it is a more complicated one because $f_t(\tau_1, \tau_2)$ has two variables rather than just one. In addition, forward rates are of great importance in the context of many valuation models, even for credit risk models. For this purpose, forward rates for infinitesimally small periods are used, which may be defined in the following way:

$$f_t(\tau) = \lim_{\Delta t \to 0^+} f_t(\tau, \tau + \Delta t) \qquad (5.17)$$

If the limit expression exists, $f_t(\tau)$ is often referred to as the *instantaneous forward rate*. It can be interpreted as an interest rate that can be stipulated today and that applies to a logical second, beginning at time τ. In order to ensure its existence, we therefore presume that the discount function $R_t(\tau)$ is differentiable.

Given continuous compounding, we derive a very simple result for it:

$$\begin{aligned}
f_t(\tau) &= \lim_{\Delta t \to 0^+} f_t(\tau, \tau + \Delta t) \\
&= \lim_{\Delta t \to 0^+} \left[-\frac{\ln R_t(\tau + \Delta t) - \ln R_t(\tau)}{(\tau + \Delta t) - \tau} \right] \\
&= -\lim_{\Delta t \to 0^+} \left[\frac{\ln R_t(\tau + \Delta t) - \ln R_t(\tau)}{\Delta t} \right] \\
&= -\frac{d \ln R_t(\tau)}{d\tau} \\
&= -\frac{R_t'(\tau)}{R_t(\tau)}
\end{aligned} \qquad (5.18)$$

According to formula 5.18, instantaneous forward rates are related to the slope of the discount function. The function of instantaneous forward rates is another equivalent expression for the term structure of interest rates. Hence, formula 5.18 can be unequivocally solved for $R_t(\tau)$, although it is a first-order differential equation:

$$R_t(\tau) = \exp\left(-\int_0^\tau f_t(s)\, ds\right) \qquad (5.19)$$

Figure 5.5 completes the set of equivalent relationships between the discount function, the function of spot rates, and the function of instantaneous forward rates.

Please note that, according to the formula at the very bottom of figure 5.5, a spot rate can be interpreted as a simple arithmetic average of instantaneous forward rates for the respective time period $[0, \tau]$.

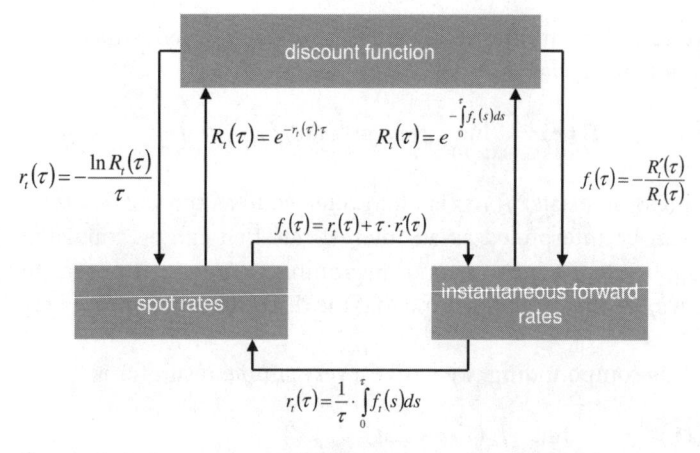

Fig. 5.5: Equivalent concepts of the term structure of interest rates

5.2 Obtaining the Term Structure of Interest Rates

To derive the current term structure of interest rates, it is common market practice to use a so-called *bootstrapping algorithm*, which is based on the term structure of swap rates. The bootstrapping mechanism can be derived from the valuation procedure of plain-vanilla interest rates swaps. The value of a receiver swap can be expressed as $V^{\text{swap}} = V^{\text{fixed leg}} - V^{\text{floating leg}}$, with $V^{\text{fixed leg}}$ and $V^{\text{floating leg}}$ being the values of the fixed and the floating leg (we incorporate the repayment of the notional amount). For the bootstrapping algorithm, we only need the fixed leg, as the floating leg has an initial value of 1. $V^{\text{fixed leg}}$ is given by (the term c_n denotes the respective swap rate for term of n):

$$\begin{aligned} V^{\text{fixed leg}} &= \sum_{i=1}^{n} c_n \cdot \Delta \tau_i \cdot R(\tau_i) + R(\tau_n) \\ &= \sum_{i=1}^{n-1} c_n \cdot \Delta \tau_i \cdot R(\tau_i) + (1 + c_n \cdot \Delta \tau_n) \cdot R(\tau_n) \end{aligned} \quad (5.20)$$

In this equation, we assume that the effective date of the swap coincides with the valuation date (no forward swap). In financial markets, swap contracts usually have an effective date of t plus two days. In case the bootstrapping algorithm should be adjusted to reflect this period, the term $-R(\tau_0)$ has to be added to $V^{\text{fixed leg}}$. Here, τ_0 is the forward start period, that is, the time to the effective date. Nevertheless, we ignore this term subsequently. In the second line of the valuation formula for the fixed leg, we separated all terms depending on the final discount factor $R(\tau_n)$. Using the conditions $V^{\text{floating leg}} = 1$ and $V^{\text{swap}} = 0$, we can solve for the last discount factor $R(\tau_n)$.

$$R(\tau_n) = \frac{1 - \sum_{i=1}^{n-1} c_n \cdot \Delta\tau_i \cdot R(\tau_i)}{(1 + c_n \cdot \Delta\tau_n)} \qquad (5.21)$$

Equation 5.21 illustrates that we can derive the discount factor for the maturity date τ_n, provided the swap rate c_n for the term τ_n is known and we already derived all previous discount factors $R(\tau_i)$ $(i = 1, 2, \ldots, n-1)$. Based on this result, the bootstrapping algorithm works as follows:

1. Get market data for money market instruments (i.e., Euribor or Libor rates) and swap rates for various maturity dates.
2. Currently, swaps are liquidly traded across the entire swap curve for major currencies (maturities between two and fifty years). If this is not the case, fill the swap gaps (maturity brackets for which a liquid swap quote is not available) by interpolating between liquidly traded contracts.
3. The short-term discount factors (one year and below) can be derived directly from money market contracts, as these products already refer to zero-coupon-bond investments.
4. Solve equation 5.21 for the first swap with a maturity of two years assuming that the fixed leg pays its coupon annually. For the first discount factor $R(\tau_1)$, use the 12M-Euribor (or 12M-Libor) rate. Continue this algorithm with consecutive swap rates, resorting to previously derived discount factors. This process assumes that coupons are paid only at the maturity dates of the previous contracts.

5.3 The Yield to Maturity

One of the major results of fixed income valuation theory is that there is typically no unique interest rate that applies for all maturities. Every term τ has its own spot rate $r_t(\tau)$. Consequently, a spot rate $r_t(\tau)$ can be interpreted as the yield of a zero coupon bond with maturity τ. However, most fixed income instruments in the market do have multiple cash flows, for example coupon-bearing bonds, which necessitates to discount each cash flow with the respective spot rate.

At the beginning of the chapter, we denoted future cash flows of a single investment by CF_i, which are due at time T_i $(i = 1, 2, \ldots, n)$. With $\tau_i = T_i - t$

Tab. 5.4: Example for a bootstrapping calculation

n	Source	Term (days)	DCC	Compounding method	Rate (in %)	$R(\tau_n)$	Spot rates[†]
1	12M-Eur.[‡]	365	Act/360	simple	2.23	0.9779	2.203%
2	2Y-Swap	720	30/360	discrete	2.39	0.9538	2.366%
3	3Y-Swap	1080	30/360	discrete	2.55	0.9271	2.522%
4	4Y-Swap	1440	30/360	discrete	2.70	0.8987	2.671%
5	5Y-Swap	1800	30/360	discrete	2.84	0.8688	2.814%
6	6Y-Swap	2160	30/360	discrete	2.96	0.8381	2.944%
7	7Y-Swap	2520	30/360	discrete	3.08	0.8067	3.069%
8	8Y-Swap	2880	30/360	discrete	3.20	0.7747	3.191%
9	9Y-Swap	3240	30/360	discrete	3.30	0.7429	3.302%
10	10Y-Swap	3600	30/360	discrete	3.38	0.7125	3.390%

DCC = Day-count convention
[†] in percent, continuous compounding and 30/360; [‡] 12M-Euribor

for all $i = 1, 2, \ldots, n$, the price of the security based on the spot rate curve has to be calculated as follows (assuming continuous compounding):

$$P_t = \sum_{i=1}^{n} e^{-r_t(\tau_i) \cdot \tau_i} \cdot \mathrm{CF}_i \qquad (5.22)$$

A mixture of various spot rates has to be applied to obtain the current price of the instrument. Market participants, however, care a great deal about a single yield measure in order to describe the return of an investment with multiple cash flows. This is where the well-known yield-to-maturity measure comes into play.

The *yield to maturity* y is defined as the unique discount rate for all maturities that reprices the bond, that is, to generate the currently observed price P_t. Hence, the following equation must be fulfilled (assuming continuous compounding):

$$P_t = \sum_{i=1}^{n} e^{-y \cdot \tau_i} \cdot \mathrm{CF}_i \qquad (5.23)$$

In general, the equation cannot be explicitly solved for more than two future cash flows. In these cases, numerical procedures (e.g., Newton-Raphson approach, bisection method) have to be applied to solve the equation for y, the yield to maturity.

It should be noted that the yield to maturity is nothing else but the internal rate of return of the cash flow stream $\{\mathrm{CF}_i\}_{i=1,2,\ldots,n}$, including an initial cash outflow which amounts to the current price P_t. It refers to the discount rate that generates a net present value (NPV) of zero for the entire series of payments.

Although the idea seems straightforward and the calculation is trivial in practice, the concept has several shortcomings that are particularly related to the economic interpretation. The main question is: Is it possible to interpret the yield to maturity as an effective yield of a fixed income investment?

We can give an answer to this question by considering a fixed income investment with an initial price P_t. If the yield to maturity had the meaning of an effective yield, the end value of the invested amount at time T_n would be

$$P_t \cdot e^{y \cdot T_n} = \left[\sum_{i=1}^{n} e^{-y \cdot \tau_i} \cdot \mathrm{CF}_i\right] \cdot e^{y \cdot T_n}$$

$$= \sum_{i=1}^{n} e^{y \cdot (T_n - \tau_i)} \cdot \mathrm{CF}_i \qquad (5.24)$$

Equation 5.24 reveals an implicit assumption of the yield-to-maturity concept. If taken as an effective yield, the cash flows CF_{T_i} have to be reinvested at the rate y to obtain the projected terminal value which is consistent with the effective yield. However, it is questionable whether this reinvestment rate is actually attainable for each of these cash flows. A comparison to respective forward rates would reveal any discrepancy. In practice, this assumption does not typically apply, and hence the yield to maturity can be barely interpreted as an effective yield.

There is another issue that merits further discussion. Combining equation 5.22 with 5.24 renders

$$\sum_{i=1}^{n} e^{-y \cdot \tau_i} \cdot \mathrm{CF}_i = \sum_{i=1}^{n} e^{-r_t(\tau_i) \cdot \tau_i} \cdot \mathrm{CF}_i \qquad (5.25)$$

which unfortunately cannot be explicitly solved for y in general. Nevertheless, it shows that the yield to maturity y can be regarded as a complex, weighted average of the spot rates $r_t(\tau_1), r_t(\tau_2), \ldots, r_t(\tau_n)$, but a very obscure one. Its precise value is largely dependent on the structure of future cash flows. Coupon-bearing bonds with identical maturity dates but different coupons will have different yields in practice. This implication is often referred to as *coupon effect* or *coupon bias*. This is an important reason why yield curves constructed from yields of coupon-bearing bonds are not meaningful. Consequently, yields are inappropriate proxies for spot rates.

5.4 Measurement of Interest Rate Risk

The term structure of interest rates is subject to changes over time, which also may have an effect on the prices of fixed income securities. The market value changes of fixed income investments may represent a significant return component compared to the interest income, particularly for investors who do not plan to hold the security to its maturity. This is referred to as *interest rate risk*, or simply *market risk*.

Interest rate risk may also arise in the context of floating rate securities, as their coupon payments are linked to some reference rate like the Libor or the Euribor, which may change over time. In this case, interest rate risk is associated with cash flow changes in place of marked-to-market changes. In practice, the existence of interest rate risk is largely determined by how a fixed income investment is funded or refinanced, or which benchmark is used to measure the performance of the investment. For example, if a floater investment is funded with a corresponding floating rate liability, there is no interest rate risk, as the cash flow variability is eliminated by a contrarian position.

In the following, we solely focus on marked-to-market changes, as many accounts consider price changes to be the most important source of uncertainty in their overall investment performance.

Measuring interest rate risk involves two complementary tasks. First, one has to define one or more risk factors that drive the market. In addition, one has to estimate the extent of how these risk factors may vary over time, which is often related to the term volatility. In a second step, one has to assess how a specific financial instrument is subject to the preassigned risk factors, that is, how its market value may change as a result of a change in risk factors. This is typically done by applying so-called sensitivities.

The most common approach in fixed income markets assumes the existence of only one risk factor, which is related to parallel shifts of the spot rate curve. In fact, at least 75 percent of the price variability of fixed income securities can be explained by parallel curve shifts. This explains the great popularity of this methodology in practice, associated with the concept of *duration* and *convexity*, which we will now introduce.

The starting point is the well-known pricing equation for a discretionary fixed income security based on spot rates (assuming continuous compounding):

$$P_t = \sum_{i=1}^{n} e^{-r_t(\tau_i)\cdot \tau_i} \cdot \text{CF}_i \tag{5.26}$$

We now introduce a spread variable s, which is considered to have an initial value of zero. Hence, the equation

$$P_t = \sum_{i=1}^{n} e^{-[r_t(\tau_i)+s]\cdot\tau_i} \cdot CF_i \qquad (5.27)$$

still holds. The spread variable can be regarded as the risk factor. A positive s, for example, represents an upward shift of the spot rate curve. We now analyze the sensitivity of the security's price towards immediate parallel curve shifts by calculating the first derivative of the pricing formula with regard to s at $s = 0$:

$$\begin{aligned}\left.\frac{dP_t}{ds}\right|_{s=0} &= \sum_{i=1}^{n} (-\tau_i) \cdot e^{-[r_t(\tau_i)+s]\cdot\tau_i} \cdot CF_i \\ &= -\sum_{i=1}^{n} \tau_i \cdot e^{-r_t(\tau_i)\cdot\tau_i} \cdot CF_i \qquad (5.28)\end{aligned}$$

To provide formula 5.28 with economic meaning, we define the *duration* (or: *Macaulay duration*) of this fixed income investment as follows:

$$\text{Dur}_t = \frac{\sum_{i=1}^{n} \tau_i \cdot e^{-r_t(\tau_i)\cdot\tau_i} \cdot CF_i}{\sum_{i=1}^{n} e^{-r_t(\tau_i)\cdot\tau_i} \cdot CF_i} \qquad (5.29)$$

The duration can be interpreted as a weighted arithmetic average of the future cash flows' terms, using the discounted cash flows as the weighting scheme for these future dates. Please note that the denominator of the duration Dur_t is simply the current price P_t of the security. Hence, equation 5.28 can be rewritten using the duration:

$$\left.\frac{dP_t}{ds}\right|_{s=0} = -\text{Dur}_t \cdot P_t \qquad (5.30)$$

We can restate this simple equation for a more realistic, discrete setting:

$$\frac{\Delta P_t}{P_t} \approx -\text{Dur}_t \cdot \Delta s \qquad (5.31)$$

Accordingly, the duration expresses the relationship between parallel spot rate curve shifts and relative price changes of the fixed income security. For example, if the duration amounts to 5 (years), an upward parallel shift of the spot rate curve by one percentage point would cause the price of the fixed income security to drop by approximately 5 percent.

Please note that using the relationship in practice only renders an approximate result, as it is only true for infinitesimally small parallel curve shifts. Nevertheless, the approximation should be appropriate for small parallel curve shifts.

The price of a fixed income security with known cash flows always has a negative relationship to the level of the spot rate curve. For example, a downward shift of the spot rate curve ($s < 0$), associated with lower discount rates, leads to an increase of the theoretical price P_t, as the time value of future cash flows rises. Figure 5.6 illustrates this relationship.

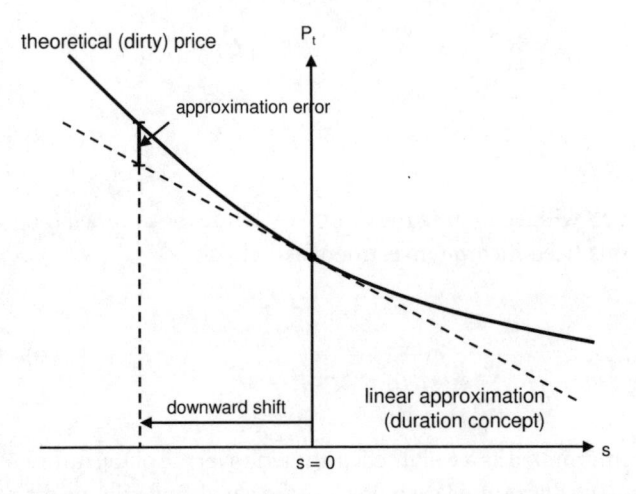

Fig. 5.6: Non-linear relationship between price and spot rate curve shift

Although the direction of the price effect is clear, the relationship is far from being a linear one. The duration concept introduced before represents a linear approximation based on the current price P_t and the current spot rate curve. It can be shown that the approximation error, defined as the difference between the correct theoretical price and the estimated price based on the duration, is always positive. This means that using the duration always leads to an underestimation of the new price, irrespective of the direction of the spot rate curve shift, as shown in figure 5.6.

This phenomenon is often referred to as *convexity*. Technically, it is often described as the second-derivative term of the following Taylor expansion:

$$dP_t = P_t + \frac{dP_t}{ds} \cdot ds + \frac{1}{2} \cdot \underbrace{\frac{d^2 P_t}{ds^2}}_{\text{convexity}} \cdot ds^2 + \ldots \quad (5.32)$$

Taking the convexity term into account when estimating the effect of a spot rate curve shift via the duration approach improves the result, but is nevertheless not precise because higher-derivative terms of the Taylor expansion are ignored.

Many fixed income textbooks differentiate between duration (Macaulay duration), modified duration, and effective duration. In the following, we would like to shed some light on the differences among these concepts. In the derivation shown above, there is no discrepancy between duration and modified duration due to the fact that we presumed continuous compounding. But if one works with a discrete compounding convention and the yield-to-maturity concept, some differences compared to the previous results will arise.

Presuming that each year is divided into $m \in \mathbb{N}$ subintervals of equal length and y denotes the yield to maturity of that instrument in accordance with that compounding convention, the following equation is true:

$$P_t = \sum_{i=1}^{n} \left(1 + \frac{y}{m}\right)^{-m \cdot \tau_i} \cdot \text{CF}_i \tag{5.33}$$

We do not need to introduce the shift variable s, as we can directly calculate the first derivative with regard to y:

$$\frac{dP_t}{dy} = -\left(1 + \frac{y}{m}\right)^{-1} \cdot \sum_{i=1}^{n} \tau_i \cdot \left(1 + \frac{y}{m}\right)^{-m \cdot \tau_i} \cdot \text{CF}_i \tag{5.34}$$

The respective (Macaulay) duration would be:

$$\text{Dur}_t = \frac{\sum_{i=1}^{n} \tau_i \cdot \left(1 + \frac{y}{m}\right)^{-m \cdot \tau_i} \cdot \text{CF}_i}{\sum_{i=1}^{n} \left(1 + \frac{y}{m}\right)^{-m \cdot \tau_i} \cdot \text{CF}_i} \tag{5.35}$$

Please note that continuous compounding has been replaced by discrete compounding, and the yield to maturity is used instead of the actual spot rate curve. Hence, equation 5.34 can be rewritten in the following way:

$$\frac{dP_t}{dy} = -\underbrace{\left(1 + \frac{y}{m}\right)^{-1} \cdot \text{Dur}_t}_{\text{ModDur}_t} \cdot P_t \tag{5.36}$$

The bracket term is often merged with the (Macaulay) duration and is referred to as *modified duration* ModDur_t. The modified duration acts more as a sensitivity measure, while the duration (without the bracket term) should more be interpreted as an average term of future cash flows. The basic considerations concerning the duration concept remain unchanged. However, there is a slight difference in the interpretation. The more textbook-style approach shown above measures the sensitivity of the fixed income security with regard to a variation of the yield to maturity y instead of considering parallel shifts of the spot rate curve.

Some practitioners avoid dealing with formulas to calculate a sensitivity measure like the modified duration. They simply resort to recently observed market data (dirty price, yield to maturity) to extract a sensitivity number. This is often referred to as *effective duration* and *effective convexity*, as demonstrated in the following example.

Example 5: Calculating the Effective Duration and Convexity

For a specific bond, we observed the following yield and price information within a short period of time (initial yield: 5.00 percent). Please note that the yield changes are assumed to be equally spaced, that is, the difference between all three observations amounts to 10 bp (4.9 versus 5.0 percent and 5.0 versus 5.1 percent).

Yield	4.90%	5.00%	5.10%
Observed price	111.1374	110.7552	110.3746

In this case, the modified duration can be estimated in accordance with the following formula (The superscript + [−] indicates a figure after the yield increased [decreased] by Δy):

$$\text{effective (modified) duration} = \frac{P_t^- - P_t^+}{2 \cdot P_t^0 \cdot \Delta y}$$

$$= \frac{111.1374 - 110.3746}{2 \cdot 110.7552 \cdot 10 \text{ bp}}$$

$$\approx 3.44$$

A similar formula applies to the effective convexity:

$$\text{effective convexity} = \frac{P_t^+ + P_t^- - 2 \cdot P_t^0}{2 \cdot P_t^0 \cdot (\Delta y)^2}$$

$$= \frac{110.3746 + 111.1374 - 2 \cdot 110.7552}{2 \cdot 110.7552 \cdot (10 \text{ bp})^2}$$

$$\approx 7.22$$

What will be the price of the bond when assuming a yield increase of 25 bp? The answer can be obtained by considering:

$$\frac{\Delta P_t}{P_t^0} = -\text{modified duration} \cdot \Delta y + \text{convexity} \cdot (\Delta y)^2$$
$$\approx -3.44 \cdot 25 \text{ bp} + 7.22 \cdot (25 \text{ bp})^2$$
$$\approx -0.8564\%$$

Based on the initial value $P_t^0 = 110.7552$, the estimated price after the 25 bp yield increase amounts to 109.8067.

As long as we focus on securities with given cash flows, effective duration should be close to the theoretically correct levels of the modified duration. Differences may arise due to the selection of discrete price observations in practice as shown in the example. Effective duration and convexity numbers, on the other hand, have a big advantage. They take possible optionalities of fixed income securities, like call or put features, into account. The modified duration formula we have presented above implicitly assumes that cash flows are known and unchangeable. In practice, a shift in the term structure of interest rates often involves a probability change that the embedded derivative will be exercised in the future.

For example, let us consider a security that currently trades at 99 and is callable by the issuer before maturity at its par amount. If interest rates decline across the board, the security's price should increase. However, this increase is largely offset by the call feature, as the probability that the option is exercised by the issuer notably surges. Figure 5.7 illustrates the price of such a callable bond against a general interest rate level.

There are two important insights that can be inferred from the figure. First, the effective duration of a callable bond is lower than a comparable noncallable bond due to the possibility of early redemption. Second, callable bonds typically have a segment in the price function which is associated with negative convexity. This is attributable to the fact that such bonds have an upper price boundary, given by the redemption price that is stipulated in the call provisions.

Irrespective of the compounding convention chosen, the (modified) duration always measures the price sensitivity of a fixed income instrument in relative terms, that is, in relation to the current price level. However, some investors may be interested in the change of the market value of a specific position, measured in currency terms. Apparently, this is a one-banana problem, which can

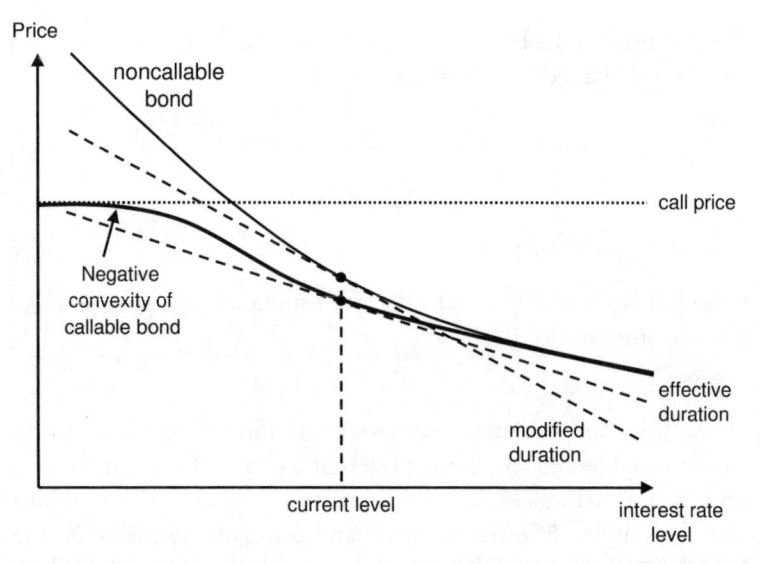

Fig. 5.7: Callable bonds and negative convexity

be easily accomplished by reorganizing formula 5.31 (presuming continuous compounding):

$$\Delta P_t \approx -\text{Dur}_t \cdot P_t \cdot \Delta s \tag{5.37}$$

It has become market standard to calculate the *price value of a basis point* (PVBP) by assuming a marginal curve shift (or a yield-to-maturity shift) of one basis point. Hence, the PVBP is simply defined as

$$\text{PVBP}_t = \text{Dur}_t \cdot P_t \cdot 0.0001 \tag{5.38}$$

Please note that this measure is still neither related to the notional amount nor to the current market value of a specific investment. As fixed income securities are typically quoted in percentage points of the notional amount (N), the following adjustment is required to arrive at the *dollar value of a basis point* (DV01):

$$\begin{aligned}\text{DV01}_t &= \text{Dur}_t \cdot \frac{P_t}{100} \cdot 0.0001 \cdot N \\ &= \text{Dur}_t \cdot P_t \cdot N \cdot 10^{-6}\end{aligned} \tag{5.39}$$

The market value MV_t of the position is simply given by $N \cdot P_t/100$, so the following alternative expression applies:

$$\text{DV01}_t = \text{Dur}_t \cdot \text{MV}_t \cdot 10^{-4} \tag{5.40}$$

We close this section by raising the duration concept to a portfolio level. Although we introduced this sensitivity measure on a single-instrument basis, it is easy to apply it to a portfolio of various fixed income instruments. Under the assumption that each of these instruments is subject to the same risk factor (parallel spot rate curve shifts), we simply have to add up the DVo1s. Given m fixed income instruments with $\mathrm{DVo1}_j$ ($j = 1, 2, \ldots, m$), we obtain the portfolio DVo1 as

$$\mathrm{DVo1}_{t,PF} = \sum_{j=1}^{m} \mathrm{DVo1}_{t,j} \qquad (5.41)$$

Considering equation 5.40, we arrive at an expression for the portfolio duration $\mathrm{Dur}_{t,PF}$:

$$\mathrm{Dur}_{PF,t} = \frac{\sum_{j=1}^{m} \mathrm{Dur}_{t,j} \cdot \mathrm{MV}_{t,j}}{\sum_{j=1}^{m} \mathrm{MV}_{t,j}} \qquad (5.42)$$

Accordingly, the portfolio duration can be attained by calculating a weighted average of instrument-specific durations. The weight is the proportion of the portfolio that a security comprises with regard to the current market value $\mathrm{MV}_{t,j}$.

Please note that this relation strictly holds only in the case of continuous compounding and assuming parallel shifts of the spot rate curve as the common risk factor. As already pointed out, the modified duration concept based on discrete compounding and considering yield-to-maturity variations (instead of spot rate curve shifts) is often used in practice. Equation 5.42 does not hold exactly for modified durations, but it should be a good approximation in practice.

However, it is questionable whether uniform yield-to-maturity variations can be taken as granted. If the yield to maturity of bond A increases by 10 bp, is it sensible to assume the same for bond B? Nevertheless, the problem is similar to ignoring spot rate curve movements other than parallel shifts.

6
Spread Measures

6.1 Basic Considerations

Managing credit risk on a single-name or portfolio level does not always start with the actual underlying risk, namely the likelihood of a default event. In fact, fair value changes of credit-risky financial instruments are the focus of the management process rather than considering possible default consequences. Hence, one is required to define an underlying variable that enables the comparison of credit risk across different instruments. This is where so-called credit spreads come into play.

The vast majority of market participants implicitly agree on using credit spread measures to achieve this goal. This is the preferred approach within this market, although there might be theoretical limitations to this concept, which we will discuss in the course of this chapter.

The basic idea of a credit spread is to measure the compensation an investor receives for incurring the credit risk embedded in a specific financial instrument, irrespective of its legal form. Hence, it should apply to credit-risky securities (e.g., bonds and loans from corporates and sovereigns) as well as to unfunded derivative instruments, including credit default swaps, total return swaps, and collateralized debt obligations, just to name a few. In practice, a number of alternative spread measures are used in certain circumstances and sometimes interchangeably, which causes confusion every once in a while within the investment community. After we have introduced them, we will discuss their various strengths and weaknesses.

Before we discuss these alternative concepts, we should note that a spread measure is always related to a specific instrument type. Regular credit-risky securities like bonds and loans with a single specific obligor are typically the starting point despite their multiple risks, primarily changing interest rates and default potential. Thus, isolating the credit risk component in terms of a spread is not as straightforward as for many unfunded products like CDS. Measuring the spread for an unfunded product is rather simple, as the spread payment is typically a directly observable feature of the respective contract. For example, a 5Y CDS contract on DaimlerChrysler may cost the protection buyer a spread

Active Credit Portfolio Management. J. Felsenheimer, P. Gisdakis, and M. Zaiser
Copyright © 2006 WILEY-VCH Verlag GmbH & Co. KGaA, Weinheim
ISBN: 3-527-50198-3

of 80 bp per year, payable on a quarterly basis. However, some cases arise in practice that do not facilitate direct access to such spread information:

- Specific CDO tranches, especially equity tranches (often referred to as first-loss tranches), typically feature a regular spread payment (e.g., 500 bp) and a one-off payment to be received by the protection seller upon initiation of the contract. This upfront payment represents compensation in addition to the ongoing spread.
- Bespoken (tailor-made) credit derivatives may be subject to regular spread payments other than on a quarterly basis. Even one-off payments in advance or at the end of the term or irregular payment dates may apply.

From the perspective of a credit-risky security, the basic idea is to measure its return relative to some default-free benchmark return, although it is actually impossible to specify a default-free security. For example, there is always a chance, however slight, that a huge meteorite destroys all life on earth, ending all prospects of repayment (although repayment would likely be a secondary concern in such a situation). Return measures are typically stated in terms of a standard period, most of the time on a per-year basis to facilitate comparisons. Against this background, it is no surprise that the market cites spreads in terms of basis points, a hundredth of a percentage point.

There is one important issue that should be mentioned before we start our detailed discussion of alternative spread measures. Consider a corporate bond issue with a time to maturity of five years. If we use one of the several procedures to extract a spread measure in order to assess the implied credit risk, we obtain a single spread level for the whole remaining life of this bond. However, credit risk may change over time, and particularly default probabilities may be different for each of the five years until maturity. The extracted spread, in any case, is a kind of average assessment of credit risk until maturity. Just focusing on a single bond will not generate a spread for each separate year or selected period of time. It should be clear that we cannot extract five different spreads from only one bond price without stipulating additional intertemporal default probability assumptions. Therefore, spreads implied by a single bond price are often referred to as *par spreads*; similarly it is common to calculate a *par yield* for a bond that assumes a flat interest rate curve.

Nevertheless, there are other approaches that take into account changing credit risk over time. However, these methods are more complex, but are basically based on similar considerations. We postpone this discussion to a later chapter when we elaborate on intensity-based models that allow for discretionary patterns of credit risk over time.

Last but not least, let us summarize some desirable properties for spread measures:

1. A credit spread measure should be related to the credit risk of the respective issuer as perceived by the market. Other factors should be largely eliminated from the respective number in order to isolate the market perception of default risk.
2. A spread measure should enable the comparison between ...
   - Different securities issued by a company or sovereign agency (intracorporate comparisons); they may differ with respect to maturity, coupon, and seniority,
   - Securities of different issuers (intercorporate comparisons),
   - Different instruments (securities vs. derivatives), e.g., a cash bond versus a CDS.
3. A credit spread should always be non-negative, provided that there are no arbitrage opportunities, as a negative spread would imply a credit quality superior to the risk-free benchmark. A natural point of origin is eligible.
4. A credit spread measure should be applicable to every kind of credit-risky security, which could be quite problematic when considering convertible bonds, as they are subject to both credit and equity risk.

As we will see in the course of this chapter, it is not an easy task to fulfill all of these requirements simultaneously. Therefore, one has to admit that there is no ideal spread measure. Nevertheless, the investing community is familiar with the spread concept, although one should be able to realize its limitations.

6.2 Yield Spreads

A very common and obvious way to calculate a spread would be to compare two yields with each other. The *yield spread* (also often referred to as *yield–yield spread*) is based on two yield-to-maturity measures: one for the respective credit-risky security and another one for a comparable risk-free bond. Simply calculating the difference between these two yields leads to the yield spread:

$$s = y_{\text{risky}} - y_{\text{no risk}} \qquad (6.1)$$

One aspect should be clear, namely how to calculate the yield to maturity. Please note that the yield to maturity reflects the internal rate of return of a series of cash flows arising for the respective investment, presuming that all cash flows are safe, i.e., are not subject to default risk. Given continuous compounding and security cash flows denoted by CF_{T_i} due at $T_1, T_2, \ldots, T_n = T$ with current (dirty) price P_t, the yield to maturity y_risky is the solution to the following equation:

$$P_t = \sum_{i=1}^{n} e^{-y_\text{risky} \cdot \tau_i} \cdot \mathrm{CF}_{T_i} \quad \text{with } \tau_i = T_i - t \tag{6.2}$$

Simple numerical procedures can be applied, for example, a one-dimensional root-searching algorithm, to solve the equation for y, the yield to maturity. The solution is always unique, as the cash flow stream of a bond or loan is normal. Alternative compounding conventions are possible as well, but should be used consistently when calculating yield spreads.

A more profound question concerns the design of a comparable risk-free bond. In practice, it would be a rare coincidence to find a risk-free security with an identical cash flow structure. Hence, practitioners typically resort to more or less adequate solutions to this problem. The following list gives an overview of these approaches:

1. Find a high-quality government bond (denominated in the same currency) with a similar maturity as the respective credit-risky security and use its current yield to maturity as the benchmark rate $y_\text{no risk}$.
2. If no such bond with an identical maturity exists, use an interpolation procedure to estimate a benchmark yield to maturity (often referred to as *I-spread* or *interpolated spread*).
3. Given the (risk-free) spot rate curve (or the discount function respectively), calculate the theoretical (dirty) price of a risk-free bond with an identical cash flow structure according to

$$\begin{aligned} \widehat{P}_{t,\text{no risk}} &= \sum_{i=1}^{n} e^{-r_t(\tau_i) \cdot \tau_i} \cdot \mathrm{CF}_{T_i} \\ &= \sum_{i=1}^{n} R_t(\tau_i) \cdot \mathrm{CF}_{T_i}. \end{aligned} \tag{6.3}$$

Subsequently, perform the yield-to-maturity calculation procedure for this synthetic risk-free bond, i.e., determine $y_\text{no risk}$ that solves the following equation:

$$\widehat{P}_{t,\text{no risk}} = \sum_{i=1}^{n} e^{-y_\text{no risk} \cdot \tau_i} \cdot \mathrm{CF}_{T_i} \tag{6.4}$$

It is apparent that the first approach provides an ad hoc solution with a lack of objectivity. Even the second one should be taken with a pinch of salt. As already discussed in our introductory chapter on interest rate considerations, a yield is a kind of obscure average of current spot rates that refer to different future points of time. Hence, a yield to maturity for a coupon bond is largely contingent on the remaining term and the coupon rate of the respective issue. Against this background, an interpolated yield based on the yields of two (risk-free) government bond issues with different maturities and different coupon rates prevents a sensible economic interpretation.

Nevertheless, both calculation procedures enjoy great popularity in practice. For example, *Bund spreads* are very popular for euro-denominated bonds, which is attributable to the importance of German government bonds (*Bundesanleihen*, *Bundesobligation*, etc.), which are considered to be almost perfectly default-free, although one cannot take this for granted forever. Unfortunately, Bunds typically possess a yield to maturity that is considerably lower than ultra-high-quality corporate bonds due to a convenience yield, as it enables its holder to refinance the bond position over the repo market at a lower rate.

Against this background, it is no surprise that many market participants prefer the Libor or Euribor swap curve as the benchmark rather than Bund yields. The spread based on this benchmark curve is often referred to as *midswap spread* and is usually lower than the respective Bund spread due to the swap spread. We view these swap spreads as problematic, because they involve a mixture of two different obscure spot rates' average calculations, that is, the yield to maturity and the swap rate.

From a theoretical perspective, the third approach overcomes the objections with regard to questionable objectivity and the meaning of interpolation procedures. However, it is arguable whether a risk-free bond with an identical cash flow structure as the credit-risky security (the synthetic risk-free bond) would actually trade at the price $\widehat{P}_{t,\text{no risk}}$, which is then taken to extract the yield $y_{\text{no risk}}$. This is particularly problematic if the cash flow structure deviates significantly from other typical outstanding risk-free bonds. Nevertheless, we prefer the third approach when talking about yield spreads.

Figure 6.1 clarifies the third approach by means of net present value (NPV) curves. Such a curve displays the net present value of the cash flow stream, including the initial cash outflow amounting to the current price P_t, against the respective uniform discount rate. The higher the discount rate, the lower the NPV, as the time value of future cash inflows decreases. Hence, the slope should always be negative. The yield to maturity is given by the point of intersection

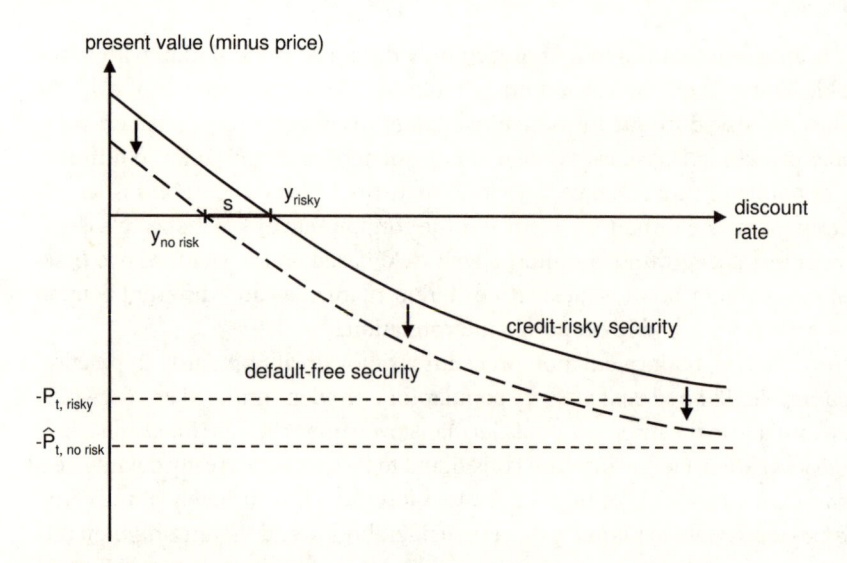

Fig. 6.1: Net present value curves

of the NPV curve with the abscissa, representing a discount rate that generates an NPV of zero.

The first step, the creation of a synthetic, default-free security with identical cash flows, is reflected by a parallel downward shift of the original NPV curve (dashed curve). Please note that the payment structure is not altered with the exception of the initial price paid for it ($\widehat{P}_{t,\text{no risk}}$), which should be higher due to the lack of default risk. Therefore, the yield to maturity $y_{\text{no risk}}$ for this synthetic security will definitely be lower than y_{risky}, which ensures that the resulting spread s is always non-negative.

What are the merits of the yield spread approach in general? Obviously, the simplicity of calculation should be emphasized, although numerical procedures must be used to generate a yield to maturity. On the other hand, YTM measures are easily accessible via several data providers like Bloomberg and Reuters. The interpretation of yield spreads seems to be straightforward, since a yield difference corresponds to the common notion of a spread.

However, there are several shortcomings worth mentioning. In this section, we implicitly presumed that the timing and extent of each cash flow is known in advance. Under this assumption, it is possible to calculate a YTM measure. When dealing with floating rate notes or securities with embedded options (e.g., callable or putable bonds), the yield-to-maturity definition cannot be applied due to unknown cash flows. How do practitioners typically react when these problems are present?

- A YTM calculation is typically suppressed for floating rate instruments. However, one could project future cash flows by consulting respective forward rates implied by the current spot rate curve. Although this is a poor forecast for true future spot rates in general, the use of forward rates is consistent with arbitrage-free valuation.
- Callable or putable securities are usually not accessible for yield-to-maturity measures in a sensible way. Often, measures like yield-to-worst or yield-to-best are applied in order to obtain a superficial notion of the respective instrument. However, such measures are typically not appropriate to evaluate the return compared to a plain-vanilla security, because the optional component may significantly affect the result.

Besides all these practical issues, there is one major objection that pervades the whole yield spread concept. As it is based on the YTM measure, yield spreads share the weaknesses of the yield-to-maturity concept. As illustrated in chapter 5, the YTM concept assumes that all cash flows during the remaining life of the security can be reinvested at a constant rate equal to the resulting yield. This assumption cannot be sustained in practice. In addition, the yield to maturity is a kind of obscure average of several spot rates, complicating a straightforward interpretation of the result.

6.3 Z-Spreads

One possibility to overcome the shortcomings of the yield-to-maturity concept is to apply the so-called *zero-volatility spread* (*Z-spread*). In practice, it is also often referred to as the *option-adjusted spread* (OAS), although this label is somewhat confusing. At the end of this section, we will explain the origin of these names.

The basic idea of the Z-spread approach is quite simple, but it differs notably from the yield spread approach discussed earlier. Instead of assuming a flat spot rate curve (a constant discount rate) as is the case for the yield-to-maturity concept, we take the current default-free spot rate curve for granted, irrespective of its actual shape. In order to incorporate default risk for a fixed income security, we perform an (upward) parallel shift of the current spot rate curve until the resulting present value of future cash flows is equal to the currently observed price of the credit-risky security $P_{t,\text{risky}}$. Figure 6.2 illustrates this idea:

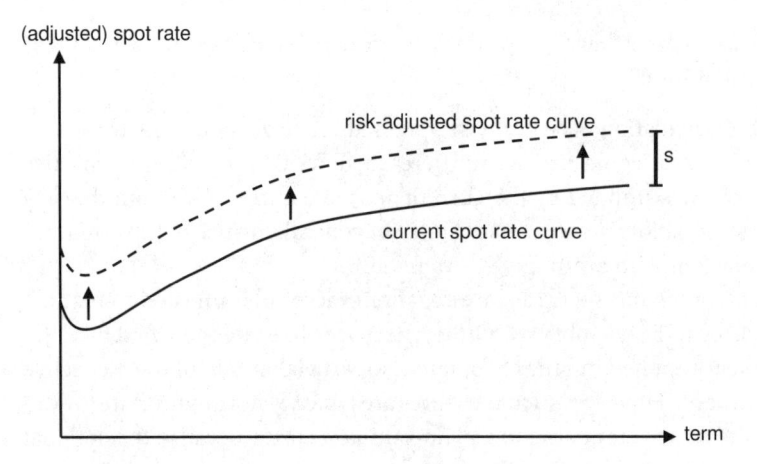

Fig. 6.2: Finding the Z-spread

Mathematically, the curve shift is done by adding a constant spread s to each spot rate. The following equation reflects the idea provided continuous compounding:

$$\begin{aligned} P_{t,\text{risky}} &= \sum_{i=1}^{n} e^{-[r_t(\tau_i)+s]\cdot\tau_i} \cdot \text{CF}_{T_i} \\ &= \sum_{i=1}^{n} e^{-r_t(\tau_i)\cdot\tau_i} \cdot e^{-s\cdot\tau_i} \cdot \text{CF}_{T_i} \\ &= \sum_{i=1}^{n} R_t(\tau_i) \cdot e^{-s\cdot\tau_i} \cdot \text{CF}_{T_i} \end{aligned} \qquad (6.5)$$

To find the right s, numerical procedures have to be applied that are quite similar to those applied for the YTM calculation. The numerical value of s that equates both terms in equation 6.5 is called the Z-spread of the respective credit-risky security.

Conditional on choosing continuous compounding for spot rates, the last row of equation 6.5 provides another helpful insight: Calculating the risk-adjusted present value of a cash flow that is subject to default risk involves discounting with the adequate risk-free spot rate as well as incorporating another discounting procedure, in this case by multiplying with $e^{-s\cdot\tau_i}$. Therefore, the resulting Z-spread s constitutes a discounting component that is separable from the well-known risk-free discounting. Unfortunately, the factorization of these two separate components only holds under continuous compounding. Nevertheless, this idea influences several valuation models for credit instruments.

From this discounting perspective, one could raise the question why a uniform spread s applies as opposed to the risk-free discounting term, where the discount rate is adjusted to the respective time horizon. As stated at the beginning of this chapter, focusing on a single credit-risky instrument does not allow one to differentiate between period-specific default risk, as we can extract only one spread from one price. Hence, the Z-spread concept assumes that the spread to be applied is the same for each individual cash flow. Alternatively, the Z-spread can be viewed as an obscure average of different spread levels, which unfortunately cannot be observed directly. This confirms our notion that an extracted spread is a kind of average assessment of credit risk until maturity (a par spread).

The term spread reveals that it is always about relative measures. In case of a Z-spread, the measurement is performed relative to a risk-free benchmark curve, while yield spreads are based on a comparison with a comparable default-free security. Therefore, Z-spreads are more abstract numbers, but they are theoretically more adequate than resorting to YTM measures with their implausible assumptions.

At this point, we may be tempted to resume the discussion of how to make the term risk-free curve operational. Similar to yield spreads, it is possible to apply a treasury curve (e.g., spot rates extracted from Bund issues) or a Libor/Euribor curve. Within the euro zone, using the treasury curve typically results in higher Z-spreads than when using the money market curve. As already noted, this is largely attributable to the convenience yield of government bond issues. Therefore, when stating Z-spreads, it is highly recommended to know what kind of risk-free curve is being utilized. It has become market standard to measure the Z-spread against Libor.

Some shortcomings of yield spreads also apply to Z-spread. The concept can only be applied to fixed rate coupon bonds without any embedded options, such as callable or putable features. Unknown cash flows of floating rate securities could basically be projected via respective forward rates. However, such an approach did not become popular in credit markets under the name Z-spread, but rather surfaced under *discount margin* and *zero discount margin*. We will return to these concepts in the context of floating rate instruments.

Now that we have discussed the mechanism of Z-spreads, we close this section with a discussion of the origin of its name. As already noted, Z-spreads are often referred to as option-adjusted spreads. To understand the idea of this more general concept, consider a fixed income security with embedded options, for example, a call feature that enables the obligor to repay the debt at a specific price prior to maturity. As the execution of this option is largely determined by the interest rate environment at the time of a possible early repayment, one has to apply option pricing models to extract its intrinsic value. This is typically done by modeling interest rate processes. Applying these models requires one to alter the cash flows of the respective security, depending on whether the option is exercised or not. As a result, the OAS refers to the spread of the security that is not attributable to embedded optionalities, and hence should describe the remaining default risk. If we stipulate the interest rate volatility for the option pricing model to be zero, the cash flows would be known and the security with embedded options degenerates to a plain-vanilla fixed coupon instrument (except for the default risk). Hence, the OAS becomes a Z-spread.

To keep these two names separate, we will use the term option-adjusted spread only in the context of securities afflicted with optionalities. When considering bullet bonds or loans, we will refer to the Z-spread.

6.4 Asset Swap Spreads

Yield spreads suffer from the crude assumptions of the YTM concept, while Z-spreads, in contrast, are rather an abstract and artificial construction, although they are theoretically more stringent. Either approach is subject to arbitrariness, as the benchmark (treasury vs. interbanking curve or instrument) is not automatically determined by the respective concept.

The asset swap spread represents a third alternative to measure the intrinsic credit risk of a fixed income security, allowing for a sensible economic interpretation due to the recourse to actual available financial contracts. In addition, the benchmark is clearly and unambiguously defined.

Consider the following situation: A fixed coupon bond investor is usually subject to several risk sources, i.e., default risk but also interest rate risk, as we presume that his position is funded based on the 3M-Euribor. As we try to focus on default risk, we assume that he simultaneously enters into a swap contract that allows him to turn the fixed coupon payments into a floating leg that matches his funding cash flow stream (3M-Euribor plus spread s). Therefore, the only remaining degree of freedom for the swap contract is the spread s, which is paid by the counterpart. This parameter is fixed at initiation in order to attain a fair contract for both parties (initial present value should be zero). Please refer to Figure 6.3.

Such a payer swap, which has to match the bond or loan investment in terms of maturity and size / timing of the coupon payments, is often referred to as an *asset swap*. The combined position of a fixed rate bond or loan with an asset

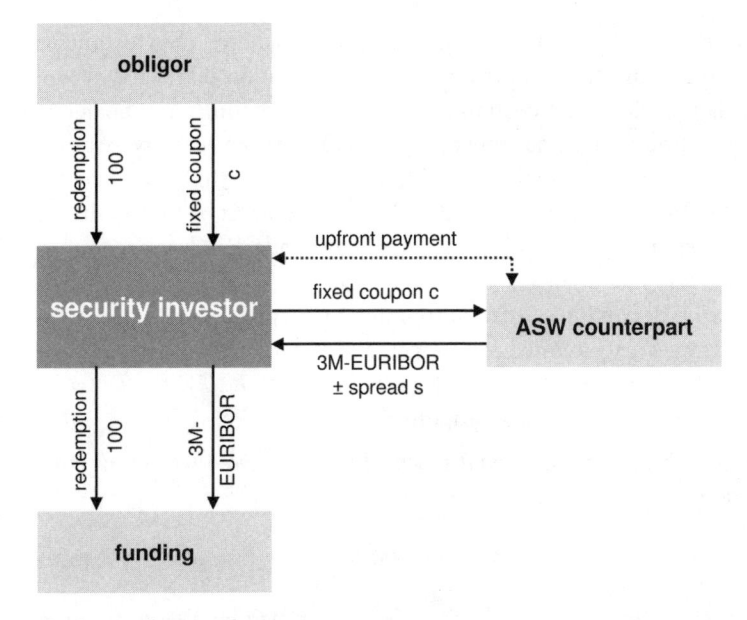

Fig. 6.3: Mechanism of a par asset swap

swap contract is called an *asset swap package*. The spread s, which is paid as a component of the swap's floating leg, forms the *asset swap spread* (ASW spread). Hence, the ASW spread can be understood as the spread over Euribor/Libor paid for an asset swap package.

However, there is an aspect that merits further discussion. The aforementioned trading scheme only works when the credit-risky security trades at par, as the funding position (3M-Euribor flat) implies an initial payout that is equal to the notional amount of the investment. It is apparent that the bond or loan trades off-par in the majority of cases. However, this problem can be solved by stipulating an upfront payment in the swap contract. For example, assume that the credit-risky instrument trades at 102, two percentage points above par. Hence, the investor needs an additional €2 per €100 of notional amount. The easiest way would be to enter into a tailor-made swap contract that incorporates a respective upfront payment. In our case, the investor (fixed-leg payer) would receive €2 assuming a notional amount of €100, transforming the credit-risky security into a *par floater*. For below-par investments, the ASW counterparty in lieu of the investor would receive a corresponding upfront payment.

In practice, the broker providing the security and the ASW counterparty often are identical. Hence, the investor simply obtains the credit-risky security for par value (100) without explicitly stipulating an upfront payment. This technique is obviously tantamount to the upfront payment separation discussed above. However, the latter reflects the economic content of generating a par floater.

After having introduced the concept of asset swaps spreads, we now focus on the question of how to calculate the spread level s. According to Figure 6.3, the asset swap spread s must be chosen so that the swap contract has zero value at initiation. Needless to say, the upfront payment has to be taken into account as well as the fixed and floating leg.

In the following derivation of the appropriate ASW spread level s, the price of the credit-risky security (quoted as a percentage of par) is denoted by $P_{t,\text{risky}}$. The payment dates of the swap's floating leg are denoted by $T'_1, T'_2, \ldots, T'_m = T$. The swap comprises the following components:

1. The present value of the *upfront payment* to be received by the investor (fixed rate payer) is stated as:

$$P_{t,\text{risky}} - 100(\%) \tag{6.6}$$

2. The present value of the *fixed leg* can be determined by discounting the cash flows of the fixed rate security. We include the redemption amount in order to facilitate the calculation of the floating leg. The discounting is done with a risk-free term structure of interest rates:

$$\widehat{P}_{t,\text{no risk}} = \sum_{i=1}^{n} R_t(\tau_i) \cdot \text{CF}_{T_i}. \tag{6.7}$$

3. If there were no spread s, the present value of the *floating leg* would be 100 (measured in %) at initiation, provided that we include the redemption amount in the same manner as for the fixed leg. However, we have to add the present value of the additional spread cash flows. Hence, we get:

$$100(\%) + 100(\%) \cdot s \cdot \sum_{j=1}^{m} R_t(\tau'_j) \cdot (T'_j - T'_{j-1}) \tag{6.8}$$

with $\tau'_j = T'_j - t \ (j = 1, 2, \ldots, m)$ and $T'_0 = t$

Please note that the sum expression is simply the present value of a (finite) annuity.

At initiation, the swap should have a present value of zero. In accordance with the above-mentioned considerations, the following equation must be applicable:

$$\underbrace{(P_{t,\,\text{risky}} - 1)}_{\text{upfront payment}} - \underbrace{\widehat{P}_{t,\,\text{no risk}}}_{\text{fixed leg}} + \underbrace{\left[1 + s \cdot \sum_{j=1}^{m} R_t(\tau_j') \cdot (T_j' - T_{j-1}')\right]}_{\text{floating leg}} = 0$$

$$\Leftrightarrow \quad s \cdot \sum_{j=1}^{m} R_t(\tau_j') \cdot (T_j' - T_{j-1}') = \widehat{P}_{t,\,\text{no risk}} - P_{t,\,\text{risky}}$$

$$\Leftrightarrow \quad s = \frac{\widehat{P}_{t,\,\text{no risk}} - P_{t,\,\text{risky}}}{\sum_{j=1}^{m} R_t(\tau_j') \cdot (T_j' - T_{j-1}')} \qquad (6.9)$$

What a result! The ASW spread s can be calculated explicitly in complete form, i.e., without applying any numerical procedures. In addition, there is an obvious similarity to yield spreads. We use the (dirty) price of a synthetic default-free bond with an identical cash flow stream in order to derive the spread s. However, this is done without the internal-rate-of-return (IRR) approach by simply dividing the price difference between this synthetic security and the credit-risky one by the present value of an annuity.

Nevertheless, there is a clear difference from the yield spread approach. The formula is based on real tradable financial instruments instead of calculating an obscure yield measure. In addition, there is no need to discuss which risk-free benchmark curve applies. As the concept is based on the idea of transforming a fixed rate security into a par floater via an asset swap, the spot rates derived from swap rates constitute the only valid benchmark.

Although the concept is based on a sensible notion and clean theoretical considerations, there are several shortcomings that should be taken into account. First, asset swap packages have become unfashionable over time, as many credit investors are hedging their interest rate exposure from a macro perspective with highly liquid futures contracts. Second, entering into a swap contract leads to additional transaction costs (bid–ask spread for swaps), increasing the range of possible ASW spread levels that are consistent with the concept.

However, the main practical problem for credit-risky securities arises from possible unwinding costs associated with the default case. If the investor suffers from the obligor's financial distress in a way that the obligor is no longer able to pay the fixed rate coupon, the investor would be forced to terminate the swap contract with his counterpart. As the interest rate environment changes over time, the asset swap will typically have an intrinsic value, which could be either positive or negative. This intrinsic value has to be settled in case of unwinding the contract via a termination fee. At first glance, this seems to be a nonsystematic risk. However, in practice there will be a correlation between the termination fee and the default of the obligor. But it is very hard to assess the extent of this effect.

As long as we refrain from lower credit qualities, the possible bias should be very limited. Unfortunately, another more profound problem may arise. Consider what happens to the ASW spread if we hypothetically increase the coupon of a credit-risky security given an unchanged credit quality (whatever that actually means). First, the price $P_{t,\,\text{risky}}$ will be higher. On the other hand, the price of the synthetic risk-free security with identical cash flows ($\widehat{P}_{t,\,\text{no risk}}$) will increase as well, but to a greater extent (in absolute terms), as the risk-free discounting has a less effective impact than risk-adjusted discounting. Therefore, the difference in the numerator of formula 6.9 would increase, while the denominator remains unchanged. The asset swap spread thus would rise, although we initially assumed an unchanged credit quality.

In a nutshell, the ASW spread does not completely isolate credit risk, as it is largely affected by the instrument's price level. Against this background, comparing the credit risk of two securities by means of the ASW spread could be misleading if their currently quoted prices diverge significantly. In general, we recommend abstaining from the ASW concept if the security trades significantly off-par. In such a case, we prefer the Z-spread approach, as it does not share this weakness of scale dependency.

Last but not least, it should be mentioned that the asset swap spread is a measure that is not limited to non-negative numbers. Since the Euribor or Libor curve acts as the benchmark, the ASW spread of a high-quality security can even be negative. We already pointed out that restricting spreads to non-negative numbers is a desirable property in order to measure the extent of default risk compared to a non-defaultable benchmark. A negative spread, however, would turn this interpretation upside down.

6.5 Spread Measures for Floaters

Up to this point, the spread measures presented were primarily related to fixed rate securities without any optionalities. Now we would like to extend the field of application to floating rate bonds and loans, particularly those that are based on Libor or Euribor reference rates. Constant maturity instruments such as notes referring to a 10Y swap rate but paying an amount relating to it on a three-month frequency, are not within the scope of this section, as they do not account for a big market share in practice in the context of credit-risky securities.

As mentioned several times before, the three basic spread concepts, the yield spread, the Z-spread, and the ASW spread, are basically accessible to floating rate instruments. Applying the yield spread and Z-spread would simply require one to project future unknown cash flows by means of forward rates, which can be deduced from the current spot rate curve. Even the ASW spread concept can also be transferred to floaters by replacing a standard swap contract by a swap with two floating legs. Even formula 6.9 for ASW spreads can be used for floaters by projecting future unknown cash flows by resorting to forward rates.

Unfortunately, one does not typically find yield spreads, Z-spreads, and ASW spreads in the context of floaters. However, the basic ideas of these concepts have found their way into peculiar spread measures, although they have different names. Hence, we do not have to reinvent the wheel and can deal with these spread measures directly.

Information that is easily accessible is the *quoted margin*. It simply reflects the spread over the reference floating rate (e.g., 3M-Euribor) paid by the floater. Usually, it is contractually stipulated at the date of issuance for the whole term, but it may also be subject to step-ups or step-downs in some rare cases. The quoted margin suffers from one striking shortcoming. It obviously reflects the credit quality of the issuer at the time of issuance but not the current state. Any changes of credit quality that occur in the meantime will affect the quoted price. For example, a floating rate note that was issued at par and experienced a deterioration of credit quality will trade significantly below par. If the floater was issued at par, the difference between the current price and the par value is the missing link to updated spread information. Thus, simply stating the quoted margin would be inappropriate.

To overcome this limitation, we have to return to our three basic measurement ideas. Two very popular spread measures for floaters are based on the notion of Z-spreads: the *discount margin* and the *zero discount margin*. Hence, the concept is to add a spread to the respective benchmark curve in order to reprice the bond. Consequently, numerical procedures must be utilized to obtain the spread number. When dealing with floating rate notes, one has to make an assumption of how to estimate future unknown cash flows. The discount margin and the zero discount margin differ in how to model the benchmark curve and how to project these future cash flows:

- The discount margin concept assumes a flat underlying benchmark curve for discounting purposes, based on the current Euribor or Libor rate for the respective frequency of coupon payments. In accordance with this crude assumption, future unknown cash flows are projected based on the current Euribor/Libor rate plus the contractually specified spread.
- The zero discount margin concept does not make these assumptions by taking the currently observable term structure of interest rates for granted instead of assuming a flat benchmark curve. Accordingly, future cash flows are estimated by utilizing forward rates inferred from the spot rate curve.

From a theoretical point of view, the discount rate is at a disadvantage due to its unrealistic assumptions. Applying forward rates to project future unknown cash flows can be justified in two different ways. On the one hand, forward rates can be interpreted as unbiased estimators of future spot rates according to the so-called *expectations theory*. On the other hand, it is a well-known fact from no-arbitrage valuation that the valuation of floating rate payments is done by substituting the unknown future spot rate by the current forward rate for the respective period of time. This is because an FRN investor could turn any unknown floating cash flow into a fixed payment by entering into a *forward rate agreement*. The amount of the fixed payment has to be chosen consistent with the current forward rate.

The zero discount margin concept has another property that underpins its viability. If the floater is currently quoted at par, then the zero discount margin is equal to the quoted margin.

In a similar manner, it would be possible to apply the yield spread and the ASW spread concept to floaters. However, this is seldomly done in practice. Thus, we skip these approaches.

6.6 Spreads and the Real Economy

The previous section introduced the spread concept from a purely technical perspective. Irrespective of the chosen concept, credit spreads are always extracted from observable security prices. Hence, a spread reflects the implied market expectation with regard to the credit risk of a specific instrument. Now, we would like to shed some light on the economic substance of the spread concept. Although this should rather be done within the scope of credit risk models, which will be introduced in the forthcoming chapters, we provide some empirical evidence with regard to spread behavior from a market perspective.

During the last few years, several academics and practitioners addressed the topic of how spreads are related to economic reality. Although the area under investigation seems clear, we have to differentiate between the following questions:

1. What are the major economic factors influencing the current spread *level* of credit-risky instruments? What is the contribution of these factors to the spread level?
2. What economic factors have an impact on spread *changes* over time?
3. Do spreads carry additional information that may be helpful to forecast other economic variables?

It seems clear that these issues are somewhat interrelated. However, it is strictly necessary to distinguish spread levels from spread level changes over time. In addition, the direction of causality (Which one was first, the chicken or the egg?) has severe implications for the results.

A fundamental publication that focuses on the first question is the article of Elton et al. (2001).[21] The authors perform a multi-stage econometric analysis to prove the existence of three components that contribute to the spread level:

- A component representing compensation for the expected default loss
- A tax premium that arises due to the characteristics of the local tax system
- A risk premium for assuming systematic rather than diversifiable risk.

The first component is self-evident. An investment in a credit-risky security must at least offer a compensation for the actual default risk. The tax premium, however, is a US-specific issue that is attributable to the fact that corporate bonds, unlike government bonds, are subject to state taxes, which can be significant in practice. In European countries there is, to the best of our knowledge, no such difference and hence no justification for a tax premium at all.

Elton et al. observed that expected default losses account for only a surprisingly small fraction of the observed credit spreads (no more than 25 percent of the spread level). A tax premium does not apply, so that the remaining part of the spread is assumed to be an additional risk premium beyond the compensation for the expected default loss.

But is there a justification for the existence of such a premium at all? It is a well-known insight from modern capital market theory, particularly the *capital asset pricing model* (CAPM), that a risk premium should only be paid for systematic risk. On the other hand, non-systematic (or idiosyncratic) risk is diversifiable (i.e., it can be eliminated) on a portfolio level, and hence requires no risk premium. Therefore, we have to find evidence of systematic risk.

A single-period, two-state default model as shown in figure 6.4 provides an easy way to recognize the dependency on systematic risk. Let us assume that the (real) probability of a default amounts to p, the so-called *probability of default*, which would result in a fixed payoff of V^{default}. Thus, $1 - p$ denotes the probability that no default (fixed payoff $V^{\text{no default}}$) will occur, often called the *survival probability*. As we find ourselves in a single-period context, the risk-free discount rate is supposed to be r (assuming simple compounding).

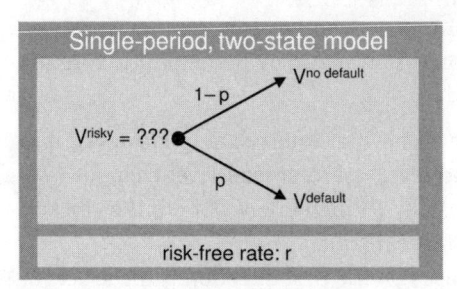

Fig. 6.4: A simple single-period, two-state default model

What is the value of this credit-risky security today? In a risk-neutral world, i.e., assuming that every investor only cares about expected return but not risk, one simply would have to calculate the risk-free discounted expected value of future payments, in this case (the tilde indicates this hypothetical situation):

$$\widetilde{V}^{\text{risky}} = \frac{1}{1+r} \left[p \cdot V^{\text{default}} + (1-p) \cdot V^{\text{no default}} \right] \tag{6.10}$$

It should be noted that no risk premium applies in a risk-neutral world. However, the real world is not risk-free. Investors do take the risk of their investments into account. In this case, the valuation equation 6.10 has to be adjusted:

$$V^{\text{risky}} = \frac{1}{1+r} \left[\pi \cdot V^{\text{default}} + (1-\pi) \cdot V^{\text{no default}} \right] \tag{6.11}$$

Real-world probabilities p and $1-p$ have been replaced by *artificial probabilities* π and $1 - \pi$. It is a well-known fact from mathematical finance that these articifial probabilities exist, that is, $0 < \pi < 1$, if we assume that the no-arbitrage condition for capital markets holds. If π and $1 - \pi$ deviate from real-world probabilities p and $1-p$, the current value of the credit-risky security V^{risky} will differ from the value $\widetilde{V}^{\text{risky}}$ we hypothetically calculated for a risk-neutral world.

But what is the economic notion of different probability measures? A common way to obtain a link to the real world is to introduce the so-called *pricing* kernel χ. It enables us to return to real-world probabilities in our valuation approach without dismissing the validity of equation 6.11:

$$V^{\text{risky}} = \frac{1}{1+r} \left[p \cdot V^{\text{default}} \cdot \chi^{\text{def.}} + (1-p) \cdot V^{\text{no default}} \cdot \chi^{\text{no def.}} \right] \quad (6.12)$$

$$\text{with } \chi^{\text{def.}} = \frac{\pi}{p} \text{ and } \chi^{\text{no def.}} = \frac{1-\pi}{1-p}$$

Apparently, the pricing kernel concept is based on a tautology, i.e., the valuation equation is simply restated by incorporating the real-world probabilities p and $1 - p$. However, this simultaneously requires the introduction of state-dependent multipliers χ, which are calculated as the ratio of artificial to real-world probabilities.

This way of stating the valuation equation provides a helpful interpretation for χ: *The pricing kernel for a specific state reflects the value of a monetary unit if the economy is in the respective state.* A pricing kernel above 1 for a specific state means that the capital market assigns an above-average appreciation for a payment that takes place in that state. The opposite is true for the case $\chi < 1$.

But is there any reason to assign different weightings $\chi^{\text{def.}}$ and $\chi^{\text{no def.}}$ for our two states? The answer is yes, as this is where the correlation to real-world economic prospects comes into play. The probability of default for a credit-risky security is usually correlated with the state of the economy. Just consider that a poor economic growth environment is often associated with numerous defaults in the economy, hence increasing the probability of a default for a single security.

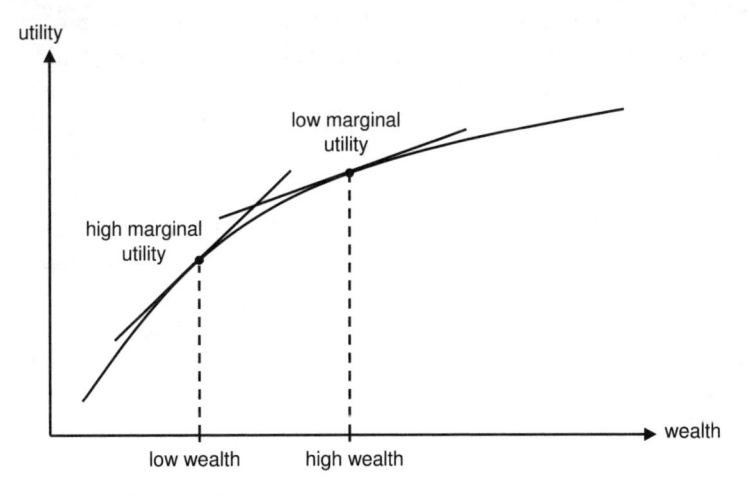

Fig. 6.5: Wealth and utility for risk-averse investors

The value of a monetary unit largely depends on the respective economic state, which can be expressed by the level of economic wealth. Based on the assumption of declining marginal utility, a common result when assuming risk-averse investors, high wealth is associated with a low marginal utility, whereas low wealth involves a high marginal utility (see Figure 6.5 for an illustration). Hence, an additional monetary unit in a sluggish economy unit offers greater value than in a situation of prosperity. This basic consideration should be reflected in the state-dependent pricing kernel χ.

If there is in fact a relationship between the default event and the economic state, as can be basically presumed, the pricing kernel of our simple two-stage model should incorporate this effect. Thus, the pricing kernel for the default state $\chi^{\text{def.}}$ should be above 1, as this state is likely associated with a poor economic state. On the other hand, no default is likely to occur when the wealth of the economy is on a high level, hence resulting in a pricing kernel $\chi^{\text{no def.}}$ below 1.

What is the consequence for the pricing of the credit-risky security? Assuming $V^{\text{default}} < V^{\text{no default}}$, which is a self-evident constraint, the resulting price V^{risky} should be lower compared to that in a risk-neutral world. Hence, $V^{\text{risky}} < \widetilde{V}^{\text{risky}}$ holds, which implies that the security's credit spread exceeds the spread that would be necessary to compensate for the default risk based on real-world probabilities. As long as there is a (negative) relationship between the likelihood of default events and the economic state, market participants require a risk premium that results in lower prices and higher spreads!

Elton et al. accepted this notion and tried to find empirical evidence for the existence of a risk premium. They detected that the remaining portion of the spread levels, which is not attributable to expected default loss and tax effects, is closely related to factors that are commonly accepted as explaining risk premiums for common stocks. If equity investments have a risk premium, which is hardly challenged in practice, credit-risky securities should have a risk premium too due to their sensitivity to market risk factors. They conclude that a large part of the risk of corporate bonds is systematic rather than diversifiable.

While Elton et al. performed their calculations for the expected default loss based on historical default rates collected by S&P and Moody's, other authors utilized alternative approaches. Nevertheless, the main results remain uncontested. Only a small fraction of corporate bond spreads is attributable to expected default losses, confirming the existence of a risk premium.

Huang and Huang (2003)[22] propose a new calibration methodology based on historical default data, resorting to a sophisticated *structural model*. We will introduce this class of credit models in a later chapter. Another interesting insight is that the fraction of the credit spread that is attributable to the expected default loss significantly depends on the credit quality of the respective security. While expected default losses account for about 20 percent of the total spread for A-rated bonds, it increases up to an amount of over 30 percent for BBBs and even higher values for junk status bonds. In addition, the authors point out that a *liquidity premium* may also apply. High transaction costs and low trading volume have to be considered when assessing credit spreads.

Dionne et al. (2004)[23], on the other hand, challenge the use of historical default data for the estimation of expected default losses. As defaults and rating transitions are rare events, a serious underestimation of default risk cannot be ruled out. Their results reveal that using alternative probabilities estimates increases the fraction of the spread attributable to default risk (36 percent for A-rated issues, 79 percent for BBBs). Nevertheless, a gap that is attributable to a risk premium still remains.

As stated at the beginning of this section, some studies focus more on spread *changes* of corporate bonds over time instead of explaining current spread *levels*. The article of Collin-Dufresne, Goldstein, and Martin (2001)[24] assesses the ability of structural models to explain corporate credit spreads. They conclude that variables that should in theory determine credit spreads have a rather limited explanatory power (only 25 percent of the observed credit spread changes). Based on this disillusioning result, the residual part of any spread change is mostly determined by a single common factor, which can be shown by performing a primary component analysis. This result argues for a systematic factor impacting spreads across the board. Avramov, Jostova, and Philipov (2004) confirm this basic observation, although they were able to increase the explanatory power to 35 percent (or even up to 67 percent for lower credit qualities) based on a structural model involving idiosyncratic volatility (extracted from stock options) and the price-to-book ratio, which reflects the growth opportunities of a firm.

If there is a single common factor that systematically affects the whole credit market, it would be helpful to explore its economic substance. One can consider several macroeconomic and financial variables as candidate proxies. According to Collin-Dufresne, Goldstein, and Martin, this attempt fails, concluding that spreads are largely driven by local supply and demand shocks that are independent of credit risk factors. Avramov, Jostova, and Philipov assert that high- and low-grade credit instruments are subject to different supply and demand forces. In practice, the demand for high-grade bonds is governed by large institutional players such as pension funds and insurance companies, where the junk bond segment involves a variety of players (hedge funds, prop desks, etc.) that try to exploit short-term profits. As a result, the high-yield segment is less vulnerable to common demand shocks. Unfortunately, this conclusion proved wrong in

2005, as many hedge funds and prop desks have implemented similar trading positions. The downgrade of Ford and General Motors to junk status in May caused a tremendous sentiment change in the market, causing a blowout of credit spreads across the board.

If one is not able to explore the economic substance of this common factor that drives credit spreads, turning the causality on its head could be a sensible reaction. Maybe this common factor incorporates some valuable information that helps to predict future economic development. This idea leads to the third question stated at the beginning of this section. For example, Chan-Lau and Ivaschenko (2001)[17] adopt this perspective and predict marginal changes in US industrial production up to twelve months in the future. They conclude that the systematic spread component has significant predictive ability for the future growth rate of industrial production. Against this background, spread information can be a valuable tool, as it acts as a leading indicator for the economic cycle and is readily available at high frequency. However, this field of application requires the absence of price bubbles and significant market frictions.

6.7 Conclusion

The variety of alternative spread concepts for credit-risky securities raises the question whether there is a superior approach that fits all needs. As we have already demonstrated in the course of this chapter, the answer unfortunately is "No". Nevertheless, we try to provide some guidance with regard to the applicability of these concepts in practice, and to identify which measure may be more appropriate than others under certain circumstances. Here we focus on fixed coupon bonds without optionalities.

A first and important observation is that market makers in the high-grade market segment primarily quote ASW spreads, while the quotation of high-yield issues is often based on Z-spreads. Although there is not really a kind of market standard with regard to which spread measure is cited, these conventions are quite reasonable from a historical perspective. In the early stages of the euro credit market, it was common practice that customers acquired asset swap packages (a combination of a fixed rate bond and a swap contract that turns the fixed rate coupon payments into a floating leg) instead of just buying a single corporate bond. Accordingly, an ASW spread best reflects the spread income that can be earned by acquiring such a package. Its advantage is related to the fact that it is based on tradable instruments.

However, the pronounced spread-widening trend during the years 2001 and 2002, accompanied by an increase in default rates, resulted in bond prices that were considerably below par, raising concerns about the (implicit) upfront payment of an asset swap package, which have already been discussed in section 6.4. In addition, we already pointed out that the ASW spread is scale-dependent, that is, the higher the bond price, the bigger the ASW spread given a specific default risk. Accordingly, the inherent credit risk of a corporate bond is underestimated in such a market environment when resorting to ASW spreads, not to mention that intertemporal comparisons of ASW spread levels lead to questionable results.

As opposed to credit markets in 2001 and 2002, we currently face a low-yield, low-spread environment, causing many (seasoned) high-grade issues to trade significantly above par. The implied market standard of stating ASW spreads should be taken with a pinch of salt. In the case that a bond trades significantly off-par, we recommend to resort to Z-spreads, although these are still not as recognized as other spread concepts.

In any case, we recommend to refrain from yield spreads such as I-spreads, although they can provide a helpful first impression about the size of compensation for incurring credit risk. Yield spreads still enjoy great popularity across different credit classes, for example in the context of asset backed securities. Nevertheless, our objections concerning this concept remain valid, particularly with regard to the shortcomings of YTM measures. Yield spreads do not take the specific shape of the spot rate curve into consideration. From this perspective, the Z-spread concept is preferable.

7
Basics of Credit Risk Models

In the following chapters, we present state-of-the-art credit risk pricing models. Although models and methods can become quite sophisticated, the basic building blocks and the economic principles behind most of the approaches are easy to understand. In the following analysis, we show that there are two quantitative factors that are of central importance for valuing single-name credit risk: the so-called survival probability function $S_t(\tau)$ and the model for the recovery payments that are conditional upon default. Using these two quantities, we can price most credit-risky contracts that refer to a single obligation (exceptions are, for example, non-linear products such as spread options). Regarding portfolio credit risk, the default dependency (a.k.a. default correlation) has to be added to the modeling framework. Against this background, portfolio derivatives, such as first-to-default baskets and collateralized debt obligations, are also considered as correlation derivatives.

The following analysis will be split into three parts. In the first part, we introduce the basic concepts such as survival probability functions and recovery modeling. We start with a brief overview of the underlying concepts (such as the probability of default and the loss given default) using a simple single-step, two-stage model. Then we expand these concepts stepwise to result in a continuous-time valuation framework. Here, the focus is on analyzing the integration of the default probabilities into pricing relations. This is followed by an analysis of the other very central building block mentioned above, the recovery treatment, which determines the modeling of the loss given default. We illustrate the different approaches and analyze them in the light of real recovery data from rating agencies.

In the subsequent chapter, we focus on three different pricing models: reduced-form models, structural models, and rating-based transition matrix models. To show the similarities and differences among these models, we choose a special presentation, in which the approaches are formulated in a way to result in the above-mentioned survival probability function and recovery rate.

Afterwards, we introduce models for aggregating single-name credit risk to a portfolio level. We do this in two steps, starting with a simple framework with uncorrelated credits and then expanding the derived findings to models with default dependency. The derived mathematical methods can be used for

Active Credit Portfolio Management. J. Felsenheimer, P. Gisdakis, and M. Zaiser
Copyright © 2006 WILEY-VCH Verlag GmbH & Co. KGaA, Weinheim
ISBN: 3-527-50198-3

pricing portfolio derivatives (FTD baskets and CDO tranches), but also serves as an introduction to the fundamentals of credit risk measurement (i.e., credit value at risk).

7.1 The Components of Credit Risk

The financial risk involved with a single credit-risky asset has two different sources. An investor who holds such a credit-risky bond faces, first, the risk that the bond experiences a default event during the holding period, leading to a significant loss, and, second, the market price of the security might change during the holding period, when the market perception of the underlying default risk changes. Note that we refer to the credit risk component of the market price, that is, the credit spread, while we do not consider effects that are attributable to changes in the risk-free yield curve. Hence, the two components of the credit risk can be considered to be *default risk*, and *spread risk* or *market price risk*.

However, these two components cannot be separated from each other easily, as the spread risk is the expression of the market's view of the corresponding default risk. But what drives the market's view of credit risk? From our previous analysis it is clear that there is not a single driving force that affects the market price for credit risk. A broad array of factors (e.g., rating changes, balance sheet information, implied equity volatilities, and market technicals such as new issuance activity and economic growth) drive the markets. Unfortunately, this is bad news because it destroys all chances of using simple models. In fact, only a few of the default models introduced below can be considered to be real default models, which try to forecast the default probability from specific structural information about the companies. These are called *structural models* and go back to the seminal work of Robert Merton.[25] In these models, the default event can be traced to an internal, company-specific factor: the value of the assets does not exceed the value of the debt, and hence the value of the equity is zero. Another advantage of this approach is that it allows for the relative valuation of debt and equity securities issued by the same company. Investors can hence identify attractive investment strategies. The downside of structural models is that they are very difficult to calibrate and sometimes result in wrong conclusions.

In contrast to the structural models, the so-called *reduced-form models* or *intensity-based models* do not explicitly explain the trigger of the default event. Default is a purely external event, it hits the company simply by accident. Moreover, even the probability of such a default event (the central issue in pricing credit risk) is not modeled explicitly, but simply extracted from traded credit spreads. However, this feature of having no specific model for the default probability is the main advantage of reduced-form models. They simply offer a very general framework to price credit risk, given the underlying probability distributions. This framework can be used either by inferring these probabilities from market prices or via more sophisticated models, such as structural models. They just have to be expressed in a way that they generate these probability distributions.

Transition matrix models try to derive the probability of default from rating migrations. However, the results can deviate substantially from market prices, as rating transitions are not the only factor that drive the markets. We only need to recall here that the market spreads segmented by rating classes are not at all stable over time. They fluctuate significantly as market conditions change.

Single-name credit risk is one thing, but the real challenge is modeling credit risk at a portfolio level. Besides security-specific factors, the correlation pattern has to be taken into account. Analogous to the separation of credit risk into default risk and spread risk at the single-name level, we have to measure two different types of correlations: the default correlation and the spread correlation. While we might have an intuitive feeling about the market price correlation (i.e., spread correlation), understanding the default dependency is a challenge of its own. Complicated mathematical methods such as copula models were introduced to tackle this field. However, some simple approaches allow interesting insights without being too mathematically complex.

> **Example 6: Moody's Definition of Default Events**
> To measure the risk of a default event, one has to clearly define what such an event exactly is. Moody's categorizes the following default events:
> - A missed or delayed interest or principal payment, including payments made within a grace period.
> - Filing for bankruptcy and related legal triggers that block the timely payments of interest or principal.
> - Consummation of a distressed exchange, for example, when the issuer offers the bondholders a new security with a diminished financial obligation, involving significant economic losses (stocks or bonds with lower coupons or par amount, lower seniority, or longer maturity).

A quick word concerning the regulatory context of modeling credit risk. In the BIS regime credit risk encompasses, besides the above-mentioned default and spread risk, also the components downgrade risk and concentration risk. Concentration risk is related to the portfolio view, as the risk of correlated default – either due to systemic reasons or to insufficient diversification – has a large impact on portfolio risk measures. However, the separation of downgrade risk and spread risk appears to be a little odd, as downgrade risk is one factor that drives the credit spreads and is hence completely reflected in the credit spread dynamics.

7.2 A Single-Step, Two-Stage Model

We start our introductory analysis with a simple single-step, two-stage model (see figure 7.1). We assume a simplified economic world, in which the payoff of a credit-risky contract depends on the outcome of a single random experiment. Moreover, the experiment has only two outcomes: the contract is either in default or it is not in default. Here, we use the commonly accepted notation: PD denotes the *probability of default*, the probability that the contract ends up in default, and LGD is the *loss given default*. As there are just two possible outcomes in this world, the probability of no default (the so-called survival probability) is simply $1 - \text{PD}$. We focus on a single-step model, so we ignore an explicit time dependency in the relevant quantities for the moment.

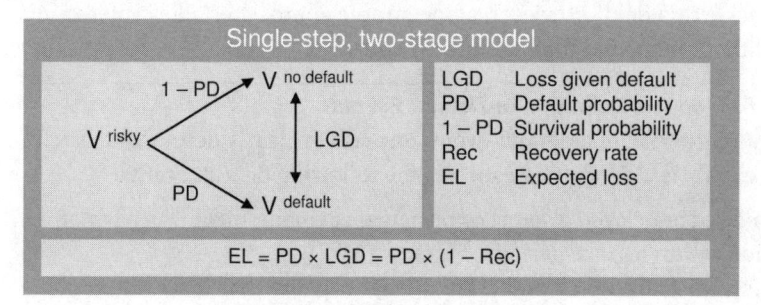

Fig. 7.1: Simplified single-step, two-stage model for credit risk

The value of the risky contract in this framework is given by the probability that the contract survives (i.e., $1 - \text{PD}$) times the value in case of no default plus the probability that the contract defaults (i.e., PD) times the value of the contract in default:

$$V^{\text{risky}} = (1 - \text{PD}) \times V^{\text{no default}} + \text{PD} \times V^{\text{default}} \tag{7.1}$$

Equation 7.1 is a general result, as it does not depend on any specific form for the payoff structure. This is indicated by the generalized expression $V^{\text{no default}}$ and V^{default}. To get an idea about the results in a specific context, we only need to think of a zero coupon bond. Neglecting any discounting effects, $V^{\text{no default}}$ would equal the face value of the bond. On the other side, the value in default V^{default} would be the recovery rate times the face value of the bond. However, by considering this simple single-step model as a single branch of a complete tree, we can make the model more complex. In such a setup $V^{\text{no default}}$ and V^{default} would be the forward prices of the underlying security (conditional on no default) and the recovery payment given a default.

However, according to equation 7.1 the value of the risky security with respect to the outcome of the random experiment is an average of the two outcomes $V^{\text{no default}}$ and V^{default}, weighted by the default and survival probability. By rearranging equation 7.1, we can isolate all terms that depend on the probability of default (PD). Moreover, by factoring out the value in case of no default $V^{\text{no default}}$ we arrive at a well-known expression on credit risk:

$$V^{\text{risky}} = V^{\text{no default}} - \text{PD} \times (V^{\text{no default}} - V^{\text{default}})$$
$$= V^{\text{no default}} \times [1 - \underbrace{\text{PD} \times (1 - \underbrace{\frac{V^{\text{default}}}{V^{\text{no default}}}}_{\text{Rec}})}_{\text{LGD}}] \qquad (7.2)$$

$$\underbrace{\phantom{= V^{\text{no default}} \times [1 - \text{PD} \times (1 - \frac{V^{\text{default}}}{V^{\text{no default}}})]}}_{\text{EL}}$$

To gain some insight into equation 7.2, we consider the value of the contract given no default to equal the value of an identical, although credit risk-free contract $V^{\text{no default}} = V^{\text{risk-free}}$. In this way, we separated the value of the risky contract in a risk-free part and the so-called *expected loss* (EL). V^{risky} is given by $1 - \text{EL}$ scaled by the value in case of no default. This means that, in the current context, we express the expected loss relative to $V^{\text{no default}}$ (or $V^{\text{risk-free}}$). The expected loss of a credit-risky contract can be derived from the difference between the values of the risky and the corresponding risk-free contract. Equation 7.2 refers to the so-called credit triangle.

$$\text{EL} = \frac{V^{\text{risk-free}} - V^{\text{risky}}}{V^{\text{risk-free}}}$$
$$= \text{PD} \times \text{LGD} = \text{PD} \times (1 - \text{Rec}) \qquad (7.3)$$

Here, LGD denotes the loss given default and Rec the recovery rate. In the two-stage model, we can measure the recovery rate as the fraction $V^{\text{default}}/V^{\text{no default}}$.

> **Example 7: Single-Step, Two-Stage Model**
>
> 1. We consider a bond that has a value of €100 at maturity if the bond does not default. In case of default, the value of the security should be €40. The probability of default over the investment horizon is 0.02. Neglecting any discounting effects, the value of the risky bond is calculated as $(1 - 0.02) \times €100 + 0.02 \times €40 = €98.8$. As €100 can also be considered as the risk-free value, the expected loss is stated as $(100 - 98.8)/100 = 1.2\%$. Moreover, the recovery rate amounts to $40/100 = 0.4$. Hence, the loss given default comes to $0.6 = 1 - 0.4$.
> 2. In the previous example, we ignored time-value-of-money effects. However, to account for these effects, we simply have to add discount factors into the suggested valuation framework. In case of a continuously compounded risk-free interest rate of 5 percent and a time horizon of one year, we obtain a discount factor of $\exp(-0.05 \cdot 1) \approx 0.95$. Hence, the present value of the €100 paid in one year would be $€95 = €100 \times 0.95$, and correspondingly the present value in default would be $€38 = €40 \times 0.95$. From these numbers we can arrive at all quantities derived above. For example, the value of the risky contract is given by $V^{\text{risky}} = 0.98 \times €95 + 0.02 \times €38 = €93.86$, which is obviously the same as discounting the value above $€93.86 = €98.8 \times 0.95$. Moreover, the expected loss is $(95 - 93.86)/95 = 1.2\%$.
> 3. The final example shows that the formulas stated above can also be used to calculate approximate default probabilities from market prices. We assume a credit-risky coupon bond with a time to maturity of 5.1 years and a current price of €97.5. Moreover, the value of a risk-free, but otherwise identical coupon bond (i.e., one with identical cash flows) should be €101.5. In addition, we assume a recovery rate of 40 percent. Using the framework derived above, we arrive at an expected loss of 3.94 percent and a (cumulative) default probability of 6.57 percent. As the remaining time to maturity is 5.1 years, we project an annualized default probability of 1.29 percent. Note that this result is a only a rough approximation.

Furthermore, equation 7.3 can be inverted to result in the default probability once we know the expected loss and the recovery rate. At first glance, this sounds a little obscure, but it becomes clear if we note that the expected loss is given by the difference between the value of the risky and the corresponding risk-free contract:

$$\text{PD} = \frac{\text{EL}}{(1 - \text{Rec})} = \frac{V^{\text{risk-free}} - V^{\text{risky}}}{V^{\text{risk-free}}} \cdot \frac{1}{(1 - \text{Rec})} \qquad (7.4)$$

The expected loss involved in a credit-risky bond is expressed as the yield spread. Hence, we can approximate a market-implied (risk-neutral) default probability from market prices by using equation 7.4.

Example 8: Default Probabilities and Credit Ratings

Rating agencies provide detailed analytic data about historical default rates. In table A.5 in the appendix, we show Moody's global annual issuer-weighted default rates, segmented by whole-letter ratings for the period between 1970 and 2004. Obviously, higher credit ratings involve lower default rates. The average default rate for a B rating was 6.21 percent, while it was only 0.17 percent for a Baa rating. Note that a Baa rating would correspond to a BBB rating in S&P's and Fitch's methodology. Besides such historical annualized data, the rating agencies also give information about cumulative default rates for different time horizons (see table A.6). The five-year cumulative default rate for a Baa rating, for example, amounts to 2.08 percent. Moreover, in addition to the whole-letter rating, the rating agencies usually provide these data also for the alphanumerical rating (Moody's, e.g., Baa3) or the rating including + or – of S&P and Fitch (e.g., BBB–). See table 1.1 for a definition of the rating categories.

However, some care is needed when assigning a default rate to a bond based on its rating, as the agencies do not only reflect the probability of default in the bond rating, but also the severity of the loss in case of a default (in other words, the loss given default). This leads to different ratings for bonds, with different subordination levels issued by the same company. This differentiation schedule is called notching. However, the probability of default is the same for all these bonds, as a company usually defaults on all bonds at the same time.

Hence, when assigning a probability of default to a company, one should prefer the issuer rating (which normally corresponds to the senior unsecured debt rating) over an individual bond's rating, especially if the bond under consideration is subordinated.

It is important to note that historical default probabilities, such as those shown in the appendix, are real probabilities, whereas for pricing purposes we need risk-neutral probabilities.

7.3 A Multi-Step Model for Zero Coupon Bonds

In the next step, we aim at extending the single-step approach to a multi-step framework by adding several single-step branches to a tree model. In fact, we illustrate the principle first by using a two-step example, in which we connect two branches. Subsequently, we will generalize the results and will switch to a mathematically more consistent nomenclature. In figure 7.2 such a tree is shown for a security that involves only one regular cash flow at maturity of the contract; in other words, it is a risky zero coupon bond. For the risk to be overly exact, we add that the security can result in a different payment structure if it defaults. But the payment that is triggered upon default is not foreseeable. The integration of more cash flows, such as coupon payments, will be shown in the next section.

Multi-step model for a zero-coupon bond

V_0^{risky} branches with probability $1-p_1$ to $V_1^{no\ default} = V_1^{risky}$, which branches with probability $1-p_2$ to $V_2^{no\ default} = V^{terminal}$ and with probability p_2 to $V_2^{default}$. V_0^{risky} branches with probability p_1 to $V_1^{default}$.

Cash-flow structure zero-coupon bond at times 0, 1, 2.

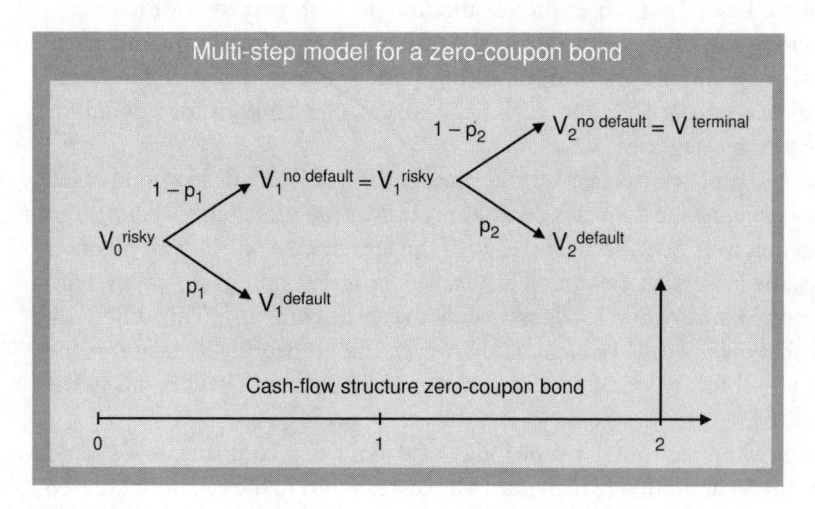

Fig. 7.2: Multi-step model for credit risk for a zero coupon

Figure 7.2 shows a tree model for two time steps. We extended the previously introduced notation to reflect several time steps. The subscripts indicate the time dependency of the different quantities. V_i^{risky} denotes the value of the risky claim at time i. Analogously, V_i^{default} is the value of the default payment in case of a default at time i. p_i is the default probability for the period between $i-1$ and i, while $1-p_i$ is the corresponding survival probability. This notation is still a little sloppy, as the values denoted by V_i refer to a point in time, while the p_i refer to a time period. Nevertheless, this simplified notation is appropriate for the current introduction, and, as already mentioned, we will develop a proper notation below. Note that although the branch model shown in figure 7.2 looks like the binomial tree implementation of a term-structure model for pricing interest rate options, it is not able to capture non-linear spread products, such as spread options. It is a purely static model, which does not include the volatility of the default probability. A tree model for spread option would at least need three stages per branch: one for the default event (in line with our model), but two for the survival case: one for upwards and one for downwards changes of p_i.[26]

Let us recapitulate the previously found results for the current example. The value of the risky claim is given as the expected value of the payoff ($V_i^{\text{no default}}$ in case of no default and V_i^{default} given a default event). The expectations are calculated using the probability of default. This can be done for each time step separately:

$$V_0^{\text{risky}} = (1-p_1) \cdot V_1^{\text{no default}} + p_1 \cdot V_1^{\text{default}}$$
$$V_1^{\text{risky}} = (1-p_2) \cdot V_2^{\text{no default}} + p_2 \cdot V_2^{\text{default}} \qquad (7.5)$$

We do not treat the time value of money explicitly. However, discounting with the risk-free rate can be implicitly integrated into the payoff $V_i^{\text{no default}}$ and V_i^{default} (this would assume that default rates and interest rates are independent).

The central idea of the multi-step model is to connect the two branches, thereby building a tree. This is done by equating the end point of the first branch with the starting point of the second, $V_1^{\text{no default}} = V_1^{\text{risky}}$. The value in case of no default after the first time step is simply the risky value over the next time step. The chain ends at the terminal payoff $V_2^{\text{no default}} = V^{\text{terminal}}$. If V^{terminal} is the repayment of the notional amount of the risky contract, the tree models a risky zero coupon bond.

Using the above-mentioned conditions to connect the two branches, we simply insert the equation for V_1^{risky} into the one for $V_0^{\text{no default}}$. The result is given by:

$$V_0^{\text{risky}} = \underbrace{(1-p_1)\cdot(1-p_2)}_{\text{survival probability for two time steps}} V_2^{\text{no default}}$$
$$+ p_1 \cdot V_1^{\text{default}} + \underbrace{(1-p_1)\cdot p_2}_{\text{unconditional default probability}} V_2^{\text{default}} \qquad (7.6)$$

Equation 7.6 can be segmented into two parts. The first line (equivalent to the first part in equation 7.1) is the value of the contract in case of no default, and the second line corresponds to the value given a default event. The combined single-step probabilities $(1-p_1)(1-p_2)$ in the first part refer to the two-period survival probability, while the probability terms corresponding to the default states are unconditional default probabilities), in other words, the probability that a default occurs in time period between 1 and 2 is conditional on surviving up to time 1. Hence, it can be calculated by multiplying the survival probability up to time 1, $(1-p_1)$, with the conditional default probability of period 2, p_2. In other words, the unconditional probability gives the probability that a default occurs exactly in this time period, not earlier and not later.

Example 9: Cumulative Default Probabilities: A Numerical Example

We analyze a zero coupon bond issued by a Baa-rated company. The maturity of the bond is three years. From table A.5 in the appendix we get the average annualized default rate of 0.17 percent. Moreover, we assume that this default rate remains constant over a three-year time horizon and that this historical probability measure is suitable for predicting future default probabilities.

The one-year survival probability is stated as $(1 - 0.0017) = 0.9983$. From equation 7.7 it follows that the corresponding three-year survival probability is $(1 - 0.0017)^3 = 0.9949$. Hence, the cumulative probability of default amounts to $1 - 0.9949$, which equals 0.51 percent. Comparing this result with the cumulative three-year probability of default in table A.6, which equals 0.98 percent, it shows that this simple cumulation of the historical annual default probability can lead to significant miscalculations of the cumulative default probability.

The reason for the difference lies in the fact that the single-period probabilities p_i, which we combine using equation 7.7, are not constant across various future time horizons. In fact, for investment-grade issuers these single-period probabilities increase, as the uncertainty about future prospects increases. Moreover, as these issuers already have a high credit quality, the chances for further improvements are lower than the risks for a deterioration of the credit quality. Hence, the probability of a default in period 3 is higher than in periods 2 and 1, and consequently the cumulated probability over three years is higher than the result of simply cumulating the period 1 probability of default.

Now it is time to generalize our approach. We consider a multi-step model with equidistant points in time τ_i with $i = 0, 1, \ldots, n$ and small but finite spacings $\Delta \tau = \tau_i - \tau_{i-1}$. The conditional default probabilities are denoted with p_i. They represent the probability that the credit defaults in the ith time interval, that is, between τ_{i-1} and τ_i provided that no default occurred up to time τ_{i-1}. The value of a risky claim at time step τ_i that runs until τ_m is stated as $V_i^{risky}(m)$. If t denotes the current date, than $V_i^{risky}(m)$ is the value of a claim at time $t + i\Delta\tau = t + \tau_i$ for a maturity date of $t + m\Delta\tau = t + \tau_m$, with $m > i$.

The survival probability $S(m)$ is defined as the product of the conditional survival probabilities $(1 - p_i)$ that are assigned to the single time intervals. Note that instead of writing $S_0(m)$ we omit the subscript to enhance readability if the circumstances are apparent.

$$S(m) = \prod_{i=1}^{m}(1 - p_i) \tag{7.7}$$

The most striking feature of the survival probabilities is that they are monotonously decreasing functions. Recall that the default probability p_i is always between 0 and 1. Hence the corresponding survival probabilities lie in this interval as well. Another interesting result of the definition of the survival probability in equation 7.7 is that it features a simple iterative structure. $S(m)$ depends on the survival probability of the previous time step via $S(m) = S(m-1) \cdot (1 - p_m)$. Using this relation, we can obtain a general expression for the above-mentioned unconditional default probability. It is the difference between the survival probabilities for the two time horizons. Hence, the unconditional probability of a default between $i - 1$ and i is given by:

$$\begin{aligned} S(i-1) - S(i) &= S(i-1) - S(i-1)(1 - p_i) \\ &= S(i-1)(1 - (1 - p_i)) \\ &= S(i-1)p_i \end{aligned} \tag{7.8}$$

The unconditional default probability – which states the probability that a default occurs exactly in the specified period – is a non-negative quantity, as the survival probability is a monotonously decreasing function (note the ordering of the survival probabilities $S(i-1)$ and $S(i)$ in equation 7.8).

Using the generalized framework, we can rewrite the result in equation 7.6 using the notation for the survival probability $S(m)$. Hence, the value of a credit-risky contract with a terminal payoff of V^{terminal} (can also be considered as a discounted payoff to account for the time value of money) is given by equation 7.9. The contract runs over m periods, and hence has a maturity date of $t + \tau_m$.

$$V_0^{\text{risky}}(m) = S(m)V^{\text{terminal}} + \sum_{i=1}^{m} (S(i-1) - S(i)) V_i^{\text{default}} \qquad (7.9)$$

The first term refers to the survival of the contract, while the second deals with the recovery payments in case of a default. Note that this is a general outcome, as we did not cite a specific recovery model. The treatment of the loss given default will be analyzed below.

Another interesting quantity is the complement of the survival probability, the *cumulative default probability*. Its definition is given by:

$$F_i(m) = 1 - S_i(m) \qquad (7.10)$$

Analogue to our previous notation, $F_i(m)$ denotes the cumulative default probability from $t + \tau_i = t + i\Delta\tau$ to $t + \tau_m = t + m\Delta\tau$ (note that here we indexed $S_i(m)$ to reflect a possible future start date for $F_i(m)$). One consequence of the definition in equation 7.10 is that $F_{i-1}(i)$ is the conditional default probability, and hence $F_{i-1}(i) = p_i$.

At the current stage of the analysis, the notation and the wording start to become a little complex. We introduced several quantities that are related to default and survival probabilities. For example, we introduced conditional default probabilities, unconditional default probabilities, and survival probabilities. It is now time to be a little more accurate with the wording, as the important underlying concepts involved may be blurred by improper wording.

Unconditional default probabilities are also known as forward default probabilities. Analogous to forward interest rates, which specify the implied interest rates for a period of time in the future, the forward default probability gives the implied default probability for a future time period. It should not be confused with the conditional default probability p_i (see table 7.1 for a summary of the notation). The differentiation between unconditional and conditional refers to the fact that the default probability for a time period between $i - 1$ and i can be measured:

- irrespective of whether the credit survived until $i - 1$, which refers to unconditional default probabilities (or forward default probabilities), and
- conditional on the survival of the credit up to time $i - 1$, which refers to conditional default probabilities.

Rearranging equation 7.8, we can obtain an expression for the conditional default probabilities p_i using the survival probability function $S(i)$:

$$p_i = F_{i-1}(i) = \frac{S(i-1) - S(i)}{S(i-1)} \qquad (7.11)$$

Example 10: Default Probability Term Structures Using Default Rate Data from Rating Agencies

Besides average annualized default rate data, the rating agencies also provide cumulative default rates for various time horizons. In table A.6 in the appendix, we provide the corresponding data from Moody's segmented by rating categories. The chart below shows the cumulative, conditional and the unconditional default probability for a Baa-rated company as a function of the time horizon.

The cumulative default probability $F(m)$ is a monotonously increasing function of the time horizon m, as the risk of a default within a ten-year period has to be no lower than that for a five-year period. $F(m)$ covers a range from 0.19 percent for 1 year to 12.05 percent for 20 years. Using equation 7.8 we can derive the unconditional probability of default. Note that the survival probability $S(m)$ needed in equation 7.8 is given by $1 - F(m)$. As an example, the unconditional probability for a default between year 2 and 3 is given by $(1 - 0.0054) - (1 - 0.0098) = 0.0044$, where 0.54% is the cumulative default probability for 2 years and 0.98% the one for 3 years. The conditional default probability can be obtained by dividing the unconditional default probability by the survival probability (see equation 7.11).

The chart shows a remarkable characteristic for the unconditional and conditional probabilities of default. They are both far from being constant over time (cf. example 9). The conditional default probabilities p_i range from 0.19% between years 1 and 2 up to a maximum level of 0.89% between years 14 and 15. For longer horizons than 15 years, the unconditional and conditional default probabilities decrease in this example.

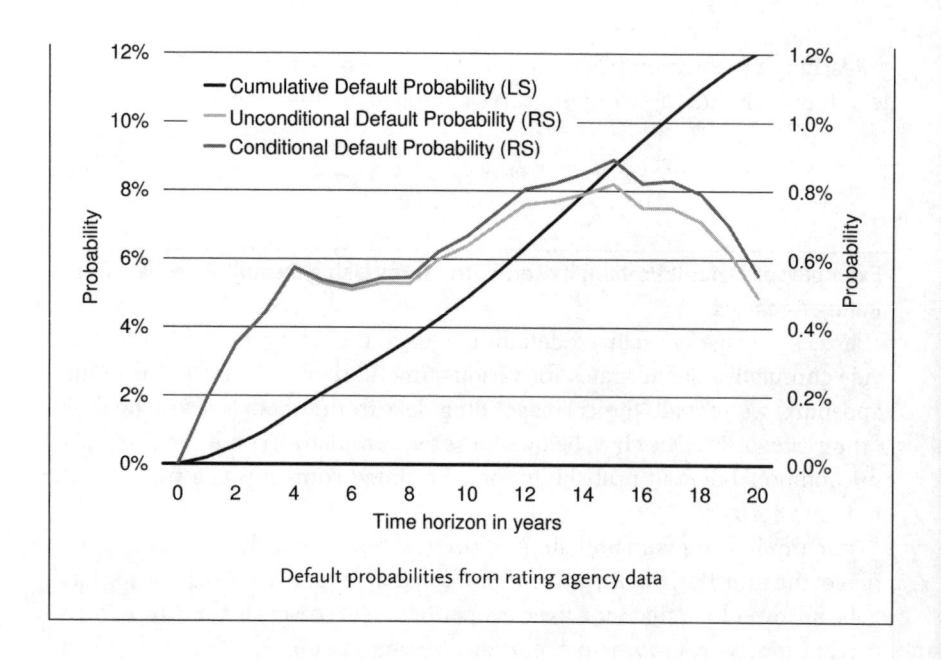

Default probabilities from rating agency data

7.4 The Multi-Step Model

In the previous section, we derived a multi-step model for a security with a single cash flow at the maturity date. This is not sufficient to model well-established instruments such as coupon bonds or credit default swaps, as they involve several payments during the lifetime. Consequently, we have to extend the multi-step model to deal with multiple payments. In figure 7.3, we show a multi-step model with m time intervals for a credit-risky instrument, which involves m payments. For the sake of simplicity, the end of the time intervals in the model coincide with the payment dates of the instrument.

As shown in figure 7.3, the value for the contract in the ith time step (the interval from τ_{i-1} to τ_i) is given by:

$$V_{i-1}^{\text{risky}} = (1 - p_i)(V_i^{\text{risky}} + V_i^{\text{cf}}) + p_i V_i^{\text{default}} \qquad (7.12)$$

By expanding V_i^{risky} in equation 7.12 iteratively and by using the survival probability function, we derive the central pricing relation for credit-risky instruments that involve multiple cash flows:

$$V_0(m) = \sum_{i=1}^{m} S(i) V_i^{cf} + \sum_{i=1}^{m} (S(i-1) - S(i)) V_i^{\text{default}} \qquad (7.13)$$

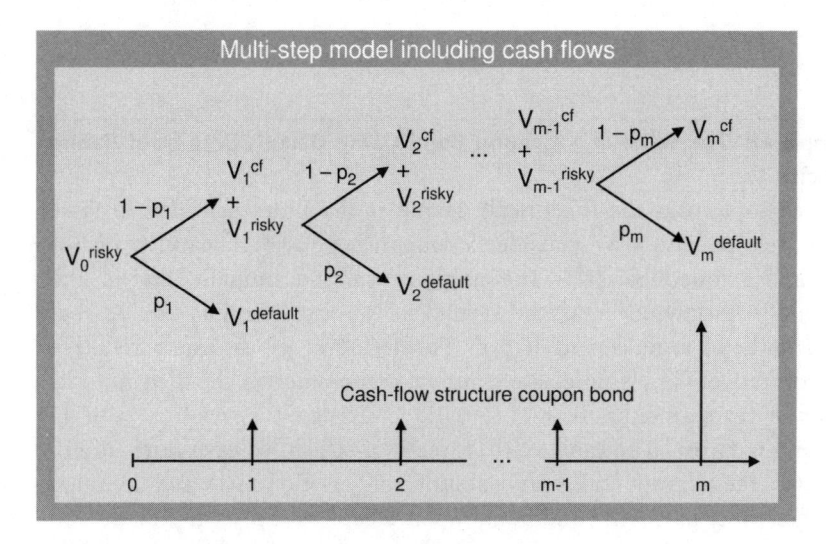

Fig. 7.3: Multi-step model for credit risk including cash flows

This result is similar to equation 7.6. The only difference is that now we multiply all cash flows with the respective survival probability. In this notation the similarity between the treatment of cash flows in interest rate and credit risk modeling becomes apparent. In credit risk modeling, the survival probabilities play a similar role as the discount factors. However, in credit risk we have to deal with an additional term: the payments that are conditional on default.

We would like to stress that equation 7.13 is the central relation in pricing credit-risky instruments. Moreover, the central quantity, which contains all relevant information about the term structure of default risk, is the survival probability function. It can be used to value regular bonds as well as credit derivatives, such as credit default swaps. It can even be used to value portfolio derivatives, such as first-to-default baskets and collateralized debt obligations. We just have to find the appropriate survival probability function and the recovery model. Admittedly, deriving the correct survival probabilities can be a difficult task. We will show below how to generalize this outcome to a continuous-time framework and its application to the most important instruments, such as bonds, credit default swaps, and portfolio derivatives.

Note that the second term in equation 7.13, the value of the recovery payments weighted with the unconditional default probabilities, will collapse to $(1 - S(m)) \cdot V^{\text{default}}$, if V^{default} does not depend on the timing of the default, as $\sum_{i=1}^{m}(S(i-1) - S(i))$ is a telescopic sum. V^{default} is time independent if the recovery payment is time independent and if we ignore risk-free discounting effects.

> **Example 11: The Value of a Coupon Bond Using Default Data from Rating Agencies**
>
> This example uses the (historical) default probabilities provided in table A.6 in the appendix. We consider a coupon bond with a maturity of five years and a coupon of 5%. The coupons are paid annually, that is, the first one in exactly one year, the second in two years, and so on. At maturity the bond is redeemed at par. Furthermore, we assume a risk-free discount rate of 5%, using discrete annual compounding; the discount factor for m years amounts to $1/(1 + 0.05)^m$. Hence, the risk-free value of the bond is €100. The value of the stream of scheduled cash flows multiplied with the corresponding survival probability is €98.1492, and the value of the recovery payment conditional upon default is €0.7051. For the latter, we used a recovery rate of 40 percent on the notional amount of the bond. The value of the risky bond is €98.8542. Hence, the expected loss is €100 − €98.8542 = €1.1458 for five years or 0.22 percent per year.
>
> In addition, we confirm that the value of recovery payment conditional upon default is $(1 - 0.9792) \times €40 = €0.8320$ if we set the discount rate at 0 percent.

7.5 Continuous-Time Approach

In the following analysis, we translate the results derived for the discrete time-step model into a continuous-time approach. The focus is on illustrating the central concepts and ideas, without going too much into mathematical details. Modeling default probabilities in a continuous-time approach essentially aims at modeling the timing of a default event using stochastic processes. For this purpose, we define the stochastic variable τ^* as the time until default. For the present point in time t, a default event occurs at date $t + \tau^*$. Regarding the loss given default, we keep our generalized approach and do not use a specific recovery assumption, but stick to our previous notation of $V^{\text{default}}(\tau)$ for the value of the claim in case of a default event. The integration of a specific recovery model into the derived results will be shown below. The central point is to characterize the probability distribution of τ^*. In order to model the default probability distribution, we introduce two functions $F_t(\tau)$ and $S_t(\tau)$:[27]

$$F_t(\tau) = \mathbb{P}(\tau^* \leq \tau) \qquad S_t(\tau) = \mathbb{P}(\tau^* > \tau) \qquad (7.14)$$

Analogous to our previously developed notation, $S_t(\tau)$ denotes the survival probability function and $F_t(\tau)$ the cumulative default probability. In the continuous-time framework, $S_t(\tau)$ expresses the probability of a default occurring later than τ, while $F_t(\tau)$ gives the probability that a default occurs not later than τ. Both functions are linked through the relation $S_t(\tau) = 1 - F_t(\tau)$. In addition, the following mathematical conditions for $F_t(\tau)$ (and $S_t(\tau)$ respectively) are required for them to describe a default probability distribution: $F_t(0) = 0$, $\lim_{\tau \to \infty} F_t(\tau) = 1$, and $F_t(\tau + \Delta\tau) \geq F_t(\tau)$ for all $\Delta\tau > 0$. These conditions basically mean that at time t we *know* that the counterparty is not in default, and thus the probability of default up to this point in time is zero, it will definitely default at some time in the future, and finally, the (cumulative) default probability is a monotonously increasing function of time. Once it reaches a certain level for a given time horizon, it can never decrease for a longer time horizon. For $S_t(\tau)$ analogous conditions apply.

The probabilities $\mathbb{P}$ in equation 7.14 do not refer to a specific probability measure, such as risk-neutral or real-world probabilities. The following results are valid for all equivalent measures. Using risk-neutral probabilities, which can be derived from market prices, will result in arbitrage-free prices.

Moreover, using the subscript t, we indicate that the quantities $S_t(\tau)$ and $F_t(\tau)$ may change over time. The time variable t refers to the real calendar time, while τ is the time to maturity. The calendar date referring to the time τ in $S_t(\tau)$ is stated $t + \tau$. As an example, if t is June 7, 2005, and τ is 1.5 years, then $t + \tau$ would be December 7, 2006. Obviously, τ refers to a specific day count convention, such as Act/360 in the current example.

We start to explore the mathematical structure of $F_t(\tau)$ and $S_t(\tau)$ by analyzing how $F_t(\tau)$ changes when we extend the time horizon τ by a small time step $\Delta\tau$ to the horizon $\tau + \Delta\tau$:

$$F_t(\tau + \Delta\tau) = \mathbb{P}(\tau^* \leq \tau + \Delta\tau)$$
$$= \underbrace{\mathbb{P}(\tau^* \leq \tau)}_{F_t(\tau)} + \underbrace{[1 - \mathbb{P}(\tau^* \leq \tau)]}_{S_t(\tau)} \cdot \underbrace{\mathbb{P}(\tau^* \leq \tau + \Delta\tau | \tau^* > \tau)}_{\text{probability for } \tau^* \in [\tau, \tau+\Delta\tau]} \qquad (7.15)$$

$$\underbrace{}_{\text{unconditional default probability}}$$

The probability $F_t(\tau + \Delta\tau)$ that a default occurs prior to $\tau + \Delta\tau$ is simply the probability that a default occurs up to time τ plus the probability that it occurs between τ and $\tau + \Delta\tau$. Equation 7.15 can be transformed into the analogous form as equation 7.8 if we rearrange the terms and substitute $F_t(\tau) = 1 - S_t(\tau)$.

$$S_t(\tau) - S_t(\tau + \Delta\tau) = S_t(\tau) \cdot \mathbb{P}(\tau^* \leq \tau + \Delta\tau | \tau^* > \tau) \quad (7.16)$$

Note that while $F_t(\tau)$ is a monotonically increasing function, $S_t(\tau)$ is a monotonously decreasing function, and hence $S_t(\tau) \geq S_t(\tau + \Delta\tau)$ for all $\Delta\tau > 0$. Therefore, $\mathbb{P}(\tau^* \leq \tau + \Delta\tau | \tau^* > \tau)$ is a positive quantity. It gives the conditional default probability between $t + \tau$ and $t + \tau + \Delta\tau$ provided that no default occurred up to $t + \tau$. It can be obtained by rearranging equation 7.16.

$$\mathbb{P}(\tau^* \leq \tau + \Delta\tau | \tau^* > \tau) = \frac{S_t(\tau) - S_t(\tau + \Delta\tau)}{S_t(\tau)} \quad (7.17)$$

Multiplying the difference $S_t(\tau) - S_t(\tau + \Delta\tau)$ on the right hand side of equation 7.17 with -1, dividing by $\Delta\tau$, and taking the limit of $\Delta\tau \to 0^+$ (assuming that $S_t(\tau)$ is differentiable) we obtain the change of $S_t(\tau)$ by τ:

$$\begin{aligned}\frac{dS_t(\tau)}{d\tau} &= \lim_{\Delta\tau \to 0^+} \frac{S_t(\tau + \Delta\tau) - S_t(\tau)}{\Delta\tau} \\ &= -S_t(\tau) \lim_{\Delta\tau \to 0^+} \frac{\mathbb{P}(\tau^* \leq \tau + \Delta\tau | \tau^* > \tau)}{\Delta\tau}\end{aligned} \quad (7.18)$$

The limit $\lim_{\Delta\tau \to 0^+} \frac{\mathbb{P}(\tau^* < \tau + \Delta\tau | \tau^* > \tau)}{\Delta\tau}$ is the so-called *hazard rate* $h_t(\tau)$. The product $h_t(\tau) \cdot \Delta\tau$ approximates the (conditional) probability of default provided that no default occurred until τ. Using the above-mentioned relation $S_t(\tau) = 1 - F_t(\tau)$, we obtain the following equations, which describe the change of $S_t(\tau)$ and $F_t(\tau)$ as a function of the time horizon τ:

$$\frac{dF_t(\tau)}{d\tau} = [1 - F_t(\tau)] h_t(\tau) \qquad \frac{dS_t(\tau)}{d\tau} = -S_t(\tau) h_t(\tau) \quad (7.19)$$

By solving these differential equations, we obtain $F_t(\tau)$ and $S_t(\tau)$ as functions of the time to maturity, depending on the hazard rate function $h_t(\tau)$:

$$F_t(\tau) = 1 - e^{-\int_0^\tau h_t(s)ds} \qquad S_t(\tau) = e^{-\int_0^\tau h_t(s)ds} \quad (7.20)$$

Both functions $F_t(\tau)$ and $S_t(\tau)$ are cumulative probabilities, with $F_t'(\tau)$ being the corresponding probability density function:

$$F_t'(\tau) = -S_t'(\tau) = h_t(\tau) e^{-\int_0^\tau h_t(s)ds} \quad (7.21)$$

Using equations 7.16 and 7.20 we can derive the unconditional default probability for the time-to-maturity interval between τ and $\tau + \Delta\tau$, stated as $S_t(\tau) - S_t(\tau + \Delta\tau)$.

$$S_t(\tau) - S_t(\tau + \Delta\tau) = e^{-\int_0^\tau h_t(s)ds} - e^{-\int_0^{\tau+\Delta\tau} h_t(s)ds}$$

$$= e^{-\int_0^\tau h_t(s)ds} \left(1 - e^{-\int_\tau^{\tau+\Delta\tau} h_t(s)ds}\right) \qquad (7.22)$$

$$\approx S_t(\tau) h_t(\tau) \Delta\tau$$

In the last line we used the approximation $e^{-x} \approx 1 - x$ and $\int_\tau^{\tau+\Delta\tau} h_t(s)ds \approx h_t(\tau)\Delta\tau$. Together with equation 7.21 we see that the unconditional default probability is $S_t(\tau) - S_t(\tau + \Delta\tau) \approx -S_t'(\tau)\Delta\tau = F_t'(\tau)\Delta\tau$. This presentation highlights the relationship between the unconditional default probability and the default density function $F_t'(\tau)$.

Table 7.1 summarizes the terminology regarding the various probability quantities and shows the relation between the discrete and the continuous-time framework. Note that in the discrete-time approach, the conditional default probability p_i in the ith time step refers to the interval from τ_{i-1} to τ_i, while the survival probability $S(m)$ was linked to the interval from 0 to τ_m.

Tab. 7.1: Summary of the default probability terminology

Type	Discrete	Continuous
Conditional default probability	p_i	$1 - \exp(-\int_{\tau_{i-1}}^{\tau_i} h(s)ds)$ $\approx h(\tau_{i-1})\Delta\tau$
Conditional survival probability	$1 - p_i$	$\exp(-\int_{\tau_{i-1}}^{\tau_i} h(s)ds)$ $\approx 1 - h(\tau_{i-1})\Delta\tau$
Survival probability	$S(m) = \prod_{i=1}^m (1 - p_i)$	$S(\tau_m) = \exp(-\int_0^{\tau_m} h(s)ds)$
Cumulative default probability	$F(m) = 1 - S(m)$	$F(\tau_m) = 1 - S(\tau_m)$
Unconditional or forward default probability	$S(i-1) - S(i)$ $= S(i-1)p_i$	$S(\tau_{i-1}) - S(\tau_i)$ $\approx S(\tau_{i-1})h(\tau_{i-1})\Delta\tau$ $= F_t'(\tau_{i-1})\Delta\tau$

The relation $p_i \approx h(\tau_{i-1})\Delta\tau$ is derived by the assumption that the hazard rate curve is piecewise constant, which results to $\int_{\tau_{i-1}}^{\tau_i} h(s)ds = h(\tau_{i-1})(\tau_i - \tau_{i-1}) = h(\tau_{i-1})\Delta\tau$ and using the approximation $e^{-x} \approx 1 - x$.

Finally, we introduce the indicator functions $1_{\{a < \tau^* < b\}}$ and $1_{\{\tau^* > b\}}$. As the name already suggests, they indicate whether a default happened in a specified time interval or not. $1_{\{a<\tau^*<b\}}$ indicates a default between a and b, while $1_{\{\tau^*>b\}}$ indicates that no default happened up to time b. Hence, the former is related to the unconditional default probability, while the latter corresponds to the survival probability. The expected value of the indicator function equals the probability of the respective event.

$$\mathbb{E}[1_{\{a<\tau^*<b\}}] = \int_a^b F'_t(\tau)d\tau \quad \mathbb{E}[1_{\{\tau^*>b\}}] = -\int_0^b S'_t(\tau)d\tau \quad (7.23)$$

At first glance, the concept of the indicator functions seems to be somewhat complicated. However, it is worth taking a closer look as it allows compact expressions for the credit risk pricing relations. To illustrate how the indicator functions work, we rewrite the pricing formula for valuing coupon-paying instruments in the discrete time-step framework (see equation 7.13) using such an indicator function. The value of a security that pays cash flows at times τ_i with $i = 1, 2, \ldots, m$ and hence with a final payment at τ_m (e.g., a coupon bond with maturity τ_m) is represented by:

$$V_t(\tau_m) = \underbrace{\sum_{i=1}^m V_i^{CF} \cdot \mathbb{E}\left[1_{\{\tau^*>\tau_i\}}\right]}_{\text{Value of risky payments}} + \underbrace{\mathbb{E}\left[V^{\text{default}}(\tau^*) \cdot 1_{\{\tau_0<\tau^*<\tau_m\}}\right]}_{\text{Value of default payments}} \quad (7.24)$$

The first term in equation 7.24 shows the sum of the value of the individual cash flows multiplied by the probability that the security survives until the payment date. This survival probability is expressed as the expected value of the indicator function $\mathbb{E}\left[1_{\{\tau^*>\tau_i\}}\right]$. As the (risk-free) values of the cash flows V_i^{CF} do not depend on the occurrence of a default event, we do not have to place it inside the expectation operator $\mathbb{E}$. This treatment contrasts with the value of the default payments, where $V^{\text{default}}(\tau^*)$ depends on the timing of a potential default. Recall that there are two unknown properties related to this default payment: Does the default occur at all, and if it occurs, when does it occur? Hence, for the value of the default payment the timing of the default event is also important, especially if we take the time value of money into account.

Using equations 7.23 and 7.21, the solution for the expected value of $\mathbb{E}\left[1_{\{\tau^*>\tau_i\}}\right]$ results in a quantity that we already know: the survival probability $S_t(\tau_i) = \mathbb{E}\left[1_{\{\tau^*>\tau_i\}}\right]$. However, for the second term, the result in continuous time looks quite complex, as we cannot separate $V^{\text{default}}(\tau^*)$ from the expectation operator.

$$\mathbb{E}\left[V^{\text{default}}(\tau^*) \cdot 1_{\{\tau_0 < \tau^* < \tau_m\}}\right] =$$
$$= \int_{\tau_0}^{\tau_m} V^{\text{default}}(s) \cdot F_t'(\tau) ds = \sum_{i=1}^{m} \int_{\tau_{i-1}}^{\tau_i} V^{\text{default}}(s) \cdot F_t'(\tau) ds \qquad (7.25)$$

In the last step, we partitioned the integral that covers the interval from τ_0 to τ_m into m time brackets, in line with the payment dates of the security. Although equation 7.25 looks rather scary, a simple assumption helps to derive a practical pricing relation. We assume that the recovery payments are only settled at regular payment dates. Note that this is still a continuous-time approach, as default events can occur at any time. We only restrict the settlement dates to a fixed time grid. As a result, we now can separate $V^{\text{default}}(\tau^*)$ from the expectation operator, which results in $\sum_{i=1}^{m} V^{\text{default}}(\tau_i) \int_{\tau_{i-1}}^{\tau_i} F_t'(\tau) ds$. Here, $V^{\text{default}}(\tau_i)$ refers to τ_i, the payment date at the end of the period to which the indicator function $1_{\{\tau_{i-1} < \tau^* < \tau_i\}}$ refers. As $F_t(\tau)$ is the cumulative default probability, the integral $\int_{\tau_{i-1}}^{\tau_i} F_t'(\tau) ds$ refers to the unconditional default probability in the interval between τ_{i-1} and τ_i. By inspecting equation 7.22 (and from our previous discrete time-step analysis) we know that this probability is given by $S_t(\tau_{i-1}) - S_t(\tau_i)$.

Now we have all credit-specific building blocks at hand to arrive at a general pricing relation for credit-risky contracts. However, for the whole analysis, we neglected the risk-free compounding effect. As already mentioned above, that affects the terms V_i^{CF} and $V^{\text{default}}(\tau_i)$. The former gives the value of the ith cash flow, which is in our notation paid at time τ_i, while the second gives the value of the (recovery) payment conditional on a default between time τ_{i-1} and τ_i. The risk-free value of the ith cash flow can be simply derived by discounting the payment by means of the discount factor. In our notation, that is expressed by $\text{CF}_i \cdot R_t(\tau_i)$. Here, CF_i denotes the amount of the ith cash flow and $R_t(\tau_i)$ the corresponding discount factor.

The value of the recovery payment conditional upon a default event is a little more tricky, as we do not know either the size of the payment and the settlement date of the payment. However, for the current purpose it is sufficient that there will be a payment, which we denote with $\text{CF}_i^{\text{default}}$. To circumvent the timing problem, we simply assume that the payment will be settled at the next scheduled payment date of the security. By assigning the subscript i to the recovery payment, we indicate that there might be a dependency of the recovery payment on the default timing. Below we will provide a more detailed analysis of the recovery problem.

Note that this approach of separating the survival probabilities and the discount factors implicitly assumes that the underlying stochastic processes driving both risk factors are independent. While this independence assumption is crucial to derive manageable pricing relations and is widely accepted for modeling purposes, it is not fully justified by economic principles. There is definitely a relation between risk-free interest rates and default rates. However, this link is subject to discussions in the market as there are several contradictory theories. However, due to the unclear relation between interest rates and default rates and the complex pricing results, it is market practice to assume independence for pricing most credit risk contracts.

Putting all the results together, we derive the following general pricing relation for credit-risky instruments:

$$V_t(\tau_m) = \sum_{i=1}^{m} \text{CF}_i \cdot R_t(\tau_i) \cdot S_t(\tau_i) + \sum_{i=1}^{m} \text{CF}_i^{\text{default}} \cdot R_t(\tau_i) \cdot (S_t(\tau_{i-1}) - S_t(\tau_i))$$

(7.26)

As this relation relies neither on a specific cash flow structure nor on a specific recovery treatment, equation 7.26 is very general. For the valuation of a cash bond, for example, the scheduled payments CF_i would refer to the coupon payments and the repayment of the notional amount at maturity, while $\text{CF}_i^{\text{default}}$ would be the recovery payment at default. If we consider a credit default swap contract, then CF_i would refer to the stipulated premium payments and $\text{CF}_i^{\text{default}}$ would be the loss given default times the notional amount, which has to be paid by the protection seller to the protection buyer.

Let us summarize the results. Assuming that interest rates and default probabilities are independent and that the (unknown) conditional payments are paid at scheduled payment dates, the value of a credit-risky contract is represented by equation 7.26. Besides the risk-free discount factors and a recovery model (see below), we only need the survival probability function $S_t(\tau)$. This quantity contains all information about the default risk we need to price risky securities (note that to derive the expected loss and subsequently the price we also need the loss given default). However, the current pricing framework should not be considered a default model because we still do not know where $S_t(\tau)$ comes from and which economic variables have an impact on this function. Nevertheless, the independence of equation 7.26 from any specific default model makes it very powerful. As the result is a general one, we can use equation 7.26 in combination with most of the explicit default models, such as intensity models, structural models, or rating-based Markov-chain models. The models just have to be derived so that the outcome is the survival probability function. The rest of the valuation process can done by applying equation 7.26.

7.6 Recovery Treatment

In the previous sections, we analyzed how the probability of a default event translates into the survival probability function, and how it is integrated into a valuation procedure. The remaining important building block, which affects the prices of credit instruments, is the loss incurred given a default event. This quantity refers to the so-called recovery payments in case of a default event. We introduced these payments, for example, in equation 7.13 by using the quantity $V_i^{default}$.

Accurately modeling recovery values on a company level is significantly more complicated than modeling default probabilities. First, due to cross-default clauses included in most contracts, a credit event for one security of a firm triggers a default on all other debt instruments of this firm. Therefore, the default probability is company-specific and not instrument-specific, while the loss severity in case of a default depends on the subordination of the corresponding claim and is therefore instrument-specific. Hence, from an analytical point of view, the evaluation of recovery rates involves not only company-related information, but also all details that refer to a specific claim. Second, as the potential recovery rate of a specific claim refers to the corresponding subordination level, a reliable recovery model would have to model the future seniority of the claim. Anecdotal evidence shows that a company's balance sheet changes dramatically when the company approaches the default point. To avoid an imminent liquidity crisis, management will try to raise new funds, which will most probably only be granted by investors or banks if the new claims are secured by certain assets. Such a collateralization of new debt obviously hurts the existing holders of unsecured debt as it reduces their recovery prospects in case of a default. In the end, determining recovery rates on a company level would require a dynamic model of the company's balance sheet, which is an extremely complicated task.

As already mentioned, the recovery rate strongly depends on the seniority of the credit exposure. As an example, in table A.8 in the appendix, we show historical recovery data provided by Moody's. The rating agency differentiates the recovery rates into seniority classes, such as senior secured and unsecured, senior subordinated, subordinated, and junior subordinated debt. Obviously, the junior subordinated class offers the smallest recovery potential, with a historical average of below 30 percent, while senior unsecured debt shows recovery rates of about 45 percent in the historical average. However, due to pari passu clauses for unsecured claims within one seniority class, which are part of standardized bond prospects, the recovery rate for all obligations in this class is the same.

In general, taking all subordination levels into account, the historical average recovery rate is 42.2 percent, with a standard deviation of 8.7 percentage points. Hence, the recovery payments are unknown in advance. But what drives this uncertainty? Clearly, the size of the payment is of major importance, but it is not the only driver. The second factor that determines the recovery value of defaulted bonds is the timing of the final settlement. In case the legal procedures to settle the loss given default run several years, the debt investor will finally get some recovery payments, but he has to wait a long time and does not get any interest payments on his claim during this procedure. Note that for regular CDS contracts the settlement issue is different to that for cash bonds. Following a grace period of up to 30 days after the default event, the CDS contracts are settled. However, this does not mean that the above-mentioned legal timing problem is not an issue for recovery modeling in the credit derivatives universe. As most contracts involve physical settlement, the protection seller receives the defaulted bonds and hence has effectively the same risk as the bondholders.

To cope with this timing problem, the recovery rate is measured by observing the prices of defaulted bonds from distressed debt markets after a grace period of several days after the default. This procedure is also adopted by some rating agencies. Moody's for example uses the 30 days post-default bid prices for the recovery estimation. Exceptions are cases in which the default trigger is the consummation of a distressed exchange, that is, when the issuer offers the bondholders a new security with a reduced financial obligation, which entails significant economic losses (stocks or bonds with lower coupons or a lower par amount, lower seniority, or longer maturity). In this case, Moody's uses trading prices of the exchanged instruments two weeks prior to exchange for the recovery estimation.

To keep things simple, we assume in our subsequent analysis that the default payment is settled immediately after the default event, that is, at the next scheduled coupon payment date. As there is only one stochastic quantity, the recovery rate, it has to reflect the uncertainty about both the size of the payment and the timing of the final settlement.

Example 12: Differences between Recovery Rates in Euroland and the US

One important driver of the recovery values is the legal jurisdiction in which the default case is settled. For example, differences between US and Euroland laws lead to differences in their historical recovery rates. Table A.8 in the appendix refers to global figures, so these differences are not evident from this data. However, the rating agencies also provide recovery data segmented by the domicile of the issuers. Moody's, for example, measured a value-weighted average recovery rate for defaults settled in the US of 35.4 percent, while for Euroland the figure was only 23.7 percent (excluding the United Kingdom and Netherlands, where the corresponding figures were 23.9 and 21.7 percent respectively).[28]

The difference in realized recoveries can be attributed in large parts to former differences between the legislative systems. In the US, the Chapter 11 rules do not acknowledge as many privileged claims as, for example, the former rules in Germany, where banks could easily force companies into liquidation to pay off their secured loan exposure. This resulted in diminished prospects for the unsecured bondholders, as there were fewer assets left to satisfy their claims.

Another reason is that the possibility of filing for Chapter 11 results in more frequent defaults in the US. Moody's recovery estimation was based on 1055 observations in the US and only 21 in Euroland (in the UK they counted 29 and in the Netherlands there were 6). However, the prospects for a company to survive under Chapter 11 legislation are quite high, because the company can restructure its business under claimholder protection. This is positive for the claims of unsecured debtholders, as an exchange of securities usually offers higher recovery values than the liquidation of the company. In Euroland, default events were less frequent, but if such an event occurred, it usually meant the liquidation of the company. Note that for a few years, Euroland has had legislation in place that is similar to Chapter 11 in the US, which will cause some convergence of the default and recovery data.

Example 13: Usage of Subordinated Bonds

The difference in recovery rates is important in case an investor analyzes the relative value of two bonds from the same company but with different subordination levels. Such differentiation is very common for bonds from financial institutions. Especially banks use the whole palette of instruments, such as covered bonds, senior unsecured debt, and subordinated debt with several seniority levels (Tier 1, Upper Tier 2, and Lower Tier 2) to optimize their capital structure with respect to constraints from the regulator, the ratings agencies, and their refinancing needs. Besides banks and other financial institutions, such as insurance companies, there is an increasing number of non-financial companies tapping the market via subordinated issues. Since they can be viewed as an intermediate instrument between debt and equity, they are also called hybrid bonds.

In an LBO transaction, a subordinated issue (a hybrid bond) can be used to partly finance the acquisition without hurting the existing bondholders too much, while investment-grade corporates might aim to stabilize their credit rating (e.g., to raise funds in the course of a major acquisition without endangering their credit rating and without the necessity of issuing new shares). If a rating agency partly recognizes a subordinated bond as equity, the company may benefit from such a bond in case the costs for this hybrid issue are lower than the corresponding costs for new equity capital. From an investor's perspective such issues are interesting, as they offer an attractive yield pick-up compared to senior issues, and the investor can gain exposure to risks with equity characteristics that might be otherwise inaccessible. As an example for the latter case, just think of a deeply subordinated bond in an LBO transaction that enables participation in such a transaction without being invested in the fund of the private equity sponsor.

A closer look at table A.8 in the appendix merits further discussions. On an individual company level, the strict priority rule would result in a different structure for the recovery rates as a function of the seniority. In case of liquidation of the company's assets, the proceeds would be distributed to the debtholders following the so-called waterfall principle. First, the claims of all senior secured debtholders would be satisfied. If the asset value exceeds their claims, the rest will be distributed to the next most senior debtholders, such as the senior unsecured debtholders and so forth. If at some stage of the process, the remaining sum of the proceeds of the asset liquidation is not sufficient to fully satisfy the claims of a corresponding debtholder, then all more subordinated claimholders would receive nothing. In figure 7.4, we show two examples for such a recovery distribution among various debt seniority levels. The data series shows the payoff structure that is in line with the strict priority rule, and the other shows a distribution that violates this rule.

As the data provided in table A.8 refer to an average of several default events, the impact of the strict priority is blurred. But investors should keep in mind

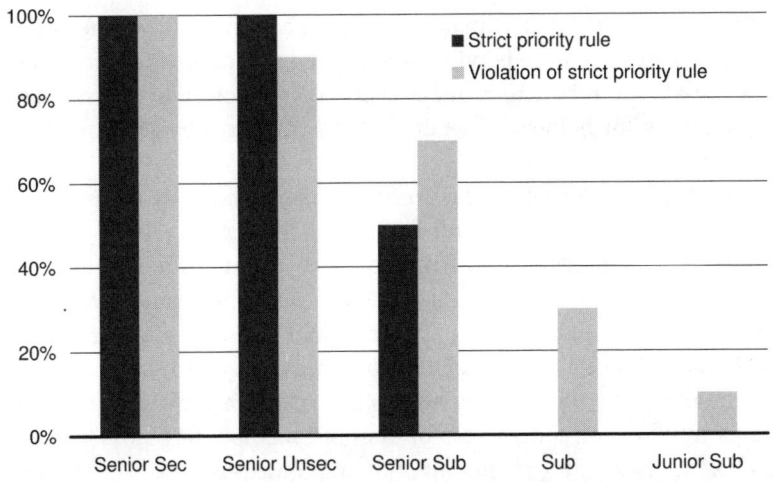

Fig. 7.4: Impact of the strict priority rule on the recovery payoff of debt instruments with different seniority levels

that from a non-zero recovery rate for subordinated debt follows that all senior debt has a recovery rate of 100 percent due to the strict priority rule. Furthermore, the aggregated recovery data in table A.8 are internally inconsistent at certain points in time. Notably in the year 1988, recoveries for senior bonds decreased with the subordination level (55.3 percent for senior secured, 45.2 percent for senior unsecured, 33.4 percent for senior subordinated, and 33 percent for subordinated). However, the average recovery rate for junior subordinated debt was higher (36.5 percent) than for the more senior subordinated debt. While this is a statistical issue rather than an error in the data, it illustrates that historical recovery data should be viewed with some care, especially if the data are used for pricing purposes.

Analyzing historical recoveries reveals that the seniority of the claim is not the only factor that drives the recovery values. In example 12, we illustrate the dependency on the legal framework. The historical recovery rates feature a significant variance across various determinants, such as industries and rating categories prior to default. In the following list, we highlight the most important factors:[28]

- *Seniority of the claim*: Due to the waterfall principle, it is obvious that the seniority of the claim has a significant impact on the recovery value. Table A.8 in the appendix gives more details.
- *Domiciles*: The legal framework in which the default case is settled has an impact on the frequency of the default events and on the distribution of

the losses across the subordination levels. The Chapter 11 regime in the US, for example, is more bondholder-oriented as it offers the companies the possibility to restructure under claimholder protection and reduces the prospects for holders of secured claims to force the company into liquidation (see example 12).

- *Industries*: The variation of recovery rates across different industries is considerable. With utilities, for example, the average value weighted recovery rate is 56.4 percent, while for telecommunication companies it is only 17.1 percent. Again, there is a fundamental and a technical argument for these differences. The fundamental view is that recovery prospects for stable, non-cyclical industries are higher on average because the underlying firm values are less volatile than for cyclical industries. Telecommunication companies, for example, incurred large losses in the past, as they have a larger amount of intangible assets.
- *Ratings prior to default*: In example 14, we illustrate the impact of the rating prior to default on the recovery prospects (see also table A.9 in the appendix). Bonds with higher ratings also tend to offer higher recovery values.
- *The type of the default trigger event*: There is a significant variation of the historical recovery rate depending on the type of the default trigger (see example 6 for the definition of a default event). Missed interest payments (which were the majority of the default events) involved a recovery rate of 26.8 percent, while in case of a Chapter 11 filing, the recovery rate was slightly higher: 30.7 percent. Grace period defaults, for example, have unsurprisingly high recovery values (54.8 percent), as these defaults are often only temporary.
- *The timing of the default event*: As shown in example 14 the recovery values (as well as the default probabilities) are highly correlated to the stage of the business cycle at default. Hence, the recovery rates vary significantly over time.

Example 14: Relationship between the Recovery Rate on the Ratings prior to Default

Credit ratings are usually expected to differentiate the relative default risk of two borrowers. An issuer with an Aa rating has a lower default risk than one with a Baa rating. However, rating agencies do not primarily assign ratings to issuers, but to specific issues. Therefore they have to take the loss severity into account. It follows that two securities issued by the same company but with different subordination levels have different credit ratings, even though they have the same probability of default. Consequently, defaulted issues that had a high rating prior to default have a significantly higher recovery rate than those with a lower rating.

In table A.9 in the appendix, we show recovery rate data compiled by Moody's, which is segmented by the rating for one to five years prior to default. For example, for an Aa-rated bond default within one year the recovery prospects are 95.4 percent, while for a Baa-rated issue the corresponding value is only 43.3 percent.

From a recovery modeling point of view, there is another important topic that has to be addressed. In the analysis above, we considered the recovery rate to be a relative quantity expressed as a percentage. To derive the recovery payment in terms of monetary units, we need a reference to multiply the recovery rate by. In table A.8 in the appendix, this reference is the amount of debt outstanding, the face value of the debt. This method is very popular for the recovery treatment. However, while this model adequately describes credit derivatives structures such as CDS, it does not always adequately reflect the economic risk for other securities, such as straight bonds if they trade far from their par value. Moreover, it leads to complicated pricing formulas.

Example 15: Recovery Treatment: Zero Coupon Bonds versus Coupon Bonds

A company issued two different bonds, a zero coupon bond and a coupon bond with a coupon rate of 10 percent. Both bonds have the same notional amount outstanding. The crucial question regarding the recovery treatment is: How will the two claims be treated in case of a default event? Let us assume that the coupon bond currently trades at par and the zero coupon bond at 80 percent. Moreover, the recovery rate is assumed to be 40 percent. As the two bonds were issued by the same company, they involve the same default probability. We analyze the relative loss given default of both bonds for two recovery assumptions: the recovery rate is stated, first, in relation to the face value of the bonds and, second, to the market value of the bonds.

In the face value framework, the recovery payment for both bonds is the same: the bondholders receive 40 percent of the notional amount. To calculate the relative LGD for both bonds, we use equation 7.2 ($LGD = 1 - V^{\text{default}}/V^{\text{no default}}$). The investor who bought the coupon bond at par loses 60 percent of his investment $(1 - 40/100)$, while the relative loss that corresponds to the zero coupon bond is only 50 percent $(1 - 40/80)$.

> In the market value framework, the recovery payment is not derived with respect to the face value but with respect to the current market value of the claim. For the coupon bond, the recovery payment in this approach is 40 percent as well, since we assumed that the bond trades at par. However, the recovery payment differs for the zero coupon bond. It is calculated as 0.4 times 80, which equals 32 percent. Hence, in this approach, the absolute recovery payment for the two claims differ, but in relative terms both bonds have the same LGD: 60 percent ($1 - 40/100 = 1 - 32/80 = 0.6$). Note that implementing such a recovery procedure in a legal framework would mean that the loss is stated in relation to the market value right before the default event.

As illustrated in example 15, the recovery payment is determined by the recovery rate and the quantity to which it refers. There are several approaches to treat the recovery payments.[29] Here is a comprehensive list of recovery models:

- *Zero recovery* (ZR): The bondholder or protection seller receives nothing in case of default. It leads to a simple pricing formula but is an unrealistic assumption.
- *Fixed recovery* (FR): The bondholder or protection seller receives a pre-specified cash payment in case of default. The resulting pricing formula is still quite simple. It is the appropriate recovery model for fixed recovery derivatives, such as digital default swaps.
- *Recovery of face value* (RFV): The bondholder or protection seller receives a fraction of the face value (par) in case of default. This is a realistic model, since the realized default loss is often quoted as a fraction of the notional outstanding. This approach is considered for the valuation of CDS contracts. Moreover, standard market practice considers this model in conjunction with the assumption of a fixed and time independent recovery rate, for example, 40 percent. In this context, the model leads to the same results as the fixed recovery model above. However, if the analyzed security is a bond that is trading significantly far from its par value, this model does not adequately reflect the economic risk. This model is sometimes also called *recovery of par*.
- *Recovery of treasury* (RT): The bondholder or protection seller receives a fraction of the value of an identical but risk-free bond in the event of default. This approach tries to tackle the above-mentioned off-par problem caused by risk-free interest rates. As an example, the loss given default of a zero coupon bond (which obviously trades significantly below

par) is calculated as a function of the corresponding risk-free zero coupon bonds (which also trades below par). In such cases, this approach might lead to more realistic results. However, the realized recovery rates for off-par instruments compared to par bonds strongly depend on the specific case and the legislative jurisdiction of the default case.
- *Recovery of market value* (RMV): The bondholder or protection seller receives a fraction of the pre-default value of the risky bond.[30] Although this model appears to be a little complicated, it gained acceptance for some problems, as it results in an easy expression for the value of a defaultable zero coupon bond. In contrast to the recovery-of-face-value model, this approach not only incorporates risk-free compounding effects for an off-par security but also takes the traded credit spread as a reason for being away from par into account. However, this model is problematic for securities that are already close to the default point and hence trade close to their market-implied recovery rate.

In a more mathematical context, these models describe what the recovery payment $CF_i^{default}$ looks like. Note that, for the sake of simplicity, we remain in the discrete framework. The above-mentioned value of the recovery payment $V_i^{default}$ is calculated by discounting the recovery payment to the valuation time: $R(\tau_i) \cdot CF_i^{default}$. This formulation refers to our previously derived general pricing relation shown in equation 7.26.

In table 7.2, we display the resulting recovery payments. For the ZR and and the FR models, the outcome is easy. It equals zero for the first case and the fixed amount X in the second. For both models, the recovery payment is deterministic.

The remaining three models involve a random component. ϕ denotes the recovery rate of the respective recovery model. In the RFV model, the recovery payment is given by the recovery rate ϕ^{RFV} times the notional amount N. This is the model used in the above-mentioned analysis of the rating agencies, as the recovery rate is stated in relation to the amount outstanding (i.e., the face value of the debt). In this model, the size of the payment does not depend on the timing of the default event, as long as the notional amount remains fixed. For an amortizing bond, the outstanding notional amount at default has to be used instead.

In the RT model, the recovery payment is derived as the fraction ϕ^{RT} of the risk-free (forward) value of the remaining cash flows. For a default event that is settled at time τ_i, all cash flows with a settlement date later than τ_i are discounted to τ_i. For this purpose, we use the forward discount factor $R(\tau_j)/R(\tau_i)$.

Last but not least, in the RMV model, the recovery rate ϕ^{RMV} refers to the risky (forward) value of the remaining cash flows, provided there has been no default until time τ_i. In the previous sections, we used the term $V_i^{no\ default}$ for this risky forward value. This model is similar to the RT model, but in addition to the risk-free discounting, it also takes the probability of default into account. For coupon bonds, the result is extremely complex, but for a zero coupon bonds it gives a nice closed-form solution, which we will show in the following section.

Note that in table 7.2, the recovery rates ϕ do have an explicit time dependency. However, such an explicit time dependency can be integrated by indexing ϕ_i with respect to the default time.

Tab. 7.2: Default payments for different recovery models

Recovery model	Recovery payment $CF_i^{default}$
Zero recovery (ZR)	0
Fixed recovery (FR)	X
Recovery of face value (RFV)	$\phi^{RFV} \cdot N$
Recovery of treasury (RT)	$\phi^{RT} \cdot \sum_{j=i+1}^{m} CF_j \cdot \frac{R(\tau_j)}{R(\tau_i)}$
Recovery of market value (RMV)	$\phi^{RMV} \cdot V_{i+1}^{no\ default}$

The RMV and the RT models differ from the RFV only in case the risky bond (for the RMV model) or the corresponding risk-free bond (for the RT model), which the calculation of the default payments refers to, trades away from par. It is obvious that both assets, the risky and the corresponding risk-free bond, cannot be priced at par at the same time. However, for securities that trade reasonably close to par, the uncertainty about the realized recovery rate will be greater than the effect from different recovery modeling. As an example, in table A.8 in the appendix the standard deviation of the realized recovery rates lies between 10.5 percent (for subordinated bonds) and 18.9 percent for junior subordinated issues.

How does the uncertainty about recovery rates affect the pricing of credit-risky securities? The short (and simplified) answer is that in standard market practice such effects are completely ignored. Market participants usually assume an average recovery rate for senior unsecured debt of 40 percent for pricing purposes, unless there are more accurate assumptions available. Even in case a default event is triggered, the market frequently assumes the 40 percent recovery at first and trades distressed debt at around the 40 percent level. In the course of the default settlement, the price for the defaulted bonds finally approaches the realized recovery values (see the Collins & Aikman case in section 4.3.3). Market prices of distressed debt reflect the market-implied recovery rate.

However, the long answer about the uncertainty of the recovery rate is that for most basic credit-risky claims (such as cash bonds and CDS) a stochastic model does not lead to significantly improved accuracy of the derived prices. This is due to the fact that these contracts have a linear payoff profile with respect to the recovery rate. Hence, using a stochastic recovery model with the corresponding distribution function in the pricing formula essentially results in multiplying the default probability by the expected value of the recovery rate. This is exactly what standard market practice does. And to be more precise, the standard expected value is 40 percent. For instruments featuring a more complex payoff profile with respect to the recovery rate (e.g., CDOs), a more consistent recovery modeling would be advisable.

The aforementioned recovery models belong to the so-called intensity-based models. However, some structural models implicitly involve a specific model for the payoff of the debtholders in case of a default event. In the classical Merton-type model, the expected loss for a debt investor is described as a short European put option on the firm's asset values with the face value of the debt as the strike price. In this framework, the recovery rate is equivalent to the payoff of the put option, that is, the difference between the strike price (face value of the debt) and the asset value at maturity. For a more detailed analysis, please refer to equation 8.10 in section 8.2.

> **Example 16: Correlation between Recovery Rates and Default Rates**
> Historical evidence shows that there is a significant negative correlation between recovery rates and default rates. The larger the number of defaults, the smaller the recovery prospects for investors on defaulted debt and vice versa.

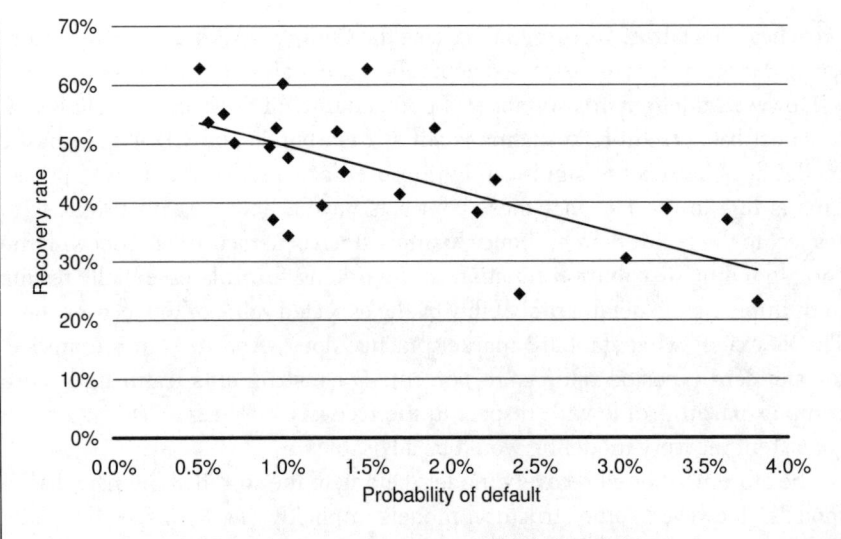

Correlation between recovery rates and default probabilities

There are at least two possible explanations for this relation, one fundamental and one technical. The first, fundamental explanation argues that both time series depend on the same underlying driving force, namely the current stage of the business cycle. In a booming economy, default rates are low and recovery prospects are high, while in a weak economy the situation is reversed. The second, technical view refers to a supply–demand argument regarding the distressed debt markets. If there is a large number of defaults at the same time, then the distressed debt market is flooded with numerous issues, driving the prices down.

7.6.1 Fitch's Recovery-Rating Methodology

Fitch recently launched its adjusted rating methodology which is based on newly introduced recovery ratings (R-ratings) and issuer default ratings (IDRs).[31,32] The new rating approach is a good example how the probability of default and the recovery rate affect the credit risk of a specific security, because it reflects these two components in a more transparent manner. Each obligation has three relevant ratings: an IDR (which refers to the default probability on an issuer level), an R-rating (which reflects the recovery prospects of the specific security) and the obligation rating (which combines both).

These R-ratings are published for all corporates, financial institutions, and sovereign issuers rated B+ and below. These ratings will be based on explicit estimates of the recovery values, using assumptions on enterprise values (either as restructuring going concern or as liquidation value), and the analysis of the capital structure for each issuer, taking contractual and structural subordination into account. R-ratings for BB and investment-grade issuers (which will not be published but can be implied from the notching of a specific security) are based on long-term average recovery expectations for each instrument type rather than on detailed analysis of the capital structure. To determine the recovery ratings, Fitch focuses on ultimate recoveries rather than on deriving a present value of the recovery payment reflecting the average time to the final settlement.

R-ratings are based on a relative scale measuring the potential recovery values in case of a default event (see table 7.3). They cover a range from R1 (highest) to R6 (lowest) and affect the notching in the obligation rating relative to the issuer default rating (IDR), which can be understood as a benchmark probability of default rating on an issuer level. It will usually be set at the issuer's current long-term credit rating or the senior unsecured debt rating. For investment-grade issues the notching is ± 2, while for speculative-grade (or high-yield) issues it is ± 3. The combined obligation rating reflects the loss severity, but it is not a pure expected loss rating. An obligation with very high recovery prospects (almost 100 percent) issued by a company in default or close to default would receive a high rating, as the expected loss (LGD $\times$ PD) would be rather limited. Such high ratings for bonds issued by companies close to default are usually not intended by rating agencies. They limit the benefit of above-average recovery prospects when notching is used. Rating agencies tend to emphasize the timeliness of the claims over potentially high recovery rates.

Fitch also revised its rating approach for defaulted and distressed debt. Instead of assigning a simple default rating, such issues can get a rating between C and CCC. In case of outstanding recovery prospects, a defaulted or distressed

Tab. 7.3: Fitch's R-ratings scale and its impact on notching for investment-grade (IG) and high-yield (HY) issues and for defaulted or distressed debt ratings

R-rating scale	Recovery prospects given default (%)	Effect of R-rating on issues			Representative securities
		IG†	HY†	defaulted/distressed	
R1	Outstanding (90–100)	+2	+3	CCC+,B–,B	Strong senior secured loans, Quasi-structured corporate instruments (e.g., *Cédulas Hipotecarias*, *Pfandbriefe*)
R2	Superior (70–90)	+1	+2	CCC,CCC+	Average senior secured loans
R3	Good (50–70)	+1	+1	CCC,CCC–	Secured bonds and loans, Mezzanine debt
R4	Average (30–50)	0	0	CC,CCC–	Senior unsecured bonds or strong subordinated bonds
R5	Below-average (10–30)	–1	–1	C,CC	Subordinated bonds or weak senior unsecured bonds
R6	Poor (0–10)	–1/–2	–2/–3	C	Preferred stock

†Indicates the number of categories the issues are notched up or down from the issuer default rating (IDR).
Source: Fitch

issue could even be rated B. The IDR for defaulted debt will be either D or RD (restricted default if the issuer defaults on some but not all issues). An example for an RD rating would have been Russia, because it defaulted on its domestic bonds but continued to service its eurobonds. The former DDD–D categories are redundant and will be phased out.

7.7 The Term Structure of Credit Spreads

We conclude our introductory analysis about basic valuation of credit risk by showing how this concept can be integrated and results in the term structure of credit spreads for defaultable zero coupon bonds. Here, we make use of the recovery of market value (RMV) model, as it results in a practical closed-form solution for the bond process.

In order to enhance clarity, we first derive the valuation formula using discrete time steps and then move on to the continuous-time version. We assume equidistant points in time τ_i with $i = 0, 1, \ldots, m$ and small but finite spacings $\Delta\tau = \tau_{i+1} - \tau_i$. Analogous to our previous notation, $F_i(m)$ denotes the cumulative default probability from $t + \tau_i = t + i\Delta\tau$ to $t + \tau_m = t + m\Delta\tau$. Between τ_i and τ_{i+1}, we assume a constant marginal default rate $F_i(i+1) = h_i\Delta\tau$. In the continuous-time limit, the marginal default rate results in the hazard rate. Using our previous knowledge that the default probability over a longer time horizon is calculated as the probability of defaulting right now plus the probability of defaulting later, we can obtain an iterative formula for $F_i(m)$:

$$F_i(m) = h_i\Delta\tau + (1 - h_i\Delta\tau)F_{i+1}(m)$$

This iterative relation is similar to equation 7.15. Its solution is given by:

$$F_i(m) = 1 - \prod_{j=i}^{m}(1 - h_j\Delta\tau) \approx 1 - \exp\left(-\sum_{j=i}^{m} h_j\Delta\tau\right)$$

In the last step, we used the first-order Taylor expansion of the exponential function $1 - x \approx e^{-x}$ for small x. Here, $(1 - h_j\Delta\tau)$ represents the probability that the credit survives the ith time step, and the product is the survival probability $S_i(m)$. Note that if the time steps $\Delta\tau$ become shorter, the sum in this equation can be substituted by an integral, which leads to the continuous-time expression $F_t(\tau) = 1 - exp(-\int_0^\tau h_t(s)ds)$ (see equation 7.20) for the cumulative default probability.

Now we can extend this discretized approach to the value $D_i(m)$ of a defaultable claim with notional amount X at time $t + \tau_m$. The terminal value is given by $D_m(m) = X$.

$$D_i(m) = (1 - f_i \Delta \tau) \left[\text{CF}_i^{\text{default}} h_i \Delta \tau + (1 - h_i \Delta \tau) D_{i+1}(m) \right]$$

The value $D_i(m)$ is the discounted expected payoff (the term in squared brackets) after one time step $\Delta \tau$. $(1 - f_i \Delta \tau)$ is the discount factor and f_i is the risk-free (forward) rate for this period. The payoff is simply the recovery payment $\text{CF}_i^{\text{default}}$ in case of default at time $t + \tau_i$ multiplied with the probability of default $h_i \Delta \tau$ in this time step, plus the subsequent value multiplied with the probability of no default $(1 - h_i \Delta \tau)$. As mentioned previously, the recovery treatment comes into play with the specification of the recovery payment $\text{CF}_i^{\text{default}}$. For recovery of face value (RFV) we define $\text{CF}_i^{\text{default}} = \phi_i^{\text{RFV}} \cdot X$, and for recovery of market value (RMV) we define $\text{CF}_i^{\text{default}} = \phi_i^{\text{RMV}} \cdot D_{i+1}(m)$ (see table 7.2). As previously indicated, using the latter leads to a closed-form expression for the credit-risky discount factor.

$$D_i(m) = (1 - f_i \Delta \tau) \left[h_i \Delta \tau \phi_i^{\text{RMV}} + (1 - h_i \Delta \tau) \right] D_{i+1}(m)$$

$$= \underbrace{(1 - f_i \Delta \tau)}_{\text{discounting}} \left[1 - \underbrace{h_i \Delta \tau}_{\text{PD}} \underbrace{(1 - \phi_i^{\text{RMV}})}_{\text{LGD}} \right] D_{i+1}(m)$$

$$= \prod_{j=i}^{m-1} (1 - f_j \Delta \tau) \left[1 - h_j \Delta \tau (1 - \phi_i^{\text{RMV}}) \right] X$$

$$\approx \exp\left(-\sum_{j=i}^{m-1} f_j \Delta \tau + h_j \Delta \tau (1 - \phi_i^{\text{RMV}}) \right) X$$

Note that the product and the sum run from i to $n - 1$. The last step m is incorporated via the claim X, since $D_m(m) = X$. In the last step, we used the first-order Taylor expansion of the exponential function $1 - x \approx e^{-x}$ for small x. Without mathematical rigor, it is quite obvious that this sequence converges to

$$D_t(\tau) = \exp\left(-\int_0^\tau f_t(s) ds - \int_0^\tau h_t(s)(1 - \phi^{\text{RMV}}(s)) ds \right) \quad (7.27)$$

$$= \exp(-r_t(\tau) \cdot \tau) \cdot \exp(-s_t(\tau) \cdot \tau)$$

Here, $(1 - \phi^{RMV}(\tau))$ is the loss given default and $s_t(\tau)$ is the credit spread. The term $h_t(\tau)(1 - \phi^{RMV}(\tau))$ can be viewed as an instantaneous loss rate. A standard simplifying assumption is that the LGD is a deterministic and a time-independent exogenous quantity: $(1 - \phi^{RMV}(\tau)) \equiv (1 - \text{Rec})$. Furthermore, we introduce the credit spread under the assumption of zero recovery:

$$\bar{s}_t(\tau) = \frac{1}{\tau} \int_0^\tau h_t(s) ds = \frac{s_t(\tau)}{1 - \text{Rec}} \qquad (7.28)$$

From this relation, we can identify a very useful expression for the survival probability as a function of the credit spread.

$$S_t(\tau) = \exp\left(-\frac{s_t(\tau)}{(1 - \text{Rec})} \cdot \tau\right) = \left(\frac{D_t(\tau)}{R_t(\tau)}\right)^{\frac{1}{(1-\text{Rec})}} \qquad (7.29)$$

We refer to the corresponding quantity $\tilde{S}_t(\tau) = S_t(\tau)^{(1-\text{Rec})}$ as the expected survival amount of the zero coupon bond using the recovery-of-market-value model.

Example 17: Approximating the Survival Probability

The senior unsecured bond of company A with a five-year maturity trades at 55 bp on a Z-spread basis. How high is the probability that company A defaults within the next five years, and what would be the fair spread for a five-year subordinated issue of the company? We can find an approximate solution to these questions using equation 7.29 and the recovery data in table A.8 in the appendix. Our first assumption is that the credit spread for the coupon bond – which is given as a Z-spread – can be used for a corresponding zero coupon bond. Second, we note that the average recovery rate for senior unsecured debt is about 45 percent and 32 percent for subordinated.

The five-year spread with zero recovery assumption comes to $55 \text{ bp}/(1 - 0.45) = 100$ bp. The corresponding survival probability amounts to $\exp(-0.01 \cdot 5) = 0.95123$. The corresponding cumulative default probability is then $1 - 0.95123 = 0.04877$. The market-implied probability of a default for company A is therefore roughly 5 percent.

In the case of the subordinated bond, the expected survival amount is $0.95123^{(1-0.32)} = 0.96657$. Solving equation 7.29 with respect to the spread, we obtain $-\ln(0.96657)/5 = 68$ bp. By the way, the same result is obtained by $55 \text{ bp} \cdot \frac{1-0.32}{1-0.45}$.

Example 18: Zero-Coupon-Bond Spreads Implied from Rating Data

The continuously compounded Z-spread can be derived from the survival probability by $s_t(\tau) = -(1 - \text{Rec}) \cdot \ln(S_t(\tau))/\tau$. In the chart below, we show the corresponding Z-spreads derived from the cumulative default rates in table A.6 in the appendix using a recovery assumption of 40 percent based on a recovery-of-market-value assumption. The chart below shows that the implied credit spread is an increasing function of the time horizon for investment-grade rating categories, while it is decreasing for credits with junk status (Caa). This is a very common phenomenon and can be explained by the fact that for highly-rated companies, the risks for a deterioration of the credit quality is higher than the chances for a further improvement. For companies close to default the situation is different. The probability that the company remains in a highly problematic situation for a longer time is limited: the company either defaults in the near term or its situation improves significantly, leading to decreasing credit spreads for longer time horizons.

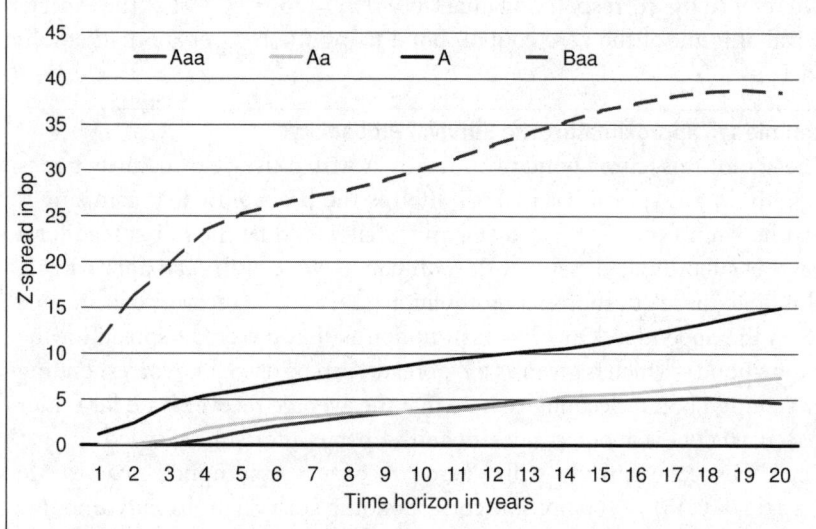

Credit spread curves inferred from rating data (investment grade)

Credit spread curves inferred from rating data (high yield)

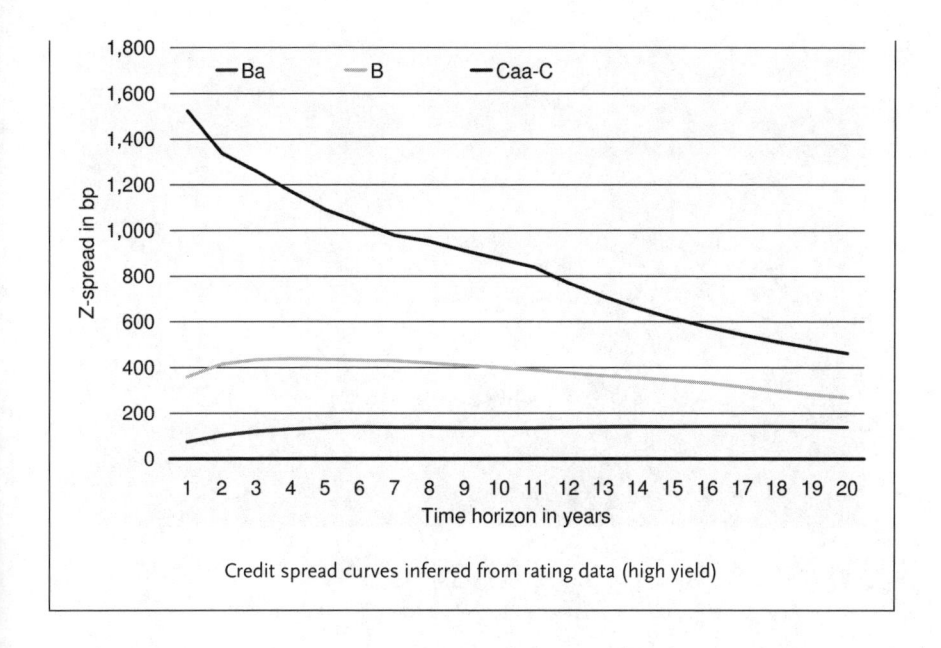

8
Single-Name Models

In the previous chapter we analyzed the basic principles of pricing credit-risky securities based on survival or default probability functions. However, one major topic remained unanswered: How can we derive the probabilities we need for valuation purposes? In the following we show that in general there are three different approaches, which may partly overlap. Note that the presentation in this section still refers to single-name credit risk. We will expand our analysis of pricing portfolio credit risk in the next chapter.

In the first approach, the *reduced-form models*, all pricing-relevant quantities (which can be for example the survival probability function or the term-structure of credit spreads) are calibrated to market prices of tradable securities. This approach allows a relative valuation of similar contracts, such as bonds versus a CDS contract, or the comparison of bonds with different maturities. Due to the reliance on market prices, these types of models implicitly ensure the no-arbitrage considerations.

The second important framework involves so-called *structural models*. Here, the probability of default – and for some models also the recovery value – are derived using option pricing technology. In case the models are calibrated to existing equity market securities, they provide the possibility to hedge the credit exposure by trading in the underlying stock and stock options. These models are also used to identify capital structure arbitrage opportunities, that is, the relative value between bonds and stocks of the same company. However, some caution concerning the use of the word arbitrage is in order. Most of the arbitrage investment strategies in credit markets (such as capital structure arbitrage [CSA]) are not actual risk-free cash-and-carry arbitrage opportunities. They should rather be viewed as risky relative value opportunities. In most cases the model approach which identifies a potential arbitrage opportunity conceals some important risks involved in the trade. Especially the structural models rely on specific dependency assumptions between debt and equity valuation of a company. In reality, however, this relation can deviate significantly from the model assumptions due to economic conditions, which are not properly captured by the model. Against this backdrop, a relative value trade should be regarded as what it is: an investment strategy which extracts a risk premium the market offers to investors who are willing to take this risk.

Active Credit Portfolio Management. J. Felsenheimer, P. Gisdakis, and M. Zaiser
Copyright © 2006 WILEY-VCH Verlag GmbH & Co. KGaA, Weinheim
ISBN: 3-527-50198-3

The third approach to derive the term structure of default probabilities involves the so-called rating-based transition matrix models (a.k.a. migration-matrix or Markov-chain models). Here, the term structure of default probabilities for a credit-risky instrument is modeled on the potential rating transitions in the future. The transition probabilities are based on historical rating transitions. Such data are provided by rating agencies (see table A.7 for a sample transition matrix from Moody's). While such models fit into the rating-oriented view of some market participants, they involve a major drawback, as pricing credit-risky securities using averaged historical probabilities neglects two major pricing-relevant factors. First, investors usually demand an extra compensation in excess of the expected loss derived in the physical probability measure (i.e., in terms of historical default probabilities). Note that an investor who just demands compensation for the expected loss in terms of historical default probability without a risk premium for the unexpected loss will in the long run only break even. Second, a purely rating-based approach cannot explain day-to-day changes of credit spreads. Credit spreads segmented by rating categories fluctuate significantly, reflecting also other relevant risk factors. However, the transition matrix models can be adjusted by factors that account for the risk premium and can therefore be calibrated to market prices. Such models are useful especially for bonds with rating-triggered features, such as coupon step-ups.

It should be noted that there are several suggestions in the literature for econometric models that are intended to fit either historical default probabilities or arbitrage-free credit spread term structures not only to the dynamics of some underlying variables, such as rating information, stock prices, and economic growth, but also to credit indices such as the CDX and the iTraxx.[24,33,34] In econometric models the functional relationship between default probabilities and the underlying risk factors is specified externally by the modeler and not driven by fundamental considerations, such as in structural models. Econometric models just identify the statistical relationship among these variables.

8.1 Reduced-Form Models

Reduced-form models (a.k.a. intensity-based models) are the most widely used models for pricing credit risk. They work directly on the default probability distribution. However, in this framework, a default is considered as a completely exogenous event. A reduced-form approach to model default risk would be "Company A has a probability of default of 1 percent per year". The 1 percent probability of default can be derived from everywhere, for instance, from historical default rates within a rating model, or it can be implied from market prices. What reduced-form models do not provide is a reasoning for the default probability. In this context, reduced-form models can simply be viewed as a general pricing framework, given a default probability distribution and, of course, a recovery model. To implement the model, the probability distributions have to be calibrated to some input data, such as historical default rates (e.g., segmented by rating categories) or to market prices.

Against this background, the whole analysis in chapter 7 can be regarded as a (static) reduced-form framework, as we did not explicitly mention where the survival probability function $S(\tau)$ comes from. In addition to our simple analysis, current state-of-the-art approaches do not only model the static probability of default for different time horizons, but also try to capture the future dynamics of the term structure of credit risk for pricing non-linear payoffs, such as bond and spread options. However, there is a major caveat with the purely probabilistic context in the reduced-form model approach when it comes to pricing. As the default probability is an external quantity, it usually does not involve prices of other tradable securities, such as stock or option prices. Hence, prices for credit-risky instruments using a reduced-form model cannot be enforced by an arbitrage-free trading strategy, as credit risk in this context is not considered as a derivative with respect to other tradable risks.

An example might help to shed some light on this problem. Just consider stock options. A stock option is a financial contract that is derived from the dynamics of the underlying stock price. From Black-Scholes technology[35] we know that one can hedge an equity option by trading the underlying stock. However, bonds and CDS contracts are already the most basic tradable assets involving a specific credit risk. So how to hedge the specific bond exposure to a company if credit risk is modeled as a completely isolated risk? There are just two possibilities: sell the bond exposure directly or short-sell another bond of the company as a hedge (alternatively, the investor could also buy protection in a credit default swap, which is effectively the same). This is what (static) reduced-form modeling is all about: a relative value framework among assets that involve a comparable source of risk. Note that such a relative valuation approach is not needed in plain-vanilla equity markets, as companies usually do not have different pure equity instruments outstanding. Of course, if we look a little deeper into the capital structure of a company, we identify all sorts of hybrid and mezzanine instruments that have both equity and debt characteristics. However, such instruments are again priced using the above-mentioned relative valuation models.

Example 19: A Simple Relative Value Analysis Involving Three Bonds
We consider a company which has three bonds outstanding.

- Bond A has a remaining time to maturity of one year, a coupon of 5%, and a market price of €99.5.
- Bond B has two years to maturity, a coupon of 6%, and a price of €100.
- Bond C has three years to maturity, a coupon of 7%, and a price of €103.

We assume that the expected recovery rate for all three bonds is 50 percent and the risk-free interest rate curve is flat at 5% (using annual compounding). We follow a very simple approach to perform a relative valuation. We first derive the expected loss per bond and divide it by the loss given default $(1 - \text{Rec})$ to approximate the cumulative probability of default. To achieve comparable quantities, we finally calculate annualized default probabilities for all three bonds.

The risk-free value of bond A can be calculated without using a spreadsheet. The bond has a single cash flow of €105 in exactly one year, which is discounted by $1/(1 + 0.05)$, which results in a risk-free value of €100. As the market price of the bond is €99.5, the expected loss is 0.5 percent of the notional amount. As the loss given default is $(1 - 0.5) = 50$ percent, the market-implied probability of default for one year is exactly 1 percent.

For bond B the corresponding calculations involve discounting the cash flows using the appropriate discount factor; for instance, the coupon payment of €6 in one year has to be discounted by $1/(1 + 0.05)$, while the final repayment of €106 is discounted by $1/(1 + 0.05)^2$. The corresponding risk-free value is €101.86. Given the market price of €100, we derive an expected loss of 1.86 percent, which results in a cumulative default probability of 3.72 percent for two years. Hence, the annualized probability of default is 1.86 percent. For bond C a similar calculation leads to an annualized probability of 1.63 percent.

This analysis reveals that bond B trades with a larger implied default probability than bond A and C. While it is understandable that the implied probability increases due to the extension in the maturity date between bond A and B, it is not reasonable that it decreases for an additional year. Hence, bond B trades cheaper compared to bond C due to potential mispricing in the market.

Example 19 illustrates how reduced-form models can be used in practice to analyze the relative value of comparable securities. In addition to the uncomplicated procedure in this example, where we simply approximated the annualized probability of default, a more sophisticated approach would target either the survival probabilities or the term structure of credit spreads, which involve both the probability and the recovery rate.

To avoid confusion about the wording *relative value*: A relative value analysis can be used in two ways: to compare market prices of traded assets to identify investment opportunities or to price a nontraded asset relative to the prices of comparable traded securities. Hence, a reduced-form model that is calibrated to market prices can be viewed as a kind of sophisticated generalized interpolation mechanism, which compares market prices for similar risks. In this context, a relative value opportunity is given if the price of one or of several securities does not smoothly fit into this generalized interpolation scheme. The major problems with relative valuation are: What are comparable risks and how large should the deviation be in order to be exploitable? Spreads of bonds with the same rating category, for example, can deviate significantly, as the rating of a bond is not the only spread driver. There are dependencies on the relative position of the bond in the capital structure, as well as industry-specific issues about bond pricing. Moreover, analyzing credit spreads for two issues of the same company but with different maturities refers to the steepness of the spread curve. But how steep can a reasonable spread curve be? These kind of questions have to be addressed in analyzing relative value opportunities (see, for example, the curve steepener and flattener trades in chapter 17).

As already mentioned, reduced-form models focus directly on the probability of default. This is done by specifying a mathematical description for the time dependency of the probability of default. While there are numerous suggestions discussed in the finance textbooks, most of the models deal in the end either directly or indirectly with a functional form of the underlying hazard rate. As a result, reduced-form models are also called hazard rate models.

There are several suggestions for specific models available in the textbooks, as well as surveys that compare the different model characteristics.[36-38] To avoid going into mathematical details, we prefer to highlight the most important characteristics of reduced-form models, and then show a generalized framework which captures the dynamics of the term structure of credit risk.

Nevertheless, there are some groundbreaking publications which the interested reader may want to review. Jarrow and Turnbull[39] suggest a discrete-time model for risky zero-coupon-bond prices. The analysis shown in chapter 7 was very much inspired by this paper. However, in contrast to our basic introduction, their model is not only a static model of default risk, but it also captures the future dynamics of credit risk and can therefore also treat non-linear payoffs such as bond and spread options. In addition, Duffie and Singleton[30] published a continuous-time term-structure model and suggested the above-mentioned recovery of market value treatment to achieve analytical tractability. They show how credit risk modeling can be integrated into an Heath-Jarrow-Morton (HJM) framework[40,41] for pricing interest rate risk. Other approaches directly model the dynamics of term structure of credit spreads.[42-44] The rating-based model suggested by Jarrow, Lando, and Turnbull[45] will be discussed in section 8.3.

The following list highlights the most important features and properties that characterize the different models. Reduced-form models can be characterized by:

- The way they deal with the timing of the default event. They can be discrete- or continuous-time models.
- Which recovery model is assumed. As discussed in section 7.6 there are several recovery models available, such as recovery of face value or recovery of market value.
- Which quantity is modeled. It can be, for example, the hazard rate, a credit spread curve (recall that there are several types of credit spreads, e.g., the asset swap spread or the Z-spread), or the bond price directly.
- Whether the default probability has a dependency on other underlying risk factors such as the term structure of risk-free interest rates, a rating process, or other economic variables, such as economic growth.
- How risk-neutral probabilities are integrated into the model. This can be done by calibrating the model to market prices or by introducing a risk premium.
- Whether it is a static or a dynamic model. A static model simply fits the term structure of credit spreads to some underlying bond prices or CDS levels, while a dynamic model also models future changes in credit spreads and therefore also involves the credit spread volatility. Such models are required if we want to price non-linear spread products such as spread options.
- The mathematical structure of the underlying stochastic process. In principle one can use the same processes as for short rate models in the interest rate derivatives world, such as arithmetical or geometrical Brownian motions or Ornstein-Uhlenbeck processes, with possibly time dependent drift or volatility functions, square-root diffusion, or even jump-diffusion processes.

- Implementation details, such as whether the model has an analytical solution or involves numerical procedures (e.g., binomial tree models or Monte Carlo simulations).

Models that incorporate the risk premium as an explicit term have the advantage that one can isolate and quantify the risk premium in the market price. However, since most of these models involve rating information, we analyze them below in section 8.3 on rating-based transition matrix models.

> **Example 20: Poisson and Cox Processes**
>
> In financial literature, reduced-form models are often described by means of stochastic processes. This is typically done by translating the random variable τ^* into a continuous default process $(X_\tau)_{\tau \in \mathbb{R}}$ with
>
> $$X_\tau = 1_{\{\tau^* \leq \tau\}} \tag{8.1}$$
>
> This stochastic process jumps from 0 to 1 at the time of default τ^* and remains at that level afterwards. The cumulative default probability can then be stated as:
>
> $$F(\tau) = \mathbb{P}(\tau^* \leq \tau) = \mathbb{P}(X_\tau = 1) = \mathbb{E}(X_\tau) \tag{8.2}$$
>
> Please note that we already made use of the indicator function at the beginning of chapter 7, however without mentioning the term stochastic process.
>
> Reduced-form models aim at modeling the hazard rate function $h(\tau)$, either deterministically or stochastically. In the following, we will introduce several standard processes that are commonly used in practice or at least mentioned in literature.
>
> A *homogeneous Poisson process* with *intensity* λ is the most simple example of a reduced-form model. Here, we simply assume that the hazard rate function $h(\tau)$ is constant, that is, $h(\tau) = \lambda$. In accordance with formula 7.20, we obtain the following expression for the cumulative default probability $F(\tau)$:
>
> $$F(\tau) = 1 - e^{-\int_0^\tau h(s)\,ds} = 1 - e^{-\int_0^\tau \lambda\,ds} = 1 - e^{-\lambda \cdot \tau} \tag{8.3}$$
>
> Accordingly, the random variable τ^* follows an *exponential distribution* with parameter λ. Please note that the expected value of τ^* under the exponential distribution is given by the reciprocal value of λ, that is, $\mathbb{E}(\tau^*) = 1/\lambda$. This obviously makes sense when considering the following example: If we assume a constant yearly (default) intensity of 1 percent, it takes a hundred years on average to observe a (default) event.

A generalization of the homogeneous Poisson process is the *inhomogeneous Poisson process*. In this case, the intensity λ is still deterministic, but it depends on the time to maturity τ. Thus, we have to specify an intensity function $\lambda(\tau)$, which should be globally non-negative. The cumulative default probability is then given by:

$$F(\tau) = 1 - e^{-\int_0^\tau h(s)\,ds} = 1 - e^{-\int_0^\tau \lambda(s)\,ds} \qquad (8.4)$$

In practice, homogenenous Poisson processes often prove inconsistent with market prices due to the fact that one is not able to reproduce, for example, upward-sloping credit curves. On the other hand, inhomogeneous Poisson processes are flexible enough to take these characteristics into account. However, one typically has to impose additional restrictions on the intensity function $\lambda(\tau)$ in order to obtain a unique solution for given market prices. A possibility would be to limit oneself to non-negative step functions, that is

$$\lambda(\tau) = \lambda_i \geq 0 \text{ for all } \tau \in [\tau_{i-1}, \tau_{i-1}[\quad (i = 1, 2, \ldots) \qquad (8.5)$$

As long as the intensity λ is deterministic, one is not able to price more sophisticated instruments like spread options. *Cox processes* fill this gap by stipulating that (λ_τ) is a stochastic process such that conditional on the realized intensity λ, (X_τ) is an inhomogeneous Poisson process. Apparently, a Cox process incorporates two stochastic sources: one that is related to the intensity λ over time, and one that is related to the occurrence of the default event conditional on the realization of λ.

By means of the law of iterated expectations, we can derive the cumulative default probability accordingly:

$$F(\tau) = 1 - \mathbb{E}\left[e^{-\int_0^\tau \lambda_s\,ds}\right]. \qquad (8.6)$$

8.1.1 Binomial Tree Models for Default Risk

In the following, we give a brief introduction to the mechanism of reduced-form term-structure modeling using a binomial tree. Due to the similarity of concepts of the hazard rate $h(\tau)$ and the instantaneous forward rate $f(\tau)$, (recall that $R(\tau) = \exp(-\int_0^\tau f(s)ds)$ and $S(\tau) = \exp(-\int_0^\tau h(s)ds)$; see equation 7.27), there is a close similarity between term-structure models for interest rates and default rates. It appears therefore reasonable to use the technology common for interest rates to model credit spread dynamics. And indeed, in focusing on binomial tree models we only need a few modifications to adjust for the default risk. Note, however, that for reasons of simplicity, we only highlight the major concept without focusing on implementational details, and we ignore interest rate effects. Nevertheless, with these concepts at hand, it is not very difficult to adjust an existing binomial tree term-structure model for risk-free interest rates (see, for example, Schönbucher[26], who presents a detailed analysis of combined interest rate and credit risk tree models).

In figure 8.1, we show a single branch of a binomial tree model for the term structure of the default probability. This branch is constructed by combining a default and a diffusion branch. In the default branch, which refers to the multi-step model derived in chapter 7, the default and survivorship case are separated. A default event occurs with probability p_1 in the first time step, while the contract survives with probability $1 - p_1$. In case no credit event occurs, the classical diffusion branch splits the dynamics of the default probability into up moves and down moves. It follows two default branches, one for the lower default probability and one for the higher default probability.

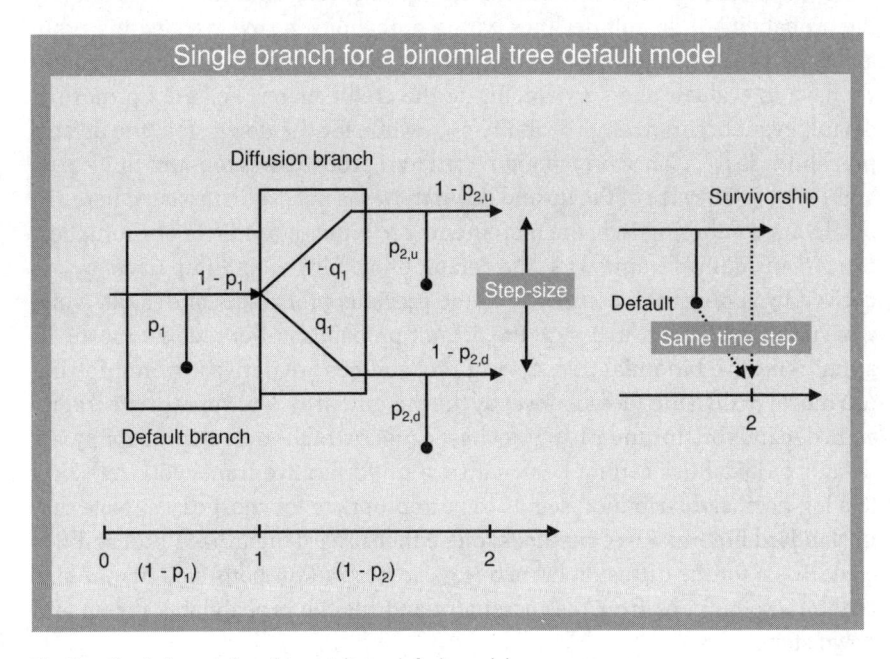

Fig. 8.1: Single branch for a binomial tree default model

Due to the combination of default and diffusion branches, the timing of the individual steps becomes a little complex. In reality, there is clearly no timing separation between changes in the credit spread curves and the evaluation of a default event. On the right hand side of figure 8.1, we indicated that default and survival paths end at the same point in time, although they look separated from a graphical perspective. We chose this presentation to make the separation of default and diffusion branching obvious.

Another difference between the binomial default model and risk-free interest rate models is that each time step ends with the evaluation of whether the credit survived or not. As a consequence, the first branching in up and down states occurs at $i = 1$ and not at $i = 0$. In the first time step, we just evaluate the probability of default without any changes. The survival probability in this step depends on the hazard rate with $1 - p_1 = \exp(-h(\tau_0)\Delta\tau) \approx 1 - h(\tau_0)\Delta\tau$. Here we assumed a piecewise constant hazard rate function $h(\tau)$ and equidistant points in time τ_i with $\Delta\tau = \tau_i - \tau_{i-1}$. Note that in this notation, the default and survival probabilities always refer to the end of the time step (i.e., p_1 is valid between 0 and 1), while the hazard rate is indicated by the beginning of the time step (i.e., $h(0)$ in the current example).

Now we focus on the diffusion branching. The hazard rate and consequently the probability of default declines with a probability q_1 and rises with a probability of $1 - q_1$. Following this split in the level of the probability of default, we have to evaluate the survivorship of the credit again. For the up move, a default event occurs with probability $p_{2,u}$, while for the down step, the default probability is $p_{2,d}$. The corresponding survival probabilities amount to $1 - p_{2,u}$ and $1 - p_{2,d}$. The size of the up and down moves is not explicitly stated here. To obtain a recombining tree, the increments can either be additive or multiplicative. In an additive framework, the default probability after an up move $p_{2,u}$ is derived by adding an increment x to the previous probability of default, while x is subtracted to arrive at $p_{2,d}$, the default probability after a down move. In a multiplicative binomial tree, default probabilities are derived by multiplying (up move) or division (down move) by the increment x. The appropriate framework depends on the underlying stochastic process of the default probability. As default probabilities cannot be negative, a multiplicative framework referring to a log-normal distribution seems to be appropriate for most cases. Note that in standard binomial tree methods, one either uses standardized probabilities q and $1 - q$ for the diffusion branch (e.g., 50 percent for both) and fits the size of the increment, or fixes the increment and fits the probabilities for up and down steps.

Tab. 8.1: Path probabilities for the fives possible states in figure 8.1

Path	Probability
Default in first step	p_1
Default in second step, up move	$(1-p_1) \cdot (1-q_1) \cdot p_{2,u}$
Default in second step, down move	$(1-p_1) \cdot q_1 \cdot p_{2,d}$
Survivorship in second step, up move	$(1-p_1) \cdot (1-q_1) \cdot (1-p_{2,u})$
Survivorship in second step, down move	$(1-p_1) \cdot q_1 \cdot (1-p_{2,d})$

After two time steps – one initial default step and one diffusion step followed by the corresponding default evaluation – the tree has five terminal points: three default and two survival states. A default event was either triggered in the first time step or in the second, and here with two different default probabilities $p_{2,u}$ and $p_{2,d}$. The survival paths end at the up and down states. In table 8.1 we show the probabilities for all five paths.

In order to obtain a term structure-consistent binomial tree (i.e., one that reprices all static, linear products, such as CDS contracts), the individual path probabilities have to reflect several constraints regarding total default and survival probabilities. The overall unconditional probability of a default in the second time step is derived as $(1-p_1)p_2$, where p_2 is the conditional default probability in the second time step (see equation 7.6). Consequently, the sum of the path probabilities resulting in a default event in the second step has to equal this probability: $(1-p_1)p_2 = (1-p_1)[(1-q_1) \cdot p_{2,u} + q_1 \cdot p_{2,d}]$. Analogously, the overall survival probability $(1-p_1)(1-p_2)$ has to equal the sum of the survival path probabilities $(1-p_1)[(1-q_1) \cdot (1-p_{2,u}) + q_1 \cdot (1-p_{2,d})]$.

In figure 8.2, we illustrate how the individual defaultable branches are combined into a binomial tree. The next diffusion branch is connected directly to the survival state. As an example, in case the credit survived the first two time steps and ended at the up state, the next diffusion branch leads to a default probability of $p_{3,uu}$ for another up move or goes down to $p_{3,ud}$ in case of a down step. Two things are worth noting at this stage. First, the probability of default is irrespective of the order of up and down steps (i.e., $p_{3,ud} = p_{3,du}$) and second, the probabilities for up and down moves do not depend on the state (i.e., they are q_2 for all down steps and $1 - q_2$ for all up steps). While the former is a consequence of the recombining tree, the latter is an assumption we made to keep the analysis as simple as possible. It can be ignored if necessary. To get an idea about the rationale of state-depending diffusion probabilities, we can think about rating transition probabilities that also depend on the current credit rating.

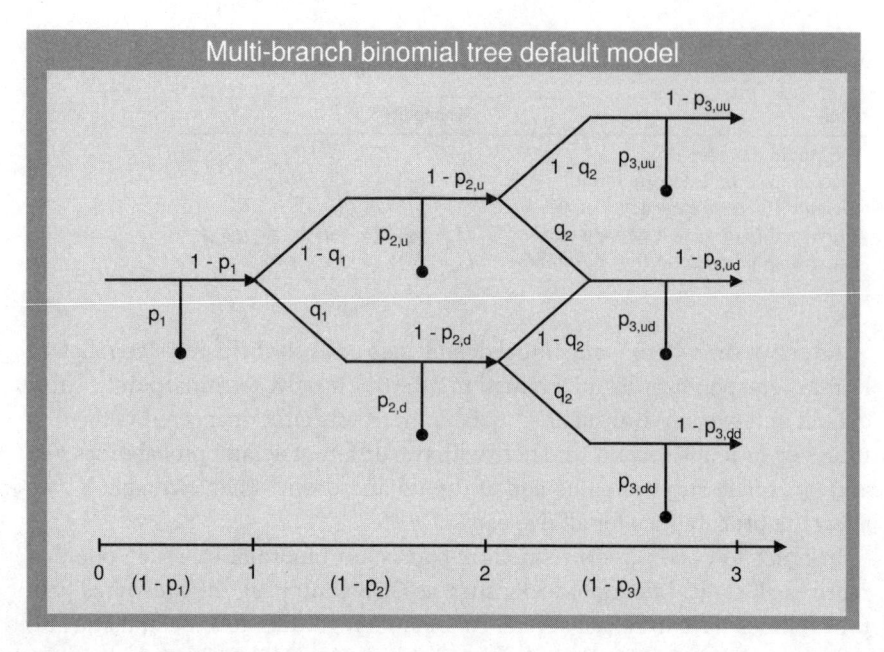

Fig. 8.2: Multi-branch binomial tree default model

To price, for example, a spread option, we have to calculate the payoff at maturity of the option. In order to do this, we need to derive the state depending on forward survival probabilities up to the maturity of the underlying. An example sheds some light. We assume that we price an option that matures after two time steps and refers to the survival probability of the third time interval. To illustrate the derivation of forward survival probability, we pick the up move; that is, we analyze the $(2, u)$ state. The corresponding forward survival probability is calculated as $(1 - q_2)(1 - p_{3,uu}) + q_2(1 - p_{3,ud})$. To price the option, we value the underlying contract using this survival probability and derive the option payoff. This is done for all possible survival states at the option's maturity. Then the payoff of the option is discounted back to the root of the tree using the survival probabilities. This means that the option buyer only receives the option payoff if the underlying credit survived up to the maturity of the option, which corresponds to the knock-out-on-default feature of most standard single-name spread options. If the option has another payoff in case of a credit event, it has to be taken into account at the default states.

This approach only models the dynamics of the default probability, while other factors such as risk-free discounting are not considered. Consequently, this model can be used to evaluate pure spread options, such as credit default swaptions. However, it is not appropriate to price credit-risky bond options that involve credit and interest rate optionalities. For such products, combined methods have to be used. An introduction to integrated credit and interest rate modeling using tree models can be found for example in Schönbucher.[26]

8.1.2 Reduced-Form Models and Illiquid Claims

Although we mentioned that reduced-form models are typically fitted to market prices, they can be used – and in fact are widely used – to price illiquid claims such as private loans. However, besides the expected loss for the individual exposure in terms of the physical (historical) probability measure, one has to incorporate a risk premium into the valuation framework, which accounts for the increase of the unexpected (portfolio) loss this individual exposure causes. Note that the unexpected loss is a portfolio quantity, while expected loss can also be defined on the level of the individual exposure. We elaborate on this topic below. A suggestion for such a pricing framework would be as follows:

- Determine the individual expected loss of the claim that has to be priced in the real probability measure, for instance, by using historical, ratings-based default probabilities and the recovery rate.
- Determine the increase of the risk budget (risk-based capital) which accounts for the incremental unexpected (portfolio) loss caused by the additional single credit-risky exposure using a credit portfolio model.
- Set a target (hurdle) rate as the cost of capital for the risk budget.

The price for the credit-risky exposure is derived from the expected loss and the cost of capital for the additional risk budget, which backs the incremental unexpected (portfolio) loss. The two crucial points in this approach are the way to determine the risk budget per single exposure and the target rate for the cost of capital. One way to determine the additional risk budget needed for pricing the risky exposure is to use an incremental value at risk. Note that the presented concept works for both risk measures, the value at risk (VaR) and the conditional value at risk (CVaR). For the moment, we focus on the VaR (see chapter 11 for an introduction to the value at risk as well as for an explanation of incremental VaR).

Let $VaR(P)$ be the value at risk of the portfolio excluding the exposure which has to be priced, while $VaR(P+A)$ is the respective conditional value at risk of the portfolio including the additional credit-risky exposure A under consideration. Hence, $VaR(P+A) - VaR(P)$ is the incremental VaR attributable to exposure A.

To arrive at the incremental risk budget that is needed to secure the additional exposure A, the incremental VaR has to be multiplied with the capital factor that was specified by management for calculating risk-based capital. Finally, this incremental risk budget is multiplied by the target rate to obtain the cost of capital, which has to be earned by the credit-risky exposure on top of the individual expected loss.

However, in contrast to pricing in the standard no-arbitrage framework, this method incorporates diversification effects of the specific portfolio into the pricing relation, as the incremental VaR depends on the structure of the portfolio and takes the correlations among the assets into account. As a result, a large and well-diversified portfolio will allow for more aggressive pricing than a small portfolio that already has a high exposure to similar risks. In the end, this framework refers to the economy-of-scale principle in risk management. Nevertheless, this approach results in the simple rule: price all risks that can be hedged at the cost for the hedge. All remaining risks that cannot be hedged have to be valued based on the cost of the incremental risk-based capital that backs the additional risks.[46]

8.2 Structural Models

Structural models date back to the seminal work of Robert Merton.[25] In contrast to reduced-form models, they derive the default probability directly from information about the company's capital structure. The central quantity that is modeled is the firm or enterprise value. Consequently, structural models are also known as Merton-type models, or firm- or enterprise-value models. There are several models discussed in the financial literature (see Cossin and Pirotte[36] or Giesecke[37] for a summary). They can be broadly classified into two groups: the classic Merton-type approach[25] and the so-called first-passage-of-time framework which dates back to Black and Cox.[47]

The classic Merton approach assumes a firm with a very simple capital structure. The liability side comprises a single zero coupon bond with maturity τ. The asset value is modeled as a geometrical Brownian motion. At maturity, the model implicitly assumes that the company's assets are liquidated and the proceeds are distributed among bond- and stockholders following the strict priority rule. The company's debt is repaid first; and only if the asset value exceeds the face value of the debt, the remaining proceeds are distributed among the stockholders. If the asset value does not exceed the face value of the debt, the bondholder suffer a loss that amounts to face value minus asset value and the stockholders miss out. Therefore, the payoff structure for the stockholders equals that of a European call option on the assets, with the face value of the debt as the strike price. This enables us to use standard Black-Scholes methodology to price the value of the equity (the European call option) and to derive the value of the defaultable debt as the risk-free value of the debt minus the value of the put option. Note that the payoff of the underlying options is only evaluated at maturity of the single debt instrument. The complete balance sheet is modeled with a finite time horizon τ, which corresponds to the maturity date of the firm's liability. Therefore, we can use standard European option pricing formulas.

This approach is based on four main assumptions (besides the usual ones like frictionless markets, risk-free borrowing, etc.):

- The payoff structure resembles that of a European call option. Consequently, default can only happen at maturity. A drop of the asset value below the strike price followed by an increase above the barrier again will not trigger a default event.
- The capital structure of the company is significantly simplified. There is only one single debt instrument considered. Effects from a debt structure with different time horizons (short-term versus long-term debt) or from debt instruments with different seniority classes (senior, subordinated, and hybrid capital) are completely ignored.
- The asset value follows a geometrical Brownian motion (standard assumption to use Black-Scholes methodology).
- Default risk and interest rate risk are independent, because the Black-Scholes pricing framework assumes deterministic interest rates.

Not surprisingly, model improvements tackle one or more of these assumptions. The already mentioned first-passage-of-time models deal with the restriction of the classic Merton approach to European options. In the Black-Cox approach, the option payoff resembles that of a barrier option. Default is triggered when the asset value hits a default barrier for the first time. Other improvements, such as the KMV model[48] introduce more realistic capital structures with several debt instruments (e.g., short- and long-term debt with different seniority classes, etc.) or use more sophisticated stochastic processes for the asset value (e.g., jump-diffusion models) to obtain more realistic characteristics of the pricing framework. Nevertheless, structural models have some important advantages as opposed to other pricing approaches:

- The default event is endogenously modeled and can therefore be explained by the model. It is not exogenous, as for example in the reduced-form model framework.
- In contrast to reduced-form models, which have to be calibrated to market prices for credit risk, they allow the valuation of claims for which reliable market prices are not available.
- They can be used for analyzing the relative value of debt and equity securities issued by a company. As a consequence, they can be used for cross asset hedging, that is, to hedge credit exposure by trading stocks and stock options.
- They are the basis for the so-called factor models to integrate default dependency into portfolio models for credit risk.

Unfortunately, they also involve major deficiencies, which we will also discuss here:

- The basic structural models are too simplistic for real markets, and current state-of-the-art models are conceptually and mathematically very complex.
- The models are difficult to parametrize and often produce significantly incorrect results.
- Most models cannot properly capture short-term credit spreads. They tend to be too low. Models that fix these deficiencies are again quite complex.
- Structural models rely on assumptions about a specific capital structure. As a consequence, they cannot properly account for changes in the capital structure.
- They do not explicitly take major credit drivers into account, such as rating changes.

In the following analysis, we show how to derive the most important mathematical characteristics of structural models. However, we will focus on a specific approach towards structural models, which allows to assess the relative value of debt and equity instruments. If they are calibrated to existing equity market securities, they provide the possibility to hedge the credit-risky exposure by trading the underlying stocks and stock options. Moreover, they can also be used to identify capital structure arbitrage (CSA) opportunities; the relative value between bonds and equity share of the same company.

The above-mentioned relative valuation approach embedded in the structural models can be used in two ways: cross asset hedging and capital structure arbitrage. In a standard structural model, which is calibrated to stock market prices, the spread for risky debt depends on a couple of equity-related factors, such as the share price and implied option volatilities. In such a model, we assume a CDS spread of s^{Model}. This spread depends (among others) on the share price E, the implied equity volatility σ, the time to maturity τ of the CDS contract, and the risk-free interest rate r. The key question is whether this spread is the same as the market spread. If it is in line with the market spread, relative pricing of equity and debt markets equals the fair value (no arbitrage opportunities) and vice versa.

$$s^{\text{Model}}(E, \sigma, \tau, r, \ldots) \begin{cases} = s^{\text{Market}}(\tau) & \text{markets in line} \\ \neq s^{\text{Market}}(\tau) & \text{markets out of line} \end{cases} \quad (8.7)$$

It follows that if debt and equity markets consistently price the various securities of a company, a structural model can be used to derive hedge ratios for credit exposure with respect to equity products. An example would be to hedge a CDS contract with an equity put option. Both instruments will (hopefully) move in line. On the other hand, in case the model indicates inconsistencies in the relative valuation of equity and debt, an investor might be interested in extracting a risk premium by implementing an offsetting position in the securities involved. However, it should be noted that most deviations in the relative debt–equity valuation are driven by reasonable underlying economic conditions, which might be hidden from the model. In case of a debt-financed M&A activity, for example, the credit spreads for the company will blow out, as the additional debt will lead to a deterioration of the credit quality of the company. On the other hand, the stock price of the company might surge, if the market views this acquisition as a value creator. The resulting price changes – credit spreads up and stock prices up – will trigger capital structure arbitrage signals in most structural models. However, in reality there is no arbitrage opportunity, as the relative price changes are reasonable from an economic point of view. This example should be interpreted as a warning. Capital structure arbitrage is almost never a real risk-free cash-and-carry arbitrage. As already mentioned, it should be viewed as a risky relative value opportunity. Moreover, such a trade usually involves complex risks and has to be carefully analyzed. It is most often driven by a fundamental story, which refers to specific financial issues of the company.

In the previous sections, we showed that the central quantity which has to be modeled is the survival probability $S(\tau)$. Recall that it gives the probability that the credit survives up to a maturity of τ. In the family of structural models, this survival probability is derived through debt–equity linkage. In the following analysis, we present a simple model which helps us to generate the link between debt and equity. In this framework, we extract an expression for the survival probability $S(\tau)$, which depends on the corresponding asset value A and the asset volatility σ^A. For the moment, let us assume that we can observe the asset value A and the asset volatility σ^A. The company has just one zero coupon bond outstanding with a face value of F, a time to maturity of τ, and a credit spread of $s(\tau)$. For reasons of simplicity, we assume a flat risk-free interest rate r. We denote the risky discount factor by $D(\tau)$. This leaves us with the basic Black-Scholes[35] methodology:

$$
\begin{aligned}
D(\tau) &= F e^{-(r+s(\tau))\cdot\tau} \\
&= F e^{-r\cdot\tau} - p(A, F, \sigma^A, r, \tau) \\
&= F e^{-r\cdot\tau} - \left[-A\cdot N(-d_1) + F e^{-r\cdot\tau}\cdot N(-d_2)\right]
\end{aligned}
\tag{8.8}
$$

$$
\text{with } d_1 = \frac{\ln\left(\frac{A}{F}\right) + \left(r + \frac{(\sigma^A)^2}{2}\right)\cdot\tau}{\sigma^A\sqrt{\tau}} \text{ and } d_2 = d_1 - \sigma^A\sqrt{\tau}
$$

$N(x)$ is the cumulative standard normal distribution function. Note that we neglect the effect from dividend payments in the option pricing formula. Using this expression, we can calculate the value of a credit-risky zero coupon bond of the company under consideration. In this approach, the value of the put option equals the present value of the expected loss. According to equation 7.2, the value of such a risky zero coupon bond can be split up into the default probability and the loss given default. The value of no default equals the product of the face value of the debt and the risk-free discount factor, which accounts for the time value of money, or $V^{\text{no default}} = F e^{-r\cdot\tau}$.

As mentioned before, the crucial variable is the survival probability, while the basic Merton methodology refers to the expected loss. Consequently, we have to divide the expected loss into loss given default (LGD) and the default probability (which provides us finally with the survival probability). Separating the face value and discount factor from equation 8.8 is an easy task, but differentiating between default probability and the loss given default requires a closer look at the payoff profile of a plain-vanilla put option. In the Merton framework, the probability of default is related to the probability that the asset value A hits the default barrier F. In option pricing theory, this simply refers to a binary put (zero value in case the asset value is above the strike price and value equals one in case the asset value is below the strike price). The value of a binary put option can be calculated by using standard Black-Scholes methodology:

$$
\text{binary put} = e^{-r\cdot\tau}\cdot N(-d_2) \tag{8.9}
$$

Putting equation 8.9 in equation 8.8, we can rewrite the pricing formula for the risky debt using the default probability instead of the loss given default. This results in:

$$D(\tau) = Fe^{-r\cdot\tau} - F\underbrace{e^{-r\cdot\tau} \cdot N(-d_2)}_{\text{binary put}} \left[-\frac{A}{F} \cdot \frac{N(-d_1)}{N(-d_2)} e^{r\cdot\tau} + 1 \right]$$

$$= Fe^{-r\cdot\tau} \left[1 - \underbrace{N(-d_2)}_{\text{default probability}} \underbrace{\left[1 - \underbrace{\frac{A}{F} \cdot \frac{N(-d_1)}{N(-d_2)} e^{r\cdot\tau}}_{\text{recovery rate}} \right]}_{\text{loss given default}} \right] \qquad (8.10)$$

As we divided expected loss into default probability and LGD, we linked the Merton world with basic credit risk terminology. In figures 8.3 and 8.4 we show the survival probability and the recovery rate derived from the Merton framework. We point out that higher implied volatility refers to lower survival probability, which – in general – declines when the maturity rises. Moreover, we show that the implied recovery rate is far from being stable. In contrast to the general assumption of 40 percent recovery value in basic CDS valuation, both volatility and maturity inversely affect the recovery rate.

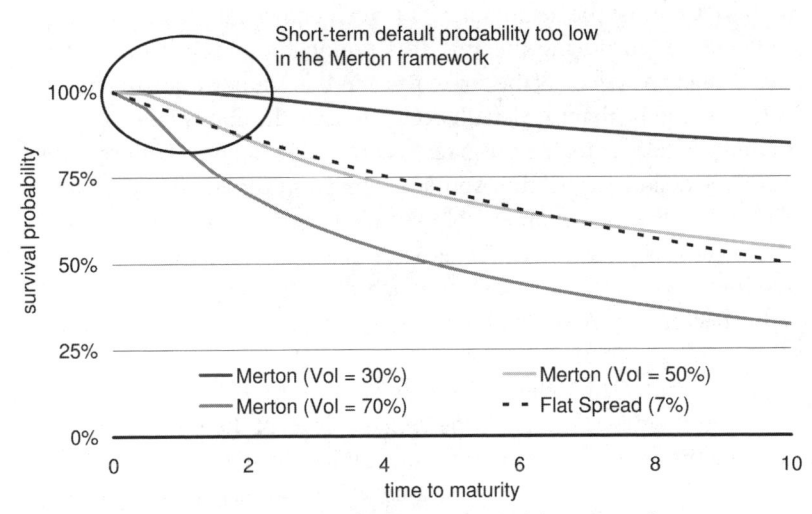

Fig. 8.3: Merton approach versus classic credit risk methodology: survival probabilities

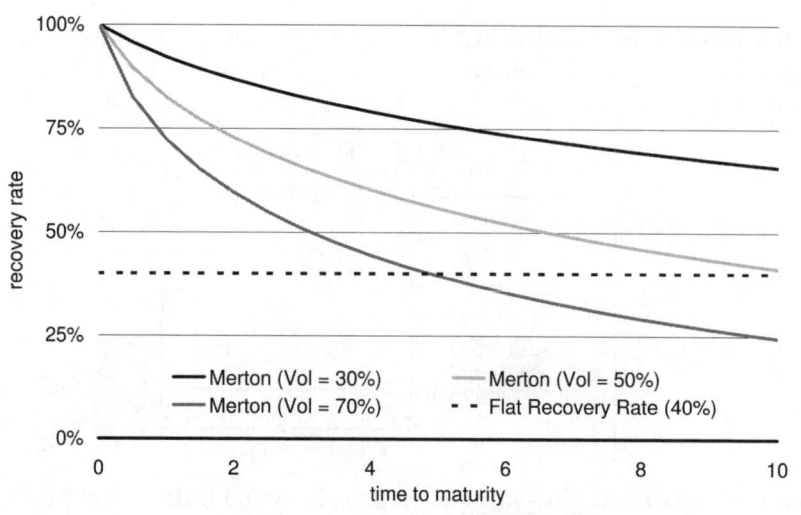

Fig. 8.4: Merton approach versus classic credit risk methodology: recovery rates

A basic shortfall of the initial Merton approach is that the firm's asset value process and the corresponding volatility cannot be observed directly. Hence, we use the stock price E and the stock price volatility σ instead of the asset value and asset volatility. For exchange-listed companies, we can obtain reliable stock prices. However, when using the equity of a firm as a proxy for the asset value, we have to adjust the default barrier (which equals the strike price in the terminology of option pricing theory). It is no longer appropriate to use the face value of the firm's debt as the strike price in this framework. An apparent modification would be that the default occurs in case the equity falls to zero. If a firm's equity value is zero, the company is certainly in default. Unfortunately, in this case, the default probability would be zero from a mathematical point of view. The probability for a geometrical Brownian motion (with an initial value greater than zero) to reach a value of zero is zero.

Consequently, we prefer a model in which default is triggered in case the equity value declines by a certain amount, for example minus 70 percent. This means that a default at time τ occurs if $E(t = \tau) \leq L \cdot E(t = 0)$, for example, with L = 30 percent. Thus, the strike price is given by $L \cdot E(t = 0)$. We set $F = L \cdot E(t = 0)$, with L being the (percentage) level of the initial stock price which triggers the default. Including the default barrier in the equation for the survival probability, and substituting the asset value and asset volatility with the corresponding equity quantities, we derive equation 8.11.

$$S(\tau) = N(d_2)$$

$$\text{with } d_2 = \frac{\ln\left(\frac{1+r^E}{L}\right) + \left(r - \frac{\sigma^2}{2}\right) \cdot \tau}{\sigma\sqrt{\tau}} \qquad (8.11)$$

$$\text{and } 1 + r^E = \frac{E(t)}{E(0)}$$

This is the most basic debt–equity model, which formulates the default probability as a dependent variable of the (cumulated) equity return process r^E and the corresponding return volatility σ. The equity return r^E is considered as a cumulated return, as it refers to the initial equity value $E(0)$ and not to the one of the previous time step $E(t - \Delta t)$. Moreover, r^E is assumed to be normally distributed (which corresponds to a log-normally distributed stock price), with the initial value of r^E being zero. The default barrier L refers to the leverage of the firm, directly determined by the debt-to-asset ratio, expressed in the following equation:

$$L = \frac{\text{debt}}{\text{assets}} = \frac{1}{1 + \frac{\text{equity}}{\text{debt}}}$$

The default barrier L lies between zero and one. The higher the debt-to-asset ratio, the lower the debt–equity ratio, and hence the lower the equity cushion which protects a bondholder from default. A high level of L refers to a small distance to default regarding the equity value and a high level of credit risk, respectively. In case L is 30 percent, default is triggered when the cumulated equity return is −70 percent, that is, the share price drops by 70 percent compared to the initial value.

That said, we can use the strike level L to calibrate the model to market quotes. Against this backdrop, L can be considered as the implied leverage ratio. Moreover, by allowing L to be a function of τ, we can fit the whole credit spread term structure by adjusting the time-dependent default barrier.

There is another interesting topic regarding the default barrier, because it incorporates balance sheet information. If L is a dynamic quantity, we can circumvent a crucial shortfall of the Merton framework. Corporate activities that affect the balance sheet, might have a different impact on share prices and credit spreads. For example, a debt-financed acquisition boosts the equity value and rewards shareholders, but at the expense of bondholders.

With $L(\tau)$ being a function of τ, we can extract the market's expectation of the future development of the default barrier within this model framework. As

Tab. 8.2: Translation of standard credit risk terminology into the Merton framework

Standard credit risk terminology	Merton models
Default probability	$N(-d_2)$
Survival probability	$N(d_2)$
Recovery rate	$\frac{1+r^E}{L}\frac{N(-d_1)}{N(-d_2)}e^{r\cdot\tau}$
Implied hazard rate	$-\frac{1}{2\sigma\sqrt{\tau}}\frac{N'(d_2)}{N(d_2)}\left[-\frac{1}{\tau}\ln\left(\frac{1+r^E}{L}\right)+\left(r-\frac{\sigma^2}{2}\right)\right]$

a side remark, L should also be related to the issuer's credit rating taking the aforementioned analysis into account.

The previous analysis dealt with the classical Merton approach using European options. In the following, we show how this approach can be translated into a first-passage-of-time framework. Here, the survival probability $S(\tau)$ can be obtained analytically from a so-called one-touch put option (OTP). For the value of a one-touch put option – in other words, an American-style, digital, out-of-the-money put option – a closed form Black-Scholes solution is available. This option pays one cash unit as soon as the stock price hits the strike price. In our previous approach using a European digital put, default could only be noticed at maturity. Using the American-style version, a default event will be triggered as soon as the equity value hits the default barrier. Equation 8.12 states the value of the one-touch put option:

$$\text{OTP}(\tau) = \left(\frac{L}{1+r^E}\right)^{\frac{2r}{\sigma^2}} \cdot N(-d_5) + \left(\frac{1+r^E}{L}\right) \cdot N(-d_1)$$

$$\text{with } d_1 = \frac{\ln\left(\frac{1+r^E}{L}\right) + \left(r + \frac{\sigma^2}{2}\right)\cdot\tau}{\sigma\sqrt{\tau}} \qquad (8.12)$$

$$\text{and } d_5 = \frac{\ln\left(\frac{1+r^E}{L}\right) - \left(r + \frac{\sigma^2}{2}\right)\cdot\tau}{\sigma\sqrt{\tau}}$$

Regarding the variables d_1 and d_5, we used the notation given in Paul Wilmott's book.[49] In order to use the one-touch put option in our previously derived credit risk pricing framework, we have to extract the survival probability from the option value. This is done by exploiting the similarity of the option payoff with the default leg in an EDS contract. An EDS can be considered as a CDS contract, where the trigger event does not refer to a pure credit event but to a drop of the corresponding stock price by a large amount (usually 70 percent). In contrast to regular CDS contracts, which involve an uncertain payoff at default due to the unknown recovery rate, an EDS has a prespecified payoff (usually 50 percent).

Hence, the result in equation 8.12 has to be scaled to pay the loss given default, since the value of the one-touch put option is given with respect to a payoff of 1. Using the discrete CDS pricing model from equation 10.4 we obtain:

$$(1 - \text{Rec}) \cdot \text{OTP}(\tau_n) = (1 - \text{Rec}) \cdot \sum_{i=1}^{n} R(\tau_i)[S(\tau_{i-1}) - S(\tau_i)]$$
$$\text{OTP}(\tau_n) = \sum_{i=1}^{n} R(\tau_i)[S(\tau_{i-1}) - S(\tau_i)] \quad (8.13)$$

In the second line of equation 8.13, we eliminated the loss given default $(1 - \text{Rec})$. We now can obtain the survival probability $S(\tau_i)$ via a simple bootstrapping algorithm. Therefore, we first split the summation from $i = 1$ to n into one from $i = 1, 2, \ldots, n - 1$ and the remaining term for n:

$$\text{OTP}(\tau_n) = \sum_{i=1}^{n-1} R(\tau_i)[S(\tau_{i-1}) - S(\tau_i)] + R(\tau_n)[S(\tau_{n-1}) - S(\tau_n)] \quad (8.14)$$
$$= \text{OTP}(\tau_{n-1}) + R(\tau_n)[S(\tau_{n-1}) - S(\tau_n)]$$

In the second step, we rearrange this equation in order to find an expression for the survival probability function $S(\tau_n)$.

$$S(\tau_n) = S(\tau_{n-1}) - \frac{\text{OTP}(\tau_n) - \text{OTP}(\tau_{n-1})}{R(\tau_n)} \quad (8.15)$$

This algorithm is similar to the bootstrapping procedure to derive discount factors from swap rates, where the current discount factor depends on the solution of the previous ones (see equation 5.21).

To value credit-risky contracts within this framework, one first has to bootstrap the survival probabilities $S(\tau_i)$ for each payment date τ_i given the value of the one-touch put option $\text{OTP}(\tau_i)$. In the second step, these survival probabilities can be used in our previously derived pricing framework. Another application is to invert this procedure. Given the market value of a credit-risky contract (bond, CDS, or EDS) and an assumption for the default trigger level for the stock price, we can derive the implied volatility for the structural model. This volatility can be compared to real implied volatilities in equity derivatives markets, for example to analyze capital structure arbitrage opportunities.

Note that the only relevant information about the underlying asset which affects the current survival probability function $S(\tau)$ is the implied option volatility. The current underlying price has no influence, as the pricing formula in equations 8.11 (standard Merton approach) and 8.12 (first-passage-of-time model) always refer to a relative strike price (not a fixed one as is the case in plain-vanilla equity options), which is given by a fraction of the current price. Note that these equations always depend on the fraction $\frac{1+r^E}{L}$ with $1 + r^E = \frac{E(t)}{E(0)}$ and not on absolute levels of $E(t)$ and a strike price of K.

The analysis above refers to a discrete-time approach. In a continuous-time framework equation 8.13, which relates the value of the one-touch put option to the value of a default leg of a credit derivatives contract, has to be modified according to the continuous-time CDS pricing relation in equations 10.1a to 10.3a.

$$\text{OTP}(\tau) = \int_0^\tau h(s) \cdot S(s) \cdot R(s) ds$$

$$\text{with } S(\tau) = e^{-\int_0^\tau h(s) ds}$$

Here, $h(\tau)$ is the hazard rate function. This equation has to be solved with respect to $S(\tau)$, which gives the continuous-time version of the survival probability function. As the solution is rather complicated and does not lead to additional insights, we refrain from deriving it explicitly.

8.3 Rating-Based Transition Matrix Models

Reduced-form models completely refrain from the underlying economic setting by simply calibrating these models to market prices of tradable securities and derivatives (relative valuation approach). Rating-based models, on the other hand, try to establish a link to observable default-related information in credit markets, namely rating assessments from external rating institutions. While reduced-form models emanate from the rationale that the default process is based on a two-state space (non-default versus default), rating-based models extend the view to a state space comprising more than two states that represent rating classes. This enables us to explicitly incorporate credit rating information into the valuation process.

At first glance, the rationale seems promising, since historical transition probabilities for the various rating classes are provided by rating agencies on a regular basis. However, one has to keep in mind that we need risk-neutral probabilities (or pseudo probabilities, risk-adjusted probabilities) instead of real-world probabilities in order to price credit-risky instruments. Hence, the main task is to derive these martingale probabilities from historical default rates, which typically involves a complex calibration process associated with several assumptions concerning the structure of the risk premium.

But is this effort worthwhile? The answer clearly depends on the field of application. Rating-based models are useful in the context of pricing and hedging credit-risky instruments with embedded options that depend on an underlying credit rating. For example, bonds whose coupon is adjusted in response to a rating action (e.g., step-ups and step-downs) cannot be priced in standard structural or reduced-form models. Rating-based models fill this gap. However, these models can also be applied for risk management purposes. For example, one can compute the probability of being in a given credit class after a fixed time interval when starting from a particular credit class. This can be done by either using risk-neutral probabilities or resorting to historical transition probabilities, depending on the objective of the analysis.

In the following, we provide a brief introduction to rating-based models but refrain from discussing details with regard to possible calibration procedures. For additional details, please refer to Jarrow, Lando, and Turnbull,[45] Das and Tufano,[50] Kijima,[51] and Kijima and Komoribayashi.[52]

Rating-based models typically presume a time-discrete economy, enumerating the periods by $t = 0, 1, 2, \ldots$ with $t = 0$ denoting the current period. This is done for simplicity's sake, although it is not difficult to derive a continuous limit. In addition, we introduce a finite *state space* $R = \{1, 2, \ldots, K\}$. This set reflects the possible credit classes, with 1 being the highest rating (e.g., AAA) and $K - 1$ being the lowest rating (e.g., C). The last state, K, represents the default state.

If we consider a specific credit-risky instrument, for example a corporate bond, we can describe its rating class $i \in R$ for each period $t = 0, 1, 2, \ldots$ by means of a process $(x_t)_{t=0,1,2,\ldots}$, with $x_t \in R$ for all $t \in \{0, 1, 2, \ldots\}$. We impose a first assumption with regard to this process: It should be *Markovian* (or: it fulfills the *Markov property*). This can be mathematically expressed by:

$$P(x_{n+1} = j \mid x_0 = i_0, x_1 = i_1, \ldots, x_n = i) = P(x_{n+1} = j \mid x_n = i) \quad (8.16)$$

Formula 8.16 implies that only the state $i \in R$ at time n and not the entire history is relevant for determining the probability of being in state $j \in R$ at time $n+1$. In other words, the probability of being in state j in the next period solely depends on where we are now but not where we have been before. A process $(x_t)_{t=0,1,2,\ldots}$ that fulfills the Markov property is said to be a *Markov chain*. Formula 8.16 also reveals that we have to deal with conditional probabilities, however only conditional on the state of the preceding period.

We add a second major assumption, namely the *time-homogeneity* of the process $(x_t)_{t=0,1,2,\ldots}$. Formula 8.16 does not reveal whether the conditional probability $P(x_{n+1} = j \mid x_n = i)$ is constant over different base periods n. Time-homogeneity simply means that this probability does not vary over time, formally:

$$p_{i,j} = P(x_{n+1} = j \mid x_n = i) \quad \text{for all } i,j \in R \text{ and } n = 0,1,2,\ldots \quad (8.17)$$

Under this assumption, the term $p_{i,j}$ can be interpreted as the probability that the Markov chain which is currently in state $i \in R$ will be in state $j \in R$ next period.

As the indices i and j can take values in the set of R, it is comfortable to pool them in a $K \times K$ matrix $\mathbf{Q}$, which is often referred to as a *transition matrix*:

$$\mathbf{Q} = \begin{pmatrix} p_{1,1} & p_{1,2} & \cdots & p_{1,K} \\ p_{2,1} & p_{2,2} & \cdots & p_{2,K} \\ \vdots & \vdots & \ddots & \vdots \\ p_{K,1} & p_{K,2} & \cdots & p_{K,K} \end{pmatrix} \quad (8.18)$$

In accordance with probability calculus, the transition matrix should fulfill the following properties:

$$p_{i,j} \geq 0 \quad \text{for all } i,j = 1,2,\ldots,K \quad (8.19)$$

$$\sum_{j=1}^{K} p_{i,j} = 1 \quad \text{for all } i = 1,2,\ldots,K \quad (8.20)$$

All entries in the transition matrix must be non-negative and the rows add up to one.

Please note that a time-homogeneous Markov chain is completely described by the quadratic transition matrix $\mathbf{Q}$. If time-homogeneity would not be presumed, we would need a transition matrix for each single period.

For a rating-class process, as in our case, it seems reasonable to assume that the default state ($i = K$) is an *absorbing state*. That is, once the state K is reached, the process will remain in this state forever. Hence, the transition matrix $\mathbf{Q}$ is supposed to have the following structure:

$$\mathbf{Q} = \begin{pmatrix} p_{1,1} & p_{1,2} & \cdots & p_{1,K-1} & p_{1,K} \\ p_{2,1} & p_{2,2} & \cdots & p_{2,K-1} & p_{2,K} \\ \vdots & \vdots & \ddots & \vdots & \vdots \\ p_{K-1,1} & p_{K-1,2} & \cdots & p_{K-1,K-1} & p_{K-1,K} \\ 0 & 0 & \cdots & 0 & 1 \end{pmatrix} \qquad (8.21)$$

The special structure of the last row indicates that K is an absorbing state. Hence, if the process reaches this state, there is no possibility to leave this state at a later period.

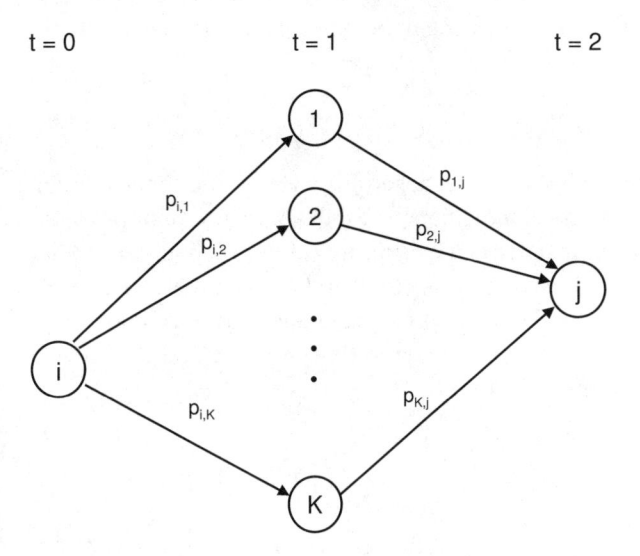

Fig. 8.5: How to calculate a two-period transition probability

The transition matrix $\mathbf{Q}$ provides information about one-period transition probabilities. But one should also be able to calculate a similar transition probability for two or more periods. First, let us consider the two-period case. According to figure 8.5 and probability calculus, the probability amounts to

$$p_{i,j}(2) = \sum_{k=1}^{K} p_{i,k} \cdot p_{k,j} \quad \text{for all } i,j = 1, 2, \ldots, K \qquad (8.22)$$

The 2 in brackets on the left hand side of the equation indicates that this is a two-period transition probability. Formula 8.22 reveals that this calculation of the two-period transition probability is identical to the operation done when multiplying matrix **Q** with itself. Hence, the matrix $(p_{i,j}(2))_{\{i,j=1,2,...,K\}}$ is simply given by $\mathbf{Q} \cdot \mathbf{Q} = \mathbf{Q}^2$. Transition probabilities for more than two periods can be analogously calculated by raising the matrix **Q** to the power of n (the n-fold matrix product of **Q**), where n denotes the number of periods.

Fortunately, the matrix **Q** can be easily filled with empirical data, for example based on Moody's Special Comment "Default and Recovery Rates of Corporate Bond Issuers, 1920-2004"[16] and S&P's RatingsDirect Research "Quarterly Default Update And Rating Transitions".[53] It is no surprise that nonzero entries of the historical matrix **Q** tend to be concentrated around the diagonal, with movements of two credit ratings or more in a year being rare or nonexistent.

We already pointed out that the survival probability S is of major importance in the context of valuation. For our time-homogeneous Markov chain, the n-period survival probability is given by

$$S(n) = 1 - p_{i,K}(n) \tag{8.23}$$

which can be easily derived by taking the absorbing state K into consideration.

The bad news is that empirical transition probabilities are not appropriate for valuation purposes as already stated at the beginning of this section. One rather needs risk-neutral probabilities instead of real-world probabilities. Hence, we have to determine a one-period transition matrix $\tilde{\mathbf{Q}}$ under the equivalent martingale probability measure, that is, the transition probabilities $\tilde{p}_{i,j}$ have to incorporate a risk premium:

$$\tilde{\mathbf{Q}} = \begin{pmatrix} \tilde{p}_{1,1} & \tilde{p}_{1,2} & \cdots & \tilde{p}_{1,K-1} & \tilde{p}_{1,K} \\ \tilde{p}_{2,1} & \tilde{p}_{2,2} & \cdots & \tilde{p}_{2,K-1} & \tilde{p}_{2,K} \\ \vdots & \vdots & \ddots & \vdots & \vdots \\ \tilde{p}_{K-1,1} & \tilde{p}_{K-1,2} & \cdots & \tilde{p}_{K-1,K-1} & \tilde{p}_{K-1,K} \\ 0 & 0 & \cdots & 0 & 1 \end{pmatrix} \tag{8.24}$$

Elements in matrix $\tilde{\mathbf{Q}}$ must be non-negative if and only if the respective real-world probability in matrix **Q** is also non-negative:

$$\tilde{p}_{i,j} > 0 \iff p_{i,j} > 0 \tag{8.25}$$

Otherwise, $\tilde{\mathbf{Q}}$ would not represent an *equivalent* probability measure.

In addition, Jarrow, Lando, and Turnbull[45] assert that these martingale probabilities $\tilde{p}_{i,j}$ can even depend on the entire history of the process. Thus, the process is neither required to be Markovian nor to be time-homogenenous, although we established these assumptions for the real-world model.

The apparent complexity of the resulting valuation model complicates the calibration process for the model. In other words, it is a challenging task to deduct the implied transition probabilities from market prices. This is typically done by imposing additional assumptions with regard to the structure of the risk premium. In addition, the calibration procedure requires a larger quantity of pricing data for a specific obligor. We refrain from discussing the various approaches available in the scientific community. For details, please refer to Jarrow, Lando, and Turnbull,[45] Das and Tufano,[50] Kijima,[51] and Kijima and Komoribayashi.[52]

Other models, for example Lando,[54] Arvanitis, Gregory, and Laurent,[55] and Nakazato,[56] even increase the degree of model complexity by introducing stochastically varying transition probabilities.

8.3.1 Redefining the Default Event

We illustrate some details of rating-based transition matrix models using a very simple but instructive example. The proposed model allows a simple marked-to-market valuation using Markov-chain models by redefining the default event.

At first glance, pure buy-and-hold investors are not price sensitive (spread sensitive). As long as there is no default, price changes in their bond exposure do not affect their investment decision, as their assets redeem at par. However, there are many portfolio managers that are restricted to invest only in the investment-grade universe. While there is only a very low probability of investment-grade default, the risk of a downgrade to junk status is obviously much higher. In case there is an investment restriction with respect to the credit quality (only high grade), investors have to redefine the default event. The risk is related to a downgrade to junk status, forcing high-grade investors to liquidate their positions, resulting in a negative P&L in general.

To model the risk for such restricted high-grade investors, we divide the problem into three parts:

- First, we derive the probability that a bond will be downgraded to junk status. This can be done by using the already presented Markov-chain approach based on a rating migration matrix. This probability corresponds to the default probability in a conventional credit risk analysis. We refer to this quantity as PE, the probability of the (restriction) event.

- Second, we have to determine the loss given such a restriction event (LGE). It can be approximated by the difference between the investment-grade and the high-yield spreads multiplied by the modified duration.
- Third, both quantities (PE and LGE) will be combined to result in a fair spread level using a simple CDS pricing model.

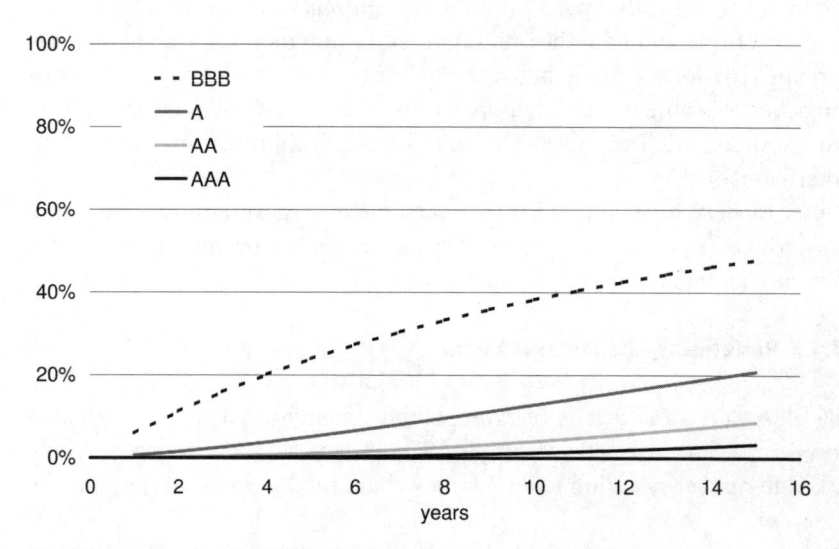

Fig. 8.6: Cumulated probability for a downgrade to speculative grade

In table A.7 in the appendix, we show the historical rating migration matrix from Moody's. It is based on rating transitions for a period from 1970 to 2004. However, as we are solely interested in the probabilities for a downgrade to sub-investment grade, we have to truncate the migration matrix and merge all non-investment-grade categories into the high-yield state. In this model, the high-yield state is the absorbing state, as we are modeling the probability of a downgrade to junk status. This assumption reflects our redefined default event, as the investor has to sell the bond on this event and will therefore not gain in case the bond reenters the investment-grade universe.

Note that dealing with the transition matrix in table A.7 involves an important subtlety. The last column records the probability of a withdrawn rating (WR state). To use this matrix, we have to exclude this state from further consideration and re-normalize the transition matrix. This is a common procedure and reflects the fact that a rating withdrawal (for investment-grade bonds) usually does not hurt investors, as they are triggered by bond redemption, M&A, and so on. This normalization is done by dividing the remaining values of each row by the sum of all probabilities, excluding the WR status. This ensures that the transition probabilities in each row in the adjusted matrix add up to 1. Alternatively, one can use already adjusted matrices, which are also sometimes provided by the rating agencies. In addition, transition matrices are provided by the rating agencies for the alphanumerical rating scale as well.

The introduction of the high-yield state into the migration matrix means that we have to consider all transitions from high grade to Ba, B, Caa–C and the default state. This raises the question of how to deal with real defaults (i.e., with migrations to the default category).

Regarding the default event, we assume – in line with buy-and-hold investors – that a real investment-grade default does not happen. In inspecting the migration matrix, this assumption may seem justified as the annualized default probability for an A-rated company to default is 0.02 percent and 0.16 percent for a Baa-rated company. Moreover, as the data provided by the rating agencies are usually annualized probabilities, we assume that these investment-grade defaults are not direct defaults but happen through an interim downgrade to junk status.

In figure 8.6, we show the cumulated probability of a downgrade to junk status. We calculated it for the given transition matrix by using the previously introduced Markov-chain model. We derive the n-period transition matrix $\mathbf{Q}_n$ from a single-period matrix $\mathbf{Q}_1$, by raising $\mathbf{Q}_1$ to the power of n (Hint: in Excel this can be done by using the worksheet function MMULT).

The last column (high-yield state) in each matrix $\mathbf{Q}_n$ gives the cumulated n-period probability for a downgrade to the high-yield status. For the single period we can derive this directly from the normalized version of table A.7 in the appendix. The probability for a downgrade to junk status from AAA is 0.03 percent, while for BBB it is 5.92 percent. Note that these probabilities are normalized to reflect the exclusion of the rating withdrawals and therefore do not equal the values in table A.7 in the appendix.

A short example sheds some light on the mechanics of the Markov-chain models. We focus on an AAA-rated credit and aim at deriving the cumulated downgrade probability over two periods. This cumulated probability is given as the probability for a direct junk status downgrade in the first period (0.03 percent) plus the probability of a downgrade to AA in the first period (7.24 percent) times the probability for a HY-downgrade from AA in the second period (0.08 percent), plus the probability of a downgrade to A in the first period (0.77 percent) times the probability for a high-yield downgrade from A in the second period (0.63 percent), and so on. In other words, we calculate the probability for a whole chain of rating transitions to the high-yield state for a specific time horizon.

In the next step, we have to determine the loss that occurs in case a bond is downgraded to junk status. We approximate this LGE (loss given event) as the marked-to-market loss due to the spread widening accompanying the downgrade. This is done by multiplying the modified duration with the spread difference between a high-grade rating category (e.g., AA) and high yield.

Figure 8.7 shows the time series of credit spreads for high yields, for the non-financials high-grade average (NFI HG) and the respective rating qualities (NFI AAA to NFI BBB). The latter were obtained for the iBoxx € universe. The spread differences between high grade and high yield is mainly driven by the high-yield spread. The wider the latter, the wider the high grade–high yield spread difference, the larger the marked-to-market loss in case of a downgrade to junk status.

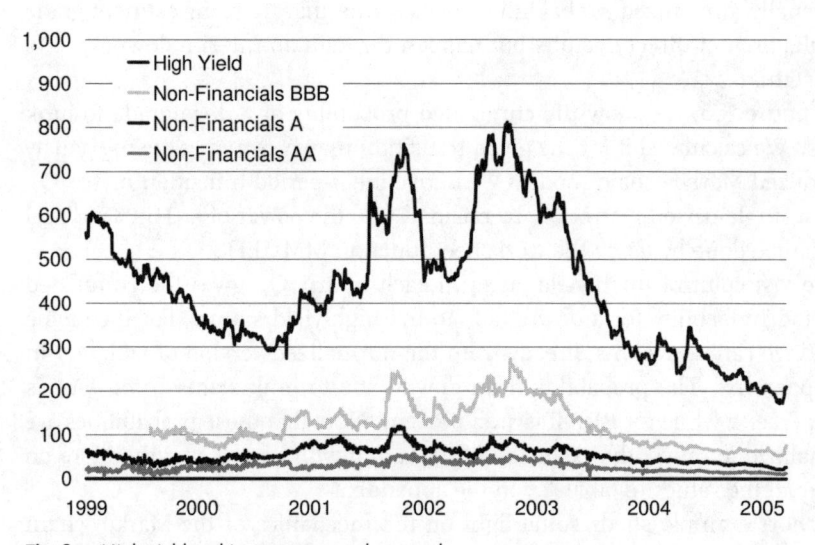

Fig. 8.7: High-yield and investment-grade spreads

Now all building blocks are available to derive an appropriate spread level for the risk stemming from a possible downgrade to junk status: the probability of a downgrade event and the loss given this event. Using a simple CDS valuation procedure, we obtain the spread curve as shown in the two charts below.

In figure 8.8, we used the current high grade–high yield spread difference, which varies between 2.1 percent for AAA–high yield and 1.3 percent for BBB–high yield. Using an average modified duration of 5 results in a loss of

10.5 percent to 6.7 percent. As an example, the calculation results in a spread of 55 bp for a five-year BBB exposure. This rather small value comes from the fact that the approximated LGE is quite low due to the tight high-yield spreads at the time of the valuation. However, on the bases of a historical average the five-year BBB spread would be twice as high. This result illustrates the fact that a buy-and-hold investor with investment restrictions (regarding the credit quality) is subject to spread risk as this can be easily translated in the risk of a downgrade to junk.

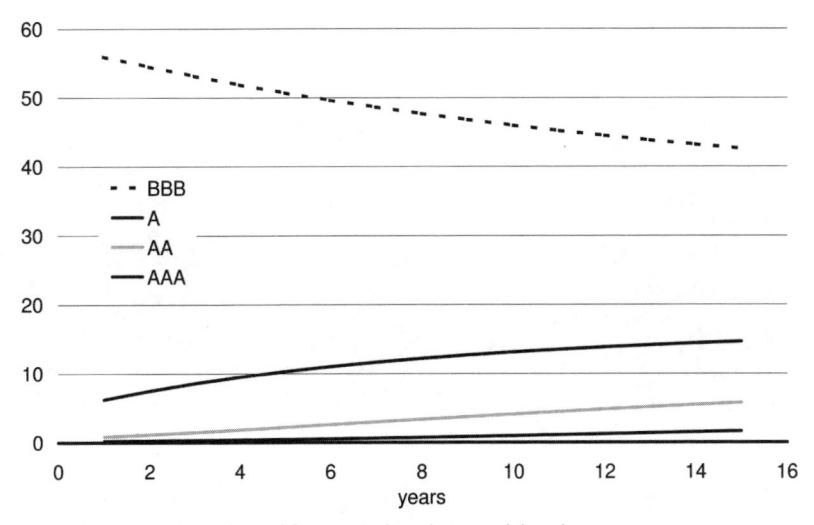

Fig. 8.8: Spread curves derived from a Markov-chain model, with a marked-to-market loss given by current high grade–high yield spread differences

9
Portfolio Models

Our previous analysis was focused on the valuation of single-name credit risk using various pricing approaches. In the following, we introduce pricing methods for credit-risky products in which the payoff, and therefore the value, depends on the portfolio loss distribution. In general, this product family covers a wide range of instruments, from securitized structures like ABS and MBS to derivative contracts, such as first-to-default baskets and single-tranche CDOs. To keep the following analysis straightforward, we will focus on derivatives structures. Nevertheless, most of the results can be transferred to the corresponding cash instruments without major problems.

Portfolio derivatives are synthetic structures that focus on aggregated credit risks on a portfolio level. Portfolio derivatives encompass n^{th}-to-default baskets and CDO tranches, but also tradable CDS indices, such as the iTraxx, and spread options written on these indices. However, the corresponding valuation mechanism for CDS indices is uncomplicated because CDS indices can simply be considered as portfolios of single-name CDS contracts. To value these contracts, we only have to calculate the sum of the values of the underlying CDS contracts. The derivation of the portfolio loss distribution is not necessary, because the value of the index contract only depends on the expected value of the portfolio loss distribution. This expected value, however, does not depend on the shape of the portfolio loss distribution, as we will shortly see. As a consequence, default dependency does not play a role here. The only major difficulty involved is the quotation mechanism, which differs from the one for single-name CDS contracts. While standard CDS contracts are quoted by the size of the premium payments (upfront payments are not involved, as the initial value of a standard contract is zero), a CDS index quotation translates the upfront payment involved into a spread measure, as the premium payment is fixed in advance. A similar argument applies to index spread options. Their value is not influenced significantly by the default correlation. For more details on this topic, please refer to the corresponding CDS index and options section in the chapter 10.

As we will shortly demonstrate, the values of the other two portfolio derivatives, the nth-to-default baskets and the CDO tranches, are strongly affected by the shape of the default distribution. As a consequence, modeling the default dependency is of central importance.

The following analysis is structured in the following steps. We begin by highlighting the differences and the similarities of nth-to-default baskets and CDO tranches. We will illustrate how the portfolio loss distribution affects the pricing. Note that at this stage of the analysis, we ignore term-structure effects and will concentrate on a single time period. In the next step, we introduce basic methods to derive the portfolio loss distribution under the assumption of independent credits, which means that the default correlation is zero. After introducing a general framework, we will show how to derive approximate solutions, which can be implemented in a spreadsheet calculation without major effort. Subsequently, the default dependency will be introduced into the model framework, and we will analyze the effect of default correlation on the portfolio loss distribution. In the last step, we show how our single-period framework has to be adjusted to integrate term-structure effects. We then present two valuation examples: one demonstrates an implementation for a first-to-default basket (using a so-called heterogeneous model) and the other focuses on the *homogeneous large portfolio model* for valuing standardized CDO tranches. We conclude the model presentation with a critical assessment of the widely used homogeneous portfolio assumption. Finally, we briefly discuss the issue of price discovery versus model competition. This raises the question of whether current correlation markets are driven by supply and demand or dominated by sophisticated pricing models.

Note that this presentation concentrates on the portfolio loss distribution and not on details of the derivative instruments. We only refer to them in a very basic way, because it helps to understand the scope of the modeling. Throughout the analysis, we consider a portfolio of m credits. Our basic assumptions are that all involved exposures have the same notional amount in the portfolio (i.e., are equally weighted) and share the same recovery rate. These are common assumptions for n^{th}-to-default baskets and (synthetic) CDO tranches. The idea of these assumptions is that, for the calculation of the portfolio loss distribution, we only need to derive the probability of n defaults in the pool. The associated loss for n defaults is then stated as $n \cdot (1 - \text{Rec}) \cdot N/m$, where the notional amount N corresponds to the volume of the entire pool, and N/m is the volume per exposure. For cash CDOs, the above-mentioned constraints of equal weightings and an average recovery rate might have to be lifted. This will have an effect only at one step of the following analysis. We will briefly indicate below how to cope with this problem. Finally, for some models we will apply additional assumptions such as an average probability of default for the underlying obligations. This will be highlighted below.

9.1 The Loss Distribution and its Impact on Portfolio Derivatives

The basic valuation procedure for portfolio derivatives, such as n^{th}-to-default baskets and CDO tranches, is similar to that for single-name credit risk. The only difference is that the survival probability for these contracts refers to a different type of risk. While a single-name contract is triggered if the single reference obligation defaults, an nth-to-default contract is triggered if the nth credit within a reference pool defaults. Therefore, the survival probability $S^{[n]}$ for an nth-to-default basket refers to the nth default.

$$V^{[n],\text{risky}} = S^{[n]} \times V^{\text{not triggered}} + (1 - S^{[n]}) \times V^{\text{triggered}} \qquad (9.1)$$

We indicate that a quantity refers to the nth default by using the superscript $[n]$. Nevertheless, knowing $S^{[n]}$ we can use the same valuation methodology as for single-name credit risk. Both contracts, the single-name and the nth-to-default basket, bear a binary risk profile: the contract either survives or default is triggered. An intermediate outcome between both final states, such as if the contract partly defaults, is impossible. This however, is different for a CDO tranche. Here, the contract can be also partly triggered. This is the case if, for example, 50 percent of the tranche notional amount is eroded by defaults. The value of the CDO does therefore not depend on a survival probability but on a survival amount $\hat{S}^{[a,b]}$. This quantity states the non-defaulted fraction of the underlying pool. Please note that there is an important subtlety involved here, as the recovery value of a defaulted obligation also belongs to the survival amount. The value of a CDO tranche $V^{[a,b],\text{risky}}$ with attachment point a and detachment point b (i.e., the lower and upper borders of the CDO tranche) is a function of the survival amount $\hat{S}^{[a,b]}$.

$$V^{[a,b],\text{risky}} = f(\hat{S}^{[a,b]}) \qquad (9.2)$$

In the simplest case of a zero coupon structure, this function would equal $\hat{S}^{[a,b]} \cdot N$, with N being the tranche notional amount.

As already mentioned, an nth-to-default basket is triggered when the nth default occurs in the pool. As an example, a 10th-to-default contract written on a basket of 20 constituents survives 9 defaults. The structure resembles that of a digital put option on the number of defaults. The survival indicator is 1 if the number of defaults is below the trigger level, while it is 0 if the number of defaults is at or above the trigger level. For CDO tranches the analogy to the option world is slightly different. The survival indicator is 1 if losses in the pool are below the attachment point (the lower border of the tranche) and 0 if they exceed the detachment point (the upper border of the tranche). Between the two points it decreases linearly. This resembles the payoff of a put spread option. In figure 9.1, we illustrate the two structures pictorially. Note that we refer to the abstract concept of survival indicators here, because the payoff of the derivatives is usually not the same as the payoff of the above-mentioned options. In case of an nth-to-default basket, the contract pays the recovery rate and not zero. Nevertheless, we can derive the quantities $S^{[n]}$ and $\hat{S}^{[a,b]}$ using this analogy.

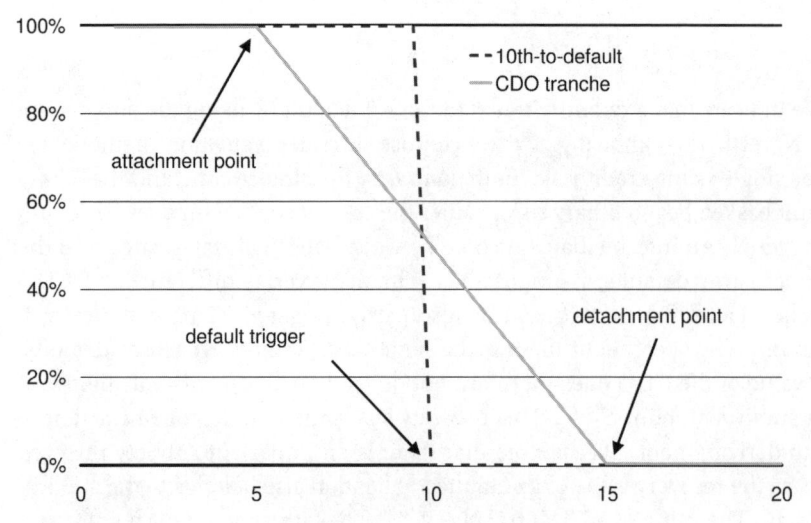

Fig. 9.1: Payoff profile for an nth-to-default basket and a CDO tranche

Figure 9.1 deals with an illustrative example with a highly unusual structure of a 10th-to-default basket and a CDO tranche, with attachment points 5 to 15 defaults, both on a pool of 20 equally weighted constituents. To keep the analysis simple, the tranche refers to a number of defaults and not losses. Nevertheless, we can transfer this profile onto the more common CDO structure using loss fractions by dividing attachment and detachment points by the number of constituents and multiplying the result by the average loss given default in the pool. The put spread option payoff which will be used to derive the survival amount $\hat{S}^{[a,b]}$ of a CDO tranche shown in figure 9.1 is stated in equation 9.3.

$$\text{Payoff}_{[a,b]}(x) = \frac{1}{b-a}[\max(b-x,0) - \max(a-x,0)] \quad (9.3)$$

To derive the survival probability $S^{[n]}$ for an nth-to-default basket and the survival amount $\hat{S}^{[a,b]}$ for a CDO tranche, we have to combine the payoffs with the corresponding probability distribution. For an nth-to-default basket this means we have to multiply the payoff for zero default by the probability of zero default, the payoff for one default by the probability of one default, and so on. In the following, $\pi(i)$ denotes the probability of i defaults in the underlying pool. Using this definition, we obtain a simple relation for the survival probability $S^{[n]}$. It is defined as the probability that less than n default events happen in the underlying basket:

$$S^{[n]} = \sum_{i=0}^{n-1} \pi(i) \quad 1 - S^{[n]} = \sum_{i=n}^{m} \pi(i) \quad \text{with } 0 \leq n \leq m \quad (9.4)$$

Note that in equation 9.4, the left sum runs from 0 to $n-1$, while in the right equation the $\pi(i)$ terms are added from n up to the number of constituents in the basket m. Therefore, the survival probability of a first-to-default basket is the probability of zero defaults $S^{[0]}$. As for the single-name credit risk, the complement of the survival probability $1 - S^{[n]}$ states the probability that the contract is triggered.

For CDO tranches, the corresponding relation is a little more complex. We distinguish between two different situations depending on the mathematical expression of the loss probability. We already introduced $\pi(i)$, the probability of i defaults in the basket. If we treat the CDO also as a finite pool of credits, in which all underlyings have the same exposure and the same recovery, we can use $\pi(i)$ for the valuation of CDO tranches as well. All we have to do is to reflect that a CDO tranche is usually written in terms of losses and not in terms of *numbers of defaulted constituents*. Hence, we have to take the loss given default into account. In this context, the survival amount $\hat{S}^{[a,b]}$ can be derived by the following equation:

$$\hat{S}^{[a,b]} = \sum_{i=0}^{m} \text{Payoff}_{[a,b]}\left(\frac{i}{m}(1-\text{Rec})\right) \cdot \pi(i) \quad (9.5)$$

Here, the loss incurred with n defaults is $\frac{n}{m}(1-\text{Rec})$, which we use as the argument in the payoff function. However, for non-equally weighted portfolios (i.e., those with different exposures to the underlyings) or where individual recovery rates have to be assigned, the $\pi(i)$, which states the probability of i defaults, is not appropriate. We might need a probability density function $\tilde{\pi}(x)$ with $0 \leq x \leq 1$, quantifying the probability density of exactly x percent losses. In this case, we use the following integral to quantify $\hat{S}^{[a,b]}$:

$$\hat{S}^{[a,b]} = \mathbb{E}\left(\text{Payoff}_{[a,b]}\right)$$
$$= \int_0^1 \text{Payoff}_{[a,b]}(x) \cdot \tilde{\pi}(x) dx \qquad (9.6)$$

Note that in this setup, x is the loss fraction including the loss given default and not the defaulted volume. Nevertheless, both the survival probability $S^{[n]}$ for n^{th}-to-default baskets and the survival amount $\hat{S}^{[a,b]}$ for CDO tranches depend on the full portfolio default probability $\pi(i)$. Note that the following analysis will be mainly based on the discrete probability $\pi(i)$. However, it is not difficult to transfer the results to deal with the continuous version $\tilde{\pi}(x)$.

In figure 9.2, we present example structures for the default probability function $\pi(i)$. All distributions have the same average default probability. They only differ on the basis of the default correlation parameter. It is interesting to note that the shape of the curves changes dramatically for different default correlations. Combining these charts with the payoff structures shown in figure 9.1 it becomes obvious that the survival probability $S^{[n]}$ and the survival amount $\hat{S}^{[a,b]}$ depend on the shape of the default density and therefore on the default correlation.

In the following, we will address the mathematical derivation of the default probability $\pi(i)$, excluding and including default correlation.

9.2 Independent Defaults

We start our analysis of the portfolio default probability function $\pi(i)$ with independent defaults using a simple two-asset example. Credit A has a probability of default of p_A and credit B one of p_B. Note that in contrast to our single-name analysis in figure 7.2, the subscripts now denote the reference company and not the time periods. We only consider a single, fixed time horizon (e.g., one year) for the default probabilities p_X ($X \in \{A, B\}$) and ignore term-structure effects. Their inclusion in the model framework will be shown later. Moreover, we assume that default events for both companies occur independently. In other words, default correlation is zero. Furthermore, the exposure to both assets in

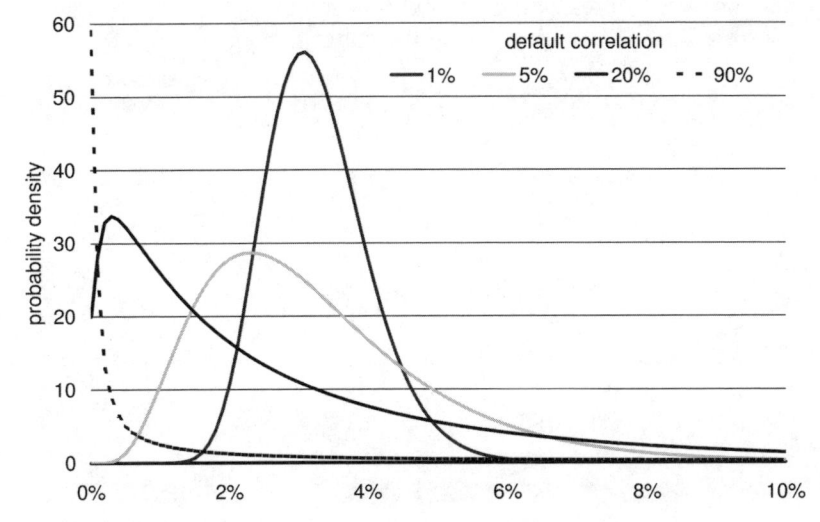

Fig. 9.2: Default probability function $\pi(i)$ for various default correlations

the portfolio is equally weighted and we assume the same recovery rate for both credits.

We are interested in determining the probabilities of zero, one, or two defaults in the portfolio of the two credits, that is $\pi(0)$, $\pi(1)$, and $\pi(2)$. As already stated, the loss incurred for a given number of defaults is simply the number of defaults times the LGD times the exposure (due to the same size and recovery rate). In figure 9.3, we show a simple branch model that illustrates how these probabilities are derived given the underlying single-name default probabilities.

The consecutive default branches refer to the different credits. Although we analyze the effect of each credit one-by-one, we do not care about different timings of default events. The order in which the individual branches are connected does not play any role. This simply refers to counting the number of defaulted credits at maturity regardless of when the default occurred.

The probability of zero defaults is stated as the probability that credit A survives times the probability that credit B survives: $(1 - p_A) \cdot (1 - p_B)$. The probability of two default events is derived as the probability that A defaults times the probability that B defaults: $p_A \cdot p_B$. For exactly one default, there are two realizations. Either A defaults and B survives, or vice versa. The corresponding probability of exactly one default is therefore the sum of the probabilities of these two realizations: $p_A \cdot (1 - p_B) + (1 - p_A) \cdot p_B$.

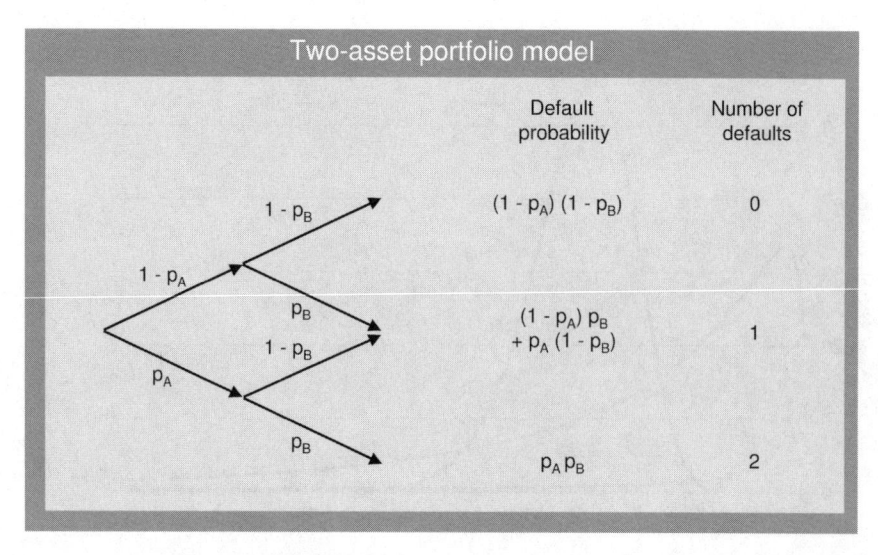

Fig. 9.3: Two-asset portfolio model

Using these results, we can derive some general characteristics of portfolio risk distributions. First, the sum of the probabilities of zero, one, and two defaults has to be 100 percent, because there are no other outcomes possible. Second, the expected value for the number of defaults is simply the sum of the individual default probabilities $p_A + p_B$. In table 9.1, we illustrate these results. The first column in table 9.1 records the number of defaults. In the second column we show the expanded probabilities, and in the third we present the product of the number of defaults and the corresponding probabilities. From this presentation, it is clear that the probabilities sum up to 1 (second column, last line) and that the expected number of defaults is given by $p_A + p_B$ (sum over the elements of the last column).

Tab. 9.1: Number of defaults and respective probability

n[†]	$\pi(n)$[‡]	$n \cdot \pi(n)$
0	$1 - p_A - p_B + p_A p_B$	0
1	$p_A + p_B - 2 p_A p_B$	$p_A + p_B - 2 p_A p_B$
2	$p_A p_B$	$2 \cdot p_A p_B$
$\sum$	1	$p_A + p_B$

[†] No. of defaults; [‡] probability of n defaults

Please recall that for pricing purposes we were interested in the survival probability, which is the complement of the default probability. However, the probabilities $\pi(i)$ themselves are not the complements of the survival probabilities. As an example, $\pi(1) = p_A \cdot (1 - p_B) + (1 - p_A) \cdot p_B$ states the probability that exactly one default occurs in the pool. The complement to this number is $1 - p_A \cdot (1 - p_B) - (1 - p_A) \cdot p_B$, which results in the probability of either zero or two defaults. However, n^{th}-to-default baskets are usually triggered when the nth credit in the basket defaults. Note that this is different from exactly n defaults, because the derivatives contract is also triggered if more than n credit defaults occur. So what we need is a cumulative default probability function. *Cumulative* in the current context refers to the number of defaults and not to a cumulation across time.

> **Example 21: Two-Asset First-to-Default Basket**
> A simple example will shed some light on the cumulative default probability in the context of portfolio losses. We consider a first-to-default basket on a portfolio of two assets A and B with the corresponding default probabilities p_A and p_B. The probability that this contract is triggered is the sum of the probabilities that exactly one default occurs $\pi(1)$ plus the probability that exactly two defaults occur $\pi(2)$. The only outcome under which the FTD survives is that there are zero defaults that is $\pi(0)$. It follows that the survival probability of the FTD is stated as $1 - \pi(1) - \pi(2) = 1 - p_A - p_B + 2p_A p_B - p_A p_B$, the complement to the default probability.

As shown in example 21, we need to add several $\pi(i)$ to quantify the probability that an nth-to-default basket is triggered. This result was also derived above in equation 9.4, which stated a general notation for survival and default probabilities in the nth-to-default framework. Moreover, the example in figure 9.1 illustrated how to derive the underlying probabilities $\pi(i)$. Unfortunately, generating analytic expressions for $\pi(i)$ using this tree framework is appropriate only for small basket sizes. For larger baskets this approach in not feasible, as the number of terms needed to evaluate the $\pi(i)$ terms grows rapidly with the size of the basket. Although the number of end points in a recombining tree is only $m + 1$ for m constituents, the number of possible paths through the tree, which determines the number of terms to be considered, amounts to 2^m. Spreadsheet calculations for basket sizes greater than 10 constituents become very unwieldy, as 1024 terms have to be evaluated.

However, there are some tricks to deal with this scaling problem. The simplest solution is appropriate for first-to-default baskets. In this case, the number of paths in the tree that we have to evaluate shrinks to one because the survival probability of the contract is the probability of zero default. Therefore, it can be derived as $\prod_X (1 - p_X)$. If we do not need the rest of the distribution, this is indeed the best way. Unfortunately, using this trick helps neither for second- or third-to-default baskets, which however are not frequently traded, nor for CDO tranches. For the latter, deriving the full distribution is imperative. However, we can derive the full probability distribution either numerically or analytically by applying additional assumptions to the model, which allow us to find manageable analytical solutions. Using numerical techniques either leads to iterative procedures for the construction of the loss distribution (see, for example, methods from Hull and White[57], Gregory et al.[58], and Anderson et al.[59]) or to Monte Carlo simulations.[26]

Although the numerical techniques are not difficult to implement (here especially the Hull-White model has to be mentioned) and work quite well, we concentrate on the derivation of the analytical solutions by applying additional assumptions, as this leads, in our view, to further insight into the modeling framework. Following the derivation, we will address the limitations and errors stemming from the additional assumptions by comparing the simplified analytical solutions with exact numerical results.

The major difficulty with the scaling problem discussed above was the sheer number of different terms one has to evaluate as the number of constituents grows. A simple assumption helps to reduce the number of terms dramatically. Instead of using heterogeneous default probabilities p_X for all the constituents, we simply use an average default probability $\bar{p}$ in the tree model. This approach refers to a homogeneous portfolio assumption. Although the homogeneous pool assumption causes some problems (see section 9.8), it is very useful, as it results in a simple relation for the probability $\pi(i)$ of i defaults in a pool of m constituents. The result is the famous probability function of the binomial distribution:

$$\pi(i) = \frac{m!}{i!(m-i)!} \bar{p}^i (1-\bar{p})^{m-i} \qquad (9.7)$$

This is an interesting outcome because, using the assumption of a homogeneous pool, the probabilities $\pi(i)$ can be simply calculated from the binomial distribution. Furthermore, for larger pools, that is, $m \to \infty$, we can use other approximations for the binomial distribution, such as the Poisson or the normal distribution, to arrive at numerical results. All three distributions play a central role in credit risk management. As already stated, the binomial distribution is appropriate for analyzing smaller pools, that is, for pricing n^{th}-to-default baskets. The Poisson distribution is the central building block in the *CreditRisk+* framework, an actuarial portfolio risk model, and finally, the normal distribution is used in the *homogeneous large portfolio* approximation, which goes back to Vasicek.[60,61] In table 9.2, we summarized the central features of the three distributions.

Tab. 9.2: Probability functions and their properties for quantifying the portfolio default probabilities $\pi(i)$

	Probability function	Expectation value	Variance
Binomial	$\frac{m!}{i!(m-i)!}\bar{p}^i(1-\bar{p})^{m-i}$	$m\bar{p}$	$m\bar{p}(1-\bar{p})$
Poisson[†,‡]	$\frac{\lambda^i}{i!}e^{-\lambda}$	λ	λ
Normal[†]	$\frac{1}{\sigma\sqrt{2\pi}}\exp(-\frac{(x-\mu)^2}{2\sigma^2})$	μ	σ^2

[†] for $m \to \infty$; [‡] $\lambda = m\bar{p}$

In order to approximate $\pi(i)$ (i.e., the probability of i defaults) for a large but finite pool with m constituents and an average default probability of $\bar{p}$ using the Poisson distribution, the λ parameter has to be set to $m\bar{p}$. For using the normal distribution, we set $\mu = m\bar{p}$ and $\sigma^2 = m\bar{p}(1-\bar{p})$.

Nevertheless, it is important to note that the remainder of the derivation of the full portfolio default probability function (i.e., the integration of the default dependency below) can be treated irrespective of a specific technique to derive the uncorrelated portfolio default probability function $\pi(i)$. To refer to a general procedure to generate the probability $\pi(i)$ of i defaults in the basket, we introduce $\Xi(i, p_A, p_B, \ldots)$. It can be a Monte Carlo simulation, a numerical solution such as the Hull-White model, or a binomial distribution. In the latter case, we would write more appropriately $\Xi(i, \bar{p})$ as all individual default probabilities p_X are the same. For the remainder of the analysis, it is sufficient to know that we have an appropriate *portfolio loss generator* $\Xi(i, p_A, p_B, \ldots)$.

For cash CDO tranches, our simplified approach with equally weighted constituents (same notional amount for all underlyings) and average recovery rates might not be applicable. Nevertheless, we can use most of the concepts shown in this chapter. The only step we have to modify is the generation of the portfolio default density. For unequally weighted pools with different recovery rates for each obligor, determining the probability $\pi(i)$ of i defaults is not sufficient, as

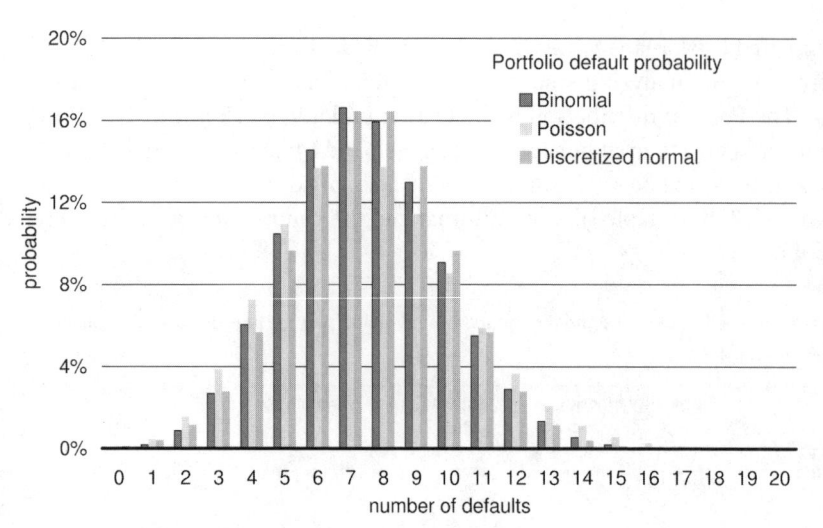

Fig. 9.4: Resulting probabilities using various portfolio default distributions for $m = 30$ and $\bar{p} = 25\%$

defaults of different obligors cause different losses. In this scenario, we have to either calculate average exposures and average recovery rates, resulting in the same setup as shown above, or we have to determine the loss density $\tilde{\pi}(x)$ directly, without using $\pi(i)$ as an intermediate step. The loss density function $\tilde{\pi}(x)$ states the probability of a certain loss of, for example, 3 percent in the underlying pool, instead of referring to a certain number of defaults. Our simple portfolio loss generators (binomial and normal distribution, etc.) are not the proper tools for this task. We have to use either a Monte Carlo simulation or a numerical model, which is capable of dealing with different exposures and recovery rates in the pool. Here, the Hull-White model is an appropriate candidate.

9.3 Default Dependency

Default dependency (related to default events) or default correlation (related to reasonably-defined random variables) is the central topic in modeling portfolio derivatives. Therefore, these products are also called correlation derivatives. Default correlation is the main factor that affects prices and sensitivities of tranches. As a consequence, these products are usually traded at separated correlation trading desks.

What does default correlation actually mean? Recall that in our introduction of credit risk pricing models, we stated that credit risk bears two sorts of risks: default arrival risk and spread risk. The first point reflects the risk that a default occurs in the holding period of an asset, involving large losses. The second refers to the risk that the market price for the default risk might change. Default correlation addresses the dependency in the default arrival risk. The modeling aims at quantifying the joint probability that credits A and B default.

Following Li[27], default dependency can be understood either as a discrete default correlation or as a survival time correlation. The first is based on a single period, for example, one year. The latter is the more general concept, since we can easily calculate the discrete correlation once we have the joint distribution of the individual survival times. Single-name default modeling aims at quantifying the distribution of the time until default for a single obligor. In this context, default dependency modeling deals with the joint probability distribution of time until default. In equation 7.14, we defined the cumulative default probability as $F_A(\tau) = \mathbb{P}(\tau_A^* \leq \tau)$, with τ_A^* being the random time until default for credit A. In this context, the joint cumulative default probability function for credits A and B is stated as $F_{A,B}(\tau_A, \tau_B) = \mathbb{P}(\tau_A^* \leq \tau_A, \tau_B^* \leq \tau_B)$. The human lifetime in an illustrative example. The probability that two persons die within the next hour will be rather small, unless they sit in the same car and approach a wall with high speed. The probability that the same two persons die within the next hundred years is almost 100 percent regardless of whether they sit in the same car or not.

The mathematical tool to describe joint distributions is the *copula approach*. These are functions that link individual marginal distributions to a joint distribution. There are several copulas discussed in literature that seem to be applicable to credit risk: Gaussian, Student-t, or the class of Archimedean copulas (see David Li's article[27] and Philipp Schönbucher's book for an introduction to copula models in credit risk). We implicitly use the Gaussian copula in the HLPGC model, which is described more detailed in section 9.6.

But how should one measure the default correlation and parametrize the model? A first guess would be to analyze the correlation between spread changes of two credits in order to measure the default correlation. However, this is not the best approach and it is not market standard. Confusion may arise due to the term *correlation*, which is somewhat misleading. The more precise expression is *default dependency*. A simple example illustrates the problem. We assume a model economy with just two competing companies. Let's further assume that they have a comparable market share and economic strength, so that we cannot predict which company will prevail. Any piece of information that influences the specific market will affect spreads of both companies in the same manner. This results in a high level of spread correlation. But what happens if one of these companies defaults? Will the other company default as well? Or will this event result in a strengthening of the surviving company due to a rising market share? The latter case indicates that a high level of spread correlation does not necessarily imply a high level of default dependency. Consequently, there are two sources of correlation: default occurrence risk and spread risk. The first gives rise to the concept of default dependency or default correlation, which is central to the valuation of credit portfolio derivatives.

The market standard for integrating default dependency or default correlation into the pricing relations are the so-called factor models. In this concept, one or more factors control the default dependency in an economy. The central concept behind this approach is based on a simplified structural model. In a structural model, default is triggered if the firm value – in other words the asset value – falls below the default barrier. In the classical Merton approach, this barrier is the face value of the debt. To achieve a certain level of default dependency between two firms, one assumes correlated dynamics of the firm values.

The value of firm A's assets is denoted by A_A, which is modeled as a normally distributed random variable. For B, the corresponding asset value is A_B. To incorporate the default risk, we need the default barriers K_A and K_B that trigger the default. As in the previous analysis, we ignore that the default probabilities p_A and p_B are time-dependent for the moment to facilitate the analysis. However, the integration of the time dependency is not difficult. We only need to allow a time dependency in the default barriers K_A and K_B. A default event occurs if the asset value falls below the default barrier. This default condition is expressed in the following relation:

$$A_X \leq K_X \Rightarrow \text{default} \quad (X \in \{A, B\}) \tag{9.8}$$

In this equation, A_X is stochastic, while K_X is deterministic. For the sake of completeness, we add that A_X and K_X would depend on the time to maturity if we would consider time-dependent probabilities. Recall that the major problem with structural models was that it is very difficult to fit the model parameters, such as the asset value and the default barrier, to achieve reasonable default probabilities. The trick of this approach is that we do not need to know the real values of A_X and K_X explicitly. We only need the condition that the probability of A_X hitting the default barrier K_X equals the already known default probability p_X:

$$\mathbb{P}(A_X \leq K_X) = p_X \quad (X \in \{A, B\}) \tag{9.9}$$

We are free to specify a distribution function for A_X that meets our view of the asset distribution. The model approach does not rely on a specific one. Nevertheless, the results of the dependency modeling depend on this distribution function. A common method is to set the absolute value of A_X to zero and assume that A_X is standard normally distributed. However, to keep our analysis general, we assume that A_X is distributed by $G(x)$, an arbitrary distribution function. Below, we will present an example using the standard normal distribution $\Phi(x)$. We can now use the inverse of the arbitrary cumulated distribution $G^{-1}(x)$ to calculate the default barrier K_X from p_X.

$$K_X = G^{-1}(p_X) \tag{9.10}$$

It is interesting to note that in this approach we inverted the concept of structural models. Usually, a classical structural model attempts to derive the credit spread from asset value and asset volatility. The default barrier is estimated from balance sheet data, such as the debt-to-equity ratio. Here, the asset value is set to zero, the asset volatility is standardized to 1, and the default boundary is derived from spread data and not vice versa.

In order to model the default dependency, we assume that the joint firm-value distributions involve a certain level of correlation $\rho(A_A, A_B) = \rho_{AB}$. However, there is a broad debate among market participants as to how to properly parametrize these correlations. Standard time series analysis is not feasible, as the firm values are usually not available. That is, by the way, the main problem of all structural models. A common solution is to calculate the correlations of the corresponding equity returns and simply assume that equity and firm-value correlation are identical. This is done in the standard CreditMetrics approach for measuring credit portfolio risk. More sophisticated approaches translate equity prices into firm values before deriving the correlations. A very crude way would be to simply add the face value of the corporate debt to the equity value. KMV, which provides another widely used credit portfolio model, uses another approach. In the structural model framework, the equity value E is derived as a call option on the firm's assets A, with the debt F being the strike price and σ_A the asset volatility: $E = \text{call}(A, F, \sigma_A)$. By making some simplifying assumptions about the capital structure of the company, we can back out the asset value A from traded equity prices. The central difficulty is that the asset volatility σ_A is also not available. KMV uses an iterative technique to calibrate σ_A in their model.

However, such generalized default dependency models are used in portfolio risk measurement, rather than in pricing. We indicated that CreditMetrics and KMV use it to derive joint default probabilities. Unfortunately, the size of the correlation matrix grows rapidly with the number of constituents, that is, it comprises $n(n-1)/2$ correlations. For example, this approach for modeling the joint default probability distribution of the iTraxx basket with 125 constituents (i.e., for pricing a CDO tranche) would require 7750 pairwise correlation parameters. This is hardly feasible. Consequently, the size of the correlation matrix has to be reduced significantly. This can be done using factor models. This approach maps the individual exposure into groups such as industries and regions. The default dependency is then modeled by providing the correlation of the firm value to a group-specific factor.

State-of-the-art pricing models rely on the factor approach to model default dependency. Furthermore, it is common market practice to use only one factor, that is, to rely on a single-factor model. The economic rationale is that the asset value A_X of the obligor X features a correlation ρ_X to a common market factor M, maybe representing the state of the business cycle:

$$A_X = \sqrt{\rho_X} \cdot M + \sqrt{1-\rho_X} \cdot \epsilon_X \quad \text{with } 0 \leq \rho_X \leq 1 \qquad (9.11)$$

The random variable ϵ_X describes the idiosyncratic, firm-specific default risk. Although all asset values are correlated with a common risk factor M, the individual defaults are independent, conditional on the level of the market factor M, since ϵ_X themselves are independent. If the correlation parameter is zero ($\rho_X = 0$), there is no effect from the market factor. The portfolio risk is completely driven by individual credit risks. If $\rho_X = 1$, the default risk of the company X is solely driven by the market factor M; then firm-specific factors do not play any role. Equation 9.11 states that the asset values A_X are conditional on the systematic risk factor M, driven by the independent distributed random variables ϵ_X. By using the default trigger definition of equation 9.8, we obtain:

$$\sqrt{\rho_X} \cdot M + \sqrt{1-\rho_X} \cdot \epsilon_X \leq K_X \text{ or}$$
$$\epsilon_X \leq \frac{K_X - \sqrt{\rho_X} \cdot M}{\sqrt{1-\rho_X}} \qquad (9.12)$$

From equation 9.12 we can derive the probability of a default $p_{X|M}$ conditional on the level of the risk factor M:

$$p_{X|M} = \mathbb{P}\left(A_X \leq K_X | M\right) = \mathbb{P}\left[\epsilon_X \leq \frac{K_X - \sqrt{\rho_X} \cdot M}{\sqrt{1-\rho_X}} \bigg| M \right] \qquad (9.13)$$

To arrive at an explicit relation for the default dependency structure we need to specify distribution functions for ϵ_X and M. For the sake of generality, we assume that ϵ_X follows the distribution $H(x)$ and M follows the distribution $Q(x)$. Note that stipulating the distribution functions for ϵ_X and M implicitly determines the distribution function for A_X (see equation 9.11). Therefore, the distribution function $G(x)$ for A_X cannot be chosen arbitrarily. $G(x)$ is determined by $H(x)$ and $Q(x)$.

Applying the distribution function $H(x)$ to equation 9.13 we obtain an expression for $p_{X|M}$:

$$p_{X|M} = H\left(\frac{K_X - \sqrt{\rho_X} \cdot M}{\sqrt{1-\rho_X}}\right) = H\left(\frac{G^{-1}(p_X) - \sqrt{\rho_X} \cdot M}{\sqrt{1-\rho_X}}\right) \qquad (9.14)$$

Using equation 9.14, we can calculate the individual default probabilities $p_{X|M}$ conditional on the level of the market factor M. However, this is not yet exactly what we need to know for valuing correlation derivatives. Above, we showed that we need the probability $\pi(i)$ that i defaults occur in the underlying pool. This quantity can be derived by, first, calculating the probability $\pi(i|M)$ of i default conditional on M and, second, calculating the expected value of this quantity. $\pi(i|M)$ is derived using one of the above-mentioned methods to generate a distribution function based on the single-name probabilities: $\pi(i|M) = \Xi(i, p_{A|M}, p_{B|M}, \ldots)$. In equation 9.15, $q(M)$ is the probability density function for the market factor M, or $q(M) = Q'(M)$, provided M is continuously distributed.

$$\pi(i) = \int_{-\infty}^{+\infty} \pi(i|M) q(M) dM \qquad (9.15)$$

To summarize, we generated the portfolio default distribution function $\pi(i)$ by performing the following steps:

1. Derive the individual default probabilities p_X for the underlying exposure X for a given time horizon.
2. Calculate the conditional default probabilities $p_{X|M}$ which depend on the correlation parameters ρ_X. This involves the specification of the asset value distribution $G(x)$ and the distribution $H(x)$ for the individual default driver ϵ_X. For pricing purposes, market participants frequently use so-called flat correlation. This means that one average correlation parameter ρ is used for all constituents.
3. Obtain the probability $\pi(i|M)$ of i defaults conditional on the level of the market factor M using one of the above-mentioned distribution generators $\Xi(i, p_{A|M}, p_{B|M}, \ldots)$. If a simplified approach is used (e.g., the

binomial distribution based on a homogeneous portfolio assumption), one has to adjust the preceding steps to deal with the homogeneous probability of default $\bar{p}$, which can, for example, be derived by averaging over the individual probabilities p_X in the first step.

4. Calculate the unconditional probability $\pi(i)$ of i defaults by integrating the product of the conditional probabilities $\pi(i|M)$ and the probability density of the market factor denoted by $q(M)$. For this step, we have to specify the distribution function $Q(M)$. The integral will have to be solved numerically in most cases, for example, by approximating it as a sum over discrete steps in the realization of M.

The specification of asset value distribution $G(x)$, the distribution function of the individual default driver $H(x)$ and the distribution function for the market factor $Q(x)$ determine a specific default dependency model. As mentioned above, it is common practice to use the standard normal distribution for ϵ_X and M, which are assumed to be independently distributed. According to equation 9.11, A_X will also follow a standard normal distribution. This results in a so-called Gaussian copula model.

To price a portfolio derivatives contract an additional step has to be implemented. We have to evaluate the survival probability function $S^{[n]}$ for the nth-to-default basket or the expected survival amount $\hat{S}^{[a,b]}$ for a CDO tranche. Here, we use the payoff functions for the two instrument types defined above.

9.4 Term-Structure Effects

The previous analysis was attributed to a single period, without dealing with term structure effects for $\pi(i)$ and consequently for $S^{[n]}$ and $\hat{S}^{[a,b]}$. However, portfolio derivatives involve several cash flows, and we have to consider therefore multiple time horizons for the survival probabilities. To be more specific, we need the survival probability function to depend on the time to maturity τ: $S^{[n]}(\tau)$ and $S^{[a,b]}(\tau)$. There are at least two approaches to deal with this time-dependency issue: a simple one, which involves the scaling of a single-period survival probability function, and a more complex one, in which the full probability distribution is derived for each time step. To keep the notation simple, we focus on the survival probability function $S^{[n]}(\tau)$ for an nth-to-default basket. The derivation for the corresponding survival amount $S^{[a,b]}(\tau)$ for CDO tranches is analogous.

For the simple scaling approach, we only calculate the survival probability function $S^{[n]}(\tau_m)$ up to the maturity date of the contract τ_m by explicitly using the model derived above. The additional values $S^{[n]}(\tau_i)$ for the time intervals τ_i are simply calculated by scaling $S^{[n]}(\tau_m)$:

$$S^{[n]}(\tau_i) \approx (S^{[n]}(\tau_m))^{\frac{\tau_i}{\tau_m}} \quad \text{for } i = 0, 1, 2, \ldots, m$$
$$= e^{-\gamma_n \tau_i} \quad \text{with } \gamma_n = -\frac{1}{\tau_m} \ln(S^{[n]}(\tau_m)) \tag{9.16}$$

In the last line of equation 9.16, we show that this approach essentially means to transfer the survival probability up to the maturity date into a time independent hazard rate γ_n for a default event in the underlying pool. In terms of a CDO tranche, the hazard rate that corresponds to the survival amount $\hat{S}^{[a,b]}$ would refer to an instantaneous loss rate, which already accounts for the recovery rate. From a mathematical point of view, this time evolution of the survival probability does not follow the outlined processes, which is mathematically inconsistent. Nevertheless, it is suitable and frequently used for simple and approximative analysis.

To arrive at the full probability distribution for each time step, we have to expand the previous analysis to time-dependent default probabilities. However, this is not a difficult task. We start with time-depending default probabilities $p_X(\tau)$. This time-dependency requires that the default barrier $K_X(\tau)$ is a time-dependent function as well (see equation 9.9). Assuming that the default correlation parameter ρ_X is time independent and that the stochastic process that drives M has zero drift, we can derive a time-dependent variant of equation 9.14 resulting in the time-dependent conditional default probabilities $p_{X|M}(\tau)$. These can now be used in the algorithm outlined above to arrive at a probability distribution for each time step.

9.5 Valuing First-to-Default Baskets

To turn the theoretical analysis into a practical example, we derive the fair spread of a 5Y first-to-default basket using the simplest heterogeneous model to generate the portfolio default density: multiplying the survival probabilities for all constituents. We consider a basket with five constituents, an average recovery rate of 40 percent, and an average (flat) default correlation parameter ρ of 0, 20, 50 and 90 percent. The five-year credit spreads for the underlyings and the corresponding default probabilities are given in table 9.3. We used an approximation to derive the cumulated default probabilities:

$$p_X(\tau) = 1 - \exp(-\text{spread} \cdot \tau/(1 - \text{Rec})) \, .$$

Tab. 9.3: Pool data for a first-to-default basket

Credit	5Y spread [bp]	$p_X(5)$ [%]
A	50	4.08
B	55	4.48
C	60	4.88
D	70	5.67
E	80	6.45
SOS	315	–

Rec = 40%; SOS = sum-of-all-spreads

As shown above, the survival probability for a first-to-default basket is simply the probability of zero defaults; it can be derived as:

$$\pi(0) = \prod_{X=A,B,\ldots,E} (1 - p_X(5))$$

In the uncorrelated case this results in 76.91 percent using the values of $p_X(5)$ in table 9.3. To integrate the correlation, we have to derive the default probabilities $\pi(0|M)$ conditional on M, for which we use equation 9.14. To keep the analysis simple, we choose the standard normal distribution function for the distribution functions $H(x)$ and $Q(x)$, and accordingly for $G(x)$. This refers to the so-called Gaussian copula model.

To derive the probability $\pi(0|M)$ of zero default conditional on M, we simply use the equation above with the conditional default probabilities $p_{X|M}$: $\pi(0|M) = \prod_X (1 - p_{X|M}(5))$. To derive the conditional default probabilities $p_{X|M}(5)$, we have to apply the respective correlation parameter ρ. In table 9.4, we compiled the values for $\pi(0|M)$ and the corresponding densities $q(M)$ for $M = -5, \ldots, 5$. This was done for three different levels of the default correlation ρ. Recall that in the current example, $q(M)$ is the standard normal density function $\phi(M)$. The unconditional probability of zero defaults $\pi(0)$ is approximately derived as the weighted sum of the conditional probability of zero defaults $\pi(0|M)$ using the corresponding $q(M)$ as weightings: $\pi(0) = \sum_M \pi(0|M) \cdot q(M)$. To transfer the $\pi(0)$, which states the survival probability, into a credit spread, we use the relation spread $= -\ln(\pi(0))/5$, which corresponds to the approximation in equation 9.16.

It is interesting to note that $\pi(0|M)$ as a function of the default correlation ρ starts as a flat curve for $\rho = 0$ and changes its shape to a Heavyside function for increasing default correlation. For 90 percent default correlation, the survival probability is 0 percent for a level of the market factor below -1 and 100 percent

Tab. 9.4: Intermediate and final results for the valuation of an FTD basket for various default correlation levels

M	$q(M)$	$\pi(0\|M)$ [%]			
	[%]	$\rho=0\%$	$\rho=20\%$	$\rho=50\%$	$\rho=90\%$
-5	0.0001	76.91	0.10	0.00	0.00
-4	0.0134	76.91	1.51	0.00	0.00
-3	0.4432	76.91	9.85	0.09	0.00
-2	5.3991	76.91	32.00	9.36	0.03
-1	24.1971	76.91	61.63	60.61	91.68
0	39.8942	76.91	84.13	94.80	100.00
1	24.1971	76.91	95.06	99.76	100.00
2	5.3991	76.91	98.81	100.00	100.00
3	0.4432	76.91	99.77	100.00	100.00
4	0.0134	76.91	99.97	100.00	100.00
5	0.0001	76.91	100.00	100.00	100.00
$\pi(0)$		76.91	79.04	82.99	92.13
Spread		315.00	282.28	223.81	98.33
%-SOS		100.0	89.6	71.1	31.2

Rec = 40%; SOS = sum-of-all-spreads

for a level of M above -1. The spread also shows the well-known behavior for FTD baskets. For 0 percent default correlation, the FTD spread equals the sum-of-all-spreads (SOS), while for increasing default correlation the FTD spread declines to the level of the highest constituent. In our example, the spread for 90 percent default correlation is 92.13 bp, compared to a level of 80 bp for credit E.

Note that for this calculation, some crucial simplifications have been made. For example, we used a very coarse integration grid for the market factor M with only 11 points ($M = -5, 4, \ldots, 5$). This causes unreliable results, especially for large default correlations, because $\pi(0|M)$ changes rapidly around $M = -1$. For real calculation one should use smaller step sizes. Moreover, we switched from the credit spread into the default probability and back using a simple rule of thumb. For serious pricing, a proper bootstrapping of the default probabilities from the CDS term structure has to be implemented, as well as a correct pricing algorithm to derive the par spread of the swap contract. Nevertheless, the illustrated concepts give a reasonable back-of-the-envelope approximation.

9.6 Valuing CDO Tranches with the HLPGC Model

The most frequently used model to evaluate CDO tranches is the so-called homogeneous large portfolio model in conjunction with a Gaussian copula for the default dependency. The model, which is sometime called the *homogeneous large portfolio Gaussian copula* (HLPGC) model, dates back to the simple Vasicek model for portfolio credit risk.[60,61] It is a factor model, such as introduced above, using a simplified firm-value approach to model the default dependency. It has only a few parameters and can easily be implemented in a spreadsheet. Due to its simplicity, it is a good candidate for tutorial purposes and serves as a vehicle to explore basic features of default correlation – although it appears too simplistic to serve as a real pricing model. However, major market participants agreed to use it for price quotation.

We start with the most immediate question: What does *homogeneous large portfolio Gaussian copula* mean? The answer to this question already reveals a lot about the characteristics and the (crude) approximations of the model.

- *Homogeneous*: This addresses the constituting credits of the underlying pool. It is assumed that they all have the same size, the same time-dependent default probability $\bar{p}$, the same recovery rate Rec, and the same correlation parameter ρ. Moreover, the default probability is usually calculated using the same simple approximation as in the FTD example above: $\bar{p} = 1 - \exp(-\text{spread} \cdot \tau/(1 - \text{Rec}))$. The reason for these assumptions is to reduce the number of parameters we need for the model. And the reduction is significant, especially if the pool is large (see also the next point): instead of $m(m+1)$ parameters in the general case we just need three. This means that the number of parameters is independent of the size of the pool, which is of advantage especially for large pools. The approach is to take some kind of portfolio average for each parameter. The economic impact of this approximation can be severe. To lift it means that we have to implement a more complex procedure to solve for the probability $\pi(i) = \Xi(i, p_A, p_B, \ldots)$ that is capable of dealing with more than just one average default probability (heterogeneous portfolios), for example, the Hull-White model.
- *Large*: This addresses the size and the granularity of the pool. We assume that the pool is sufficiently large, that it has infinite constituents. Thus, the expected loss function is continuous. Consider a small pool with 10 equally-sized constituents. Here, the expected loss function is not continuous, since a single default causes a loss of 10 percent (we as-

sume 0 percent recovery). The advantage behind this approximation is that we can handle the continuous distribution functions analytically (i.e., the Gaussian distribution, see next point). Since CDOs are usually written on quite large pools (for smaller ones n^{th}-to-default baskets are more common), this assumption is not too critical. Dropping this assumption means using a discrete distribution function (such as the binomial distribution) instead of a continuous function.

- *Gaussian copula*: This topic is the heart of modeling the default dependency structure. With Gaussian copula we indicate that the default correlation is incorporated via correlated stochastic processes for the firm values that involve the Gaussian distribution function. In the framework derived above this means that $H(x)$ and $Q(x)$, and accordingly $G(x)$, represent standard normal distributions. This type of default correlation is widely used (it is, for example, similar to the CreditMetrics approach) and well accepted.

Having said a lot about the characteristics of the model, we try to summarize some model criticism concerning economic properties, which we neglect, and ask whether we can adjust the model to account for them.

- *Spread dispersion*: It is a harsh approximation to assume that all credits in the pool have the same credit spread and hence the same default probability. The spread dispersion in the pool will affect the calculated prices. We will address this topic separately. Unfortunately, this is one of the basic assumptions of the model.
- *Bilateral default correlation*: The average pool correlation approach, which we adopt by using the discussed model, does not account for bilateral correlation effects. To shed some light on the limitations, we just have to think about economic scenarios that involve individual correlations, for example, sector or regional correlation or company–subcontractor relations.
- *Term structure of credit spreads*: Usually one uses a flat spread level in the model, but this approximation is not necessary. We can easily calculate the default probability using an average term structure, if we have one.
- *Uncertainty of recovery*: Assuming statistical independence between recovery rates and default probabilities, we can incorporate the recovery uncertainty in the model without major problems.
- *Spread correlation*: Since spreads are modeled as a non-stochastic, average value, we integrate a spread correlation. However, spread correlation does not affect prices of tranches in a critical way.

Now we will address the mathematical characteristics of the homogeneous large portfolio model. We consider an infinitely large pool of equally weighted single-name credits. For the practical implementation, we assume that the portfolio of 125 names which makes up the iTraxx index is large enough to be treated as infinite. For CDS indices, such as the iTraxx, there are standardized tranches available in the market. We assume that the average spread in the portfolio is 40 bp. Furthermore, we consider an average recovery rate of 40 percent. The analyzed CDO tranche has a time to maturity of five years. The corresponding average default probability for five years is given by $\bar{p} = 1 - \exp(-\text{spread} \cdot \tau/(1 - \text{Rec}))$. In the current example it is 3.28 percent. The next step is to turn this unconditional default probability into a conditional default probability $\bar{p}_{|M}$ using the same procedure as for the first-to-default basket above. We use equation 9.14 together with the average default probability $\bar{p}$ and the standard normal distribution function $\Phi(x)$ for $G(x)$, $H(x)$, and $Q(x)$.

Following the evaluating of the conditional default probability $\bar{p}_{|M}$, our usual procedure was to derive the probability $\pi(i|M)$ of i defaults in the basket (or $\tilde{\pi}(x|M)$ of x percent defaults), using the distribution generator $\Xi(i, \bar{p})$. However, in this model framework, we do not need this step. The fraction of companies that are expected to default in the underlying pool is already given by $\bar{p}_{|M}$, as we assumed an infinitely large portfolio. Therefore, we can immediately calculate the payoff of the tranche conditional on the level of the market factor M using the payoff definition in equation 9.3 and derive the unconditional survival amount $\hat{S}^{[a,b]}$ by integrating the product of the $\bar{p}_{|M}$ and the density function of M. We only have to multiply $\bar{p}_{|M}$ by the loss given default $(1 - \text{Rec})$ to arrive at the expected loss fraction:

$$\hat{S}^{[a,b]} = \int_{-\infty}^{+\infty} \text{Payoff}_{[a,b]}(\bar{p}_{|M} \cdot (1 - \text{Rec})) \cdot \varphi(M) dM \qquad (9.17)$$

In table 9.5, we compiled the intermediate results of our example valuation of a 3–6% mezzanine tranche for a default correlation parameter of 0, 5, 20, and 90 percent. We stated the conditional survival amounts $\hat{S}^{[a,b]}_{|M}$ and the corresponding probabilities for the market factor M. The unconditional survival amount $\hat{S}^{[a,b]}$ is derived as a weighted sum of the conditional survival amounts, using the $q(M)$ as weighting factors: $\hat{S}^{[a,b]} = \sum_M \hat{S}^{[a,b]}_{|M} \cdot q(M)$. To transfer the $\hat{S}^{[a,b]}$, which states the survival amount, into a credit spread, we use the relation spread $= -\ln(\hat{S}^{[a,b]})/5$, which corresponds to the approximation in equation 9.16.

Tab. 9.5: Intermediate and final results for the valuation of a 3–6% mezzanine CDO tranche for various default correlation levels

M	$q(M)$	$\hat{S}^{[a,b]}_{|M}$ [%]			
	[%]	$\rho=0\%$	$\rho=5\%$	$\rho=20\%$	$\rho=90\%$
-5	0.0001	100.00	0.00	0.00	0.00
-4	0.0134	100.00	0.00	0.00	0.00
-3	0.4432	100.00	0.00	0.00	0.00
-2	5.3991	100.00	47.39	0.00	0.00
-1	24.1971	100.00	100.00	80.93	100.00
0	39.8942	100.00	100.00	100.00	100.00
1	24.1971	100.00	100.00	100.00	100.00
2	5.3991	100.00	100.00	100.00	100.00
3	0.4432	100.00	100.00	100.00	100.00
4	0.0134	100.00	100.00	100.00	100.00
5	0.0001	100.00	100.00	100.00	100.00
$S^{[a,b]}$		100.00	96.70	89.53	94.14
Spread		0.00	67.06	221.18	120.69

Rec = 40%; a=3%, b=6%
$\hat{S}^{[a,b]}_{|M} = \text{Payoff}_{[a,b]}(\bar{p}_{|M} \cdot (1 - \text{Rec}))$

The resulting spread shows the well-known behavior of the 3–6% mezzanine tranche. It first increases with rising default correlation and then declines for a larger ρ. For $\rho = 0$, the tranche spread is zero, because the survival amount $S^{[a,b]}$ is 100 percent. This is due to the fact that the default risk only depends on the individual default probabilities, which are 3.28 percent. Multiplying this default probability with the LGD of 60 percent ($= 1 - \text{Rec}$), we arrive at an expected loss of 1.97 percent. This is below the 3 percent attachment point of the mezzanine tranche. It can therefore not be eroded under these circumstances.

The presented procedure deviates from the general pricing framework for CDO tranche, which we outlined above, as we did not derive the probability $\pi(i)$ of i defaults or $\tilde{\pi}(x)$ of x percent defaults in the pool. Nevertheless, we can derive the corresponding probability density function $\tilde{\pi}(x)$ and use it in the previously outlined pricing framework.

$$\tilde{\pi}(x) = \sqrt{\frac{1-\rho}{\rho}} \exp\left(\frac{1}{2}(\Phi^{-1}(x))^2 - \frac{1}{2\rho}(\Phi^{-1}(\bar{p}) - \sqrt{1-\rho}\phi^{-1}(x))^2\right) \tag{9.18}$$

For details regarding the derivation of $\tilde{\pi}(x)$ in terms of the homogeneous large portfolio model, see Philipp Schönbucher's book[26].

Note that for the calculation shown in table 9.5, some crucial simplifications have been made. Similar to our previous n^{th}-to-default example, we used a very coarse integration grid for the market factor M and an approximation to switch from the credit spread into the default probability and back using a simple rule of thumb. For correct pricing, one has to use proper bootstrapping and valuation methods. Nevertheless, the illustrated concepts give a reasonable back-of-the-envelope approximation.

9.7 Spread Dispersion

In the previous analysis, we focused on the homogeneous large portfolio model, which was established as the market standard for quoting standardized CDO tranches on CDS indices, such as the iTraxx. It assumes that all constituents in the underlying pool have the same average spread. However, the spread blowout in May 2005, which drove the iTraxx Europe index up to 60 bp (on May 17), illustrated impressively that the average spread assumption for a disperse pool is not always justified. As a consequence, this occasion triggered discussions about how such a blowout might affect prices of related CDO tranches. The blowout was driven by idiosyncratic rather than systematic risk, reflected in a rise of the spread dispersion in the pool (see figure 9.5). But how does this translate into default probabilities and market quotes of iTraxx tranches? This topic can be analyzed using the analogy between CDO tranches and first-to-default baskets.

Just consider the following example: An investor has to choose between two first-to-default investments, one with a homogeneous pool (i.e., all underlyings have the same credit spreads), and one with a disperse pool (i.e., the underlyings have different spreads). However, the heterogeneous pool has the same average spread as the homogeneous one. Moreover, we assume independent defaults among the pool, or in other words a default correlation of zero. At first glance, one would prefer the homogeneous pool, as the heterogeneous at least has one constituent with a larger spread and hence a higher default risk. The larger the dispersion, the larger the spread of this (or these) outlier(s).

Two questions arise: Is this intuitive result mathematically justified, and How can we translate this idea to CDO tranches? We start with the simplest first-to-default basket: one with two constituents. We assume that the two constituents have default probabilities of p_A and p_B and corresponding survival probabilities of $(1 - p_A)$ and $(1 - p_B)$. We compiled model results in table 9.6.

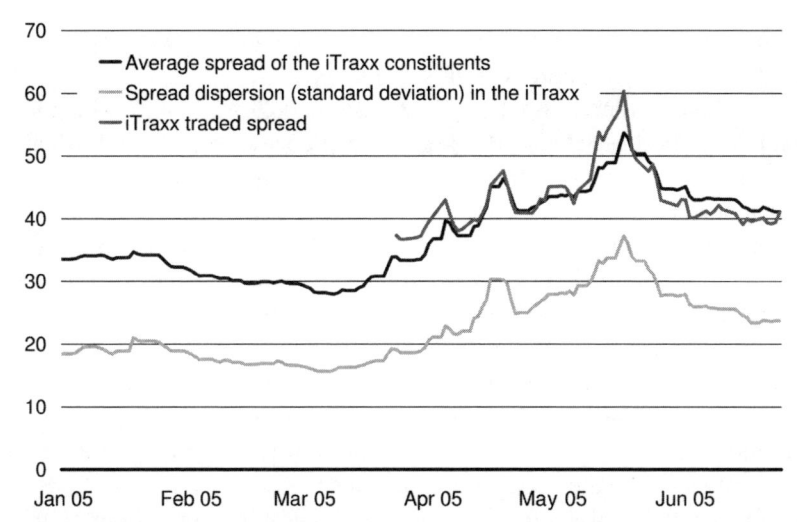

Fig. 9.5: The blowout in the iTraxx Europe index was accompanied by a sharp increase in the spread dispersion

Tab. 9.6: Impact of the homogeneity assumption on the probabilities $\pi(n)$ in a two-asset portfolio

i	Heterogeneous	Homogeneous	Difference
0	$(1-p_A)(1-p_B)$	$(1-\bar{p})^2$	$0.25(p_A - p_B)^2$
1	$p_A(1-p_B)$ $+(1-p_A)p_B$	$2\bar{p}(1-\bar{p})$	$-0.5(p_A - p_B)^2$
2	$p_A p_B$	$\bar{p}^2$	$0.25(p_A - p_B)^2$

The second column in table 9.6 records the probability of exactly i defaults in the two-asset basket using the individual default probabilities (note that we assume independent defaults). This is the same approach as shown in figure 9.3. For example, the probability that exactly one default occurs is given by the probability that the first credit survives and the second defaults, plus the probability that the first defaults and the second survives. In the following, we refer to it as the heterogeneous portfolio. The third column presents the results for the homogeneous portfolio, or the one in which all constituents have the same average default probability $\bar{p}$. The last column gives the difference between both approaches using the relation $\bar{p} = 0.5(p_A + p_B)$.

The result looks promising, as it justifies our gut feeling. The probabilities of zero and two default(s) are higher for the homogeneous case, as the difference is always positive. In contrast, the probability of one default is lower, while the cumulated difference for 0 and 1 defaults is still negative.

Moreover, the differences in table 9.6 depend on $0.25(p_A - p_B)^2$, which is the variance of p_A and p_B. Hence, the larger the variance among the individual default probabilities, the larger the difference between the homogeneous and the heterogeneous case.

However, the current two-entity model excluding default dependency is rather simplistic. As we are interested in CDO tranches, we have to include effects stemming from larger portfolio sizes and from default dependency. To illustrate these effects, we analyze a portfolio including 30 entities, with default probabilities 10 percent and 20 percent equally distributed among the constituents. Figure 9.6 shows the difference of the cumulated default probabilities ($\sum_{i=0}^{n} \pi(i)$) for the homogeneous (all entities with a probability of 15 percent) and the heterogeneous model up to the number of n defaults.

We performed the analysis for zero correlation and for a correlation of 20 percent. The result shows that the probability of zero defaults is higher for the homogeneous model. The positive exaggeration of the homogeneous model is increasing up to three defaults, but thereafter, the difference in the cumulated default probability is sharply decreasing. At about five defaults (equivalent to 16.6 percent defaults), the difference between both approaches is zero.

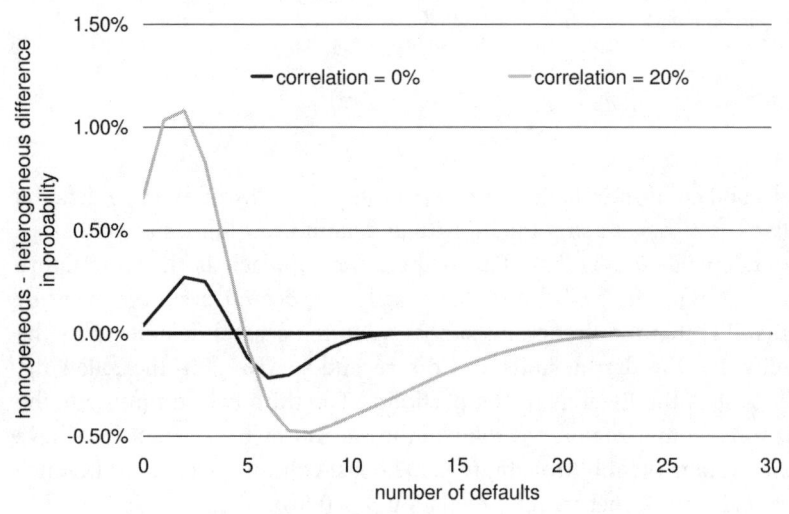

Fig. 9.6: Difference between homogeneous and heterogeneous approach in the default density $\pi(n)$ for a portfolio of 30 constituents

This means that our gut feeling is correct in case of a very thin equity tranche. However, if the equity piece becomes larger, the difference between both approaches diminishes and can even reverse. Even worse, the difference depends on several quantities, such as the dispersion in the pool and the default correlation. Hence, we cannot derive a simple rule of thumb for the outcome.

What can we learn from this analysis for tranche pricing? Using the above-mentioned framework, we investigated the default probability structure (as a function of the number of defaults) for the iTraxx and the CDX for spread levels as of May 17, 2005. In figure 9.7, we show the default probability distribution for both indices using a heterogeneous model, in other words one reflecting spread dispersion correctly. The iTraxx has a much higher probability of zero defaults than the CDX, which is in line with the corresponding average spread levels (iTraxx 54 bp, CDX 83 bp). In figure 9.7, we also show the difference between homogeneous and heterogeneous of the cumulated default probability functions. For five defaults, the function equals roughly the 0–3% tranche and the difference is almost zero, which means that the upfront payment is independent of dispersion. Below five defaults, there is a notable difference between the homogenous and the heterogeneous approach.

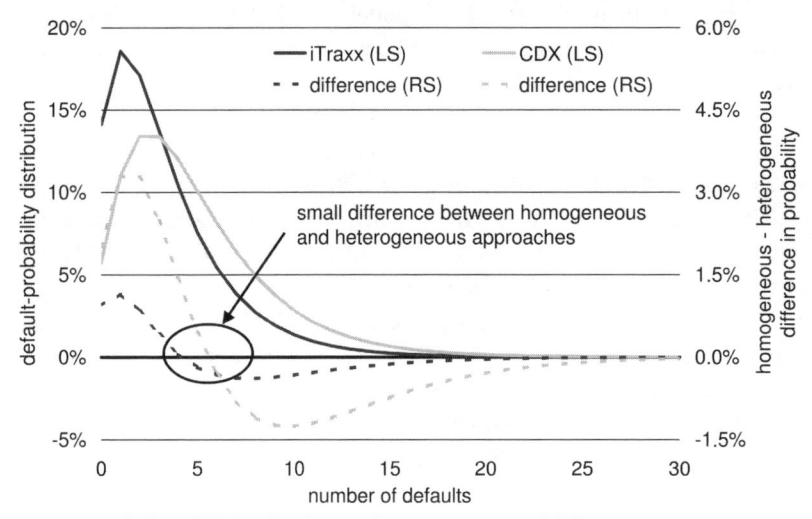

Fig. 9.7: Default-probability distribution (heterogeneous) and difference between homogeneous and heterogeneous for the cumulated probability distribution (iTraxx and CDX levels of May 17, 2005) assuming an average default correlation of 10 percent

9.8 Price Discovery versus Model Competition

One of the interesting topics regarding default correlation currently discussed by the financial community is *price discovery* versus *model competition*. This discussion is closely linked to the maturation of the whole market. In early stages of the development of a market, prices are derived by models. A proper model, which covers all (or most of the important) risks, results in sound hedging parameters and good prices.

Thus, market participants who have access to such a model have a good chance to outperform their competitors. Such models are usually complex and only specialized market participants can handle them, which makes the whole thing rather intransparent. This obviously puts a limitation on the further development of the market, since investors will only enter the market if the value of their position does not depend on obscure models.

If the market becomes more liquid, prices are no longer driven by models but by supply and demand. This means that the real price is one which the market participants can agree upon. This adds transparency, since one can mark-to-market a position without a complicated model and without model risk. So, does this mean that the market rules and models are not needed? A clear "No" is the answer. In fact, there is no conflict between price discovery and model competition. In the current market environment we need both.

On one hand, the pricing mechanism for products has to be flexible enough that prices can fluctuate according to the market consensus. On the other hand, we need a model to identify all risks and quantify their impact on prices. In other words, risk managers have to hedge all risks involved in the transaction they do not want to take. And therefore they need a model that is capable of calculating sensitivities. This is especially true for the arranger of such single-tranche CDO transactions. Since the arranger just sold the risk of a specific tranche to an investor, he has to hedge the risks of the remaining capital structure, and therefore needs sophisticated models. So there is a model competition on the side of the CDO arrangers. The company with the best model can offer the most competitive prices for single-tranche CDOs and can thus gain a larger market share.

The investor's point of view on models is somewhat different. Models should be simple and robust. The major task is to isolate the relevant risk factor: the correlation risk. And we need to identify its economic drivers. That will allow us to compare default correlation across different products, sectors, and regions.

And it will help us to find an answer to the question whether correlation is a new asset class (such as volatility). In addition, we can identify price inconsistencies and arbitrage opportunities.

10
Valuation of Credit Derivatives

The focus in this chapter is to shed some light on the most important credit derivatives. For this purpose, we refer to previously derived concepts such as the survival probability function. We will highlight important sensitivities and, if available, standard tools for analyzing these products. The family of credit derivatives can be classified into single-name and portfolio derivatives. Plain-vanilla credit default swaps that refer to a single reference obligor, for example, belong to the single-name products, while n^{th}-to-default baskets and collateralized debt obligations are examples of portfolio derivatives. However, some derivative contracts, such as credit default swaptions, may refer to single names as well as to a portfolio of CDS, that is, to options on CDS indices. The latter – CDS indices – belong to the portfolio derivatives as well. However, they differ from n^{th}-to-default baskets and CDOs, as their value does not depend on the default correlation in the underlying pools. The corresponding pricing relations are less sophisticated. To avoid confusion about the names of the various portfolio derivative structures, we adopt the following convention. We address the plain-vanilla portfolio derivatives that simply transfer the risks of the whole underlying portfolio (e.g., the iTraxx index contracts) as *CDS index swaps* or simply *CDS indices*. We do not use the name CDS basket in order to avoid confusion with n^{th}-to-default baskets, which are also sometimes called simply default baskets.

In this chapter we first analyze plain-vanilla credit default swaps. We highlight the standard pricing equations, show how to infer survival probabilities from market data, evaluate forward CDS contracts, and introduce Bloomberg's CDSW tool. This is followed by an analysis of options on credit-risky products, focusing on pricing equations for single-name credit default swaptions and options on credit indices. We then explore credit indices, such as the iTraxx and the CDX. Here, we show how the theoretical value of a CDS index is defined and how it can be approximated by a simple weighted average of the underlying CDS spreads. Subsequently, we introduce pricing relations for n^{th}-to-default baskets and CDO tranches using portfolio risk pricing models. Here, we also explain the two corresponding Bloomberg functions CDSM and CDSN. We conclude the chapter with an introduction of two more exotic credit derivatives: constant maturity CDS and equity default swaps.

Active Credit Portfolio Management. J. Felsenheimer, P. Gisdakis, and M. Zaiser
Copyright © 2006 WILEY-VCH Verlag GmbH & Co. KGaA, Weinheim
ISBN: 3-527-50198-3

10.1 Credit Default Swaps

In the following analysis, we show how a CDS contract can be valued using the pricing framework derived earlier. A CDS contract comprises two legs: a premium leg (PL) and a default leg (DL). The value of a CDS contract from the perspective of a protection seller is calculated as the value of the premium leg minus the value of the default leg:

$$V_{PS}^{CDS} = V^{PL} - V^{DL}$$

Throughout our analysis, we take the perspective of the protection seller (PS), that is, the investor who receives the premium payment in exchange for being prone to the default risk. Therefore, the value of the premium leg (the stream of premium payments the investors receives) has a positive sign, while the value of the default leg (the payment the investor has to make in case of a default event) has a negative sign. From a protection buyer's (PB) point of view this relation would be obviously reversed: $V_{PB}^{CDS} = -V^{PL} + V^{DL}$.

Moreover, the default leg usually comprises two components. The main component is the so-called default payment that settles the LGD, which is (1 − Rec). The second component is the accrued premium upon default. It refers to a specific detail in common CDS contracts. In case of a default event, the protection seller receives the fraction of the premium payment that was accrued since the last premium payment date. Therefore, the value of the default leg is stated as $V^{DL} = V^{DP} - V^{AP}$, with V^{DP} being the value of the default payment and V^{AP} the value of the accrued premium. Both are conditional upon the default event.

The separation into two legs, the premium leg and the default leg, closely resembles the valuation procedure of a plain-vanilla interest rate swap (IRS). For the IRS, the fixed and the floating leg are also treated separately. Some market participants use the analogy between CDS and IRS and understand the premium leg of the CDS as the fixed leg of the contract, while the default leg is then the floating leg.

There is another implication of the separation into premium and default leg. As we will see below, markets established several modifications of plain-vanilla credit default swaps, such as contracts where the premium is paid as a single upfront payment instead of a running spread (e.g., if the reference entity is close to default) or the so-called constant maturity CDS contracts. Most of them only involve modifications with respect to the structure of the premium leg, while the default leg remains the same as in the standard CDS contracts. Hence for valuation purposes, we only have to adjust the valuation of the premium leg.

We begin by deriving a pricing algorithm within the discrete-time framework, which has been established as the common market practice. This is followed by an illustration of the bootstrapping algorithm to derive the survival probability function $S(\tau)$ within this discrete-time framework. The implied survival probability function is needed for valuing other derivatives contracts, such as forward CDS, n^{th}-to-default baskets, or CDO tranches. Please recall that $F(\tau) = 1 - S(\tau)$ is the cumulative default probability, which is the central building block for valuing portfolio derivatives. Subsequently, we introduce the valuation of forward CDS contracts and show the central sensitivity figures needed for risk management purposes. Then we briefly illustrate how credit default swaps can be valued in a continuous-time framework, which refers to the well-known Hull-White model.[62] Finally, we show how market participants analyze CDS contracts using Bloomberg's CDSW function.

10.1.1 Discrete-Time Model

The discrete-time CDS pricing algorithm we show in this section has established itself as a kind of market standard. It is referred to as the *JPMorgan model*[63] and is available in Bloomberg's CDSW tool, which we will also describe below. In the discrete-time framework, we can derive the CDS value using equation 7.26 in our introduction to credit pricing models. We reiterate this equation and indicate the relation to the CDS contract.

$$V(\tau_m) = \underbrace{\sum_{i=1}^{m} \text{CF}_i \cdot R(\tau_i) \cdot S(\tau_i)}_{V^{\text{PL}}}$$
$$+ \underbrace{\sum_{i=1}^{m} \text{CF}_i^{\text{default}} \cdot R(\tau_i) \cdot (S(\tau_{i-1}) - S(\tau_i))}_{-V^{\text{DL}}} \qquad (7.26\text{a})$$

To transfer this equation into a real pricing algorithm, we only have to specify the structure of the contractual cash flows CF_i in the premium leg and the payment conditional upon default $\text{CF}_i^{\text{default}}$ in the default leg. Note that in equation 7.26a, the second term has a positive sign, while in the CDS pricing relation the value of the default leg is subtracted. This is reflected in the subsequent analysis by a negative default payment $\text{CF}_i^{\text{default}}$. It is important to recall that the derivation of equation 7.26 required several approximations, such as that default events are settled at the next regular payment date (see above for details). Note that besides the survival probability function $S(\tau)$ we need the risk-free discount function $R(\tau)$ for the valuation. The latter can be derived by bootstrapping a swap curve (see section 5.2).

The regular payments CF_i are simply the contractual CDS rate $c(\tau_m)$ times the accrual period $\Delta\tau_i = \tau_i - \tau_{i-1}$. The CDS rate $c(\tau_m)$ usually refers to the maturity date τ_m of the CDS contract. Hence, the value of the premium leg is derived by substituting $CF_i = c(\tau_m) \cdot \Delta\tau_i$ in equation 7.26a:

$$V^{PL} = \sum_{i=1}^{m} c(\tau_m) \cdot \Delta\tau_i \cdot R(\tau_i) \cdot S(\tau_i) \tag{10.1}$$

Here, $R(\tau)$ is the risk-free discount function and $S(\tau)$ the survival probability. Note that the sum starts at $i = 1$. Following our definition of the accrual factor, the first period covers the interval $\Delta\tau_1 = \tau_1 - \tau_0$ where τ_0 is the time until the effective date of the contract. For a plain-vanilla CDS this period is usually two days. Nevertheless, a frequently used assumption is $\tau_0 = 0$, or that the effective date equals the valuation date. Moreover $S(0) = 1$, since the survival probability for a zero-length period for a credit that does not start in default obviously equals 1. Regarding the payment dates τ_i, market participants follow the ISDA 2003 documentation.[8] According to these rules, CDS contracts have standard payment and maturity dates: March 20, June 20, September 20, and December 20 (with "Following" as business day convention; see table 5.1). Every three months, contracts roll over to the next date. Accordingly, coupons on the contracts are paid quarterly.

For the derivation of the payment $CF_i^{default}$ conditional upon default we have to consider the two above-mentioned components: the default payment $(1 - Rec)$ and the accrued premium upon default. The default payment is the most important component, while the effect from the accrued premium has the order of 1 percent of the default payment, depending on the recovery rate and the CDS rate. Nevertheless, the accrued premium causes some troubles, but we solve the problems by applying a simple assumption.

To determine the accrued payment upon default, we have to know exactly at which date the default occurred. Consequently, for the derivation of this exact date, we would need a default probability distribution with an accuracy of a single day. Unfortunately, this refers to a continuous-time model. In the discrete-time approach we do not have a default probability for each individual day in the accrual period, but just one for the whole period. Of course, we could derive such a probability distribution by fitting a hazard rate function, but this would lead to a significant complexity in the calculation. Therefore we assume that default occurs on average in between two premium payment dates τ_{i-1} and

τ_i. The accrual factor comes to: $\frac{\tau_i - \tau_{i-1}}{2} = \frac{\Delta \tau_i}{2}$. This is known as the *mid-point approximation*.

As a result, we split the default payment CF_i^{default} introduced in equation 7.26a into the default payment $(1 - \text{Rec})$ that the protection seller has to pay and the accrual payment $c(\tau_m) \cdot \frac{\Delta \tau_i}{2}$ which the protection seller receives.

$$V^{\text{DP}} = (1 - \text{Rec}) \sum_{i=1}^{m} R(\tau_i) \cdot (S(\tau_{i-1}) - S(\tau_i)) \qquad (10.2)$$

$$V^{\text{AP}} = \sum_{i=1}^{m} c(\tau_m) \cdot \frac{\Delta \tau_i}{2} \cdot R(\tau_i) \cdot (S(\tau_{i-1}) - S(\tau_i)) \qquad (10.3)$$

Recall that the unconditional default probability between τ_{i-1} and τ_i (i.e., the probability that a default occurs in this time interval) is given by the change in the survival probability function $S(\tau_{i-1}) - S(\tau_i)$. This difference is always non-negative, because the survival probability $S(\tau)$ is a monotonously decreasing function of τ.

Putting the above-mentioned components together, we arrive at the formula for the value of a CDS contract.

$$\begin{aligned}V^{\text{CDS}} &= V^{\text{PL}} - V^{\text{DL}} = V^{\text{PL}} + V^{\text{AP}} - V^{\text{DP}} \\ &= \sum_{i=1}^{m} c(\tau_m) \cdot \Delta \tau_i \cdot R(\tau_i) \cdot S(\tau_i) \\ &+ \sum_{i=1}^{m} c(\tau_m) \cdot \frac{\Delta \tau_i}{2} \cdot R(\tau_i) \cdot (S(\tau_{i-1}) - S(\tau_i)) \\ &- (1 - \text{Rec}) \sum_{i=1}^{m} R(\tau_i) \cdot (S(\tau_{i-1}) - S(\tau_i))\end{aligned} \qquad (10.4)$$

A standard CDS contract does not involve upfront payments, as its initial value is zero. This condition is satisfied when the CDS rate $c(\tau_m)$ used in equation 10.4 is set at the par-CDS rate. The par-CDS rate can therefore be derived by solving equation 10.4 with respect to $c(\tau_m)$ under the condition $V^{\text{CDS}} = 0$:

$$c(\tau_m) = \frac{(1 - \text{Rec}) \sum_{i=1}^{m} R(\tau_i) \cdot (S(\tau_{i-1}) - S(\tau_i))}{\sum_{i=1}^{m} \Delta \tau_i \cdot R(\tau_i) \cdot S(\tau_i) + \sum_{i=1}^{m} \frac{\Delta \tau_i}{2} \cdot R(\tau_i) \cdot (S(\tau_{i-1}) - S(\tau_i))} \qquad (10.5)$$

We already mentioned that V^{AP}, the value of the accrued premium conditional upon default, acts just as a small correction to the value of the default leg. Its relative size compared to the value of the default payment V^{AP} can be approximated as $c(\tau_m)\Delta\tau/2(1-\text{Rec})$. For a spread of 50 bp, an accrual period of $1/4$ and a recovery rate of 40 percent, its value is 0.1 percent of the value of the default leg. Hence, we can safely ignore it in most calculations, especially when the involved spreads are small. This leads to a nice approximation of the par spread for a CDS contract:

$$c(\tau_m) \approx \frac{\overbrace{(1-\text{Rec})\sum_{i=1}^{m} R(\tau_i) \cdot (S(\tau_{i-1}) - S(\tau_i))}^{\text{expected loss}}}{\underbrace{\sum_{i=1}^{m} \Delta\tau_i \cdot R(\tau_i) \cdot S(\tau_i)}_{\text{risky annuity}}}$$

The par-CDS spread can be approximated by dividing the expected loss by the *risky annuity*, defined by:

$$A(\tau_0, \tau_m) = \sum_{i=1}^{m} \Delta\tau_i \cdot R(\tau_i) \cdot S(\tau_i). \qquad (10.6)$$

Note that for $\tau_0 > 0$, $A(\tau_0, \tau_m)$ is the *risky forward annuity*. Neglecting the value of the accrued premium upon default V^{AP}, the risky annuity $A(\tau_0, \tau_m)$ can be used to calculate the change of the value of a CDS contract with respect to the deal spread, keeping the survival probability function fixed. This means that we can approximate the value of an off-par CDS by multiplying the difference in its CDS rate to the par rate with the risky annuity $A(\tau_0, \tau_m)$:

$$\Delta V^{CDS} \approx \Delta c(\tau_m) \cdot A(\tau_0, \tau_m) \qquad (10.7)$$

It is worth mentioning that equation 10.4 collapses to a very simple relation if we assume zero interest rates, or $R(\tau) = 1$, and an average payment period $\Delta\tau$:

$$V^{CDS} = c(\tau_m) \cdot \Delta\tau \sum_{i=1}^{m} S(\tau_i) + \left(c(\tau_m)\frac{\Delta\tau}{2} - (1-\text{Rec})\right) \cdot (S(\tau_0) - S(\tau_m))$$

Here, we used the fact that $\sum_{i=1}^{m}(S(\tau_{i-1}) - S(\tau_i))$ is a telescopic sum. The only elements that remain are the first and the last: $S(\tau_0) - S(\tau_m)$. The approximated risky annuity for zero interest rates is $\Delta\tau\sum_{i=1}^{m} S(\tau_i)$. The corresponding par spread is given by:

$$c(\tau_m) = \frac{(1 - \text{Rec}) \cdot (S(\tau_0) - S(\tau_m))}{\Delta\tau \sum_{i=1}^{m} S(\tau_i) + \frac{\Delta\tau}{2}(S(\tau_0) - S(\tau_m))} \approx \frac{\overbrace{(1 - \text{Rec}) \cdot (S(\tau_0) - S(\tau_m))}^{\text{expected loss}}}{\underbrace{\Delta\tau \sum_{i=1}^{m} S(\tau_i)}_{\text{risky annuity}}}$$

(10.8)

Finally, it is worth mentioning that equation 10.4 can be used to price other swap-like structures, such as unfunded n^{th}-to-default baskets. We only have to adjust the survival probability function, which has to be related to the probability of the nth default: $S^{[n]}(\tau)$ (see below).

Example 22: Simple CDS Analysis

This example illustrates a simple CDS valuation within a spreadsheet calculation. We use equation 10.4. The main idea in this example is to approximate the survival probability function $S(\tau)$, the central pricing quantity, by a simple relation:

$$S(\tau) = \exp\left(-\frac{\text{spread}}{1 - \text{Rec}} \cdot \tau\right)$$

Here, spread is the market spread that corresponds to the maturity date for the CDS under consideration. As an example, when analyzing a 5Y CDS contract, we use the 5Y market spread for the survival probability. This means that the approximation assumes a flat hazard rate function of spread/(1 − Rec). Moreover, we assume – for the sake of simplicity – that the CDS contract has a yearly payment schedule. The figure below shows a spreadsheet example. The spreadsheet is divided into five parts. In the deal information part, we can set up the CDS contract by specifying the notional amount, the time to maturity, and the deal spread. In the market data part, we can specify the market spread, the recovery rate, and the risk-free discount rate. The remaining two parts contain calculation data.

	A	B	C	D	E	F	G
1							
2		Deal Information			Market Data		
3		Notional	10,000,000		Market spread	100	
4		Maturity	5		Recovery rate	40.00%	
5		Deal spread	101.00		Interest rate	5.00%	
6							
7		Results			Hazard rate	1.67%	
8		Value	4,156		PL / Annuity	4.1119	
9		Par spread	100.00		AP	0.0346	
10					DP	0.0415	
11							
12		Indicator	Time	Discount Factor	Survival Probability	Cond. Fwd. PD	
13		1	0	1.00000	1.00000		
14		1	1	0.95123	0.98347	1.65%	
15		1	2	0.90484	0.96722	1.63%	
16		1	3	0.86071	0.95123	1.60%	
17		1	4	0.81873	0.93551	1.57%	
18		1	5	0.77880	0.92004	1.55%	
19		0	6	0.74082	0.90484	1.52%	
20		0	7	0.70469	0.88988	1.50%	
21		0	8	0.67032	0.87517	1.47%	
22		0	9	0.63763	0.86071	1.45%	
23		0	10	0.60653	0.84648	1.42%	
24							

=EXP(-F5*C20)   =EXP(-F7*C20)   =E20-E21

=SUMPRODUCT(B14:B23,E14:E23,D14:D23)

Simple CDS valuation model

In the large calculation area, the indicator column is defined to manage the maturity date of the calculation. An `if` statement compares the entry in the time column with the maturity date. If the time is greater than maturity then the indicator is zero. The indicator is used in the following sums as a switch for different maturity dates. The discount factor is derived as $\exp(-\text{interest rate} \times \text{time})$ and the survival probability as $\exp(-\text{hazard rate} \times \text{time})$. The conditional forward default probability is the difference of the survival probability between two time steps.

Now, we can calculate the premium leg (PL), the accrued premium upon default (AP), and the default payment (DP). All three can be easily calculated using the worksheet function `sumproduct`. For example, PL can be calculated by `sumproduct(indicator,discount factor,survival probability)`. The arguments refer to the respective columns. Note that the considered areas encompass all numbers in the columns except for the first one, which corresponds to the time zero. Here, we derived PL and AP without multiplying with the coupon rate. In this way, we can use PL and AP for both the calculation of the value of the contract as well as for the par spread. The value of the contract is then derived as notional amount × ((deal spread/10000) × (PL + AP) − DP). Division by 10000 adjusts for the basis point specification of the spread. The par spread is calculated as DP / (PL + AP) × 10000.

It is interesting to note that the result is quite accurate. The value of a contract with the deal spread and market spread being the same is almost zero, although the approximation of the introduced approximation survival probability function is quite crude. We can now use this example to calculate other characteristics, such as sensitivities, off-par values, and so on. We can now confirm that notional amount × annuity × 1 bp is a good approximation for the value difference between 101 bp in the deal spread and 100 bp in the market spread. Note that the results improve when we use quarterly payment periods instead of yearly.

10.1.2 Obtaining the Survival Probability Curve

All above derived equations depend on the survival probability function $S(\tau)$, which is, as already mentioned, the central quantity to price credit risk. In chapter 8, we introduced several models that help to derive this quantity, such as structural models and rating-based transition matrix models. In principle, we could use each of them. As an example, deriving the survival probability from a structural model that was fitted to stock market prices, such as implied option volatilities, we can value a CDS contract in the cross asset framework, such as for purposes of a capital structure arbitrage strategy.

Nevertheless, in the current credit market, CDS contracts are liquidly traded for a broad range of obligors and maturities. Therefore, we can invert the valuation procedure shown in equations 10.4 and 10.5 and back out the implied survival probabilities from CDS quotes, which can then be used to price other credit-risky instruments such as bonds, n^{th}-to-default baskets, and CDO tranches. This is the same idea as in swap markets. The swap rates are used to derive a risk-free discount factor curve that is used for pricing other securities. We can choose between two different ways to derive the survival probability function:

1. We can fit a hazard rate curve such that it reprices traded contracts.
2. We can use a bootstrapping algorithm similar to the one presented for the fixed income universe (see section 5.2).

The former can be implemented, for example, by assuming a piecewise constant hazard rate curve. Standard CDS contracts have maturities of 1, 2, 3, 5, 7, and 10 years. For example, the survival probability for up to two years may be derived as $S(2) = \exp(-h_1(1-0) - h_2(2-1))$. This has to be done numerically, because the CDS valuation procedure involves the sum over several of these exponential functions, which cannot be solved for the corresponding hazard rate. Nevertheless, the solver function in Excel is sufficient for this procedure. From a mathematical perspective, a piecewise constant hazard rate function h_i would result in the following substitution in equation 10.4: $S(\tau_i) = e^{-h_i \cdot \tau_i}$. For a constant h_i between the standard CDS maturities, this procedure results in a log-linear interpolation between the survival probability values. The disadvantage of a piecewise linear hazard rate curve is that the unconditional default probabilities $S(\tau_{i-1}) - S(\tau_i)$ have large jumps at the points where the hazard rate jumps to a new level, which does not make a lot of sense from an economic point of view.

The bootstrapping algorithm can be implemented without using a numerical solver. This algorithm is similar to the procedure for deriving the discount factor curve from swap rates (see section 5.2). The bootstrapping procedure is a stepwise algorithm to determine the term structure of the survival probability function $S(\tau)$ from par-CDS spreads. However, there is also a drawback involved: the par-CDS curve has to be interpolated in order to fill the swap gaps. We will return to this point below. To derive the bootstrapping procedure, we start with equation 10.4 and separate the nth term in each sum.

$$
\begin{aligned}
V^{\text{CDS}} = \\
&\left. \begin{array}{l} c(\tau_m) \cdot \sum_{i=1}^{n-1} \Delta \tau_i \cdot R(\tau_i) \cdot S(\tau_i) \\[6pt] + c(\tau_m) \cdot \sum_{i=1}^{n-1} \frac{\Delta \tau_i}{2} \cdot R(\tau_i) \cdot (S(\tau_{i-1}) - S(\tau_i)) \\[6pt] - (1 - \text{Rec}) \sum_{i=1}^{n-1} R(\tau_i) \cdot (S(\tau_{i-1}) - S(\tau_i)) \end{array} \right\} \text{from 1 to } n-1 \\[10pt]
&\left. \begin{array}{l} + c(\tau_m) \cdot \Delta \tau_m \cdot R(\tau_m) \cdot S(\tau_m) \\[6pt] + c(\tau_m) \cdot \frac{\Delta \tau_m}{2} \cdot R(\tau_m) \cdot (S(\tau_{n-1}) - S(\tau_m)) \\[6pt] - (1 - \text{Rec}) \cdot R(\tau_m) \cdot (S(\tau_{n-1}) - S(\tau_m)) \end{array} \right\} n^{\text{th}} \text{ (last) term}
\end{aligned}
$$

The first three lines in this equation correspond to a CDS contract which runs from τ_0 to τ_{n-1} (note that the sums run up to $n-1$), while the last three lines give the corresponding term for the last, the nth, time step. Now we solve this equation for the survival probability $S(\tau_m)$ under the condition that the value of a par CDS is zero ($V^{\text{CDS}} = 0$):

$$S(\tau_m) = \frac{A+B+C}{-c(\tau_m)R(\tau_m)\frac{\Delta \tau_m}{2} - (1-\text{Rec})R(\tau_m)}$$

with:

$$A = c(\tau_m) \sum_{i=1}^{n-1} R(\tau_i) S(\tau_i) \Delta \tau_i$$

$$B = c(\tau_m) \sum_{i=1}^{n-1} R(\tau_i) \left(S(\tau_{i-1}) - S(\tau_i)\right) \frac{\Delta \tau_i}{2} + c(\tau_m) R(\tau_m) S(\tau_{n-1}) \frac{\Delta \tau_m}{2}$$

$$C = -(1-\text{Rec}) \sum_{i=1}^{n-1} R(\tau_i) \left(S(\tau_{i-1}) - S(\tau_i)\right) - (1-\text{Rec}) R(\tau_m) S(\tau_{n-1})$$

(10.9)

Bootstrapping the survival probability using equation 10.9 is an iterative process. The survival probability $S(\tau_m)$ depends on the previous survival probabilities $S(\tau_i)$, with $i = 1, 2, \ldots, n-1$, and the par-CDS rate $c(\tau_m)$ for a time to maturity τ_m. Unfortunately, we need survival probabilities for each payment date τ_i, but we do not have par-CDS rates for all these time horizons. We will hardly find liquid quotes for a 2.25-year contract. So we have to fill the swap gaps between the liquidly traded contracts by interpolating. The easiest way to do this is by a linear interpolation in the par-CDS curve, which however, leads to non-continuous unconditional default probabilities $S(\tau_{i-1}) - S(\tau_i)$. However, compared to the large jumps in the piecewise constant interpolation of the hazard rate curve (see above), the result for the linear interpolation in the CDS rates looks less problematic. Note that by interpolating the CDS rate curve linearly, the implied hazard rate curve will also show an almost linear interpolation.

We demonstrate the initial step of this procedure. The survival probability $S(\tau_1)$ can be derived by solving the following equation with respect to $S(\tau_1)$:

$$V(\tau_1) = c(\tau_1) \Delta \tau_1 R(\tau_1) S(\tau_1)$$
$$+ c(\tau_1) \frac{\Delta \tau_1}{2} R(\tau_1)(S(\tau_0) - S(\tau_1))$$
$$- (1-\text{Rec}) R(\tau_1)(S(\tau_0) - S(\tau_1))$$

Using the par condition $V(\tau_1) = 0$ and a contract that does not start in default $S(\tau_0) = 1$ (recall $\tau_0 \approx 0$) we get:

$$S(\tau_1) = \frac{(1 - \text{Rec}) - c(\tau_1)\frac{\Delta \tau_1}{2}}{(1 - \text{Rec}) + c(\tau_1)\frac{\Delta \tau_1}{2}}$$

However, it should be noted that the implied survival probabilities depend on the recovery rate. As a consequence, market participants consistently use a recovery rate assumption of 40 percent for almost all contracts. Bootstrapping the survival probability function with respect to one recovery assumption and pricing a contract using another recovery assumption may lead to terribly wrong results. Investors should do this only if they really know what they are doing!

10.1.3 Forward CDS Valuation

A forward CDS is a contract that offers protection with respect to a reference obligor for a future period of time. As an example, an investor who sells protection via a 1Y-into-5Y forward CDS agrees to take the default risk between years 1 and 6 (i.e., a five-year period) starting from the trading date and, in exchange, receives the contracted premium payments over the five-year period. Hence the effective date of the contract is the trading date plus one year, while the maturity date is the trading date plus six years. The premium is paid during the forward period. This means that the forward contract expires without involving any further payments if the reference obligor defaults before the effective date. This is called a *knock-out-on-default* feature.

Valuing a forward CDS contract is not difficult. We can use equations 10.4 and 10.5 directly. The only difference compared to the standard CDS contract is that the time to the effective date is greater than zero: $\tau_0 > 0$. In other words, we only need to adjust the payment grid τ_i with $i = 0, 1, \ldots, n$ to reflect the forward periods. Note that the survival probability up to the effective date no longer equals 1 but is $0 < S(\tau_0) < 1$ for $\tau_0 > 0$. To reflect the fact that the effective date is in the future, we refer to a forward CDS rate as $c(\tau_0, \tau_m)$. However, the value of a forward CDS contract depends on the underlying CDS curve and therefore its value changes when spreads change.

Why are forward CDS contracts important? First, they offer an interesting payoff profile, as the contract is sensitive to spread changes but (usually) does not involve default risk in the forward period. Hence, forward CDS contracts are interesting tools for investors who are willing to trade spread changes but do not want to take outright default risk. Second, forward CDS contracts are central building blocks for other derivative instruments, such as constant maturity CDS and credit default swaptions.

A forward-like payoff profile can also be constructed via two offsetting positions. Consider the following example: sell 6Y protection for a premium of 100 bp and buy 1Y protection for 30 bp. As a consequence, the investor has no default risk in the first year, as the default legs of both contracts offset each other. He only has a default risk between year one and year six. However, the premium leg of this position differs from that of a normal forward CDS contract. The investor receives a net payment of 70 bp (= 100 bp − 30 bp) in the first year, while he receives 100 bp for the remaining five years.

A normal forward CDS contract involves no premium payments in the forward period but only in the period in which protection is offered. Therefore, the forward CDS spread will be higher. However, we can roughly estimate the par spread for a forward CDS contract from this example. It will be about 114 bp, or 14 bp (= 70 bp / 5) higher than the par spread of the 6Y contract. To arrive at a more serious estimate, we have to divide the present value of the net premium payments for the first year, 70 bp · $R(1)$ · $S(1)$, by the risky forward annuity $A(\tau_0, \tau_m) = \sum_{i=1}^{m} \Delta\tau_i R(\tau_i) S(\tau_i)$, with $0 < \tau_0 < \tau_m$.

Constructing a forward-like payoff profile using two standard CDS contracts can nevertheless be an attractive alternative, because forward CDS markets are not as liquid as the plain-vanilla ones.

To be a little more formal, a forward CDS par rate $c(\tau_0, \tau_m)$ can be approximated from the corresponding standard CDS rates $c(\tau_0)$ and $c(\tau_m)$, using the risky annuity for the period between trading date and effective date $A(0, \tau_0)$ and the risky forward annuity $A(\tau_0, \tau_m)$. Note that this approximation neglects the effect from the accrued premium at default.

$$c(\tau_0, \tau_m) \approx c(\tau_m) + [c(\tau_m) - c(\tau_0)] \cdot \frac{A(0, \tau_0)}{A(\tau_0, \tau_m)} \qquad (10.10)$$

The forward rate $c(\tau_0, \tau_m)$ can be derived from the above-mentioned example or by the using the connection rule

$$\underbrace{c(0, \tau_m) \cdot A(0, \tau_m)}_{V^{PL} \text{ for entire period}} = \underbrace{c(0, \tau_0) \cdot A(0, \tau_0)}_{V^{PL} \text{ until effective date}} + \underbrace{c(\tau_0, \tau_m) \cdot A(\tau_0, \tau_m)}_{V^{PL} \text{ of forward contract}} \qquad (10.11)$$

as well as the fact that $A(0, \tau_m) = A(0, \tau_0) + A(\tau_0, \tau_m)$, where $0 < \tau_0 < \tau_m$.

10.1.4 CDS Sensitivities

The analysis and management of CDS contracts requires the calculation of the central sensitivities. The most important among these is the SpreadDV01, that is, the change in value when the market spreads change by 1 bp. DV01 means "dollar value of a basis point". To derive this number, the whole CDS curve is shifted by 1 bp, while the deal spread, that is, the stipulated premium, is kept unchanged. From a mathematical point of view, the original CDS contract is valued using an implied survival probability curve that was derived from the shifted CDS spreads. This concept is comparable to the DV01 calculation in the swap market. Most state-of-the-art tools provide this information.

However, we have several possibilities to approximate this sensitivity:

- Perhaps the best approximation for the SpreadDV01 is to use the risky annuity: $N \cdot 0.0001 \cdot A(\tau_0, \tau_m)$, where N is the notional amount of the contract and 0.0001 is 1 bp.
- Approximate the derivative of the pricing equation for CDS contracts with respect to the spread curve by substituting all $S(\tau_i)$ by $-\frac{\tau_i}{1-\text{Rec}} \cdot S(\tau_i)$. Multiply this derivative with the notional amount and 0.0001 to arrive at the SpreadDV01. This approach can be understood as differentiating the CDS pricing equation with respect to the hazard rate curve h_τ. Note that hazard rate, credit spread, and recovery rate are related to each other via the credit triangle.
- The simplest and crudest approximation is to use $-N \cdot 0.0001 \cdot \tau_m \cdot S(\tau_m)$, where τ_m is the maturity date of the contract and $S(\tau_m)$ the survival probability until maturity. In case a properly implied survival probability is not available, we can even approximate it using the credit triangle: $S(\tau_m) \approx e^{-\text{spread} \cdot \tau_m / (1-\text{Rec})}$.

Although the last approximation is quite crude and should not be used for real investment purposes, it helps to understand intuitively how the SpreadDV01 depends on the spread level. The term $\tau_m \cdot S(\tau_m)$ corresponds to an average life of the contract. Obviously, the average life of the CDS will be shorter for higher credit spreads, because the risk of a default event is higher. Consequently, the sensitivity of the CDS contract to a spread change of 1 bp will be lower for high spreads than for low spreads. However, the exact sensitivity (and the change of the sensitivity with the market spread) depends on the structure of the whole spread curve: the level, the steepness, and the curvature.

Excursus 6: Risky Duration and Convexity: Analogies between CDS and Fixed Income Securities

Duration and convexity are well-established key figures for fixed income securities. They are sensitivities of the value of a bond towards changes in the discount curve. We can derive analogies for these key figures for CDS contracts. Consider a CDS contract with a maturity τ_m. The stipulated deal spread is denoted by $\tilde{c}$, while the current market spread for a CDS with time to maturity τ_m is stated as $y = c(\tau_m)$. Therefore, the value of the CDS contract under consideration does not equal zero if the deal spread and the market spread differ: $\tilde{c} \neq c(\tau_m)$. We can approximate the value of the CDS contract $V(y)$ depending on the market spread y by using the following survival probability function in conjunction with equation 10.4 (see also example 22).

$$\text{value: } S(\tau) \to \exp\left(-\frac{y}{1-\text{Rec}} \cdot \tau\right)$$

This simply assumes that the hazard rate can be expressed as $c(\tau_m)/(1-\text{Rec})$. With this substitution, we can derive a closed form for risky duration and risky convexity. Recall that the risky duration is the change of the value $V(y)$ by a change in y: risky duration $= \frac{dV(y)}{dy}$. Note that – in contradistinction to the modified duration as yield sensitivity for fixed income instruments – there is no division by $V(y)$ in this definition. The reason for this difference is that, here, we consider absolute changes of the value whereas the modified duration expresses relative price changes. Analogously, the risky convexity can be expressed as the second derivative of $V(y)$ with respect to y: risky convexity $= \frac{d^2V(y)}{dy^2}$. After the substitution for the value above, we derive a closed expression for risky duration and convexity by the following similar substitutions in equation 10.4:

$$\text{risky duration: } S(\tau) \to -\frac{\tau}{1-\text{Rec}} \cdot \exp\left(-\frac{y}{1-\text{Rec}} \cdot \tau\right),$$

$$\text{risky convexity: } S(\tau) \to \left(\frac{\tau}{1-\text{Rec}}\right)^2 \cdot \exp\left(-\frac{y}{1-\text{Rec}} \cdot \tau\right).$$

Note that y is given as the par spread $c(\tau_m)$ for the time to maturity τ_m of the CDS contract. Hence, we can easily approximate key figures of a CDS contract, such as the risky duration and convexity simply by using $c(\tau_m)/(1-\text{Rec})$ as the hazard rate.

Another sensitivity figure is the (IR)DV01, which states the sensitivity to changes in the risk-free interest rate curve. However, the interest rate sensitivity of a par-CDS contract is zero. For off-par contracts there is a sensitivity towards changes in the risk-free curve, but compared to the SpreadDV01 it is rather subdued. We only have to recall that economically a CDS contract behaves like a package of a risky floater and a risk-free floater. The interest rate sensitivity of these instruments is quite limited.

10.1.5 Continuous-Time Model

In addition to the discrete-time framework, CDS contracts can also be valued in a continuous-time approach.[26,62] In equation 7.24, we derived the corresponding pricing relation. We reiterate this equation below and identify the relation to both legs of the CDS.

$$V(\tau_m) = \underbrace{\sum_{i=1}^{m} V_i^{\text{CF}} \cdot \mathbb{E}\left[1_{\{\tau^* > \tau_i\}}\right]}_{V^{\text{PL}}} + \underbrace{\mathbb{E}\left[V^{\text{default}}(\tau^*) \cdot 1_{\{\tau_0 < \tau^* < \tau_m\}}\right]}_{-V^{\text{DL}}} \qquad (7.24\text{a})$$

Recall that τ^* is the time until default. Again, the premium leg is uncomplicated. We simply substitute $V_i^{\text{CF}} = c(\tau_m)\Delta\tau_i$ and derive the same results as in equation 10.1.

$$V^{PL} = \sum_{i=1}^{m} c(\tau_m)\Delta\tau_i R(\tau_i) \mathbb{E}\left[1_{\{\tau^* > \tau_i\}}\right] = c(\tau_m) \sum_{i=1}^{m} \Delta\tau_i R(\tau_i) S(\tau_i) \qquad (10.1\text{a})$$

The expected value of the default indicator function results in the survival probability function: $\mathbb{E}\left[1_{\{\tau^* > \tau_i\}}\right] = S(\tau_i)$ (see also equation 7.23). The default leg again comprises two parts, the default payment and the accrued premium. So $V^{\text{default}}(\tau^*)$ in equation 7.24 is substituted by the corresponding terms that reflect these two components. For the default payment, we insert $(1 - \text{Rec})R(\tau^*)$, which results in

$$\begin{aligned} V^{DP} &= \mathbb{E}\left[(1-\text{Rec})1_{\{\tau_0 < \tau^* < \tau_m\}} R(\tau^*)\right] = (1-\text{Rec})\mathbb{E}\left[1_{\{\tau_0 < \tau^* < \tau_m\}} R(\tau^*)\right] \\ &= (1-\text{Rec})\int_{\tau_0}^{\tau_m} F'(s)R(s)ds = (1-\text{Rec})\int_{\tau_0}^{\tau_m} h(s)S(s)R(s)ds \end{aligned} \qquad (10.2\text{a})$$

We can take the loss given default $(1 - \text{Rec})$ out of the expectation integral, because we assume that the recovery rate is deterministic and time-independent. The second part of the default leg, the accrued premium upon default V^{AP}, is calculated as the expected value of the accruals at the default time τ^*.

$$V^{AP} = \mathbb{E}\left[\sum_{i=1}^{m} \frac{\tau^* - \tau_{i-1}}{\tau_i - \tau_{i-1}} c(\tau_m) \Delta\tau_i 1_{\{\tau_{i-1} < \tau^* < \tau_i\}} R(\tau^*)\right]$$

$$= c(\tau_m) \sum_{i=1}^{m} \Delta\tau_i \int_{\tau_{i-1}}^{\tau_i} \frac{s - \tau_{i-1}}{\tau_i - \tau_{i-1}} F'(s) R(s) ds \qquad (10.3a)$$

$$= c(\tau_m) \sum_{i=1}^{m} \Delta\tau_i \int_{\tau_{i-1}}^{\tau_i} \frac{s - \tau_{i-1}}{\tau_i - \tau_{i-1}} h(s) S(s) R(s) ds$$

The term $\frac{\tau^* - \tau_{i-1}}{\tau_i - \tau_{i-1}}$ is the fraction of the coupon period until the time of default τ^*. Unfortunately, the resulting integral is quite complicated, since the terms $h(s)$, $S(s)$, $R(s)$ depend on the integration variable s, which refers to the default time τ^*. Hence we cannot get the risk of the integrals in equations 10.2a and 10.3a. The rest of the valuation procedure is similar to equations 10.4 and 10.5 derived above. The value of the CDS contract is calculated as $V^{CDS} = V^{PL} + V^{AP} - V^{DP}$.

The pricing relation derived in the continuous-time framework can also be used directly to value forward CDS contracts. The default indicator function is stated as $1_{\{\tau_0 < \tau^* < \tau_m\}}$, which captures defaults between τ_0 and τ_m. $\tau_0 > 0$ would refer to the default leg of a forward CDS. The same arguments apply for the indicator function for the premium leg in equation 10.1a and for the accrued premium in equation 10.3a.

However, solving these equations and fitting them to market prices involves some really nasty integrals. If we do not use a very simple relation for the hazard rate function, numerical procedures will be necessary.

10.1.6 Bloomberg's CDSW Function

Bloomberg provides a credit default swap calculator, which can be invoked by the command CDSW. Figure 10.1 shows an example for DaimlerChrysler (DCX). The screen is split into three parts. In the right part, named "Spreads", market data information such as the spread curve and the zero curve can be entered. Note that the spread curve is usually provided based on ISDA dates

(March 20, June 20, September 20, and December 20). In the current example, September 20, 2010 corresponds to the 5Y contract, having a par spread of 122 bp. Next to the par spreads, CDSW provides the implied cumulative default probability $1 - S(\tau)$. Below the curve information, one can set the recovery rate. In the upper part of the Spreads section, one can specify the discount curve. In this example, we used the generic Bloomberg swap curve.

In the second part, named "Deal Information", we have to specify the CDS contract. The most important data are notional amount, effective date, maturity date, and the deal spread. The latter is set to 122 bp, which corresponds to the 5Y par spread given in the "Spreads" section. To obtain the standard CDS payments dates, one should select IMM as the date generation method. Most other attributes contain standard entries, such as the quarterly payment frequency.

The third part in the CDSW function is the "Calculator" section. Here, the investor can specify the calculation model. It is common market practice to use the JPMorgan model,[63] which corresponds to the discrete-time model derived above. Other options are discounted spreads and a modified Hull-White model, which corresponds to our continuous-time model. However, we do not recommend using the discounted spread model. The field "Replication Spread" states the par spread of the analyzed contract given the par spread curve in the Spreads section. In the current example it is 122 bp, which we already entered in the field "Deal Spread" in the "Deal Information" section. The valuation in figure 10.1 refers to a par-CDS contract. Hence, the value of the contract is zero. This can be seen in the field "Market Value", which is zero. Finally, on the right hand side of the "Calculator" part, we see that the SpreadDV01 is €4,648.97.

The CDSW calculator can be used to determine sensitivities that are important information for managing a credit-risky position. Another important case for the calculator is the valuation of off-par contracts. A seasoned CDS contract for example will only accidentally trade at par. It is more likely that the deal spread deviates from current par spreads. The investor is then able to analyze the P&L of his position by using such a valuation tool. Moreover, in case a seasoned position should be unwound, both participants have to agree upon a closing price, the so-called back-end payment. Such a transaction involves a calculation of the cash settlement one counterparty has to pay to the other. For this purpose it is common market practice to use CDSW.

First, the two counterparties have to choose the appropriate interest rate curve, for example the Bloomberg generic swap curve. Then they agree upon the par-CDS spread for the remaining time to maturity of the contract. And finally, the cash price is calculated using this par spread. Note that there is one

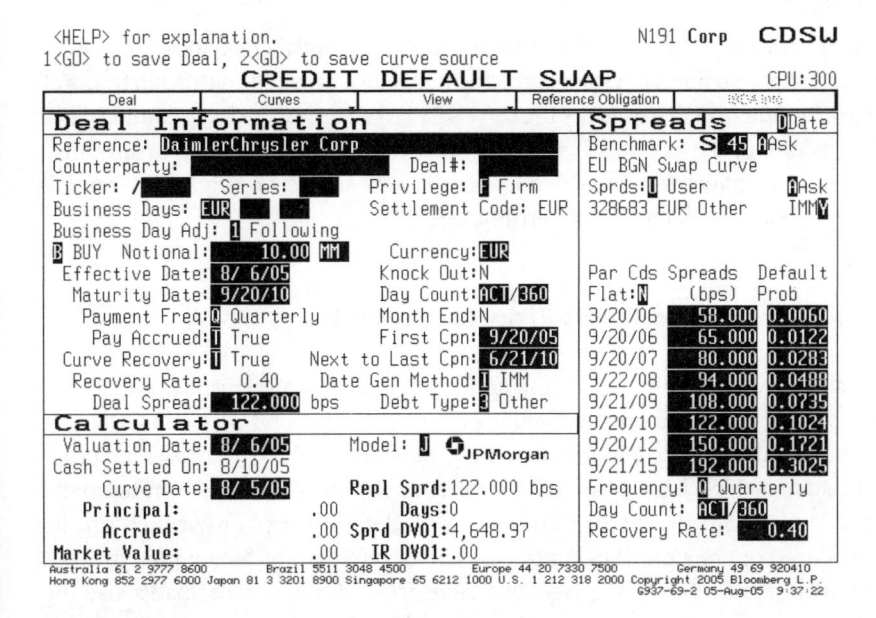

Fig. 10.1: Bloomberg's credit default swap calculator CDSW

subtlety involved in this process. The cash price is usually calculated using the agreed par spread as a flat spread curve. This facilitates the transaction, because otherwise the two counterparties would have to agree upon several spread levels. Note that the investor does not necessarily have to unwind a seasoned position with the initial counterparty. He can also unwind it with another bank that offers a better price, for example. The investor will then simply hand over the contract to the new bank, which will then be the new counterparty for the initial counterparty.

The other possibility to close a seasoned CDS position is to enter into an offsetting contract. The advantage of this procedure is that the offsetting contract does not have to match the initial contract exactly, which enables the investor to trade in a corresponding liquid on-the-run maturity bracket. Consider an investor who sold protection on a company for a spread of 100 bp. After a few months, the market spread tightened 20 bp. The investor could now buy protection in a contract that is slightly longer than the initial, but has to pay only 80 bp. He would keep both contracts until maturity and would earn a spread income of 20 bp. In case of a credit event, the investor simply passes through the cash or physical delivery.

Unfortunately, these two transactions leave him with a risky position. First, the offsetting position does not perfectly match the seasoned contract in terms of maturity date, which expresses the convexity risk. Second, he has a counterparty risk, as one of the offsetting positions involves buying protection. And third, in case of a default event he will no longer receive the 20 bp spread differential, because both contracts will be terminated.

10.2 Options on Credit-Risky Instruments

As outlined in section 2.6.4, the notion of credit options covers a wide range of instruments: bond options, options on single-name and portfolio CDS contracts (so-called credit default swaptions), and even options on correlation products, such as FTD baskets and CDO tranches. In the following, we refer to the latest category in the credit universe, credit default swaptions, which can be considered options on CDS contracts. The designation of the option type (call or put) is a little confusing (see also table 10.1). Market participants use the same notation as for interest rate swaptions by referring to the premium leg of the CDS. A payer credit default swaption refers to an option to buy protection at a specified CDS rate at maturity; in other words, it is a put option on the value of the credit risk. It is referred to as payer default swaption, because the investor has to pay the premium in the underlying CDS. A receiver swaption refers to selling protection. The analogy to stock options can be somehow misleading when we use the common perspective of an investor who sells protection (and receives the premium payments). The value of such a CDS position declines if the CDS spread increases. Hence, a receiver option offers a positive payoff in case the spread increases. However, for increasing spreads, the value of the CDS decreases. A receiver swaption can therefore be considered as a put option on the credit risk. To avoid confusion, we prefer thinking about credit default swaptions in terms of CDS rates (payer/receiver), rather than in terms of CDS values or credit risk (put/call).

Tab. 10.1: Credit default swaption notation

Swaption type	CDS protection	premium pmts	Risk perspective
payer	buying protection	paying	put
receiver	selling protection	receiving	call

The most common and therefore most liquid contracts are 3M-into-5Y European-style swaptions, meaning that the option expires in three months and will deliver a 5Y CDS contract. For liquid names, option prices are quoted for a number of strike rates, which allows for the valuation of out-of-the-money options.

Credit default swaptions can be traded on single-name and on index basis. A single-name credit default swaption is an option to enter into a standard single-name CDS contract, while its index counterpart is an option to enter into a CDS index contract, such as the iTraxx. Both instruments are quite similar, but there is an important difference. While standard single-name credit default swaptions do not offer default protection until the option's expiration (knock-out-on-default feature), options on credit indices are not knocked by a default event in the underlying basket and hence provide default protection also during the lifetime of the option.

The following introduction to credit default swaption pricing is structured in two parts. The first part shows the standard pricing framework for single-name credit default swaptions. In the second part, we highlight the changes in this framework that we have to implement when pricing index swaptions. Note that in this analysis, we present a modified Black-76 model,[64] which established itself as a kind of market standard for credit default swaptions.[65] Nevertheless, there are numerous other approaches discussed in financial textbooks. Most of these refer to the reduced-form framework as introduced in the defaultable binomial tree model in section 8.1. For a more detailed analysis, the interested reader might refer to the papers of Hull and White[66], Jamshidian[67], Brigo[68], Schmidt[42,43], and Gisdakis.[44]

10.2.1 Single-Name Credit Default Swaptions

The most important feature of standard single-name credit default swaptions (a.k.a. CDS options) is that they offer protection against spread changes and not against default risk, as most of the single-name swaptions are so-called knock-out-on-default contracts. However, it is apparent that credit default swaptions have to be European-style rather than American or Bermudan. As an example, think of an American-style spread option – one which can be exercised at any time. The owner of a payer option, which refers to buying protection, can – and surely will – exercise his option shortly before default when financial distress of the reference credit has already become apparent. Hence, an American-style option is one that includes default protection due to technical reasons, unless there are strict rules that circumvent the aforementioned exercise strategy. For receiver default swaptions (selling protection), the knock-out-on-default feature is not required. The holder of the option will not exercise it in case of a default event, because this would mean selling protection on an already defaulted name. A receiver default swaption will only be exercised if the reference spread is tighter than the strike spread, not wider.

To derive a pricing relation for credit default swaptions, we have to think about the payoff for such an option. We use a 3M-into-5Y payer swaption as an example. This option has an expiration of three months and the holder can enter into a 5Y CDS contract at expiration. Suppose the strike K of the option was fixed at 100 bp. This means that we have the option to buy protection on the reference obligor with a CDS rate of 100 bp. In other words, the investor pays an annual fee of 100 bp for the default protection. If the market spread at expiration of the option is 80 bp, he would not exercise the option, because he could buy protection for 80 bp directly. However, if the spread were trading at 120 bp, he would exercise, because he would get the protection 20 bp cheaper than the current spread level. In terms of present value, the payoff would be 20 bp times the annuity of the 5Y CDS contract. Here we used equation 10.7 to derive the change in value. The mathematical description of the payoff structure including the knock-out-on-default is shown in table 10.2.

Tab. 10.2: Credit default swaption payoff including knock-out on default

Type	No default	Default
Payer	$\max[(c(\tau_0, \tau_m) - K) \cdot A(\tau_0, \tau_m), 0]$	0
Receiver	$\max[(K - c(\tau_0, \tau_m)) \cdot A(\tau_0, \tau_m), 0]$	0

Note that in table 10.2, $c(\tau_0, \tau_m)$ is the forward spread for a CDS contract with time to maturity τ_m and an effective date τ_0, and $A(\tau_0, \tau_m)$ is the corresponding annuity. Obviously, τ_0 will be zero at the expiration date of the option. This is a similar payoff structure as for plain-vanilla interest rate swaptions. Hence, we can use similar techniques for pricing credit default swaptions. We only have to account for the knock-out-on-default feature. It is standard market practice to quote swaption prices (for interest rates as well as for credit default swaptions) in terms of the Black-76 model[64] (see JPMorgan's credit option pricing model[65]).

$$V^{\text{payer}} = A(T_0, T_m) \cdot [c(T_0, T_m) \cdot N(x) - K \cdot N(x - \sigma\sqrt{T_0})]$$
$$V^{\text{receiver}} = A(T_0, T_m) \cdot [-c(T_0, T_m) \cdot N(-x) + K \cdot N(-x + \sigma\sqrt{T_0})] \quad (10.12)$$
$$\text{with } x = \frac{\ln(\frac{c(T_0, T_m)}{K})}{\sigma\sqrt{T_0}} + \frac{1}{2}\sigma\sqrt{T_0}$$

$N(x)$ is the standard normal distribution function, $c(T_0, T_m)$ the forward swap rate, K the strike rate, and σ the Black-76 swaption volatility. Using the risky annuity instead of the risk-free one implicitly accounts for the knock-out-on-default feature, because the expected payoff is discounted using the survival probability in addition to the risk-free discount factor. In this way, the value of the option is derived as a fraction of the notional amount on which the swaption is written. It is usually quoted in terms of basis points.

In equation 10.12, we use the forward CDS rate $c(T_0, T_m)$ for the period between the expiration of the option and the maturity of the underlying CDS. Moreover, $A(T_0, T_m)$ is the corresponding forward annuity. The Black-76 model assumes that the forward CDS rate follows a geometrical Brownian motion and is therefore log-normally distributed. Consequently, the Black-76 parameter σ corresponds to the annualized volatility of the log returns of the CDS spread.

> **Example 23: Log-Return Volatility of the 5Y CDS Spread for DaimlerChrysler**
>
> To get an idea about the magnitude of the Black-76 volatility parameter σ that we need in equation 10.12, we calculate the annualized historic volatility for the 5Y CDS spread of DaimlerChrysler. This can be done by using the following estimation:
>
> $$\hat{\sigma} = \text{StDev}\left[\ln\left(\frac{c_{i+1}(T_m)}{c_i(T_m)}\right)\right] \cdot \sqrt{250}$$
>
> For the DaimlerChrysler 5Y CDS rate (Bloomberg-Ticker CDCX1E5), the historical log-return volatility is about 54 percent. We use the Excel function StDev on the log returns of the 5Y CDS rate time series. Multiplying with $\sqrt{250}$ results in an annualized volatility, assuming 250 trading days per year on average. Note that we did not equate the Black-76 volatility parameter σ with the historical volatility. For option pricing, we need the future volatility; the historical one is just a rough proxy for this quantity.

10.2.2 Index Swaptions

Options on CDS indices, such as the iTraxx and the CDX, are very similar to single-name credit default swaptions. A payer swaption on an index, for example, is an option to buy protection in the underlying index for a given strike spread (see section 10.3 for the pricing of a CDS index). The only difference is that options on CDS indices usually do not have a knock-out-on-default feature and therefore offer protection against default risk during the lifetime of the option. Therefore, the valuation framework shown in equation 10.12 has to be modified. Table 10.3 summarizes the payoff structure for a credit default swaption without a knock-out-on-default feature.

Tab. 10.3: Credit default swaption payoff excluding knock-out on default

Type	No default	Default
Payer	$\max[(c - K) \cdot A, 0]$	$\max[(c - K) \cdot A + \text{LGD}, 0]$
Receiver	$\max[(K - c) \cdot A, 0]$	$\max[(K - c) \cdot A - \text{LGD}, 0]$

$c = c(\tau_0, \tau_m)$ and $A = A(\tau_0, \tau_m)$

The payoff of a credit default swaption in case of no default is apparently the same as for the option including a knock-out feature. However, in case of a default event, the option does not expire valueless but integrates the loss given default. For a payer swaption (buying protection), the investor receives the normal payoff of the option plus a payment which compensates the loss given default (LGD), while for a receiver swaption (selling protection) he has to pay the default compensation. It is important to note that the LGD payment cannot be separated from the payoff. For example, an investor cannot choose to receive the default compensation and not to enter in the remaining index swap contract at the same time. He has to either accept both parts of the payoff or not execute the option at all. Such a split strategy would be profitable if the remaining index after a default were trading below the strike price of the option. We only have to think about an investor who entered into a payer swaption contract (buying protection) shortly at a time when a potential default event for one participant was already apparent; therefore the index spread already traded at high levels. Excluding the culprit after default will result in a tighter index spread. Hence, the option investor has to calculate whether the whole payoff (default compensation plus marked-to-market loss in the remaining index) is positive. Only then will he exercise the option.

As a consequence, simply calculating the value for the corresponding knock-out-on-default option and adding the cost for the default protection during the option's lifetime will misprice the contract. Such an approach would treat the default compensation and the option payoff as two separable contracts, which could be exercised differently. As demonstrated above, this is not the case.

Fortunately, it is not difficult to integrate the default compensation into the valuation formula. The present value of the expected loss (recall that EL = PD × LGD) during the lifetime of the option can be approximated as $c(\tau_0) \cdot A(0, \tau_0)$, because in a par-CDS contract the value of the premium payments equals the value of the default leg (excluding effects from the accrual upon default; see equation 10.5). Here, $c(\tau_0)$ is the par spread for a CDS with the same time to maturity as the option (i.e., τ_0) and $A(0, \tau_0)$ is the risky annuity for this CDS contract. Since we have to evaluate the loss at the expiration date of the option, we have to compound the present value of the expected loss $c(\tau_0) \cdot A(0, \tau_0)$ up to the expiration date by dividing by the risk-free discount factor $R(\tau_0)$. Hence, we can integrate the settlement of the LGD into the payoff by adjusting the forward CDS rate $c(\tau_0, \tau_m)$:[65]

$$c_{\text{adj}}(\tau_0, \tau_m) = c(\tau_0, \tau_m) + c(\tau_0) \cdot \frac{A(0, \tau_0)}{R(\tau_0) \cdot A(\tau_0, \tau_m)} \qquad (10.13)$$

Putting the pieces together, pricing index swaptions with no knock-out feature can be done by equation 10.12. One only has to use the default-loss-adjusted forward CDS rate $c_{\text{adj}}(\tau_0, \tau_m)$ shown in equation 10.13 instead of the non-adjusted one.

10.3 CDS Indices

A CDS index, such as the iTraxx Europe Benchmark, can be regarded as a portfolio of single-name CDS contracts. But in terms of valuation, its constituting CDS contracts are treated differently from standard market practice, since they are traded on an off-par basis. In fact, they all have identical premium legs, which means that deal spreads, maturity, and payment dates are the same for all index members. The value of the basket from the perspective of a protection seller is simply the (weighted) sum of the value of its constituent.

$$V^{idx} = \sum_{j=1}^{k} w_j \cdot V_j^{CDS} = \sum_{j=1}^{k} w_j \cdot \left(V_j^{PL} + V_j^{AP} - V_j^{DP}\right) \qquad (10.14)$$

Bear in mind that in the approximated CDS pricing model the value of the swap legs (i.e., the terms V_j^{PL}, V_j^{AP} and V_j^{DP}) depend linearly on the survival probabilities (cf. equation 10.4). Under the assumptions that (1) all default events occur on average in the middle of an accrual period and defaults are settled on scheduled payment dates, and (2) all counterparties have the same recovery value, we can derive the quantity $S^{idx}(\tau_i)$ as the weighted sum of the single-name survival probabilities. In addition, we use the fact that the deal spreads $c(\tau_m)$ and the payment dates τ_i are the same for all underlyings. $S^{idx}(\tau_i)$ corresponds to the survival probability function in the single-name valuation procedure, but it is not the survival probability of the portfolio. It can rather be viewed as the expected loss across the whole portfolio under the assumption of zero recovery.

$$S^{idx}(\tau_i) = \sum_{j=1}^{k} w_j \cdot S^j(\tau_i) \qquad (10.15)$$

By inserting equation 10.15 into equation 10.4 we can derive the following formula for the (theoretical) price of the CDS basket:

$$\begin{aligned} V^{idx} &= \sum_{i=1}^{m} c(\tau_m) \cdot \Delta\tau_i \cdot R(\tau_i) \cdot S^{idx}(\tau_i) \\ &+ \sum_{i=1}^{m} c(\tau_m) \cdot \frac{\Delta\tau_i}{2} \cdot R(\tau_i) \cdot \left(S^{idx}(\tau_{i-1}) - S^{idx}(\tau_i)\right) \\ &- (1 - \text{Rec}) \sum_{i=1}^{m} R(\tau_i) \cdot \left(S^{idx}(\tau_{i-1}) - S^{idx}(\tau_i)\right) \end{aligned} \qquad (10.16)$$

This pricing algorithm is very similar to equation 10.4. The only difference is the survival probability $S^{idx}(\tau)$, which now accounts for portfolio losses rather than single-name events. However, for valuing CDS indices, it is common practice to skip the value of the accrued premium upon default (i.e., the second line in equation 10.16).

The value V^{idx} of a CDS index swap refers to the difference between the current and the stipulated spread $c(\tau_m)$, which is fixed at the issue date of an index series and does not change over time. If the current spread level trades above this fixed spread, a protection seller receives the present value of this difference as an upfront payment. In addition, he receives the premium payments $c(\tau_m)$ as a running spread. The price of the index swap is quoted as the flat CDS par spread, which resembles the same value as V^{idx}, given the contracted premium leg. This trading mechanism is more similar to the cash bond universe than to the CDS universe. An investor receives a fixed cash flow in exchange for taking the risk, and the credit-specific component of the price is quoted as a spread.

In fact, equation 10.15 is quite useful, since it allows us to calculate various other quantities given the par spread curves of the underlyings. Besides the par spread curve of the basket, we can calculate forward prices for the basket, which is necessary for valuing options on the index swaps.

Although the illustrated valuation approach is not very difficult to understand, it is a little complex to implement. Most market participants prefer an easy algorithm that can be implemented within a simple spreadsheet calculation. An approximation of the theoretical value is arrived at by simply computing the average of the underlying spreads. However, this approach involves three basic problems: a dispersion bias, a maturity mismatch, and a quotation bias:

- The *dispersion bias* is based upon the fact that an iTraxx swap pays a uniform spread for all index constituents, while regular CDS contracts pay individual spread levels. However, this problem can be resolved by using a weighted instead of an unweighted average of single-name spread levels, which leads to a significant discrepancy in calculation, especially when the dispersion of individual spreads is large. As long as the spread dispersion within an index is limited, this bias is negligible.
- The *maturity mismatch* refers to a lack of appropriate single-name CDS quotations owing to the fact that the rollover of iTraxx indices occurs only every six months, while regular CDS contracts roll quarterly. This problem always appears during the second quarter in an index contract's life and can only be solved by using certain interpolation approaches.
- The *quotation bias* is attributable to initially fixed spread levels, while entering into a iTraxx swap is always accompanied by an upfront payment to compensate for the intrinsic value. In order to convert quoted spreads into this amount (via Bloomberg's CDSW tool), several partial unrealistic assumptions are necessary. However, the resulting quotation bias is negligible as long as the difference between theoretical spread and strike spread level is limited.

Even when accounting for these issues, there still may be discrepancies with where the index market trades. These deviations are often referred to as the *basis to theoretical* or *skew*. Recent history has shown that this skew can be quite substantial; for example, quoted spreads for the 10Y iTraxx Crossover swap exceeded theoretical levels by about 20 bp, given that market levels are driven by supply and demand rather than by sophisticated models. From a theoretical point of view, bid–offer spreads and liquidity considerations allow such deviations to a certain extent. For a more detailed analysis please refer to Felsenheimer, Gisdakis, and Zaiser.[69]

10.4 n^{th}-to-Default Baskets

The value of an nth-to-default basket swap contract can be simply derived by using the analogy to a normal CDS contract. The protection seller receives a premium until the specified default event occurs (i.e., the nth default) or until maturity of the contract. If there is a default, he has to pay the default loss $(1 - \text{Rec})$ to the protection buyer, who in return pays the accrued premium until default. The contract is then terminated. The valuation algorithm resembles that for the standard CDS valuation with some modifications. Consequently, we can value n^{th}-to-default baskets using a modified version of equation 10.4. We only have to use the survival probability with respect to the nth default $S^{[n]}(\tau)$ instead of the single-name survival probability $S(\tau)$. Moreover, the contract spread $c^{[n]}(\tau_m)$ obviously depends on the trigger level of the basket.

$$V^{[n]} = \sum_{i=1}^{m} c^{[n]}(\tau_m) \cdot \Delta\tau_i \cdot R(\tau_i) \cdot S^{[n]}(\tau_i)$$
$$+ \sum_{i=1}^{m} c^{[n]}(\tau_m) \cdot \frac{\Delta\tau_i}{2} \cdot R(\tau_i) \cdot \left(S^{[n]}(\tau_{i-1}) - S^{[n]}(\tau_i)\right)$$
$$- (1 - \text{Rec}) \sum_{i=1}^{m} R(\tau_i) \cdot \left(S^{[n]}(\tau_{i-1}) - S^{[n]}(\tau_i)\right)$$

We defined the survival probability function of nth-to-default baskets in chapter 9. It is important to note that this valuation of nth-to-default baskets integrates an average recovery rate. The previous derivation of $S^{[n]}(\tau_i)$ concentrated only on the default probability, which is the probability for a certain number of defaults. It does not provide any information about which credit defaults. Therefore, we have to use an average recovery rate. If company-specific recoveries need to be integrated, we have to use a portfolio model that provides not only the probability $\pi(n)$ of n defaults, but also the probabilities of default per constituent.

Since the valuation framework for single-name CDS and n^{th}-to-default baskets is very similar, most of the conclusions that are valid for CDS are also valid for n^{th}-to-default baskets. For example, we derive the par spread of the basket by the valuation formula with respect to the basket spread $c^{[n]}(\tau_m)$. Similar to the CDS, we infer the level of the central risk factors that drive the spread from market prices. For default baskets, the central quantity is the default correlation. Consequently, we derive the market-implied default correlation by adjusting the default correlation so that the model reprices the market levels. Unfortunately, we have to solve this problem numerically.

In table 10.4, we show four standardized 5Y FTD baskets from the iTraxx universe. Usually market makers quote in their runs the spread levels for underlyings, the *sum-of-all-spreads* (SOS) of the basket, and the bid–offer spreads for selling and buying protection in the baskets. The SOS is a central quantity, as the spread for an FTD will trade within the range from the highest spread in the basket and the SOS. Therefore, bid–offer quotes are also presented as a percentage of the SOS. Finally, the market-implied default correlation for mid quotes is also shown in table 10.4.

Tab. 10.4: Examples for standardized iTraxx first-to-default baskets (5Y)

Automobiles		Diversified		HiVol		Crossover	
Continental	22.5	Bayer	29.5	BAT	50.0	ABB	112.5
Peugeot	33.5	FT	39.5	BT	46.5	Ahold	145.0
Renault	25.8	HVB	22.5	ICI	67.5	Alcatel	115.0
Valeo	23.0	MKS	109.5	MKS	109.5	Corus	360.0
VW	22.5	Suez	30.5	Vivendi	62.5	EMI	165.0
		VW	57.5				
SOS	260.5		289.0		336.0		897.5
Bid	197.0		228.0		262.0		664.0
Offer	224.0		254.0		292.0		726.0
% SOS Bid	76%		79%		78%		74%
% SOS Offer	86%		88%		87%		81%
Implied Corr	35%		29%		29%		27%

Single-name and basket spreads are stated in bp.

However, there is one major difference in managing defaults compared to single-name CDS, because the value of default baskets depends on more than one risk factor. Therefore, we have to derive sensitivities with respect to spread changes and with respect to the implied correlation. In figures 10.2 and 10.3, we show Bloomberg's basket default swap calculator. This tool has two important screens, one in which one specifies the basket contract (i.e., effective date, maturity date, and the number of defaults that trigger the default of the contract) and one in which we have to specify the basket constituents.

On the basket screen, we can derive the spread sensitivity (i.e., the SpreadDV01) for the whole basket. It states the value change per basis point change in the

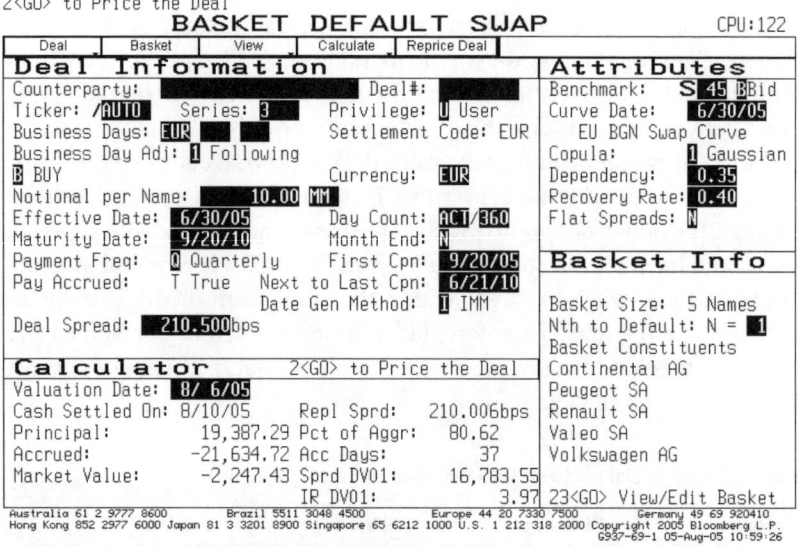

```
<HELP> for explanation.                                  N191 Corp    CDSN
2<GO> to Price the Deal
                    BASKET DEFAULT SWAP                        CPU:122
     Deal    |   Basket   |   View   |  Calculate  | Reprice Deal
   Deal Information                              Attributes
 Counterparty:                    Deal#:         Benchmark:    S 45 B Bid
 Ticker: /AUTO   Series: 3    Privilege: U User  Curve Date:    6/30/05
 Business Days: EUR           Settlement Code: EUR  EU BGN Swap Curve
 Business Day Adj: 1 Following                   Copula:       1 Gaussian
 B BUY                        Currency:  EUR     Dependency:    0.35
 Notional per Name:    10.00 MM                  Recovery Rate: 0.40
 Effective Date: 6/30/05    Day Count: ACT/360   Flat Spreads: N
 Maturity Date:  9/20/10    Month End: N
 Payment Freq:  Q Quarterly   First Cpn: 9/20/05    Basket Info
 Pay Accrued:   T True  Next to Last Cpn: 6/21/10
                        Date Gen Method: I IMM   Basket Size:  5 Names
 Deal Spread:   210.500 bps                      Nth to Default: N = 1
                                                 Basket Constituents
   Calculator           2<GO> to Price the Deal  Continental AG
 Valuation Date: 8/ 6/05                         Peugeot SA
 Cash Settled On: 8/10/05    Repl Sprd:  210.006bps  Renault SA
 Principal:        19,387.29 Pct of Aggr:  80.62 Valeo SA
 Accrued:         -21,634.72 Acc Days:       37  Volkswagen AG
 Market Value:     -2,247.43 Sprd DV01: 16,783.55
                             IR DV01:        3.97 23<GO> View/Edit Basket
Australia 61 2 9777 8600       Brazil 5511 3048 4500       Europe 44 20 7330 7500       Germany 49 69 920410
Hong Kong 852 2977 6000 Japan 81 3 3201 8900 Singapore 65 6212 1000 U.S. 1 212 318 2000 Copyright 2005 Bloomberg L.P.
                                                                    G937-69-1 05-Aug-05 10:59:26
```

Fig. 10.2: Bloomberg's basket default swap calculator CDSN

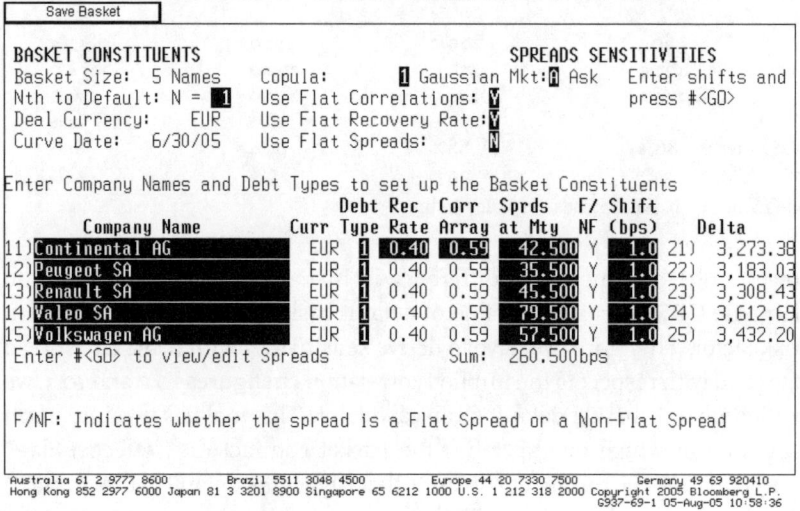

```
<HELP> for explanation.                                  N191 Corp    CDSN
Enter Basket Information, or <Menu> to return the Deal Page and Reprice
                 BASKET SETUP/SENSITIVITIES
   Save Basket

 BASKET CONSTITUENTS                        SPREADS SENSITIVITIES
 Basket Size:  5 Names   Copula:    1 Gaussian  Mkt: A Ask  Enter shifts and
 Nth to Default: N = 1   Use Flat Correlations: Y         press #<GO>
 Deal Currency:    EUR   Use Flat Recovery Rate: Y
 Curve Date:   6/30/05   Use Flat Spreads:       N

 Enter Company Names and Debt Types to set up the Basket Constituents
                          Debt  Rec   Corr   Sprds   F/  Shift
         Company Name     Curr Type   Rate   Array   at Mty  NF  (bps)    Delta
 11)Continental AG         EUR  1    0.40   0.59    42.500  Y   1.0  21) 3,273.38
 12)Peugeot SA             EUR  1    0.40   0.59    35.500  Y   1.0  22) 3,183.03
 13)Renault SA             EUR  1    0.40   0.59    45.500  Y   1.0  23) 3,308.43
 14)Valeo SA               EUR  1    0.40   0.59    79.500  Y   1.0  24) 3,612.69
 15)Volkswagen AG          EUR  1    0.40   0.59    57.500  Y   1.0  25) 3,432.20
 Enter #<GO> to view/edit Spreads        Sum:    260.500bps


 F/NF: Indicates whether the spread is a Flat Spread or a Non-Flat Spread

Australia 61 2 9777 8600       Brazil 5511 3048 4500       Europe 44 20 7330 7500       Germany 49 69 920410
Hong Kong 852 2977 6000 Japan 81 3 3201 8900 Singapore 65 6212 1000 U.S. 1 212 318 2000 Copyright 2005 Bloomberg L.P.
                                                                    G937-69-1 05-Aug-05 10:58:36
```

Fig. 10.3: Bloomberg's CDSN (basket setup and single-name sensitivities)

basket. Here, the spread for all underlyings are shifted in parallel. Hence, this information can be used to assess the risk of a broad market change, such as when all single-name spreads move parallel to one another. However, the value of the basket also depends on the spread dispersion. This means that the value of the basket will change, even when spreads of two underlyings move in the opposite direction, keeping the average spread constant (see also chapter 9 for an analysis of the sensitivity of the portfolio default density with respect to dispersion). For this purpose, the CDSN tool provides SpreadDV01s for the individual underlyings on the basket constituents screen (see delta column in figure 10.3). It is interesting to note that the sum of the single-name deltas corresponds approximately with the SpreadDV01 for the whole basket.

Excursus 7: Upper and Lower Bounds for First-to-Default Baskets

As stated before, the fair spread level of a first-to-default basket should always lie within a clearly defined range. The lower bound for the FTD spread is defined by the spread level of the most risky basket constituent. On the other hand, the sum-of-all-spreads acts as an upper bound for the FTD spread. In the following, we provide a justification for this range.

Let us consider that the basket comprises m different reference obligations, enumerated by $i = 1, 2, \ldots, m$. Without loss of generality, we assume $s_1 \leq s_2 \leq \ldots \leq s_m$. For simplicity's sake, we presuppose that each reference obligation is subject to the same recovery rate $R_i = \bar{R}$. In accordance with the simple credit triangle approximation, $s_i = p_i \cdot (1 - R_i)$, the probabilities of default p_i are also ordered (i.e., $p_1 \leq p_2 \leq \ldots \leq p_m$).

The bounds for the FTD spread can be derived by considering extreme situations. First, let us assume a setting where all default events (we denote them by B_i for all $i = 1, 2, \ldots, m$) are mutually exclusive. In other words, if a default event B_i occurs, no other reference obligation in the basket can default. This can be mathematically expressed by:

$$\mathbb{P}(B_i \cap B_j) = 0 \text{ for all } i \neq j \text{ and } i, j \in \{1, 2, \ldots, m\}$$

The following Venn diagram illustrates this theoretical case based on a basket encompassing five names. Please note that the default events do not overlap.

sample space

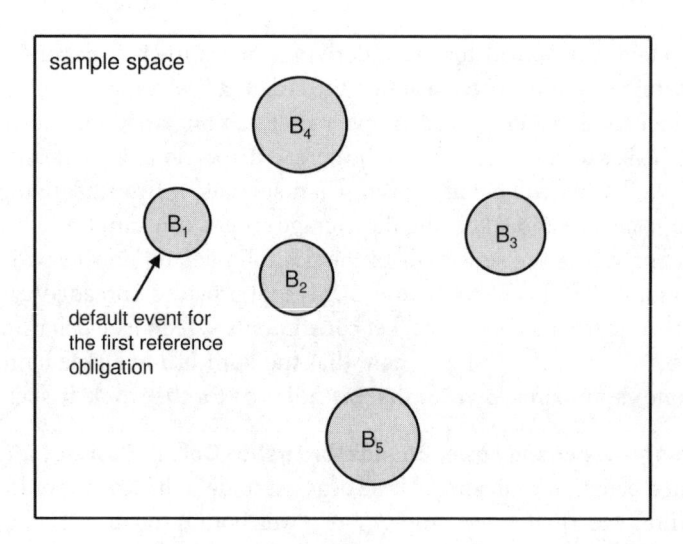

B₄

B₁ ← default event for the first reference obligation

B₂

B₃

B₅

Venn diagram for mutually exclusive default events

Based on these assumptions, we can infer the probability that the FTD contract defaults:

$$\begin{aligned} p_{\text{FTD}} &= \mathbb{P}(\text{at least one default}) \\ &= \mathbb{P}(B_1 \cup B_2 \cup \ldots \cup B_m) \\ &= \mathbb{P}(B_1) + \mathbb{P}(B_2) + \ldots + \mathbb{P}(B_m) \\ &= \sum_{i=1}^{m} p_i \end{aligned}$$

When we again resort to the credit triangle, we obtain the fair spread of the first-to-default basket:

$$\begin{aligned} s_{FTD} &= p_{\text{FTD}} \cdot (1 - R_{\text{FTD}}) = \left(\sum_{i=1}^{m} p_i \right) \cdot (1 - \bar{R}) = \sum_{i=1}^{m} p_i \cdot (1 - \bar{R}) \\ &= \sum_{i=1}^{m} s_i \end{aligned}$$

Accordingly, we obtain the sum-of-all-spreads as the fair spread level for the first-to-default basket. In this extreme and unrealistic case, the FTD contract is tantamount to a portfolio of single-name CDS contracts due to the fact that the probability for two or more defaults amounts to zero.

Now let us consider another extreme situation. We assume that the default events overlap in such a way that if a reference obligation i defaults, all others names j with a default probability of at least p_i will default as well. This can be mathematically expressed as follows:

$$\mathbb{P}(B_i \cap B_j) = \mathbb{P}(B_i) = p_i \text{ for all } i < j$$

Alternatively, one could state:

$$\mathbb{P}(B_j \mid B_i) = 1 \text{ for all } i < j$$

This case can also be illustrated by a Venn diagram, which also provides an alternative description for this setting, namely $B_1 \subset B_2 \subset \ldots \subset B_m$:

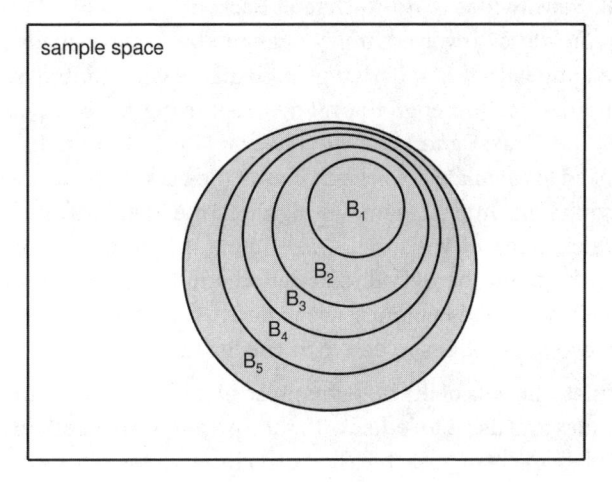

Venn diagram for nested default events

We can again infer the probability that the FTD contract defaults under these special assumptions:

$$\begin{aligned} p_{\text{FTD}} &= \mathbb{P}(\text{at least one default}) \\ &= \mathbb{P}(B_1 \cup B_2 \cup \ldots \cup B_m) \\ &= \mathbb{P}(B_m) \text{ since } B_i \subset B_m \text{ for all } i = 1, 2, \ldots, m \\ &= p_m = max\{p_1, p_2, \ldots, p_m\} \end{aligned}$$

The probability of default for the FTD contract coincides with the highest PD among the basket constituents. The basket product can thus be hedged by simply entering into a single-name CDS contract referring to this name. Accordingly, the FTD spread should be identical to the spread of this single-name CDS, i.e., $s_{\text{FTD}} = max\{s_1, s_2, \ldots, s_m\}$.

In practice, the true relationship will somewhat lie between these two extremes. This leads us to the conclusion that the fair spread level of a first-to-default basket will lie between these two bounds:

$$max\{s_1, s_2, \ldots, s_m\} \leq s_{\text{FTD}} \leq \sum_{i=1}^{m} s_i$$

Excursus 8: Sensitivities of nth-to-Default Baskets

Hedging spread risk involved in n^{th}-to-default baskets is usually performed by delta hedging with the underlying single-name CDS contracts. However, another approach is to hedge the market risk using a corresponding CDS index (e.g., the iTraxx) and leave the idiosyncratic risk unhedged. In both cases, we need to calculate the sensitivities of the basket contract with respect to the hedging instrument. Here, we highlight the methodology for hedging a first-to-default basket with the iTraxx. Leaving the default risk and the dependency between the default correlation and the spread level aside, we can use a delta-adjusted beta measure to derive the hedge ratio.

There are two possibilities to derive the hedge ratio:

- Calculate the beta of the average spread of the basket constituents versus the index and use it together with the SpreadDV01 of both instruments.
- Calculate the beta of each basket constituent versus the index individually and use the single-name SpreadDV01 of the FTD basket to derive a hedge ratio.

We explore both possibilities using the standardized HiVol FTD basket and the iTraxx HiVol index as an example. For the first variant, we derive the beta of the average spread of the basket constituents with the index (0.45, see table below). To arrive at the correct hedge ratio we have to multiply the beta with the quotient of the SpreadDV01 of the FTD (16.44) and of the iTraxx index (4.46). This results in a ratio of 1.65.

HiVol FTD basket data

HiVol FTD	Spread	Beta vs. HiVol	SpreadDV01	Beta contr.
BAT	47.0	0.11	3.18	0.34
BT	43.5	0.21	3.15	0.65
ICI	57.5	0.79	3.27	2.59
MKS	111.5	0.59	3.60	2.11
Vivendi	52.5	0.54	3.23	1.74
Average	62.4	0.45	16.44	
HiVol (mid)	66.5	1.00	4.46	
SOS	312			
FTD (mid)	257			
% SOS (mid)	82%			
Implied Correlation	31%			

In the second approach, we multiply each individual beta by the individual SpreadDV01 to arrive at a beta contribution. As an example, for MKS (beta of 0.59 and SpreadDV01 of 3.60) this results in 2.11. The sum over the beta contribution of all constituents (here 7.44) has to be divided by the SpreadDV01 of the hedge instrument (i.e., the iTraxx HiVol index, 4.46). The resulting hedge ratio of 1.67 is very close to the previously derived one.

As a consequence, for baskets with a limited spread dispersion we can use the simple variant (beta of the average spread of the constituents) to derive hedge ratios between indices and FTD baskets. The DV01 sensitivities can be derived using Bloomberg's basket default swap calculator CDSN.

10.5 Collateralized Debt Obligations

As for the nth-to-default basket, we can derive the valuation formula for an unfunded (swap-like) CDO tranche from equation 10.16. However, some modifications have to be applied. In contrast to an NTD basket, a CDO tranche contract is not terminated if the first default hits the tranche. The contract stays alive until maturity, unless the losses incurred from defaults with the underlying portfolio completely erode the tranche notional. If a default hits a tranche, the investor has to cover the loss and the tranche notional is reduced by the loss incurred. However, the investor will keep receiving premium payments on the remaining amount of the tranche notional.

We characterize tranche-specific quantities of a CDO tranche by its attachment point a and detachment point b (e.g., $V^{[a,b]}$). Note the different notation for n^{th}-to-default baskets and CDO tranches. A quantity that refers to a default basket is characterized by one index (e.g., $S^{[n]}(\tau)$), while the corresponding notation for a tranche has two (e.g., $\hat{S}^{[a,b]}(\tau)$).

$$V^{[a,b]} = \sum_{i=1}^{m} c(\tau_m) \cdot \Delta\tau_i \cdot R(\tau_i) \cdot \hat{S}^{[a,b]}(\tau_i)$$
$$+ \sum_{i=1}^{m} c(\tau_m) \cdot \frac{\Delta\tau_i}{2} \cdot R(\tau_i) \cdot \left(\hat{S}^{[a,b]}(\tau_{i-1}) - \hat{S}^{[a,b]}(\tau_i) \right) \quad (10.17)$$
$$- \sum_{i=1}^{m} R(\tau_i) \cdot \left(\hat{S}^{[a,b]}(\tau_{i-1}) - \hat{S}^{[a,b]}(\tau_i) \right)$$

There are two things that are noteworthy: First, instead of a survival probability $S(\tau)$ we use the expected survival fraction $\hat{S}^{[a,b]}(\tau)$, and second, the $(1 - \text{Rec})$ before the default payment term is missing. This is due to the fact that the recovery rate is already accounted for in the derivation of $\hat{S}^{[a,b]}(\tau)$.

The first term $\sum_{i=1}^{m} c(\tau_m) \cdot \Delta\tau_i \cdot R(\tau_i) \cdot \hat{S}^{[a,b]}(\tau_i)$ corresponds to the premium leg. An investor will receive the premium payments at times τ_i with a coupon of $c(\tau_m)$ written on the non-defaulted (surviving) amount $\hat{S}^{[a,b]}(\tau_i)$ at τ_i. The accrual factor is $\Delta\tau_i$. By discounting each payment with the risk-free discount factor $R(\tau_i)$ we obtain the present value of the payment. The next term $\sum_{i=1}^{m} c(\tau_m) \cdot \frac{\Delta\tau_i}{2} \cdot R(\tau_i) \cdot (\hat{S}^{[a,b]}(\tau_{i-1}) - \hat{S}^{[a,b]}(\tau_i))$, which corresponds to the accrual payment, accounts for the fact that the premium paid at time τ_i is usually calculated on the notional outstanding at time τ_{i-1}, which is $\hat{S}^{[a,b]}(\tau_{i-1})$. Hence, the investor receives half of the premium, which corresponds to the expected loss $\hat{S}^{[a,b]}(\tau_{i-1}) - \hat{S}^{[a,b]}(\tau_i)$. Note that $\hat{S}^{[a,b]}(\tau)$ is a decreasing function of time. Finally, $\sum_{i=1}^{m} R(\tau_i) \cdot (\hat{S}^{[a,b]}(\tau_{i-1}) - \hat{S}^{[a,b]}(\tau_i))$ is the value of the contingent (default) payment, which has to be paid by the protection seller to settle any default losses.

In the following, we show basic valuation and analysis methods for CDO tranches based on the liquid and traded standardized iTraxx CDO tranches. Here, we introduce the market approach towards default correlation and highlight the central sensitivities.

10.5.1 Standardized iTraxx Tranches

Beside the iTraxx Europe Benchmark and its sector subindices, there are also tranched iTraxx products available. These are quite similar to unfunded CDO transactions but with an important difference: While most CDOs are illiquid private transactions specifically designed to fit the needs of a portfolio manager and bought by buy-and-hold investors, iTraxx tranches are standardized, tradable, and highly liquid.

These tranches have a standardized capital structure based on a liquid underlying. They are designed to attract both medium-term-oriented investors and traders injecting liquidity into the market. Because there is a liquid market for the underlying – on a single-name and index level – the exposure to tranches can be hedged without exorbitant transaction costs. Since short selling for the tranches as well as for the underlying is possible, investors can efficiently implement arbitrage and relative value strategies. Time series of traded tranche spreads can, for example, be downloaded from Bloomberg (see table A.3 in the appendix).

CDO tranches from the iTraxx family belong to the class of single-tranche CDO (STCDO) structures. In contrast to fully-tranched CDOs with a complete capital structure, a STCDO is a specific tranche on a specific pool of assets an investor wants to acquire. The CDO manager compiles the reference pool and sells the risk of the designated tranche (i.e., he buys protection), with specified upper and lower tranche boundaries (attachment and detachment point) to the investor (i.e., he sells protection). Consequently, the CDO manager has to hedge the risk for all remaining tranches.

From an investor's point of view, the iTraxx CDO tranches offer leveraged exposure to the credit market and thus attractive spread levels without the need to invest in low single-name credit quality. The impact of defaults on the tranche value depends strongly on the subordination level of the specific tranche. A mezzanine tranche for example offers significant spread enhancement compared to the iTraxx Europe Benchmark index, accompanied by a protection against immediate risk of credit defaults. Even if they are not directly affected, also the value of higher protected tranches can change significantly if there is a credit event. This is related to the fact that credit protection of the tranche deteriorates with reduced subordination.

The main risk factor – besides the underlying credit spreads – is default correlation among the reference entities. A high default correlation indicates a higher risk of joint defaults, which may erode higher protected tranches of the capital structure. The value of the tranches and, accordingly, the spread paid to investors is highly sensitive to default correlation. Therefore, trading CDO tranches is often referred to as *correlation trading*. An unhedged position in a CDO tranche indicates a market view on individual credit spreads and default risk in the underlying credits and a view on joint default risk in the pool. Usually, default correlation is an input parameter for a complex model that results in a price. For iTraxx tranches it is the other way around. Due to high liquidity in the market, prices (i.e., tranche spreads) are driven by supply and demand. Consequently, the level of default correlation can be extracted from these prices. Thus, the name of the game is price discovery (implied correlation) rather than model-based pricing.

However, due to the standardization of the underlying CDS portfolio, it is rather difficult to provide customized protection using the iTraxx CDO tranches. They may not be suitable as a tool to hedge joint defaults of a specific portfolio. Main players will be correlation-trading desks and credit hedge funds that actively trade correlation risk. Additional market participants are bank proprietary desks, bank loan portfolio managers, and insurers who want to gain leveraged exposure to credit risk.

In figures 10.4 and 10.5, we show Bloomberg's CDO pricing tool CDSM and the corresponding screen for the basket setup. The calculation deals with a 3–6% tranche with an implied (compound) correlation of 3 percent. While the deal spread is struck at 100 bp, the current fair spread is calculated as 73.9 bp, given the default correlation of 3 percent and the average pool spread of 35 bp (see figure 10.5).

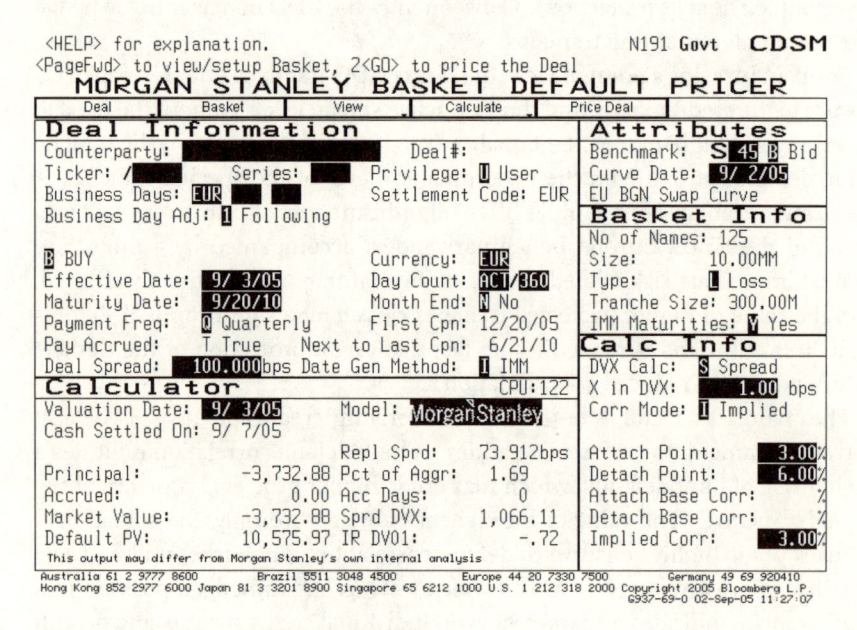

Fig. 10.4: Bloomberg's CDO calculator CDSM

<HELP> for explanation. N191 Govt **CDSM**
53<GO> to setup Spread Curves, <Menu> to return to the Deal

BASKET SETUP/SENSITIVITIES CPU:122

Deal Info | Spread Curves | Calculate DVXs

Type: Loss Currency: EUR IMM: Yes Flat Notional: No Flat Recovery: No Flat Spreads: No

	Company Name	Notional	Recovery (decimal)	Sprd at Mty (bps)	Partial Dvx	Hedge Amount
1	VLVY	80000.00	0.40	35.000	-8.28	-17488.12
2	BMW	80000.00	0.40	35.000	-8.28	-17488.12
3	MICH	80000.00	0.40	35.000	-8.28	-17488.12
4	CONT	80000.00	0.40	35.000	-8.28	-17488.12
5	DCX	80000.00	0.40	35.000	-8.28	-17488.12
6	GKN	80000.00	0.40	35.000	-8.28	-17488.12
7	PEUG	80000.00	0.40	35.000	-8.28	-17488.12
8	REN	80000.00	0.40	35.000	-8.28	-17488.12
9	VLOF	80000.00	0.40	35.000	-8.28	-17488.12
10	VW	80000.00	0.40	35.000	-8.28	-17488.12
11	ACC	80000.00	0.40	35.000	-8.28	-17488.12
12	ELT	80000.00	0.40	35.000	-8.28	-17488.12
13	ALLD	80000.00	0.40	35.000	-8.28	-17488.12
14	ALT	80000.00	0.40	35.000	-8.28	-17488.12
15	BOTP	80000.00	0.40	35.000	-8.28	-17488.12
16	BAT	80000.00	0.40	35.000	-8.28	-17488.12
Total:	125	10000000.00		4375.000	-1035.54	-2186014.44

Australia 61 2 9777 8600 Brazil 5511 3048 4500 Europe 44 20 7330 7500 Germany 49 69 920410
Hong Kong 852 2977 6000 Japan 81 3 3201 8900 Singapore 65 6212 1000 U.S. 1 212 318 2000 Copyright 2005 Bloomberg L.P.
G937-69-0 02-Sep-05 11:28:12

Fig. 10.5: Bloomberg's CDO calculator CDSM (basket setup)

10.5.2 Compound and Base Correlation

The prices for CDO tranches based on the iTraxx Europe Benchmark index are quoted as bid–ask spreads for a tranche with a given maturity (usually five years). There are quotations available for the following standardized tranches: Equity (0–3%), BBB (3–6%), AAA (6–9%), Junior Super Senior Low (9–12%), and Junior Super Senior High (12–22%). The numbers in parenthesis give the attachment and detachment (a.k.a. exhaustion) points of the tranches. The quotation for the equity tranche is slightly different, since the investor receives a fixed running coupon of 500 bp and an upfront payment (see table 10.5).

In case there is a market price (= tranche spread), we can convert it into an average pool correlation using the simple HLPGC model, which can be considered a kind of market standard for this purpose. This is called compound or implied correlation and most CDO arrangers quote it in tandem with tranche spreads. Beside the *compound correlation*, there is another correlation measure, which is frequently used in conjunction with CDO tranches: *base correlation*. We will elaborate on this concept and other aspects of price quotation using a numerical example.

Tab. 10.5: Tranche sensitivities

Tranche	Spread (in %)	Base correlation	Compound correlation	Fair spread	Spread leverage**	Delta†	Delta† (idx adj.)	ΔV‡ (−5bp)	ΔV‡ (+5bp)
0–3%	20.4% + 500 bp*	26.97%	26.97%	10.27%	29.34	−88.6	−17.8	4.7%	−4.3%
3–6%	106 bp	37.63%	9.19%	106 bp	3.03	−42.9	−8.6	1.9%	−2.3%
6–9%	42 bp	45.27%	17.12%	43 bp	1.23	−15.2	−3.1	0.7%	−0.8%
9–12%	28 bp	51.15%	23.72%	27 bp	0.78	−9.0	−1.8	0.4%	−0.5%
12–22%	17 bp	64.35%	34.90%	17 bp	0.50	−4.8	−1.0	0.2%	−0.3%

* According to market standards, the price for the equity tranche is quoted as an upfront payment of 20.4% and a running spread of 500 bp.
** The spread leverage is calculated as fair spread / index spread (35 bp).
† Delta is calculated as the change of tranche value with respect to the underlying index change given current levels. The index-adjusted delta is delta(tranche) / delta(index).
‡ ΔV (−5 bp) gives the change in tranche value, if the underlying index changes by 5 bp.

In the following, we assume 5Y single-tranche CDO contracts with an underlying index value of 35 bp and a risk-free interest rate of 0 percent. We generate results by using the HLPGC model (please refer to section 9.6). Table 10.5 presents sample data for long positions (selling protection) on the specified tranches.

In the first column, tranches are specified by their lower (attachment point) and upper (detachment point) borders. Then we state the tranche spread (note that the equity tranche is quoted as a running spread of 500 bp and as an upfront payment of 20.4 percent), followed by compound and base correlation.

The compound correlation is calculated as the (implied) correlation, which reprices the specific tranche in terms of the HLPGC model. For example, the spread of 106 bp for the BBB (mezzanine) tranche can be reproduced using an average pool correlation of 9.19 percent. The base correlation is the (implied) correlation of the corresponding equity tranche with the same detachment point (upper border). In this case, it is the 0–6% tranche, which has an implied correlation of 37.63 percent. Please note that compound and base correlation for the equity (0–3%) tranche are obviously identical. (A short hint on our notation: we use the terms *compound correlation* and *base correlation* as stated above, whereas *implied correlation* is used in a more general sense, since both correlation figures are implied in prices.)

In figures 10.6 and 10.7, we highlight compound and base correlation for the indicated example. The characteristic structure of the compound correlation is

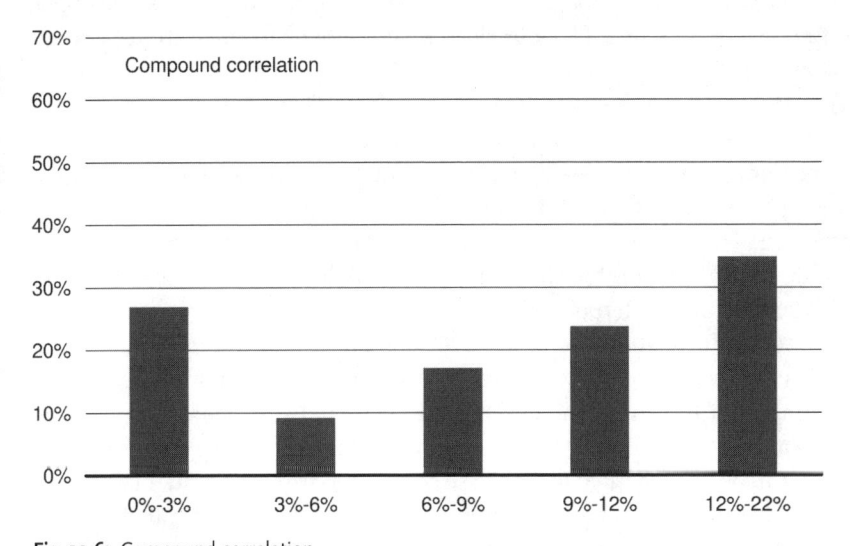

Fig. 10.6: Compound correlation

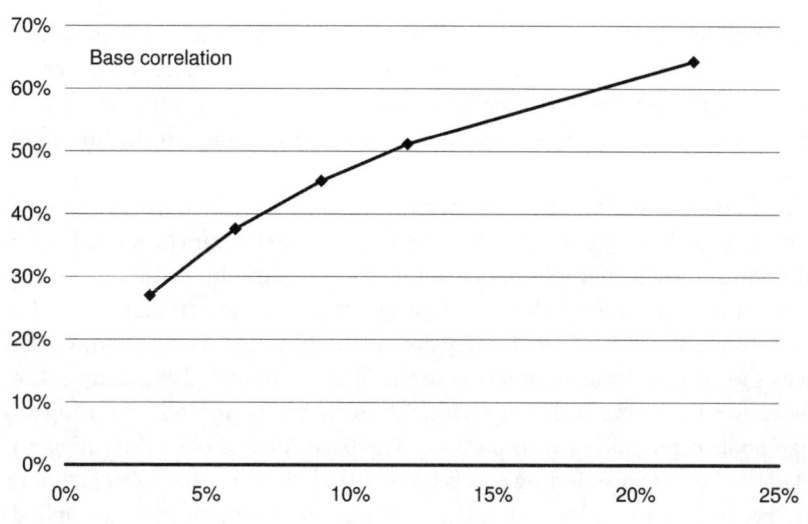

Fig. 10.7: Base correlation

frequently called the *correlation smile*. To plot it, we use a column diagram and not an interpolated scatter chart, since each tranche has to be viewed separately. We can compare the correlation levels among the tranches and can conclude for example that the compound correlation for the equity tranche is higher than the one for the BBB tranche, but there is no meaningful way of interpolating the correlation of the 0–3% and the 3–6% tranche. Since both points (the upper and the lower) are shifted, it is unclear what happens to correlation between these two points.

The situation is different for base correlation. Since only the detachment point is shifted and the attachment point for all equity tranches is kept fixed (at 0 percent), there is a meaningful way of interpolating between two points. The 4.5 percent base correlation is between the 3 percent and 6 percent base correlation. Thus, once we know the base correlation for a few tranches, we can calculate the correlation for all other equity tranches between the lowest and the highest point by interpolation.

Compound correlation and base correlation are related to each other via the expected survival amount (see equation 9.5). The expected survival amount of a compound tranche is the difference of expected survival amounts of the corresponding equity tranches, adjusted by the thickness of the tranches. This relation can be used to calculate the base correlation from the sequence of compound correlations in a bootstrapping algorithm: for the first tranche, compound and base correlation are the same. For the second tranche, calculate the market-implied expected survival amount of the base tranche as the (thickness-adjusted) sum of expected survival amounts of the first two tranches and solve for the correlation parameter, which reproduces this expected survival amount. Thus, we receive the base correlation and the expected survival amount of the second equity tranche. To analyze the senior tranches, we repeat this procedure with the next compound tranche.

Using the pricing framework derived in section 9.6, we can also infer the price of an off-the-run tranche, such as a 4–8% tranche. This is clearly an advantage of this quotation mechanism. From compound correlation we cannot derive this price directly.

But compound correlation is not useless. In fact, the curious structure says a lot about the market's view of risk, which we cannot derive directly from base correlation. Let us briefly discuss the smile structure (for more details please refer to the section below on sensitivities of CDO tranches). A high level of correlation shifts default probability from the equity to higher tranches in the capital structure. Thus, a high level of correlation results in a reduced equity tranche spread. The dependency of the mezzanine tranche on the level of correlation is less obvious. For a low correlation, the tranche spread increases with increasing correlation, but for higher levels of correlation it decreases with increasing correlation. The spread dependency of senior tranches is contrary to those of equity tranches. A high level of risk means a high level of clustered (large) losses, which might also affect senior tranches. Thus, a high correlation means higher spreads for senior tranches.

> **Excursus 9: Correlation: Why is there a Smile?**
> On the back of this analysis, the shape of correlation structure is understandable. Since there is a high demand in the market to sell protection in equity and mezzanine tranches, equity correlation goes up (which reduces the tranche spread) and mezzanine correlation goes down (which reduces the corresponding tranche spread as well). There is little demand for higher protected tranches. Thus, correlation is high for this side. Due to the supply–demand imbalance across the capital structure (high demand for low tranches, low demand for high tranches), equity and mezzanine tranches are (relatively) more expensive from an investor's point of view than other tranches.
> There is another argument why the right branch of the correlation chart is upward sloping. Since senior tranches are very well protected, the risk of a default event which might hit them is negligible. The fair spread would be therefore approximately zero. But since there will not be anybody out

there who would like to take the risk of joint defaults for zero reward, the correlation has to be at a level where these tranches pay at least a basis point or so. Concerning the modeling aspect, there is an ongoing discussion in the financial community of how to model this correlation smile in compound correlation within a more sophisticated model.

10.5.3 Sensitivities of iTraxx Index Tranches

As seen before, the pricing of credit index tranches requires more sophisticated valuation techniques than index swaps. This increased complexity in pricing is generally accompanied by higher difficulties when trying to hedge index tranche positions. Sensitivity measures for relevant risk factors are a convenient way to accomplish this task.

Needless to say, there are many investors in index tranches who just want to take an open position in order to express their market view (or just to receive the carry in case of a long position in credit risk) without following a hedge strategy (a perfect hedge would mean no risk, and no risk would mean no return, except for arbitrage opportunities). Nevertheless, even an investor in unhedged tranches should have an idea of how his position reacts when risk factors vary. This is why we now focus on the topic of index tranche sensitivities.

What are relevant risk factors for tranched index products? First of all, we have to differentiate between risks that emerge in reality and those incorporated in the used valuation model. There are possibly risk factors that, for simplicity's sake, are not covered by the model. Even if the model includes the respective risk factor, there is no guaranty that reality and the model coincide. All this is a consequence of what is called *model risk*.

We already depicted the HLPGC model as a simple way to model portfolio credit risk. A couple of restrictive assumptions of this model reduce the number of parameters to a minimum, leaving only a handful of risk factors:

- A change in the uniform spread level for the index constituents (reflecting the default probability given the uniform recovery rate)
- A change in the uniform correlation parameter
- A change in the uniform recovery rate.

Apparently, there are many other risk factors in reality, particularly those that are due to the dispersion of single-name spreads, recovery rates, and pairwise correlations. For example, it is definitely useful to know how the present value of an index tranche reacts if we assume an individual credit spread blowout in contrast to a pool-wide spread movement (see section 9.7). Sensitivities concerning different risk factors can only be calculated on the background of a pricing model. This kind of sensitivity therefore cannot be analyzed within the HLPGC model. Nevertheless, we think that presenting sensitivities based on the HLPGC model gives a good indication of how iTraxx index tranches work in practice.

A risk factor that has not been mentioned yet is the default risk. A default causes an immediate loss for the equity tranche and reduces the subordination of other tranches, thus lowering the present value of such a contract. Usually this kind of risk is presented independently from spread risk. It should be emphasized that spread risk is nothing else but a latent expression of default risk. Both types of risk are inextricably linked together given a fixed recovery rate. Nevertheless, asking both questions of how an index tranche behaves when spreads widen and defaults occur is legitimate. Measuring these sensitivities very often discloses that they are not complementary. An effective hedge against default risk may involve an open position in spread risk and vice versa.

Option pricing theory often refers to what is called *theta risk*, which measures the change in present value of a contract solely due to elapsing time until maturity. We like to point out that time is not a risk factor, as time will pass anyway. But the theta measure is important when considering credit-risky positions, because it particularly incorporates the carry issue to the examination. In the majority of cases, a hedging strategy for a tranched product featuring a negative carry should mostly be avoided.

As mentioned earlier, our calculation of sensitivities is based on the HLPGC model, which will give us a reasonable insight into how iTraxx tranches work. For the sake of comparability, we always start with the same parameter setting.

We focus on iTraxx Europe tranches with a maturity of five years. Let's consider a flat term structure of interest rates with an interest rate level of zero and a uniform recovery rate of 40 percent (Rec = 0.4) associated with a spread level of 60 bp (clean spread level is then 100 bp). If we assume a uniform correlation parameter ρ of 0.3 as a starting point, the tranches should have the following fair spread levels:

Tab. 10.6: Fair spread levels of iTraxx Europe tranches (5Y)

Tranche	Equity	BBB	AAA	Junior	Senior
Losses	0–3%	3–6%	6–9%	9–12%	12–22%
Fair spread	1,194 bp	467 bp	219 bp	114 bp	37 bp

It should be noted that showing the fair spread for an equity tranche (here: 1,194 bp) does not comply with the quotation for this piece in practice as stated before (always a constant premium of 500 bp plus the quoted upfront payment in terms of the notional amount). We treat the equity tranche the same way as the other tranches to make them comparable. Nevertheless, the special quotation mechanism and fixing of the premium leg for the equity tranche does not substantially change the risk characteristics of it.

However, we will not only focus on how the present value of a fixed contract changes due to a variation of risk factors. As an alternative view, we always depict the impact of changes to fair spread levels. This approach enables us to calculate sensitivities in terms of basis points, which provides clear and favored measures when looking at the market behavior itself. For example, one might be interested in the magnitude of a spread change for a tranche product provided that the spread of the underlying index increases by 1 bp.

Sensitivities to a Common Spread Movement

At first, we will have a look at how a common spread widening or tightening affects the present value of already existing tranches that carry fixed spread levels based on table 10.6 and the fair spread levels of such tranches. Just remember that individual spread changes are not within the scope of the used HLPGC model. That is why we focus on equal spread changes across all names of the

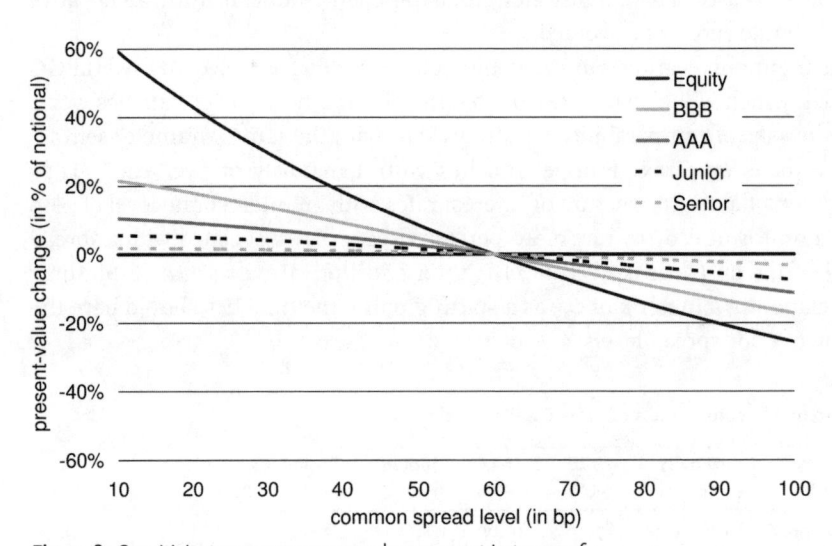

Fig. 10.8: Sensitivity to a common spread movement in terms of present-value change . . .

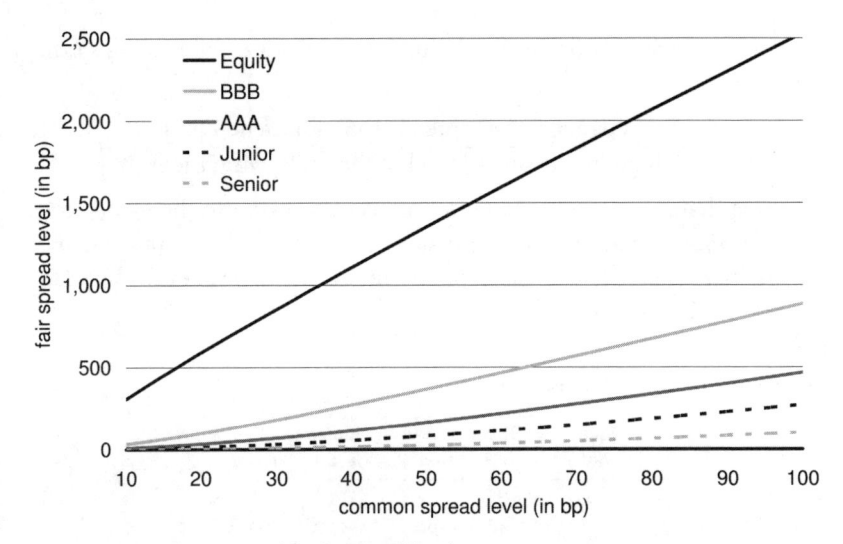

Fig. 10.9: ...and in terms of the fair spread level

underlying index. In figures 10.8 and 10.9, we show the impact of an overall spread change in the range of 10 to 100 bp.

Note that calculating a sensitivity with respect to a certain risk factor (e.g., the spread movement) is based on the assumption that all other parameters are fixed. For correlation trading, the crucial point is which correlation remains fixed; the implied compound correlation or the base correlation? Unfortunately, the two different approaches lead to significant differences, especially for the mezzanine (3–6%) tranche.

The delta in a *fixed base correlation* view (which is the market standard) means that we consider the 3–6% as a long position in a (virtual) 0–6% equity tranche plus a short position in the real equity (0–3%) tranche. In this context, the delta is around 5, while in the *fixed compound correlation* framework the delta is roughly 9. In the following analysis, we refer to the latter concept.

As one would expect, an increasing spread of the underlying index leads to decreasing present values of already existing contracts and rising fair spread levels for tranched products based on the index. However, the magnitude of present value and spread changes differs across tranches. The equity tranche shows the highest sensitivity towards spread changes in the underlying index. Apparently this is not surprising, because the first loss tranche incorporates additional default risk to the largest extent, followed by higher tranches in turn.

Figure 10.9 enables us to calculate sensitivities in terms of basis points simply by extracting the slope of each curve. The slope of such a curve at a certain point (we use a starting point of 60 bp for the underlying index) defines the *spread delta*, which is

$$\Delta_{i,\text{spread}} = \frac{\text{change in fair spread level of tranche } i \text{ [bp]}}{\text{change in fair spread level of the underlying index [bp]}}$$

Please note that this measure is non-dimensional owing to the same scale unit in the numerator and the denominator. We computed the spread deltas for each iTraxx Europe tranche based on an initial spread level of 60 bp. The results are listed in table 10.7.

Tab. 10.7: Spread sensitivities for iTraxx Tranches

Tranche Losses	Equity 0–3%	BBB 3–6%	AAA 6–9%	Junior 9–12%	Senior 12–22%
Spread delta	23.9	10.1	5.7	3.4	1.3
Spread PV delta [% / bp]	−0.80	−0.46	−0.27	−0.16	−0.06
Hedge ratio	16.6	9.5	5.6	3.4	1.3

As we can see, the equity tranche exhibits a spread delta of 23.9. This means that a 1 bp spread level increase in the underlying index leads to a spread blowout of 23.9 bp for the first loss piece. This demonstrates the leveraged exposure of tranched products in comparison to plain-vanilla index investments. But be careful! A delta of 23.9 does not mean that one needs a notional amount in the underlying index that is 23.9 times the notional amount of the tranche in order to eliminate the risk of spread changes. Three reasons for this are:

- Eliminating the risk of spread changes requires that the present value of the hedged item and the hedging instrument, and not their fair spread levels, move in line! Usually, the impact on present values resulting from a 1 bp spread change (often referred to as SpreadDV01) is different for an index swap and for a tranche based on this index. Thus, the spread delta is inappropriate when building up a hedging relationship.
- The charts above already showed that the slope of the curves is not constant. Different spread levels in the underlying index are accompanied by different delta values, which means that the notional amount of the hedging instrument regularly has to be adjusted according to the current delta values.
- The spread delta concept deals with the fair spread levels for index tranches. This is the wrong approach for an existing position featuring a fixed spread level, whereas the change in present value should be in the limelight when tracking a position.

In order to solve the hedging problem, a few modifications to our spread delta concept have to be implemented. First of all, we have to define a delta measure that involves present value changes for a contract with a fixed spread level. For these purposes, we use the slope of the chart in figure 10.10 and call it *spread PV delta*. It is defined by:

$$\Delta^{PV}_{i,\text{spread}} = \frac{\text{change in present value of tranche } i \text{ [fractions of notional]}}{\text{change in fair spread level of the underlying index [bp]}}.$$

Please note that this measure is independent from the size of the respective contract, because the present value change in the numerator refers to the nominal amount. Furthermore, we need to know how the underlying index swap reacts with regard to a spread level change. Applying the HLPGC model to a virtual 0–100% tranche, which corresponds with a regular index swap contract, solves this problem. Now we can calculate our spread PV delta above for this special tranche:

$$\Delta^{PV}_{\text{swap,spread}} = \frac{\text{change in present value of the swap [fractions of notional]}}{\text{change in fair spread level of the underlying index [bp]}}$$

In our example we had a spread PV delta for the index swap of about −0.048 percent. Thus, if the spread level increases by 1 bp, the present value of an index swap contract (long credit risk) declines about €4,830 given a notional amount of €10 mn. Consequently, we derive the desired hedge ratio by computing the ratio of both spread PV deltas:

$$\text{hedge ratio} = \frac{\Delta^{PV}_{i,\text{spread}}}{\Delta^{PV}_{\text{swap,spread}}} = \frac{\text{change in present value of the tranche } i}{\text{change in present value of the swap}}$$

We added the spread PV deltas for iTraxx tranches and corresponding hedge ratios (dividing spread PV deltas by −0.048 percent) to table 10.7. In general, hedge ratios do not coincide with spread deltas, particularly for tranches with lower subordination (equity and BBB tranches). However, our obtained spread deltas offer a good approximation for tranches with higher subordination.

According to table 10.7, an equity tranche investor who wants to eliminate the risk of spread changes has to build up a contrarian index swap position with a notional amount that is 16.6 times the size of the tranche contract. Unfortunately, this raises additional issues that have to be taken into account:

- Apparently, the hedged position is not carry neutral! The premium spread of the equity tranche (1194 bp) is not totally offset by the hedging instrument (16.6 × 60 bp = 996 bp).

- Even though spread neutrality can be assumed, there is a lack of neutrality towards default risk! Notice the amount that disappears given a single default within the iTraxx Europe index (suppose a recovery rate of 40 percent as assumed for our pricing model):
  - Equity tranche: $\frac{1}{125} \cdot (1 - 0.4) \cdot \frac{1}{3\%-0\%} \cdot 1 = 16.0\%$
  - Index swap hedge: $\frac{1}{125} \cdot (1 - 0.4) \cdot \frac{1}{100\%-0\%} \cdot 16.6 = 8.0\%$

  Here, the first term is: the proportion of a single name within the index; the second term: the loss given default; the third term: the allowance for the thickness of the tranche; and the fourth term: the notional multiplier.
- As already mentioned, the hedge position has to be adjusted, since spread PV delta and hedge ratios are not constant particularly with regard to spread level changes of the underlying index. However, this phenomenon is not unusual when trying to manage the risk of non-linear contracts, as are index tranches.

The latter is evident on closer examination of the sensitivity graphs (see figures 10.8 and 10.9) in which the pronounced non-linearity of the curves is recognizable. In the figures 10.10 and 10.11, we clarify this aspect by drawing delta PV spreads and delta spreads, respectively, against the common spread level.

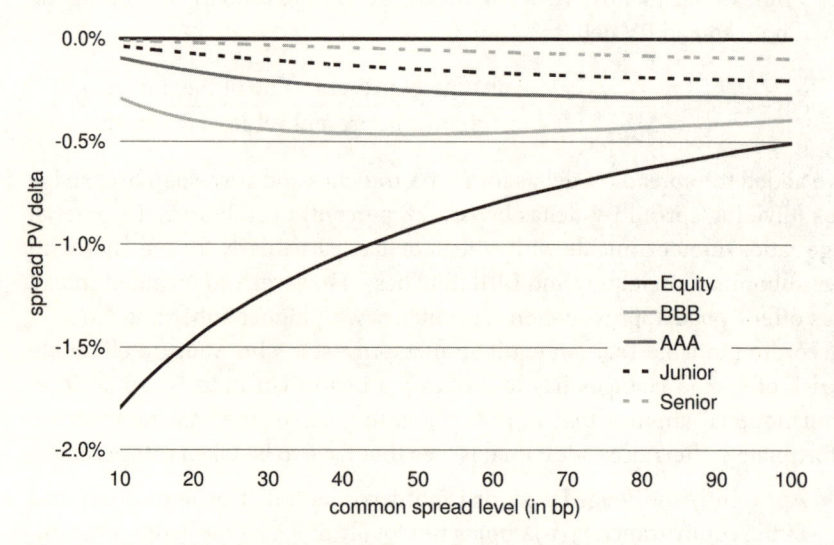

Fig. 10.10: Spread PV deltas subject to different common spread levels

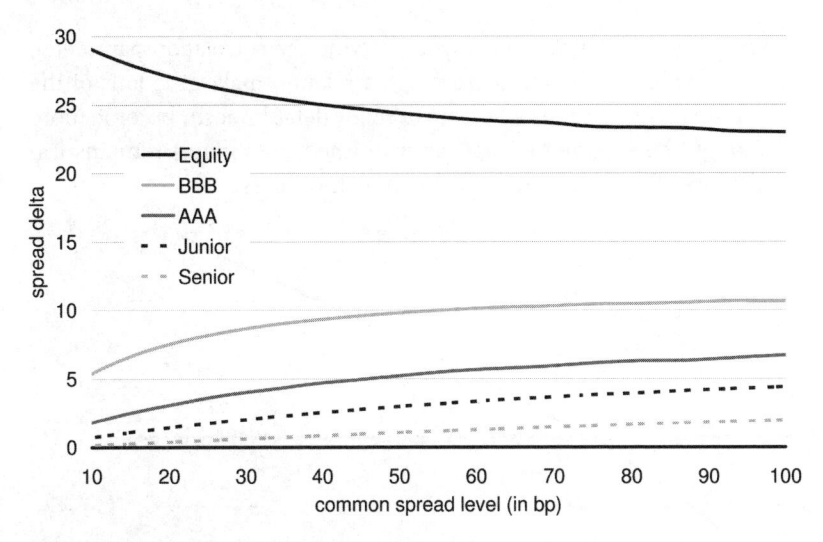

Fig. 10.11: Spread deltas subject to different common spread levels

In addition to the fact that deltas change when altering the common spread level, we see different curve progressions for each tranche. The equity tranche shows the greatest change in delta (often referred to as gamma) combined with a decreasing spread sensitivity for higher spread levels. For the record, the iTraxx Europe BBB tranche achieves its maximal spread PV delta (in absolute terms) for a spread level of about 48 bp. However, the remainder (the other subordinated tranches) exhibit a rising spread sensitivity for higher spread levels. In a nutshell, the possible gamma problem has to be taken into account, particularly for tranches with a low subordination level (especially first loss tranches).

Sensitivity to the Correlation Parameter

After delving into the subject of how common spread movements affect the pricing of iTraxx tranches, we now continue with the impact of changes in the correlation parameter for the HLPGC model. Initially, we would like to emphasize the already discussed issue that the correlation parameter could only be understood as a rough surrogate for default correlation in reality.

In practice, this measure is rather used for quotation purposes than for pricing, as we already pointed out (please refer to the concept of implied correlation). Nevertheless, varying this parameter within the HLPGC model gives us an idea of how iTraxx tranches react concerning correlation risk.

We already elaborated on how the correlation parameter changes the pool loss distribution for the underlying index. While the expected loss of the pool loss distribution remains unchanged when varying the correlation parameter, the shape of distribution alters. Increasing correlation makes the tails of the loss distribution fatter. Settings where no or many defaults occur become more likely. Although the expected loss of the pool (the whole index) remains unchanged, the loss allocation with respect to tranches varies.

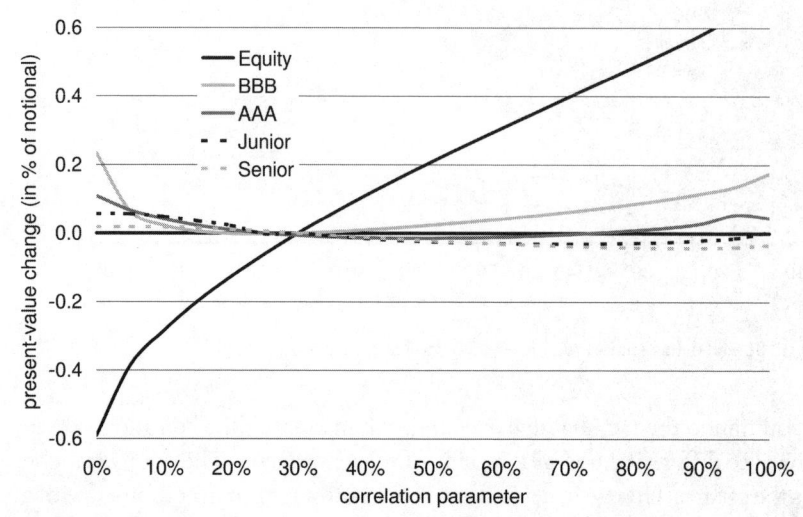

Fig. 10.12: iTraxx sensitivity to a change in correlation in terms of present value ...

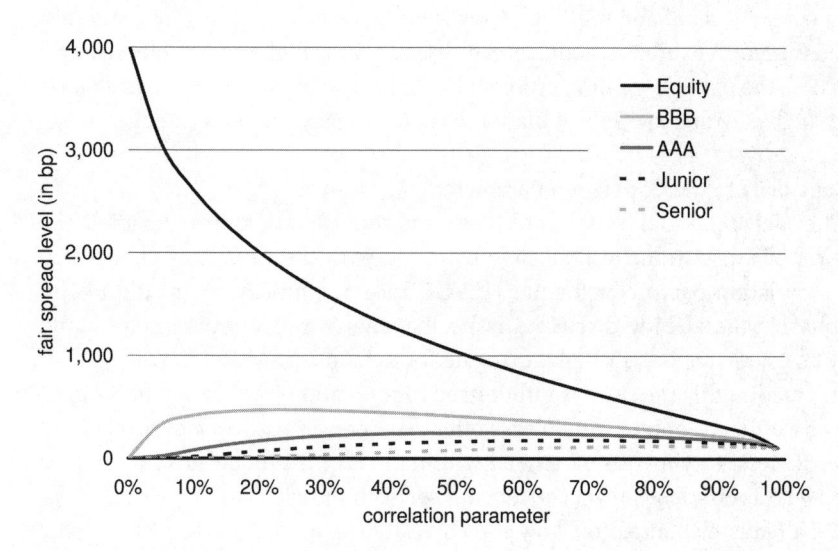

Fig. 10.13: ... and in terms of fair spread levels

As an increasing correlation parameter involves fatter tails of the pool loss distribution, one would expect the fair spread of the equity tranche to decline due to an increased probability of zero losses. On the other side, the fair spread level for the senior tranche is expected to rise because joint default scenarios become more likely. Figures 10.12 and 10.13 confirm that the equity tranche shows the highest sensitivity. However, effects for mezzanine tranches are less intuitive. Both figures exhibit intervals with rising spreads and others involving declining spreads.

Sensitivity to the Recovery Rate

Eventually, an analysis of how a change of the uniform recovery rate affects iTraxx Europe tranches is still missing. The market convention for recovery rates (40 percent) is usually taken for granted, while reality often proves to be different. Hence, investors should be aware of the fact that the expected recovery rate is a market risk factor that is expensive to hedge (e.g., via digital default swaps).

In this paragraph we outline how changes in expectations affect the present values of already existing iTraxx tranches and their fair spread levels in the same manner we did before. Figures 10.14 and 10.15 impressively show that different recovery rates (0 to 100 percent) have a substantial pricing impact with the highest sensitivity for the equity tranche. It is needless to say that tranche spreads converge towards zero if the recovery rate draws near 100 percent.

In order to retrace the effect of a change in the expected recovery rate, let us consider the BBB tranche (3–6% tranche). Given a decline from 40 percent to 30 percent, we have to differentiate between the following effects:

- While the contractual subordination level of the BBB tranche is fixed to a fraction of 3 percent of the notional amount, the effective subordination level, measured in terms of necessary default cases until the prior tranches (here: the equity tranche) erode, increases. A recovery rate of 40 percent implies a loss of 60 percent $\times$ 1/125 = 0.48 percent per default for the iTraxx benchmark index. Thus, 7 defaults are needed until the equity tranche (0–3%) is exhausted and the BBB tranche is affected. However, if we assume a recovery rate of 30 percent (implying a loss of 0.56 percent per default), only 6 defaults would be needed.
- Second, reducing the recovery rate from 40 percent to 30 percent also means a jump in the uniform spread level for the index constituents from 60 bp to 70 bp provided a constant clean spread of 100 bp. This setting is accompanied by a shift in the pool loss distribution owing to a higher expected loss for the iTraxx Europe Benchmark index.

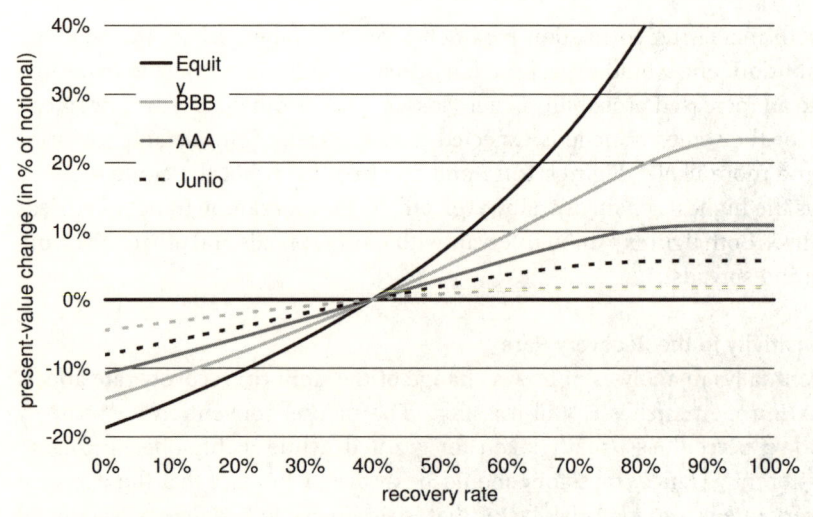

Fig. 10.14: iTraxx sensitivity to a change in the expected recovery rate in terms of present value ...

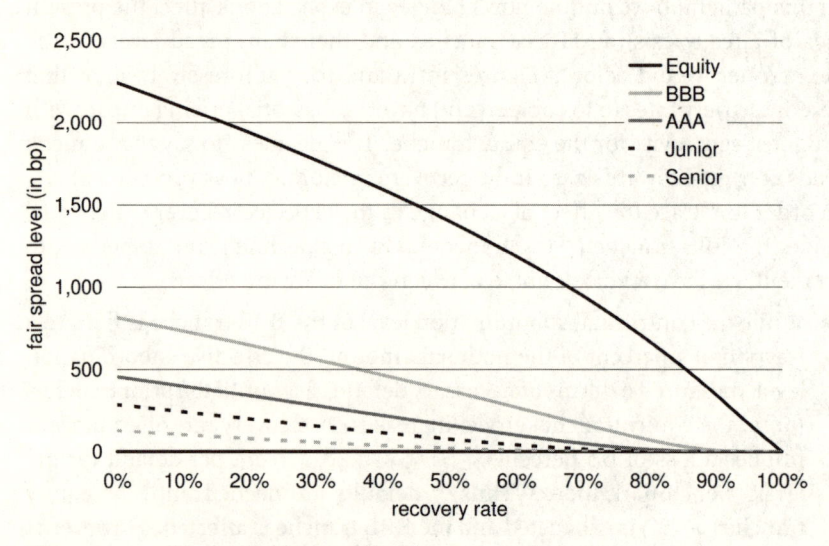

Fig. 10.15: ... and in terms of fair spread levels

A Few Words Concerning the Passage of Time

As previously mentioned, the passage of time is no risk factor by itself, because time progresses anyway. Nevertheless, it is necessary for an investor to know how his position evolves over time, focusing on contractual cash flows and marked-to-market changes. He should be aware of the following aspects assuming all other risk factors to be constant:

- From a pure cash flow perspective, the protection seller receives quarterly premium payments according to the initially stipulated spread level provided that no default occurs.
- Second, the pool loss distribution shifts to the left, attributable to the fact that the expected loss declines through the passage of time. Less time to maturity means a lower probability of experiencing enough defaults that erode the tranches.
- In addition to the latter, a diminishing probability of (additional) defaults or losses due to the passage of time has the following consequence. While the equity tranche still suffers from a potential danger of defaults, the chance of a loss (default risk) for subordinated tranches diminishes. The closer we get to the maturity, the more of the (remaining) default risk has to be borne by the equity tranche and not by subordinated tranches.

10.6 Exotic Derivatives

10.6.1 Equity Default Swaps

We already introduced equity default swaps (EDS) in section 2.5.3. They have similar characteristics as credit default swaps.[10] An investor who sells protection receives regular premium payments until the specified trigger event occurs or until the final maturity is reached. If the trigger event occurs, the protection seller pays a recovery payment that is fixed in advance. If the trigger event does not occur, the contract expires without a default payment. There are two structural differences between EDS and CDS: the trigger event and the recovery payment. The differences in the recovery payment are easy to integrate into the valuation framework. In contrast to standard CDS contracts, EDS have a prespecified default payment (usually 50 percent of the notional amount), while the recovery payment for a CDS is unknown in advance. For valuation purposes, we only have to use the specified recovery payment in the pricing algorithm.

The differences in the definition of the trigger event are more difficult to cope with. A CDS contract is triggered if one of the specified default events occurs (bankruptcy, failure to pay, or restructuring). An EDS, however, is triggered if the share price of the reference company falls below a certain barrier. Usually this default barrier is set to 30 percent of the initial value. Hence, the value of the EDS depends on the probability that the stock price hits the barrier. However, this payoff structure resembles that of a far-out-of-the-money option. In fact, EDS can be considered as far-out-of-the-money one-touch put options with regular premium payments instead of a single initial payment. A one-touch put option is an American-style binary option, that is, the payoff is triggered immediately if the share price touches the strike level. This is exactly what we used in equation 8.12.

Putting the pieces together, we can value EDS contracts using equation 10.4. For the recovery rate, we simply use the specification in the contract, while the survival probability function can be inferred from prices of far-out-of-the money one-touch put options. Hence, EDS are frequently considered as credit–equity hybrids. They are stock options in a CDS format. Furthermore, due to the very low default barrier, the risk involved in an EDS is similar to a CDS contract. The probability that CDS and EDS contracts are triggered in conjunction is quite high.

Equity default swaps are used as building blocks for more complex structures. *First-to-trigger baskets* are comparable to FTD basket with EDS as underlyings instead of CDS contracts. Similarly, EDS are also used as portfolio additions in CDO structures, especially for yield enhancement purposes. Moreover, market participants can also invest in EDS indices, comparable to the iTraxx CDS index. The difference is that the underlyings of EDS indices are EDS contracts and not CDS. Finally, EDS contracts can also be structured on equity indices, which are called index EDS. Here, the trigger event refers to a drop in the equity index. Attractive trading strategies can be developed by combining EDS indices and index EDS contracts. As an example, hedging an EDS index with an index EDS would effectively result in a strategy that trades the far-out-of-the-money correlation of the index members.

10.6.2 Constant Maturity Structures

Constant maturity default swaps (see also section 2.5.5) are comparable to their interest rate analogues. They appear in financial markets in various structures. For example, they refer to single-name CDS as well as to portfolio derivatives such as CDO tranches. The differences between the plain-vanilla derivatives and the corresponding constant maturity instruments lies in the specification of the premium leg. In contrast to the plain-vanilla derivatives, constant maturity swaps involve variable premium payments. Hence, they can be considered as spread floaters.

As an example, we consider a CMCDS with a time to maturity of seven years, where the variable payments are indexed to the 5Y rate. Ignoring the accrued premium upon default, the default leg of the CMCDS is the same as the one of a standard 5Y CDS contract. The protection seller has to pay the loss given default (1 − Rec) to the protection buyer in case a default occurs. However, while in a normal CDS contract the protection seller receives fixed premium payments, in a constant maturity variant he receives a fixed fraction of the 5Y CDS rate valid at the fixing dates. Therefore, the value of the premium leg in a CMCDS is calculated as

$$V^{CM,PL} = \sum_{i=1}^{m} PR \cdot \mathbb{E}[c(\tau_{i-1}, \tau_{i-1} + \tau_{CM})] \cdot \Delta\tau_i \cdot R(\tau_i) \cdot S(\tau_i) \qquad (10.18)$$

Here, $c(\tau_{i-1}, \tau_{i-1} + \tau_{CM})$ is the forward CDS rate for a period between τ_{i-1} and $\tau_{i-1} + \tau_{CM}$ and PR is the *participation rate*. The constant maturity of the spread index is denoted by τ_{CM}. In the above-mentioned example, τ_{CM} would be the 5Y par spread. Equation 10.18 involves two technical subtleties. The first one is that the fixing of the payments refers to τ_{i-1}, while the premium payment is at τ_i, that is, at the end of the accrual period. This payment structure is called *in-advance fixing*. In case fixing and payment dates are identical (i.e., τ_i in our notation), the fixing is called *in-arrears*. In contrast to the fixed income universe, where both methods are well known, constant maturity CDS usually use the in-advance fixing method shown in equation 10.18.

The second subtlety is related to the expected value of the forward rates $\mathbb{E}[c(\tau_{i-1}, \tau_{i-1} + \tau_{CM})]$. Due to the mismatch between the length of the forward period τ_{CM} and the lengths of the accrual period $\Delta\tau_i = \tau_i - \tau_{i-1}$ (in the above-mentioned example the forward period was five years, while the accrual period is three months for a standard CDS contract), the expected value under the risk-neutral probability measure is not necessarily identical to the forward rate $c(\tau_{i-1}, \tau_{i-1} + \tau_{CM})$. Therefore, a static replication of the premium leg trading in the standard CDS contracts is not possible. We have to add a convexity adjustment. Using standard textbook finance (see for example Hull's book[70]) we find that the expected value of the forward swap rate can be approximated by using the forward rate and a convexity adjustment:

$$\mathbb{E}[c(\tau_0, \tau_m)] \approx \underbrace{c(\tau_0, \tau_m)}_{\text{forward swap rate}} - \underbrace{\frac{1}{2}c^2(\tau_0, \tau_m)\sigma^2 \tau_0 \frac{V''(c(\tau_0, \tau_m))}{V'(c(\tau_0, \tau_m))}}_{\text{convexity adjustment}}$$

However, for the sake of simplicity, we neglect the effect from the convexity adjustment in the following analysis. Now we aim to derive the participation rate PR. To do so, we think of a combination of a normal and a constant maturity CDS contract. Selling protection in the CMCDS and buying protection in the CDS results in a cancellation of the default leg; therefore this package is free of any default risk. By equating the value of the premium leg in equation 10.4 and the premium leg in equation 10.18 we derive:

$$\text{PR} \approx \frac{\sum_{i=1}^{m} c(\tau_m) \cdot \Delta\tau_i \cdot R(\tau_i) \cdot S(\tau_i)}{\sum_{i=1}^{m} \text{PR} \cdot c(\tau_{i-1}, \tau_{i-1} + \tau_{\text{CM}}) \cdot \Delta\tau_i \cdot R(\tau_i) \cdot S(\tau_i)} \qquad (10.19)$$

This formula is an approximation for the participation rate PR, as we neglect the convexity adjustment, which, however, is not difficult to integrate. The participation rate will be below that of an upward sloping curve, exactly like that of a flat curve and above one of a downward sloping curve. Note that in interest rate CMS contracts, the usage of a participation rate is less common. Normally, we use a spread to account for the slope effect in the swap curve.

For a normal spread curve, the participation rate is between 60 and 80 percent. The steeper the curve, the smaller the PR. In addition, this participation rate will be reduced by approximately 1 to 3 percentage points due to the convexity adjustment. The size of the adjustment depends on the spread level, the spread volatility, the duration, and the convexity of the CDS contract. The combination of a CDS and a CMCDS results in a position that is more sensitive to changes in the steepness of the curve rather than to the level of the curve. Moreover, a CMCDS has a sensitivity to spread up to the maturity of $\tau_m + \tau_{\text{CM}}$, that is, the maturity of the contract itself plus the forward period of the constant index. Up to now, CMCDS are the only practical possibility to gain exposure to an instrument with a variable spread. Consequently, investors use it to invest long in credit risk in a spread-widening environment.

10.6.3 Digital Default Swaps and Recovery Swaps

Digital default swaps (see also section 2.5.2) are innovative products with interesting characteristics.[9] DDS are comparable to standard CDS contracts. The only difference is that the loss given default, which corresponds to the default payment in the CDS contract, is known in advance. Selling protection in a DDS involves the risk of losing the full notional amount, which is secured by the contract, as the recovery rate is fixed in advance at 0 percent.

From a purely mathematical perspective, valuing DDS is straightforward. We just have to use standard CDS valuation models with a fixed recovery rate of 0.

In this framework, the value of a DDS contract is calculated as the premium leg minus the value of the default leg (ignoring accrued premium upon default). The value of the premium leg is derived as the PV of the stream of payments times the corresponding survival probability, while the value of the default leg reflects the expected loss taking an LGD of 100 percent into account.

However, the central element in this valuation is the survival probability function. In plain-vanilla CDS markets, this quantity is derived from market spreads using a bootstrapping approach similar to the one in interest rate swap markets, involving an explicit assumption for the recovery rate. As this quantity is hard to determine, market participants simply use a standardized recovery rate of 40 percent. The remaining uncertainty about the recovery rate has only a limited impact on a CDS contract (the quantity is eliminated at first in the bootstrapping algorithm but then reenters in the valuation procedure). As long as the recovery assumption in the bootstrapping procedure and in the valuation algorithm coincide, there is no major problem. But for DDS, this is exactly what happens. The survival probability is derived from CDS contracts involving recovery payments, and then included in the DDS valuation.

In the following, we show how to derive the central equation to deduce the value of DDS. This is done by exploiting the similarities between standard CDS and DDS. Moreover, the analysis reveals that RDS are closely related to CDS and DDS.

We start our introduction of the valuation of DDS with a simplified version of the standard CDS valuation formula 10.4:

$$V^{CDS} = \sum_{i=1}^{m} c^{CDS}(\tau_m) \cdot \Delta \tau_i \cdot R(\tau_i) \cdot S(\tau_i)$$
$$- (1 - \text{Rec}^{CDS}) \sum_{i=1}^{m} R(\tau_i) \cdot (S(\tau_{i-1}) - S(\tau_i)) \qquad (10.20)$$

For the sake of simplicity, we ignored the term $V^{AP} = \sum_{i=1}^{m} c(\tau_m) \cdot \frac{\Delta \tau_i}{2} \cdot R(\tau_i) \cdot (S(\tau_{i-1}) - S(\tau_i))$, which accounts for the value of the accrued premium paid in the case of a credit event. However, it is not difficult to integrate this term into the presented framework. We simply have to add V^{AP} to the value V^{CDS}.

In addition, Rec^{CDS} in equation 10.20 denotes the recovery rate that determines the loss given default. This quantity is unknown in advance. Note that for the valuation of CDS contracts, the survival probability function $S(\tau)$ is usually inferred from the par-CDS spread curve using a bootstrapping algorithm, under the assumption of a specific level of the recovery rate (see section

10.1.2). Since traded CDS spreads mirror the market's view about the expected loss rather than the default probability itself, the implied survival probability depends on the recovery assumption used in the bootstrapping procedure.

We can derive the value of a corresponding DDS contract by using an appropriate recovery rate in equation 10.20. For the moment, we stick to a general approach and assume that the DDS contract pays a fixed recovery of Rec^{DDS}, instead of simply using the market standard of zero recovery. The following steps do not depend on a specific value for Rec^{DDS}, because, as we will see below, any changes will be reflected by the relation between the notional amounts invested in the DDS and the CDS. The valuation equation for a DDS is identical to equation 10.20. We only have to substitute CDS by DDS. The central idea in valuing DDS contracts is to consider a portfolio of a DDS contract (selling protection) with respect to a notional amount of N^{DDS} and a CDS contract (buying protection) based on a notional amount of N^{CDS}.

$$N^{DDS} \cdot V^{DDS} - N^{CDS} \cdot V^{CDS}$$
$$= \left[N^{DDS} \cdot c^{DDS}(\tau_m) - N^{CDS} \cdot c^{CDS}(\tau_m) \right] \cdot \sum_{i=1}^{m} \Delta\tau_i \cdot R(\tau_i) \cdot S(\tau_i)$$
$$- \left[N^{DDS} \cdot (1 - \text{Rec}^{DDS}) - N^{CDS} \cdot (1 - \text{Rec}^{CDS}) \right] \sum_{i=1}^{m} R(\tau_i) \cdot (S(\tau_{i-1}) - S(\tau_i))$$

(10.21)

In the next step, we adjust the relative notional amount N^{DDS} and N^{DDS} so that the resulting premium payments of the portfolio of DDS and CDS are zero:

$$\left[N^{DDS} \cdot c^{DDS}(\tau_m) - N^{CDS} \cdot c^{CDS}(\tau_m) \right] \cdot \sum_{i=1}^{m} \Delta\tau_i \cdot R(\tau_i) \cdot S(\tau_i) = 0$$

(10.22)

$$N^{DDS} = N^{CDS} \cdot \frac{c^{CDS}(\tau_m)}{c^{DDS}(\tau_m)}$$

Now we substitute this relation in equation 10.21. The term for the value of the premium payments drops out due to the definition of the relative notional amounts of DDS versus CDS. The remaining value of the portfolio only depends on the value of the underlying default legs.

$$N^{CDS} \cdot \left[V^{DDS} \cdot \frac{c^{CDS}}{c^{DDS}} - V^{CDS} \right] =$$
$$- N^{CDS} \left[\frac{c^{CDS}}{c^{DDS}} \cdot (1 - \text{Rec}^{DDS}) - (1 - \text{Rec}^{CDS}) \right] \cdot \sum_{i=1}^{m} R(\tau_i) \cdot (S(\tau_{i-1}) - S(\tau_i))$$
$$(10.23)$$

In the last step, we only have to require that $V^{DDS} \cdot c^{CDS}/c^{DDS} - V^{CDS} = 0$, that is, that the value of the portfolio of DDS and CDS is 0. This translates into the requirement that the expected loss of the portfolio should be zero, which corresponds to the fact that the values of the (notional amount-adjusted) default legs of the DDS and the CDS contracts have to offset each other. In the following equation, we derive a condition for the recovery rates and spread levels, which satisfied the requirement of zero value.

$$\frac{c^{CDS}}{c^{DDS}} \cdot (1 - \text{Rec}^{DDS}) - (1 - \text{Rec}^{CDS}) = 0$$
$$\Rightarrow \text{Rec}^{CDS} = 1 - \frac{c^{CDS}}{c^{DDS}} \cdot (1 - \text{Rec}^{DDS}) \qquad (10.24)$$

Equation 10.24 states a relation between the recovery rate in the CDS contract Rec^{CDS} and Rec^{DDS} in the DDS contract. The last step is to set the value for the recovery rate of the DDS at zero. For simplicity reasons, market participants use zero recovery: $\text{Rec}^{DDS} = 0$. Consequently, the value of a portfolio comprised of a DDS and a CDS has an initial value of zero when the expected recovery rate used in the CDS contract follows equation 10.25.

$$\text{Rec}^{impl} = 1 - \frac{c^{CDS}}{c^{DDS}} \quad \Leftrightarrow \quad c^{DDS} = \frac{c^{CDS}}{1 - \text{Rec}^{impl}} \qquad (10.25)$$

This is an impressively simple outcome. The relation between the par spread c^{DDS} of the DDS and the par spread c^{CDS} of the CDS is related to the implied recovery rate Rec^{impl}. This is nothing other than the well-known credit triangle. The par credit spread of a DDS is derived as the par spread of a plain-vanilla CDS contract divided by one minus the implied recovery rate.

Since plain-vanilla CDS contracts refer to the expected loss rather than to the default probability, valuing DDS with respect to the corresponding CDS contracts involves the implementation of a view regarding the implied recovery rate. This dependency is perfectly illustrated by equation 10.25. Moreover, a recovery default swap RDS can be split into two contracts, a DDS contract and a corresponding CDS contract. The relative notional amounts of both contracts are adjusted so that the RDS does not involve any premium payments. The relation between the par spreads of the underlying DDS and CDS determined the implied recovery rate.

Let us summarize the derivation above, which leads to the conclusion that we can simply use the credit triangle to derive the par spread of a digital default swap. The analysis was based on the following three steps:

1. We considered a portfolio of a DDS and a CDS, with different notional amounts.
2. We adjusted the notional amount of both contracts so that the premium legs canceled each other.
3. We derived an implied recovery rate by requiring that the value of the portfolio is zero, which corresponds to the fact that the expected loss in both (notional amount-adjusted) contracts has to be equal.

11
Portfolio Risk Measurement

11.1 Risk Measures

11.1.1 Market Risk versus Credit Risk

Before measuring credit risk on a portfolio level, we first have to define which kind of risk we want to take on. As previously mentioned, credit-risky securities involve basically two sources of risk: the default arrival risk and the risk of spread changes. In the former, we are concerned whether a default event occurs within the holding period, while the latter deals with market price changes. Measuring risk in terms of price changes refers to the concept of the *market value at risk* or market VaR. The default risk, on the other hand, can be quantified by the so-called *credit value at risk* or credit VaR. In the following, we will briefly describe the two concepts. For a more detailed analysis, please refer to Jorion[71], Matten[72], or Gundlach and Lehrbass.[73]

As already mentioned, the market VaR measures the risk of changes of market prices. When dealing with credits, we are obviously interested in the credit specific component of the price dynamic, which we have to isolate from the interest rate component. The central building block is that all securities in the portfolio have to be subjected to a marked-to-market valuation. Therefore, buy-and-hold or hold-to-maturity strategies, which ignore price changes to a large extent cannot be integrated in a market VaR framework. This approach is more suitable (and recommended) for trading-oriented portfolios comprised of liquid assets. As we concentrate on daily price changes, the market VaR applies to a short- or medium-term risk horizon. Usually we assume a holding period of one to ten days. The appropriate holding period in a VaR calculation is driven by the time horizon a risk manager needs on average to liquidate a position or to acquire a hedge. For liquid assets such as bonds or CDS contracts, this can be done – under normal market conditions – within a few days, if not within a few hours. However, since liquidity usually dries up in the course of a crisis, market VaR figures with a longer time horizon (e.g., ten days) should also be taken into account.

The most famous method to calculate the market VaR of a portfolio is the so-called delta-normal VaR. Here, we only consider linear sensitivities of the

Active Credit Portfolio Management. J. Felsenheimer, P. Gisdakis, and M. Zaiser
Copyright © 2006 WILEY-VCH Verlag GmbH & Co. KGaA, Weinheim
ISBN: 3-527-50198-3

portfolio towards the risk factors/credit spreads (hence the word delta) and, in addition, we assume that the underlying risk factors follow a normal distribution (hence the word normal). In addition, we assume that the joint distribution of all credit spreads can be described by using a covariance matrix. Under these assumptions, we can use standard procedures for measuring market risk. It is important to note that the correlation measurement in this approach refers to spread correlation and not to default correlation. The latter belongs to the concept of credit VaR, as we will see below.

Unfortunately, there is a major drawback in this approach. The size of the covariance matrix needed for the risk measurement can become very large, even for a medium-sized portfolio. To reduce the number of risk factors, it is common practice to map the individual risky assets into risk classes. Here, we can use rating categories, industries, sectors, and maturity brackets to arrive at reasonable risk classes. When we group single names into rating categories, we have to integrate the risk of rating migrations into this framework. For a completely disaggregated approach this is not needed, because on a single-name level the risk of rating changes is well reflected in the spread dynamics.

Another interesting feature with market VaR is that we can distinguish between spread VaR and interest rate VaR within the same framework. We only need to map each security to two risk factors: the credit spread and the interest rate curve. In this framework, we can even integrate the correlation between spread and interest rate VaR.

In contrast to the market VaR, credit VaR focuses on longer time horizons, such as one year. A credit VaR framework is needed for buy-and-hold investment strategies, especially when dealing with illiquid assets. The central building block for measuring credit VaR is the portfolio loss density $\tilde{\pi}(x)$ (see chapter 9 for an introduction to portfolio models). As previously noted, this quantity depends on the individual default probabilities, the recovery rates, and the default correlation. For some instruments we also need to model the exposure at default. In the next section, we show how to arrive at risk figures once we have derived the portfolio loss density.

Besides the difference in the time horizon and the correlation measurement – both are related to the different nature of the underlying risk – there is another, more technical difference that we have to take into consideration. The credit VaR is usually defined as the difference between the unexpected and the expected loss. The expected loss is given by the expected value of the portfolio loss distribution. In the market VaR framework, one usually assumes that the expected value of the distribution is zero (in relative terms) or that it equals the current value of the portfolio (in absolute terms). In other words, we assume zero drift in the portfolio. Here, the VaR is the difference between the current value of the portfolio and the quantile of the distribution that refers to the required confidence level. The justification of the zero-drift assumption is related to two important issues: first, we consider a short time horizon (i.e., several days), and second, the return on the underlying assets is small. For market VaR these assumption are usually applicable. Nevertheless, deriving a market VaR for a longer time horizon (e.g., three months or one year), we have to take the drift into consideration.

11.1.2 Value at Risk and Conditional Value at Risk

In the following, we will primarily concentrate on credit VaR. Nevertheless, most of the concepts can be transferred to the market VaR approach without major difficulties. As previously stated, a VaR measure always refers to a specific time horizon. For the credit VaR, a one-year period seems to be appropriate. To facilitate the following analysis, we do not explicitly mention the corresponding time horizon for the VaR figures, but the reader should keep in mind that these figures implicitly refer to a specific time horizon (e.g., one year).

The standard finance textbook uses two related concepts to quantify financial risks. The value at risk (VaR) and the conditional value at risk (CVaR) (a.k.a. expected shortfall or tail value at risk). The VaR states the maximum loss which is incurred in the reference time horizon for a given confidence level. The CVaR, on the other hand, quantifies the expected loss conditional on exceeding the VaR. Both concepts can be used to express portfolio risk in a single number. As an example, most portfolio managers implement risk limiting measures by means of VaR or CVaR. From an economic point of view, the CVaR has some attractiveness because it quantifies the expected loss that is incurred given a tail event. In other words, it answers the question "How bad is bad?". Moreover, especially the CVaR is frequently used for optimizing the risk–return profile of a credit portfolio because CVaR – in contrast to VaR – is a coherent risk measure (see Artzner[74,75] for a definition of coherent risk measures), and it is more stable in optimization routines from a numerical point of view. For a general introduction to risk measures such as VaR and CVaR, the reader might refer to Jorion's book on value at risk.[71] A more detailed description regarding the concept of the CVaR and its application to credit risk and portfolio optimization can be found in the papers of Uryasev.[76–78] Finally, an interesting application of these concepts to credit portfolios can be found in Jobst and Zenios.[29,79]

Note that the abbreviation CVaR is not used consistently in the literature. Some authors use it for the credit value at risk, others, such as Jorion[71] use it to denote the component VaR (see section 11.1.3). However, in line with the most common notation, we use CVaR to denote the conditional value at risk.

The VaR and CVaR concepts can in principle be applied to market and credit risk measurement. In the following, we refer to the credit VaR. Nevertheless, all findings can be easily transferred to the market VaR concept.

The central building block for deriving the VaR and the CVaR, and hence for quantifying the credit risk on a portfolio level, is the portfolio loss density function. Previously, we introduced the discrete distribution $\pi(i)$ as the probability of i defaults in the portfolio. It is suitable for pricing portfolio derivatives such as n^{th}-to-default baskets and CDOs in which all underlyings are equally weighted. However, for risk measurement purposes of real investment portfolios it is less suitable, because it does not distinguish among the defaulted credits as it simply deals with the number of defaults. In case we want to use this approach, we have to assume an average exposure and an average recovery rate for all underlyings. Note that the above-mentioned relation of the VaR figures to a specific time horizon comes into play at the stage of the portfolio loss density. Its shape differs for different time horizons.

As introduced in chapter 9, $\tilde{\pi}(x)$ denotes the portfolio loss density. The probability of a loss between x and $x + \Delta x$ is approximately given by $\tilde{\pi}(x)\Delta x$. This time, x is the loss in monetary units. Nevertheless, all relations can be derived also in terms of percentage of the portfolio volume. Note that in terms of the discrete function $\pi(i)$ the corresponding loss would be $(1 - \text{Rec}) \cdot i \cdot N/m$, with i being the number of defaults, N the overall notional amount of the portfolio and m the number of credits in the portfolio. As mentioned above, we assume an average trade size of N/m.

Once we know the portfolio loss density $\tilde{\pi}(x)$, it is rather easy to derive the VaR and the CVaR. We only need to calculate two related quantities. The first is the cumulated loss distribution $\tilde{\Pi}(y)$:

$$\tilde{\Pi}(y) = \int_0^y \tilde{\pi}(x)dx \qquad (11.1)$$

It states the probability for a loss of up to y. Here, y is also given in terms of monetary units. It is apparent that the probability for a loss up to N – the total exposure in the portfolio – equals one, that is, $\tilde{\Pi}(N) = 1$.

The second important quantity is the expected loss conditional on exceeding a loss of z, which we denote as $\text{CEL}(z)$.

$$\text{CEL}(z) = \frac{\int_z^N x \cdot \tilde{\pi}(x)dx}{\int_z^N \tilde{\pi}(x)dx} = \frac{\int_z^N x \cdot \tilde{\pi}(x)dx}{1 - \widetilde{\Pi}(z)} \qquad (11.2)$$

Knowing these two functions ($\widetilde{\Pi}(y)$ and $\text{CEL}(z)$), which depend on the portfolio loss density $\tilde{\pi}(x)$, we can easily derive the VaR and the CVaR. Another important quantity is the expected loss. It is simply the expected value of the loss density function $\tilde{\pi}(x)$.

$$\text{EL} = \int_0^N x \cdot \tilde{\pi}(x)dx \qquad (11.3)$$

Comparing equations 11.3 and 11.2, and using the fact that $\widetilde{\Pi}(0) = 0$, it becomes apparent that the expected loss can be easily derived from the conditional expected loss function for $z = 0$: $\text{CEL}(0) = \text{EL}$.

Figure 11.1 depicts the methodology graphically. Path A corresponds to equation 11.1 and aims at calculating the VaR, while path B corresponds to equation 11.2 and deals with the CVaR.

From a mathematical perspective, a credit value at risk with a confidence level of a (e.g., 90 percent) – which we denote by $\text{VaR}(a)$ – is calculated as the difference between the unexpected loss and the expected loss. Note that this is in contrast to normal market risk measurement, where we do not take the expected loss into account. Using equation 11.1, we can derive the unexpected loss as $\widetilde{\Pi}^{-1}(a)$. Therefore, the value at risk $\text{VaR}(a)$ with a confidence level of a is derived as

$$\text{VaR}(a) = \widetilde{\Pi}^{-1}(a) - \text{EL} \qquad (11.4)$$

> **Example 24: Deriving $\widetilde{\Pi}(y)$ and $\text{CEL}(z)$ in terms of a discrete portfolio default distribution $\pi(i)$**
>
> Let us assume that we derived the discrete portfolio default probability function $\pi(i)$. It states the probability of i defaults in the portfolio. We can transfer this into a portfolio loss distribution by assuming that all underlying credits have the same exposure N/m, with N being the total portfolio notional and m the number of constituents.

The cumulated loss probability is derived as

$$\Pi((1 - \text{Rec}) \cdot n \cdot N/m) = \sum_{i=1}^{n} \pi(i)$$

The conditional expected loss can be derived as

$$\text{CEL}((1 - \text{Rec}) \cdot n \cdot N/m) = (1 - \text{Rec}) \cdot N/m \cdot \frac{\sum_{i=n+1}^{m} i \cdot \pi(i)}{\sum_{i=n+1}^{m} \pi(i)}$$

Due to the fact that the expected loss equals CEL(0), and because the sum over all $\pi(i)$ equals 1, we can derive the expected loss as

$$\text{EL} = (1 - \text{Rec}) \cdot N/m \cdot \sum_{i=1}^{m} i \cdot \pi(i)$$

These derivations can be easily implemented in a spreadsheet calculation, using the Excel worksheet functions sum and sumproduct.

For calculating the CVaR, we need the expected loss conditional on a loss exceeding the VaR. Using the framework derived above, it is given by CEL(VaR(a)) = CEL($\widetilde{\Pi}^{-1}(a)$). In analogy to the VaR, the CVaR is usually stated as the difference between the conditional expected loss and the (total) expected loss of the portfolio:

$$\begin{aligned}\text{CVaR}(a) &= \text{CEL}(\text{VaR}(a)) - \text{EL} \\ &= \text{CEL}(\text{VaR}(a)) - \text{CEL}(0)\end{aligned} \quad (11.5)$$

The process sketched in figure 11.1 illustrates these relations. As already mentioned, we start with the portfolio loss density and derive the cumulated portfolio loss distribution $\widetilde{\Pi}(y)$ (path A) and the conditional expected loss CEL(z) (path B). To obtain the 90 percent VaR, we follow the horizontal, dashed line starting at the 90-percent level (upper right chart in figure 11.1). The unexpected loss is depicted as the loss on the corresponding x-axis, where this line crosses the cumulated loss distribution function. For the VaR we also need the expected loss, which is given as the CEL(0). The latter is shown in the lower right chart in figure 11.1 at the level where the conditional expected loss crosses the y-axis. To facilitate the illustration, we added the bisecting line in the chart. In general,

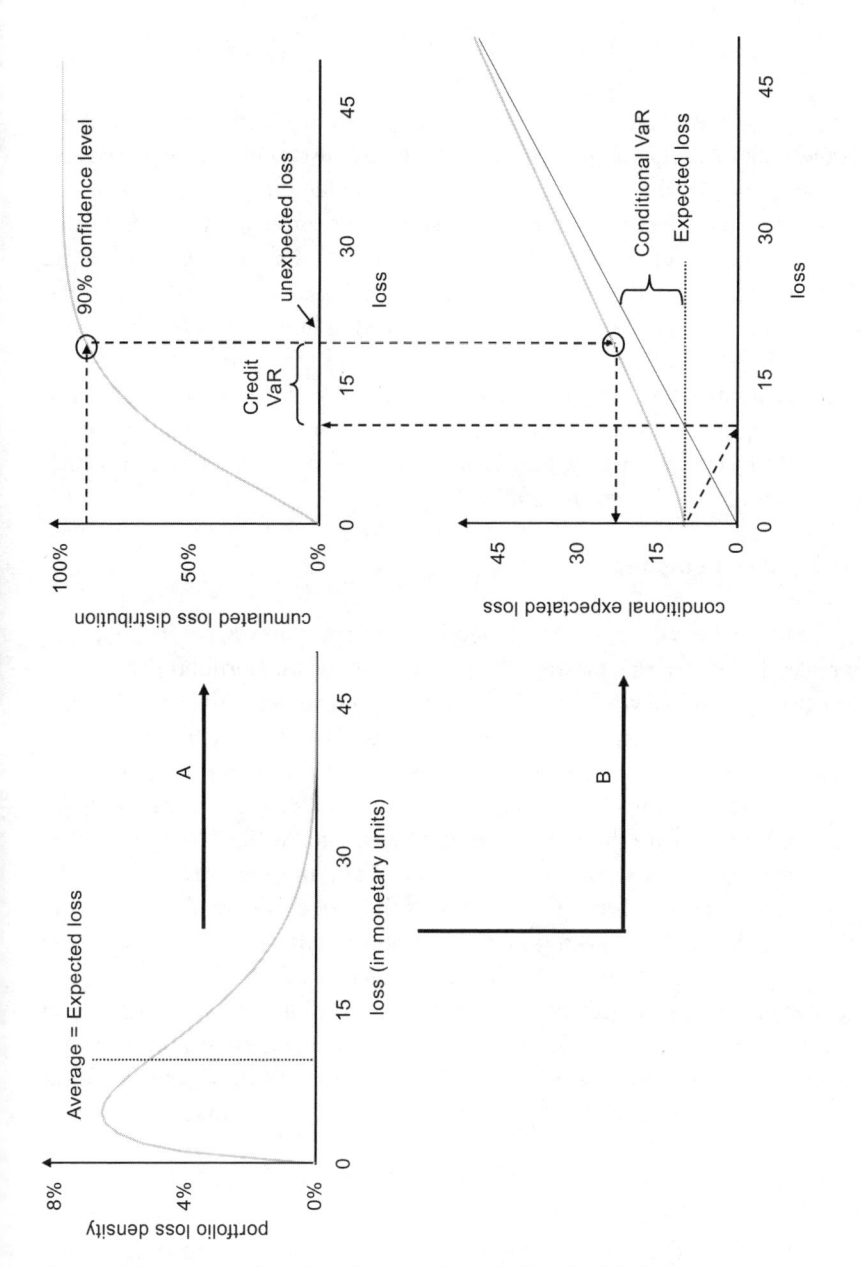

Fig. 11.1: Value at risk and conditional-value at risk definitions for default risk

the conditional expected loss approaches this bisecting line when z approaches N.

To arrive at the CVaR, we elongated the vertical line which characterized the unexpected loss of the upper chart until it crosses the conditional expected loss function (note that the x-axis of all three charts are identical). The value on the y-axis of the lower right chart at the crossing point corresponds to CEL(VaR), the expected loss conditional on exceeding the VaR. Finally, the CVaR is the difference between CEL(VaR) and the expected loss, i.e., CEL(0). Note that the distance of the CEL(y) function to the bisecting line depicts the difference between the VaR and the corresponding CVaR. For high confidence levels, this difference approaches zero, which means that VaR and CVaR measures result in similar figures. The lower the confidence level, the higher the impact from the CVaR concept. Since the CEL(y) function is always above the bisecting line, the CVaR is always greater than the VaR.

11.1.3 Risk Components

To manage the risk on a portfolio level, we need to know more than just the aggregated VaR or CVaR figures. If we want to shape the portfolio risk profile, we need to quantify how an individual exposure contributes to the portfolio VaR. A simple question a portfolio manager might ask is "How much does the VaR of my portfolio change if I remove exposure A?". Unfortunately, VaR and CVaR are complicated non-linear functions. The impact of changes in the portfolio on the risk figures are therefore difficult to estimate. Jorion[71] suggests three related concepts: marginal VaR, component VaR, and incremental VaR. All three concepts deal with the composition of the VaR driven by the underlying risks. Note that in the following we concentrate on VaR. Nevertheless, all these concepts can be transferred to CVaR without major differences.

The *marginal VaR* quantifies the change in the portfolio VaR driven by a small change in the exposure to a given underlying. From a mathematical perspective, it is the partial derivative of the VaR with respect to the component weight in the portfolio: marginal VaR = $\frac{\partial \text{VaR}}{\partial w_A}$, with w_A being the weight of the component A.

The *component VaR* is derived by multiplying the marginal VaR by the real exposure in the portfolio: component VaR = $\frac{\partial \text{VaR}}{\partial w_A} \cdot w_A$. It is thus the linear approximation of the change in the VaR when a specific component is deleted from the portfolio. Although the linearity assumption which lies behind this approach might not be justified (especially for small portfolios where the impact of an individual exposure to the portfolio VaR is large), the component VaR has some advantages. First, we can derive it from the marginal VaR, and second, we can almost completely disaggregate the portfolio risk in its components. Under certain circumstances (i.e., using a delta-normal VaR) the component VaR figures exactly add up to the portfolio VaR.[71]

Last but not least, the *incremental VaR* exactly quantifies how the portfolio VaR changes due to a specific position. In contrast to the component VaR, we do not use a linear approximation here, but derive the impact of a specific component directly: incremental VaR = VaR(P + A) − VaR(P), with VaR(P) being the VaR of the portfolio excluding exposure A. Due to the non-linearity of the VaR, the incremental VaR figures do not add up to the portfolio VaR.

11.2 Credit Portfolio Models

As indicated above, the central task to calculate the credit value at risk is the construction of the portfolio loss density. There are four major models discussed by the financial community. The CreditMetrics model,[80] proposed by JPMorgan, combines a rating-based transition matrix approach with a Merton-based default correlation framework. The KMV model[48] links a structural model with historical default frequencies. Credit Suisse proposed CreditRisk+[81], a model that is based on an actuarial approach and solely deals with default risk. It assumes that the portfolio loss can be adequately described by a Poisson distribution. Last but not least CreditPortfolioView[82,83], which was introduced by the consulting firm McKinsey, is a credit portfolio model in which default probabilities are driven by macroeconomic variables, such as economic growth, unemployment rates, and the level of interest rates. In the following, we briefly outline the CreditMetrics model and the KMV model. For a detailed analysis and comparison of all four approaches, the reader might refer to the review article by Crouhy, Galai and Mark.[84]

Credit portfolio models usually construct the portfolio loss density in two stages. First, one has to derive the credit risk on the level of the individual assets, and second, these risks have to be aggregated to the portfolio level. The CreditMetrics approach uses a rating-based transition matrix model to capture default and migration risk. For migration to the default state, the loss given default has to be modeled as well. For the other rating categories, the dynamics of the corresponding credit spreads (as an average spread per rating category) can also be integrated.

For the second step, the integration of the default correlations, the CreditMetrics approach uses a simplified structural model similar to the factor model introduced in section 9.3. To be more specific, the CreditMetrics approach does not only model the default dependency (i.e., the default correlation), but the complete joint migration probabilities. In this framework, the default correlation is only a special case where the joint probability of two credits migrating to the default state is quantified. To arrive at the complete joint transition probability matrix, the model extends the previously introduced factor model. Instead of partitioning the asset distribution into two parts – the default and the survival part – as in the default dependency models,[60,61] we define one segment per rating class. The ranges of the segments in the asset distribution are defined on a quantile basis (see figure 11.2).

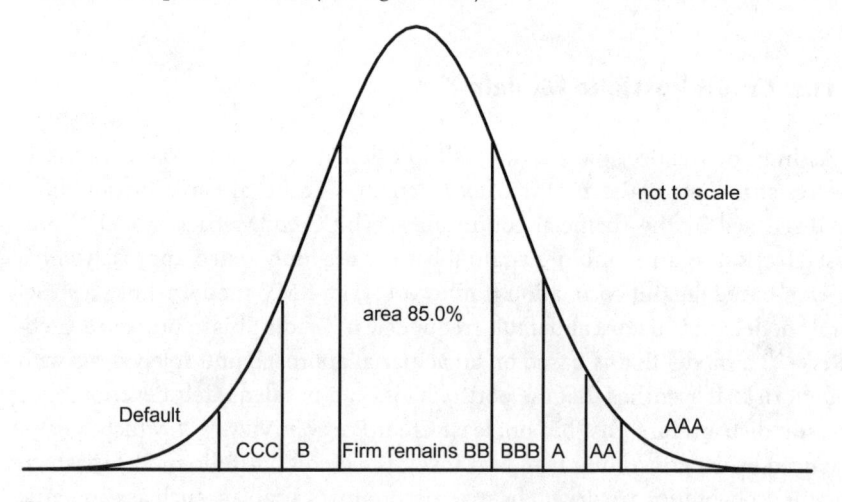

Fig. 11.2: Partitioned standard normal distribution for a BB credit

Once we have the joint transition probabilities for all credits, the dynamics of the credit spreads per rating category, and the recovery rates for the defaulted credits, we can derive the portfolio loss distribution using Monte Carlo simulation techniques.

In contrast to the CreditMetrics model, which can be considered as a reduced-form model, the KMV model uses a structural framework to arrive at the default probabilities. However, in this framework the default probabilities, which are called expected default frequencies (EDF), are not directly calculated from asset values and asset volatilities. The EDF estimation is based on the following three steps. First, the asset value and the asset volatility, which are usually not directly accessible, have to be derived from equity prices and historical volatilities. In the second step, these data are used to calculate the so-called distance to default (DD) by relying on a structural model. In the last step, the EDF is estimated by scaling the distance to default into actual default probabilities (i.e., the EDFs). For this purpose, KMV uses a large database with historical information, including default events.

In contrast to the simple Merton model, where the capital structure of the firm is comprised of only two instruments (equity and a zero coupon bond) the KMV model assumes a more complex liability structure. Besides equity, the firm has short-term debt (which is considered to be identical to cash), long-term debt (modeled as a perpetuity) and convertible preferred shares. Based on these assumptions, the model infers the asset value and the asset volatility from equity prices and equity volatility. Note that the model relies on historical volatilities rather than on implied volatilities from option markets. To derive the asset value and volatility, we only have to recall that the equity value in a structural model is calculated as a call option on the underlying asset value. Since we know the equity value from the stock market, we can back out the underlying asset value by inverting the call option formula.

Regarding the structural model, KMV uses a first-passage-of-time model to derive the distance to default. As introduced in the section about structural models, default is triggered in such a framework when the asset value falls below a certain barrier. Based on historical data, KMV assumes a default barrier that is given by the short-term debt plus one half of the long-term debt. To calculated the distance to default (DD), the model assumes that asset values follow a log-normal process, with a specific growth rate. Then, the DDs are mapped into the EDFs for each time horizon. For valuation purposes, the EDFs have to be transformed into risk-neutral EDFs. Finally, the portfolio loss distribution is constructed using correlated asset returns, similar to the CreditMetrics approach.

Part III

Management

12
Principles of Credit Portfolio Management

12.1 The Role of ACPM in the Asset Allocation Process

In this chapter, we introduce the role of active credit portfolio management in a global asset allocation process. The construction of an optimal cross-asset-class portfolio is not straightforward, as it depends on various constraints, such as the investor's risk aversion and specific asset–liability management (ALM) considerations, such as the matching of assets with future obligations. As an example, the optimal asset allocation for a health insurance company might differ significantly from that of a life insurance company due to the different liability structure. While the health insurance firm might want to hedge its exposure to inflation in the medical and healthcare business, a life insurance company will emphasize a matching of ultra-long-term liabilities with appropriate assets. Due to the inherent complexity of the global asset allocation process, we do not want to delve into the minutiae of this topic but, within this chapter, just highlight the central principles and their impact on active credit portfolio management.

We start our analysis by outlining a generalized asset allocation process. As illustrated in figure 12.1, this process can be structured into the following fundamental building blocks:

- Definition and analysis of the constraints (i.e., ALM considerations, the regulatory framework, the individual risk aversion, and general strategic issues).
- Selection of the underlying asset classes that should be part of the asset allocation optimization procedure.
- Dependency analysis of the underlying asset classes (i.e., the long- and short-term correlations due to fundamental and technical relationships).
- Finding the optimal strategic (long-term) global asset allocation, that is, the weightings for the individual asset classes.
- Decision about and implementation of short- and medium-term tactical modifications and adjustments of the strategic asset allocation.

The strategic asset allocation is strongly influenced by individual issues, such as asset–liability considerations, risk aversion, the regulatory framework, and

Active Credit Portfolio Management. J. Felsenheimer, P. Gisdakis, and M. Zaiser
Copyright © 2006 WILEY-VCH Verlag GmbH & Co. KGaA, Weinheim
ISBN: 3-527-50198-3

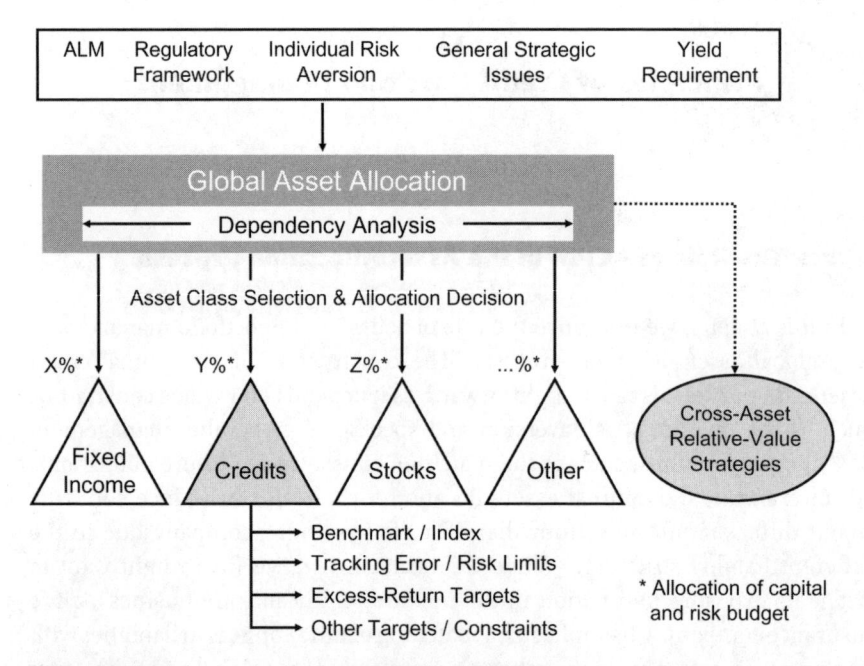

Fig. 12.1: Credit risk management in the global asset allocation process

other strategic considerations of general importance. While the last three topics will normally remain intact for longer time horizons, the ALM constraints can change quite rapidly, triggering potential allocation adjustments (see below for a detailed discussion about time scales). However, this obviously depends on the structure of the liability side. It can be a predictable stream of fixed payments (as with bank portfolios), or a stochastic stream of payments (as with insurance companies). Another prerequisite of the global asset allocation is the decision about which asset classes have to be considered in the analysis. As shown in figure 12.1, these will obviously be fixed income securities, credits, and equities. Moreover, other asset classes, such as emerging market bonds, commodities, and also cash can be included in the analysis. Another important topic that has to be discussed is currency risk, as some investors might want to match their potential FX risks in their asset allocation.

After defining the global constraints and choosing a set of asset classes, the global asset allocation has to be implemented by assigning weightings to the individual asset classes. This is the central and most costly part of the global asset allocation. This process can be either structured top-down or bottom-up, and it can involve fundamental economic considerations, as well as complex mathematical modeling, to find an optimal allocation. Moreover, the optimal allocation is very much affected by the asset price correlation and consequently, dependency analysis plays a major role in this process. However, for our purposes, it is not important how this analysis and the optimization of the allocation are achieved. What we need to know is: What is the effect for credit portfolio management?

In the context shown in figure 12.1, allocation means to specify the X, Y, and Z percentages. Although this point seems to be evident at first glance, there are some important subtleties. In modern asset allocation procedures, global asset management has to assign at least weightings for two different quantities to the individual asset classes: the amount of investment capital and the size of risk budget, which underlies the managed risk in the mandate (e.g., for the allowed tracking error). This is especially important if the global asset management decides that the portfolio managers should manage actively the underlying asset classes. *Risk budgeting* is a transfer of the concept of risk-based capital from bank book management to global asset allocation procedures. The risk of each portfolio (either with respect to the benchmark or in absolute terms) is measured using suitable techniques (e.g., in terms of value at risk or conditional value at risk), and has to be covered by enough risk budget. Using a benchmark-oriented risk measure, global asset management can also assess the quality of the portfolio manager's excess returns: high tracking errors require high excess returns! Another strong argument for using such a risk budgeting mechanism in addition to the allocation of invested funds is the usage of credit derivatives, which do not involve initial cash flows but can bear significant risks. Note that taking correlation among the various asset classes into account, the risk budgets for the individual asset classes do not necessarily have to sum up to the global risk budget. In case of positive correlation, the sum of the individual risk budgets has to be lower than the global risk capital, due to risk acceleration stemming from the positive correlation. For negatively correlated risks, the individual asset classes act as hedges for each other and therefore reduce the overall risks. Consequently, the sum of the individual risk budgets can be larger than the total risk-based capital.

The distinction between a strategic and a tactical asset allocation process (to keep the following analysis straightforward and simple, we ignore other concepts, such as dynamic asset allocation, etc.) lies in the different time scale of the allocation decisions. The strategic asset allocation concentrates on the long-term investment strategy, whereas the tactical asset allocation on a short-term one.

The main drivers of strategic asset allocation decisions are long-term correlation patterns and individual strategic issues of the specific investor, such as (stationary) asset–liability considerations. It aims at identifying an optimal mixture of the underlying asset classes (i.e., the one with the highest expected return) given the investment constraints (liability structure, risk limitations, etc.). The strategic asset allocation defines the investment basis an investor is committed to. This involves longer periods of time, usually covering several business cycles. Note that a long-term commitment does not necessarily mean a buy-and-hold strategy, as asset allocation refers to asset classes as a whole, while the term buy-and-hold usually refers to an individual asset, like a specific bond or stock.

In the strategic asset allocation, the investor decides which principal asset classes he wants to consider in his global allocation. Main input factors are the long-term time series of asset returns, which are necessary to derive expected returns, return volatility, and return correlation patterns. This is the domain of fundamental analysis, as these long-term correlations are mainly driven by basic economic factors. A very simple example of such fundamental dependencies involves risk-free interest rates. Obviously, they affect the prices of all fixed income securities (government bonds, high-yield or high-grade credits, and emerging market bonds): rising yields mean declining prices. However, the correlation between price changes for fixed income securities and stocks is a little more complex. But this is what strategic asset allocation is all about.

In contrast to strategic asset allocation, which frames the long-term picture, the tactical asset allocation focuses on timing issues of the investment process, on market technicals, and on short-term decoupling of long-term correlation patterns. Tactical (i.e., short- to medium-term) considerations sometimes argue for temporary modifications of the strategic allocation. Hence, tactical and strategic decisions operate on different time horizons. In addition, strategic allocation tends to be top-down driven, while tactical decisions are often impacted by bottom-up considerations. Although this distinction is not always applicable, it helps to understand the different issues of the investment process.

For the purpose of our generalized analysis (recall that we are just interested in the role of ACPM in the investment process), global asset management operates at two levels of the global asset allocation process:

- It requires decisions about the long-term (strategic) allocation, and
- It decides about short to medium-term (tactical) adjustments or modifications of the global allocation.

In the framework outlined in figure 12.1, these modifications or adjustments of the strategic asset allocation can be implemented in three different ways.

1. The amount of capital invested in a specific asset class can be changed. This involves the redistribution of larger parts of funds from one asset class to another, for instance, a position in one portfolio (e.g., stocks) has to be liquidated and invested in another (e.g., credits). Such adjustments involve high transaction costs and might disturb the long-term strategy of the portfolio manager. Changes on this scale are usually not performed very frequently for cost reasons.
2. One can change the amount of risk budget that is allocated to each asset class. Modifications at this level will force the portfolio manager from whom the risk budget is withdrawn to move closer to the benchmark, while the manager who receives the budget can now increase his deviations. These procedures can be used to change the beta sensitivities of the underlying portfolios. The asset class in which the risk should be reduced will be structured to a low-beta portfolio, while the other one will be changed to a high beta. While this procedure will also trigger adjustments in portfolio allocation of each asset class, the costs for such shifts might be smaller, as such adjustments can be implemented without liquidating large parts of the funds by using derivatives, for example. However, such procedures violate to a degree the independence of the portfolio manager, as he has to implement a specific deviation from his benchmark. Hence, this will trigger at least significant communication and coordination costs.
3. The risk profile of the global asset allocation can be changed without touching the strategic asset allocation, that is, the invested capital and the risk budget weightings. At the right side of figure 12.1, we introduced an additional investment portfolio, that for cross asset relative value strategies. By implementing trades like short stocks/long credits, the risk profile of the global allocation can be modified. In this sense, this portfolio would act like a hedge fund.

From this analysis it follows that, besides credit risk considerations on the global allocation level, there are two areas in the asset allocation framework where an active credit portfolio management is involved: the benchmark- or index-oriented portfolio management and the cross asset relative value strategies. In figure 12.1, we indicated both areas by means of the gray-shaded blocks. Now we will focus on these two topics.

Benchmark- or index-oriented portfolio mandates belong to the standard techniques of portfolio management. For the portfolio manager, it usually involves the following targets:

- The specification of the *benchmark*, which might be, for example, a bond index such as the iBoxx € high-grade index. Alternatively, the benchmark can also be an absolute return target.
- Global asset management will also specify the *tracking error targets*, such as an average and a maximum tracking error. Besides these frequently used methods, other risk limiting measures can be implemented. As already mentioned, the risk limitation can be implemented by a risk budgeting mechanism. In this framework, global asset management specifies a risk measurement (e.g., value at risk or conditional value at risk) and a factor to determine the required risk budget (or risk-based capital) for a given level of risk. As global asset management also assigns a risk budget to each asset class – in addition to the amount of invested capital – the risk, which can be taken by the portfolio management, is essentially limited. This mechanism resembles the risk-based capital management techniques well-known from bank capital management. However, a central topic of this framework is the way the portfolio risk is calculated. Besides the already mentioned tracking error, one can also use value at risk concepts for this purpose. To achieve an effective benchmark-based risk measure, the managed portfolio is integrated in an ALM framework. The projected future cash flows of the invested assets make up the asset side of the hypothetical balance sheet, while the projected cash flows of the benchmark index make up the liability side. If the invested portfolio closely tracks the benchmark, then the value at risk will be small, whereas it will be large if the deviations are large.
- In addition to the benchmark and risk limitation, there might also be *excess return targets* specified. In case of the above-mentioned risk budgeting framework, the excess return targets can be clearly quantified. They are given by the expected return on the risk budget allocated to the asset class. Hence, the portfolio manager is expected to deliver a high excess return in case he implemented a high-risk portfolio allocation, while the excess return can be small for a strategy that closely tracks the benchmark. Note that for total return funds, value at risk based risk limitation and risk–return-oriented performance measurement techniques are essential.
- Finally, global asset management can also specify other constraints and targets that are not part of the benchmark and index rules, such as a

maximum exposure per issuers, the maximum amount of cash in the portfolio balance, or a specific portfolio duration.

One issue concerning index-based investment strategies should be raised here. This frequently used management technique has also often been criticized as being too rigid. The main criticism is that it forces portfolio management into investment strategies that are too passive. Moreover, the portfolio manager may have to be rewarded for an excess return, even if the absolute value of the portfolio suffered significant losses. However, we believe that this criticism does not properly reflect the role of an index-oriented portfolio construction in a global asset allocation process. In this management framework, the global risks of a specific asset have to be addressed on the global asset allocation level and not at the level of the individual portfolio manager. However, if the global strategic asset allocation process lacks this level of cross asset risk management, index-oriented investment strategies may of course not be appropriate.

Nevertheless, benchmark investment strategies fit perfectly the above-mentioned top-down oriented asset allocation framework. Moreover, the framework offers a clearly structured mandate for the portfolio manager, the basic portfolio construction can be easily implemented, and the performance of portfolio managers can be tracked. In addition, by using risk–return-based performance measures, the size and the quality of the portfolio manager's excess return can also be benchmarked. A note regarding the quality of the excess return: besides risk–return adjustments to the performance, the correlation of the excess returns to the benchmark return is another important part of the manager's performance. The quality of the excess return is high if the excess returns are stable and uncorrelated with the returns of the underlying benchmark. A positive correlation means that the portfolio manager simply increased the beta of the benchmark: the excess return is high when the benchmark return is high, and it is low when the benchmark return is low.

Now, we concentrate on cross asset relative value strategies, which can be viewed as a kind of hedge fund in the asset allocation framework. From a credit risk management point of view, it involves alternative investment and trading strategies such as capital structure arbitrage (long credit versus short equity and vice versa). These cross asset strategies can be implemented based on single-name considerations, as is done in classical capital structure arbitrage approaches, or the risk manager can use aggregated index derivatives for his relative value strategies, playing an equity index derivative (i.e., an ETF) against a credit index derivative such as the iTraxx.

These cross asset strategies can be driven either by asset allocation considerations (changes in the ALM constraints, etc.) or by index-based capital structure arbitrage strategies. We outlined such an innovative investment approach in a credit derivatives special publication.[85] Another business case for the cross asset relative value portfolio will be alternative investments, such as structured credit products (first-to-default baskets and CDO tranches) and equity–debt hybrids (such as equity default swaps). Since these derivatives-oriented investment strategies can be highly flexible, the global asset allocation can be easily and quickly adjusted. This is especially important for scenarios in which long-term correlation patterns break down, such as during the correlation crisis in May 2005.

A final remark on duration risk in the global asset allocation process: The above-mentioned distinction between (risk-free) fixed income securities and credits has one important side issue: duration risks, as both asset classes involve similar risks. To avoid offsetting (and inconsistent) duration allocations across the underlying asset classes, driven by different views concerning the optimal duration allocation, global asset management might give explicit instruction about interest rate sensitivities in the credit portfolio. This can be implemented by limiting the deviation in the duration allocation or by specifying an interest rate-hedged credit benchmark, that is, one in which the benchmark performance is calculated when interest rate risks are swapped, for example, to the 3M-Euribor. Such a portfolio would resemble a floater benchmark.

12.2 Management Styles: Passive or Active

Generally, one can distinguish between two portfolio management styles: passive and active. The passive style is characterized by pure index tracking, while the active approach tries to outperform the benchmark by allocation decisions that differ from the benchmark. In the following, we briefly analyze these two management styles.

12.2.1 Passive Management

In the most common passive management style, the portfolio manager attempts to closely follow the benchmark in terms of the realized returns. However, a pure replication of the benchmark is in most cases simply impossible, as the transaction costs for a portfolio that tracks a broad market index with hundreds of constituents will be significant. Hence, the portfolio manager will try to optimize the portfolio allocation in terms of minimizing the tracking error and the transaction costs. Besides such an index-oriented passive portfolio management, other techniques can also be considered as passive. In stock portfolio management, we are familiar with strategy-oriented funds. These are investment techniques that follow a predefined investment strategy, for example, focusing on stocks with specific P/E ratios, and so on. Such strategy-oriented management techniques are not frequently used in bond portfolio management.

With a passive management style, the main issue for the portfolio manager is the analysis of the benchmark. For this purpose a top-down approach is most suitable. The benchmark constituents are grouped into segments, sectors, rating qualities, and maturity brackets. The portfolio manager then picks those single issues that in total resemble the overall benchmark in terms of the above-mentioned groupings. As an example, from the top-down perspective, the index might have 30 percent telecoms, 20 percent utilities, 10 percent automobiles, and so on. The portfolio manager then chooses single-name issues that fit into these relative weightings.

Instead of constructing a portfolio based on alpha-strategies, the portfolio manager can also track the benchmark by implementing a core–satellite strategy using an appropriate CDS index (e.g., the iTraxx or the CDX). This means that the core market risk is acquired by investing in the CDS index, while the remaining tracking error between the CDS index and the benchmark is reduced by single-name or sector additions, either in the bond market or in the CDS market.

In any case, specific characteristics of bond markets make pure replication strategies very costly.

- The index constituents change more frequently in bond than in stock indices, which therefore requires triggering the necessity of permanent adjustments.
- In contrast to the stock market, the bond market includes illiquid bonds, which are placed with buy-and-hold investors. Acquiring and/or selling such issues might involve significant transaction costs.
- Transaction costs for small trading volumes are high. This makes a simple replication especially for small portfolios very costly, as it involves buying bonds below standard ticket sizes. However, due to reinvestment needs of coupon payments, the ticket size problem can also be an issue for larger portfolios.

In addition to considerations regarding transaction costs, there are other issues that can make pure replication unattractive. Fixed income assets are especially interesting due to a predictable cash flow stream, leaving credit risk and bond options aside for the moment. Hence, a credit portfolio can be structured so that it perfectly matches future obligations. Usually, a pure replication strategy will not match a specific liability structure. Moreover, the portfolio management mandate might also contain constraints that limit the exposure to specific risk categories, for example, quality constraints. A passive management might involve marked-to-market losses in case a bond has to be liquidated due to the violation of these constraints.

12.2.2 Active Management

Investment strategies in an active management context can be grouped into three categories: market timing, sector, and security selection strategies. In a *market timing strategy*, the portfolio manager adjusts the beta and the risky duration (see below) of the total portfolio depending on his current expectations of future market developments. If the manager has a bullish view, he will increase the portfolio beta or the risky duration, while he will reduce the beta in a bearish environment. The beta allocation can be implemented either on a single-name basis (choosing high or low beta credits) or using appropriate portfolio derivatives: credit indices such as the iTraxx, options on single names or indices, FTD baskets, or standardized CDO tranches.

A brief remark on risky duration: the sensitivity of the portfolio towards spread changes can be adjusted by the beta allocation and by changing the duration. For credit-risky bonds, the duration accounts for both changes in the risk-free yield curve and changes in the credit spread.

The *sector and security selection* strategies involve the search for undervalued assets followed by an attempt of forecasting rotation. Note that in credit portfolio management, the term *sector* is slightly more general as it encompasses product segments (e.g., covered bonds, financial and non-financial credits), regions, industries (e.g., telecoms, utilities, and automobiles), maturity brackets, or ratings qualities. A selection strategy is implemented by overweighting, marketweighting, or underweighting a sector, a single-name, or a specific security. In an index-oriented approach, an overweight position means a larger fraction of the specific risk (i.e., the sector, the single name, or the specific security) is taken on than in the benchmark, while an underweight position accepts a smaller exposure to this risk. Marketweight exposure is in line with the corresponding weight in the reference index.

As in the case with the passive portfolio management, the central activity in an active benchmark-oriented portfolio management is the analysis of the benchmark. The best starting point for an active strategy is an overall marketweight portfolio. In this context, *optimal* refers to the above-mentioned minimization of tracking error and transaction costs. The active management component is the deliberate deviation from this marketweight portfolio.

Active management procedures also refer to continuous adjustments rather than buy-and-hold strategies. Current new product developments and innovations facilitate such a continuous process, without involving huge transaction costs. As an example, using CDS indices (e.g., iTraxx and CDX), first-to-default baskets, and CDO tranches allow the acquisition of specific portfolio risks without implementing hundreds of single-name transactions. Hence, active management also involves similar techniques and efforts as passive management. Moreover, bond markets are still bearing pricing inefficiencies, offering significant outperformance opportunities.

12.3 Quantitative and Fundamental Credit Research

The evolution of credit markets caused strong progress in credit research. Besides the fundamental approach (focusing on balance sheet analysis), quantitative tools and models gained in importance, especially in the derivatives universe. As both approaches have their specific advantages, a combination of both methods offers value for investors: believe in models but trust your analysts.

The key problem in credit portfolio management is the negatively skewed risk and return profile. This means that the investor is faced with the possibility of a 100 percent loss, while the maximum profit is limited to the (discounted) coupon payments and redemption. Also, in a well-diversified portfolio, one single blowout could significantly influence the performance of the whole portfolio. If we consider a credit portfolio including 100 constituents, on average delivering a spread of 50 bp over government bonds, the maximum return of the portfolio is 50 bp p.a. over risk-free return until maturity. If only one bond will lose 50 percent (an often seen phenomenon in 2002), the excess return of the portfolio drops to zero.

The key problem of credit portfolio management is managing default risk, as a default has a significant impact on the overall portfolio performance given the negatively skewed risk and return profile of credits (limited upside potential). That said, credit research is not a luxury good; it is rather a prerequisite for generating excess returns in highly complex and heterogeneous markets. The question is if the focus should be on qualitative or quantitative research.

Fundamental credit analysis is a major input for credit portfolio management as credit fundamentals, for example the credit metrics and the business strategy of a company can be used to determine related risks. This is especially the case for more complex high-yield issuers, as subordination structures have to be considered. In addition, off-balance sheet items (pension liabilities) need to be analyzed by an accounting professional. Even if there are evaluation models, these need to be serviced by someone with knowledge of accounting. This is also true if the capital structure changes, e.g., caused by new debt issues, equity write-offs, and asset disposals. Last but not least, fundamental analysis adds value in determining recovery rates, a major input for credit risk models.

Nevertheless, quantitative research gained significantly in importance against the background of (1) investors who demand new approaches, (2) the ongoing progress of developing new models and (3), most importantly, the efficiency of credit markets, which improved steadily. Rising efficiency triggers a decline in bid–ask spreads and reduces the opportunity to earn *windfall profits*, e.g., via market power.

Both approaches (fundamental and quantitative) have their specific advantages, while there is also another side of the coin. Fundamental analysis is focused on specific companies and provides no technique to evaluate the fair bond price, as pricing is directly linked to a relative value comparison. A prerequisite for the optimization of credit portfolios and the evaluation of structured products is the impact of a single asset's risk and return profile on the portfolio and on the structured product, respectively, using statistical methods based, for example, on correlation analysis. In this context, a problem of quantitative models is the use of historical data, which could change in the course of the investment horizon, making a previously optimal portfolio suboptimal. In addition, a purely quantitative analysis does not account for significant fundamental developments, like a change in the capital structure of the company. Despite the fact that credit risk models will gain in importance for credit portfolio managers, the fundamental credit analysis will remain a prerequisite for an adequate risk statement because it provides additional insights that cannot be delivered by quantitative tools.

Pricing single credits and especially evaluating more complex instruments require a combination of both methods. A way to implement this combination when optimizing credit portfolios is to link a bottom-up with a top-down approach. This means that the fundamental view of credit analysts leads to a recommendation for a single issuer, reducing the universe of names that have to be included in a portfolio by interpreting a sell recommendation as a zero weight of the name in the portfolio. Then, the portfolio can be optimized from a top-down view with respect to the sector, the quality, and the duration view. Adding bonds to portfolios also requires several quantitative figures, among others beta factors, Z-scores, and breakeven numbers. These data are the basis to calculate aggregated indicators such as sector betas.

12.4 Diversification in Credit Portfolios

A major topic of portfolio construction in general is the optimal degree of diversification. The concept of diversification is simply to spread an investment over a large number of securities in order to reduce idiosyncratic risk. Besides the optimization process (which takes the optimal risk–return profile of a portfolio into consideration), there is a preceding process regarding the principle of diversification. Depending on the portfolio approach (top-down versus bottom-up), the first step of successful portfolio management is to expand the universe of instruments or specific bonds which have to be optimized.

Although credit portfolios face many kinds of risks, we focus in the following on credit risk only. Diversification means focusing on alpha rather than on generating beta returns, that is, on how to diversify idiosyncratic risks. For example, the diversification of the underlying pool of credits is a key investment parameter for a CDO investor. The homogeneity or heterogeneity of the universe has a significant impact on the risk–return profile of a CDO tranche, while spread dispersion is a crucial indicator in this context.

Following Dynkin, Hyman, and Konstantinovsky[86], the key questionnaire for diversification includes several points:

- How many bonds (from each quality class) should be included in the portfolio? This corresponds to the optimal degree of diversification, a well-known concept from optimizing equity portfolios. Unfortunately, this concept is more complex on the credit side as, in contrast to equities, there is often more than one debt instrument of a specific issuer available. That said, focusing on the issuer might be insufficient to derive the optimal degree of diversification for a credit portfolio.
- With respect to the performance of the portfolio, the risk–return profile depends on the number of instruments in the portfolio. In other words, a credit portfolio manager is searching for the number of bonds that maximize the information ratio, which is simply the arithmetic average

of excess returns divided by the standard deviation of excess returns (for more details please refer to Goodwin[87]).
- A rather practical question is what percentage of the market should be covered by credit research? Limited resources of an asset manager argue for restricting the potential universe of instruments that can be included in a portfolio. Again, this also depends on the portfolio construction approach (top-down versus bottom-up). For example, the analysis of sub-investment-grade issues is more complex and requires more effort from the analysts. Limited resources therefore argue for a concentration on a more homogeneous universe, for example investment-grade credits.

The clarification of the topics above can be seen as a basic step in the credit portfolio construction and optimization process. In the following, we highlight the step-by-step checklist:

- First of all, regulatory issues have to be considered. For example, an investor who is allowed to trade credit derivatives increases the potential universe of instruments significantly as there are more reference obligors traded in CDS than in cash, and there are CDS quotes across the whole maturity curve for almost every name. The number of trading as well as potential hedging strategies rises dramatically for investors who are able to trade credit derivatives compared to cash-only investors. Enlarging the universe of tradable assets allows the construction of more efficient portfolios, accompanied by higher complexity of the optimization process, as more additional constraints have to be incorporated.
- The research capacity is a key factor of determining the universe of instruments: The wider the universe and the higher the complexity of products, the larger the necessary input from analysts. This is closely coupled with the basic portfolio construction approach. A top-down-managed portfolio is rather quantitatively allocated, screening single instruments by using quantitative indicators, which means the marginal cost of analyzing an additional instrument is rather small. In contrast, adding one instrument to the covered universe in a bottom-up-managed portfolio process requires the establishment of a coverage process, including a detailed analysis of the additional instrument. Thus, enlarging the universe is more costly in a bottom-up approach as is the case in a top-down-managed portfolio.
- Based on regulatory constraints and given the research capacity, the next step includes the determination of the tradable universe (high-yield, high-grade, and other credit-risky assets), which also serves as the benchmark for the portfolio.

When the universe is fixed, the question arises of how many bonds should be included in the portfolio to achieve the optimal degree of diversification. The basic principle is simply that adding one instrument provides the investor with a marginal diversification gain as idiosyncratic risk in the portfolio declines. On the other hand, including an additional security in a portfolio produces costs (e.g., transaction costs and monitoring costs). The optimal degree of diversification is reached when the marginal gain equals the marginal costs of an additional unit out of the universe of instruments available. A rule of thumb is that credits are more heterogeneous than equities are (as idiosyncratic risk explains more of the total variance of a credit than is on average the case for equities). Assuming an optimal degree of diversification of 15 percent in equity portfolios, we believe the figure in credits lies between 20 and 25 percent.

12.5 Credit Risk Management in an ALM Environment

The previous analysis was primarily focused on the role of credit risk management in an asset management context. Nevertheless, active credit portfolio management is also of central importance for asset–liability management (ALM). Historically, ALM and credit risk management were considered to be two different tasks, concentrating on different risk factors, with separate risk management technologies and reporting lines. While asset–liability management was primarily focused on managing interest rate risks stemming from interest rate and liquidity gaps, credit risk management obviously monitored and managed the default risk associated with the asset side of the balance sheet. (For further reading with respect to credit risk in terms of managing bank capital see, for example, Matten[72], Bessis[88], and Smithson[89]).

In the banking industry, for example, the only contact between both reporting lines was global bank capital management. The total amount of the available risk budget of the bank had to be divided and assigned to each risk management unit. The most basic approaches simply partitioned the total amount of the risk capital, so that the individual risk budgets added to the total amount, while more advanced methods also took correlations among the risk factors into account. Similar to the assignment procedure of the risk budget in the global asset allocation, a positive correlation resulted in the sum of the individual risk budget that was lower than the global risk capital, while for negative correlations the allocation of the risk budget could be more aggressive. This whole procedure resembles the approach in the long-term oriented strategic asset allocation. Once the risk budgets were assigned and the managers' targets were defined, there was no more interaction between managing interest rate and credit risk. Short-term adjustments due to tactical considerations could not be implemented in this framework.

From a historical point of view, the separation of credit risk and interest rate risk management was understandable. For interest rate risk, there were plenty of derivative instruments and techniques available to manage the exposure. Swaps, futures, and options were already plain-vanilla tools for interest rate risk managers. However, managing credit risk without appropriate derivatives was a binary affair: take it or leave it. Once the exposure was on the balance sheet it was difficult and costly to get rid of it again. Passive risk management procedures, relying on sophisticated rating systems to identify and avoid unwanted risks, were the key to successful risk management. While company analysis is still a major performance driver, credit risk management can be significantly more active these days, as current markets offer a large set of appropriate tools for managing credit risk as well (e.g., credit derivatives).

The next step of the evolution in modern risk management aims at integrating interest rate and credit risk management in an asset–liability framework.[90] As we showed above, interest rate risk (and other sources of market risks) and credit risks are not completely separable. They are interdependent. Unfortunately, this dependency is not stable across time. In the current market environment, correlation patterns evolve continuously. As a result, asset price correlations can even change signs: a former hedge might even add to the risk of a portfolio. This argues against using static risk management procedures and makes integrated risk management, using state-of-the-art technology, essential.

12.6 Credits in the Global Asset Allocation

12.6.1 Increasing Importance of Credit-Risky Instruments

We already discussed the rising importance of credit risk from an economic point of view. We stated that credit-risky instruments are the appropriate asset to match the inherent risk of an economy, which we named growth risk, highlighting that in the end it is primarily corporate credit risk that is the central risk factor. Besides corporate credit risk, any other financial instrument (sovereign debt, stocks, ABS, etc.) reflects only an isolated part of the overall risk of an economy. A tradable tranched index swap including all companies of an economy would be the preferable tool for trading and managing overall risk. Such an index also includes financial institutions, which means that interest rate risk (which is still the plain-vanilla banking business) is also a part of the overall index through the performance of banks. Against this backdrop, we conclude that credit risk rather than interest rate risk is the major risk factor for financial institutions (not only for banks but also for insurance companies). From this point of view, credit risk management is still underestimated.

12.6.2 Credits, Government Bonds, and Equities

A key question for umbrella funds is how to structure a risk and return optimized portfolio, including credits, stocks, and government bonds. In the following, we explain how credits reduce diversification costs in an overall portfolio and note that credits add value not only in a modest growth scenario.

Regarding global portfolios, which include a broad range of asset classes, optimizing the asset mix requires an analysis of single drivers for every asset class and correlation patterns among all assets and asset classes. While there are many possible input factors that could be used to feed factor models, interest rates are still in the limelight for a large number of market participants, especially insurance companies.

Focusing on government bonds and stocks, the traditional mechanism is that declining interest rates go hand-in-hand with rising stock prices. The two major arguments are: first, declining interest rates reduce refinancing costs and support capital expenditures, boosting future company profits, which lead to a higher share price. Second, declining interest rates will trigger allocation shifts from government bonds into equities. This was (and probably still is) the main theme in most financial-economics textbooks. However, the problem is that this mechanism has been suspended since the bursting of the equity bubble in March 2000. From 1990 until March 2000, there was an inverse relationship between share prices and interest rates, which fits with common theory. In contrast, since March 2002 (all-time high in many European stock indices), the picture changed dramatically. Interest rates and share prices show a high positive correlation in the aftermath of the equity markets' plunge.

Does the monetary mechanism still work? In our view, it does. However, the world is now more complicated. The fact is that the sensitivity of economic growth to interest rates may evolve over time not only due to structural changes but also to micro-fundamental developments (like overwhelming indebtedness of the private sector or banks that have to repair their balance sheets and could not continue their intermediary function). Without going into detail, a major impact from the evolving correlation for financials markets is the fact that the length of the time series is decisive for the outcome of any correlation analysis.

This is the reason why many investors prefer to focus on scenario analysis rather than on historical data.

Despite this problem, credits have a very attractive risk and return profile due to their three return components: the credit return, the curve return and accrued income. While the former is (mostly) positively correlated to equity returns, the latter are the fixed-income-like performance components. What we call the offsetting process is the fact that – on a total return basis – credits are the real safe havens in the fixed income world as the credit and the curve return are negatively correlated. In the case of bullish macroeconomic environment, the curve return is negative due to rising interest rates, while the credit return will be positive on the back of spread tightening and vice versa.

Hence, in a portfolio context, single return components of credits are negatively correlated to other asset classes, particularly stocks and government bonds. Hence, credits can be used as a substitute for a combined equity and safe-haven portfolio to a certain extent. This is especially the case for sub-investment-grade issues, as the equity-part of high-yield bonds exceeds that of investment-grade credits. Having said this, credits have a positive impact on the overall diversification process as they add a significant portion of diversification gains to a portfolio. Moreover, adding credits in an umbrella fund allows fund managers to reduce diversification costs. Using credits is a simple and favorable way to reduce diversification costs while keeping the gains of diversification. Based on structural approaches, credit portfolio manager can use equity derivatives for hedging reasons or to optimize the portfolio structure.

Regarding historical patterns, credits offer value in a modest growth environment, which is even more the case in global portfolios, as we stated above. In any case, credits should always have a weight above zero in an umbrella fund. From a purely theoretical standpoint, credits can replace the portfolio's risk and return contribution of safe havens due to the fact that the return components of government bonds can also be found in credits. Under the assumption that every maturity profile can be displayed by credits, one can construct a portfolio including equities and credits that has exactly the same risk and return profile as a portfolio including government debt and equity. Due to the equity-related risk component of credits (the spread return), the correlation between equities and credits is higher than between the former and sovereign bonds. This means that the equity share could be reduced in an equity/credit portfolio compared to a governments/equity portfolio, generating the same risk and return profile.

To summarize the advantages of credits in an umbrella fund: (1) there might be arbitrage opportunities on a macro level as there is more than one alternative to reach a specific risk and return profile due to the substitute character of credits; (2) diversification costs in the equity exposure can be reduced, since credits already provide natural diversification effects; (3) in a CAPM approach, adding credits to an umbrella fund can move the portfolio to the preferred utility curve of the investor.

12.7 Building Blocks of Credit Portfolio Management

There are three general risk management principles for both financial and non-financial risks: a global perspective (consider all risks), integrated management (consider the interaction and dependency of risks), and a continuous process (never stop thinking about your risks). Risk management is a complex task. Hence, successful portfolio management is an art and a science. Both soft and hard facts are important determinants for a sustainable performance of the portfolio. A correct forecast – like making the right call – is only one side of the coin. Nevertheless, this part has a lot to do with experience, knowledge about markets, and the portfolio manager's gut feeling. On the other hand, the impact of forecasts on the performance of the portfolio belongs to the scientific part of portfolio management. This essentially means that the portfolio manager has to know the key sensitivities and characteristics of the portfolio under management.

The general procedures for successful portfolio management can be grouped into the following building blocks.

1. Define the target quantities of the portfolio that have to be managed.
2. Determine the quantifiable risk factors that affect the portfolio.
3. Analyze the economic variables that drive the risk factors.
4. Derive a view of the future direction of the economic variables and the corresponding impact on the risk factors.
5. Calculate the sensitivities of the portfolio with respect to the risk factors.
6. If necessary, perform a portfolio optimization analysis that integrates the current portfolio characteristics and sensitivities, your view on the future development of risk factors, and the dependency structure (e.g., the historical correlation) among the risk factors.
7. Adjust the portfolio characteristics so that their sensitivities correspond to your above-mentioned view of the future development of the risk factors, taking the results of the optimization analysis into account.
8. Implement a performance analysis that allows a detailed attribution of realized returns and projected risks with respect to the specific risk factors.

In the following few paragraphs, we discuss and elaborate on these building blocks. As this discussion is meant to be a general introduction that highlights the central arguments and major tasks, we do not claim to provide a comprehensive analysis for each topic. As a result, we prefer to ask the important questions rather than to give exhaustive answers. For most of the points below, there are several specialized books available that focus on the details of solutions. Nevertheless, we think that there is added value for the reader if we broadly outline the basic portfolio management considerations.

12.7.1 Step 1: Investment Targets

At first glance, the specification of investment targets seems to be easy: "Earn a sufficient return on the invested capital without taking too much risk." Although this simple claim is absolutely true, it is much too vague to serve as a rational portfolio management process. The above-mentioned expression contains several core features of rational portfolio management that have to be exactly specified:

- Sufficient return: How can one exactly specify this return and how much is sufficient? These questions are closely related to the scope of portfolio management. As introduced above, there are in principle two different links to active credit portfolio management in a global asset allocation process: index- or benchmark-oriented investment management and relative value cross asset strategies (hedge fund type of investments). In case of a benchmark-oriented portfolio, the appropriate return measurement will be the excess return over the total return of the benchmark. As previously mentioned, benchmark-oriented management is sometimes considered to be a double-edged sword. Anecdotal evidence demonstrates that managers of benchmark-oriented portfolios can successfully outperform their benchmark, although they probably lose money if the benchmark incurs significant losses. Nevertheless, it is a common technique to construct investment portfolios, as it fits seamlessly in with global asset allocation management. Global asset management decides about the exposure to certain asset classes, while the scope of portfolio managers of each asset class is to track and hopefully to beat the benchmark indices. In the case of cross asset relative value and total return strategies, there is no index that has to be tracked. The benchmark is simply a specified minimum return that has to be earned by the portfolio. Finally, the question of *sufficient* return has to be addressed. Using modern risk–return management techniques, the return is sufficient if it exceeds the cost of capital for the assigned risk budget (or risk-based capital). Please recall that in the previously outlined cross asset allocation process, management assigns investment capital and a risk budget to each asset class. Moreover, for index tracking, other criteria for the quality of excess return, such as a low correlation between the excess return and the total return of the fund, may be applicable.

- Invested capital: What is the invested capital? This question appears to be strange at first, as the invested capital is simply the sum that was needed to acquire the assets in the portfolio. But in reality such an approach might cause trouble if the risky exposure in the portfolio is leveraged either directly or through the use of unfunded credit derivatives. As an example, entering into a standard CDS contract does not involve any upfront cash exchanges. Hence, the investor does not need capital to acquire these assets. However, in the case that the investor sold protection to the market via CDS, the counterparty will demand collateral to back the claim in case of a default. At this stage, the situation becomes confusing. Just think of a CDS contract that pays a 50 bp premium. If the return were simply defined as the premium income divided by the notional amount and therefore neglected a liquidity effect in this setup, then such an investment would be completely unattractive. Under normal market conditions, a risk-free money market account earns a return higher than 50 bp. While in this setup it is quite clear that a liquidity effect has to be considered, the possibility of separating the risks involved from the real cash investment through the use of unfunded derivatives makes a pure return-on-invested-capital approach inappropriate. To address these problems, we introduced above the risk budget (see section 12.1). The reference used to calculate the portfolio return (the invested capital in the above-mentioned claim) has to be adjusted by the risk budget that backs the risks involved in the portfolio.

- Without too much risk: How much is too much and which kind of risks should be taken? While the above-mentioned two topics are manageable without involving too many mathematical procedures, measuring the risk of a portfolio is a tough task, especially for credit portfolios, as the probability distributions and the dynamics of the underlying risk factors are fairly complex. So what does risk limitation mean in an asset class involving the risk of large losses (in case of a default event)? This is an old question and the most basic answer is diversification. However, capturing diversification effects on a portfolio level in a mathematical framework means to model asset price correlations and default dependencies. Besides well-established procedures, such as single-name and industry limitations for the investment exposure, a portfolio manager should be able to quantify and manage the absolute level of risk. The portfolio value at risk is a frequently used risk measure. It gives the maximum loss that is not exceeded in a pre-specified time horizon for a given level of confidence. For example, a 99 percent ten-day value at risk of 5 percent says that with a probability of 99 percent the maximum loss incurred within ten days will not exceed 5 percent. It is also interesting to consider what this quantity does not tell us, namely: What is happening in the 1 percent case when the loss exceeds the 5 percent level? What is the expected loss in this case? Unfortunately, in credit risk the corresponding losses for such a rare event can be significantly large. Hence, we need a measure that is able to capture this possibility. A risk quantity that measures this conditional loss is the so-called conditional value at risk (a.k.a. expected shortfall). Most portfolio managers do not only limit the value at risk but also the conditional value at risk. Finally, an important part of risk limitation deals with the question of which risks should be avoided. For example, most investors do have rating limitations. Companies that do not belong to a certain level of credit quality are not allowed in the portfolio. Hence, investment-grade portfolio managers have to liquidate their exposure to fallen angels within a certain time period after their downgrade to junk status. Moreover, some portfolio managers are restricted to a certain level of interest rates risk; they have to maintain a specified duration, while they might be allowed to deviate from their benchmark to a larger extent with the credit exposure.

12.7.2 Step 2: Risk Factors

A central task is to determine the quantifiable risk factors. These are factors that directly determine the value of the assets under consideration, such as interest rates (i.e., risk-free bond yields and swap rates), exchange rates, implied volatilities, credit spreads, and implied correlation. Credit-risky portfolios usually involve a huge number of risk factors. In contrast to risk-free fixed income portfolios, there is not only one yield curve (per currency) driving the performance, but each asset is associated with a specific reference entity, for which the credit risk has to be reflected. Moreover, in contrast to equity portfolios, there is not only one single asset (i.e., one stock) per reference entity, but a whole set of bonds and credit default swaps with different maturities. Moreover, if the portfolio contains portfolio derivatives, such as first-to-default baskets or CDO tranches, implied default correlations will be added to the list of risk factors. The asset price correlation is an important risk factor, too, as it is needed for risk measurement purposes. Hence, the sheer number of underlying risk factors and the complexity of their dynamics cause significant challenges for credit portfolio management. Note that economic variables, such as economic growth, do not have a direct pricing impact and are not considered as direct risk factors. Their contribution to the management process will be shown below.

12.7.3 Step 3: Economic Variables

The economic variables that drive the risk factors need to be analyzed. For example, the short end of the government yield curve is driven by monetary policy, while the long end mainly reflects long-term growth prospects. Another example regarding credit spreads: deleveraging activities (i.e., repayment of debt) are credit supportive and will therefore trigger a spread tightening. However, sometimes it is difficult to determine the impact of an economic variable on the risk factors. A high oil price, for example, can be supportive for oil producing companies, whereas it might hurt oil consuming industries.

12.7.4 Step 4: Forecasting and Scenario Assessment

In the next step, an outlook on the future direction of economic variables and their corresponding impact on risk factors should be formulated. A proper forecast statement contains the direction of the movement, the size of the projected change, and the time horizon the forecast refers to. A call like "The iTraxx spread is expected to rise by 7 bp from a current level of 40 bp within the next three months" completely expresses the view of the investor with respect to the iTraxx credit index. However, as the real world dynamics tend to deviate from forecasts, the risk assessment is an integral part of the forecast. Accordingly, the investor should add a statement about risks to his forecast that stem from the uncertainty about future dynamics. This is done by analyzing base-case, worst-case, and best-case scenarios and by assigning probabilities to these scenarios. A simple example for such a scenario framework would be "The iTraxx will tighten by 5 bp with a probability of 60 percent and it will widen by 25 bp with a probability of 40 percent." The expected value for this scenario set is 7 bp.

12.7.5 Step 5: Sensitivities

The sensitivities of the portfolio with respect to the risk factors (see step 2) is important information that a portfolio manager needs for his work. For fixed income instruments, crucial sensitivities are yields and duration. For credit derivatives, such as credit default swaps, the corresponding quantities are the deal spread (i.e., the size of the premium payments) and the basis point value of the credit spread (a.k.a. SpreadDV01). The sensitivity topic belongs to the engineering part of the portfolio management process. For some instruments, there is a significant amount of different sensitivities to capture, and the calculation of the sensitivities can be quite difficult. We only have to think about a CDO tranche that refers to a portfolio of 100 underlying credits. We need the spread sensitivities (i.e., the SpreadDV01) for all underlying credits and, in addition, the appropriate correlation sensitivities.

As previously introduced (see for example section 10.1.4), a *sensitivity* is defined as the change in value of the asset with respect to a specific risk factor, given that all other factors are kept fixed. In a mathematical framework, this corresponds to the derivative of the value with respect to the risk factor. However, the underlying assumption "all else equal" causes difficulties for some products. In the case of a CDO tranche, this means that we have to keep the default correlation fixed, but, as mentioned above, there are different correlation measures (base and compound correlation), and hence there are different sensitivities that belong to different models. Such tasks make the quantification of sensitivities challenging even for experienced financial analysts.

Another problem stems from the necessity to obtain aggregated figures. An investor needs to know how much the value of his portfolio changes if a benchmark index changes by a certain amount. Such an analysis involves asset price correlation and argues for a beta assessment, a technique well known from equity portfolio management. Finally, as the number of key figures can be huge, we need aggregation and disaggregation (drill-down) schemes to extract the appropriate and important data and to avoid an information overload. This argues for a well-organized and hierarchical reporting structure, from a highly aggregated top-level report with only few key figures down to detailed single-name information.

Note that the current value of the portfolio does not depend on the asset price correlation. These quantities are only needed to measure the value at risk on the portfolio level. Consequently, a price sensitivity cannot be calculated. Nevertheless, the risk sensitivity (change of the VaR with respect to the correlation) can be an interesting source of information for the portfolio manager.

12.7.6 Step 6: Portfolio Optimization Analysis

When thinking about optimization techniques, it is important to differentiate between strategic portfolio allocation and day-to-day portfolio adjustments. Strategy-oriented full portfolio optimization using mathematical procedures is usually not an everyday task. As most optimization techniques involve long-term correlations, it is more suitable for a strategic allocation that concentrates on longer time horizons. As indicated above, a mathematical portfolio optimization analysis is performed on the level of the global asset allocation, especially when dealing with the strategic view. However, the implementation of a – from a strategic point of view – optimal portfolio will not be a one-time event, as tactical issues, such as market-timing, will require temporary adjustments.

An optimal strategy is one that balances all important scenarios weighted by the corresponding probabilities and takes the underlying investment constraints into account. It offers maximum outperformance potential for a given level of risk. The result of such an analysis is an optimized exposure to the desired risk factors. In addition, advanced portfolio optimization techniques suggest an efficient set of trades that also take the transaction costs into account.

A prerequisite for portfolio optimization techniques is a quantifiable risk measurement that adequately models the individual underlying risk factors (e.g., single-name risks) as well as the dependency structure among the risk factors. For a credit-risky portfolio, capturing the risk of default events is essential. As default risk refers to a highly skewed probability distribution (high probability for zero losses and small probability of large losses), standard optimization techniques that rely on Gaussian-shaped symmetrical distributions, such as the standard value-at-risk measure, are not the best method. A better and more coherent method would be the conditional value at risk. Another important issue for an efficient analysis is the integration of major investment constraints in the mathematical optimization. This can encompass, for example, regulatory as well as individual limitations, such as a minimum rating quality.

As the dependency of the projected payoff, the dynamics of the underlying risk factors, and the impact of the constraints on the profile of the portfolio can be quite complicated, a mathematical optimization procedure that captures all these factors will be necessary. Unfortunately, most reliable portfolio optimization procedures will be very time-consuming as they will in most cases involve Monte Carlo simulations. And moreover, the quality of the results strongly depends on the quality of the input data (garbage in, garbage out), especially as asset price correlations, which tend to be faulty, matter.

Nevertheless, mathematical optimization techniques can also be of value on an asset management level. First, a correct mathematical model that integrates all relevant price dependencies helps to analyze the central portfolio characteristics, especially in the credit derivatives world with its complicated price relations. As an example, a simulation – as it is performed in an optimization analysis – offers additional insight into the impact of a specific trade on the risk profile of the portfolio. Second, it is an important piece of information for the portfolio manager to know how the efficient frontier of his specific market looks and where his portfolio is located in the risk–return plot, especially if his performance is judged in terms of risk and return. And third, a portfolio optimization approach forces the portfolio manager to make a scenario-based expression of his fundamental views. Recall that a scenario-based approach is the most honest way to express a specific view. However, as already mentioned, for most day-to-day decisions of a portfolio manager, full mathematical optimization would be overkill, if applicable at all.

12.7.7 Step 7: Portfolio Adjustments

The implementation of portfolio adjustments and the optimization analysis are closely related. Nevertheless, we separated the implementation of the portfolio adjustments from the portfolio optimization procedure to highlight that not all actions regarding portfolio adjustments are triggered by mathematical optimization. On the contrary, complex mathematical models can be harmful, if the resulting impulses cannot be understood by the portfolio manager. Hiding behind mathematical models without intuition about their characteristics and potential risks is indeed dangerous.

Nevertheless, most transactions are driven by linear considerations, which can be easily captured by the portfolio manager without the necessity of a complex mathematical framework. Here, the portfolio will be adjusted so that its sensitivities correspond to the above-mentioned view of the future trend of the risk factors. In other words, the portfolio characteristics are reshaped in a way that the portfolio provides the desired payoff given the anticipated movement of risk factors. However, as already mentioned, the re-shaping of the portfolio characteristics can be a complicated task, as one has to consider various restrictions and constraints. Very common and rational constraints are, for example, single-name limits. Constraints that are driven by asset–liability considerations can be more subtle. A life-insurance company might face the constraint that the portfolio has to earn a certain return over a given time horizon.

12.7.8 Step 8: Performance Analysis

The detailed ex post analysis of the realized performance is another important building block for successful portfolio management. It should be viewed as a central tool for analyzing portfolio characteristics, rather than as a simple benchmarking of the management qualities. A reasonable performance analysis is split into three parts:

- The *return attribution analysis* splits the total return into the components stemming from the underlying risk factors, that is, the risk-free yield curve and the credit spread.
- The *ex post risk analysis* reviews the underlying risk factors to arrive at risk-adjusted performance measures.
- The *performance explanation* rationalizes the returns based on realized changes in the underlying risk factors.

While the first two points are related to mathematical procedures and standardized reporting techniques, the last refers to the management activities and the discussion of the performance drivers. The importance of such a performance explanation and discussion should not be underestimated. However, the analysis should be focused on identifying the major performance drivers. It justifies or challenges the investment strategy and helps to find mistakes in the implementation. As an example, it might reveal that the management correctly forecasted the direction of a specific risk factor, but the portfolio underperformed because the strategy was not properly implemented or did not consider other related issues that negatively impacted the total return. On the back of such an analysis, the portfolio manager can rethink and improve his investment decisions and learn about new factors that impact his performance.

A performance attribution analysis is needed on an aggregated portfolio level, as well as a performance breakdown into segments, sectors, rating qualities, maturity brackets, and single names.

A close monitoring and continuous performance measurement is especially necessary for risky trading strategies, which bet, for example, on a specific relative performance of two assets. In such cases, the performance has to be tracked on a day-to-day basis and the risk manager has to watch for stop-loss triggers and return targets.

Another important aim of the return attribution analysis is back-testing a value-at-risk measure. Focusing on market risk measurement, the realized one-day loss should not exceed the 99 percent one-day VaR more than 2.5 times per year. Otherwise, the risk measure does not properly reflect the portfolio risk, as the 99 percent one-day VaR predicts a loss being greater than the VaR in only 1 percent of the trading days, which is 2.5 assuming 250 trading days per year.

Finally, a risk-adjusted performance analysis assesses the quality of the excess returns the portfolio manager provides. Besides the target return on the assigned risk budget, the stability of the excess returns are in the focus. Excess returns that are uncorrelated with the total return of the benchmark are a sign of strong management qualities, as the portfolio manager provides excess return in bull and in bear markets. Moreover, the source of the excess return is another important piece of information. Was an outperformance mainly driven by a successful alpha management (i.e., the ability to select undervalued assets) or by a proper management of the market timing?

12.8 Key Portfolio Figures

In this section, we divide the process of constructing, managing, and benchmarking credit portfolios into three parts:

- The top-down allocation level starts at the *top level*, including the decision for different asset classes (high yield, high grade, ...), the macro-allocation process and basic construction principles, for example, the determination of key figures for portfolio management. On the valuation side, the top level covers the most important figures, namely the VaR, the average spread, the spread sensitivity, the duration, and the performance of the overall portfolio.
- Portfolio management and construction on the *medium level* is concerned with sector and quality allocation, implementing the macro view on a more detailed level. For example, a very defensive macro allocation would be reflected in a defensive industry allocation, that is, preferring low beta sectors (utilities) versus high beta sectors (industrials, automobiles). Regarding qualities, a defensive allocation would be mirrored by an overweight position in higher-rated names, while such a portfolio carries only limited exposure to high-yield bonds.
- Last but not least, single-name selection in the asset management process is done on the *bottom level*. This is in line with the traditional bottom-up approach, including an in-depth company analysis as well as a relative value approach regarding specific instruments. In contrast to managing equity portfolios, there is an additional management level in the credit world, as there is in general more than one credit-risky instrument for a specific name available.

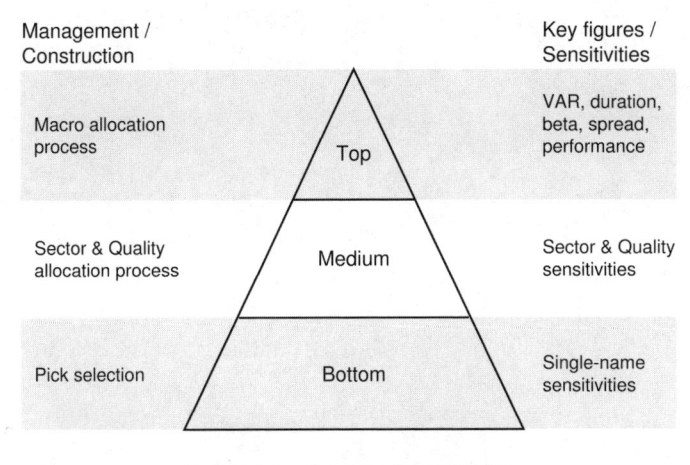

Management / Construction		Key figures / Sensitivities
Macro allocation process	Top	VAR, duration, beta, spread, performance
Sector & Quality allocation process	Medium	Sector & Quality sensitivities
Pick selection	Bottom	Single-name sensitivities

Performance Analysis, Benchmarking & Return Attribution Analysis

Fig. 12.2: Key principles of portfolio management

13
Portfolio Allocation

In chapter 12, we described the effect of including corporate bonds in umbrella funds and argued that credit-risky instruments offer value due to the substitutive character of credits for both equities and risk-free fixed income securities. In this section, we focus on the sector and quality allocation within the credit universe, which has a significant impact on the risk–return profile of a portfolio and, last but not least, on the performance. This is true for beta-managed rather than for alpha-managed portfolios. We choose the iBoxx € universe because the sector classification (Dow Jones) coincides with equity indices, which allows us to use information from equity markets which can be directly transferred to the credit spectrum. In the following, we derive an optimal allocation based on a simple Markowitz approach and we identify tools which support the sector and quality allocation.

From a macro perspective, the cyclical nature of credit markets argues for the importance of sector allocation as is the case in equity markets. This is underpinned by historically significant performance differences among specific industries through the business cycle. This is also true regarding the quality allocation, while the basic differentiating factor with respect to qualities is the rating of a company. This might be misleading as company ratings, in general, lag behind market moves and therefore an optimizing quality allocation using ratings can significantly differ from an optimal quality allocation using implied ratings. Optimizing the sector and quality allocation, in any case, is only one part of the puzzle to creating an efficient portfolio. This becomes obvious when we look at the heterogeneity of sector constituents. For example, the iBoxx € Automobiles & Parts contains AAA-rated companies like Toyota and also BBB-rated issuers like Michelin. Deriving an optimal industry allocation taking aggregated sector spreads into account also means simplifying and ignoring additional information which is available in the spreads of the sector constituents. Against this background, a practical alternative is calculating spread betas (with respect to the respective quality and industry spread) for all names within the target index, which provides additional information about the risk profile of the portfolio.

13.1 Indices

13.1.1 The Function of Indices

There are two major functions of indices in general. An index is designed to replicate a target market properly in order to reflect performance and risk figures of a specific asset class. Moreover, an index provides a benchmark for index trackers; it requires a transparent calculation procedure that allows a portfolio manager to track his portfolio versus the benchmark.

Benchmark investors can directly compare the sector and quality risks of their portfolio to the respective index. In table 13.1, we show the reference universe, the iBoxx € Non-Financials by industry and by rating brackets, together with a model portfolio.

Tab. 13.1: The iBoxx € Non-Financials universe by sector and quality

Quality Allocation	iBoxx	Portfolio	Deviation
AAA/AA	12.5%	4.2%	−8.3%
A	51.8%	49.2%	−2.6%
BBB	35.7%	46.6%	+10.9%

Sector Allocation	iBoxx	Portfolio	Deviation
Automobiles & Parts	9.7%	9.8%	+0.1%
Basic Resources	2.0%	1.8%	−0.2%
Chemicals	4.6%	4.9%	+0.3%
Construction & Materials	3.5%	4.5%	+1.0%
Food & Beverage	1.8%	2.0%	+0.2%
Health Care	1.9%	0.5%	−1.4%
Industrial Goods & Services	8.4%	4.4%	−4.0%
Media	2.0%	2.5%	+0.5%
Oil & Gas	4.7%	4.4%	−0.3%
Personal & Household Goods	5.4%	7.3%	+1.9%
Retail	4.7%	6.2%	+1.5%
Technology	0.3%	0.0%	−0.3%
Telecommunications	26.3%	28.1%	+1.8%
Travel & Leisure	0.7%	0.2%	−0.5%
Utilities	24.1%	23.4%	−0.7%

In this section, we focus on the iBoxx € index universe as a well-known and often-used benchmark for euro-denominated credit portfolios. We explain in detail the construction of the iBoxx, followed by an index analysis of the RDAX, a bond index including the DAX30 companies. A comprehensive analysis of the target index is a prerequisite for calculating sensitivities of credit portfolios as well as tracking and benchmarking these portfolios versus a respective benchmark.

13.1.2 The iBoxx € Index Universe

The iBoxx € index family covers the investment-grade fixed income market for euro-denominated bonds, while seven major financial institutions (ABN AMRO, Barclays Capital, BNP Paribas, Deutsche Bank, Dresdner Kleinwort Wasserstein, Morgan Stanley, and UBS Investment Bank) provide prices for all bonds that are included. Deutsche Börse as the index provider is responsible for calculating and publishing index figures.

There are four major advantages of the iBoxx € index construction and calculation mechanism:

- Price contribution: The median price concept (iBoxx consolidated prices), which is based on prices for every bond from seven contributors, makes sure that indicative index quotes almost match executable prices. This strengthens the function of iBoxx indices as a benchmark for performance analysis. Moreover, the median concept eliminates the risk of inventory-related pricing. This means that pricing single issues by a price contributor might be related to the position of a specific bond in the trading books. For example, if a bank carries a huge amount of a specific bond that should be reduced, the price might be below the theoretically fair value of the bond. Last but not least, due to the heterogeneity of the universe (in mid-2005 there were more than 350 issues in the iBoxx € Non-Financials subsegment) and given the fact that a lead manager has pricing commitments, no single bank prices all bonds with the same conscientiousness.
- Transparency: The index provider calculates and releases all important data for every constituent on a daily basis. This allows portfolio managers to replicate all index data, analyze index changes or performance figures exactly, and calculate spreads for all bonds. Single bond data released by the index provider include the bond structure, risk figures (time to maturity, modified duration, convexity), and daily index weightings.
- The iBoxx € universe is the already established basis for pricing derivative instruments. There are even exchange traded funds (ETFs) outstanding, while the iTraxx Corporate index in Series 1 and 2 was constructed on the basis of iBoxx non-financial criteria.
- The iBoxx € universe is unique with respect to the comprehension of euro fixed income assets. The index universe is divided into subsec-

tors, which makes benchmarking much easier as quality, maturity, and industry-specific indices are available.

The iBoxx family comprises an overall index and four major subindices. The sovereigns index group includes euro-denominated sovereign debt issued by governments in the eurozone, with subindices by geography and by maturity. The iBoxx € Non-Sovereigns index covers all non-sovereign bonds, which are further divided into sub-sovereigns, collateralized debt, and corporates subindices. The corporates indices are classified into investment-grade non-financials and financials, including overall rating and maturity indices. Moreover, there is a breakdown into sectors based on the Dow Jones STOXX SM family, which is well-known from equity indices. The financial sector is divided into senior and subordinated debt.

Selection Criteria for iBoxx € Corporates

The selection criteria for the iBoxx € index family includes the bond type, the rating of an issuer, the time to maturity, and the outstanding amount of an issue. In the following, we focus on the criteria that are relevant for the iBoxx € Corporates universe, ignoring specific criteria for other asset classes, such as soft bullet features in the collateralized debt index.

- *Bond type*: The iBoxx € Corporates universe includes only euro-denominated bonds, ignoring the issuer's domicile. Eurobonds issued by US companies are included, while bonds denominated in US dollars from European companies are not. Included are straight bonds (fixed coupon bonds), rating-driven bonds (step-up and step-down feature), and dated or callable bonds (including fixed-to-floater characteristics) only in the financials universe. Hybrids from the non-financials world are excluded (as of August 2005).
- *Rating*: All iBoxx € Corporates bonds must be categorized as investment grade and must be rated by at least one of the following rating agencies: S&P (minimum rating BBB–), Moody's (minimum rating Baa3), or Fitch (minimum rating BBB–). The bond is put into a classification based on its lowest rating if it has been rated by at least two agencies. There is no differentiation of rating notches, for example, BBB+, BBB, and BBB– are all consolidated to BBB. In the financials universe, every bond is classified as a senior or a subordinated issue; the latter are divided into iBoxx € Tier 1, iBoxx € Upper Tier II, iBoxx € Lower Tier II, and iBoxx € Other Subordinated.

- *Time to maturity*: All index constituents must have a minimum remaining time to maturity of at least one year as of the respective rebalancing date.
- *Outstanding amount*: To ensure liquidity of the underlying index members, the minimum amount outstanding has to be €500 mn.

Index Calculation

The index provider consolidates all prices from the contributing banks, entering the index calculation in real time as consolidated bid quotes. Bonds that are not in the iBoxx € universe for the current month but will be included at the next rebalancing date enter the indices at their ask price. An index is calculated if at least one available bond matches all index criteria. The following day count conventions are taken into account when calculating the iBoxx € indices: Act/Act, Act/360, and 30/360, while the settlement convention for all iBoxx € indices is $t + 0$. Indices are calculated as basket indices based on real bonds, and all indices are published as price and total return indices.

13.1.3 Analyzing the RDAX

On May 9, 2005, Deutsche Börse AG launched a new corporate bond index, the RDAX, which is designed to track the performance of bonds issued by DAX companies. Subsequent to the outstanding success of the iTraxx index family, whose first series was introduced in June 2004, the RDAX is the next logical step, as it covers the high-grade cash bond market of the biggest listed German companies in place of the European focus of the iTraxx Europe FTD baskets. In contrast to iTraxx indices, the RDAX should not be considered as a perfect diversification tool for euro-denominated credit portfolios, but rather as a tool to track a specific region (Germany) and company-size market bracket. In addition, the RDAX provides a basis for many cross-asset-class instruments, as it is directly linked to its peer on the equity side, the DAX universe.[91]

One of the major features of the RDAX is that it resorts to index construction principles of the DAX index and the iBoxx € universe simultaneously. Only issuers that belong to the illustrious DAX 30 circle come into consideration. However, only bond issues that fulfill the iBoxx € criteria (euro denomination, investment-grade rating, time to maturity exceeding one year, benchmark size of at least €500 mn, etc.) qualify for the index. With the focus on corporate bonds of DAX companies plus the strict selection criteria, Deutsche Börse will ensure both the high quality of the index and liquidity of the index components.

In May 2005, the RDAX comprised 94 corporate bonds from 21 DAX companies, but it is subject to a monthly adjustment. A price and a total return index are available.

According to Deutsche Börse AG, the RDAX index serves issuers as a basis for structured financial products and certificates, offering interesting investment opportunities by combining corporate credits and equities in a cross-asset-class approach, even for retail investors. The term *structured financial products* simply means that there will be credit derivatives based on the index, which also reflects the rising importance of credit derivatives for real money accounts.

Selection Criteria

The RDAX is based on issued corporate bonds of the DAX 30 companies that qualify for the iBoxx € benchmark indices. These selection criteria are applied to ensure high liquidity and quality for each of the underlying bonds. In the following we provide some details with regard to the construction principles and their consequences for the indices.

The index calculation is done in two steps: First, one has to determine which objects, in this case corporate bonds, are included in the index basket. In a second step, the index calculation is done based on a predefined index formula. In this paragraph, we will focus on the first issue, the selection criteria of the RDAX, which comply with the internationally accepted EFFAS standards.

The RDAX solely includes corporate bonds from companies that belong to the DAX index at the time of the rebalancing, which is done on a monthly basis. In addition, eligible bonds from the iBoxx € benchmark indices particularly have to meet the following criteria:

- an investment-grade rating, that is, a rating of at least BBB– or better,
- a time to maturity of at least one year,
- an outstanding issuing volume of at least €500 mn.

As the DAX and iBoxx € composition changes over time, a regular adjustment of the basket components is necessary. This is done on a monthly basis at the end of each month. This procedure includes the application of the selection criteria (index composition), but other steps as well that will be discussed in the course of the index calculation. A new membership list of the RDAX is published by Deutsche Börse AG on the last business day of each month.

Index Calculation

Two indices are calculated by Deutsche Börse AG, namely a price index and a total return index. The index calculation is done according to the Laspeyres index concept, with individual prices weighted in accordance with the outstanding volume of the respective issue. The monthly rebalancing procedure as already noted in the context of selection criteria is also used to adjust the weighting scheme, which is held constant until the next rebalancing date.

The RDAX index calculation is done with so-called iBoxx consolidated prices, which are a result of a two-step consolidation process. In the first step, real-time bid and ask quotes from ten leading investment banks are put into a filter process, which includes a plausibility check (non-negativity, bid quote lower than ask quote, reasonable bid–ask spread, timeliness of prices). In the second step, the remaining quotes are aggregated by calculating a mean that is robust to outliers (a kind of compromise between an arithmetical average and median, depending on the number of available prices). This procedure is separately applied to bid and ask quotes. For details, please refer to the "Guide to the RDAX Index", which was published by Deutsche Börse.[92]

The calculation for the price and total return index is basically performed by using bid quotes. However, there is an important exception. If an eligible bond becomes a member of the index after not having been included in the previous month, it enters the index at its ask price. This rule enables investors to track the index, as it incorporates transaction costs incurred by the investor. As bond quotations are typically clean prices, accrued interest must be added for the total return index. The same applies for coupon payments that have already been paid since the last rebalance date.

Basically, each bond issue of the index is weighted in accordance with its amount outstanding, with a cap of 20 percent applying for each included issue. Deutsche Börse AG does not only provide a price and a total return index, but also some analytics, including average yield, average (modified) duration, average convexity, average coupon, average time to maturity, and volume numbers like nominal and market value.

The Index Composition (as of May 9, 2005)

In the following, we analyze the composition of the RDAX in comparison with the iBoxx € Corporates index. This is particularly done with respect to quality and industry allocation. Despite significant differences between these indices in the number of constituents and their structure, the RDAX offers sufficient diversification with regard to credit risk.

The basket of underlying corporate bonds comprises 94 issues from 21 issuers in May 2005. The remaining nine DAX names either have had no outstanding bond issues that meet the iBoxx criteria (e.g., SAP and Infineon) or they possessed a non-investment-grade rating (e.g., TUI and Fresenius). On the other hand, the iBoxx € Corporates universe is based on 736 cash bonds from 274 issuers at this time. Please note that the iBoxx € Corporates is not restricted to German companies. Even non-European companies that tap the market for euro-denominated bonds are covered by the index. In addition, comparing the volume of both indices draws the same picture with regard to the proportion. In May 2005, the RDAX covers an outstanding notional amount of €113.6 bn vs. €640.4 bn in the iBoxx € Corporates. The average time to maturity of the index amounted to 6.25 years, which was lower than the number for the iBoxx € Corporates index (7.49 years).

In May 2005, the biggest issuer in the RDAX universe is Deutsche Telekom with a market cap of almost 19 percent (see table 13.2). Also Deutsche Bank was playing in the double-digit league (with a market share of 12.64 percent), while Siemens was ranked only 11th, although the company is the biggest name in the DAX equity universe. It is obvious that single-name weightings in the RDAX do not correspond to those of the DAX. At first glance, this seems to be a severe mistake for equity–debt players. Although this is basically true from a single-name perspective, we view this structural difference as negligible as both indices offer a considerable degree of diversification for their respective market segment.

There are a few names that have only one liquid bond outstanding, including BASF, Continental, Deutsche Börse, Henkel, Linde, and Munich Re. As of May 2005, the market cap of these six issuers amounted to only 5.40 percent, less than a third of Deutsche Telekom. Therefore, there is a huge dispersion within the RDAX universe, also reflected in the fact that the issuer weightings range between 0.44 percent and 18.90 percent at introduction!

The RDAX apparently offers a good mix of high-quality issues (AA) and lower qualities within the high-grade universe (BBB). Hence, the average rating of the RDAX underlying issues is A. The iBoxx € Corporates, in contrast, has a mixture of AAAs with a share of 3 percent. In other respects, the quality structure of RDAX and iBoxx € Corporates is quite similar.

The industry allocation is characterized by a large share of financials (33.1 percent), but which is still below the level in the iBoxx € Corporates (45.7 percent). The German automobile sector takes a large fraction of the RDAX (20.2 percent) due to DCX, BMW, and VW versus 9.0 percent in the iBoxx € Corporates. Nevertheless, the RDAX offers good diversification from an industry perspective.

Tab. 13.2: Initial RDAX composition in May 2005

Company	Weights [%] RDAX	Weights [%] DAX	Stock price	5Y CDS level	ASW	Ratings Moody's/S&P/Fitch
Deutsche Telekom	19.7	8.7	14.64	34/37	41.54	Baa1/A–/A–
Deutsche Bank	10.3	7.5	61.85	16/17	40.30	Aa3/AA–/AA–
Volkswagen	9.5	1.6	33.18	73/78	66.11	A3/A–/A–
Allianz	8.5	7.2	92.50	21/25	39.95	Aa3/AA–/A+
RWE	7.8	4.8	46.86	19/22	25.39	A1/A+/A+
DaimlerChrysler	6.6	5.9	30.96	132/137	90.09	A3/BBB/BBB+
HypoVereinsbank	4.9	2.4	18.91	27/30	44.58	A3/A–/A–
E.ON	4.8	10.3	66.30	18/21	14.74	Aa3/AA–/AA–
Commerzbank	4.7	1.7	16.10	20/22	21.30	A2/A–/A–
Bayer	4.5	4.2	26.22	30/35	31.99	A3/A/ –
Siemens	4.1	10.3	56.27	21/24	12.99	Aa3/ – /AA–
BMW	3.3	2.4	33.31	26/31	28.42	A1/ – / –
Munich Re	2.9	3.6	84.39	24/28	106.48	A2/A–/A+
Deutsche Post	2.0	1.9	18.20	22/32	28.01	A1/A/A+
ThyssenKrupp	1.7	1.3	14.30	105/110	111.92	Baa2/BBB–/BBB+
Metro	1.5	1.3	40.23	50/55	46.63	Baa1/BBB/BBB
Henkel	0.9	0.9	71.00	26/31	42.14	A2/A–/ –
BASF	0.8	6.3	52.12	22/25	11.86	Aa3/AA–/AA–
Linde	0.6	0.9	53.13	50/55	23.72	A3/BBB+/ –
Continental	0.5	1.7	54.90	55/60	29.61	Baa1/BBB+/ –
Deutsche Börse	0.4	1.5	63.15	5/15	9.56	Aa1/AA/ –
SAP	–	5.6	126.50	18/28		
Schering	–	2.0	53.60	22/32		
Adidas-Salomon	–	1.3	128.50	34/41		
MAN	–	1.0	32.25	60/70		
Infineon	–	0.9	6.89	285/340		
Lufthansa	–	0.9	10.02	59/64		Baa2/BBB/ –
Altana	–	0.7	46.76	24/33		
TUI	–	0.7	19.33	179/194		– / – / –
Fresenius	–	0.5	64.03	220/320		Ba2/BB–/ –

Source: Deutsche Börse

Historical index analysis

As the RDAX covers a subset of the iBoxx € Corporates, its spread dynamics are closely related to the iBoxx as well as the iTraxx. Regarding the spread sensitivities at introduction of the RDAX, the beta of the RDAX relative to the iBoxx is 0.73, while the respective beta relative to the iTraxx is 1.03. This means that the RDAX features a reduced systematic risk compared to the iBoxx € Corporates (beta < 1), while it is roughly in line with the iTraxx Europe Benchmark index.

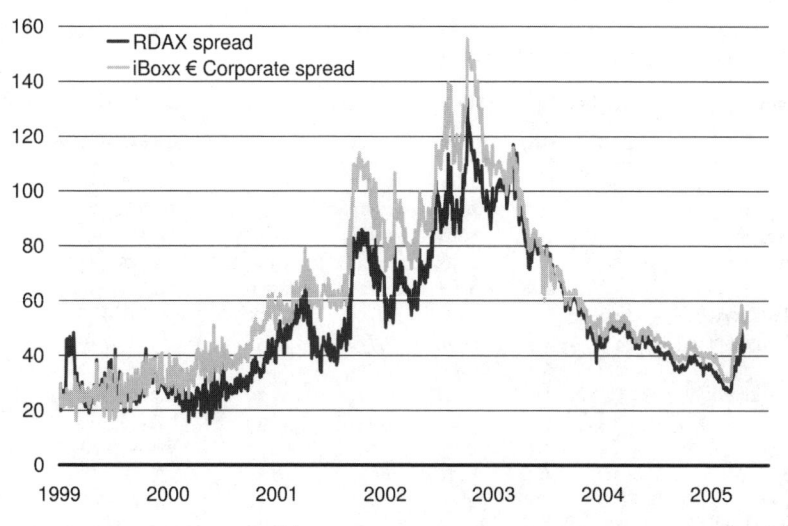

Fig. 13.1: Spread comparison of the RDAX versus the iBoxx € Corporates

The correlation of the RDAX index with its iBoxx counterpart is demonstrated in figure 13.1. Both indices move largely in tandem, as the RDAX is a subindex of the iBoxx € Corporates index (financials plus non-financials).

13.2 Sector Allocation in a Markowitz Framework

In a low spread environment, sector and quality allocation is of central importance for credit investors. Markowitz-based portfolio optimization provides some in-depth insights into the historical risk structure regarding credit and curve specific allocation. As a baseline, our analysis shows that credit investors should aim at co-optimizing credit and curve exposure in a portfolio context. This is also an important input factor for implementing hedging strategies, for example, as the sector-specific correlation matrix underpins an optimized sector or segment hedge.

Some methodological concerns on applying the classical Markowitz technique for credit risk should be noted. The analyzed risk–return figures (historical average and volatility for credit returns) are appropriate for normally distributed returns. Taking default events into consideration, credit returns feature non-normal distributions. However, as we focus on an investment-grade universe in this analysis, default risk is more related to downgrade action to junk status rather than to direct investment-grade defaults. This migration risk is well reflected in price and spread changes, which are by and large normally distributed. Moreover, spread moves of heterogeneous credit portfolios or indices are normally distributed rather than single-name spreads.

In table 13.3, we show the correlation matrix for the credit returns (as part of the total return) for the iBoxx € Non-Financials industries. We approximated the credit returns as

$$\text{spread} \times \text{elapsed time} + \text{change in spread} \times \text{sensitivity}$$

on the basis of a day-to-day time series, starting in April 2003 until March 2005. From a hedging perspective, the idea behind this is to use the sector-specific correlation matrix to optimize sector-related hedging strategies. In case sectors are highly correlated, a cross-sector hedge might be appropriate as the impact on the hedge efficiency is relatively low, while transaction costs can be reduced.

Tab. 13.3: Credit-return sector correlation matrix

	TEL	UTI	ATO	IGS	RET	HCA	MED	BAS	TEC	CHE
TEL	1.00	0.83	0.59	0.22	0.51	0.77	0.74	0.61	0.77	0.80
UTI		1.00	0.63	0.31	0.58	0.91	0.53	0.46	0.58	0.90
ATO			1.00	0.22	0.43	0.53	0.30	0.28	0.31	0.62
IGS				1.00	0.04	0.28	0.09	0.12	−0.09	0.30
RET					1.00	0.51	0.28	0.28	0.38	0.48
HCA						1.00	0.52	0.51	0.60	0.86
MED							1.00	0.23	0.91	0.52
BAS								1.00	0.28	0.41
TEC									1.00	0.56
CHE										1.00

The main result from the correlation matrix above is that the credit return correlation covers a wide range between +0.91 (between Utilities and Health Care) and −0.09 (Industrial Goods & Services and Technology). While the former is due to the fact that both sectors are dominated by (highly correlated) high-quality issues, the latter is more artificial, as (in our example) the technology sector comprises of just one issuer. In general, the column chart of the pairwise correlation shows a bimodal structure, with one maximum around +0.15 (low correlation) and one at +0.60 (medium correlation). This means that – in contrast to the similar analysis regarding rating categories – the segmentation by industry is more structured, which consequently offers investors better diversification opportunities.

Hence, the optimal portfolio allocation from a Markowitz analysis changes dramatically if we allow short selling in the optimization process, which is reflected in the efficient frontier for credit returns including and excluding short selling, which we show in figure 13.2. For a given level of risk (measured by the variance of credit returns), the expected credit return can be significantly higher if investors are able to build up short positions. Besides the correlation structure, this is due to the fact that sector-specific credit returns and volatilities cover a wide range. Thus, shorting a sector with a low return to finance one with a higher return results in a portfolio with a significantly improved risk–return profile.

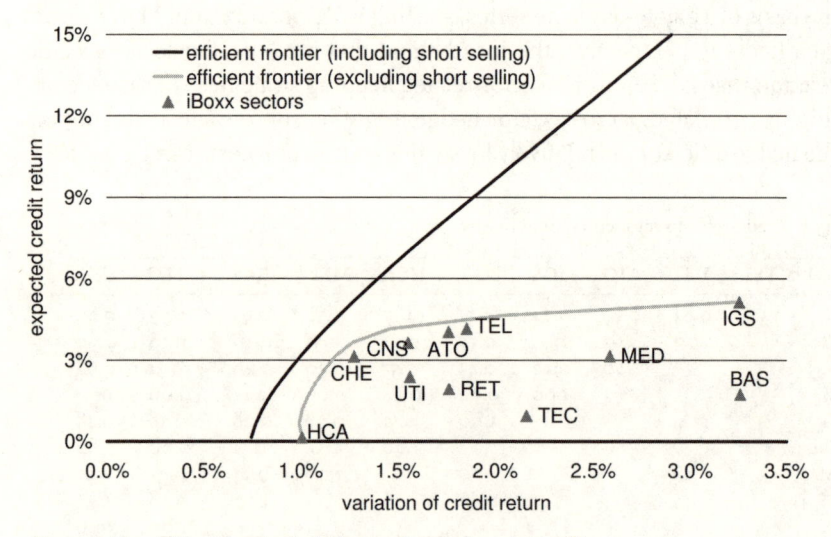

Fig. 13.2: The efficient frontier including and excluding short selling

Shorting credit risk can be viewed from two different angles. A benchmark investor will be short in a specific sector if he allocates fewer resources in this sector compared to the benchmark. However, for non-benchmark-oriented investors who want to boost their risk–return profile, shorting credit risk on a sector level can be implemented using the iTraxx Europe Benchmark index swap (shorting a whole sector using the repo market includes significant transaction costs).

In figure 13.3, we show the portfolio composition along the Markowitz frontier for the five largest iBoxx € Non-Financials sectors (Telecommunications, Utilities, Automobiles & Parts, Industrial Goods & Services, and Retail). This chart gives the percentage for each constituent in the respective efficient portfolio. As an example, a portfolio with a (historical) annual volatility of 2.3 percent has an exposure of 50.3 percent to Utilities, 43.4 percent to Retail, and 6.3 percent to Automobiles & Parts. At the low-risk end of this chart, the Retail sector is represented with a high share. With increasing portfolio risk, we subsequently add Utilities, Automobiles & Parts, and Telecommunications. On the high-risk side, Industrial Goods & Services dominates the portfolio, while exposure to all other sectors diminishes.

This analysis shows that an optimal low-risk portfolio has an overweight position in Retail and Utilities, while it underweights more volatile sectors such as Automobiles & Parts and Industrial Goods & Services. Note that the efficient branch in this portfolio with a smaller number of constituents starts around a credit return volatility of 3 percent.

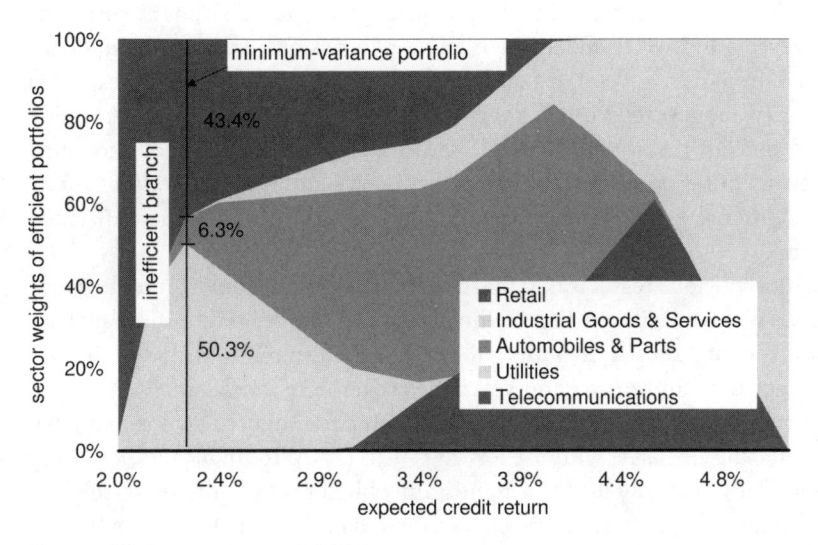

Fig. 13.3: Minimum-variance portfolios

13.3 Quality Allocation

For the quality optimization, we start with a portfolio segmentation with respect to rating categories. To keep the amount of data at manageable levels, we use full rating brackets only (AAA, AA, A, and BBB). Moreover, we distinguish between two performance categories: credit and curve return.

In the credit-return analysis, we analyzed the historical time series of credit returns (as a part of the total return) with respect to the rating category segmentation. The expected (historical average) credit returns vary between 0.1 percent p.a. for AAA credits and 1.6 percent p.a. for BBBs, while the corresponding volatilities cover a range from 1.1 to 1.8 percent. As these numbers reflect only the credit risk and not interest rate risk, they are related to the numbers for a portfolio of unfunded CDS contracts. As the effect from risk-free compounding is eliminated completely, the returns are well below average bond yields. It is interesting to note that the expected return and volatility of the risk-free funding part is much larger: 6.6 percent expected return and 3.0 percent volatility. All numbers are calculated for a five-year historical period.

To account for funding effect, we added the 3M-Euribor to each credit return. In general, we assumed that all credits in the underlying portfolio are swapped against the 3M rate – eliminating the intrinsic interest rate risk on the corporate bonds level – and we re-added the interest rate risk as a separate component via a risk-free (e.g., sovereign bonds) exposure. In this framework, expected (historical average) credit returns vary between 4.6 percent p.a. for AAA credits and 6.2 percent p.a. for BBBs, while the corresponding volatilities remained between 1.1 to 1.8 percent. Taking interest rate risk into consideration results in an additional 4.6 percent in terms of expected returns for the BBB-rated spectrum.

The most obvious result is that the difference in the efficient frontier between portfolios with and without short selling is smaller for the credit-return analysis than for the total return, including the funding effect. This is due to the fact that expected credit returns and volatilities cover only a very small range and are strongly correlated (see table 13.4 with correlation figures for the analysis). Thus, shorting the asset with the lowest return (AAA) to finance a more risky position (BBB) does not lead to a significantly higher return, driven by the limited (absolute) diversification effect. For the total return analysis the situation is different, as expected return and volatility of the additional interest rate part differ from the credit return and is, in addition, negatively correlated. Thus, financing a (interest rate) risky position by shorting a swapped AAA asset adds value to the portfolio. In any case, this is exactly what leveraged interest rate exposure (i.e., through swaps) means.

Moreover, the total return profile features a pronounced inefficient branch, while for the credit-return analysis, this inefficient part of the portfolio characteristic is rather small. This is especially interesting if we analyze the composition of the portfolio along the Markowitz frontier. As indicated in figure 13.4, the percentage of each segment for a portfolio with a specific expected return is provided. As an example, an unfunded portfolio with an expected credit return of 0.5 percent would comprise 16.8 percent AAAs, 67.6 percent AAs, 8.7 per-

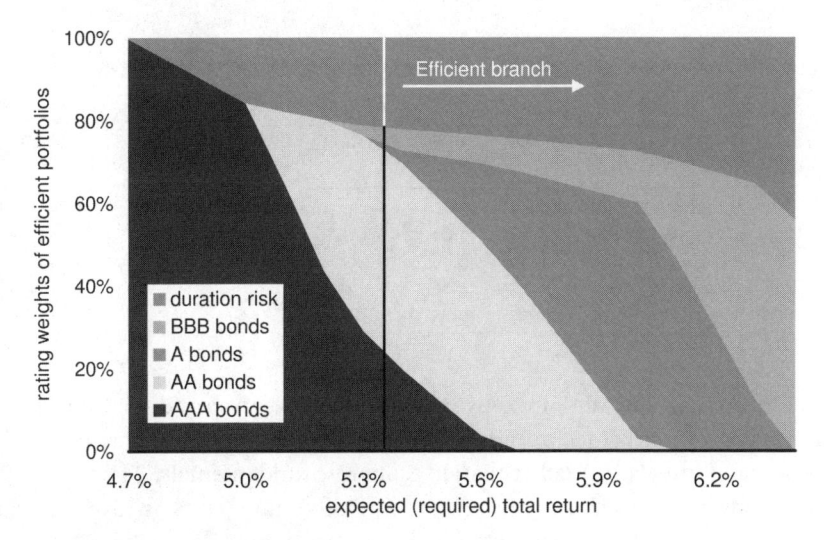

```
                                    Efficient branch
100% ┤
     │
 80% ┤
     │
 60% ┤
     │
 40% ┤  ■ duration risk
     │  ■ BBB bonds
     │  ■ A bonds
 20% ┤    AA bonds
     │  ■ AAA bonds
  0% ┤
     └────┬──────┬──────┬──────┬──────┬──────┬──
        4.7%   5.0%   5.3%   5.6%   5.9%   6.2%
              expected (required) total return
```

Fig. 13.4: Efficient quality allocation

cent As, and 6.9 percent BBBs. From figure 13.4, we can additionally conclude that this portfolio has a historic volatility of about 1.1 percent.

In figure 13.4, the label "efficient branch" indicates the part of the portfolio frontier that is considered to be efficient in Markowitz terms. All portfolios left of this line show a decreasing return for increasing risk, which is obviously inefficient. Consequently, investors prefer to allocate to the right of this line.

The striking result is that, from a portfolio selection point of view, a large exposure to AAA (and also AA) credits without lower rating qualities is inefficient. Moreover, the higher the expected return – and consequently the higher the risk – the larger the exposure to duration risk. This reflects the fact that a non-hedged sovereign portfolio is riskier than a high-grade corporate bond portfolio in which the interest rate risk is swapped away, at least in terms of spread risk.

In table 13.4, we highlight the correlation matrix for the total return analysis (credit returns plus 3M-Euribor to add the funding effect) for the segmentation by rating categories. As one would intuitively assume, the more distant the rating classes, the lower the correlation. In addition, the correlation for higher rating qualities is higher (AAA versus AA: 0.90) than for lower ones (A versus BBB: 0.74). The correlation between credit returns and interest rate (risk-free duration) risk is negative. This reflects the fact that, in contrast to the current situation, on a long-term average basis (recall that we analyzed a five-year period) increasing economic growth prospects trigger rising interest rates

Tab. 13.4: Correlation matrix of credit returns (including funding effect via 3M-Libor) for rating categories and a credit-risk-free asset

	AAA	AA	A	BBB	Duration
AAA	1.00	0.90	0.85	0.60	−0.52
AA	0.90	1.00	0.89	0.62	−0.56
A	0.85	0.89	1.00	0.74	−0.56
BBB	0.60	0.62	0.74	1.00	−0.45
Duration risk	−0.52	−0.56	−0.56	−0.45	1.00

but tightening credit spreads. A positive correlation between spreads and yields is more related to market technicals (for example, a liquidity overhang and a supply–demand imbalance) rather than to economic fundamentals. Moreover, a low-yield environment can trigger allocation shifts into credits as investors want to enhance their returns by increasing credit exposure.

13.4 Tools to Derive the Optimal Allocation

Optimization of the quality and sector allocation using a Markowitz approach is a rather time-intensive process. Moreover, the optimal allocation is not constant over time. Adjusting the portfolio for all minor changes is not practical because of transaction costs (primarily bid–ask spreads). In this section, we discuss tools which can be used to identify value on a sector or quality level. This is especially important in times of high volatility, which makes a continuous adjustment of the credit allocation necessary, while continuously changing the portfolio on a single-name basis is too costly.

For the fund manager, another problem of optimizing credit portfolios arises, namely the constant inflow of fresh money which has to be invested. A manager will not adjust the entire portfolio to invest fresh money, but rather allocate it to single names within attractive sectors and qualities. Therefore, active credit portfolio management means actively searching for investment opportunities and identifying attractive valuation levels within the target universe. The development of sector baskets in the iTraxx spectrum can be understood as a very important step towards an active industry allocation. They allow the portfolio manager to implement sector adjustments efficiently and at low transaction costs.

13.4.1 Alpha and Beta

In figure 13.5, we plot sector betas versus sector alphas. We obtain both parameters by a simple regression of the sector spread versus the market spread (overall index). Alpha simply reflects the intercept and beta the slope of the regression line, as indicated in the following equation (with ϵ_{sector} hopefully being white noise):

$$s_{sector} = \alpha_{sector} + \beta_{sector} \cdot s_{market} + \epsilon_{sector} \qquad (13.1)$$

The idea behind this is to separate the systematic and the unsystematic component of the sector spread. While beta measures the sensitivity of a specific sector with regard to the whole market, alpha refers to the remaining spread level of a sector that cannot be explained by systematic risk. The higher the beta, the higher the market dependency of a sector. Empirically, it can be measured as the intercept of a regression line, which describes the relationship between a specific industry spread (y-axis) and the market spread (x-axis). The slope can be regarded as the respective beta measure. In figure 13.5, we perform this analysis for all iBoxx € Non-Financials sectors. The iBoxx € sectors Automobiles & Parts, Oil & Gas, and Travel & Leisure are primarily driven by systematic risk (high-beta, low-alpha sectors), while Technology, Construction & Materials, and Basic Resources are driven by alpha (high-alpha, low-beta sectors). Chemicals and Industrials Goods & Services show a beta near one and an alpha close to zero. This means that both sectors behave rather in line with the overall market, that is to say, the iBoxx € Non-Financials index.

How can we use this analysis in practice? Let us assume an investor has a bearish stance towards credits as a whole. He will then prefer sectors which have a low beta (and hence are affected by an overall spread widening to a lesser extent) and a high alpha. In our analysis, the Technology sector looks quite attractive from this point of view.

13.4.2 The Shortcomings of a Beta Analysis

Betas calculated on historical data face the problem that the underlying assumption is that the world will remain unchanged, that is, that historical betas will also be realized over the investment horizon. In the following, we show how betas can change over time, especially in case of an external shock. For this reason, we analyze the iBoxx € universe with respect to betas before and after the exclusion of Ford and General Motors from the index universe in June 2005 due to multiple downgrades to junk status.

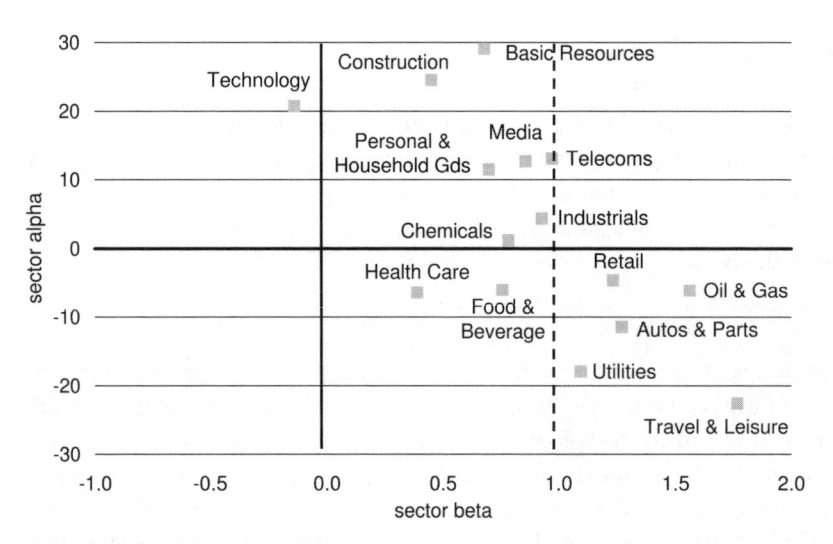

Fig. 13.5: Alphas and betas

The multiple downgrade action of Ford and General Motors to junk status caused a historical structural break for the iBoxx € universe. As the high-beta issues of F and GM left the iBoxx € in June 2005, the risk characteristics of the iBoxx € Non-Financials index changed considerably. The exclusions triggered significant structural differences in terms of beta factors (based on daily spread changes between January and June 2005). The beta factor for the Automobiles & Parts industry declined from 4.42 to 1.46. Consequently, the beta factors for the rest of the pack were subject to an average increase of 144 percent, which is solely attributable to the significant decrease in overall market risk. The exclusion of F and GM from the iBoxx € universe reduced heterogeneity. Industry betas within the iBoxx € Non-Financials range from 0.49 (Health Care) to 1.46 (Automobiles & Parts) compared to the era when F and GM were included, with sector betas ranging from 0.19 to 4.42.

Beta as a measure of systematic spread risk is subject to many decisions, for example, with regard to the underlying timeframe and the applied estimation procedure. Typically, an OLS (ordinary least squares) approach based on daily spread changes is used to estimate the corresponding beta factor. An alternative approach would be to use spread levels. Although this approach is not the market standard, it might be appropriate from a hedging perspective as the medium- to long-term relationship rather than daily changes is in the limelight of the estimation procedure (e.g., consider a portfolio manager who wants to hedge against systematic spread movements).

Our empirical results show discrepancies that are quite considerable for many iBoxx € industries. We also found evidence for a systematical bias, generally leading to higher betas (based on spread levels) for riskier industries and lower betas for less riskier sectors.

Where do these differences come from? The following list of possible explanations is not exhaustive:

- Serial correlation (auto correlation) of the time-series spread data
- A medium-term trend in the respective sector, which partially means a decoupling from market spread levels (relative value considerations)
- A spurious correlation between the market spread level and the spread level of the respective industry; that is, there is a third variable in the background influencing both the market spread and the average industry spread.

Although we do not want to delve into theoretical issues, we would like to stress a major practical aspect. A portfolio manager should consider which beta measure to use. From a theoretical point of view, a beta coefficient which refers to daily or other periodical changes is desirable. In a hedging context, however, the relationship among spread levels might be more appropriate when estimating betas. The favorable process, in any case, is to calculate alternative numbers and to assess the sensitivity towards market spread movements not solely on one measure.

The beta factor is a measure of systematic spread risk, which is a primary factor that should be taken into account from a portfolio perspective, as the unsystematic risk can be largely diversified. Therefore, it appears self-evident to relate this risk measure to the respective return (the current spread level). Without taking correlation into consideration, a rule of thumb would suggest to focus on sectors which provide higher expected returns and carry lower systematic risk.

13.4.3 Aggregated Z-Scores

Single-name Z-scores measure the difference between the current spread and the average spread (we use 60 days for our analysis) and in units of standard deviations, making different bonds with different spread levels comparable. Normally, this number is between +2 (significantly cheap) and −2 (significantly expensive). The Z-score provides an answer to the question of how an investor is being compensated in terms of potential spread tightening for taking spread risk. This concept can be easily transferred to a sector or quality level. One alternative is to calculate Z-scores using aggregated spread data for specific sectors, rating classes, or maturity brackets. The other alternative is to compare the positive and negative Z-scores of the constituents of a specific subindex (by sector, by rating, or by maturity). A shortcoming of the concept of Z-scores is that it does not prove to be a good indicator for the dearness or cheapness of a corporate bond during periods of more pronounced spread trends as the concept is based on a mean-reverting process.

In figure 13.6, we analyze the maturity brackets for the iBoxx € Non-Financials in April 2005. The light gray part shows the cheap spectrum, that is, the percentage of subindex constituents that carry a positive Z-score, and the dark gray part reflects the percentage of negative Z-scores. In this analysis, longer-dated issues (seven years and above) look more attractive compared to shorter-dated issues.

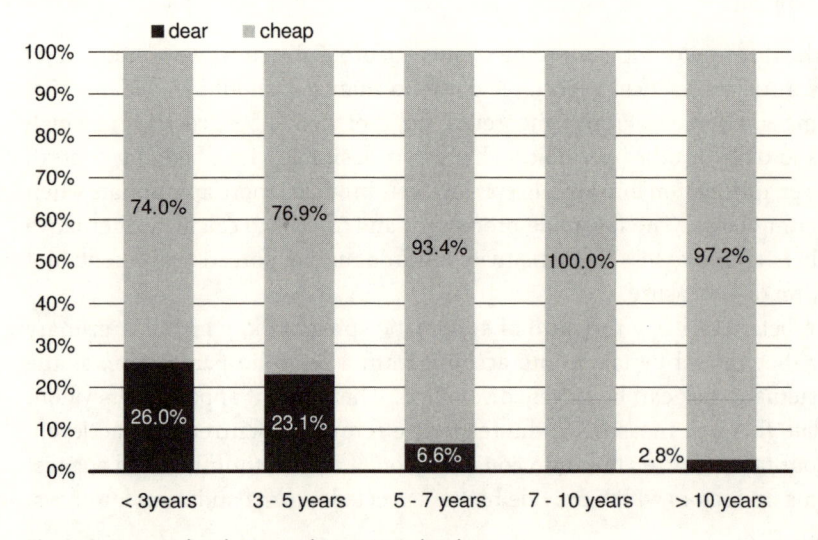

Fig. 13.6: Z-score distribution within maturity brackets

This analysis can be also implemented on a sector and quality level and provides a useful tool in the allocation process.

13.4.4 Equity Volatility as a Tool in the Allocation Process

While we discussed structural models in detail in section 8.2, Merton's idea can also be helpful in identifying value on a sector level. In the following, we show how implied equity volatilities can be used to derive a relative value measure in combination with average industry spreads.

We follow the simple idea of interpreting equity volatility as a risk factor for credits because the existence of spillover effects from equity to credit markets is a basic rationale of Merton-type models. High equity volatility within an industry should typically be accompanied by higher spread levels as a compensation for higher systematic risk. In figure 13.7, we plot the average spread of the iBoxx € Non-Financials index in April 2005 versus historical equity volatility in the Euro STOXX equity universe, based on the ICB classification scheme (which applies to both universes).

The motivation is to identify sectors that carry low systematic risk (and consequently, have a low implied equity volatility) but offer an attractive return (provide a high spread income). An industry located at the top left of the chart offers value from this particular point of view.

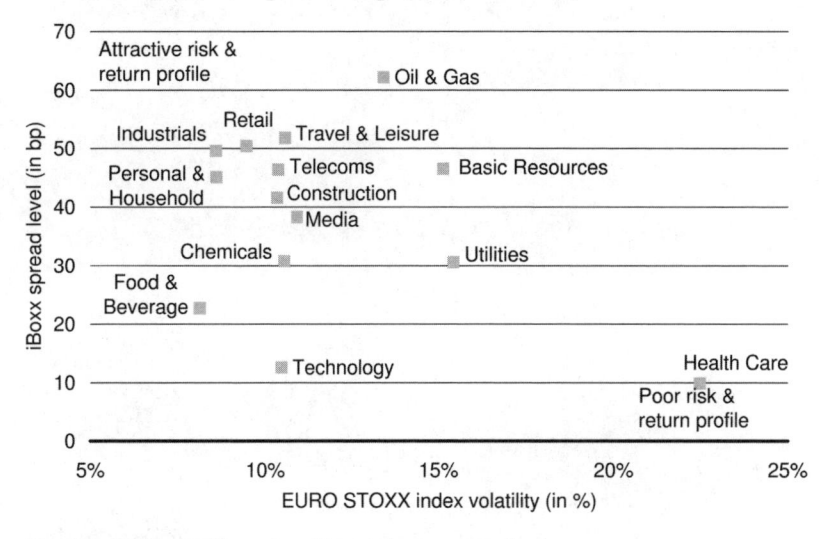

Fig. 13.7: Equity volatility and credit spreads on a sector level

14
Performance Measures

The investment objective of a fund is to achieve excess returns versus the target index (the benchmark). In chapter 15, we discuss the return attribution analysis of credit portfolios, with excess return being the crucial indicator reflecting the relative performance of a portfolio versus the benchmark. However, excess return is not the appropriate measure to determine the quality of a fund manager. To properly rank the performance of a fund versus the target index, we need more information. Excess return can be generated by taking excessive additional risk, and hence the outperformance of a portfolio might be in contrast to the optimization process. Thus, a portfolio that outperformed the index is not necessarily the optimal portfolio from a risk–return perspective. For example, a portfolio manager who is allowed to buy investment-grade and high-yield bonds can generate more credit return by shifting the allocation towards more risky and higher yielding junk bonds. In a bullish market environment, this strategy will lead to an outperformance compared to a more balanced portfolio, but will significantly underperform the index target if spreads start to widen. Against this backdrop, return as the only indicator for relative performance is not sufficient to measure the quality of a portfolio manager. *Modern portfolio theory*[93] is consequently also incorporating risk measures.

Most performance measures are based on historical data with practical implementation using ex post results, while theoretical discussions focus on ex ante values. However, implicitly or explicitly, it is assumed that historical results have at least some predictive capability. For basic applications, it suffices for future values of a measure to be related monotonically to past values: portfolio A had a higher historic measure than portfolio B, and it is assumed that it will have a higher future measure. In a Markowitz' mean-variance paradigm, we assume that the mean and standard deviation of the distribution of one-period return are sufficient statistics for evaluating the prospects of a portfolio. Comparisons are based on the first two moments of a distribution and do not take into account possible differences among portfolios in other moments of the distributions. In addition, we ignore different levels of investor utility.

In the following, we briefly discuss popular performance measures that are well known from portfolio theory. Our objective is not to provide a detailed overview of all measures discussed in the portfolio management community, as there is enough literature that outlines this topic in detail. We will rather focus on the specifics of a credit portfolio when using performance measures that were initially created to examine equity portfolios. Although corporate bonds are exposed primarily to interest rate and credit risk, we recommend to split duration from credit risk management. A credit portfolio manager is basically paid for managing credit risk properly, and therefore we discuss how to use traditional performance measures when valuing the credit-risk-specific performance isolated from additional risk factors.

14.1 Tracking Error

The *tracking error* is quantified as the annualized standard deviation of the differences in returns between the portfolio and the target index (standard deviation of the excess return):

$$\text{TE} = \sigma \left(r_{\text{Portfolio}} - r_{\text{Benchmark}} \right) \tag{14.1}$$

It quantifies how closely a manager's return pattern follows that of a benchmark index. The tracking error is constructed for index funds that replicate a specific target index. Initially, tracking error is defined for total return indices, while we can simply apply the concept to credit risk by using excess credit returns instead of total return data. Therefore, tracking error is an important performance measure for instruments that replicate a specific credit index, for example, performance notes based on the iTraxx performance, or exchange traded funds (ETFs) that are linked to the iBoxx universe (e.g., the iShares iBoxx EUR ETF).

The tracking error indicates how closely a fund is tracking the index. The closer the weightings of the portfolio constituents are to the index weightings, the smaller is the tracking error. Against this background, cash holdings and outflows or inflows in corporate bond funds are increasing the tracking error. Using the iBoxx as a target index (which is calculated on bid prices), index in- and exclusions have to be taken into account, while transaction costs (broker commission and bid–ask spreads) will trigger additional tracking costs, which, in general, increase the tracking error.

Especially for credit portfolios, reaching a tracking error of zero is almost a mission impossible. Fund expenditures through transaction fees, missing the full-investment restriction (there will be naturally a cash balance), the OTC character of corporate bonds and derivatives (the credit portfolio manager will not be able to execute a trade at the same price the index is calculated), rounding effects (the fund will be definitely smaller than the target index) and the continuously rebalancing of the target index (for example, iBoxx indices experience a monthly adjustment).

Nevertheless, the tracking error is a useful performance measure, not only from the viewpoint of a client, but also for the portfolio manager, as it shows the additional risk taken by the fund in terms of achieving excess return. Following El-Hassan and Kofman[94] (2003), the "tracking error can either be the investment goal, or an investment constraint. This leads to the following two interpretations of tracking error: A passive strategy that seeks to reproduce as closely as possible an index or benchmark portfolio by minimizing the tracking error of the replicating portfolio, or an active strategy that seeks to outperform an index or benchmark portfolio, while staying within certain risk boundaries defined by the benchmark."

14.2 Sharpe Ratio and Treynor Ratio

The *Sharpe ratio* (SR) measures the portfolio's excess return relative to the total variation of the portfolio and is named after Nobel Laureate William Sharpe[95–97]:

$$SR = \frac{r_{\text{Portfolio}} - r_{\text{risk-free}}}{\sigma_{\text{Portfolio}}} \tag{14.2}$$

As mentioned above, performance measures are based on historical data, while a practitioner would prefer an ex ante measure. The Sharpe ratio can be defined both ex ante and ex post and is based on Markowitz's mean variance framework and the CAPM model, as the slope of the capital market line equals the ex ante Sharpe ratio.

The Sharpe ratio measures the expected return per unit of risk for a zero investment strategy, reflecting how much risk has to be taken for generating a certain return.

The Sharpe ratio attempts to summarize an unbiased prediction of performance with a single number, which requires a substantial set of assumptions for justification. Such assumptions are likely to hold at best approximately in practice, and the use of unadjusted historic (ex post) Sharpe ratios as surrogates for unbiased predictions of ex ante ratios is subject to serious question. However, we appreciate it as a measure that takes into account both risk and expected return over any alternative that focuses only on the latter.

For certain investment decisions, the ex ante Sharpe ratio can provide important inputs. When choosing one from among a set of funds to benefit from the performance of a particular market sector, it makes sense to favor the one with the highest predicted Sharpe ratio, as long as the correlation of funds available with other relevant asset classes is reasonably similar. This is the major shortfall of the Sharpe ratio, as it does not take correlation into account. If an investment decision is part of a broader allocation process, correlation between different assets within the overall portfolio is a crucial part of the optimization process. With this respect, correlation measures have to be used to supplement comparisons among different investment opportunities based on Sharpe ratios.

When analyzing investment strategies, however, it makes sense to allocate funds with respect to the preferred additional risk levels of the investment, which can be predicted by Sharpe ratios for the excess returns. Sharpe ratios might provide useful guidance as the ratio determines the expected additional return per unit of additional risk, providing a convenient summary of two important aspects of any strategy involving the difference between the return of a fund and that of the target index.

The concept of measuring the costs for excess return by the excess risk that has to be carried, tries to solve a principle problem of credit portfolio management. When isolating the credit-specific performance of a portfolio (by splitting credit risk and interest rate risk management), generating additional spread income is the most obvious strategy to outperform the benchmark. In a buy-and-hold approach, a portfolio manager earns spread carry until maturity and is not exposed to marked-to-market risk; almost independent from the spread development until maturity as long as no default occurs. This is the major reason for the domination of simple yield enhancement strategies by using credits as additional performance generators or by moving down the quality curve in the search for higher-yielding assets. However, these strategies often do not consider the additional risk that has to be taken when reducing the quality of the underlying portfolio. When analyzing a credit portfolio on a marked-to-market basis, the Sharpe ratio can provide interesting insights into the risk and return profile of the investment strategy.

Replacing the standard deviation (total risk) in the equation for the Sharpe ratio with a systematic risk component, the portfolio beta, results in the *Treynor ratio* (TR):

$$TR = \frac{r_{Portfolio} - r_{risk-free}}{\beta_{Portfolio}} \qquad (14.3)$$

Like the Sharpe ratio, the Treynor ratio is a measurement of the returns earned in excess of those that could have been earned on a risk-free investment.

However, the Treynor ratio also does not quantify the value added, if any, of active portfolio management, since it is only a ranking criterion. A ranking of portfolios based on the Treynor ratio is only useful if the considered portfolios are subportfolios of a broader, fully diversified portfolio. If this is not the case, portfolios with identical systematic risk but different total risk will be rated the same.

Despite the fact that the Treynor ratio suffers from the same shortfalls as the Sharpe ratio, using systematic instead of total risk is only a practicable approach in credit portfolio management when the underlying universe is homogeneous. Is the target universe a heterogeneous one, then idiosyncratic risk factors, which are not covered by the Treynor ratio, have to be the focus of portfolio optimization. Using ex post data might be misleading when dividing into beta and alpha risk as the latter carries a tail-event character. This is reflected in the fact that spread histories show that there are jumps in case of an issuer-specific event (for example an LBO bid). In normal times without issuer-specific events, credits behave lemming-like, without significant deviations between the spread trends of single bonds or instruments.

14.3 Information Ratio

As is the case with the Sharpe and the Treynor ratios, the *information ratio* tries to summarize the mean-variance properties of a portfolio in one single number. The information ratio is based on historical data and is defined as the excess return of a portfolio versus the target index divided by the standard deviation of the excess return (tracking error). It measures the average excess return in units of volatility of excess returns:

$$\text{IR} = \frac{r_\text{Portfolio} - r_\text{Benchmark}}{\sigma(r_\text{Portfolio} - r_\text{Benchmark})} \qquad (14.4)$$

The information ratio is an ideal figure to value alpha risk, which is also a major task of constructing credit portfolios. Following Goodwin[87], the most straightforward interpretation of the information ratio is one in which the portfolio manager is confined to the universe of the benchmark index and must maintain the same level of systematic risk as the target index. This means that the systematic risk (beta) equals one. The manager can implement alpha bets by under- or overweighting individual bonds relative to the benchmark index weight. The information ratio is therefore also known as the *alpha-omega ratio*.

A common approach in practice is to fix the estimated beta at 1 and to focus on alpha, because the information ratio depends on both alpha and beta. If the primary task of a credit portfolio manager is actively searching for alpha, the impact from the beta component on the information ratio does influence the valuation of the manager.

Empirical evidence on the information ratio regarding a manger's ability to generate excess return shows that the information ratio is a powerful tool for assessing the quality of an actively managed portfolio, while a rule of thumb suggests never to rely exclusively on any single measure.

14.4 Summary

All the presented performance measures are an attempt to express the quality of a managed portfolio in one single number. The basic assumption of a mean-variance framework is especially problematic regarding credit portfolios. However, all ratios mentioned above are easy to implement and provide additional insight for the investment as well as for the monitoring process. As every ratio has a specific shortfall, the basic rule is to use all ratios available, while avoiding to take only one ratio into consideration.

Although interest rate risk has a significant impact on the total return of a cash portfolio, we define credit portfolio management as managing credit risk only, hedging for excess duration risk versus the benchmark. Keeping the portfolio duration neutral versus the target index will generate additional costs, and credit portfolio management in practice also includes managing interest rate risk, at least to a certain extent. However, all the ratios discussed previously can be applied to credit risk and credit return only, simply by implementing a performance attribution analysis, isolating the credit-specific return from other risk factors.

Last but not least, the construction principle within the portfolio management process also determines the use of performance measures. In the case of a merged top-down/bottom-up approach, where taking beta risk from a top-down view is merged with managing alpha risk from a bottom-up view, the information ratio can provide interesting information for the performance of the pick selection process. The Sharpe ratio is constructed to evaluate the total risk, while the Treynor ratio quantifies excess returns using the systematic risk component (beta). Although these measures can be applied for evaluating active portfolio management, the tracking error matches the requirements of investors in passively managed funds and index-linked instruments.

15
Performance Analysis

A detailed performance analysis plays an important role in portfolio management, as monitoring return generation allows a deep insight into the structure and sensitivities of the portfolio. The following analysis is split into two parts. First, we introduce the total return concept and show how to aggregate total returns over longer time periods. In the second part, we show how total returns can be split into performance components. The latter can be a complicated task, since the value of a credit-risky security is a complex function involving several quantities: the risk-free spot rate curve, the credit spread curve, and the time to maturity. Nevertheless, by using some approximations a return attribution analysis can be implemented without involving complicated numerical routines.

15.1 Return Accumulation

The total return $\text{TR}(t_{i-1}, t_i)$ of a fixed income security over a period from t_{i-1} to t_i is calculated as the total P&L, denoted by $\Delta V(t_{i-1}, t_i)$, divided by the value V_{i-1} of the security at time t_{i-1}:

$$\text{TR}(t_{i-1}, t_i) = \frac{\Delta V(t_{i-1}, t_i)}{V(t_{i-1})} \tag{15.1}$$

Calculating the total P&L refers to dirty prices, including accrued interest. In the following, we write $V^d(t)$ for the dirty and $V^c(t)$ for the corresponding clean price observed at time t. Note that this definition of total return does not depend on whether a risky or a risk-free fixed income security is considered. The total P&L $\Delta V(t_{i-1}, t_i)$ in the period from t_{i-1} to t_i is calculated as the change in dirty value plus the sum of all cash flows which are due during this period:

$$\Delta V(t_{i-1}, t_i) = V^d(t_i) - V^d(t_{i-1}) + \sum_{t \in]t_{i-1}, t_i]} \text{CF}^I_t + \text{CF}^P_t \tag{15.2}$$

Here, CF^I_t and CF^P_t are the interest and principal payments which are due at time t. We assume that the period between t_{i-1} and t_i is small (i.e., a few days).

Active Credit Portfolio Management. J. Felsenheimer, P. Gisdakis, and M. Zaiser
Copyright © 2006 WILEY-VCH Verlag GmbH & Co. KGaA, Weinheim
ISBN: 3-527-50198-3

We can therefore ignore compounding effects on cash flows within this period. Recall that the dirty value V^d of a security can be derived by discounting its future cash flows at an appropriate discount rate. For credit-risky instruments, the discount rate has to incorporate the credit spread.

To aggregate total returns over a longer time horizon (e.g., to derive a YTD total return from daily returns), single-period returns have to be linked multiplicatively. The total return between t_0 and t_n is depicted by:

$$\text{TR}(t_0, t_n) = \left[\prod_{i=1}^{n} (1 + \text{TR}(t_{i-1}, t_i)) \right] - 1 \quad (15.3)$$

15.2 Return Attribution Analysis

The total return $\text{TR}(t_{i-1}, t_i)$ can, in principle, be split into the following two components: a *market value component*, which results from changes in market parameters (i.e., the spot rate curve and the credit spread curve) and the *time value component*, which accounts for changes in the bond's time value.

The first component is easy to understand. Obviously, the price of a bond changes with changes in the level of the risk-free discount curve and with changes in the credit spread curve. The time value component, on the other hand, encompasses several effects: a compounding effect, a pull-to-par effect, and a roll-down effect stemming from the yield curve as well as from the term structure of credit spreads. A simple method to arrive at a reasonable return attribution analysis is to disaggregate the total return into the following three components:

- *Curve return*: the performance derived from the movements of the underlying risk-free yield curve.
- *Credit return*: the performance from credit spread changes.
- *Time value component*: the performance resulting from accrued income, including the pull-to-par-effect.

Although the approximation of the time value effect as accrued interest plus pull-to-par is quite crude, it gives reasonable results and is easy to calculate. Besides contractual data (such as the coupon rate, the compounding period, the maturity date) the only thing we need is the dirty price of the bond, which can be obtained from the market. Complicated numerical procedures (i.e., discounting) are not necessary.

The following analysis is divided into two steps. In the first step, we aim at isolating the time value component in the total P&L, while in the second step, we disaggregate the remaining market value component into the curve and the credit return. We start by dividing the dirty value $V^d(t)$ of the security at time t into its clean value $V^c(t)$ and the respective accrued interest $AcI(t)$:

$$V^d(t) = V^c(t) + AcI(t) \qquad (15.4)$$

Inserting this definition into equation 15.2, one can divide the total P&L $\Delta V(t_{i-1}, t_i)$ into a clean P&L and realized interest income:

$$\Delta V(t_{i-1}, t_i)$$
$$= [V^c(t_i) + AcI(t_i)] - [V^c(t_{i-1}) + AcI(t_{i-1})] + \sum_{t \in]t_{i-1}, t_i]} CF_t^I + CF_t^P$$
$$= \underbrace{V^c(t_i) - V^c(t_{i-1}) + \sum_{t \in]t_{i-1}, t_i]} CF_t^P}_{\text{clean P\&L}} + \underbrace{AcI(t_i) - AcI(t_{i-1}) + \sum_{t \in]t_{i-1}, t_i]} CF_t^I}_{\text{interest income}}$$

$$(15.5)$$

The clean P&L is the change in the clean value of the bond plus the sum of all principal cash flows that are due in the time period, while interest income is the change in the accrued interest plus the sum of all interest cash flows. The interest income is the realized part of the coupon an investor earns by holding the security from t_{i-1} to t_i.

In this way, we separate the compounding effect in terms of accrued interest. The clean P&L can be defined as the residual quantity after subtracting the interest income from the total P&L. The clean P&L incorporates changes in the market value of the bond and other time value components such as the pull-to-par and curve roll-down effects. For bonds which trade far from par, the pull-to-par effect can be substantial. To eliminate it from the clean P&L we can use the simplifying assumption that the difference to par will vanish linearly until the maturity of the bond τ_m:

$$\text{PtP} \approx \frac{100 - V_t^c}{\tau_m} \cdot (t_i - t_{i-1}) \qquad (15.6)$$

Note that the pull-to-par effect will reduce the bond value in case it trades above par and it will increase the value if it is below par. In our simplified approach, we approximate the time value component $\Delta \text{TV}(t_{i-1}, t_i)$ of the total return as the sum of the interest income and the pull-to-par effect:

$$\Delta \text{TV}(t_{i-1}, t_i) \approx AcI(t_i) - AcI(t_i) + \sum_{t \in]t_{i-1}, t_i]} \text{CF}_t^I$$
$$+ \frac{100 - V_t^c}{\tau_m} \cdot (t_i - t_{i-1}) \quad (15.7)$$

On the other hand, the corresponding market value component $\Delta \text{MV}(t_{i-1}, t_i)$ is given by the clean P&L minus the pull-to-par effect:

$$\Delta \text{MV}(t_{i-1}, t_i) \approx V^c(t_i) - V^c(t_{i-1}) + \sum_{t \in]t_{i-1}, t_i]} \text{CF}_t^P$$
$$- \frac{100 - V_t^c}{\tau_m} \cdot (t_i - t_{i-1}) \quad (15.8)$$

What remains is to divide the market value component into the curve and the credit return. To derive a reasonable separation without involving complicated equations, we approximate the curve return from the change in the risk-free yield curve multiplied by the modified duration. The credit return is calculated as the difference between the market value component $\Delta \text{MV}(t_{i-1}, t_i)$ and the curve return. The risk-free yield for a bond with a remaining time to maturity τ valid at time t is given as $y_t(\tau)$. Consequently, the curve return for a risky bond is approximated by:

$$\text{curve return} \approx -\text{ModDur} \times (y_{t_i}(\tau_m) - y_{t_{i-1}}(\tau_m)) \quad (15.9)$$

Note that this equation approximates the curve return (i.e., in relative terms). To arrive at the absolute change in value, in terms of monetary units, we have to multiply it by the value of the bond at the beginning of the period. Here, τ_m is the remaining time to maturity for the credit-risky bond. The negative sign stems from the fact that the value of a bond decreases when the yield increases. It is important to note that $y_t(\tau)$ is a yield curve for coupon-bearing bonds (e.g., the government curve or the swap curve) and not the spot rate curve. Since a yield curve is usually comprised of discrete time to maturities, we might have to interpolate to arrive at the required yield $y_t(\tau_m)$.

> **Example 25: A Simple Return Attribution Analysis**
> We assume a credit-risky bond that pays an annual coupon of 5% and has a remaining time to maturity of 5.1 years. At maturity it redeems at par and currently has a modified duration of 4.3. We analyze the total return for a

period of one week, which corresponds to 0.019 years (=7/365). Moreover, there is no cash flow due within the valuation period. The value of the bond at the beginning of the period was €99.5, while it was €99.7 at the end. During this time period, the corresponding risk-free yield increased by 10 bp.

The total P&L of the bond is €0.2, while the total return is 20.1 bp. The interest income can be calculated as the coupon rate (5%) times the valuation period (7 days) times the par value (€100): €0.096 or 9.6 bp. The pull-to-par effect is calculated as €0.002 or 0.2 bp. Adding both components results in the time value component €0.098 or 9.8 bp. Consequently, we arrive at a market value component of €0.102 or 10.3 bp.

In order to divide the market value component into curve and credit return, we multiply the modified duration of 4.3 by the 10 bp yield change, which results in a curve return of −43 bp (recall the negative sign in equation 15.9). As a result, the credit return amounts to 53.3 bp. Since for straight bonds the sensitivity to changes in the risk-free yield and to the spread curve is identical, we can conclude that this credit return corresponds to a spread change of 12 bp.

16
Hedging Credit Risk

After having discussed the portfolio management process from a more general and operational perspective, we now demonstrate how to use the various available credit instruments in the context of active credit portfolio management. However, we have to distinguish between different motives when discussing the use of credit-risky instruments, namely the *hedging motive*, which focuses on reducing or eliminating some sources of risk of an already existing position, and the *trading motive*. While hedging is based on the notion of common risk factors that account for stable correlation patterns between two or more instruments, trading strategies depend on temporary inefficiencies of the capital market that hopefully will vanish over time and therefore generate short-term profits. These will be discussed in the following chapter.[98]

Nevertheless, both hedging activities and many trading strategies resort to so-called *sensitivities*, which measure the dependency of an instrument's fair value on risk factors that seem to be of particular interest. They provide guidance to set up the hedge (or the trade idea) in the right way; that is, they enable us to calculate an appropriate hedge ratio, which simply reflects the proportion of notional amounts for the used financial instruments.

16.1 Hedging on a Single-Name Level

In the following, we will provide a stepwise introduction of elements that are crucial in the context of hedging cash bond portfolios. First, we start with hedging single-name exposure that is subject to several risk sources in practice, particularly interest rate and credit risk. However, we will primarily focus on the subject of hedging credit risk, while the reader is invited to consult fixed income textbooks that address possible hedging strategies for interest rate risk.

16.1.1 Basic Considerations

The simplest setting, considering just a single cash bond investment, is a good starting point to introduce basic concepts with regard to hedging credit

Active Credit Portfolio Management. J. Felsenheimer, P. Gisdakis, and M. Zaiser
Copyright © 2006 WILEY-VCH Verlag GmbH & Co. KGaA, Weinheim
ISBN: 3-527-50198-3

risk. When talking about credit risk, it is necessary to differentiate between two aspects that are nevertheless inextricably connected to each other:

- Credit risk can be understood as the possibility of an adverse default case (*default risk*).
- In addition, market perception of the magnitude of default risk and the risk aversion of market participants may change over time, causing marked-to-market changes to a credit-risky position (*spread risk*).

It should be noted that the latter can only exist if there is a default risk as an underlying risk source. However, the variety of instruments in credit markets allows one of these two facets to come to the fore. For instance, CDO tranches typically have different hedge ratios with respect to default and spread risk, as we will discuss later in the context of trading strategies. In the following, we will clearly distinguish between these two aspects by referring to default and spread risk, respectively.

The type of investment and the kind of investor should also be taken into account when determining which aspect of credit risk has to be considered, maybe even both. For example, a credit investor who is only allowed to buy cash bonds with a rating of at least AA–, default risk usually appears to be far in the distance. Although a (multiple) downgrade action is within the realm of possibility, the default case can be ruled out, at least for a limited investment horizon. On the other hand, such an investor, provided he is not a buy-and-hold investor, may face spread risk, as adverse rating actions will usually trigger wider credit spreads and hence marked-to-market changes. If he plans to settle his position prior to maturity or cannot rule out a possible sale in the secondary bond market, his P&L is subject to credit spread changes.

Even an investor who plans to maintain his cash bond investment until maturity but is required to mark-to-market his position due to accounting rules may be subject to credit spread changes that affect his accounting profit. However, a loss attributable to spread changes in one period will definitely be compensated for in future accounting periods. Consequently, this just yields a time displacement of earnings. Against this background, accounting rules are in conflict with economic reality. Hence, accounting standard setters usually offer the possibility to classify these investments as held-to-maturity, a category that allows entities to refrain from showing mark-to-market changes in the income statement. Investors who like to apply these provisions need to have "the positive intention and ability to hold (the cash bond) to maturity" (please refer to the chapter 18 for details). However, buy-and-hold investors in lower credit qualities have to cope with credit risk, namely default risk.

16.1.2 Hedging Default Risk

If default risk is the only relevant factor for a single cash bond investment (e.g., a buy-and-hold investor), the hedging procedure seems straightforward by buying protection via a CDS contract. However, there are a few issues that should be taken into consideration.

First, the term of the CDS contract should be close to the remaining maturity of the cash bond. Although choosing off-market terms may be a solution, it is often accompanied by wider bid–ask spreads, and hence leads to higher transaction costs. Consequently, one has to perform a trade-off between term congruency and transaction costs. 5Y credit default swaps feature the highest liquidity, followed by 3Y, 7Y, and 10Y contracts.

Another problem that may result from hedging a bond exposure by a single-name CDS contract is a discrepancy between the bond investment and the reference obligation specified in the CDS agreement. For example, both debt instruments may differ with regard to seniority, maturity, and coupon payments, which would have a significant impact on respective bond prices. If, in case of a default, the investor's bond dropped from 100 to a price of 60, causing a loss in the cash bond position of 40, while the reference obligation of the CDS slumped to a price of 50, the investor would gain an amount of $-40 + 50 = 10$. With the benefit of hindsight, this result indicates an overhedging of the outstanding cash bond exposure. Consequently, an adjustment of the notional amount of the CDS contract may be advisable to avoid excessive hedging costs. In practice, differences arising from the reference obligation, as long as they are not related to seniority, are typically negligible but cannot be ruled out.

Even if default risk with regard to the reference obligation is eliminated, credit risk remains due to the fact that the CDS counterparty may not be able to fulfill his contractual obligation in case of default. Hence, the creditworthiness of the counterparty and the default correlation between the reference obligation and the CDS counterparty are of major importance when assessing the effectiveness of such a hedging instrument.

There may be other cases as well that require an adjustment of the CDS's notional amount. This is due to the fact that a regular CDS contract refers to the par value (100) of the bond by stipulating that the protection seller has to pay an amount of 100 in exchange for the reference entity that the protection buyer delivers in case of physical settlement. Thus, the protection buyer effectively receives compensation which amounts to 100 − recovery rate (in percent). On the other hand, the loss in the cash bond investment amounts to the difference between the price paid for it and the recovery rate. If the paid price deviates from

100 (an *off-par investment*), a CDS contract with a notional amount equal to the bond's notional amount results in an overhedged (below par) or underhedged (above par) position.

To avoid these difficulties, one has to adjust the CDS's notional amount in accordance with

$$\text{NA}_{\text{Bond}} \cdot (P - R) = \text{NA}_{\text{CDS}} \cdot (100 - R) \tag{16.1}$$

with NA_{Bond} = cash bond's notional amount, NA_{CDS} = notional amount of the CDS contract, R = recovery rate (in percentage points), and P = price paid (dirty) for the cash bond (in percentage points).

Solving this equation for NA_{CDS} renders the required notional amount for the CDS contract:

$$\text{NA}_{\text{CDS}} = \frac{P - R}{100 - R} \cdot \text{NA}_{\text{Bond}} \tag{16.2}$$

According to this result, a cash bond that has been acquired above par ($P > 100$) requires a notional amount for the CDS contract that exceeds the notional amount of the cash bond. The opposite holds for below-par cash bond investments.

> **Example 26: Hedging Default Risk for DCX 7% 03/2011**
>
> A credit investor acquired the DaimlerChrysler 7% 03/2011 issue on August 12, 2005, investing in a notional amount of €10 mn. In accordance with market convention, the spot trade is settled on August 17, 2005. On this date, the bond trades at 117.4 (clean price). Since the last coupon payment took place on March 21, 2005, accrued interest applies for 149 days, resulting in a dirty price of $117.4 + 2.86 = 120.26$.
>
> Simultaneously, the investor considers protecting himself from being hit by a possible DaimlerChrysler default. Due to the significant off-par investment in the DCX issue, one should adjust the notional amount of the CDS contract accordingly. For lack of detailed information, the investor assumes a recovery rate of 40 percent in case of a default.
>
> According to formula 16.2, the notional amount of the DCX CDS contract should be:
> $$\text{NA}_{\text{CDS}} = \frac{120.26 - 50}{100 - 50} \cdot €10 \text{ mn} = €14.052 \text{ mn}$$

There is another special case that should be noted. If one assumes a recovery rate of zero, the equation becomes

$$\text{NA}_{\text{CDS}} = \frac{P}{100} \cdot \text{NA}_{\text{Bond}} \tag{16.3}$$

The term on the right hand side is simply the amount invested in the cash bond. In this extreme case, the investor should choose a notional amount for the CDS contract that equals the invested amount.

As the recovery rate is of major importance when determining the hedge ratio (ratio of notional amounts), one needs an educated guess for R. In any case, just taking a value of 40 percent as usually applied to perform single pricing calculations (e.g., calculating the termination fee by means of the CDSW function on Bloomberg) could lead to inefficiency with regard to the hedging relationship. Extracting implied recovery rates from digital default swaps or recovery default swaps may be a good approximation in practice. However, one should be aware that implied recovery rates may significantly deviate from realized values. Please note that the recovery rate R ultimately is a random variable and is not a predetermined parameter. Hence, hedging default risk for an off-par cash bond investment by means of a standard CDS contract will typically be an imperfect hedge due to recovery risk, which is one component of default risk.

Although the adjustment of the CDS's notional amount for off-par cash bond investments seems rather straightforward, it may not be appropriate over time. To demonstrate this, let us reconsider the above-par investment in the DCX issue depicted in the example box above. It should be clear that the pull-to-par effect applies in the course of time, attributable to the fact that the bond pays a coupon that is significantly above the internal rate of return observed at initiation. Provided that there is no default event during the first years and the recovery rate assumption remains unchanged, the notional amount of the CDS contract will be too high, as the advantage of an above-market coupon rate has already been realized to some extent. Hence, the cash bond position is overhedged, arguing for a gradual reduction of the CDS's notional amount over time.

Another issue is related to asset swap packages. Sometimes investors enter into an asset swap contract in order to obtain a par floater instead of an off-par, coupon-paying bond. At first glance, it seems clear that no adjustment of the CDS's notional amount is required in this case. However, this proves wrong. On the one hand, the difference between the (dirty) price paid and the par value is offset by an upfront payment in the swap contract. If a default occurs shortly after initiation, the swap contract still exists and has a significant positive or negative market value due to the initial upfront payment, which would lead to a notable termination payment. Hence, an asset swap package simply shifts the off-par investment problem to the swap contract, but it is not resolved.

16.1.3 Hedging Spread Risk

In practice, many investors are subject to spread risk instead of default risk, that is, they try to hedge their position against marked-to-market changes that are attributable to a variation of credit spreads. As already mentioned, such an objective may arise from one of the following situations:

- The investor plans to sell his cash bond position prior to maturity.
- The investor basically plans to keep his position until maturity, but he might be forced to liquidate it due to factors that are beyond his sphere of influence, such as a liquidity bottleneck or a limitation with regard to the external rating of his investment.
- The investor can be classified as a buy-and-hold investor, but his position is evaluated on a regular basis (marked-to-market portfolio).

Hedging the risk of spread changes is not as easy as eliminating default risk. It is not sufficient to enter into a CDS contract with a notional amount that equals the face value of the cash bond, even if the bond has been acquired for a price of 100. In order to offset marked-to-market changes of a cash bond (hedged item) with a corresponding hedging instrument (here: single-name CDS), one has to cope with sensitivities. The idea of sensitivities is to measure the extent of marked-to-market changes due to the underlying risk factors of both instruments, the hedged item and the hedging instrument. If one knows these numbers, it is an easy task to calculate a hedge ratio that leads to the required notional amount for the hedging instrument.

But what are the underlying risk factors for cash bonds and single-name CDS contracts? As cash bonds are subject to several sources of risk (interest rate and credit risk), the set of risk factors comprises the whole risk-free term structure of interest rates and the whole credit curve for the respective name (alternatively: the hazard rate function or survival probabilities over time and assumptions concerning the recovery rate). As we focus on hedging spread risk, we still have a huge set of risk factors concerning credit risk from a theoretical point of view. The same applies for single-name CDS contracts, although these contracts are also subject to interest rate risk, although typically to a lesser extent in comparison to cash bonds with fixed coupons.

From a practical perspective, working with a big number of risk factors is impractical and, in addition, useless if only one hedging instrument is available. Hence, one has to specify a risk factor that is able to explain a large share of actual marked-to-market changes for both instruments. A common way is to

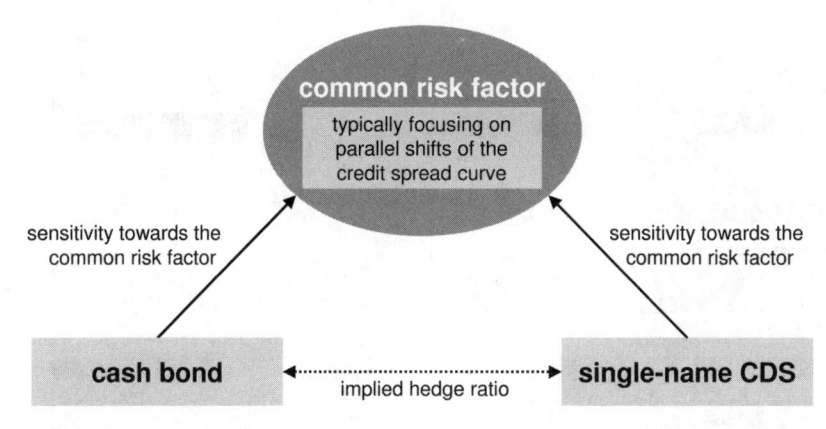

Fig. 16.1: The basic hedge concept for spread risk

focus on parallel shifts of the spread curve, thus reducing the set of risk factors to just one item. Figure 16.1 illustrates this basic idea.

This leads us to a sensitivity measure called *SpreadDV01*, which measures the change in market value (present value) when the spread curve is increased by one basis point. Apparently, the underlying concept is similar to the *DV01* concept introduced in chapter 5, whereas here it is related to spread curve movements instead of considering shifts of the risk-free spot rate curve. Calculating a market-value change requires the stipulation of a notional amount for the respective financial instrument. If we compare these sensitivities across different instruments, we should ensure that they are being calculated based on the same notional amount.

Fortunately, Bloomberg provides risk measures via the functions

- YAS <GO> ("Yield and Spread Analysis") and
- CDSW <GO> ("Credit Default Swap"),

which allow the sensitivity calculation for cash bonds and CDS contracts.

As the credit spread can be regarded as an integral part of the respective discount curve (at least when considering Z-spreads), results from plain-vanilla duration analysis can also be applied to parallel shifts of the credit spread curve.

The YAS screenshot in figure 16.2 shows how to extract sensitivity measures for cash bonds. The section "Risk and Hedge Ratios" offers three numbers that may be of use in a hedging context: the modified duration, the risk, and the convexity. The best figure for our purposes is provided by the value of *risk* (see column "workout" for bonds without optionalities), which is, according to Bloomberg's definition, 100 times the price change of a basis point change

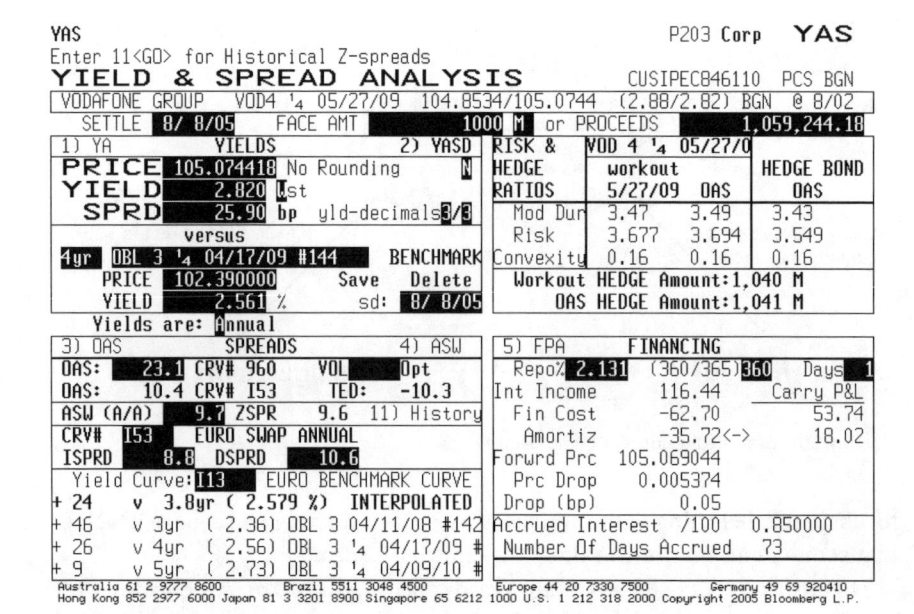

Fig. 16.2: A screenshot of Bloomberg's YAS tool

in the yield curve. For the example below (VOD 4.25% 05/2009) and given a notional amount of €10 mn, a 1 bp upward parallel shift of the credit spread curve would result in a market value decrease for the cash bond position of approximately

$$\frac{3.677}{100} \cdot \frac{\text{€10 mn}}{100} = \text{€}3677$$

From a CDS perspective, the case is straightforward. After having fed the CDSW screen (cf. figure 16.3) with the contract specification (take a notional amount of €10 mn), the maturity date, and the deal spread, one can gather the *SpreadDV01* directly from the respective line within the *Calculator* area. In the present case, a 1 bp upward parallel shift of the credit spread curve would result in a market value increase of €4,807.94.

If one has obtained both SpreadDV01s (for the cash bond and the CDS), it is a simple step to calculate the hedge ratio by dividing both numbers by each other:

$$\frac{\text{€}3677.00}{\text{€}4648.72} \approx 0.791$$

Hence, an investor who wants to protect his VOD 4.25% 05/2009 position (notional amount €10 mn) with regard to credit spread changes may enter into

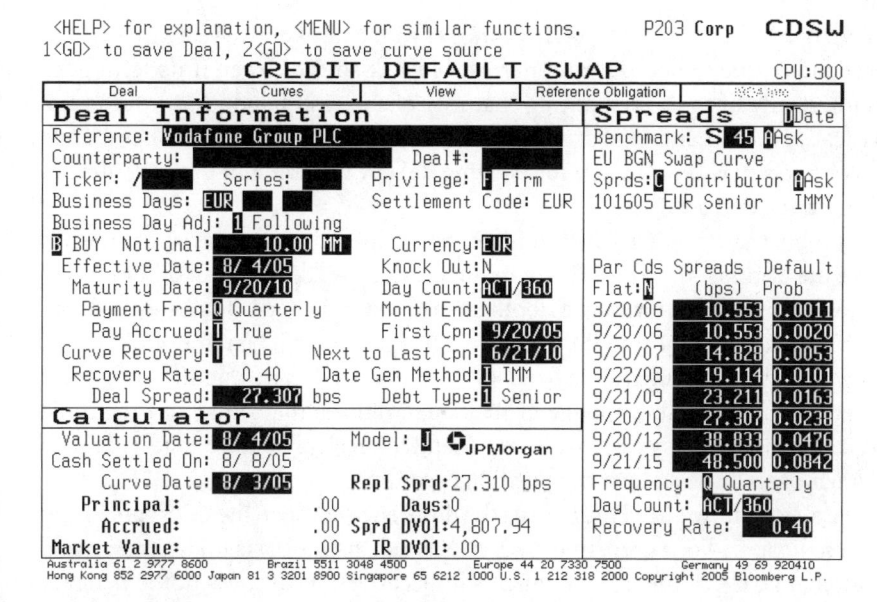

Fig. 16.3: A screenshot of Bloomberg's CDSW tool

a 5Y CDS contract on Vodafone Group PLC with a notional amount of about €7.91 mn.

As we have already discussed the most common approach to hedge a cash bond position against credit spread changes on a single-name basis, we now shed some light on difficulties raised by such a hedging approach. The hedge efficiency is subject to the following considerations:

- The interest rate risk is still alive, though not the focus of this chapter.
- Which term to choose for the CDS contract?
- Are adjustments of the hedge ratio necessary in the course of time?
- Possible effects from a spread discrepancy between CDS and cash bond markets (*basis risk*).
- Possible effects from non-linear price relationships (*convexity risk*).

In the example above, we took a CDS term of five years for granted. However, this choice is not necessarily self-evident. Typically, one would try to choose a CDS maturity that is close to the remaining term of the cash bond. Although we solely consider parallel spread curve movements, the shape and steepness of the credit curve may change over time. Against this background, matching maturities will help to minimize hedge inefficiencies arising from these effects. In practice, one has to make a trade-off between CDS liquidity and the prevention of term effects. A CDS contract with a term of five years may be the best choice due to liquidity and narrow bid–ask spreads, even if its term does not perfectly fit to the remaining maturity of the cash bond. In any case, we basically recommend to abstain from tailor-made CDS contracts. These kinds of contracts may be adequate for hedging default risk, but not in the context of eliminating spread risk.

Another issue concerns the stability of the hedge ratio in the course of time. To state the obvious, the *SpreadDV01* gradually declines, keeping all other market factors constant. However, as both instruments, hedged item and hedging instrument, are subject to this effect, the hedge ratio will be rather unaffected. However, if the maturity date for both instruments deviates significantly from one another, a possible change of the hedge ratio in the course of time must be considered. In any case, we recommend to recalculate the hedge ratio on a regular basis and to adjust the position accordingly.

We already introduced the *basis* as the difference between the CDS spread and the credit spread of a corresponding cash bond. As the basis for a single name may change over time, this could also impact the effectiveness of the hedging relationship. Hence, it is good to know the leading sign and the magnitude of the basis before entering into a hedge. Beyond the issue of an efficient repo market for the cash bond, there are several other topics that affect the basis in practice, such as market liquidity and technical factors like supply and demand imbalances. Please refer to section 17.3.5 for an in-depth analysis concerning the basis.

16.2 Hedging on a Portfolio Level

Hedging credit risk on a portfolio level basically poses the same challenges as on a single-name basis. However, the main focus changes to hedging spread risk, as eliminating default risk should basically be done by considering the underlying single-name risks as demonstrated in section 16.1.2. On the other hand, the recent introduction of credit index products like iTraxx index swaps offers an opportunity to address the topic of hedging spread risk from a macro perspective.

In the following, we start with some basic considerations with regard to hedging systematic spread risk. Subsequently, we focus on a setting where we try to hedge spread risk of a single cash bond by means of buying protection in an iTraxx index swap. This serves as a preparation for the general portfolio case. We close the section with a discussion of how to choose the right hedging instrument in a portfolio context, taking various important decision criteria into account.

16.2.1 Basic Considerations

At first glance, it seems impudent to hedge an existing credit portfolio by buying protection in an iTraxx index swap, particularly against the background that the composition of the iTraxx basket will typically not be a good fit for the underlying credit portfolio. However, there are a few reasons that encourage the application of such an approach.

First of all, credit indices like the iTraxx Europe Benchmark index have narrower bid–ask spreads owing to high liquidity, hence reducing transaction costs to a minimum compared to the vast majority of single-name CDS contracts. The extraordinary liquidity of these instruments also contributes to a reduction of basis risk, one of the major risk sources we highlighted in the last section.

Hedging single-name credit risk via a credit index product means to eliminate just the *systematic spread risk*, that is, the component of the spread movement that is attributable to overall market changes. There is a clear economic rationale behind joint spread movements, namely the general economic outlook and the change in risk aversion of market participants due to supply and demand imbalances in the market, just to name a few. In fact, a credit index like the iTraxx Europe Benchmark is a good proxy of the overall market (at least: investment-grade credit risk), as it provides well-diversified access to high-grade credit risk.

After having eliminated the systematic spread risk, a fraction of the spread movements remains, which is referred to as idiosyncratic (or unsystematic) spread risk. Figure 16.4 illustrates the idea behind a hedge of systematic spread risk.

16.2.2 Hedging Systematic Spread Risk for a Single Cash Bond

In preparation for the general portfolio case, we discuss a setting where we try to hedge systematic spread risk of a single cash bond by means of buying protection in an iTraxx index swap. However, we first need a model to describe the relationship between the cash bond instrument and the market.

The interaction of idiosyncratic and systematic credit risk is usually modeled on a spread basis, subject to an additive link between both factors. Against the background of well-known CAPM results, the following approach is applied:

$$s_i = \alpha_i + \beta_i \cdot s_M + \epsilon_i \qquad (16.6)$$

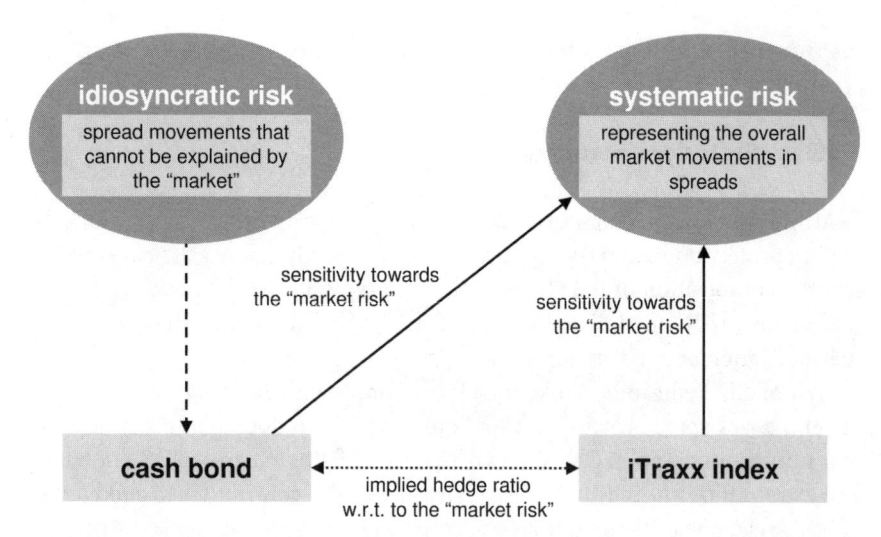

Fig. 16.4: The hedge concept for systematic spread risk

The expression s_i refers to the spread level of obligor i, while s_M is the average spread level of the market.

This approach assumes a linear relationship between the s_i and s_M with constant parameters α_i and β_i, which is subject to a stochastic error term ϵ_i, as shown in figure 16.5. This expression represents the idiosyncratic credit risk of name i. The parameter β_i can be interpreted as a sensitivity measure of name i's spread s_i with regard to the market spread s_M. For instance, a beta of 2 means that name i's credit spread experiences an average increase of 2 bp given an increase of 1 bp for the market spread.

Please note that this model cannot be inferred from any sophisticated valuation model, but is rather a simple attempt to reproduce an observation that can regularly be made in practice. Quoted spreads from various credit-risky instruments often move in tandem, leaving the impression that credit spreads are largely driven by "the market in general".

As the parameters α_i and β_i cannot be observed directly, they have to be estimated in an econometric procedure. For these purposes, we need a few more assumptions to obtain the parameters from historical spread time series, namely:

- The stochastic error term ϵ_i features a mean of zero (otherwise, α_i would be ambiguous) and has a constant variance (which means that the possible magnitude of idiosyncratic risk does not change over time). In addition, the error term ϵ_i is not autocorrelated; observing its value at any point in

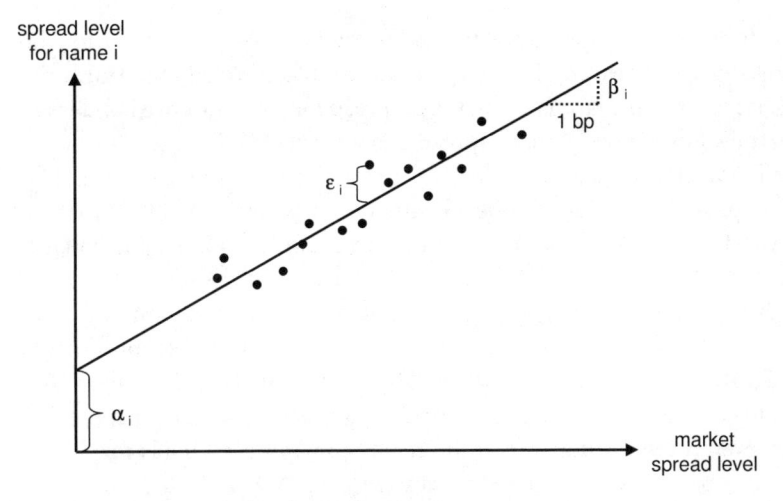

Fig. 16.5: The regression idea of estimating betas

time does not enable us to predict the idiosyncratic risk component for any future period.
- The idiosyncratic risk, represented by ϵ_i, and the market spread s_M are not correlated, in other words, both factors can be completely separated from each other.

These assumptions can also be expressed mathematically (t indicates the respective time of observation:

$$E\left(\epsilon_{i,t}\right) = 0 \text{ for all } t \tag{16.7}$$

$$\text{Var}\left(\epsilon_{i,t}\right) = \sigma^2 \text{ for all } t \tag{16.8}$$

$$E\left(\epsilon_{i,t} \cdot \epsilon_{i,\tau}\right) = 0 \text{ for all } \tau \neq t \tag{16.9}$$

$$E\left(\epsilon_{i,t} \cdot s_{M,t}\right) = 0 \text{ for all } t \tag{16.10}$$

Given this simple spread model and the assumptions above, a regression analysis (ordinary least squares [OLS] approach) can be applied to obtain an estimate for the parameters. Please note that the resulting values from this procedure are only estimates and may be subject to the underlying time frame used for the estimation.

We still have to consider how to measure the market spread. From a theoretical point of view, the best solution would be to calculate an average spread of all credit-risky bonds outstanding. However, such a procedure is quite time-consuming. As we aim at hedging a cash bond position via a credit index swap, we resort to the quoted spread for the index product as a good proxy for the whole credit (derivatives) market. As a result, we recommend to perform the time-series regression analysis using the Z-spread for the respective bond issue and the iTraxx Europe Benchmark spread, respectively.

In the following, we take the VW 4.5% 01/2010 issue as an example. Figure 16.6 depicts the result of the beta estimation procedure, provided that we use the most common instrument in the iTraxx familiy as a hedging instrument, namely the iTraxx Europe Benchmark. Based on time-series data from May 16 until August 5, 2005, we obtain a beta of 1.1232, which indicates that the Z-spread of the VW issues reacts slightly stronger to market movements than the iTraxx Europe Benchmark itself. The coefficient of determination (R^2) amounts to circa 91 percent, which is exceptionally good for such an approach. However, even if the relationship of the regression approach holds for the future, about 9 percent of the spread variation for the VW 4.5% 01/2010 issue cannot be explained by market movements and contributes to possible hedge inefficiencies.

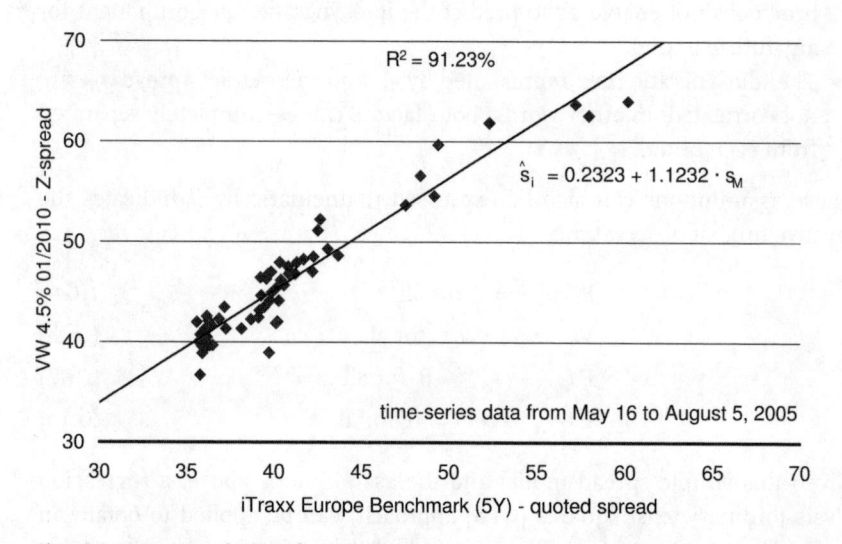

Fig. 16.6: Estimating the beta for the VW 4.5% 01/2010 issue

However, the time series for these two spread instruments (cf. figure 16.7) illustrates that the estimation result may be affected by large idiosyncratic factors like the GM/Ford turmoil in May 2005. Hence, we recommend to carefully choose the period that acts as the basis for the estimation procedure.

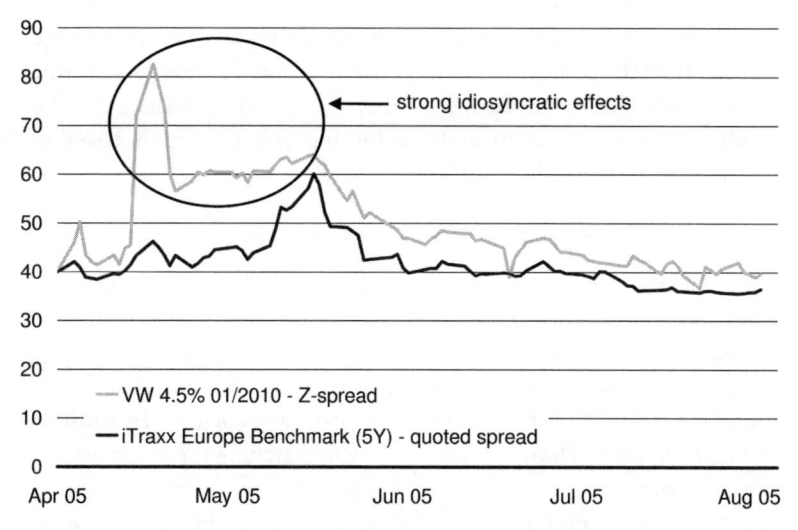

Fig. 16.7: External idiosyncratic shocks may distort the estimation

Again, the final is step is to calculate the hedge ratio based on *SpreadDV01* measures for both instruments, the hedged item (cash bond) and the hedging instrument. However, the sensitivity of name i's credit spread s_i with regard to the market spread s_M has to be taken into account, as a 1 bp market spread change is, on average, accompanied by a β_i bp change in name i's spread. Hence, the hedge ratio calculation must be modified as follows (the hat on the beta measure indicates the usage of an estimated value for it):

$$\text{hedge ratio} = \frac{\text{SpreadDV01 of bond issue}}{\text{SpreadDV01 of the iTraxx}} \cdot \hat{\beta}_i \qquad (16.11)$$

We return to our VW 4.5% 01/2010 case with a SpreadDV01 of €4,237 given a notional amount of €10 mn, while we take the Series 3 of the iTraxx Europe Benchmark (5Y) as the hedging instrument with a SpreadDV01 of about €4,543. According to the results of the above regression analysis, a beta of 1.1232 has to be taken into account. Hence, we get a hedge ratio of

$$\frac{€4237}{€4543} \cdot 1.1232 \approx 1.048$$

Provided a notional amount of €10 mn for the VW issue, one would need a notional amount of €10.48 mn in the iTraxx Europe Benchmark index to eliminate systematic spread risk.

As figure 16.7 already suggested, some of the model assumptions may be violated in practice. Particularly the relationship does not seem to be stable over time as anticipated, or may be subject to idiosyncratic effects for longer periods, which raises the problem of autocorrelation. Against this background, we recommend to reassess the hedge position on a regular basis. Another possibility that is often cited is to perform the regression analysis based on daily spread *changes* instead of spread levels:

$$\Delta s_i = \alpha'_i + \beta'_i \cdot \Delta s_M + \eta_i \qquad (16.13)$$

Please note that the error term ϵ_i has been replaced by η_i, nevertheless with the same assumptions concerning the stochastic properties as for ϵ_i. However, the regression (with $\alpha'_i = 0$ typically being stipulated in advance) often renders unstable results due to delay effects (sometimes a certain CDS might be illiquid and its quote is not adjusted until further turnover takes place). In addition, the coefficient of determination is often too low to conclude the existence of a stable market impact.

In the context of hedging spread risk by means of a single-name CDS, we already pointed out that the hedge efficiency may be subject to the *basis*, which relates to the spread differential between the cash bond and the credit derivatives market. When considering index swaps, hedge inefficiencies from a change of the basis are still possible, but to a lesser extent due to the high diversification of the underlying basket. Nevertheless, one has to cope with the *skew*, which has already been introduced in the context of index swap valuation. A deviation of the quoted index swap spread from its theoretically correct level may contribute to hedge inefficiencies, at least temporarily. Hence, we recommend to keep an eye on the skew when entering into or unwinding an index swap like the iTraxx Europe Benchmark.

16.2.3 Hedging Systematic Spread Risk for a Credit Portfolio

Although the hedge efficiency on a single-name basis may not trigger exuberant enthusiasm, the above considerations are expected to lead to better results when considering portfolios consisting of various bonds. In this case, diversification becomes effective with a reduction of the idiosyncratic spread component. It is a well-known fact from portfolio selection theory that the idiosyncratic risk declines when the number of instruments included in the portfolio increases. A similar idea can be applied to credit-risky portfolios, where the combination of default risk from various obligors results in a reduction of idiosyncratic spread risk from a macro perspective, as illustrated in a very simplified manner in figure 16.8. If one increases the number of different credits within the portfolio (provided a given portfolio size), the idiosyncratic risk diminishes due to diversification, while the systematic spread risk basically remains unchanged.

total spread risk
of the
credit portfolio

idiosyncratic spread risk

systematic spread risk

n

number of different names in portfolio

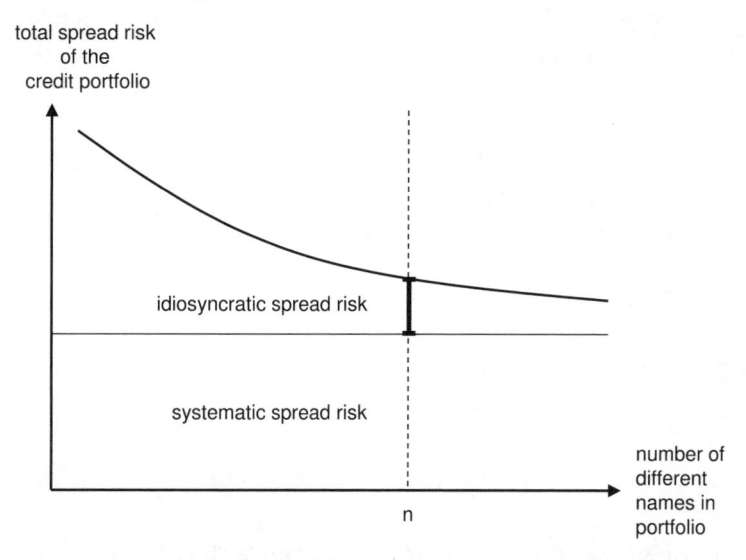

Fig. 16.8: Exploiting diversification for credit portfolios

But how to apply the notion of section 16.2.2 to cash bond portfolios? This can be basically done in two different ways. One self-evident possibility would be to rerun the already known procedure for each single bond issue within the portfolio and then to add up the required notional amounts for the hedging instrument. Although this procedure is quite annoying and time-consuming for largely diversified portfolios, it offers the opportunity to select an appropriate beta estimation period for each portfolio constituent on an individual basis, resulting in stable and reliable beta estimates.

Another way would be to perform an ad hoc calculation on a portfolio level, based on a SpreadDV01 measure for the whole portfolio and a portfolio beta β_{PF}. In the following, we discuss how this portfolio beta can be estimated in a similar regression approach as in the case with a single cash bond, namely:

$$s_{PF} = \alpha_{PF} + \beta_{PF} \cdot s_M + \epsilon_{PF} \qquad (16.14)$$

It is needless to say that ϵ_{PF} is expected to fulfill the same stochastic properties as ϵ_i in section 16.2.2. If we want to estimate α_{PF} and β_{PF} in a regression approach, we first have to clarify how to define the spread level of the portfolio, denoted by s_{PF}.

We can give an answer to this question by starting from a single-name level and aggregate the presumed, underlying equations of how single-name spreads are determined until we finally arrive at a portfolio level. Provided that single-name spreads are determined by

$$s_i = \alpha_i + \beta_i \cdot s_M + \epsilon_i \text{ for all } i = 1, 2, \ldots, n \qquad (16.15)$$

as before (n denotes the number of bond issues in the portfolio), the expected marked-to-market (present value) change of the credit portfolio resulting from an (infinitesimally small) change of the market spread s_M would be:

$$\begin{aligned} \text{E}(\Delta \text{PV}_{\text{PF}}) &= \text{E}\left(\sum_{i=1}^{n} \Delta \text{PV}_i\right) \\ &= \sum_{i=1}^{n} \text{E}(\Delta \text{PV}_i) \\ &= \sum_{i=1}^{n} \text{E}(\Delta s_i) \cdot \text{SpreadDVo1}_i \end{aligned} \qquad (16.16)$$

Considering the stochastic properties of ϵ_i and formula 16.15, one obtains

$$\text{E}(\Delta s_i) = \beta_i \cdot \Delta s_M \text{ for all } i = 1, 2, \ldots, n \qquad (16.17)$$

Accordingly, the expected PV change of the credit portfolio approximately amounts to

$$\text{E}(\Delta \text{PV}_{\text{PF}}) = \Delta s_M \cdot \sum_{i=1}^{n} \beta_i \cdot \text{SpreadDVo1}_i \qquad (16.18)$$

Please note that this expression is based on the notion that the credit portfolio consists of various single items. However, from a aggregated perspective, we would implicitly define the portfolio beta β_{PF} by the following equation:

$$\text{E}(\Delta \text{PV}_{\text{PF}}) = \Delta s_M \cdot \beta_{\text{PF}} \cdot \text{SpreadDVo1}_{\text{PF}} \qquad (16.19)$$

$$\text{with } \text{SpreadDVo1}_{\text{PF}} = \sum_{i=1}^{n} \text{SpreadDVo1}_i \qquad (16.20)$$

Equating formula 16.18 with 16.19 thus shows us how to calculate the portfolio beta from a theoretical perspective:

$$\beta_{\text{PF}} = \frac{\sum_{i=1}^{n} \beta_i \cdot \text{SpreadDVo1}_i}{\sum_{i=1}^{n} \text{SpreadDVo1}_i} \qquad (16.21)$$

Consequently, the portfolio beta can be calculated as a weighted average of single-name betas, which refer to the credits included in the credit portfolio. Although this seems to be a self-evident result, one should explicitly note the fact that the SpreadDVo1s of the portfolio constituents act as weightings instead of just resorting to the notional amount or the market value of the respective single-name investment.

When resorting to formula 5.40, we obtain an alternative expression for the portfolio beta, which makes use of to the market value and the modified duration of the portfolio constituents:

$$\beta_{PF} = \frac{\sum_{i=1}^{n} \beta_i \cdot MV_i \cdot ModDur_i}{\sum_{i=1}^{n} MV_i \cdot ModDur_i} \qquad (16.22)$$

Example 27: How To Calculate the Portfolio Beta

An investor maintains a credit portfolio with a notional amount totaling €50 mn, which comprises five bond issues as shown in the following table:

Calculating the portfolio beta (data from 08/12/2005)

Issue	Notional amount	Dirty price	Mod. dur.	Spread DVo1	Beta
DCX 6.125% 03/2007	€10 mn	107.76	1.51	1,627	2.62
AUTSTR 5.0% 06/2014	€5 mn	110.43	7.09	3,915	0.72
TITIM 6.5% 04/2007	€12 mn	108.40	1.58	2,055	0.35
DT 6.625% 03/2018	€8 mn	127.46	8.81	8,983	0.78
RWE 5.375% 04/2008	€15 mn	108.78	2.46	4,013	0.11

We can calculate the SpreadDVo1 of each single cash bond based on the following data: notional amount (column 2), dirty price (column 3), and modified duration (column 4). One simply has to use formula 5.39, namely

$$DVo1_t = Dur_t \cdot P_t \cdot N \cdot 10^{-6}$$

to obtain the SpreadDVo1 values shown in column 5. The betas in last column stem from an estimation procedure, which has been performed for each single bond. According to 16.21, the portfolio beta β_{PF} amounts to

$$\beta_{PF} = \frac{2.62 \cdot 1,627 + 0.72 \cdot 3,915 + \ldots + 0.11 \cdot 4,013}{1,627 + 3,915 + \ldots + 4,013} \approx 0.74$$

If one considers the linear structure of the portfolio regression relationship as shown in formula 16.14, the construction principle for the portfolio beta β_{PF} is carried forward to the portfolio spread s_M in order to grant the model consistency. Finally, this renders (we skip the mathematical proof):

$$s_{PF} = \frac{\sum_{i=1}^{n} s_i \cdot \text{SpreadDV01}_i}{\sum_{i=1}^{n} \text{SpreadDV01}_i} = \frac{\sum_{i=1}^{n} s_i \cdot MV_i \cdot \text{ModDur}_i}{\sum_{i=1}^{n} MV_i \cdot \text{ModDur}_i} \qquad (16.23)$$

This result has an immediate practical implication: The average spread level of a credit portfolio is often calculated based on the constituents' market values (or: the market capitalization). However, this approach proves incorrect in the context of deriving the portfolio beta via a single portfolio regression approach. The calculation of the average portfolio spread should rather be done by incorporating the modified duration ModDur_i for each included instrument. This result also represents a justification for the weighting scheme that applies to the iTraxx Europe Corporate index, namely weighting the iBoxx € Non-Financials issuers with the product of the market capitalization and modified duration for each outstanding cash bond.

Now that we have estimated the portfolio beta β_{PF} based on the regression equation shown in formula 16.14 and the correct definition of the portfolio spread s_{PF}, the calculation of the hedge ratio can be done in accordance with the single-name hedging case:

$$\text{hedge ratio} = \frac{\text{SpreadDV01}_{PF}}{\text{SpreadDV01 of the iTraxx}} \cdot \hat{\beta}_{PF} \qquad (16.24)$$

16.2.4 Finding the Right Hedging Instrument

Buying protection in a credit index swap may be an appropriate measure to protect one's credit portfolio from adverse systematic spread changes. Since the market offers a variety of instruments that may be eligible for this purpose, primarily linear index swaps, one has to come to a decision with regard to the hedging instrument. As we will see, there are several decision criteria that have to be taken into account. Beyond the requirement to keep the negative carry of the protection buyer position as small as possible, one should additionally consider the hedge effectiveness and transaction costs associated with each eligible hedging instrument.

Finding the right hedging tool can be quite complex in practice, as it is not always possible to achieve the optimal satisfaction level for all decision criteria at the same time (conflict of interest). However, one should try to attain a satisfactory solution with regard to all requirements, or to make one specific criteria a top priority.

In our view, a credit portfolio manager should consider the following factors:

- The *effective cost of insurance* should be minimized to avoid an extensive loss caused by the running negative spread. When entering into a protection buyer position, one has to pay a fixed spread that accrues over time. When comparing different index swaps, one should take the different required notional amounts of the possible hedging instruments into account. As already demonstrated, one first has to determine the beta and the SpreadDV01 of the respective index swap and the SpreadDV01 of the portfolio in order to obtain the required hedge ratio (and notional amount). Because the SpreadDV01 of the portfolio is constant, one can easily perform a comparison based on the following measure, which should be minimized:

    effective cost = ask spread of the instrument × hedge ratio

    The importance of this consideration clearly depends on the expected time horizon until the hedging instrument will be unwound. The longer the holding period, the more one should take this criterion into account.

- The *hedge efficiency* is of utmost importance for any hedging relationship, and particularly for a hedge of systematic spread risk. For example, this could be measured by resorting to the unexplained portfolio spread variance of the regression approach used to estimate the portfolio beta. The share of the portfolio spread variance that cannot be explained by spread movements of the hedging instrument is simply given by $1-R^2$, hence the complementary measure of the coefficient of determination. The lower the unexplained share (or: the higher the coefficient of determination), the better the prospect to efficiently hedge future spread movements of the portfolio.

- The *similarity of composition* with regard to the credit portfolio and the potential hedging instrument is another consideration that may be of importance. Although the hedging relationship is based on the notion of eliminating systematic spread risk, a similar basket may be helpful to increase the hedge efficiency. In addition, the index swap could even offer protection with regard to default risk, at least to some extent. But how should one assess this criterion quantitatively? Although there are several statistical methods available to compare two distributions concerning

structural differences, one has to stipulate the granularity of the examination (single-name versus industry versus sector). Since this aspect is, in our view, largely covered by the criteria of hedge effectiveness, we refrain from a detailed discussion.
- *Transaction costs* associated with entering and unwinding the index swap should also be considered when finding the right hedging instrument. This can be simply measured by the bid–ask spread of the instrument, but it should also be related to the required notional amount of the respective hedging instrument in order to allow comparison across these instruments. In addition, the SpreadDV01 (which is largely related to the term of the contract) should also be taken into account, as a 1 bp bid–ask spread has different marked-to-market implications for different terms and SpreadDV01s. Accordingly, we should calculate:

relative transaction costs = bid–ask spread × hedge ratio × SpreadDV01

The narrower the (relative) bid–ask spread, the more favorable the respective hedging instrument. Despite the fact that the bid–ask spreads for iTraxx index swaps are quite small (please refer to table 16.1 for details), transaction costs should be taken into account, particularly when allotting a limited time horizon for the hedging relationship.
- A *maturity mismatch* between the credit portfolio and the hedging instrument may also cause hedge inefficiencies in practice. If the average remaining maturity of the credit portfolio deviates significantly from the term of the hedging tool, the hedge may suffer from credit curve movements other than parallel shifts. In our view, the impact of a curve flattening or steepening is of minor importance compared to general shifts of the spread level. Nevertheless, putting up with a maturity mismatch will, at least to some extent, leave one's mark in the measurement of hedge efficiency.

In table 16.2 we performed a comparison of the most liquid iTraxx index swaps with regard to their eligibility to hedge the systematic spread risk of a standard credit portfolio, in this case the iBoxx € Non-Financials. The hedge ratio for each instrument is calculated based on the beta of the iBoxx € Non-Financials with regard to the respective iTraxx index and the SpreadDV01 of the instrument and the portfolio (either assuming a notional amount of €10 mn; the modified duration of the iBoxx index amounts to about 4.485 years).

Apparently, a hedge against systematic spread changes by means of the 10Y iTraxx Europe HiVol involves the lowest (negative) carry (–39.5 bp). In addition,

Tab. 16.1: Bid–ask spreads for the most liquid iTraxx Europe index swaps

Index	Term	Spread level (08/12/2005)	Range of bid–ask spread
Benchmark	5Y	36.5 bp	0.25–0.5 bp
Benchmark	10Y	56.5 bp	0.5–1.0 bp
Non-Financials	5Y	39.5 bp	2.0–3.0 bp
HiVol	5Y	66.5 bp	0.5–1.0 bp
HiVol	10Y	98.5 bp	2.0–3.0 bp
Crossover	5Y	284.5 bp	2.0–7.0 bp

the tracking performance versus the iBoxx € Non-Financials index proved best for the period used for the estimation procedure (March 21 to April 8, 2005). However, the relative transaction cost of 1.1 bp (= 3 bp × 0.3691) exceeds that of its peers, but only to an immaterial extent. Against this background, one could arrive at the conclusion that the 10Y iTraxx Europe HiVol is the right instrument for this hedging case. But the maturity mismatch between the credit portfolio (modified duration of about 4.5 years) and the iTraxx index swap (10Y) may pose a problem in a scenario of a pronounced flattening or steepening of the credit curve.

In any case, we recommend to perform similar calculations based on the actual credit portfolio composition and based on the most recent time series for the portfolio and the possible hedge instrument data. One should take into account that beta may gradually change over time and thus alter the eligibility of the various iTraxx index swaps.

Even when considering the iTraxx Europe HiVol (10Y) in order to hedge the iBoxx € Non-Financials portfolio, one has to accept a negative spread of 39.5 bp in the case above. An alternative would be to resort to iTraxx instruments other than index swaps, particularly standardized CDO tranches based on the iTraxx Europe Benchmark index. For example, if one considers buying protection in the 5Y iTraxx Europe 3–6% tranche (presuming a tranche delta of 4 versus the iTraxx Europe Benchmark [5Y] index swap), one arrives at a total hedge ratio of $1.9344 \times \frac{1}{4} = 0.4836$. If the ask spread of the instruments amounts to 74 bp, one obtains an effective cost of 74 bp × 0.4836 ≈ 35.8 bp.

Tab. 16.2: A comparison of possible hedging instruments in the iTraxx universe (April 11, 2005)

iTraxx Europe	Term	Beta	Spread DV01	Hedge ratio	Offer spread	Hedge carry	Relative tr. cost	Unexplained variance
Benchmark	5Y	2.069	4.797	1.9344	40	−76.9	4.5	33.2%
Benchmark	10Y	1.376	8.316	0.7417	61	−45.2	5.6	23.9%
Non-Financials	5Y	1.361	4.774	1.2785	44	−56.2	5.8	22.5%
HiVol	5Y	0.801	4.723	0.7602	74	−45.2	3.6	18.5%
HiVol	10Y	0.657	7.978	0.3691	107	−39.5	8.8	16.2%
Crossover	5Y	0.220	4.244	0.2320	285	−66.1	3.1	18.1%

At first glance, this result argues for the use of iTraxx CDO tranches when hedging credit portfolios against systematic spread movements. However, there are a few shortcomings that should be mentioned. First, CDO tranches are non-linear credit products that require a regular adjustment of the hedging position in case of pronounced market movements. In addition, the valuation of such an instrument, and thus its quoted price, does not solely depend on the underlying market spread (in our case the 5Y iTraxx Europe Benchmark). In particular, changes in market-implied correlations can lead to significant marked-to-market changes, which challenges the desired hedge efficiency.

17
Trading Strategies

On the back of the accelerating number of instruments in the credit universe, the variety of potential trading strategies is increasing significantly. We discuss the most popular trading strategies below, starting with cash instruments and show how to identify relative value. Then we focus on the credit derivatives universe, which offers a broader variety of trading opportunities compared to the cash market. Trade ideas in the credit derivatives universe are divided into trading single names, trades including portfolio CDS, basis and skew trading, and correlation trades (FTD baskets and STCDOs). We conclude with the basic idea behind capital structure arbitrage and CPPI strategies.

For a straightforward discussion of trading strategies in the credit derivatives universe, we stick with the same modus operandi for every trade:

1. We start with the rationale behind the trade.
2. We then discuss how to implement the trade.

17.1 Trading Cash Bonds

The scope of the cash universe with respect to trading strategies is limited. As the repo market is still rather illiquid and as there are a limited number of corporate bonds that are repo-compatible, we do not cover short strategies, which can only be implemented by using the repo market. Consequently, directional spread bets can be only implemented through long positions. The key question is how to find attractive issues. While pure credit fundamentals can be taken into consideration when choosing the name from a strategic point of view, trading ideas are related to a *relative value analysis* (RVA). RVA means using quantitative indicators, primarily based on spread levels, to derive the current relative value of a bond (compared to its own history, to similar names, or to an index). Despite fundamental analysis, a bond can be cheap or dear versus a specific comparable, e.g., another bond of the issuer or a similarly rated company from the same industry. This relative value perspective is crucial for curve trades (playing the credit curve of an issuer) or switch ideas.

Active Credit Portfolio Management. J. Felsenheimer, P. Gisdakis, and M. Zaiser
Copyright © 2006 WILEY-VCH Verlag GmbH & Co. KGaA, Weinheim
ISBN: 3-527-50198-3

Here, we repeat briefly the most important RVA measures, which we explained in section 2.1. The simple idea behind this is identifying over- and undervalued securities.

The crucial figure in an RVA is the spread of a specific bond, which is derived by market prices and underlying assumptions, such as those concerning the yield curve and calculation methods. As we highlighted in section 2.1, adequate spread measures in an RVA framework are the asset swap spread and the Z-spread. As both have specific shortcomings and advantages, it depends on the specific bond and on the incentive of the trade as to which spread measure is the most appropriate one. We refer simply to spread (without determining which one we use) in the following explanations.

Besides the spread of a bond, there are several indicators that can be used within an RVA (as we already explained in section 2.1):

- The Z-score takes the difference between the current spread with its trailing average and measures it in units of standard deviations, making different bonds with different spread levels comparable. Normally this number is between +2 (significantly cheap) and −2 (significantly expensive).
- The beta of an individual bond compares the issue to a reference universe, also calculated on a spread basis. A beta greater (or smaller) than 1 means that if the spread of a reference index increases by 1 bp, the spread of the bond will increase more (or less) than 1 bp on average. Betas are usually calculated versus the overall universe, versus the respective rating class, and versus the sector in which the bond is included.
- Breakeven spread changes represent the number of basis points the spread of a bond can widen over a set period of time before the total return on the credit exceeds that of an investment in a risk-free asset, under the assumptions of an unchanged risk-free curve and an unchanged spread to the risk-free curve during the investment horizon. For example, a one-month breakeven of 5 bp means that if the spread to the risk-free curve will widen about 5 bp in one month, the excess return of the bond versus the risk-free investment is zero (the total return of both investments is exactly the same). Breakeven figures are based on the well-known horizon analysis in fixed income markets (roll-down effect).

All these indicators are based on historical data, which means that any trade idea using traditional RVA implicitly incorporates that the world will remain unchanged during the investment horizon. Nevertheless, RVA can provide very interesting insights into the relative pricing, the performance potential, and the risk of a corporate bond. In practice, a bullish investor will prefer a bond that carries a higher spread and that has a higher beta, a lower Z-score, and a higher breakeven figure.

Besides taking directional spread risk in a single bond, playing the credit curve of a frequent issuer (which has several bonds outstanding) is a typical relative value trade. For example, switch ideas including bonds of the same obligor but with different maturities offer the advantage that the idiosyncratic risk component affects both involved instruments in (almost) the same manner.

The basic intention behind switch ideas of bonds with a different maturity but issued by the same company is exploiting the steepness of the credit curve of a company. Credit curves are normally upward sloping, as the risk of default (i.e., the uncertainty about the future credit metrics) increases with time. Only in the distressed debt market or in case of a heavily negative news flow for a company can we observe an inverse credit curve (which is downward sloping). However, demand–supply imbalances (this idea refers to market segmentation theory, a basic approach that tries to explain the slope of the risk-free spot rate curve) can have a significant impact on the credit curve. This might lead to a very flat (or steep) credit curve of an issuer, which argues for selling long-dated paper and shifting exposure into shorter-dated bonds (and vice versa). As we excluded repos in the context of trading ideas due to a lack of liquidity, a curve trade in the cash bond market means selling one issue (which is currently on the book) and buying another bond of the same obligor with a different maturity. Moreover, liquidity restrictions have to be considered when implementing curve trades, as different bonds (although from the same obligor) can differ dramatically with respect to liquidity in secondary markets. Liquidity, in general, is closely linked to the amount issued and is reflected in the bid–ask spread. A large bid–ask spread argues for low liquidity and vice versa.

The same is true for relative value switches between different obligors. These trades rest upon a relative mispricing between two names, in general within the same sector or the same quality class. While typical relative value measures (Z-scores, betas, etc.) can be used to extract value between two names, also a fundamental valuation is necessary to account for the fact that there is a deviating unsystematic risk in bonds of different issuers (in contrast to playing the credit curve of the same issuer).

Unfortunately, relative value opportunities do not last forever, and theoretically they disappear in an efficient market. Therefore, a continuous monitoring of spreads in the secondary market is necessary to exploit market anomalies. At the same time, above-mentioned relative value measures – which can send important signals, while being the basis of relative value ideas – have to be calculated.

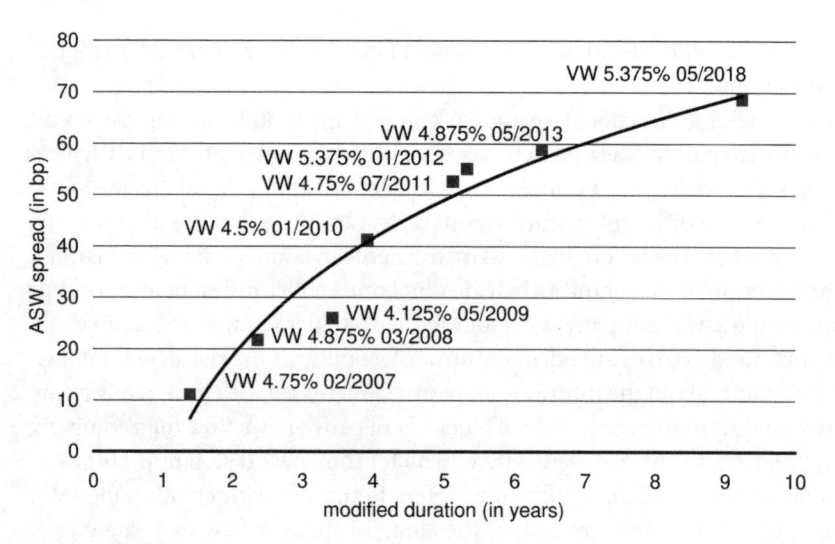

Fig. 17.1: Example of an issuer curve

Relative value trades between different issuers and also curve trades reduce systematic spread risk and the risk of a parallel shift of the credit curve of an issuer. However, these trades are not risk free. A very steep credit curve can steepen further and a spread difference between two issuers might be far from the historical average, but there is no compelling reason why the spread difference will not even become larger. If the asset swap spread (which, in a first step, turns a straight bond into a par floater) is used to calculate relative value measures, one ignores the fact that the cash flows (coupon payments) will most likely occur at different points in time, which can be an issue for asset–liability accounts. In the end, ASW spreads do not take into consideration whether a bond trades at a discount (below par) or at a premium (above par). This also can be a topic for a portfolio manager.

17.2 Trading Strategies with Single-Name CDS

Besides the unfunded nature of credit default swaps, they offer another huge advantage when implementing trade ideas: CDS allow for the easy implementation of both long (selling protection) and short positions (buying protection). This is especially true for trades that combine a short and a long position. Moreover, the standardization of CDS contracts (maturities, calculation methods) makes relative value trades much more efficient.

We introduced a comprehensive overview of CDS valuation in section 10.1. In practice, this can be easily done with the help of, for example, the CDSW function in Bloomberg, which allows the calculation of the P&L impact of a spread move. The SpreadDV01 of a CDS contract determines the impact from a one basis point spread move on the P&L of the CDS position. For example, a SpreadDV01 of 4,500 means that the protection buyer (equal to a short position) will gain €4,500 (0.045%) on a €10 mn CDS position in case of a spread widening of one bp.

In general, trades that combine short and long CDS positions can be set up in two ways: spread neutral or delta neutral (DV01-neutral).

- *Spread neutrality* means that in a long–short trade, the notional amount of the involved contracts is chosen in a way that the trade is spread-carry neutral. Let us assume that 5Y protection on name A and B is quoted at 50 bp and at 100 bp, respectively. Betting on an outperformance of name A versus name B, while keeping the trade spread neutral, would include selling protection on name A on a notional amount of X and buying protection on name B on a notional amount of $0.5 \times X$. The premium cash flows of the two positions offset each other (-0.5×100 bp $+ 50$ bp) and the trade generates profit in case name A outperforms name B on a spread basis.
- The alternative to a spread-neutral trade is *delta neutrality* (or SpreadDV01-adjusted trades). The notional amounts of involved CDS contracts are adjusted to keep the SpreadDV01s neutral, focusing on generating profit via a positive spread carry. In general, this is the mechanism used in curve and correlation trades. Let us assume that 5Y protection on name A is quoted at 50 bp with a SpreadDV01 of 4,000 and 10Y protection on the same name is quoted at 110 bp with a SpreadDV01 of 8,000 (this is a simplification; in reality SpreadDV01s are not proportional to the contract term). Betting on a stable slope of the credit curve and being hedged versus parallel shifts of the spread curve of name A would include buying 5Y protection on a notional amount of X and selling 10Y protection on a notional amount of $0.5 \times X$. This trade is P&L neutral in case of a parallel shift of the credit curve and generates a positive spread carry of 10 bp on the notional amount $0.5 \times X$.

17.2.1 Plain-Vanilla CDS Trades

The basic trade, which is also involved in all combined positions, is outright buying or selling protection via CDS. The intention of this trade is taking directional spread risk, that is, anticipating spread widening or spread tightening in a name. Finding opportunities in the CDS universe is based on the same idea as is the case in the cash universe. Relative value analysis, which we discussed with respect to the cash market, can be easily translated into the CDS world.

However, there is a major difference between cash bonds and CDS regarding the termination of a trade. In the cash universe, a purchase of a bond, which should be sold later on, can be easily performed with different counterparties. This is simply the case as all cash flows associated with the bond are shifted at the purchase of the bond from the seller to the buyer (including accrued). In the CDS world, an offsetting transaction is necessary to lock in the profit (or loss) of a transaction. Let us assume that an investor enters a long protection position at a spread X on issuer A which is executed with counterparty 1. The trade generates profit in case of a spread widening. If protection is becoming more expensive (spread widening), the protection buyer can now sell protection at a spread Y, with Y being greater than X, performed with counterparty 2. Consequently, the investor locked in the spread difference between Y and X, which he receives on a quarterly basis (CDS standard). Adding the discounted spread payments up to maturity is the expected profit of the position. The problem is, however, that this is only true for the premium leg of the CDS contract. In case of default, the future spread income will be lost, as both contracts (the long and the short position) will be settled, matching each other perfectly. Against this background, terminating the CDS contract will be the proper way to close the trade. Termination means that both initial counterparties agree to terminate the contract. Future premium legs will be discounted and prepaid (back-end payment).

17.2.2 Switch Ideas

Switch ideas in the CDS market are based on the same idea as in the abovementioned cash trade. An investor is betting on the outperformance of one obligor (sell protection) versus another obligor (buy protection), while reducing systematic spread risk (which is assumed to affect both positions in a similar way). Due to the standardization of CDS contracts, duration mismatch, which is often a problem when performing switch ideas in the cash universe, can be ignored. The simple implementation of short positions underpins the execution of switch ideas using CDS.

In general, these trades are set up on a delta-neutral basis. That said, an investor is selling protection on an undervalued name at spread X and buying protection on an overvalued name at spread Y. If X exceeds Y, the trade generates a positive spread carry and creates additional performance in case of a relative spread widening of Y versus X. Due to the highest liquidity of the 5Y segment, switch ideas will be primarily performed in this maturity bracket without taking additional curve risk on the book (5Y short versus 5Y long).

17.2.3 Curve Trades

We already discussed the idea behind curve trades with respect to cash bonds. In the CDS market, the maturity standardization allows one to easily implement curve trading strategies. 1Y, 3Y, 5Y, 7Y, and 10Y CDS contracts are actively traded on more liquid names. The credit curve of an issuer reflects the implied default probabilities (please refer also to hazard rates in chapter 7) for different maturities and is, in general, upward sloping as the risk of default increases over time. However, the steepness of the credit curve varies over time and might offer attractive trading opportunities.

There are two basic curve trades: steepeners and flatteners.

- The rationale behind curve steepener trades is that the investor expects a steepening of the credit curve, that is, an outperformance of the short end versus the long end of the credit curve. A steepening of the credit curve goes, in general, hand-in-hand with spread widening, that is, a bearish market environment. In an optimized credit cycle, a steepening of credit curves indicates the beginning of a general spread widening trend, and hence a steepener fits with an anticipated trend reversal in credit markets from a bullish into a bearish scenario. A steepener includes buying protection on a longer-dated CDS contract and selling protection on a shorter-dated CDS contract. The combined position will generate a profit in case of a *bear steepener* (the short end of the curve tightens) and in case of a *bull steepener* (the long end of the curve widens).
- The rationale behind curve flattener trades is that the investor anticipates a flattening of the credit curve, that is, an outperformance of the long end versus the short end of the credit curve. A flattening of the credit curve is in general driven by a more bullish view on credits and consequently goes hand-in-hand with spread tightening. In an optimized credit cycle, a

flatter credit curve marks the end of a spread tightening cycle, and hence a flattener fits with an anticipated trend reversal in credit markets from a bearish into a bullish scenario. A flattener includes buying protection on a shorter-dated CDS contract and selling protection on a longer-dated CDS contract. The combined position will generate a profit in case of a *bear flattener* (the short end of the curve widens) and in case of a *bull flattener* (the long end of the curve tightens).

17.3 Portfolio Derivatives Trades

In this section, we discuss trading ideas which involve (linear) portfolio derivatives. As shown in the model section, a linear portfolio CDS is a basket of equally weighted single-name CDS which act also as the basis for portfolio trades. In the following, we will use the most liquid and transparent portfolio CDS, the iTraxx baskets. The principle remains the same for other portfolio derivatives, but its standardized character makes the iTraxx universe the most used portfolio CDS. In addition, time series are available back to June 2004.

The iTraxx universe offers the opportunity to implement various trading strategies, including plain-vanilla intra-iTraxx trades (e.g., name versus sector and sector versus sector trades) as well as more sophisticated cross asset strategies and correlation strategies (iTraxx default baskets and tranches). It can also be used as the risky asset in CPPI strategies. Without claiming completeness, we describe the basic thinking of implementing and analyzing the payoff structures of such trading strategies.

17.3.1 Single Name versus Sector or Market

Through a combined single-name CDS and portfolio CDS position, an investor tries to exploit an under- or overvaluation of a single name versus a target index (in which it is included), betting on directional idiosyncratic spread risk.

Using relative value and/or fundamental analysis, an investor might conclude that a specific name is relatively dear compared to an index. Then the investor buys protection on the name and sells protection on the target index and vice versa in case the investor considers a specific name as undervalued (trades cheap versus the index). Combining single-name and portfolio derivatives is set up in a SpreadDV01-neutral way in general (using the same maturity bracket, DV01s of different names or indices deviate only slightly). Consequently, these kinds of trades are rather spread focused, betting on a relative outperformance or underperformance of a name compared to the target index and/or generating positive spread income.

17.3.2 Core–Satellite Strategies

We see the establishment of a liquid credit index (like iTraxx instruments) as a perfect tool for smaller clients to implement core–satellite strategies. A core–satellite investment strategy in the credit universe includes building up exposure to a market by buying a well-diversified index (the core investment), while reducing or increasing idiosyncratic or sector risks (satellites). This is an attractive strategy especially for smaller clients who do not have the support of a group of analysts to analyze each particular name in the universe.

The implementation of this approach is straightforward due to the equal-weighted nature of iTraxx indices. The only restriction could be an investment volume that is too low to hedge for single index constituents. Assuming a €5 mn long position in the iTraxx Europe Benchmark implies that the investor carries single-name exposure of €40,000. This is not a sufficient size for a CDS contract. A similar problem arises even in the case of a sector hedge. An investor who wants to hedge against sector-specific risk in automobiles (which amounts to 8 percent) of the iTraxx Europe Benchmark has to buy protection on a notional amount of €400,000. Besides the bid–offer problematic (which prevents a theoretically perfect hedge), the price for a small notional amount may differ from the price for tradable sizes.

Let's assume an investor who wants to sell protection on the iTraxx Europe Automobiles 5Y index for a notional amount of €10 mn. However, the investor has a negative view on VW, which has a 10 percent stake within the index. A delta neutral overall position requires a €1 mn long protection position in VW. We assume a current spread of the iTraxx Europe Automobiles of 45 bp and 5Y protection for VW trades at 80 bp. In case VW spreads widen by 10 bp, the iTraxx position would generate a loss of €4,650, while the long protection position in VW would generate a profit of €4,515 (using the CDSW function in Bloomberg; standard settings). However, this trade is not spread neutral in general. An investor has to pay 80 bp on €1 mn, while he receives 45 bp on €10 mn. That said, the costs for hedging one-tenth of the index exposure does, in general, not equal 10 percent of the amount received for the long investment in the iTraxx, which is related to the fact that usually spread dispersion exists. Only in case all sector constituents trade with the same CDS spread would the above-mentioned hedge be carry neutral.

17.3.3 Sector and Segment Trades

In the previous example, we pointed out hedging and trading strategies on a single-name basis. The incentive for such a single-name hedge is to eliminate or to bet on idiosyncratic risk. Such pure alpha bets are primarily embedded in bottom-up portfolio management processes. Investors who implement instead a beta-managed top-down approach to run their credit portfolios would prefer to use subindices to reduce and/or build up additional exposure to single industries.

As all subindices of the iTraxx Europe Benchmark carry similar strike spreads (please refer to the index description section 2.6), the dispersion on an industry level is much smaller than on a single-name basis. Hence, the divergence between delta and carry neutrality is much smaller regarding benchmark–sector trades.

Beta management on a sector level includes the active weighting of single industries in case the investor expects an out- and/or underperformance potential of single sectors. An iTraxx Europe Benchmark investor who is bullish on telecom bonds (20/125) and bearish on the automobile sector (10/125) could switch from the latter to the former by buying protection on automobiles in the amount of 10/125 of the notional amount, while selling protection on telecoms in the same amount. Assuming all indices are trading at their initial strike spread of 45 bp, the trade position is nearly (ignoring dispersion effects) delta and carry neutral. In case the auto sector widened by 10 bp, the overall index should approximately widen by 0.8 bp. Multiplied by the notional amount, the PV impact on the overall position is nearly zero. A spread tightening of the telecom sector by 10 bp would generate a gain on the total position of $30/125 \times 10$ bp in spread terms. In terms of PV (assuming an initial notional amount of €10 mn), a 10 bp tightening (only) in telecoms would generate a profit of €3,714 in the former automobile position (notional amount of €800,000), a profit of €7,463 in the iTraxx Europe Benchmark position (€10 mn), while the long protection position in the auto sector remains unaffected.

The iTraxx universe also offers the opportunity for relative value trades on a segment level, as there is a high-grade and a high-yield basket swap tradable. The motivation for trading market segments is primarily driven by relative value analysis and a bet on a directional market trend, without an exact view with respect to the timing of the trend. Taking directional risk is based on the historical spread difference between two market segments and the assumption of a mean-reverting process of this spread difference (in other words, assuming that this difference will not hold forever). In case the spread difference significantly deviates from the historical average, an investor can bet on a return to the average spread by selling protection on the undervalued segment and buying protection on the overvalued segment. This trade is clearly coupled to a directional market view that one segment will underperform another. A bullish investor will implement a long position in the more risky segment and sell the more defensive segment and vice versa in case of a bearish market view. This trade is set up spread neutral or spread positive in general, which reduces the importance of the timing of the decision. In case an investor is bullish and implements the above-mentioned trade, a positive or neutral spread carry means that the costs of carry of the trade are at least zero in case the spread between both segments will remain unchanged. The faster the expected market move occurs (spread tightening), the faster the trade generates money, while the investor only loses money on a marked-to-market basis if the intersegment spread moves in the opposite direction.

Investors who want to benefit from an underperformance of lower qualities can purchase credit risk in the high-grade universe, while implementing a short position in the high-yield index. An investor can sell protection in the iTraxx Europe Benchmark 5Y swap at 29.5 bp with a notional amount of 12.7 times the notional amount of the iTraxx Europe Crossover contract. This leaves a positive carry of 188.65 bp with respect to the notional amount of the iTraxx Europe Crossover contract. This position is largely delta neutral, as the beta of the Crossover index with regard to the Benchmark is quite high. He can sell protection in the iTraxx Europe Benchmark 5Y swap at 29.5 bp with a notional amount of 6.3 times the notional amount of the iTraxx Europe Crossover contract. Thus, the trade is carry neutral but is not completely hedged with regard to market spread risk.

17.3.4 Trading the Skew

The so-called skew (also known as the basis to theoretical) refers to the difference between the quoted spread of an index swap contract (e.g., the iTraxx Europe Benchmark) and the theoretically fair value spread level. The fair value spread level is derived from the sum of CDS spreads of all index constituents. The skew allows for a comparison between single-name and basket CDS markets within the credit derivatives universe. As we showed in section 10.3, the existence of the skew is theoretically verified. A rule of thumb is that the higher the spread level, the higher the skew (e.g., the skew in the iTraxx Crossover index exceeds the skew in the iTraxx Europe index), while the skew in case of rather subdued spread levels of the index and the index members (e.g., for high-quality credits from the AA segment) is almost negligible.

The iTraxx universe developed into the most liquid unfunded credit product, even exceeding liquidity in the single-name CDS market. The skew is also attributable to liquidity in basket swaps compared to the liquidity in single-name CDS contracts. In a bullish market environment, the skew is declining (the skew can become negative) as investors who want to build up credit exposure significantly will use the most liquid instrument, the credit index/basket. This drives the index spread tighter, while the (indicative) pricing adjustment of the spreads of the index constituents will be delayed. In contrast, a bearish market sentiment argues for an increasing skew as the index will be sold (buying protection) first. In figure 17.2, we demonstrate that the skew is not stable over time. This means that trading the skew can be an attractive trading opportunity, also providing a tool for arbitrage players.

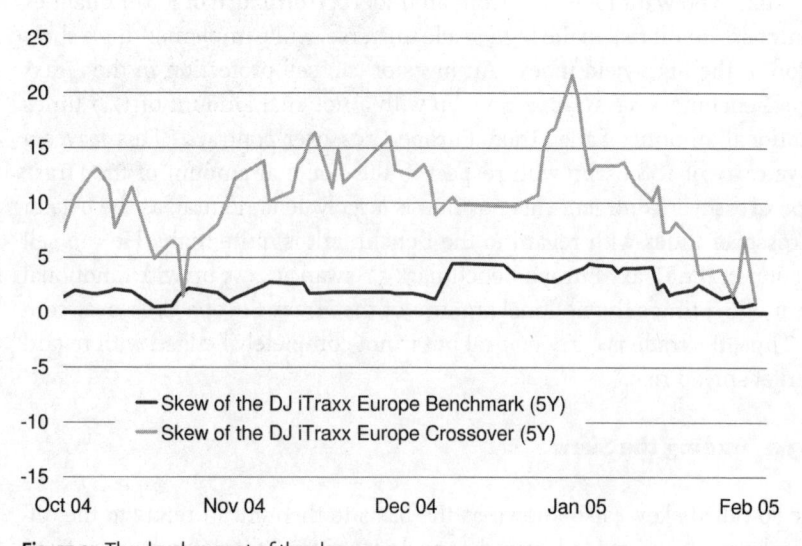

Fig. 17.2: The development of the skew

There are two trading strategies directly focusing on the skew. If the skew reached levels that are theoretically not verified, an investor can directly take skew risk by trading the underlying names versus the overall index. Taking transaction costs into account, this trade only makes sense in case of a limited index (e.g., an iTraxx sector basket), which includes very liquid names. In case the skew is in highly positive terrain, buying protection on the single names is cheaper than buying protection on the index. Consequently, the investor will buy protection on the single names and sell protection on the index, taking a directional view on a declining basis. If the basis declines, the long position (selling protection on the index) will outperform the short position (buying protection on the index constituents) in any case. The combined position is immune to the general trend of credit spreads as the skew is completely isolated.

Also arbitrage players have a look at the skew, which offers the opportunity to implement a delta-neutral carry trade. Assuming that the skew is sufficiently large and positive, arbitrage players would set up the above-mentioned trade (purchasing protection on single names and selling protection on the index), betting on positive spread income rather than on a decline of the basis. The spread income of this trade is positive, while spread risk and default risk are (almost) eliminated when the risk assessment is taken at maturity of the trade. However, arbitrage is somewhat misleading as this trade suffers from market-value fluctuations of an even stronger market anomaly. Even in case the skew is irrationally large, there is no law which prevents the skew from becoming even larger. The risk of this trade is simple skew risk, namely the risk that market anomalies might even aggravate. This was exactly the case with the crisis in 1998, when market-value changes forced the hedge fund LTCM (Long Term Capital Management) to close positions, which certainly would have generated a profit at maturity.

17.3.5 Basis Trades

In section 16.2, we highlighted the principles of hedging cash portfolios using portfolio derivatives. A major risk factor of these hedging strategies is the *basis*, which is the difference between the CDS level and the asset swapped cash bond spread. On a single-name level, the basis can also be a reason to enter a trade by implementing opposite positions in the cash bond and in the credit derivatives market.

Although CDS and cash bond spreads are primarily driven by the same idiosyncratic risk factors at first glance, there are fundamental and technical reasons for the deviation between CDS quotes and cash bond spreads. In the following, we analyze different factors that influence the basis.

In general, the basis is positive, which is underpinned by theory (see table 17.1) and verified from a historical perspective. However, the basis is also driven by the underlying market trend and by liquidity. This is consistent with the arguments we discussed with respect to the skew. As CDS have a front-running character, a bullish market environment argues for a declining basis (which even can beat down the basis into negative terrain) and a bearish market environment

Tab. 17.1: Basis drivers

Impact	Basis effect	Comment
Counterparty risk	↓	Additional risk in bilateral CDS contracts
Funding issues	↓	Above Libor funding/unfunded nature of CDS
Market structure	↓	Short positions implemented in CDS markets
Volatility/Convertible trading	↑	Convertible players hedge credit risk via CDS
Market sentiment	↑↓	Front-running nature of default swaps
Cheapest-to-delivery option	↑	Delivery option favors default swaps
Repo anomalies	↑	Repo optionality of the cash investors
Profit realization	↑	Offsetting trade: Investor remains long
CPN stepups	↓	Step-up features favor cash investors
Technical default risk	↑	Different default definitions for cash and CDS

argues for a widening basis. Basis trades offer an interesting opportunity to extract value from swings in the pricing relation between cash bonds and CDS. In case the default swap trades below its cash peer, a negative basis trade (buying the bond and buying protection) position is usually attractive. If the basis is positive, a positive basis trade (selling the cash bond and selling protection) would be the appropriate trade. In any case, those trades are not risk-free! The risk is reflected in basis swings, related to the above-mentioned factors.

17.3.6 First-to-Default Baskets

First-to-default baskets (FTD) are the most basic correlation instruments and have been rather tailor-made products at the beginning of the correlation market. The advent of the standardized iTraxx FTD baskets increased the liquidity in this market significantly. In the following, we discuss how these products – involving spread and correlation risk – can be used for interesting investment strategies.

The basic risk of an FTD basket is that the underlying obligors experience a credit event, regardless of which one. Hence, it is quite obvious that such an FTD contract is more risky than a single-name CDS: the latter involves only risk with respect to one default trigger, while the FTD basket refers to several default triggers.

It is true that an FTD basket itself is not a diversified investment (if investors seek such an investment they should consider iTraxx baskets), but it is an important building block for diversified investment strategies. In the following, we illustrate such strategies based on two examples: one with selling protection and one with buying protection in the FTD.

We start the analysis with a simple example and will subsequently derive two real trading opportunities using the standardized iTraxx FTD baskets. Think of a portfolio of three names: credit A has a spread of 50 bp, credit B one of 100 bp, and credit C one of 150 bp. We assume an average recovery rate of 50 percent. The time to maturity of the contract is five years. In table 17.2, we compiled the important data for the FTD basket valuation, separated by single-name and basket data.

The probability of default for each underlying was approximated by $PD \approx 1 - \exp(\text{spread}/(1 - \text{recovery rate}) \times \tau)$, with τ being the time to maturity. Hence, the PD for credit A with a spread of 50 bp cumulated up to the maturity of five years is 4.88 percent. On the right side of table 17.2, we give the probability for exactly 0, 1, 2, and 3 defaults separately. These numbers were derived using the Hull-White model for default baskets in conjunction with a single-factor, Gaussian-copula default dependency model. Inputs to the model are the single-name PDs and an average default correlation. We calculated the basket for 10 percent and 90 percent default correlation. For an FTD basket, the central quantity is the survival probability of basket (i.e., the probability of zero defaults). For 10 percent default correlation the survival probability amounts to 74.83 percent, while for 90 percent correlation the survival probability for the FTD basket is higher: 84.20 percent.

Tab. 17.2: Single-name and default-basket data

	Single-name data		Basket data		
	Credit Spread	Probability of default (PD)	Number of defaults	PD for 10% correlation	PD for 90% correlation
A	50 bp	4.88%	0	74.83%	84.20%
B	100 bp	9.52%	1	22.17%	7.28%
C	150 bp	13.93%	2	2.85%	4.53%
SOS	300 bp		3	0.15%	3.99%
Recovery	50% avg.		FTD spread	290 bp	172 bp
			% of SOS	96.64%	57.33%

Finally, we have to reconvert the survival probability of the basket to a basket spread. We approximate this step simply by inverting the above-mentioned approximation to derive the PD from the credit spread. This results in spread $\approx -(1 - \text{recovery rate}) \times \ln(1 - PD)/\tau$. Here $(1 - PD)$ is the survival probability, or 74.83 percent for the 10 percent FTD basket.

The calculation results in an FTD spread of 290 bp for the 10 percent correlation basket and in a spread of 172 bp for the 90 percent basket. Here, we can see the important characteristics of FTD baskets. Their spreads remain within the range of the highest spread in the underlying basket (in this case 150 bp for credit C) for a correlation that approaches 100 percent and the sum-of-all-spreads (SOS, here it is 300 bp) if the default correlation is zero. Therefore, most market makers quote the FTD basket spread also as a percentage of the SOS. Based on these examples, there are two investment strategies.

- Strategy 1 (sell FTD protection): If the default correlation is low, an investor can get exposure to the names in the basket by investing in an FTD basket. The basket spread will be close to the sum-of-all-spreads. Hence, investing €100 in the FTD basket generates a similar spread income as investing €100 in each underlying name (amounting to an investment of €300). That said, the risky exposure of the FTD basket strategy is significantly lower (only one third). In our example, the trade would generate a spread income of 290 bp (10 percent default correlation), which equals roughly 97 percent of the sum-of-all-spreads.
- Strategy 2 (buy FTD protection): If the implied default correlation is higher than the investor anticipates, he can cheaply hedge an exposure in credits A, B, and C with an FTD basket. While the hedge costs in basis points are only slightly higher than the spread of the most risky basket constituent (credit C trades at 150 bp), it refers to all names in the basket. Implementing such a strategy would involve selling protection on all underlying credits, and buying protection on the FTD basket. In our example, this would generate a spread income of 128 bp (= 300 bp–172 bp). This is only slightly below the spread income the investor would earn on an outright long position in credits A and B.

One disadvantage in customized FTD baskets is that bid–ask spreads can be quite large, as liquidity is limited. However, if the investor feels comfortable with a standardized basket, then he can choose FTD baskets available for the iTraxx universe. This family offers baskets for each iTraxx sector: autos, consumer, energy, industrials, TMT, financials senior/sub, and a diversified basket (across all sectors), a HiVol, and a crossover basket.

As an example, the diversified basket in the iTraxx Series 3 spectrum (consisting of Bayer, France Telecom, HypoVereinsbank, Marks & Spencer, Suez, and Volkswagen) pays an FTD spread that is 79 percent of the SOS in July 2005. Hence, the investor can get exposure to these names and earns about 80 percent of the spread income for an investment in all names, but has just a sixth of the exposure.

17.3.7 iTraxx Tranches versus Default Baskets

Synthetic CDO tranches and n^{th}-to-default (NTD) baskets are similar financial products. In contrast to single-name derivatives like CDS they are based on a portfolio of credit-risky assets. For a portfolio manager, they provide good protection against the risk of an adverse clustering of defaults at lower costs than hedging all individual exposures with single-name CDS. A protection seller might achieve an attractive premium and gain leveraged exposure to a portfolio of credits, which might be inaccessible otherwise. For both derivative structures, default correlation is the name of the game in order to model the payoff profile and the value. But for valuation purposes, a superficial analysis of the structures may lead to poor results, since a CDO tranche is not just a bunch of NTD baskets. The NTD basket involves the probability of a certain number of defaults, while for CDO tranches one needs the probability of an accumulated realized loss. A simple example sheds some light on the differences.

Regarding the mechanism of a first-to-default basket, the legal construction as well as the trigger event are similar to a single credit default swap (for analyzing default baskets, we recommend to use the CDSN function on Bloomberg). In case of a credit event, the protection seller pays

$$(1 - \text{recovery rate}) \times \text{notional amount of the defaulted issue}$$

to the protection buyer (cash settlement), or the protection buyer hands over deliverable obligations and receives the notional amount (physical settlement). Following the first default, the FTD contract is terminated and the protection buyer loses any further protection for the other basket constituents. As the protection buyer is only insured against the first default, the basket spread is below the sum of the CDS levels of all basket credits. A basket is attractive for both counterparties. From the protection buyer's standpoint, the protection fee is cheaper compared to CDS on single names, while the protection seller gains leveraged exposure to a basket of credits as it enables the investor to earn a higher yield than any of the credits in the basket. In any case, the protection seller has to closely monitor his delta and gamma positions, as these are highly sensitive to price changes of the underlying credits and can be interpreted as additional risk components.

Besides the risk of default, the issuer of a default basket is exposed to spread swings (as he carries a short position in credit risk), which could be hedged by selling protection via CDS. In case the spread of one or more portfolio constituent changes, the protection buyer's initial position is over- or underhedged. For the implementation of optimal hedging strategies, the hedge ratio needs to be determined (i.e., Which notional amount must be sold?), and this requires knowing the spread delta of the position. Besides the problem of determining portfolio Greeks, using historical data, or modeling those stochastic processes, negative spillover effects on the spread of the remaining issues could cause a loss when the position is unwound in case of a default of one basket constituent. Another possibility for an investor in an FTD to hedge against default is to buy protection for a combination of NTD baskets (please refer to the following paragraph), including similar credits. The problem of this strategy is to find counterparties who are willing to sell protection on similar baskets.

Besides the difficulty of determining sensitivities for a delta hedge, hedgers via long protection also carry a long position in gamma (sensitivity of the delta with respect to spread changes). In case of spread widening of a basket credit, the delta will rise and the basket is overhedged. Hence, the hedger will try to sell protection at wider levels. In case of narrowing spreads, the basket is underhedged and the hedger will buy back protection at lower levels. Therefore, accelerating spread volatility favors the hedger and could help compensate for the negative carry of a hedged FTD basket. However, the possibility of dynamic hedging is overestimated as adjustment trades to spread changes are limited because of the (at least for the time being) lack of liquidity for individually structured products and CDS on exotic names in secondary markets. Moreover, due to the small deal size of baskets (single-digit million area), dynamic hedging requires the investor to sell or buy credit risk in very small portions (let's say €20,000), which is not realistic. By the way, maturity mismatch could be another problem, as CDS markets lose significant liquidity regarding non-standardized maturities.

Usually, CDO tranches and NTD baskets focus on different portfolio sizes. A typical NTD basket contains up to ten reference entities, while the portfolio underlying a CDO transaction might be larger, up to a few hundred credits (e.g., the recently established tranched iTraxx products). For our analysis, we assume a portfolio of ten single-name CDS contracts. For the sake of simplicity, we further assume that all CDS are written on the same volume (i.e., 10 percent of the total volume) and involve a uniform, non-stochastic recovery rate of say 40 percent. These assumptions are crucial for the following discussion, given their impact on the pricing of CDOs and default baskets.

The similarity of both structures becomes obvious if we make clear that the first-to-default CDS is related to the first 10 percent volume of the portfolio, the second to 10 to 20 percent volume, and so on. Thus, a naive (or rule-of-thumb) approach would suggest that a hypothetical 10–40% tranche of a CDO is the same as a portfolio of a second-, third-, and fourth-to-default CDS. If we knew the spread of the NTD baskets, we could easily calculate the fair spread of the tranche by taking the average spread of the related NTD baskets.

Why is this approach wrong? The first and most obvious reason is recovery. Tranche derivative products are usually defined in such a way that just the realized losses eat into the tranches. The first default hits the first-to-default CDS, but since there will be a recovery payment, the loss of the first default will not completely extinguish 10 percent of the outstanding portfolio notional amount. So there will be something left from the 0–10% tranche after the first default. One difference lies in the fact that, in the case of a default, the first-to-default investor has to pay the notional amount, receives the recovery, and the game is over. While the tranche investor suffers a decline in the outstanding balance, he still receives the premium on the rest of the tranche. Clearly, we could adjust the tranches to cover this problem. In our example, we would define a 0–6% tranche. But then we will face the next problem: the uncertainty of the recovery payment. Most probably, it will not be exactly 40 percent, but will deviate from the expected value quite substantially. But since we want to stick to our example, we suppress all these recovery problems with a brave assumption: zero recovery.

We admit that this is unrealistic but it helps to explain a second problem. We compare the portfolio of a second-, third-, and fourth-to default CDS with the 10–40% tranche. Now let there be two defaults that strike our portfolio and both derivative structures suffer. Since there will be no recovery, both lose a third of their volume. What is the difference between the portfolio of NTD baskets and the tranche? The CDS investor says goodbye to his second-to-default swap. On his remaining portfolio, he now receives the average of the spread of third- and the fourth-to-default swap, which will certainly be lower than the average spread just before the default, since the NTD spread decreases with an increasing number of assets. Additionally, he earns this reduced spread on a reduced outstanding notional amount. He gets punished on the spread and on the volume. In comparison to that, the situation for the tranche investor seems to be more comfortable; he just faces a loss on the tranche volume. The spread he receives on the remaining volume is fixed.

We conclude that investment strategies have different payments in the premium leg but the same realization in the default leg. These different payments will be reflected in the pricing. Thus, for pricing a CDO tranche we cannot just take the average price of the corresponding NTD baskets. From a modeling point of view, the NTD involves modeling the number of defaults, while for the CDO tranches the accumulated realized loss is of high importance.

While there is no rule of thumb with respect to the spread difference between a default basket portfolio and a tranche product (including the same credits), in our example the spread on the tranche is lower than the average spread of the basket portfolio.

17.3.8 Playing the Steepness of the iTraxx Curve

With the introduction of Series 3 in March 2005, there are now four maturities in the iTraxx universe (3Y, 5Y, 7Y, and 10Y). Investors can easily implement their view towards the average steepness of credit curves. The motivation behind this is consistent with single-name steepener or flattener trades, which we highlighted above. In the following example, we anticipate the flattening of credit curves, with the short end underperforming the long end (e.g., due to rising risk aversion). In the following, we depict the mechanics of a possible flattener trade utilizing the 5Y and the 10Y iTraxx Benchmark swaps.

Before introducing a possible trading constellation, we should be aware of which criteria could be important in such a context. The trade should not involve a downside risk in case of default, which means that the long position in credit risk (selling protection) shall not exceed the short position (buying protection). Additionally, the trade should not generate negative spread carry in order to avoid any negative cash flows. If possible, the P&L impact of a parallel shift of the iTraxx credit curve should be minimized. However, accomplishing all three objectives with only two contract types is usually not possible due to a missing degree of freedom. This is why we start with the first two goals and assess the third one afterwards.

Against this background, a possible trading structure may look like this:

- Buy protection in the 5Y iTraxx Benchmark swap at 37.5 bp (ask quote).
- Sell protection in the 10Y iTraxx Benchmark swap at 50 bp (bid quote). The notional amount of this contract is adjusted to carry neutrality, amounting to 37.5/50 = 0.75 times that of the first contract.

The concept behind the trade is to gain from a spread widening at the short end (5Y) while anticipating rough stability in the 10Y bracket. Even though a 10Y credit index swap shows a longer duration and therefore a higher sensitivity to spread changes than the 5Y contract, the maturity mismatch is to a large extent offset by the reduced notional amount (0.75 versus the proportion of duration of about 0.59). In the following table we point out the structure of the trade:

The first two scenarios correspond to settings where the spread curve performs a parallel shift upwards and downwards. The impact on the total PV is

Tab. 17.3: Different scenarios for a trading recommendation*

	Current spreads	Trade position	Scenario 1 upward shift	Scenario 2 downward shift	Scenario 3 40% flattening
5Y iTraxx swap	36.5 / 37.5	Buy protection	42.0	32.0	42.6
10Y iTraxx swap	50.0 / 52.0	Sell protection	56.0	46.0	51.0
MTM 5Y swap			+22,464	−27,456	+25,459
MTM 10Y swap			−37,806	+25,204	−6,301
Total MTM			−15,342	−2,252	+19,158

*Indicative levels for October 1, 2004. The calculation is based on a notional amount of €10 mn for the 5Y and €7.5 mn for the 10Y contract. The computation of marked-to-markets changes (MTM) is subject to spread changes immediately after initiation of the trades. MTMs are calculated on mid levels.

rather limited due to the above-mentioned partial duration neutrality. Scenario 3 assumes a decline of the credit curve steepness by 40 percent, leaving the 10Y level unchanged. In this case, the trade generates significant profits, which can be realized by termination of both contracts.

17.4 Spread Options: Single and Complex Strategies

The iTraxx Europe index also acts as an underlying for spread options. Options allow investors to implement simple hedging strategies (portfolio insurance/protective put), and also more complex strategies (straddles, strangles, butterflies, etc.). Standardized spread options are available for the iTraxx Europe and the iTraxx Crossover. There are payer options (calls) and receiver options (puts), with different strike prices (for example 30, 35, 40, 45, 50 for the iTraxx Europe Series 4), as well as straddles (combining receiver and payer options). The expiration dates are scheduled on three, six, and nine months at the introduction date of a new series. Spread options are quoted in bp, with implied at-the-money volatility (ATM volatility) also being quoted.

Hedging strategies for credit portfolios (portfolio insurance strategies) or long positions in iTraxx indices (protective put) could be easily implemented. Trading strategies include complex strategies like straddles, strangles, butterflies, condors, and so on. These strategies are well known from equity derivatives markets and hence we abstain from a detailed analysis.

We already discussed in section 10.2 that the major problem is linked to the pricing of the option. An exact definition of an investor's risk positions (the Greeks: delta, gamma, vega, and theta) requires an appropriate pricing model. A possible approach is to use the Black-Scholes framework, extended by a stochastic jump process to cover the problem that credit spread swings are not log-normally distributed. While the Black-Scholes approach is widely accepted, the problem lies, in our view, in determining the parameters for the jump process. Jump intensity and jump width, the two major parameters for a jump process vary significantly over time. Estimating jump processes depends heavily on the market environment. As long as there is no standard model to price spread options, investors are exposed to model risk. An investor may calculate the theoretically fair price of the option correctly, but all other market players use different models and calculate different prices. In this case, P&L realization would be affected.

We divide option strategies into directional trades and volatility trades:

- Directional trades: Option strategies can be implemented to take leveraged exposure to directional spread swings. An investor who wants to benefit from a spread widening trend would purchase out-of-the-money payer options; and in case of expected spread tightening, receiver options are the appropriate instrument. The payoff profiles of directional strategies using spread options equal those of plain-vanilla long/short equity option strategies. The option investor can take a leveraged view on credit spreads.
- Volatility trades: As correlation is the crucial parameter of correlation instruments, volatility is crucial for option valuation. Using spread options, an investor can take volatility exposure. If an investor anticipates a more pronounced spread swing (betting on increasing volatility) without knowing the direction of the move, a long straddle strategy pays off. If an investor assumes stable spreads or a decline in volatility, he will sell a straddle (receiving the option premium).

17.5 CPPI Strategies Including iTraxx Indices

Given the well-diversified nature of the iTraxx Europe, the index family could be seen as an interesting risky asset within constant proportion portfolio insurance (CPPI) strategies. In combination with risk-free instruments, an interesting payoff profile could be generated.

The CPPI was introduced in the late 1980s for fixed income and equity instruments, implementing a dynamic asset allocation over time. In a first step, the investor sets a floor equal to the lowest acceptable value of the portfolio.

This determines the *cushion* as the excess of the portfolio value over the floor, which defines the amount allocated to the risky asset by multiplying the cushion by a predetermined multiple (dependent on the riskiness of the asset). Both the floor and the multiple are functions of the investor's risk tolerance and are exogenous to the model, while the total amount allocated to the risky asset is known as the *exposure*. The remaining funds are invested in the risk-free asset, usually AAA-rated government bonds. The higher the multiple, the more the investor will participate in a price increase of the risky asset, while a higher multiple means that the portfolio will approach the floor faster in case of a sustained price drop. As the cushion approaches zero, so does the exposure. This prevents the portfolio value from falling below the floor.

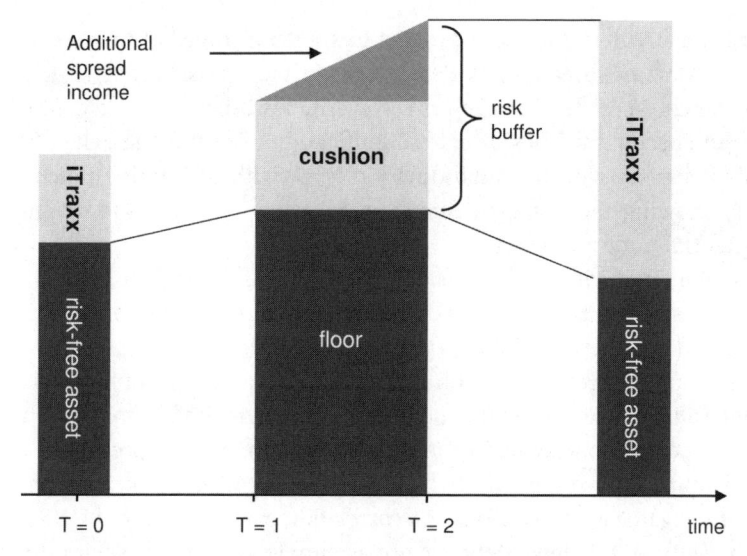

Fig. 17.3: Mechanism of a CPPI strategy using the iTraxx as the riky asset

The major ingredients for a CPPI strategy are a risky asset and a risk-free asset. Therefore, one may think about combining corporate credits and government bonds in such a strategy. While this would lead to a relatively high multiple (as the total return variance of credits is relatively low, i.e., compared to equities), a well-diversified credit index reduces management costs as idiosyncratic risk is already eliminated to a large extent. Dealing with company-specific risk is not the major competence of a CPPI manager.

17.6 Correlation Trading

The standardization of tranched index products (iTraxx tranches) provides a liquid instrument to trade correlation (joint default probabilities), and correlation becomes a separate asset class. There are strong interdependencies between pure spread trading and correlation trading as reflected in the correlation crisis of May 2005, which had a significant impact on credit spreads. In section 10.5, we discussed in detail the mechanism and sensitivities of tranches, focusing on the most liquid instrument in this area, the iTraxx universe (to which we refer in the following). As the understanding of tranche behavior is crucial for setting up trading ideas in the correlation market, we briefly highlight the basic relationships:

- Spread sensitivities: All tranches react to spread changes in the underlying in the same direction. Wider spreads in the iTraxx Europe trigger wider tranche spreads and vice versa. Nevertheless, the spread delta (the DV01) of specific tranches deviates significantly. The tranche delta obviously increases with the subordination level, with the equity tranche (0–3%) showing the highest delta. Spread deltas are crucial to set up delta-neutral trade strategies.
- Correlation sensitivities: The impact of correlation is rather difficult to determine as specific tranches react differently to changes in the correlation parameter (e.g., the probability of joint defaults). For a detailed sensitivity analysis, please refer to section 10.5.3, while a simple rule of thumb is that the value of the equity tranche is positively correlated to correlation (a higher correlation parameter is consistent with tighter spreads, i.e., a lower upfront payment), while higher tranches (AAA, Junior, and Senior) are negatively correlated to the correlation parameter. For the BBB tranche (3–6%), the dependency is not as simple as it changes with the magnitude of correlation. For a low correlation parameter, the sensitivity is negative, while it declines at very high correlation and then behaves like the equity tranche.

Table 10.5 in section 10.5.2 depicts tranche sensitivities, correlation figures, and the P&L impact of spread changes. To calculate tranche deltas properly, traders quote in general the delta exchange (the current spread level of the underlying).

As mentioned above, tranches offer leveraged exposure to credit risk, in our example leveraged exposure to the iTraxx Europe universe. Directional spread risk can be taken by unhedged tranche investments. Assuming a delta of 20 for the equity tranche, the P&L impact from an equity investment equals twenty times the P&L impact of a plain-vanilla index investment. A 1 bp spread widening in the iTraxx Europe generates 0.045 percent profit in a long protection position in the iTraxx Europe, but around 0.9 percent in a short equity position. However, taking directional spread risk through tranched products is rather the exception, while tranches are often used for hedging purposes. The major application for tranched instruments is taking a position on correlation, with the basic implementations being tranche versus index and tranche versus tranche trades. The availability of five liquid tranches in the iTraxx universe offers several potential combinations within the iTraxx index world. In the following, we highlight the basic mechanism of these trades without covering each possible combination.

- Tranche versus index trade: The simplest trade to exploit correlation swings is playing a specific tranche versus the underlying index. An investor who wants to benefit from rising correlation without being exposed to changes in the underlying index spread can buy the equity tranche (sell protection) and hedge spread risk via selling protection on a delta-adjusted amount in the iTraxx Europe. In contrast, benefiting from a declining correlation parameter includes buying protection on the equity piece and selling protection on the index. These trades generate profits when the correlation increases or decline, but it is immune to spread swings. This trade can also be implemented by using other than the equity tranche. Two major risk factors are coupled with these kinds of trades. In the first, changes in spread dispersion within the underlying index (please refer to section 9.7) have a diverse impact on correlation and on deltas, making the trade vulnerable to spread swings. This is exactly what happened in the correlation crisis in May 2005. Second, nonlinearity is the buzzword for correlation traders and means that deltas are not stable over time and change with shifts in the underlying spread. Delta neutrality is only guaranteed for infinitesimal small changes in the index spread, with gamma (the delta of the delta) being the remaining risk factor involved in these trades.
- Tranche versus tranche: The principles of a tranche versus tranche trade equals the above-mentioned mechanism of a tranche versus index trade. Adjusting the notional amount of both positions generates delta neutrality, while achieving positive spread carry combined with taking a long or short correlation position is the main task. This is the appropriate trading strategy for pure correlation gamblers, as the tranches will be chosen in a

way that they react in the same way on the expected correlation move. For example, an investor who will build up a long correlation position without taking direction spread risk would buy the equity piece and hedge spread risk through a short mezzanine position. In case correlation increases, the equity piece will benefit, while the mezzanine tranche will suffer.

17.7 Capital Structure Arbitrage Trades

Typically, capital structure arbitrage involves building up long and short positions in securities (or their derivatives) at different tiers within an issuer's capital structure, maintaining a generally neutral overall exposure to the issuer but exploiting pricing inefficiencies. Instruments included in capital structure arbitrage are primarily senior and subordinated debt, credit derivatives, equity and equity derivatives, as well as convertibles. The basic motivation behind capital structure arbitrage is to benefit from the disparity in prices among the various related securities in anticipation that over time all tiers and classes will become more efficiently priced relative to one another. In the following, we concentrate on debt–equity trades, exploiting pricing anomalies between credit and credit derivatives on the one hand, and equity and equity derivatives on the other hand.

With respect to capital structure arbitrage between high-yield bonds and equity, the capital structure arbitrageur uses a structural model to measure the richness and cheapness of the CDS spread. The model, typically a variant of Merton (1974), predicts spreads based on a company's liability structure and its market value of equities. When the arbitrageur finds that the market spread is substantially larger than the predicted spread, a number of possibilities can be entertained. He might think that the equity market is more objective in its assessment of the price of credit protection, and the CDS market is instead gripped by fear. Alternatively, he might think that the market spread is right and the equity market is slow to react to relevant information. If the first view is correct, the arbitrageur is justified in selling credit protection. If the second view is correct, he should sell equity. In practice, the arbitrageur is probably unsure, so that he does both and profits if the market spread and the model spread converge. The size of the equity position relative to the CDS notional amount is determined by delta hedging.

Unfortunately, arbitrage is not the appropriate expression as in practice, these trades bear some risks. Capital structure arbitrage trades suffer if Merton is wrong. Unfortunately, this happens very often. In section 4.4.2, we already highlighted the shortfalls of classic Merton approaches: Despite these problems there is a failure of the Merton approach which makes the model inaccurate with respect to a crucial factor: the equity–debt ratio. The change in this ratio clearly affects the outcome of the model, as a lower ratio argues for a wider spread (as the risk of a default increases) and vice versa. But the model only works if markets drive relative pricing between different instruments. In case there is a force majeure, a basic mechanism of the model is canceled. This is exactly the case if the capital structure is a goal of the financial policy of a company.

At the beginning of 2005, the most prominent example for a failure of the Merton model was the popular debt–equity trade based on GM. Despite an anticipated downgrade of GM, GM bonds offered attractive carry at the beginning of 2005 and many accounts entered a long position in GM bonds, hedged by short positions in GM shares, which traded relatively stable. Some accounts substituted the short equity position with a long volatility position using GM options. The rationale of the trade was based on the assumption that a spread blowout would be accompanied by a drop in share prices (or an increase in implied option volatility). This is true for the default case, which hits GM bonds but also drives GM shares towards zero and make the trade profitable. In contrast, this is not true in the case of restructuring. Restructuring is also a credit event in terms of CDS contracts (the CDS player is indifferent to default or restructuring as a credit event), while this might be a favorable outcome for the GM shareholder. In this case, spreads blow out and share prices stabilize or even rise. In 2004, nevertheless, this trade generated profit.

Against this backdrop, capital structure arbitrage trading requires the implementation of sophisticated quantitative tools and is primarily performed by proprietary desks of banks and hedge funds. A prerequisite is to monitor all instruments available on a company's capital structure and to derive a relative pricing relationship. There is obviously not only one specific trade strategy but rather a huge number of opportunities, which, however, work consistent with the above-mentioned principles.

17.8 Recovery Trades

Besides the probability of default, the recovery value is one of the key parameters in credit portfolio management. Managing recovery risk is consequently a major task and hence, trading the recovery value will gain in importance, especially in times when credit spreads trade at wide levels and the probability of default is high. While the recovery value is indirectly tradable with a combination of CDS and DDS contracts, recovery default swaps allow investors to take directional exposure to recovery risk.

Recovery default swaps are contracts that fix the recovery rate at the strike level in a forward-style manner and thus eliminate the recovery risk. At initiation of the contract, the counterparties only fix the strike level and the maturity of the contract. In contrast to CDS contracts, there are no premium payments. In case of a credit event, the contract is settled via physical delivery based on the contracted strike level. If no default event occurs, they expire without any exchange of cash flows. A long position in the RDS with a strike of 40 percent, for example, results in a positive payoff if the real recovery rate is above 40 percent. As the contract is forward-styled and not option-styled, it will involve a negative payoff in case the recovery rate is below the strike level.

An investor who assumes the realized recovery value will exceed (fall short of) the implied recovery rate (in standard CDx contracts priced at 40 percent) will perform a long (short) recovery swap. In case of a long recovery swap, the profit of an investor amounts to the positive difference between the realized recovery value and the strike recovery value on the notional amount.

Based on the pricing relation between CDS and DDS, the implied recovery value of the same name can be simply derived. Matching the premium leg of a DDS and a CDS via adjusting the notional amount leaves us with a simple equation for the implied recovery assumption in the CDS contract. Assuming the DDS on name A pays 200 bp (notional amount of €5 mn) and the CDS on name A pays 100 bp (notional amount of €10 mn), the implied recovery in the latter equals $1 - 100/200 = 50$ percent. As long as the recovery swap trades above (below) 50 percent, an investor can set up a CDS/DDS position and buy (sell) a recovery swap. Assuming the implied recovery rate matches the realized recovery rate in case of default, such a trade would generate a profit while being P&L neutral in case of non-default.

17.9 EDS versus CDS and the Role of DDS

The ongoing development of new instruments in credit derivatives markets offers new trading opportunities that try to exploit pricing relationships between these instruments, with equity default swaps, credit default swaps, and digital default swaps on the same reference obligor being the most prominent examples. Following a rule of thumb, and all else being equal, a DDS pays about 1.5 times the premium of a CDS, while an EDS premium amounts roughly to 3 times the respective CDS. Hence, a DDS spread amounts to half the EDS premium. Combining these instruments, one can trade deviating implied volatilities, implied recovery rates, and the expected default barrier.

As mentioned above, an EDS corresponds to a far-out-of-the-money barrier put option. In case the share price drops below a certain threshold (in general 30 percent) of the initial value, the protection seller has to pay the protection amount. In a Merton-like world, a drop of the share price would go hand-in-hand with a sharp increase of the default probability, such as a rising CDS premium. However, a drop of the share price of at least 70 percent does not equal a credit event. It might be a temporary drop that nevertheless causes a trigger event for the EDS, while the company is far from delivering any credit event! The crucial point of the story is where the default barrier is in terms of the share price.

Assuming the default barrier (when a credit event is triggered) corresponds to 30 percent, the value of the EDS equals the CDS in case the recovery rate corresponds to the protection premium for the EDS. In case the default barrier is below 30 percent, the CDS premium must be lower than the EDS premium. In general, the CDS spread amounts to one-third of the EDS spread. If we know the EDS and the CDS levels, we can also easily derive the (in the CDS spread) implied default barrier and consequently can enter a trade based on the implied barrier using the difference between the EDS and the CDS premium.

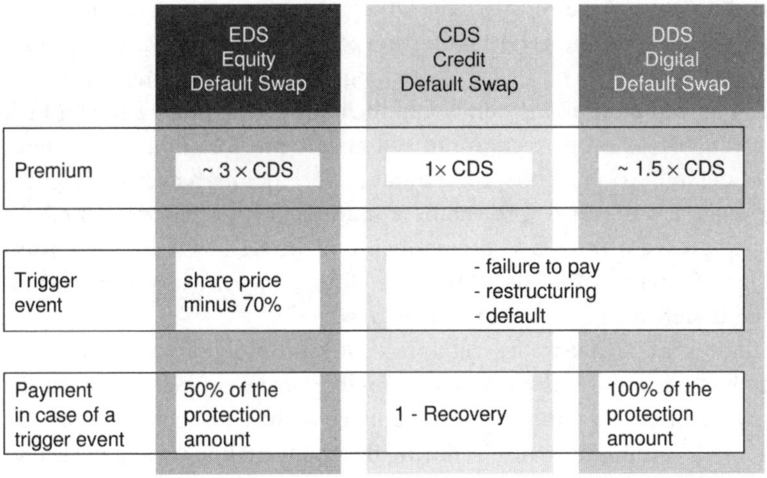

	EDS Equity Default Swap	CDS Credit Default Swap	DDS Digital Default Swap
Premium	~ 3 × CDS	1× CDS	~ 1.5 × CDS
Trigger event	share price minus 70%	- failure to pay - restructuring - default	
Payment in case of a trigger event	50% of the protection amount	1 - Recovery	100% of the protection amount

Fig. 17.4: EDS, CDS AND DDS: the weird trio!

What is the role for DDS in this respect? A DDS is a zero-recovery CDS. In case of a credit event, the protection seller has to pay 100 percent of the notional amount to the protection buyer in a cash-settled DDS contract. That means that the protection seller receives an additional premium for taking the risk of zero recovery (the recovery assumptions in CDS contracts based on non-financials amounts to 40 percent) in the default leg. The additional premium, in general, is around 50 percent of the CDS spread. DDS contracts are rather popular in the financial universe from a purely relative value point of view. Protection selling via a DDS based on a financial entity generates the same spread income as a CDS on a non-financials entity with a higher default probability, while the LGD, however, might be the same. Moreover, using DDS and CDS allows us to bet on the realized recovery value versus the basic assumption of 40 percent recovery in plain-vanilla CDS contracts. In case an investor expects the recovery value of a specific reference entity to be above 40 percent, selling protection on the CDS and buying protection on the DDS can be an attractive opportunity. If a credit event happens, the investor receives 100 percent of the notional amount, while he has to pay less than 60 percent to the protection buyer of the CDS. If the PV of the amount earned in case of a credit event exceeds the PV of the negative spread carry (as the DDS premium is above the CDS premium), the trade generates a profit. Against this background, recovery swaps are an interesting alternative.

Putting the pieces together, the combination of an EDS and a DDS might be an attractive alternative. Assuming that the DDS equals 50 percent of the premium of an EDS, we can combine a short protection position on an EDS and DDS with a long protection position on a CDS. Assuming the above-mentioned premium relations, a spread-neutral position would include, for example, €10 mn EDS and €20 mn DDS (short protection), as well as €60 mn CDS (long protection). In case of default (40 percent recovery and cash settlement) accompanied by a trigger event for the EDS (protection amount equals 50 percent), the P&L amounts to plus €9 mn (€36 mn profit from the CDS, €5 mn loss from the EDS and €20 mn from the DDS). In addition, one can also implement a PV-neutral trade which generates positive carry.

Nevertheless, EDS/CDS trades clearly face the same problems as plain-vanilla equity/debt trades do. Besides a pure Merton-like view, a couple of characteristics which might have an impact on the capital structure of a company have to be taken into account. For example, during the equity meltdown that peaked in March 2003 (Iraq war), Allianz shares lost more than 80 percent of their initial value (June 2002). This would have been the trigger event for a standardized

EDS contract. In the same period, the spread widened from 70 bp to 250 bp – a substantial increase, but far from triggering a potential credit event.

Despite the obvious problems insurance companies faced in the aftermath of the burst of the equity bubble in 2000, there are additional security systems established in the insurance sector. That said, a default scenario is more unlikely than is the case in the corporate sector, while the sector-specific problems have naturally a negative impact on the share price, which even underperformed in a weak equity market environment. By the way, the DAX index also lost more than 50 percent in the respective period. This reflects that implementing debt/equity trades using a combination of CDS and EDS contracts requires sector-specific adjustments as Merton-based approaches are not the pillar of wisdom in any case. This is also reflected in market quotes for EDS and CDS in the insurance sector: at the beginning of 2005, the 5Y CDS on AXA traded at 20 bp, while the corresponding EDS premium was at around 260 bp, 13 times the CDS! The EDS premium equals 3 times the CDS spread is just a rule of thumb, being clearly affected by sector and company-specific issues.

Finally, knowing the EDS premium and the CDS spread permits a view on the implied default barrier traded in the market. Under specific assumptions with respect to the expected distribution of the share price in a certain time frame, we can derive a market-implied default barrier. Assuming the difference between the EDS and the CDS spread, we can calculate the additional drop in the share price after it hits the EDS threshold, which is in line with the premium difference for both instruments. Hence, we can derive the share price which corresponds to the implied default barrier.

In the following we summarize the key points in the EDS/CDS/DDS framework:

- There is a pricing relationship among EDS, CDS, and DDS as the payoff profile is similar in many aspects. Knowing these relationships offers trading, arbitrage, and hedging opportunities.
- Using EDS, CDS, and DDS allows us to implement a broad variety of potential trading opportunities, like capital structure arbitrage, recovery bets, implied default barrier trades, and so on.
- EDS provides an insight into the market-implied view on the risk of a specific credit event. It answers the question: Is the market playing restructuring or default risk?
- Industry specific characteristics have to be taken into consideration. The EDS premium of, for example, insurance companies differs significantly from the respective premium of plain-vanilla corporates.

- Inherent problems include the fact that we assume that the equity of a company mirrors the asset value (which we cannot observe directly in the market). Therefore, we have to factor in equity-specific characteristics, such as whether if the underlying share could be added to the growth or to the value universe.

17.10 CDS–Cash–Repo Arbitrage

17.10.1 The Repo Market

A *repurchase agreement* (repo and reverse repo) is an agreement between two parties. The one party sells the other party a security at a specified price with the commitment to repurchase the security at a later date for another specified price. The party purchasing the security is making funds available to the seller while holding the security as collateral. A *reverse repo* is used to describe the opposite side of the repo transaction. A dealer borrowing money does a repo, and an investor lending money does a reverse repo.

The repo market allows investors to build up short positions, which is the central motivation behind repo transactions besides refinancing long positions. The possibility of shorting securities is a prerequisite of cash-and-carry arbitrage. To sum up, the major incentives to enter a repurchase agreement are:

- Financing: reducing refinancing costs of long positions
- Liquidity: Collateralized liquidity management and bridging of tight liquidity positions (on-the-run paper and bonds going special).

Besides these primary motivations, there is an additional reason for a repo transaction, the implementation of trading strategies (cash-and-carry arbitrage and hedging strategies). We focus on these in the next section.

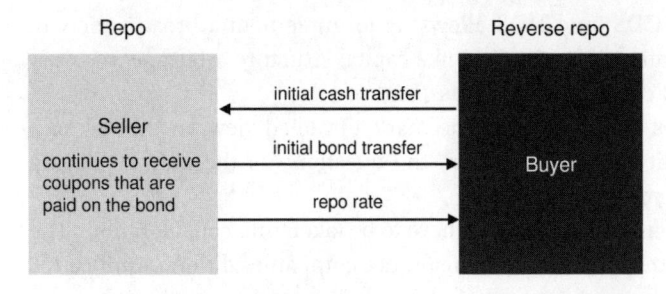

Fig. 17.5: Plain-vanilla repo deal

In figure 17.5, we show the basic mechanism behind a repo transaction. The seller has to repurchase the security (performing a repo), while the buyer purchases (and later resells the security). In other words, the buyer is performing a reverse repo. Legally, a repo is the sale and subsequent repurchase of a security; its economic effect is that of a secured loan. The buyer makes funds available to the seller and holds the security as collateral. In the case of coupon-paying corporate bonds, this coupon income is returned to the seller. The difference between the sale and the repurchase price paid for the security represents the interest on the bond. The *repo rate* is the interest the borrower has to pay the lender. Repos are quoted as interest rates.

In a repo deal, the lender is exposed to counterparty risk, that is, a default of the borrower. Therefore, the lender keeps the bond as collateral. The remaining risk is that the borrower and the issuer of the bond default simultaneously.

In a *tri-party repo*, there is a global custodian. The global custodian acts like a clearinghouse between the involved parties, keeping the security in its account, marking collateral to market, and issuing margin calls. The primary advantages of a tri-party repo are the extremely low risk (reduction of counterparty risk) and the low transaction costs for the repo counterparts.

The latest development in the repo market is the introduction of *hedge repos*, which extend the plain-vanilla repo transaction by including integrated hedging, collateral, and counterparty risk management. For this purpose, credit derivatives (CDS, TRS, FTD, CMCDS, and CDS options) will be implemented in the transaction, which is especially useful for repo transaction based on lower qualities (sub-investment-grade issues).

17.10.2 How an Arbitrage Trade Works

On the back of rising liquidity in the repo market, several institutional investors merged their short-term trading desks, including corporate bonds and credit default swaps with maturities below one year, as well as repo transactions. The reason is simply that there are relative value opportunities based on exploiting market anomalies in one of the three markets. These kinds of trading strategies are known as CDS–cash–repo arbitrage.

While the CDS market offers the opportunity to build up short and long positions, combining cash and repo transactions allows for replication strategies. Below, we highlight the basic structure of CDS–cash–repo arbitrage trading, which includes five steps (cash flow in brackets):

- Buying the corporate bond (cash outflow)
- Swapping the cash bond into floating via an asset swap package (receiving spread income)
- Buying protection via a CDS contract (paying protection fees)
- Refinancing via a repo on the corporate bond (paying repo fees).

Basically, this trade generates a profit in case the spread income of the swapped corporate bond exceeds the repo costs plus the refinancing costs plus the protection fees. In the opposite case, the trade would be implemented as follows:

- Shorting the corporate bond (cash inflow)
- Reverse repo on the corporate bond (receiving repo fee)
- Swapping the coupon income, receiving fix and paying variable (paying the remaining spread carry)
- Selling protection in the CDS market (receiving protection fees)

To sum up, using a simple replication approach, investors can exploit market anomalies by using CDS, cash bonds, and repo or refinancing transactions to generate almost risk-free returns (there is remaining counterparty risk and the risk that the bond issuer and the counterparty default simultaneously). In Figure 17.6, we summarize the payoffs of the different transactions using the first example.

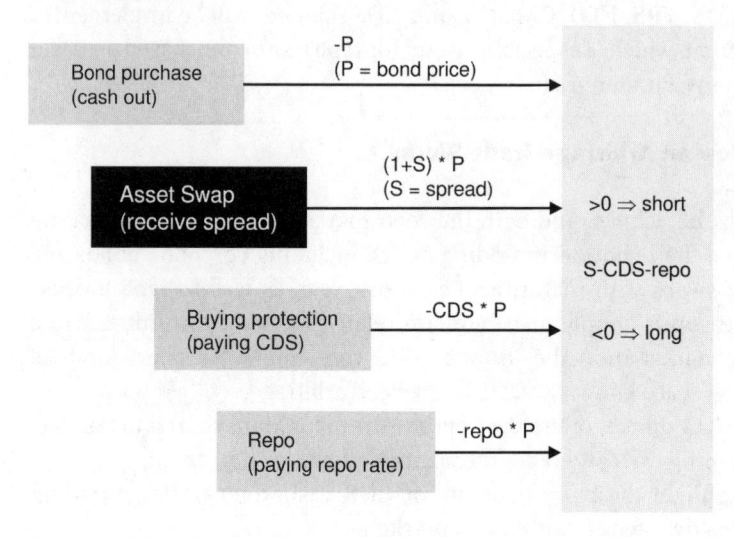

Fig. 17.6: CDS–Cash–repo arbitrage

18
Operational Issues: Accounting

After having demonstrated how to use various credit instruments in the context of credit portfolio management, we now take a more operational view. The tremendous growth of credit markets, accompanied by a variety of instruments that facilitate an efficient credit portfolio optimization, raises operational questions like accounting and regulatory issues that have to be resolved before entering the market. In this chapter, we provide guidance with the International Accounting Standards (IAS), as these have become mandatory for listed companies as of January 1, 2005. The next chapter will address regulatory issues, particularly with respect to Basel II.

Applicable accounting rules in the international arena are currently subject to significant changes. Before 2001, each country had its own accounting standards. For example, German companies had to comply with provisions of the *Handelsgesetzbuch* (HGB), which provides a rough framework for the preparation of financial statements, including the balance sheet and the income statement. In the course of European harmonization of accounting rules, International Accounting Standards, alternatively called International Financial Reporting Standards (IFRS), have been developed to achieve comparability across European companies and beyond. In the meantime, the vast majority of these rules have been made a part of legislation for public companies.

However, national accounting principles are still present. For example, German companies are still obliged to prepare individual financial statements according to German GAAP and tax laws as well. In our view, it is merely a matter of time until the different accounting rules will be abolished. Considering this fact, we focus primarily on IAS rather than on national GAAP.

The first section gives a brief overview of the basic accounting principles outlined in IAS 39, which is of major importance for credit-risky instruments. However, as we will see, IAS 39 does not exhaustively cover the topic, as it allows several exceptions with regard to *financial guarantee contracts* (or *insurance contracts*). Hence, we inevitably refer to other related accounting standards (IFRS 4 for insurance contracts and IAS 37 for financial guarantee contracts).

Subsequently, accounting rules are applied to major credit-risky instruments, particularly bonds and loans, credit default swaps, total return swaps, credit linked notes, and the iTraxx product family. In addition, we provide additional guidance with regard to more exotic products, including such instruments like options on CDO tranches.

18.1 An Introduction to IAS 39

In order to facilitate an understanding of the topic of financial instruments accounting, we focus on its fundamental principles. We provide an introduction to basic provisions of the International Accounting Standard 39, "Financial Instruments: Recognition and Measurement". However, we ignore many specific issues and exceptions to these principles for simplicity's sake.

18.1.1 The Scope of IAS 39

IAS 39 deals with the accounting of so-called financial instruments. However, IAS 39 is not the only set of provisions that addresses this topic. In fact, it can only be applied in combination with IAS 32, "Financial Instruments: Disclosure and Presentation", which includes provisions particularly concerning the notes as part of an entity's financial statement. Accordingly, we will resort to certain definitions and provisions once in a while. It must be noted that both standards IAS 32 and 39 have to be applied at the same time for periods beginning on or after January 1, 2005, or earlier (IAS 39.103).

The International Accounting Standards Board (IASB) is a non-profit organization that developed these rules with the objective to provide generally accepted accounting principles for the European Union and beyond. However, the European Union and its member states have to put these standards into legislation before they become mandatory. In the course of this process, called the endorsement, the standards may be subject to changes that are mainly attributable to the influence of certain lobbies. We will highlight these discrepancies if they pertain to the accounting of credit-risky instruments.

According to IAS 32.11, a *financial instrument* is "any contract that gives rise to a financial asset of one entity and a financial liability or equity instrument of another entity." In addition, IAS 32 and 39 differentiate between different categories of financial instruments, namely financial assets, financial liabilities, and some contracts to buy or sell non-financial items (IAS 39.1) (the latter is not within our field of interest).

However, it is not easy to distinguish between financial assets or liabilities covered by the IAS 39 and those addressed by other standards. One important exception is the area of so-called *financial guarantee contracts* (including letters of credit and other credit default contracts) (IAS 39.2 [f]). If such contracts "provide for specified payments to be made to reimburse the holder for a loss it incurs because a specified debtor fails to make payment when due under the original or modified terms of a debt instrument", then IAS 37: "Provisions, Contingent Liabilities and Contingent Assets" applies. Hence, this rule basically provides a back door for credit default swaps and similar products. We will return to this point later, as it enables credit investors to avoid fair value accounting for particular credit products. In the meantime, the IASB introduced a new standard that deals with *insurance contracts*, IFRS 4, which also encompasses financial guarantees. Hence, IFRS 4 currently applies instead of IAS 37, however with no substantial change with regard to the accounting treatment of financial guarantees.

International Accounting Standards aim at showing the entity's assets and liabilities at fair value on the balance sheet as far as possible (*fair value accounting*). With respect to financial instruments, this means that all (financial) contracts within the scope of IAS 39 have to be disclosed on the balance sheet, even for derivatives, which is in contrast to many national GAAPs where derivatives are basically treated as off-balance-sheet contracts due to their conditional characteristic. In IAS 39, however, there is no rule without exception. Hence, it takes more than four hundred pages to clarify these exceptions and to deal with the problems arising from them.

18.1.2 Categories of Financial Instruments

IAS 39 defines four different categories of financial instruments to capture the base case and the most common exceptions with regard to fair value accounting. As we will see later, these categories are not exhaustive because the standard provides additional rules for so-called *hedge accounting*, which facilitates a special treatment of specific instruments irrespective of their original category. Figure 18.1 provides an overview concerning these categories.

The allocation of financial instruments to these categories is not self-evident, as the user typically has several options. However, the attribution of a financial instrument to one of these categories should be made according to the purpose of the respective contract.

The category *at fair value through profit or loss* (aFVtPL) complies the most with the goal of fair value accounting, as we will see later. IAS 39 allows for the designation of any financial asset or liability as aFVtPL. However, one has to designate the respective instrument at initial recognition (IAS 39.9), which is an irrevocable act (IAS 39.50). Unfortunately, the fair value option is currently

At Fair Value through Profit or Loss (aFVtPL)	
Held for trading	**Designated as aFVtPL**
(1) Short-term selling or repurchasing (2) Short-term profit-taking (3) Derivatives	• Designated by the entity upon initial recognition

Held-to-Maturity Investments (HtM)
- Only for financial assets with fixed or determinable payments and a fixed maturity
- Entity has the positive intention and ability to hold to maturity

Loans and Receivables (LaR)
- Non-derivative financial assets with fixed or determinable payments
- Not quoted in an active market

Available-for-Sale Financial Assets (AfS)
- Non-derivative financial assets
- Category for items that are not designated as aFVtPL, HtM or LaR

Fig. 18.1: The four categories of financial instruments

unavailable for financial liabilities due to partial endorsement of the standard. For financial assets, the application of the fair value option is currently not restricted.

Held-to-maturity (HtM) investments require fixed or determinable payments with a fixed maturity date (IAS 39.9). While cash bond investments typically fulfill these conditions, stock purchases cannot be allocated to this category because they have no maturity date. In fact, the HtM category is a restrictive one, as it requires the ability and intention of the entity to hold to maturity. Any material violation of this provision leads to a punishment in a way that the entity is not allowed to use the category for three years. The idea of this category is to save the entity from fair value accounting for these instruments, as the fair value changes during the remaining lifetime are not of interest from an economical perspective (as long as there is no default event). Hence, fair value accounting would not be appropriate.

The same applies for *loans and receivables* (LaR), where IAS 39 abstains from fair value accounting due to a lack of market prices. In practice, this means that loans and receivables are disclosed on the balance sheet at amortized cost.

Any financial instrument that does not qualify for the categories HtM and LaR and is not designated as aFVtPL is automatically designated as *available for sale (AfS)*.

As highlighted in figure 18.1, derivatives are automatically designated as *held for trading*, and hence included in aFVtPL with the exception of those instruments that qualify for hedge accounting. However, derivatives in an accounting context have an alternative meaning compared to the market vernacular. Usually, derivatives refer to financial instruments that are subject to the risk of other asset classes in a way that their payoff or value depends on the valuation or price of another financial instrument. For IAS 39, the term *derivatives* refers to financial instruments that additionally meet the following criteria (IAS 39.9):

- No initial net investment (e.g., swaps, future or forward contracts) or an initial net investment that is smaller than would be required for other types of contracts that would be expected to have a similar response to changes in market factors (e.g., options)
- Settlement at a future date.

Hence, the IAS 39 term derivative is somewhat more restrictive compared to that in an economic point of view. For example, structured products like regular credit linked notes do in fact have a comparable net investment level (same as a direct bond investment in the respective name). Hence, such contracts cannot be designated as derivatives, although the market value of such a contract is linked to a non-issuer-related credit risk.

As stated above, IAS 39 primarily deals with financial assets and financial liabilities. However, while all four categories basically have to be considered for the asset side of the balance sheet, only one category is available for the liability side. As this division seems insufficient, the following section provides an alternative for financial liabilities, which is not covered by the four categories presented above.

18.1.3 Measurement

One would typically discuss the topic of recognition and derecognition before delving into measurement aspects. However, as the measurement of a financial instrument is closely related to the four categories introduced before, we postpone the recognition issue for the time being. Let us assume that a financial instrument is recognized on the balance sheet when bought or incurred, and derecognized when it is sold or redeemed.

When talking about measurement, one has to differentiate between the following questions:

1. What is the value to be disclosed on the balance sheet when initially recognized? (Initial Measurement)

2. What is the value to be disclosed on the balance sheet subsequently, or after initial recognition and before derecognition? (Subsequent Measurement)
3. What has to be done once the financial asset or liability has been derecognized?

The first question is the easiest to answer. At initial recognition, or at the time the financial asset is bought or one has incurred the financial liability, the asset or liability is measured at fair value (IAS 39.43). Transaction costs that are directly attributable to the acquisition or issuance of the financial asset or liability are added if the instrument does not belong to the category aFVtPL (cf. figure 18.2).

Assets

Financial Assets aFVtPL
Initially: Fair Value [IAS 39.43]
Subsequently: Fair Value [IAS 39.46]

Held-to-Maturity
Initially: FV + Transact. C. [IAS 39.43]
Subsequently: Amort. Cost [IAS 39.46(b)]

Loans and Receivables
Initially: FV + Transact. C. [IAS 39.43]
Subsequently: Amort. Cost [IAS 39.46(a)]

Available-for-Sale
Initially: FV + Transact. C. [IAS 39.43]
Subsequently: FV, but no P&L effect

Liabilities

Finanical Liabilities aFVtPL
Initially: Fair Value [IAS 39.43]
Subsequently: Fair Value [IAS 39.47(a)]

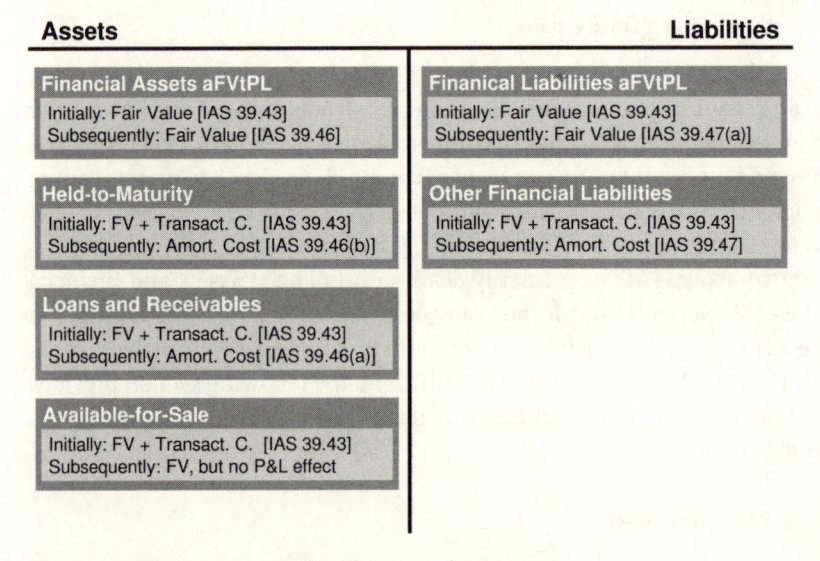

Other Financial Liabilities
Initially: FV + Transact. C. [IAS 39.43]
Subsequently: Amort. Cost [IAS 39.47]

Fig. 18.2: Basic measurement considerations under IAS 39

Although this concept seems straightforward, it is important to know what IAS 39 recognizes as fair value. IAS 39 defines the *fair value* as "the amount for which an asset could be exchanged, or liability settled, between knowledgeable, willing parties in an arm's length transaction". In the context of the initial measurement, that simply means we have to take the actual transaction price (IAS 39.AG71). However, determining the fair value at a later date can be quite tough. We will return to this point later on.

Hence, acquiring a bond or stock simply requires putting the price paid on the balance sheet, for example. Entering into a swap contract, for instance a plain-vanilla interest rate swap, typically involves no upfront payment. In this case, the carrying amount is zero at initiation and the instrument enters neither the asset side nor the liabilities side. Option-style contracts (calls, puts, caps, floors, swaptions, etc.) typically feature a premium payment at initiation, which represents the value of the option. In case one buys an option, the premium paid enters the balance sheet as an asset, while writing an option involves recognizing a liability that amounts to the premium received.

However, the initial measurement is of minor importance, as it describes the balance sheet effect for just a logical second, whereas the subsequent measurement deals with the impact on (a) the balance sheet and (b) the income statement over the course of time. With regard to the balance sheet, one has to differentiate between the fair value approach and the measurement at amortized cost. Financial assets aFVtPL and available-for-sale items are disclosed at fair value, while held-to-maturity investments and loans and receivables are subject to the so-called *effective interest method*, which accompanies measurement at amortized cost (cf. figure 18.2).

First of all, we have to return to the issue of determining the fair value of a financial instrument. As the expression "the amount for which an asset could be exchanged, or liability settled, between knowledgeable, willing parties in an arm's length transaction" does not hold water, IAS 39 (IAS 39.AG69-AG82) provides detailed guidance for implementing the fair value approach. A major conclusion is: As long as there is a published price quotation available (market price quoted by an exchange, dealer, broker, etc.), one should take it as the fair value (IAS 39.AG71). Otherwise, one has to use a valuation technique in order to establish a fair value (IAS 39.AG74). Basically, the following possibilities are appropriate:

- Recent arm's length market transaction between knowledgeable, willing parties
- Reference to the current fair value of another instrument that is substantially the same
- Discounted cash flow analysis
- Option pricing models.

If one of these techniques is commonly used by market participants and has proved valid in the past, one should adopt that technique (IAS 39.AG74).

Although fair value accounting applies for both aFVtPL items and available-for-sale assets, there is a substantial difference between both categories with regard to the effect on the income statement. As the expression "... through profit or loss" suggests, fair value changes for aFVtPL items do not only lead to an adjustment of their carrying amount on the balance sheet, but they also immediately affect the income statement (IAS 39.55[a]). AfS items, however, do not automatically entail a P&L effect from unrealized profits (IAS 39.55[b]). In fact, gains and losses arising from a change in fair value are basically recognized in equity through the so-called *statement of changes in equity*. This is a very special item in equity, which does not belong to the income statement and is often referred to as *AfS reserve*.

However, there is no rule without an exception! In case of so-called impairment losses, the entity is obliged to recognize the loss on the income statement (IAS 39.67). Possible reasons for an impairment are (IAS 39.59):

- Significant financial difficulty of the issuer or obligor
- Breach of contract (default, delinquency) with regard to interest or principal payments
- Bankruptcy or restructuring is becoming probable
- Measurable decrease in estimated future cash flows.

It should be added that a downgrade of an issuer's credit rating is basically not sufficient for impairment (IAS 39.60). For an equity instrument, a significant or prolonged decline in the fair value below its cost is also objective evidence of impairment (IAS 39.61).

If, in a subsequent period, the fair value of the instrument increases due to "an event occurring after the impairment loss was recognized in profit or loss, the impairment loss shall be reversed, with the amount of the reversal recognized in profit or loss" (IAS 39.70). Unfortunately, this provision only holds for debt instruments. Fair value gains for equity instruments in the aftermath of an impairment are recognized in the AfS reserve (IAS 39.69).

In a second step, we now delve into the topic of measuring a financial instrument at amortized cost. As we already pointed out, the carrying amount of a financial instrument when initially recognized equals the amount spent or received for it. However, abiding by this amount until the financial instrument is due or sold or redeemed is not self-evident. For an equity instrument, it makes sense to keep the carrying amount up over time. On the other hand, debt instruments are typically redeemed at par value (100), but they are bought or sold above or below par. Hence, one needs an approach to distribute the premium or discount over time. Some national GAAPs simply solve this problem by establishing a deferred item on the balance sheet at initial recognition and dissolving it proportionately until maturity. However, IAS 39 does not permit such an approach, but dictates the *effective interest method* (EIM) instead.

The following example explains the concept further. Let us assume that an entity purchases a government bond with a notional amount of €100,000, a yearly coupon of 6 percent, and five years to maturity at a price of 95.9. The first step is to calculate the effective interest rate of this fixed income investment. Please note that the effective interest rate is the internal rate of return, or the uniform discount rate that generates the current market price. In the present case, applying a simple numerical procedure renders an effective interest rate of 7.00 percent, as shown in table 18.1.

Tab. 18.1: Payment structure and internal rate of return

Year	Cash flow	Discount factor	Present value
1	6,000	$1/1.07$	5,607
2	6,000	$1/1.07^2$	5,241
3	6,000	$1/1.07^3$	4,898
4	6,000	$1/1.07^4$	4,577
5	106,000	$1/1.07^5$	75,577
Amortized cost at the beginning of year 1			95,900

Tab. 18.2: Carrying amount and interest income (IAS 39)

Year	Carrying amount (start of period)	Carrying amount (end of period)	Interest income
1	95,900.00	96,613.00	6,713.00
2	96,613.00	97,375.91	6,762.91
3	97,375.91	98,192.22	6,816.31
4	98,192.22	99,065.68	6,873.46
5	99,065.68	100,000.00	6,934.32
Sum			34,100.00

Table 18.2 shows the development of the carrying amount until maturity of the bond. At initial recognition, the carrying amount equals the purchase price. The effective interest method now presumes that the investment provides an interest income in accordance with the initial internal rate of return. Hence, the interest income for the first year amounts to

$$€95900 \times 7.00\% = €6713$$

However, as there is only a cash inflow of €6,000 during this period, the difference of €713 has to be assigned to a hypothetical value increase of the position, leading us to a carrying amount at the end of year one of

$$€95\,900 + €713 = €96\,613$$

The carrying amount at the end of the period also acts as the carrying amount for the start of the next period. For period 2 and afterwards, the procedure is repeated for the respective new carrying amount. For example, the interest income of 7 percent for the second year is then calculated based on the new carrying amount of €96,613. In fact, the carrying amount and the interest income are subject to a y-o-y increase of 7 percent, the initial rate of return, as shown in table 18.2.

Applying the effective interest method as demonstrated above is just the regular case. However, there are impairment provisions for HtM and LaR assets similar to those we already saw with regard to AfS assets (IAS 39.63). If there is objective evidence for impairment, the difference between the asset's carrying amount and its present value is recognized in profit or loss. The entity may choose between (a) the reduction of the carrying amount and (b) the use of an allowance account. IAS 39.65 states that if the impairment loss decreases afterwards, then it shall be reversed with the amount of the reversal recognized in profit or loss.

In a nutshell, IAS 39 is characterized by a mixed measurement approach; in other words, some financial instruments are recognized at fair value, while others are disclosed at (amortized) cost. The attribution of a financial instrument to one of these categories is primarily driven by the purpose of the item within the company.

18.1.4 Recognition and Derecognition

Finally, we deal with recognition and derecognition. In the preceding section, we discussed measurement issues, presuming that the recognition of the respective financial instrument has already taken place. It seems rather obvious to assume the recognition of a financial asset as soon as it is acquired and the contract is settled. However, side issues may arise that challenge the recognition or derecognition of a financial instrument in practice.

The initial recognition of a financial asset or liability is straightforward. IAS 39.14 uses the expression "the entity becomes a party to the contractual provisions of the instrument." In the context of *regular way purchases* (meaning: spot transactions), the entity even has the choice of using *trade day accounting* (date that an entity commits itself to purchase or sell an asset) or *settlement day accounting* (date that an asset is delivered to or by an entity) (IAS 39.38).

However, the method should be chosen consistently for all purchases and sales (IAS 39.AG53).

In contrast, derecognition provisions for financial assets are extensive. First of all, it is clear that a financial asset has to be derecognized when the rights to the asset's cash flows expire (IAS 39.17[a]). However, there is another possibility: the transfer of the financial asset (IAS 39.17[b]). *Transferring* of an asset means that one (1) transfers the contractual rights to receive the cash flows of the financial asset, or (2) assumes a contractual obligation to pay the cash flows to one or more recipients (IAS 39.18). In addition, derecognition of the asset requires that the entity transfers "substantially all the risks and rewards of ownership" (IAS 39.20[a]). This is evaluated by comparing the entity's exposure, before and after the transfer, with the variability in the amounts and timing of the net cash flows of the transferred asset (IAS 39.21).

Derecognition rules for financial liabilities are comparatively easy to implement. Such an instrument is removed from the balance sheet when it is extinguished, in other words, the obligation specified in the contract is discharged, canceled, or expired (IAS 39.39).

Last but not least, it should be noted that if a financial instrument is removed from the balance sheet because of derecognition, the difference between the carrying amount and the consideration received or paid is recognized in profit or loss (IAS 39.26 and IAS 39.41). In case an AfS reserve has been built up for a financial asset over time, the balance sheet item has to be dissolved and recognized in P&L.

18.1.5 Embedded Derivatives

The market for structured products has recently experienced tremendous growth. Against this background, the financial statement of companies investing in these products may feature significant leveraged exposure to non-related asset classes (e.g., equity and credit risk). Given that these companies classify hybrid instruments as HtM or even as LaR (e.g., structured promissory loans), the financial risk would not be identifiable for the reader of the financial statement. Hence, the standard setter introduced specific rules that clarify how to cope with this kind of instrument.

The basic idea of the embedded derivatives concept is to divide structured or hybrid products into

- a host contract (typically a fixed income security) and
- an embedded derivative (IAS 39.10).

The valuation and payout of the embedded derivative is subject to a specified interest rate, a financial instrument price, commodity price, foreign exchange rate, index of prices or rates, credit rating or credit index, or other variable.

Not every embedded derivative has to be separated from its host contract. A separation is mandatory if (a) the risk of the embedded derivative is not closely related to the host contract, (b) the embedded derivative would meet the definition of a derivative, and (c) the hybrid instrument is not measured at fair value with changes in fair value recognized in profit or loss (IAS 39.11). Please refer to Figure 18.3 for an illustration.

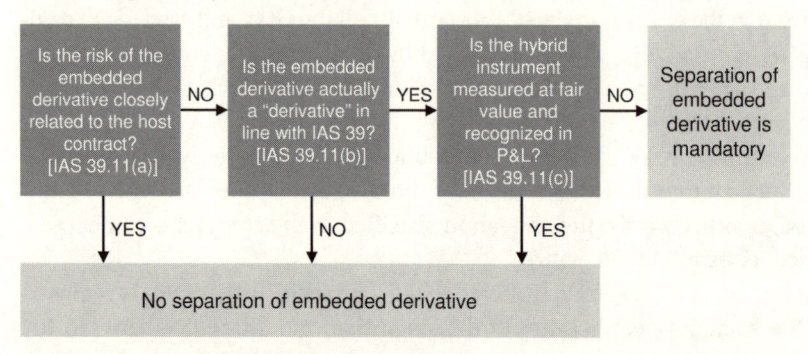

Fig. 18.3: The decision tree for separating embedded derivatives

The term *closely related* refers to the similarity of risk sources of the host contract and the embedded derivative. Typically, the host contract is a fixed income security (fixed coupon bond, floater, zero coupon bond). Risk sources related to that product are interest rate risk and the issuer's credit risk. If the embedded derivative is driven by other risk sources (equity risk, other credit risk than the issuer's, etc.) or has leveraged exposure, the embedded derivative's risk is not supposed to be closely related to the host contract. Convertible bonds, credit linked notes, and notes that are linked to commodity or equity prices are the most popular examples of not closely related risk sources.

What are the consequences of a separation? IAS 39 stipulates that the host contract is accounted for in accordance with the hybrid instrument's original category. For example, if the hybrid product is classified as HtM, the host contract (should be a fixed income instrument) will also be treated as a HtM contract (IAS 39.11). On the other hand, the embedded derivative will be recognized as aFVtPL, as it can be interpreted as a derivative in line with IAS 39. If no valuation tools are available, one can determine the fair value of the embedded derivative as the difference between the fair value of the hybrid instrument as a whole and the fair value of the host contract (IAS 39.13).

In practice, it is difficult and time-consuming to separate an embedded derivative. However, the introduction of the *fair value option* in December 2003, which allows the entity to designate each single financial instrument to disclose it aFVtPL without the duty to perform a separation procedure, provides a basis to avoid Sisyphean labor. Nevertheless, one has to accept the effect of fair value changes in the P&L in this case.

18.1.6 Hedge Accounting

As noted in the section about measurement, a major characteristic of IAS 39 is the mixed measurement approach, as fair value and cost accounting for financial instruments exist simultaneously. In a hedging context, this parallelism may lead to inappropriate income statements, as the hedged item may be recognized at amortized cost while the hedging instrument (e.g., a derivative) is disclosed aFVtPL. In order to avoid P&L asymmetries, IAS 39 provides rules that facilitate a valid reproduction of economically-driven hedging relationships (IAS 39.71 et sqq.), called *hedge accounting*. Table 18.3 gives a brief overview of basic terms and concepts of hedge accounting.

Tab. 18.3: Basic terms and concepts of hedge accounting

Concept	Explanation
hedged item	an asset, liability, firm commitment (forward contract), highly probable transaction, or net investment in a foreign operation, involving a risk of changes in fair value or future cash flows
hedging instrument	a derivative whose fair value or cash flows are expected to offset changes in the fair value or cash flows of a designated hedged item
hedge effectiveness	the degree to which changes in the fair value or cash flows of the hedged item that are attributable to a hedged risk are offset by changes in the fair value or cash flows of the hedging instrument
fair value hedge	a hedge of the exposure to changes in fair value of a recognized asset or liability that is attributable to a particular risk and could affect profit or loss
cash flow hedge	a hedge of the exposure to variability in cash flows that (1) is attributable to a particular risk associated with a recognized asset or liability or a highly probable forecast transaction and (2) could affect P&L

IAS 39 provides three types of hedging relationships. The idea of a *fair value hedge* is to balance the hedged item's fair value changes by means of fair value changes of the respective hedging instrument. Ideally, fair value changes for both instruments have opposite algebraic signs and the same absolute amount.

When setting up a fair value hedge, one has not only to designate the hedged item and the hedging instrument, but also specify the particular risk that motivates the hedge.

Any recognized financial asset or liability or an unrecognized firm commitment can be utilized as a hedged item for a fair value hedge. Figure 18.4 shows a typical situation: The company has purchased a bond with a fixed coupon (hedged item) and wants to hedge the interest rate risk by entering into a payer swap (pay fixed leg, receive floating leg). The funding position is shown for the sake of completeness and is not part of the hedging relationship.

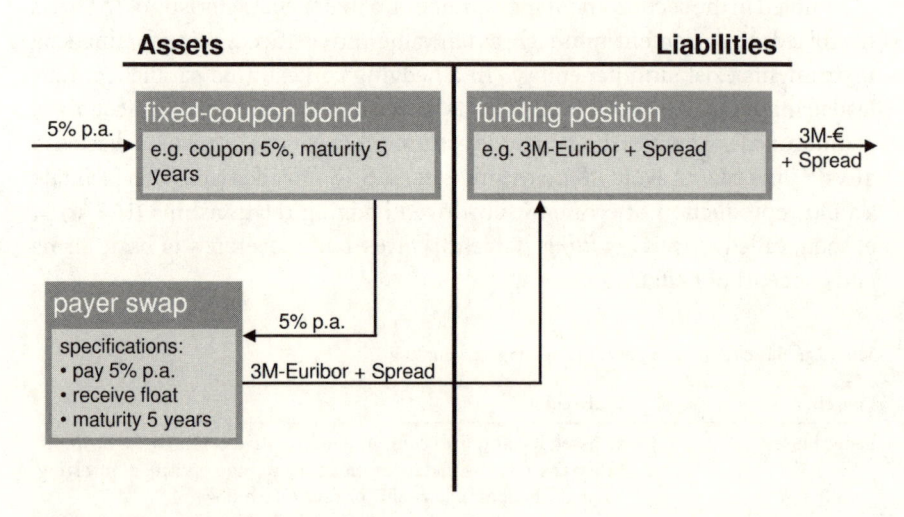

Fig. 18.4: A typical fair value hedge

In case the fair value hedge proves effective (which seems clear for the example above), IAS 39 stipulates the following accounting rules for the involved instruments:

- Marked-to-market changes of the hedged item that are attributable to the hedged risk are used to adjust the carrying amount of the hedged item and simultaneously recognized in P&L (IAS 39.89[b]).
- As the hedging instrument (a derivative) is already disclosed aFVtPL, no special treatment is necessary (IAS 39.89[a]).

This results in an avoidance of a P&L disavowal, which would otherwise be attributable to the hedged risk. A fair value hedge approach is only indicated when the hedged item is categorized as HtM, LaR, or AfS.

The *cash flow hedge* is an alternative approach covered by IAS 39 provisions. It aims at eliminating or reducing the exposure to variability in future cash flows. These cash flows may be variable cash flows from already recognized assets or liabilities (e.g., floaters), but also from highly probable forecast transactions (IAS 39.86[b]). Figure 18.5 shows a typical situation: The company has purchased a floating rate note (hedged item) and wants to hedge the risk of unstable future interest income by entering into a receiver swap (receive fixed leg, pay floating leg). The company's funding position involves fixed coupon payments and is only shown for the sake of completeness.

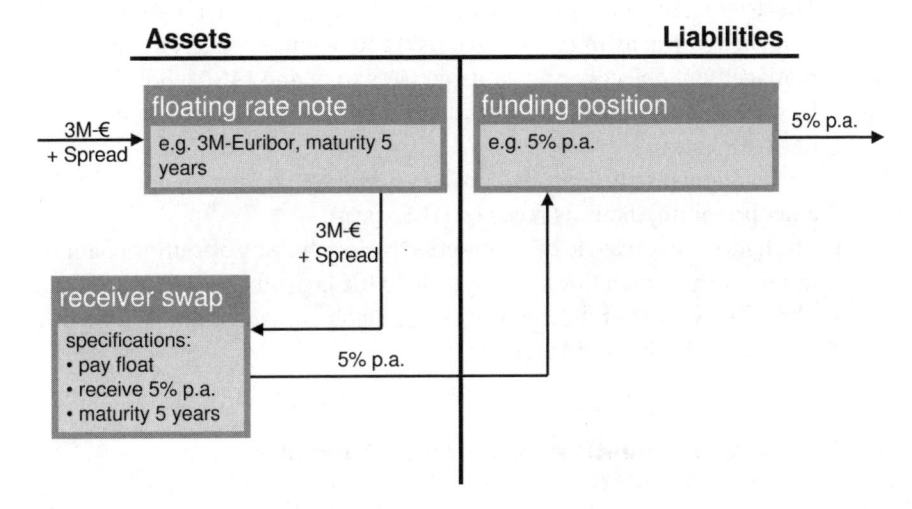

Fig. 18.5: A typical cash flow hedge

In case the cash flow hedge proves effective (which seems clear for the example above), IAS 39 stipulates the following accounting rules for the involved instruments:

- The portion of the hedging instrument's fair value change which is determined to be an effective hedge is recognized directly in equity through the statement of changes in equity (the so-called *cash flow hedge reserve*). On the other hand, the ineffective portion, if there is any, is recognized in P&L (IAS 39.95).
- The hedged item, if it is already recognized, is treated in accordance with its original category.

Apparently, the accounting consequences of an effective cash flow hedge differ substantially from those for a fair value hedge. An effective fair value hedge leads to a P&L recognition for both hedged item and hedging instrument. In contrast, an efficient cash flow hedge involves no P&L effect due to changed fair values; marked-to-market changes of the hedging instrument are put on a parking position similar to the AfS reserve.

There is also a third hedge accounting approach, namely the *hedge of a net investment in a foreign operation*. We skip this alternative due to the fact that it is not related to our specific focus on credit-risky instruments.

As hedge accounting allows one to deviate from basic IAS 39 measurement rules, one has to fulfill several conditions:

- The hedging relationship has to be formally designated at initiation (hedged item, hedging instrument, hedged risk) and requires documentation (risk management objective and strategy) (IAS 39.71 and IAS 39.88[a]).
- Hedged item and hedging instrument must involve external counterparties (IAS 39.73).
- The hedging instrument shall not be a net written option, in other words, a net premium, if any, is received (IAS 39.77).
- The hedge is expected to be highly effective in achieving offsetting changes in fair value or cash flows attributable to the hedged risk (IAS 39.88[b]).
- The effectiveness of the hedge can be reliably measured and is assessed on an ongoing basis (IAS 39.88[d],[e]).

18.2 IAS 39 Accounting for Credit Instruments

18.2.1 Bonds and Loans

Credit-risky instruments like bonds and loans typically form the starting point for any credit portfolio management consideration. Consequently, we will start with the accounting consequences for these plain-vanilla instruments, although they may be subject to some special features like call or put options and step-ups or step-downs. Afterwards, we will go to credit derivatives that play an important role in the management process of credit risk.

Credit portfolio managers typically try to achieve a consistent accounting treatment for both the basis instruments (loans and bonds) and potential hedging instruments (CDS, iTraxx products, etc.). This practice particularly aims at avoiding any volatility in the income statement that is related to the fact that multiple measurement approaches for different credit-risky instruments apply. As we have already discussed in section 18.1, IAS 39 is characterized by a mixed measurement approach; some financials instruments are recognized at fair value, while others are disclosed at (amortized) cost. Even if fair value accounting applies, it is questionable whether marked-to-market changes are recognized in P&L.

We exclude credit linked notes from the forthcoming discussion, as they are subject to special embedded derivatives provisions. Hence, we dedicate a separate section for this class of instruments.

The basic IAS 39 accounting framework for financial instruments has already been presented in the course of this chapter, which is particularly related to the various categories of financial instruments (aFVtPL, HtM, LaR, and AfS). As long as we focus on bond or loan investments rather than on issuing or incurring liabilities, each of these categories needs to be considered. Against this background, we will provide additional details that merit further discussion in the context of credit portfolios.

Bonds and loan investments are assigned to the aFVtPL category if they are either part of a trading activity or designated as aFVtPL at initiation. Trading activity should be associated with "active and frequent buying and selling" of financial instruments in order to generate profit from short-term fluctuations (IAS 39.AG14). Short selling of bonds, even if implemented in the context of simple relative value positions to exploit the basis, is always regarded as trading activity. Liabilities of any kind that are used to fund these trading activities do not automatically belong to this category (IAS 39.AG15). The option to designate any bond or loan as aFVtPL is a convenient way to benefit from fair value accounting if desired.

In contrast to following a full fair value philosophy for credit portfolios, many investors often try to avoid any impact on the income statement due to unrealized gains and losses. This can be accomplished by resorting to one of the categories AfS, HtM, or even LaR.

Available-for-sale portfolios are very common in the context of active credit portfolio management, as the HtM category is basically subject to penalties in case securities are sold prior to maturity, and the category LaR is not accessible for actively quoted instruments like corporate bonds. Unfortunately, investors have to tolerate the existence of the AfS reserve as an additional component of equity, which encompasses accumulated marked-to-market changes of the respective investments, although it does not enter the income statement.

The category "held-to-maturity", however, may be an alternative, but a very restrictive one. As already mentioned, it requires the ability and intention to hold the respective bonds or loans to maturity. IAS 39.9 additionally states that only instruments with fixed or determinable payments with a fixed maturity date are eligible for this category. It is questionable which kinds of bonds and loans qualify for such a categorization.

Some details regarding this issue can be found in the *Application Guidance* of IAS 39. Despite the fact that floating rate notes feature uncertainty with respect to the amount of future coupon payments, IAS 39.AG17 clarifies that even variable interest rate payments can satisfy HtM requirements. Accordingly, coupon-bearing bonds with step-ups or step-downs, which are triggered by rating actions, are in our view eligible for the HtM category. On the other hand, perpetuals do not qualify for HtM due to the lack of a maturity date.

A considerable share of the market for euro-denominated bonds is subject to optionalities like call or put features. Callable bonds (issuer can repay the debt prior to maturity) can be classified as HtM if the holder would recover substantially all of the carrying amount due to the fact that such a call option accelerates the effective maturity date (IAS 39.AG18). On the other hand, putable bonds (an option to be exercised by the investor) are not eligible for the HtM category because paying a premium for a put feature in a financial asset is inconsistent with expressing an intention to hold it to maturity (IAS 39.AG19).

Besides these specific issues for the HtM categorization, there is a more general question with regard to credit portfolios: Does the existence of default risk for loans and bonds have an effect on the ability to classify these securities as HtM? The clear answer is no. According to IAS 39.AG17, "a significant risk of non-payment does not preclude classification of a financial asset as held to maturity" as long as the other criteria for HtM investments are met. Hence, the quality of a credit investment does not have any effect on the classification decision. The standard setter even allows to sell the assets prior to maturity without a penalty in case "a significant deterioration in the issuer's creditworthiness" occurs (IAS 39.AG22[a]). Please note that a single downgrade action by an external rating agency does not necessarily lead to such a conclusion. On the other hand, an impairment due to the deterioration of credit quality is often regarded as sufficient.

Last but not least, the category "loans and receivables" may be another alternative, although the accounting consequences for the balance sheet and the income statement are quite similar to HtM investments. However, the category does not require the intention and ability to hold to maturity, and hence is not subject to the tainting provisions that apply to HtM investments (IAS 39.BC25). However, the category is only eligible for financial assets that are not quoted in active market (IAS 39.AG26). This means that this category is accessible for the vast majority of loans, even purchased ones, but not for actively traded bond investments.

18.2.2 Credit Default Swaps

We pass over to credit derivatives by first focusing on credit default swaps, as they represent the most important product group within the credit derivatives spectrum in terms of turnover and volume. In addition, CDS contracts act as basic building blocks for more complex credit derivatives, which we will discuss later. Against this background, accounting for credit default swaps is expected to be rather straightforward. However, as we will see below, this conclusion is premature.

Irrespective of the CDS position entered into (protection buyer or seller), one has to assess whether the contract is covered by IAS 39, as the guarantee character is apparent. As already stated, particular *financial guarantee contracts* are subject to IAS 37 (or IFRS 4), according to IAS 39.2(f) and IAS 39.3. Such contracts are excluded from the scope of IAS 39 if the contract provides "for specified payments to be made to reimburse the holder for a loss it incurs because a specified debtor fails to make payment when due under the original or modified terms of a debt instrument." This particularly means that the following conditions have to be met:

- In case of a default, the protection buyer must incur a loss in the reference obligation. Obviously, this means that he is required to hold the obligation.
- The payoff profile of the CDS must be qualified to make up the loss of the debt instrument.
- The CDS contract has to provide a reimbursement if, and only if, the specified debtor "fails to make payment when due".

Apparently, the first aspect seems inapplicable from the perspective of a protection seller, as one has to know whether the counterparty holds the reference obligation or not. In practice, no one will be able to verify this condition for long credit positions. Hence, we are convinced that no external auditor will insist upon this requirement.

As for the last two prerequisites, there are different views. For example, Auerbach and Klotzbach[99] from KPMG recently stated that the inclusion of *restructuring* as a credit event does not comply with these conditions. Hence, it would mean that practically all CDS contracts are recognized in accordance with IAS 39. However, there are other opinions as well, which currently seem to be confirmed as best practice. All three standard credit events (bankruptcy, failure to pay, restructuring) are regarded as fulfilling the required conditions. Credit events like obligation acceleration, obligation default, and repudiation /

moratorium, however, are typically not accepted. The inclusion of such credit events therefore would automatically lead to a derivatives accounting in accordance with IAS 39. In a nutshell, the only possibility to avoid IAS 39 becoming effective for CDS accounting is to refrain from additional credit events that are not market standard.

In case of a short credit position (protection buyer), the CDS should be used to hedge already existing credit risk exposure (loan or cash bond). In our view, it is not necessary that the hedge complies with risk mitigation prerequisites of Basel II, which would lead to a reduction of risk-weighted assets. If the hedge makes sense from an economic point of view (e.g., same obligor but different reference loans or bonds, different reference entities but same economic risk due to a letter of comfort or a profit-pooling contract), IAS 37 (or IFRS 4) applies.

In any case, conducting trading activities, or, entering into a CDS contract in order to render profits due to short-term spread changes, does not reflect the nature of financial guarantees. Hence, trading positions should always be accounted for in accordance with IAS 39.

The decision tree presented in figure 18.6 summarizes the crucial aspects pointed out above. However, we recommend consulting an external auditor in order to get clear guidance on credit default swaps and to avoid a rude awakening later.

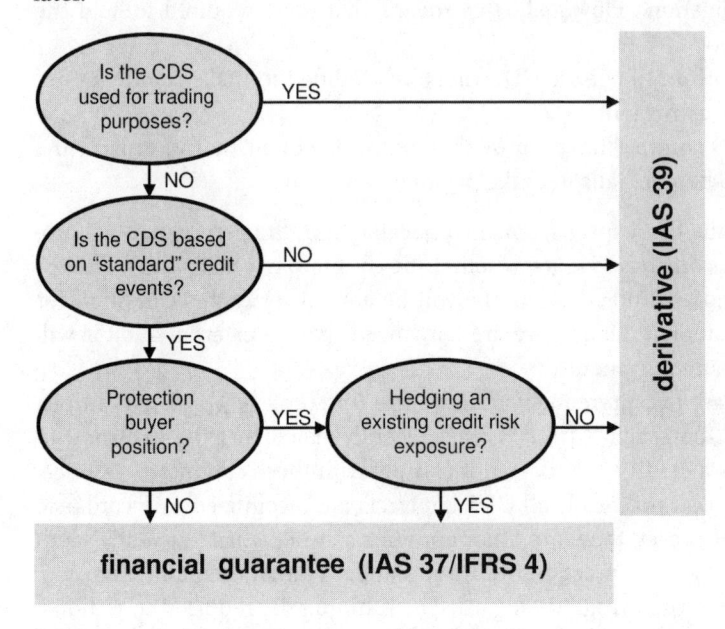

Fig. 18.6: Credit default swaps: IAS 39 or IAS 37/IFRS 4?

After having resolved whether the CDS contract is a derivative or a financial guarantee, one has to apply the respective accounting rules. In case of a financial guarantee, the CDS establishes a *contingent liability* (protection seller) or a *contingent claim* or *collateral* (protection buyer). Basically, both items are not shown on the balance sheet as long as the default case is outside the range of vision (IAS 37.31 et sqq.). However, the contingent claim or collateral has to be taken into account in case of impairment for the hedged loan or bond. If the potential loss can be retrieved by the CDS contract, an impairment is not necessary. A contingent liability may entail reserves in case the underlying credit quality experiences a dramatic deterioration.

As already stated, derivatives in line with the IAS 39 definition are categorized as aFVtPL; their fair value is disclosed on the balance sheet and fair value changes are recognized in the income statement. It should be noted that the initial present value is zero and may become positive (asset) or negative (liability) afterwards, depending on the market spread development.

What about the ongoing premium payments? One could argue that the stream of payments is an option premium with deferred payment dates. This seems reasonable, as the default case is detrimental to just one counterparty, namely the protection seller. However, it is not the usual interpretation of a credit default swap: the premium leg is swapped for the default leg. Hence, the premium payments are accounted for as interest payments, which calls for accrual accounting and recognizing the premium as interest income unless the CDS is held for trading purposes.

18.2.3 Total Return Swaps

Total return swaps belong to the basic credit derivative structures, although their importance has declined against the background of the massive growth of credit default swap products. Nevertheless, we give a short abstract of the accounting consequences.

First of all, applying the accounting provisions for financial guarantee contracts (IAS 37/IFRS 4) is out of the question, as the contract provides for payments that go beyond a reimbursement of credit-related losses. If at all, the derivatives definition in line with IAS 39 applies. However, it is arguable whether the TRS should be treated as a stand-alone contract or rather in relation to its underlying, as we will discuss in the following.

In our view, there is a recognition–derecognition issue that has to be taken into account. From an economic perspective, the protection buyer transfers all risks and rewards of the underlying asset to his counterparty. But is this transfer in line with IAS 39.17 et sqq., which would lead to a derecognition of the underlying asset in the protection buyer's balance sheet? Apparently, the protection buyer "retains the contractual rights to receive the cash flows of the financial asset, but assumes a contractual obligation to pay the cash flows to one or more recipients" (IAS 39.18[b]). IAS 39.19 stipulates additional conditions that have to be met in order to achieve derecognition, namely:

- The protection buyer has no obligation to pay amounts to the eventual recipient unless it collects equivalent amounts from the original asset (IAS 39.19[a]).
- The protection buyer is prohibited by the terms of the transfer contract from selling or pledging the original asset (IAS 39.19[b]).
- The protection buyer has an obligation to remit any cash flows it collects on behalf of the eventual recipients without material delay; no reinvestment of such cash flows should be possible (IAS 39.19[c]).

In our view, the first and the third conditions can be easily met by respective legal definitions of the TRS contract. However, the protection seller typically cannot be kept from selling or pledging the original asset by means of the total return swap. We anticipate therefore that a transfer in line with IAS 39.17 et sqq. has not taken place. A derecognition of the underlying asset does not come into question.

Accordingly, the TRS is accounted for as a regular derivative contract in line with IAS 39. Hence, the fair value (can be either positive or negative) is disclosed on the balance sheet and marked-to-market changes are recognized in the income statement. Interest cash flows (bond coupon and refinancing leg) of the contract call for accrual accounting, while compensation payments due to fair value changes are directly recognized in the income statement.

There is another case that should be considered (IAS 39.AG40[c] and IAS 39.AG51[o]). Let's assume that a company sells a financial asset to a counterparty and enters into a TRS with the same party to retrieve all cash flows and fair value changes. In such a case, derecognition of the asset is prohibited due to the fact that the company "retains substantially all the risks and rewards of ownership of the financial asset" (IAS 39.20[b]). The total return swap is just a legal contract that facilitates the maintenance of the economic property. No separate disclosure of the TRS contract is thus required.

18.2.4 Credit Linked Notes

Credit linked notes belong to the class of hybrid products, as their payoff is related to credit risk that is not (exclusively) issuer-related. Against this background, IAS 39 provisions with regard to embedded derivatives come into play. IAS 39.AG30(h) states that "credit derivatives that are embedded in a host debt instrument and allow one party to transfer the credit risk of a particular reference asset to another party are not closely related to the host debt instrument."

But this does not automatically lead to a separation of the embedded derivative, as two additional criteria have to be met. The second condition, namely that the embedded derivative is in line with the derivative definition of IAS 39, brings us back to our CDS discussion in section 18.2.2. Consequently, there is a good chance to avoid the separation. From the perspective of an investor in a regular CLN, which is not held for trading purposes, one only has to ensure that the embedded CDS contract is subject to the standard credit events (bankruptcy, failure to pay, restructuring) in order to avoid separation. (Please note: The investor implicitly is a protection seller.) The respective issuer of the note, however, must prove that he is hedging an existing credit exposure with the embedded CDS protection buyer position to be able to circumvent the separation.

In case the embedded contract matches the derivative definition of IAS 39, the separation decision finally depends on the chosen asset category. In case of held-to-maturity assets or loans and receivables (think of a credit linked promissory loan), the embedded credit derivative has to be separated and disclosed at fair value, while marked-to-market changes are recognized directly in P&L. Available-for-sale credit linked notes have to be split up as well, accompanied by recognizing fair value changes that are attributable to the embedded credit derivative in the income statement instead of the AfS reserve. Only an FVtPL categorization prevents the entity from separating the embedded derivative.

But what do the accounting consequences look like for the issuer? The results basically remain unchanged, although there are only two categories available for the liabilities side. Issues belonging to the category "other financial liabilities" are subject to a separation of the embedded credit derivative.

As mentioned before, splitting up a CLN into a host contract and an embedded derivative is an annoying procedure in practice. In addition, fair value accounting for the embedded derivative contributes to P&L volatility. However, the December 2003 version of IAS 39 provides several ways to avoid the separation of the embedded derivative:

- The IASB introduced the *fair value option*, which enables the entity to designate each single financial instrument to disclose aFVtPL. Hence, the duty to perform the separation of the embedded derivative is circumvented, but one has to accept possible P&L volatility.
- The fair value option is currently unavailable for financial liabilities due to the partial endorsement of the standard by the European Union. Thus, the only possibility for CLN issuers to avoid a separation is to implement hedge accounting. We recommend to perform a fair value or cash flow hedge, which requires an appropriate hedging instrument with an external counterparty. For instance, a single-name CDS contract would be appropriate for hedging a regular CLN with regard to credit risk.
- In place of implementing a hedge accounting approach, one could issue the CLN from a trading portfolio, if applicable. Hence, the category aFVtPL applies without the obligation to separate the embedded derivative.

18.2.5 iTraxx Products

Since its introduction in June 2004, the iTraxx product family has achieved great popularity, as it offers diversified access to credit exposure by means of a variety of different indices and products. In fact, the iTraxx Europe Benchmark index has become the most liquid instrument within the credit universe, accompanied by extremely narrow bid–ask spreads. In the following, we will point out the accounting treatment of the various product types individually. As iTraxx index swaps are of major importance and also act as the basis for more sophisticated iTraxx products, we will start with these instruments.

The iTraxx index swaps are based on a basket of reference entities (or obligations) with static weightings. Like most CDS contracts, they are settled physically in case a credit event occurs. Bankruptcy, failure to pay, and restructuring act as credit events in line with the European CDS market standard.

Hence, one could argue that their treatment in terms of IAS accounting should be similar to regular CDS contracts, particularly with regard to a possible recognition as financial guarantee contracts. However, IAS 39.3 states that financial guarantee contracts are subject to IAS 39 if they provide for payments to be made in response to changes in a credit index. In our view, this provision is not applicable to iTraxx index swaps because they are not based on a credit index. The gain or loss of an iTraxx index swap position is solely based on real economic default risk, namely credit events on constituents in the respective basket. In addition, an iTraxx index swap can be understood as a portfolio of regular CDS contracts, which does not justify an accounting treatment distinct from regular CDS contracts.

We are convinced that the IAS 39.3 provision does not apply to iTraxx index swaps. Hence, accounting consequences drawn with regard to CDS contracts can be transferred to iTraxx index swaps. But protection buyers will indeed have difficulties to prove an economic hedge of default risk. For the iTraxx Europe Benchmark index swap, one would need all 125 reference assets on the balance sheet to achieve an accounting treatment under the terms of IAS 37 (or IFRS 4).

When considering iTraxx FTD baskets or CDO tranches, it seems self-evident to designate these as derivatives in accordance with IAS 39. However, we see a good chance to transfer the CDS considerations to these products. As for iTraxx index swaps, the underlying is still not a credit index, but a portfolio of regular CDS contracts. Admittedly, FTD baskets and CDO tranches are complex products, but they still rely on credit events reflecting losses that arise "because a specified debtor fails to make payment when due" (IAS 39.2[f]). The non-linearity of payoff profiles for these instruments is, in our view, an aspect that is not relevant for assessing financial guarantee contracts. However, we recommend to consult an external auditor in order to get clear guidance with regard to these exotics.

Credit spread options based on iTraxx index swaps do have the quoted spread of the index swap (credit index) as underlying, but not the economic default risk of the reference entities. Hence, credit spread options cannot be designated as financial guarantee contracts, and hence have to be accounted for as derivatives in line with IAS 39. They have to be disclosed at fair value on the balance sheet, while marked-to-market changes have to be directly recognized in the income statement.

18.2.6 Other Instruments of Interest

Besides the instruments discussed in the preceding sections, the credit derivatives market created several exotic structures over the last few years. Despite the fact that these are still of minor importance, we provide a list to give brief guidance with regard to International Accounting Standards. It should be noted that the list is not exhaustive. In case of doubt, we recommend to apply IAS 39, that is, fair value accounting for the respective instrument.

Tab. 18.4: A non-exhaustive list for exotic credit derivatives

Instrument	Description	IAS accounting
Digital default swap	Similar to CDS except that the recovery value is fixed at the start of the trade. This specification avoids the complicated mechanism to determine the recovery rate for cash settlement.	derivative (IAS 39.9)
Recovery default swap	A forward contract with regard to the recovery rate. In case of a default, the actual recovery rate is compared to the stipulated recovery rate in the contract to determine a compensation payment (can be either positive or negative).	derivative (IAS 39.9)
Equity default swap	Actually no credit derivative, but an equity derivative (a far-out-of-the-money put option with barrier)	derivative (IAS 39.9)
Rating-triggered CDS	Similar to CDS except that the default event is defined in terms of rating classes.	derivative (IAS 39.9)
Constant maturity credit default swap	Similar to CDS except that the spread level of the premium leg is regularly adjusted in accordance with market levels	IAS 37/IFRS 4 cannot be ruled out
Option on a CDO tranche or FTD basket	Option contract that allows the buyer to enter into a CDO tranche or FTD basket	derivative (IAS 39.9)

19
Operational Issues: Basel II

Basel II (official name: "International Convergence of Capital Measurement and Capital Standards: A Revised Framework"[100]) is one of the most important operational issues that banks will face in the future. Many financial institutions have already begun to implement procedures in order to meet Basel II requirements, although the Basel II framework will not become effective until the end of 2007. This chapter provides an insight into Basel II with a specific focus on credit risk. In a final step, we will point out how the use of credit derivatives in the context of active credit portfolio management affects regulatory capital requirements.

19.1 An Introduction to Basel II

We begin by providing a brief overview with regard to the basic structure of the Basel II framework. Subsequently, we demonstrate that the capital adequacy framework from Basel I, which was introduced long before, has been carried over to Basel II. Nevertheless, the devil is in the details, as Basel II provides a variety of alternative approaches to measure a financial institution's credit risk. Hence, the focus will be on how to determine risk-weighted assets for the different approaches contained in the Basel II framework.

19.1.1 The Basic Structure

The Basel II framework offers a set of standards for establishing minimum capital requirements for financial institutions. It was prepared by the Basel Committee on Banking Supervision, whose members represent several central banks and national bank supervisory authorities. The first standard, Basel I, was published in 1988 and has been subject to several changes and refinements over the last few years. The final version was published in June 2004, so that it is up to each jurisdiction to turn the standards into legislation.

Nearly all banking markets have already been subject to capital requirements. The basic idea is that the bank's capital serves as a cushion for unexpected losses, which may arise from assuming market risk, credit risk, and other risk sources

Active Credit Portfolio Management. J. Felsenheimer, P. Gisdakis, and M. Zaiser
Copyright © 2006 WILEY-VCH Verlag GmbH & Co. KGaA, Weinheim
ISBN: 3-527-50198-3

(operational risk). Expected losses, in contrast, are not within the scope of the Basel II framework, as they should already be covered by requiring risk-adequate prices. Hence, capital requirements for a bank aim at ensuring stability of the financial system, which is accomplished by minimizing the probability of a bank filing for bankruptcy.

The 1988 Basel Capital Accord set out the first internationally accepted definition of minimum capital requirements. However, the banking industry has been subject to many changes, particularly with regard to internal credit risk management processes (e.g., internal rating models), the introduction of securitization procedures, and credit derivatives to actively manage credit-risky portfolios. Meanwhile, the Basel I accord has not kept pace with these advances. Accordingly, the development of a revised capital adequacy framework was overdue.

The main differences between Basel I and Basel II can be stated as follows:

- Newly introduced measurement approaches allow taking account of the risk that banks actually face, including internal credit risk measurement techniques.
- A variety of different approaches for measuring credit risk with different degrees of difficulty is provided. More sophisticated approaches that make use of internal risk management systems create incentives for banks due to lower capital requirements.
- A new capital charge has to be made for exposures to the risk of losses caused by operation failures (so-called operational risk).

A further major difference from Basel I arises from the new structure of the new framework. It is now based on three mutually reinforcing pillars that allow banks, supervisors, and the market to evaluate properly the various risks that banks actually face. These pillars are (cf. figure 19.1):

- Pillar 1: Minimum capital requirements, which correspond to the core of Basel I but which now offer a variety of measurement options compared to the original approach.
- Pillar 2: Supervisory review of an institution's capital adequacy and internal assessment process.
- Pillar 3: Market discipline through effective disclosure to encourage safe and sound banking practices.

The minimum capital requirements (pillar 1) can be regarded as a revision of the 1988 Basel Capital Accord's guidelines. This is done by aligning the minimum capital requirements more closely to each bank's actual risk. Pillar

2 recognizes the necessity of exercising effective supervisory review of banks' internal assessments of their overall risks to ensure that bank management is exercising sound judgment and has set aside adequate capital for these risks. Pillar 3 counts on the ability of the market to assess the quality of banks' public reporting. Accordingly, Basel II provides several provisions that state which public disclosures banks have to make with respect to their risk management. Market discipline is promoted through greater transparency and improved public disclosure.

Stability of the Financial System

Pillar 1	Pillar 2	Pillar 3
Minimum Capital Requirements	Supervisory Review of Capital Adequacy	Market Discipline
(quantitative bank capital norms)	(qualitative regulation)	(transparency norms, disclosures)

Basel II - The New Capital Adequacy Framework

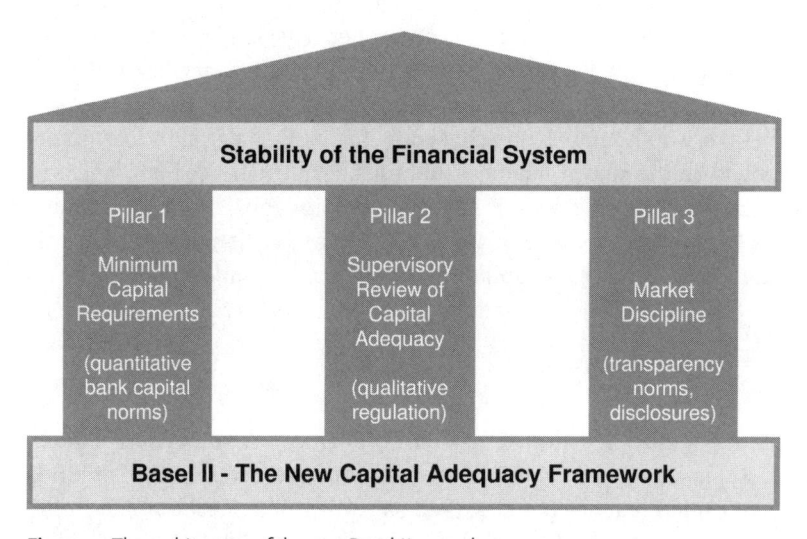

Fig. 19.1: The architecture of the new Basel II accord

Despite the fact that the Basel Committee has published a comprehensive and detailed framework (nearly 240 pages of text), several degrees of freedom remain that have to be filled by national legislation. Hence, the economic consequences of some rules are still not assessable. We will highlight these uncertainties in the course of the chapter where necessary.

Our main focus will be on the first pillar of the Basel II architecture as shown in figure 19.1. Capital adequacy requirements are always related to some source of risk; in the case of Basel II to credit risk, market risk, and operational risk. Dealing with credit-risky instruments as in the case of active credit portfolio management does not automatically mean that one just needs to consider capital requirements for credit risk. It rather depends on the purpose of these instruments. Banking book portfolios are subject to provisions relating to credit risk, while market risk is associated with trading book positions.

Basel II provides three different approaches that deal with credit risk in the banking book. The *standardized approach* as the first alternative ultimately is nothing else but a refinement of the previous (Basel I) approach, which makes use of standardized risk weights that depend on external rating assessments. However, Basel II offers two more sophisticated approaches that are referred to as the *internal ratings-based approach* (IRB approach). The basic idea of the IRB approach is to resort to internal credit risk management systems in place of external ratings. Basel II differentiates between the *foundation IRB approach*, where the probability of default (PD) is estimated by the bank, and the *advanced IRB approach*. The latter takes a more comprehensive view by estimating not only the PD, but also the loss given default (LGD) and the exposure at default (EAD) based on internal estimation procedures.

Regardless of which approach is chosen by the bank, a decision that particularly depends on the size of business and the advancement of internal credit risk management systems, the basic idea of assessing capital adequacy remains unchanged. *Regulatory capital* is related to *risk-weighted assets* (RWA), which is typically done by calculating a capital ratio. The *total capital ratio* must be no lower than 8 percent (Basel II, paragraph 40, hereafter referred to as Basel II.40), i.e.,

$$\frac{\text{Tier 1 capital} + \text{Tier 2 capital}}{\text{RWA}_{\text{total}}} \geq 8\%. \tag{19.1}$$

Shareholders' equity constitutes the Tier 1 capital with the exception of goodwill. Tier 2 capital comprises subordinated debt, loan reserves, and other kinds of long-term capital that are not classified as equity. The Tier 2 capital in the numerator of the total capital ratio is limited to 100 percent of Tier 1 capital.

The denominator is determined by multiplying the capital requirements (CR) for market risk and operational risk by 12.5 (the reciprocal of the minimum capital ratio of 8 percent) and adding the resulting numbers to the sum of risk-weighted assets for credit risk (Basel II.44):

$$\text{RWA}_{\text{total}} = \text{RWA}_{\text{credit risk}} + 12.5 \cdot [\text{CR}_{\text{market risk}} + \text{CR}_{\text{operational risk}}] \tag{19.2}$$

Simply adding up risk-weighted amounts for credit risk, market risk, and operational risk implicitly presumes that there are no diversification effects between these risk categories; these risk factors are assumed to be perfectly positively correlated, which is a very crude assumption. This worst-case scenario perspective is a basic principle of Basel II, which we will find in many other provisions that we will discuss later.

In the following section, we will focus on how to calculate the $\text{RWA}_{\text{credit risk}}$ number, which largely depends on which approach one has chosen to measure the credit risk exposure (standardized approach versus IRB approach). We will also take the regulatory capital and the capital requirements for market and operational risk for granted.

19.1.2 The Standardized Approach

As already mentioned, the standardized approach is solely an advancement of the previous Basel I approach to measure credit risk for banking book exposures. As the calculation procedure is easy to implement, the approach does not require any explicit approval by the supervisor as opposed to the IRB approach (Basel II.51). The basic idea of calculating risk-weighted assets is well-known from Basel I. One just has to multiply the amount of a credit exposure by a specific risk weight, which is expressed in percentage points. Finally, these results are summed up to obtain $RWA_{credit\ risk}$.

Within the Basel II framework, the individual risk weight largely depends on the category of the obligor (sovereigns, banks, corporates, etc.) and an external rating if available. Table 19.1 gives an overview with regard to the most common risk weights that can be found in practice.

Tab. 19.1: Risk Weights for the Standardized Approach

Rating	Sovereigns	Banks		Corporates
		Option 1	Option 2	
AAA	0%	20%	20%	20%
AA	0%	20%	20%	20%
A	20%	50%	50%	50%
BBB	50%	100%	50%	100%
BB	100%	100%	100%	100%
B	100%	100%	100%	150%
below B–	150%	150%	150%	150%
unrated	100%	100%	50%	100%

The sovereigns category also encompasses their central banks (Basel II.53). The Bank for International Settlements, the International Monetary Fund, the European Central Bank, and the European Community automatically receive a risk weight of 0 percent (Basel II.56). National supervisors may accept OECD country risk scores instead of an assessment from an external rating agency (Basel II.55). Please refer to the Export Credit Arrangement section under www.oecd.org for a consensus country risk classification, which is based on eight risk score categories. Risk scores 0 and 1 correspond to a risk weight of 0 percent, a risk score of 2 to a risk weight of 20 percent, a risk score of 3 to a risk weight of 50 percent, a risk score of 4 to 6 to a risk weight of 100 percent, and finally a risk score of 7 to a risk weight of 150 percent (Basel II.55).

With regard to claims on banks, the Basel II framework provides two options. However, the respective decision remains in the hands of the respective nation's supervisor and applies to all banks in its jurisdiction (Basel II.60). Please note that option 1 is solely based on the rating assigned to claims on the sovereign of that country rather than on the bank's individual rating, which is, in contrast, the basis for option 2 (Basel II.61 and 62).

Claims on corporates are also provided with a risk weight that corresponds to their individual rating. However, the scale for risk weights as shown in table 19.1 may be subject to changes by the national supervisor. For example, the supervisor is allowed to increase the standard risk weight for unrated claims (Basel II.67) and may permit banks to risk weight all corporate claims at 100 percent without regard to external rating (Basel II.68).

Some claims are not included in table 19.1. Retail credits, for example, typically receive a risk weight of 75 percent (Basel II.69). Claims secured by residential property are furnished with a risk weight of 35 percent (Basel II. 72), while the risk weight for other assets, such as investments in equity, amounts to 100 percent (Basel II.81).

There are more provisions that, for example, address past due loans and short-term claims. However, we will skip these here in order to facilitate readability by focusing on the most important aspects of the Basel II framework.

We close this section about the standardized approach with a problem that may arise in practice, namely the possibility of split ratings or multiple rating assessments, that is, the case that a claim is assigned different ratings by two or more external rating agencies. Basically, it is up to the bank to decide which rating agencies to take into account. If there are two assessments by two rating agencies chosen by the bank, the worse rating applies (Basel II.97). In case of three or more ratings, the second-best rating has to be taken to determine the respective risk weight.

19.1.3 The Foundation IRB Approach

The basic idea of the internal ratings-based approach, irrespective of whether one chooses the foundation or advanced IRB approach, is to rely on the bank's own internal estimates of risk components in order to determine the capital requirement for a given exposure (Basel II.211). This is done by applying a *risk-weight function*, which generates capital requirements for possible unexpected losses (Basel II.212). The shape of the risk-weight function depends on the type of exposure (retail, sovereigns, banks, corporates, etc.) and is stipulated by a few parameters, as we will see shortly.

Calculating the amount of risk-weighted assets for a specific credit exposure requires the following input factors, namely:

- The probability of default for a one-year time horizon (PD)
- The loss given default (LGD)
- The effective maturity (M)
- The exposure at default (EAD).

The first three components determine the risk weight according to the respective risk-weight function, which is then multiplied by the exposure at default (EAD) to obtain the amount of risk-weighted assets.

Implementing the foundation IRB approach requires that the bank fulfills certain minimum conditions and adheres to some disclosure requirements (Basel II.211 and many others). In addition, a supervisory approval is necessary to apply the IRB approach instead of the standardized approach.

In contrast to the advanced IRB approach, the foundation IRB approach allows the bank to develop its own estimates of PD based on internal rating systems, while the other risk components (LGD, M, EAD) are defined by respective Basel II provisions (Basel II.245 and 246).

In a very first step, banks using the IRB approach must categorize their credit exposures into the following broad classes of assets (Basel II.215):

- Corporates (debt obligation of a corporation, partnership, or proprietorship)
- Sovereigns (and their central banks, etc.)
- Banks (including some securities firms)
- Retail
- Equity.

We abstain from defining these classes, as this would take too long and also does not offer any additional insight into the mechanism of the IRB approach. However, it should be noted that some subclasses within the corporates class are established, namely project finance (PF), object finance (OF), commodities finance (CF), income-producing real estate (IPRE), and high-volatility commercial real estate (HVCRE). These are accounted for separately.

In the following, we demonstrate the mechanism of calculating risk-weighted assets (RWA) based on the most common credit risk classes *corporates*, *sovereigns*, and *banks*. First, one has to calculate a *correlation parameter*, which we denote by R, by means of the following formula (Basel II.272):

$$R = 0.12 \cdot \frac{1 - e^{-50 \cdot PD}}{1 - e^{-50}} + 0.24 \cdot \left[1 - \frac{1 - e^{-50 \cdot PD}}{1 - e^{-50}}\right] \quad (19.3)$$

Accordingly, the correlation parameter solely depends on the probability of default (PD), which is provided by the bank's internal rating system. In addition, the correlation parameter R will always lie between 0.12 and 0.24, as the two weighting factors involving PD sum up to 1. Figure 19.2 depicts how the parameter R depends on PD.

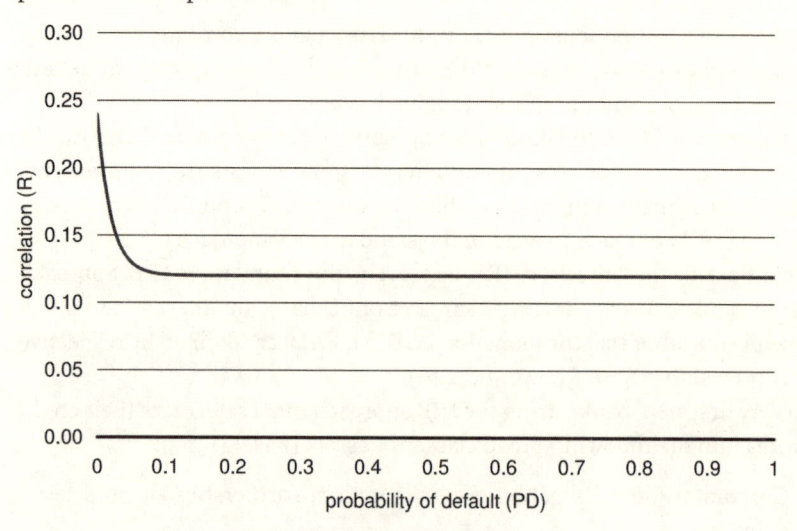

Fig. 19.2: How the PD affects the correlation parameter R

The lower the PD, the higher the correlation coefficient. There is a rationale behind this formula. If the default probability of a specific credit exposure is very small, it seems reasonable that the default case will primarily be triggered by a systemic crisis that captures numerous credit risks at the same time. Hence, the correlation of such a credit with the market should be rather high compared to a credit with a high PD, whose default is likely to occur as a result of idiosyncratic factors.

In a second step, one has to calculate the capital requirement (K) via the risk-weight function:

$$K = \left[LGD \cdot \Phi\left(\frac{\Phi^{-1}(PD) + \sqrt{R} \cdot \Phi^{-1}(0.999)}{\sqrt{1 - R}}\right) - LGD \cdot PD\right] \cdot \frac{1 + (M - 2.5) \cdot b}{1 - 1.5 \cdot b} \quad (19.4)$$

The function Φ denotes the standard normal cumulative distribution function, while Φ^{-1} is its inverse function.

Let us analyze this expression step by step. The term in squared brackets can be interpreted as the *unexpected loss* measured in percent of the exposure at default, resulting from subtracting the expected loss (LGD · PD) from the credit value at risk (CrVaR). Apparently, the CrVaR takes into account the correlation parameter R as well as a significance level of 99.9 percent. The calculation procedure is subject to a Gaussian copula approach as already discussed in the context of correlation products.

However, the result from this calculation is modified by applying an additional multiplier, which is determined by the *effective maturity* M and the *maturity adjustment b*, which has to be calculated as follows:

$$b = (0.11852 - 0.05478 \cdot \ln \text{PD})^2 \qquad (19.5)$$

In the end, one can simply calculate the amount of RWA by multiplying the resulting capital requirement K by the exposure at default EAD and the factor 12.5, which is the reciprocal of the minimum capital ratio of 8 percent:

$$\text{RWA} = 12.5 \cdot K \cdot \text{EAD} \qquad (19.6)$$

Please note that $12.5 \cdot K$ is tantamount to the risk weight, which plays a central role in the standardized approach.

Within the foundation IRB approach, the PD is the result of an internal rating process, while the other risk components (LGD, EAD, M) are given by the Basel II framework. For corporates and banks, the PD must at least amount to 0.03 percent, while there is no such floor for sovereigns. With regard to the other risk components, the following guidelines apply:

- Senior claims on corporates, sovereigns, and banks are assigned a LGD of 45 percent (Basel II.287) unless they are secured by some collateral. Subordinated claims on corporates, sovereigns, and banks are assigned a LGD of 75 percent (Basel II.288).
- Measuring the EAD is done for both on and off-balance sheet positions (Basel II.308). Netting is basically permitted for on-balance sheet loans and deposits (Basel II.309). Off-balance sheet positions are recognized by calculating the committed but undrawn amount multiplied by a so-called credit conversion factor (CCF) (Basel II.310). For example, a CCF of 75 percent applies for committed facilities, note issuance facilities, and revolving underwriting facilities.
- The effective maturity M is supposed to be 2.5 years with the exception of repo-style transactions where $M = 0.5$ is stipulated (Basel II.318).

Figure 19.3 performs a comparison between the standardized approach and the foundation IRB approach based on a senior corporate credit. We presume a large-sized company (total annual sales of over €50 mn) and the standard values for the other risk components (LGD = 45% and M = 2.5) for the calculations. Historical default rates by Moody's[16] were used to approximately match the rating classes to respective PD values.

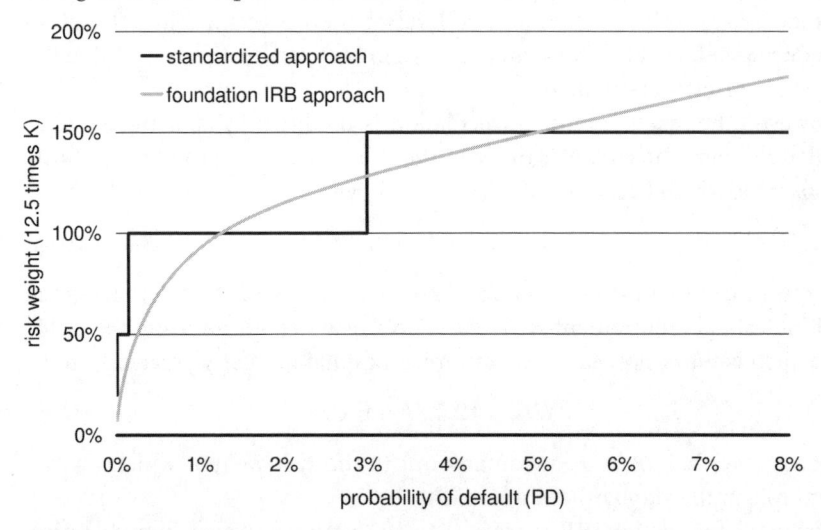

Fig. 19.3: Contrasting the standardized and the foundation IRB approach

An apparent conclusion is that the foundation IRB approach results in continuous risk weights depending on the PD. However, this conceptual benefit is undermined in practice by the bank's internal rating system, which is typically subject to a limited number of internal rating classes. In addition, none of these two approaches is superior to the other in general. In some PD areas, the standardized approach leads to a lower risk weight, and the foundation IRB approach is preferable in other areas. Nevertheless, the foundation IRB approach should typically result in lower risk weights for investment-grade credits.

After having discussed the IRB calculation methodology for claims on sovereigns, banks, and corporates, we close the section with a short guidance for other risk classes and some special cases that can be found in table 19.2.

19.1.4 The Advanced IRB Approach

Most of the facts we mentioned in the preceding section retain their validity for the advanced IRB approach. Unlike the foundation IRB approach, the

Tab. 19.2: Modifications for other risk classes

Risk class	Comment
Corporates	Firm-size adjustment for small- and medium-sized entities: For companies with reported sales of less than €50 mn per year, the correlation parameter R is reduced by up to 4 percentage points.
Corporates	Some standardized risk weights apply for specialized lending (PF, OF, CF, IPRE, HVRE) if the bank does not fulfill several requirements (Basel II.275 et sqq.).
Retail	Three different risk-weight functions apply (Basel II.327 et sqq.). Residential mortgage exposures and qualifying revolving retail exposures are assigned a constant correlation parameter of 15 and 4 percent, respectively. The parameter R varies for other retail exposures between 3 and 16 percent. Banks have to provide an estimate of the PD and LGD for each identified pool of retail exposures (PD floor: 0.03 percent).
Equity	Two approaches to calculate RWA are available: a market-based approach and a PD/LGD approach. For details, please refer to Basel II.339 et sqq.

advanced IRB approach is not only based on internal estimates for the PD, but also for other risk components (LGD, EAD and M) for each credit exposure. Please note that the distinction between foundation and advanced IRB approach is applicable to many asset classes. For some assets, however, the opportunity to decide which of these approaches to choose does not exist, such as for retail credits where both PD and LGD have to be estimated for each pool.

Below, we once again focus on claims on sovereigns, banks, and corporates. The formulas presented before remain unchanged with the exception of how to obtain the risk components LGD, EAD, and M.

While the loss given default in the foundation IRB approach can only assume a value of 45 or 75 percent, depending on the seniority of the claim, the advanced IRB approach basically allows one to derive internal estimates of LGD (Basel II.297). However, some additional requirements have to be met to be eligible (Basel II.298 and 468 et sqq.).

Similar rules apply for the exposure at default. With regard to the foundation IRB approach, we already introduced the term *credit conversion factor* (CCF). Within the advanced IRB approach, banks are allowed to use their own internal estimates of CCFs across different product types unless the exposure is not subject to a CCF of 100 percent in the foundation IRB approach (Basel II.316). For example, the standard CCF of 75 percent for commitments could be replaced by an appropriate estimate. Utilizing this option requires that the banks meet additional conditions, given in Basel II.474 et sqq.

Applying the advanced IRB approach also entails calculating the *effective maturity* instead of just taking a discretionary value for M of 2.5. In this case, the

formula
$$M = \frac{\sum_t t \cdot \text{CF}_t}{\sum_t \text{CF}_t} \tag{19.7}$$

is used, where CF_t denotes the contractual cash flows including principal, interest payments, and fees payable by the obligor in period t. In fact, this is a very similar expression as the (Macaulay) duration, differing only with respect to the missing discounting of cash flows. In any case, M must not be less than one year (with the exception of short-term exposures) or greater than five years (Basel II.320).

If a bank is not able to establish such a calculation procedure, it is allowed to use a more conservative measure of M, for example, the maturity of the respective instrument.

19.1.5 Securitization Transactions

Basel II also introduced a separate framework for securitization transactions, regardless of whether they are traditional or synthetic structures (Basel II.538). The respective provisions of Basel II apply if there are at least two different stratified risk positions or tranches reflecting different degrees of credit risk (Basel II.539 et seq.). This ruling particularly includes (single-tranche) collateralized debt obligations.

Similar to the framework for measuring capital requirements for credit risk, a standardized approach as well as an IRB approach are available for securitization transactions. However, there is no distinction between a foundation and an advanced IRB approach. Although this seems to provide some freedom of choice for the bank, the application of the framework is strictly related to the approach that is used for the respective type of underlying exposure (Basel II.566 and 606). If a bank is using a mixed model approach, that is, applying the IRB approach for some exposures and the standardized approach for other exposures in the underlying pool, it should generally use the methodology corresponding to the predominant share of exposures within the pool (Basel II.607). As we will see shortly, the label *IRB approach* in the context of securitization transactions is somewhat misleading, since it does not necessarily depend on internal rating.

Within the standardized approach, the calculation of risk-weighted assets is similar to the methodology shown in section 19.1.2, with the exception that different risk weights apply for various external rating categories (Basel II.567 et sqq.). They can be found in table 19.3.

Tab. 19.3: The standardized approach for securitization transactions

Rating	Risk weight for third-party investors	Risk weight for originating banks
AAA	20%	20 %
AA	20%	20 %
A	50%	50 %
BBB	100%	100 %
BB	350%	capital deduction
B	capital deduction	capital deduction
below B–	capital deduction	capital deduction
unrated	capital deduction	capital deduction

Apparently, the risk weight does not depend on the respective category of obligor. In addition, the risk weights are higher compared to those for the underlying exposure(s), hence meeting concerns about the more leveraged characteristic of these instruments. Ratings below BB- and unrated instruments automatically result in capital deduction, which is tantamount to a risk weight of 1,250 percent.

Originating banks who retain or repurchase securitization exposures with a BB rating (or lower) must deduct these exposures from capital (Basel II.560 and 570). Capital deduction for securitization transactions must basically be taken 50 percent from Tier 1 capital and 50 percent from Tier 2 capital (Basel II.561).

If a securitization instrument has a short-term instead of a long-term rating, a similar risk-weight scale applies. A–1/P–1 is associated with a risk weight of 20 percent, A–2/P–2 with a risk weight of 50 percent, and A–3/P–3 with a risk weight of 100 percent. All other ratings require capital deduction.

Last but not least, we would like to address an important exception from capital deduction provisions. If an unrated instrument is the most senior exposure in a securitization, the bank may apply the *look-through treatment* (Basel II.571 et sqq.). This simply means that one can resort to the average risk weight of the underlying exposures. However, that requires that the bank knows the composition of the underlying pool at all times and is able to determine the risk weights assigned to the underlying credit risk exposures.

As already mentioned, the IRB approach for securitization exposures does not necessarily depend on internal ratings. Basel II provides three alternative approaches to render risk-weighted assets:

- The ratings-based approach (RBA)
- The supervisory formula (SF)

- The internal assessment approach (IAA).

The RBA has to be used when an external or an inferred rating is available (Basel II.609). Otherwise, either the SF or the IAA must be applied.

Since it would take too long to elaborate on all these approaches in detail, we focus on the most common case, namely that the RBA applies due to the existence of an external or inferred rating. In contrast to the standardized approach for securitization exposures, the risk weight does not solely depend on the external or inferred rating of the respective instrument, but also on granularity of the underlying pool and the seniority of the position (Basel II.612).

Tab. 19.4: The RBA approach for securitization exposures, part I

Long-term rating	Risk weight for senior position	Risk weight for base risk	Risk weight for tranches backed by non-granular pools
Seniority	senior	non-senior	senior, non-senior
Granularity	$N \geq 6$	$N \geq 6$	$N < 6$
AAA	7%	12%	20%
AA	8%	15%	25%
A+	10%	18%	35%
A	12%	20%	35%
A−	20%	35%	35%
BBB+	35%	50%	50%
BBB	60%	75%	75%
BBB−	100%	100%	100%
BB+	250%	250%	250%
BB	425%	425%	425%
BB−	650%	650%	650%
below BB−	capital deduction	capital deduction	capital deduction
unrated	capital deduction	capital deduction	capital deduction

In table 19.4, the term *senior* refers to tranches that are "effectively backed or secured by a first claim on the entire amount of the assets in the underlying securitized pool" (Basel II.613). In practice, this is typically the most senior position within a securitization transaction (the *super senior tranche* of a synthetic transaction and the most senior one in the waterfall for traditional structures). The expression N is defined as the effective number of underlying exposures (Basel II.615 and 633).

A similar mapping of risk weights is also available for securitized exposures with a short-term rating, as presented in table 19.5 (Basel II. 616).

Tab. 19.5: The RBA approach for securitization exposures, part II

Short-term rating	Risk weight for senior position	Risk weight for base risk	Risk weight for tranches backed by non-granular pools
Seniority	senior	non-senior	senior, non-senior
Granularity	$N \geq 6$	$N \geq 6$	$N < 6$
A–1/P–1	7%	12%	20%
A–2/P–2	12%	20%	35%
A–3/P–3	60%	75%	75%
other ratings	capital deduction	capital deduction	capital deduction
unrated	capital deduction	capital deduction	capital deduction

19.1.6 Credit Risk Mitigation

We have so far presented various approaches within the scope of Basel II that aim at measuring capital requirements when exposed to credit risk in the banking book. In the course of time, banks have developed several techniques to eliminate or (at least) mitigate exposure to credit risk without selling the respective credit-risky asset. Even some credit derivatives, like credit default swaps on single names, serve this purpose.

In the following, we provide a brief introduction on the topic of credit risk mitigation (CRM) techniques and their consequences on measuring risk-weighted assets. We try to point out the basic mechanism of CRM and leave some details to the next section where several requirements and limitations from the perspective of the most important credit instruments, particularly credit derivatives, are discussed.

Basel II explicitly itemizes which techniques may be qualified for CRM (Basel II.109):

- Collaterals in the shape of first priority claims on cash or securities
- Netting agreements (netting loans owed to the bank against deposits from the same counterparty)
- Guarantees by third parties
- Credit derivatives (buying protection).

As one would expect, these techniques have to meet several general and specific requirements, particularly with regard to legal certainty, in order to obtain capital relief (Basel II.110). This includes minimum standards for legal documentation (Basel II.117), which "must be binding on all parties and legally enforceable in all relevant jurisdictions" (Basel II.118). In addition, the use of CRM techniques may lead to an increase of other risks, such as legal, operational, liquidity, and market risks. Hence, banks need to employ "robust procedures and processes to control these risks" (Basel II.115).

Regardless of which measurement approach is used to determine capital requirements for credit risk, there are some basic principles to credit risk mitigation, which can be summarized as follows:

1. Using CRM techniques should not render a higher capital requirement than an otherwise identical transaction where such techniques are not used (Basel II.113 and 301).
2. The effect of CRM should not be double-counted; an instrument cannot be used twice in the context of CRM to obtain capital relief (Basel II.114).
3. For guarantees and credit derivatives, the adjusted risk weight should not be less than that of a comparable direct exposure to the protection provider (Basel II.301 and 333).

In contrast to the first two principles, the third principle, which is often referred to as the *double default issue*, merits some further discussion. If we consider a single loan exposure that is (perfectly) hedged by a credit default swap referring to this borrower, one is exposed to two possible default events. Only in case of a double-default event (obligor of the loan and the counterparty of the CDS default) would one incur a loss on this position. From an economic point of view, the default correlation between the obligor and the protection seller has to be taken into account in order to assess the likelihood of such an event. Principle 3 apparently presumes the worst-case scenario by stipulating "perfectly correlated" default events, since the risk weight of the obligor is typically replaced by the risk weight of the CDS counterparty (so-called substitution approach in accordance with Basel II.141).

We start with some CRM basics within the scope of the standardized approach for measuring credit risk. A collateralized transaction requires hedging a (potential) credit exposure in whole or in part by posting a collateral that is provided either by the counterparty or by any third party on behalf of the counterparty (Basel II.119). Basel II.145 provides a comprehensive list of financial instruments that are eligible as collateral, including cash, gold, and qualified debt or equity instruments (including convertible bonds) (Basel II.145 et sqq.). In addition, the legal structure of the collateral must ensure that in case of default, the bank is able to liquidate or to take legal possession of it in a timely manner (Basel II.123). It should be clear that securities issued by the counterparty are not eligible as collateral (Basel II.124).

Basel II provides a comprehensive CRM framework for collateralized transactions (Basel II.119-138 and 145-187). Since we view this as a side issue from the perspective of active credit portfolio management, we do not delve into details. However, it should be noted that a simple approach and a comprehensive approach are available. Applying the simple approach consists of replacing the risk weight of the counterparty by the risk weight of the collateral, basically subject to a floor of 20 percent risk weight (Basel II.121, 129, and 182). The comprehensive approach involves calculating an adjusted exposure to a counterparty in order to take account of the effects of that collateral (Basel II.130), which can be quite complex in practice.

On-balance sheet netting in the context of CRM is rather simple. A bank needs a legally enforceable netting arrangement with the respective counterparty in order to calculate capital requirements on a net basis (Basel II.139 and 188).

Guarantees and credit derivatives are typically addressed under the same provisions. According to Basel II.140, they have to be "direct, explicit, irrevocable, and unconditional" in order to be eligible for CRM. If the bank meets certain minimum operational conditions with regard to risk management, the already mentioned substitution approach applies (Basel II.141), which implies that the risk weight of the counterparty is replaced by the risk weight of the guarantor (or the protection seller) for the protected portion. The risk weight for the uncovered portion remains unchanged. Some more operational requirements with regard to guarantees and credit derivatives are provided in Basel II.189-199. However, we postpone discussing consequences until the next section.

The various CRM techniques discussed in the context of the standardized approach are subject to general provisions concerning a possible *maturity mismatch*, which occurs when the residual maturity of a hedge is less than that of the underlying exposure (Basel II.143 and 202). If, in such a case, the original maturity of the credit protection arrangement is below one year, no capital relief is possible (Basel II.143 and 204). Otherwise, the following adjustment has to be made (Basel II.205):

$$P^* = P \cdot \frac{\min(5, T^{\mathrm{prot}}) - 0.25}{\min(5, T^{\mathrm{exp}}) - 0.25} \tag{19.8}$$

The term T^{exp} in equation 19.8 denotes the residual maturity of the exposure, while T^{prot} corresponds to the residual term of the credit protection arrangement. Both numbers have to be defined conservatively (Basel II.203). Hence, the (notional) amount of the credit protection arrangement P is reduced to a lower level of P^*.

Credit risk mitigation in the context of the IRB approach, regardless of whether using the foundation or the advanced IRB approach, basically starts with the CRM provisions for the standardized approach. However, several differences arise with regard to eligible instruments and particularly with regard to how the (estimated) risk components (PD, LGD, EAD, M) are affected. We will now focus on the major differences compared to our previous remarks.

In contrast to CRM for the standardized approach, the mechanism of capital relief largely depends on the respective credit class (corporates, sovereigns, banks, retail, etc.). It is no surprise that all requirements with regard to legal certainty keep their validity for the IRB approach (Basel II.213).

For claims on corporates, sovereigns, and banks, which represent the most important group within the scope of active credit portfolio management, Basel II.289 expands the set of eligible collateral (e.g., receivables and real estate). However, the simple approach for collateralized transactions is not available to banks (Basel II.290). The methodology is rather based on the comprehensive approach. The basic idea within the foundation IRB approach is to adjust the loss given default (LGD) for a senior unsecured exposure (45 percent) and retain the other risk factors (PD and EAD remain unchanged) in accordance with the formula

$$LGD^* = LGD \cdot \frac{E^*}{E} \qquad (19.9)$$

where E denotes the current value of the exposure, while E^* corresponds to the exposure value after CRM (Basel II.291). Within the advanced IRB approach, possible collateral is already taken into account when determining LGD based on own internal estimates (Basel II.297).

The treatment of guarantees and credit derivatives largely depends on whether the foundation or the advanced IRB approach is applied (Basel II.300). For the former case, the substitution approach applies as already seen for the standardized approach. This means that the risk weight of the counterparty is replaced by a new risk weight, which is derived by taking the risk-weight function of the guarantor and using a PD in line with the guarantor's credit quality (Basel II.303). If there remains an uncovered portion of the exposure, it is assigned the risk weight associated with the underlying obligor (Basel II.304). Banks that use the advanced IRB approach may adjust either PD or LGD estimates, but in a consistent manner for a given guarantee or credit derivative (Basel II.306). However, basic principle no. 3 must be applicable; the adjusted risk weight must not be less than that of a comparable direct exposure to the protection provider.

19.2 Basel II for Credit Instruments

In contrast to the introductory section of Basel II, we now focus on the instruments used for active credit portfolio management and the arising regulatory consequences. As we will see shortly, the results largely depend on the following criteria:

- Is the instrument used to incur additional credit risk (long credit, short protection), or rather applied to dispose of credit risk (short credit, long protection)?
- Is the instrument used to hedge an already existing position? (credit risk mitigation)
- Which approach is utilized to calculate capital requirements for credit risk? (standardized approach versus IRB approach)

19.2.1 Credit Default Swaps

In a first step, we focus on the consequences that arise when assuming additional credit risk by means of a credit default swap (short protection position). The standardized approach provides a simple procedure to grant comparability between on- and off-balance-sheet items. Basel II.82 states that off-balance-sheet items have to be converted into credit exposure equivalents through the use of credit conversion factors CCFs, a number we have already mentioned in the context of the IRB approach. In our case, a CCF of 100 percent applies; we obtain a credit exposure equivalent amounting to the notional amount of the CDS contract. Afterwards, the regular risk-weighting scheme of section 19.1.2 comes into play. In our view, a similar treatment applies for the IRB approach despite the fact that no specific provision concerning off-balance-sheet items can be found.

If one enters into a credit default swap in order to obtain protection for an already existing credit exposure, credit risk mitigation provisions apply. Table 19.6 summarizes the consequences from CRM in case the protection buyer position in a CDS is eligible (we presume a corporate, sovereign, or bank exposure for both IRB approaches).

However, before capital relief can be concluded for a CDS protection buyer position, one has to consider whether certain requirements that Basel II stipulates are met. First, the CDS has to be "direct, explicit, irrevocable, and unconditional" (Basel II.140). Basel II.189 states these requirements more precisely and demands that the "extent of the cover is clearly defined and incontrovertible".

Tab. 19.6: Credit risk mitigation if the CDS is eligible

Chosen approach	Consequences
standardized approach (Basel II.141 and 196)	For the protected portion, the risk weight of the counterparty is replaced by the risk weight of the protection seller (substitution approach).
	The uncovered portion retains the risk weight of the underlying obligor.
foundation IRB approach (Basel II.303 et sqq.)	For the protected portion, the risk weight of the counterparty is replaced by a new risk weight, which is derived by taking the risk-weight function of the protection seller and using a PD in line with the protection seller's credit quality (substitution approach).
	The uncovered portion retains the risk weight of the underlying obligor.
advanced IRB approach (Basel II.306)	Adjust the PD or LGD estimates in a consistent manner. The adjusted risk weight must not be less than that of a comparable direct exposure to the protection seller.

Against the background that the ISDA 2003 Credit Derivatives Definitions are the common basis for regular CDS contracts traded in the market, these legal features should be satisfied in practice.

However, if we consider a CMCDS, which adjusts the spread level of the premium leg on a regular basis in accordance with market movements, no capital relief can be claimed, since Basel II.189 explicitly excludes contracts that "would increase the effective cost of cover as a result of deteriorating credit quality in the hedged exposure."

A credit default swap can only be recognized in the context of CRM if at least the credit events *failure to pay, bankruptcy*, and *restructuring* are specified by the contracting parties (Basel II.191). Since exactly these three credit events have been established as the CDS market standard, no problem should basically arise in practice. If one of the former two credit events is not covered by the contract, there is no capital relief at all. When, however, restructuring as a credit event is not covered by the CDS, only up to 60 percent of the exposure can be recognized as protected (Basel II.192).

Although most CDS contracts are based on physical settlement in case of a default, cash settlement is sometimes stipulated as well. Basically, Basel II does not preclude cash settlement from CRM (Basel II.191[d]). However, a robust valuation process in order to estimate the loss in case of a default is required, which is typically achieved by conducting a dealer poll. We view the ISDA documentation as an adequate basis to fulfill this requirement.

As digital default swaps are cash settled and apparently do not have a "robust valuation process" to estimate the loss of the reference obligation, they do not qualify for CRM. However, consequences in practice should be limited due to the fact that DDS protection buyer positions will typically occur in the trading book instead of the banking book.

A problem that might occur in practice is related to a possible mismatch between the obligor of the underlying exposure and the reference obligation of the CDS contract. Basel II.191(g) and (h) clarify this issue. A mismatch is tolerable, "if

1. the reference obligation ranks pari passu with or is junior to the underlying obligation, and
2. the underlying obligation and reference obligation share the same obligor (i.e., the same legal entity) and legally enforceable cross-default or cross-acceleration clauses are in place."

Hence, it is not possible to achieve capital relief by hedging a subordinated credit exposure with a CDS referring to a senior obligation of the same counterparty.

There are additional legal requirements stated in Basel II.191. Since these conditions are typically met when following the ISDA documentation, we abstain from a broad discussion. Please refer to Basel II.191(c), (e), and (f) for details.

One last question remains: Which entities are eligible protection sellers for credit default swaps in order to obtain capital relief? Within the standardized approach for measuring credit risk, any sovereign or public sector entity, banks, and securities firms come into consideration. It is self-evident that only counterparties with a lower risk weight than the underlying obligor should be considered in practice. Other entities, such as corporates, will only be recognized in accordance with Basel II.195 if they are rated A– or better.

Within the foundation IRB approach (considering claims on corporates, sovereigns, and banks), the treatment of CDS within the scope of CRM is similar to the standardized approach discussed above. However, even protection sellers with no external rating are eligible. If an internally rated company has a PD equivalent to A– or better, a CDS with this counterparty may lead to capital relief. Other requirements retain their validity within the foundation IRB approach.

But the advanced IRB approach does not explicitly refer to the sophisticated provisions of Basel II.189-194. According to Basel II.307, a bank has the option to adopt the treatment of the foundation IRB approach (which is quite similar to the standardized approach), or simply "to make an adjustment to its LGD estimate of the exposure to reflect the presence of the credit derivative." The latter does not have any limitations with regard to eligible protection sellers. Basel II.488 and 489 provide some general requirements for CDS that are, however, less strict than the provisions discussed within the scope of the standardized approach.

19.2.2 Total Return Swaps

In contrast to credit default swaps, total return swaps do not only facilitate the transfer of credit risk but also the remaining market risk of the respective underlying. However, the legal structure of a TRS is totally different from the CDS documentation because cash flows and the settlement procedure do not depend on the occurrence of a credit event. Nevertheless, the treatment of a TRS is straightforward, as we will see shortly.

Entering into a TRS with the objective of assuming credit and market risk of a specific underlying instrument is, from an economic point of view, tantamount to a direct investment in the underlying, without the need to fund the position. Against this background, it is no surprise that Basel II.82 applies again, requiring the conversion of the off-balance-sheet item into a *credit exposure equivalent* via a credit conversion factor of 100 percent. Subsequently, the risk-weighting scheme of section 19.1.2 comes into play. A similar treatment applies for the IRB approach despite the fact that no specific provision concerning off-balance-sheet items can be found.

Buying protection for a specific instrument via a TRS raises the question whether capital relief can be obtained. Although the various requirements with regard to credit events in Basel II.189 et sqq. do not apply to TRS unlike CDS, Basel II.193 explicitly mentions total return swaps as eligible instruments for CRM. They only have to be "equivalent to guarantees", which simply means that Basel II.189 and 190 have to be fulfilled. Paragraph 189 has already been discussed in the context of CDS (requirements: "direct, explicit, irrevocable, and unconditional") and can be regarded as fulfilled for a regular TRS contract. Basel II.190 raises the following additional requirements:

- In case of default or non-payment, the bank is able to pursue the protection seller for any amount outstanding under the documentation governing the transaction.
- The TRS is an explicitly documented obligation assumed by the protection seller.

- The TRS covers all types of payments the underlying obligor is expected to make.

In our view, these conditions should definitely be met by any regular TRS contract. Hence, we conclude that a capital relief should be accomplished for a TRS. However, any asset mismatch would automatically forfeit this opportunity.

However, Basel II.193 provides an exception to the general conclusion: "Where a bank buys credit protection through a total return swap and records the net payments received on the swap as net income, but does not record offsetting deterioration in the value of the asset that is protected (either through reductions in fair value or by an addition to reserves), the credit protection will not be recognized". Apparently, this is one of few links from Basel II to the accounting universe. The illustrated case represents a situation where the bank tries to conceal the true economic hedging relationship between the underlying asset and the TRS in order to show sham profits. It seems reasonable that the Basel Committee on Banking Supervision does not approve capital relief in this case because the stockholders' equity would be overstated.

If the underlying asset (from the perspective of IAS 39) is designated as held-to-maturity (HtM) or as loans and receivables (LaR), capital relief for a TRS that refers to this asset would not be accessible. This is due to the fact that these two categories for financial assets neither account for regular fair value changes on the balance sheet nor recognize a reserve in equity. Conducting a fair value hedge could be a possible solution to this problem, resulting in an appropriate financial statement and allowing for capital relief.

The remaining conclusions drawn for CDS with regard to the range of eligible protection sellers and the mechanism of how to calculate the capital relief (cf. table 19.6) are also applicable to total return swaps.

19.2.3 Credit Linked Notes

Credit linked notes (CLN) seem to be a neglected class of instruments in the Basel II framework. The most instructive insight with regard to regular CLN contracts can be found in the footnotes of paragraphs 145 and 194, stating that "cash funded credit linked notes issued by the bank against exposures in the banking book which fulfill the criteria for credit derivatives will be treated as cash collateralized transactions."

Unfortunately, this statement is solely related to credit linked notes on the liabilities side of the balance sheet but does not offer any insight into the treatment of CLN investments. Consequently, we will start with a discussion regarding issued credit linked notes.

In accordance with the above-mentioned footnote, a regular CLN issue is tantamount to entering into a protection buyer CDS contract (or a guarantee) while the counterparty (protection seller) simultaneously provides a cash collateral. In the following, we presume that this embedded CDS contract is in line with the requirements discussed in section 19.2.1.

From the perspective of the standardized approach, this cash collateral is eligible (Basel II.120 and 145[a]). Accordingly, it is allowed to reduce the exposure of the underlying obligation specified in the CLN, subject to more detailed provisions, provided in paragraph 121 et sqq. of the Basel II framework. As already discussed in section 19.1.6, banks may opt for either the simple approach or the comprehensive approach for collateralized transactions, both generally subject to a 20 percent risk weight floor (Basel II.121). In any case, we presume that the legal and operational conditions of Basel II.123-126 are met.

Under the simple approach, the risk weight for the underlying credit exposure is replaced by the risk weight of the collateral instrument (Basel II.129). In order to obtain such recognition, the collateral must be pledged at least for the life of the exposure, which cannot be taken for granted in practice (Basel II.182 and 143). The residual maturity of the CLN is very often below that of the underlying credit exposure. Otherwise, one would have to stipulate a new reference obligation once the original reference obligation has become due. Although Basel II.121 establishes a minimum risk weight of 20 percent, there are some exceptions to this general rule. If the underlying exposure and the CLN are denominated in the same currency, a 0 percent risk weight can be applied (Basel II.185).

The comprehensive approach, in contrast, is based on the idea of reducing the underlying exposure amount by "the value ascribed to the collateral", and even allows a maturity mismatch (Basel II.121 and 130). While no haircut is necessary for possible future fluctuations in the value of the cash collateral, a haircut may apply when the underlying exposure and the CLN are denominated in different currencies (Basel II.131). This would effectively lead to a reduction of the collateral amount. Last but not least, one has to calculate the risk-weighted assets as the difference between the exposure amount and the (adjusted) collateral amount (Basel II.132). Please refer to Basel II.147-150 for details.

After having delved into the consequences from the perspective of the standardized approach, we need to add a short comment on the foundation and advanced IRB approach. The recognition of collateral for the foundation IRB approach closely follows the comprehensive approach to collateral in the standardized approach (Basel II.290). According to Basel II.291, one has to adjust the LGD by the already known formula

$$\text{LGD}^* = \text{LGD} \cdot \frac{E^*}{E}$$

Remember that E denotes the current value of the exposure, while E^* corresponds to the exposure value after the cash collateral has been taken into account.

Within the advanced IRB approach, the associated cash collateral of a CLN has to be incorporated when determining LGD based on own internal estimates (Basel II.297).

Finally, we return to our initial question of how to treat CLN investments as opposed to CLN issuance. From an economic point of view, a CLN investor apparently incurs two different credit risks when investing in such an instrument, namely the credit risk of the underlying reference obligation and the risk of a potential default of the CLN issuer. Hence, the double default issue, which is typically discussed in the context of CRM, arises here as well. If one considers the worst-case scenario, that is, a setting where both default events are mutually exclusive, the only possible solution would be to add up the risk weights of the issuer and the underlying reference obligation. For example, if we consider a credit linked note issued by a bank with an AA rating and which refers to DaimlerChrysler (BBB from S&P), this would result in a risk weight of 120 percent (100 percent for the underlying reference obligation and 20 percent for the issuer) in the context of the standardized approach (assuming that option 2 applies for banks).

It should be noted that the framework for securitization transactions is, in our view, not applicable, although credit linked notes are explicitly mentioned in Basel II.540. Since synthetic securitization requires "at least two different stratified risk positions or tranches that reflect different degrees of credit risk", the provisions do not apply in case of a regular CDS contract.

19.2.4 Default Baskets

Default basket products like first-to-default (FTD) and second-to-default (STD) baskets enjoy great popularity in the context of active credit portfolio management. The usage of these instruments, however, is largely affected by regulatory considerations, particularly with regard to the extent of required capital or the capital relief resulting from buying protection.

As before, we begin a discussion concerning protection seller positions in default baskets. In the context of the standardized approach, Basel II provides explicit provisions that address FTD and STD baskets. According to Basel II.208

and 210, the calculation of risk-weighted assets depends on whether an external rating for the respective instrument is accessible. If an external agency provides an external credit assessment, the risk-weight tables of the standardized approach for securitization transactions (cf. table 19.3) apply. Consequently, investing in a default basket with an external rating results in a 20 percent risk weight, even when the basket comprises only high-quality names.

If no such rating is available for a first-to-default basket, which essentially is the standard case in practice, the standard risk weights of the obligations included in the basket (cf. table 19.1) have to be aggregated up to a maximum of 1,250 percent (Basel II.208). For second-to-default baskets, the lowest risk weight can be excluded from the summation (Basel II.210). However, a risk weight below 20 percent cannot be accomplished for STD baskets.

This procedure apparently does not take into account any default correlation effects that typically exist in practice. Simply adding up the involved risk weights assumes a perfectly negative correlation between the default events, which is the worst-case scenario for a default basket investor.

Whether securing oneself an external rating for a default basket pays off from the perspective of capital requirements largely depends on the composition of the underlying basket. If the basket comprises only high-quality sovereigns with an AAA or an AA rating, the resulting risk weight would be 0 percent under the assumption that no external rating is accessible. However, resorting to an external rating leads to a lower risk weight in many other cases, although the high costs generated by requesting an external rating often nullifies the advantage of a lower risk weight.

In contrast to the standardized approach, Basel II provisions governing the IRB approach do not explicitly describe the treatment of default baskets. Hence, we anticipate an analog application of Basel II.208 and 210, namely to sum up risk weights, even though the underlyings' risk weights are calculated in accordance with the respective IRB approach, using an appropriate risk-weight function for each underlying obligor.

Buying protection in a default basket may be a low-priced alternative to buying protection via a single-name CDS contract referring to the underlying names of the basket. Although Basel II.193 lists only credit default swaps and total return swaps as eligible credit derivatives in the context of credit risk mitigation, Basel II.207 and 209 provide specific rules for default basket products as well.

Since FTD and STD baskets are typically based on the same ISDA documentation as regular CDS contracts, no additional legal or operational considerations arise compared to the issues that have already been discussed in section 19.2.1.

Basel II.207 grants capital relief for first-to-default baskets, but only for the obligor with the lowest risk weight in the basket. However, there is an additional requirement to obtain capital relief. The notional amount of the underlying obligation with the lowest risk weight must be less or equal to the notional amount of the FTD basket.

Basically, no capital relief can be achieved by entering into a STD protection buyer position. However, there are two exceptions to this general rule (Basel II.209):

- If first-to-default protection on the same basket has also been obtained, capital relief is granted for the two obligations with the lowest risk weight.
- If one of the assets within the basket has already defaulted, the STD basket effectively becomes a FTD basket. Capital relief is then granted for the (remaining) obligation in the basket with the lowest risk weight.

19.2.5 iTraxx Products

It is no surprise that the Basel II framework provides no specific rules that address the topic of the iTraxx product family. However, many instruments from the iTraxx universe are covered by respective rules, for example first-to-default baskets as discussed in section 19.2.4.

The most important iTraxx instrument type is the index swap, which may have the iTraxx Benchmark, HiVol, Crossover, and other subindices as an underlying credit basket. It seems self-evident to treat index swaps similar to regular credit default swaps. If one enters into an iTraxx Europe Benchmark swap in order to incur credit risk (sell protection), a €10 mn position is tantamount to 125 single-name CDS contracts with a notional amount of €80,000 each.

In practice it would definitely be an operational issue if one were forced to replace an iTraxx index swap by 125 single-name CDS. Hence, it may be sufficient from the bank's point of view to use the highest risk weight of the respective basket constituents to calculate the amount of risk-weighted assets for the whole iTraxx index swaps. For example, one could utilize a risk weight of 100 percent for the iTraxx Europe Benchmark index, although the average risk weight of the constituents amounts to about 66 percent. If the bank is in a position to furnish the system that performs the capital requirement calculations with an average, instrument-specific risk weight, one would obtain minimized risk-weighted assets.

When considering iTraxx index swaps in the context of credit risk mitigation, one could accordingly split up the iTraxx swap into respective single-name CDS contracts in order to obtain capital relief for various names included in the underlying credit basket. To be honest, buying protection in an iTraxx index swap typically aims at hedging systematic spread movements rather than eliminating default risk. This result is particularly reflected in the fact that the composition of the underlying iTraxx basket usually does not correspond to the banking book portfolio. However, capital requirements for credit risk within the scope of Basel II are based on unexpected losses due to default events rather than on changes of credit spreads. From this economic point of view, one should not rely on CRM techniques when utilizing iTraxx index swaps.

Basel II.193 explicitly specifies credit default swaps and total return swaps as eligible in the context of CRM, while Basel II.194 states that "other types of credit derivatives will not be eligible for recognition at this time." However, it is unclear whether iTraxx index swaps must be excluded from CRM, as they can be interpreted as a portfolio of single-name CDS contracts.

With regard to other iTraxx instrument types, we draw the following conclusions:

- Credit linked notes based on an iTraxx credit basket should be treated under the considerations of section 19.2.3. However, we see little chance to apply credit risk mitigation as discussed in the context of iTraxx index swaps.
- First-to-default baskets available on several iTraxx indices have to be treated in accordance with section 19.2.4.
- Standardized CDO tranches are subject to securitization provisions of Basel II. Within the standardized approach, capital deduction would result because no external ratings are available. Under the IRB approach, an inferred rating may prevent capital deduction for various mezzanine and senior tranches.

Part IV

Appendix

A.1 Analytics with Bloomberg and Reuters

Both Bloomberg and Reuters provide a broad range of informational and analytical pages with respect to credit markets. The most important functions are listed below. Moreover, historical time series are available, which are crucial to feed portfolio models with data and to run optimization processes.

A.1.1 Bloomberg

In table A.1, we list the major credit-relevant functions in Bloomberg. Besides analyzing various spread measures and functions regarding the credit quality of an issuer, Bloomberg offers some interesting analytical tools, which simplify life for credit derivatives investors.

Tab. A.1: Bloomberg analytics

Function	Description
Credit derivatives functions	
CDSD	Set up custom curve defaults, valuing credit default swaps
CDSI	Credit default swap indices, such as iTraxx and CDX
CDSW	Value credit default swaps of single issuers; including implied default probabilities
CDSN	Analysis and creation of default baskets; can be used for iTraxx FTD valuation
CDSM	Analysis and creation of CDO tranches; can be used for iTraxx tranche valuation
NI CDRV	News on credit derivatives
Spread valuation	
YAS	Analyzing different spread measures
ASW	Structure and value asset swaps; hedging swap cash flows for any fixed income security
RVS	Shows the history of spreads versus swaps for a single bond
OAS1	Calculating option values and pure credit spreads for bonds with option features
Credit quality functions	
CRPR	Current rating for a specific issuer and/or a specific fixed income security
RATC	Current and historical rating actions
RATD	Rating scales and definitions for various rating agencies
DDIS	Maturity distribution of a selected issuer's outstanding debt

Besides the CDSW function that can be used to price credit default swaps, there are also valuation tools for more complex derivatives available. The CDSN function allows to calculate the FTD basket spread by entering the spreads of every constituent, as well as the correlation parameter. The CDSM function can be used to value STCDOs, for example, for the iTraxx tranche spectrum. There is an upload file in Excel format to feed the model with constituent spreads. Entering the correlation parameter or the market quote generates a fair tranche spread and vice versa. Last but not least, the availability of so-called CDS Overrides offers the opportunity to extend the CDSW pricing capability to an Excel-based environment. Using CDS Overrides allows to replace input data in the CDSW framework (which have a black-box character) to individually calculate, for example, the termination fee or the upfront payment for portfolio derivatives like the iTraxx Europe Benchmark index.

The Bloomberg ticker logic for the unfunded iTraxx swap products is as follows:

ITRXEB54   iTraxx Europe Benchmark 5Y Series 4
ITRX   basic ticker name
    E   area code: E = Europe
       B   sector: B = Benchmark
         5   term: 5 for 5Y, 0 for 10Y
         4   series number: e.g., 4 for Series 4

Tab. A.2: Bloomberg tickers for iTraxx Europe Series 4 indices

	5Y index	10Y index
Benchmark	ITRXEB54 Index	ITRXEB04 Index
Financials Senior	ITRXES54 Index	ITRXES04 Index
Financials Subordinated	ITRXEU54 Index	ITRXEU04 Index
Non-Financials	ITRXEF54 Index	ITRXEF04 Index
Automobiles	ITRXEA54 Index	ITRXEA04 Index
Industrials	ITRXEI54 Index	ITRXEI04 Index
Consumer	ITRXEY54 Index	ITRXEY04 Index
Energy	ITRXEE54 Index	ITRXEE04 Index
TMT	ITRXET54 Index	ITRXET04 Index
HiVol	ITRXEH54 Index	ITRXEH04 Index
Crossover	ITRXEX54 Index	ITRXEX04 Index

A.1.2 Reuters

Besides useful functions with respect to credit relevant news – including CDx markets and a very comprehensive overview of rating actions and CDS quotes for more than 2,000 reference entities – there is also a CDS pricing tool available on Reuters.

Tab. A.3: Bloomberg tickers for iTraxx Europe Benchmark Series 4 tranches

	5Y tranches	10Y tranches
0–3%	ITRTAE54 Index	ITRTAE04 Index
3–6%	ITRTBE54 Index	ITRTBE04 Index
6–9%	ITRTCE54 Index	ITRTCE04 Index
9–12%	ITRTDE54 Index	ITRTDE04 Index
12–22%	ITRTEE54 Index	ITRTEE04 Index
3–100%	ITRTFE54 Index	ITRTFE04 Index

Reuters' CDS analysis tool calculates the CDS spread, the CDS premium and a default probability curve from CDS spreads. A CDS spread curve can be derived from the contributed spreads using credit risk models. To evaluate the basis, one can compare asset swap spreads of the bonds with the respective CDS spreads. One can compare CDS spreads against asset swap spreads using the Cox-Ingersoll-Ross model, while a credit event probability curve can be used to calibrate the credit risk models from CDS spreads. A risky curve, derived from interest rate swap prices or related straight bond, can be used to build an individual zero curve.

- Reuters provides daily market overviews of US, European, and Asian credit markets, including the cash corporate bond and the credit derivatives market. For a comprehensive overview, type in <CDV> in the news mode.
- There are real-time market quotes for the global corporate bond universe available, including single-name CDS and the whole iTraxx and CDX index universe (provided by GFI).
- The <Bondviews> function allows to search for all corporate bonds that can be sorted in a relative value analysis table. This encompasses the whole high-grade and high-yield universe.
- Based on the constituents of the <LIQUIDCREDIT> menu, term structures of aggregated credit spreads are displayed. This includes spread curves by rating class, which can be calculated using different spread measures (yield spreads and asset swap spreads).
- There is a CDS search function, which helps finding CDS quotes for specific issuers by market and by the company name of the reference obligor. In the CDS menu, issuer details are available including the capital structure of the company. There is also a link to equity markets included, which allows for a basic analysis of capital structure arbitrage trades.

- Reuters includes a CDS–ASW-basis function, where credit default swaps can be compared to cash corporate bonds. This is a crucial function to generate basis trades.
- The above-mentioned CDS valuation tool can be transferred into an Excel worksheet (drag-and-drop function).
- All Reuters real-time quotes can be linked to Excel via the RtGet() function.

Tab. A.4: Reuters RICs for iTraxx Europe indices*

iTraxx Europe ...	Series 3 maturity	RIC
Benchmark 3Y	06/20/2008	<ITRAC08MEA=ITX>
Benchmark 5Y	06/20/2010	<ITRAC10MEA=ITX>
Benchmark 7Y	06/20/2012	<ITRAC12MEA=ITX>
Benchmark 10Y	06/20/2015	<ITRAC15MEA=ITX>
Financials Senior 5Y	06/20/2010	<ITFSR10MEA=ITX>
Financials Senior 10Y	06/20/2015	<ITFSR15MEA=ITX>
Financials Subordinated 5Y	06/20/2010	<ITFSU10MEA=ITX>
Financials Subordinated 10Y	06/20/2015	<ITFSU15MEA=ITX>
Non-Financials 5Y	06/20/2010	<ITNFL10MEA=ITX>
Non-Financials 10Y	06/20/2015	<ITNFL15MEA=ITX>
Automobiles 5Y	06/20/2010	<ITAUT10MEA=ITX>
Automobiles 10Y	06/20/2015	<ITAUT15MEA=ITX>
Consumer 5Y	06/20/2010	<ITCOE10MEA=ITX>
Consumer 10Y	06/20/2015	<ITCOE15MEA=ITX>
Energy 5Y	06/20/2010	<ITENE10MEA=ITX>
Energy 10Y	06/20/2015	<ITENE15MEA=ITX>
Industrials 5Y	06/20/2010	<ITIND10MEA=ITX>
Industrials 10Y	06/20/2015	<ITIND15MEA=ITX>
TMT 5Y	06/20/2010	<ITTMT10MEA=ITX>
TMT 10Y	06/20/2015	<ITTMT15MEA=ITX>
HiVol 3Y	06/20/2008	<ITHVC08MEA=ITX>
HiVol 5Y	06/20/2010	<ITHVC10MEA=ITX>
HiVol 7Y	06/20/2012	<ITHVC12MEA=ITX>
HiVol 10Y	06/20/2015	<ITHVC15MEA=ITX>
Crossover 5Y	06/20/2010	<ITCRS10MEA=ITX>
Crossover 10Y	06/20/2015	<ITCRS15MEA=ITX>

*Start page for iTraxx data is ITRAXXCDS

A.2 Default and Recovery Data from Rating Agencies

Tab. A.5: Global annual issuer-weighted default rates (in %) by whole-letter rating, 1970-2004

Cohort year	Cohort Rating									All rated
	Aaa	Aa	A	Baa	Ba	B	Caa–C	IG	SG	
1970	0.00	0.00	0.00	0.27	4.12	20.78	53.33	0.14	8.78	2.64
1971	0.00	0.00	0.00	0.00	0.42	3.85	13.33	0.00	1.10	0.29
1972	0.00	0.00	0.00	0.00	0.00	7.14	40.00	0.00	1.88	0.46
1973	0.00	0.00	0.00	0.46	0.00	3.77	44.44	0.23	1.24	0.45
1974	0.00	0.00	0.00	0.00	0.00	10.00	0.00	0.00	1.31	0.28
1975	0.00	0.00	0.00	0.00	1.02	5.97	0.00	0.00	1.73	0.36
1976	0.00	0.00	0.00	0.00	1.01	0.00	0.00	0.00	0.87	0.18
1977	0.00	0.00	0.00	0.28	0.52	3.28	50.00	0.11	1.34	0.35
1978	0.00	0.00	0.00	0.00	1.08	5.41	0.00	0.00	1.78	0.35
1979	0.00	0.00	0.00	0.00	0.49	0.00	0.00	0.00	0.42	0.09
1980	0.00	0.00	0.00	0.00	0.00	4.94	33.33	0.00	1.61	0.34
1981	0.00	0.00	0.00	0.00	0.00	4.49	0.00	0.00	0.70	0.16
1982	0.00	0.00	0.26	0.31	2.72	2.41	25.00	0.21	3.54	1.04
1983	0.00	0.00	0.00	0.00	0.91	6.31	40.00	0.00	3.82	0.97
1984	0.00	0.00	0.00	0.36	0.83	6.72	0.00	0.10	3.32	0.93
1985	0.00	0.00	0.00	0.00	1.40	8.22	0.00	0.00	3.67	1.01
1986	0.00	0.00	0.00	1.33	2.03	11.73	23.53	0.32	5.64	1.91
1987	0.00	0.00	0.00	0.00	2.71	6.23	20.00	0.00	4.23	1.51
1988	0.00	0.00	0.00	0.00	1.24	6.36	28.57	0.00	3.59	1.37
1989	0.00	0.00	0.00	0.59	2.98	8.95	25.00	0.15	5.79	2.27
1990	0.00	0.00	0.00	0.00	3.35	16.18	58.82	0.00	10.08	3.64
1991	0.00	0.00	0.00	0.27	5.35	14.56	36.84	0.07	10.40	3.28
1992	0.00	0.00	0.00	0.00	0.30	9.03	26.67	0.00	4.85	1.33
1993	0.00	0.00	0.00	0.00	0.56	5.71	28.57	0.00	3.52	0.95
1994	0.00	0.00	0.00	0.00	0.24	3.82	5.13	0.00	1.95	0.57
1995	0.00	0.00	0.00	0.00	0.69	4.81	11.57	0.00	3.33	1.04
1996	0.00	0.00	0.00	0.00	0.00	1.44	13.99	0.00	1.67	0.52
1997	0.00	0.00	0.00	0.00	0.19	2.12	14.67	0.00	2.06	0.66
1998	0.00	0.00	0.00	0.12	0.63	4.26	15.09	0.04	3.45	1.24
1999	0.00	0.00	0.00	0.10	1.01	5.85	20.54	0.04	5.65	2.16
2000	0.00	0.00	0.00	0.38	0.89	5.49	20.04	0.13	6.14	2.41
2001	0.00	0.00	0.16	0.19	1.57	9.36	34.37	0.13	10.58	3.82
2002	0.00	0.00	0.16	1.21	1.54	4.97	30.30	0.49	8.45	3.04
2003	0.00	0.00	0.00	0.00	0.95	2.66	21.53	0.00	5.27	1.70
2004	0.00	0.00	0.00	0.00	0.19	0.65	12.33	0.00	2.23	0.72
Mean	0.00	0.00	0.02	0.17	1.17	6.21	21.33	0.06	3.88	1.26
Median	0.00	0.00	0.00	0.00	0.89	5.49	20.54	0.00	3.45	0.97
Min	0.00	0.00	0.00	0.00	0.00	0.00	0.00	0.00	0.42	0.09
Max	0.00	0.00	0.26	1.33	5.35	20.78	58.82	0.49	10.58	3.82
StDev	0.00	0.00	0.06	0.32	1.27	4.44	16.78	0.11	2.88	1.05

Source: Moody's Investor Service[16]

Tab. A.6: Global average issuer-weighted cumulative default rates (in %) by whole-letter rating, 1970–2004

Cohort rating	Time horizon (years)									
	1	2	3	4	5	6	7	8	9	10
Aaa	0.00	0.00	0.00	0.04	0.12	0.21	0.30	0.41	0.52	0.63
Aa	0.00	0.00	0.03	0.12	0.20	0.29	0.37	0.47	0.54	0.61
A	0.02	0.08	0.22	0.36	0.50	0.67	0.85	1.04	1.25	1.48
Baa	0.19	0.54	0.98	1.55	2.08	2.59	3.12	3.65	4.25	4.89
Ba	1.22	3.34	5.79	8.27	10.72	12.98	14.81	16.64	18.40	20.11
B	5.81	12.93	19.51	25.33	30.48	35.10	39.45	42.89	45.89	48.64
Caa–C	22.43	35.96	46.71	54.19	59.72	64.49	68.06	71.91	74.53	76.77
IG	0.07	0.21	0.41	0.67	0.92	1.17	1.44	1.70	1.99	2.31
SG	4.85	9.84	14.43	18.41	21.91	24.95	27.52	29.76	31.75	33.61
All rated	1.56	3.15	4.60	5.86	6.94	7.85	8.62	9.30	9.93	10.53

Cohort rating	Time horizon (years)									
	11	12	13	14	15	16	17	18	19	20
Aaa	0.76	0.90	1.05	1.13	1.22	1.32	1.42	1.54	1.54	1.54
Aa	0.69	0.84	1.01	1.25	1.38	1.52	1.73	1.92	2.20	2.44
A	1.72	1.95	2.20	2.43	2.74	3.12	3.51	3.93	4.41	4.87
Baa	5.59	6.35	7.12	7.91	8.73	9.48	10.23	10.94	11.56	12.05
Ba	22.01	24.07	26.11	28.02	29.67	31.53	33.16	34.71	35.92	37.07
B	50.99	52.85	54.62	56.35	57.72	58.80	59.11	59.11	59.11	59.11
Caa–C	78.53	78.53	78.53	78.53	78.53	78.53	78.53	78.53	78.53	78.53
IG	2.64	3.01	3.39	3.77	4.18	4.61	5.04	5.48	5.92	6.31
SG	35.47	37.27	39.05	40.71	42.13	43.65	44.87	46.00	46.89	47.75
All rated	11.14	11.75	12.37	12.95	13.51	14.10	14.65	15.18	15.68	16.13

Source: Moody's Investor Service[16]

Tab. A.7: Global average annual whole-letter rating migration matrix (in %), 1970–2004

Cohort rating	Issuer count	Terminal rating								
		Aaa	Aa	A	Baa	Ba	B	Caa–C	Default	WR
Aaa	3,179	89.48	7.05	0.75	0.00	0.03	0.00	0.00	0.00	2.69
Aa	11,310	1.07	88.41	7.35	0.25	0.07	0.01	0.00	0.00	2.83
A	22,981	0.05	2.32	88.97	4.85	0.46	0.12	0.01	0.02	3.19
Baa	18,368	0.05	0.23	5.03	84.50	4.60	0.74	0.15	0.16	4.54
Ba	12,702	0.01	0.04	0.46	5.28	78.88	6.48	0.50	1.16	7.19
B	10,794	0.01	0.03	0.12	0.40	6.18	77.45	2.93	6.03	6.85
Caa–C	2,091	0.00	0.00	0.00	0.52	1.57	4.00	62.68	23.12	8.11

Source: Moody's Investor Service[16]

Tab. A.8: Global annual average issuer-weighted defaulted bond recovery rates by seniority class in US$, 1982–2004

Default year	Senior sec	Senior unsec	Senior sub	Sub	Junior sub	All bonds
1982	72.5	34.4	48.1	32.3	–	35.0
1983	40.0	52.7	43.5	41.4	–	50.1
1984	–	49.4	67.9	44.3	–	44.4
1985	83.6	60.2	30.9	42.7	48.5	39.9
1986	59.2	52.6	50.2	42.9	–	44.3
1987	71.0	62.7	46.5	46.2	–	61.7
1988	55.3	45.2	33.4	33.0	36.5	42.9
1989	46.5	43.8	33.1	26.8	16.9	32.8
1990	35.7	37.0	26.7	19.5	10.7	27.5
1991	50.1	38.9	43.8	24.1	7.8	39.1
1992	62.7	52.1	47.9	37.8	13.5	45.5
1993	–	37.1	51.9	43.7	–	48.0
1994	69.3	53.7	29.6	33.7	–	44.5
1995	63.6	47.6	34.3	39.4	–	45.8
1996	47.6	62.8	43.8	22.6	–	43.6
1997	76.0	55.1	44.7	38.4	30.6	51.8
1998	51.8	39.5	44.2	14.1	62.0	40.4
1999	43.3	38.3	29.1	35.5	–	37.6
2000	41.7	24.4	20.3	31.9	15.5	25.7
2001	41.7	23.1	20.9	15.9	47.0	34.3
2002	49.3	30.5	25.3	24.5	–	34.6
2003	63.5	41.4	39.6	12.3	–	43.1
2004	80.8	50.1	44.4	–	–	58.5
Mean	57.4	44.9	39.1	32.0	28.9	42.2
Median	55.3	45.2	43.5	33.4	23.7	43.1
Min	35.7	23.1	20.3	12.3	7.8	25.7
Max	83.6	62.8	67.9	46.2	62.0	61.7
StDev	14.3	11.2	11.4	10.5	18.9	8.7
N	251	1,207	478	485	22	2,443

Price per US$ 100 par
Source: Moody's Investor Service[16]

Tab. A.9: Global average issuer-weighted recovery rates by whole-letter rating in US$, 1982–2004

Senior unsecured rating	Years prior to rating				
	1	2	3	4	5
Aaa	–	–	–	97.0	74.1
Aa	95.4	62.1	30.8	44.4	41.1
A	49.8	49.0	43.1	46.0	45.2
Baa	43.3	41.3	45.3	42.2	41.6
Ba	40.7	44.2	43.8	45.4	44.0
B	38.4	38.1	39.0	40.0	37.8
Caa–Ca	36.4	33.8	31.0	42.3	12.3
IG	46.0	44.4	44.1	44.3	43.2
SG	38.2	38.6	39.1	41.7	39.4
All	39.0	39.4	40.2	42.5	40.7

Price per US$ 100 par
Source: Moody's Investor Service[16]

References

1. Bank for International Settlements (BIS). *BIS Quarterly Review – International banking and financial market developments*, Bank for International Settlements (BIS), Basel, Switzerland, March 2005.
2. Fitch Ratings. Global Credit Derivatives Survey: Single-Name CDS Fuel Growth, *Special Report*, 7 September 2004.
3. Fitch Ratings. Hedge Funds: An Emerging Force in the Global Credit Markets, *Special Report*, 2005.
4. S. Rao Aiyagari and Mark Gertler. Overreaction of Asset Prices in General Equilibrium, *Academic Press for the Society for Economic Dynamics*, 2, no. 1 (1999): 3–35.
5. Fitch Ratings. Corporate Rating Methodology, *Criteria Report*, 2001.
6. Ingo Fender and John Kiff. CDO rating methodology: Some thoughts on model risk and its implications, *BIS Working paper*, 163 (2004).
7. Frank J. Fabozzi, ed.. *The Handbook of Fixed Income Securities*, McGraw-Hill, 6th edition, 2000.
8. ISDA. 2003 *ISDA Credit Derivatives Definitions*, International Swaps and Derivatives Association, New York, 2003.
9. Jochen Felsenheimer, Philip Gisdakis, and Michael Zaiser. Digital Default Swaps, *HVB Global Market Research: Credit Derivatives Special*, 2005.
10. Jochen Felsenheimer, Philip Gisdakis, and Michael Zaiser. Equity Default Swaps, *HVB Global Market Research: Credit Derivatives Special*, 2005.
11. Jerome S. Fons, Vincent J. Truglia, and Christopher T. Mahoney. The Application of Joint Default Analysis to Government Related Issuers, *Rating Methodology, Moody's Investor Service, Global Credit Research*, 2005.
12. Michael E. Porter. *Competitive Strategy – Techniques for analyzing industries and competitors*, Free Press, New York, 57th edition, 1998.
13. Scott Sprinzen, Emmanuel Dubois-Pelerin, and Ralf Kortuem. Adjusting Financials for Postretirement Liabilities, *Standard & Poor's RatingsDirect*, 2003.
14. Michael West, Falk Frey, Susie Maidment, Lisa Matalon, Edwin Wiest, Michael Mulvaney, and Junichi Yamaki. Global Auto Supplier Industry, *Rating Methodology, Moody's Investor Service, Global Credit Research*, 2005.

15 Brian Cahill, David Staples, and Julia Turner. Global Telecommunications Industry, *Rating Methodology, Moody's Investor Service, Global Credit Research*, 2005.

16 David T. Hamilton, Praveen Varma, Sharon Ou, and Richard Cantor. Default and Recovery Rates of Corporate Bond Issuers, 1920-2004, *Special Comment, Moody's Investor Service, Global Credit Research*, 2005.

17 Jorge A. Chan-Lau and Iryna V. Ivaschenko. Corporate Bond Risk and Real Activity: An Empirical Analysis of Yield Spreads and Their Systematic Components, *International Monetary Fund Working Paper WP/01/158*, 2001.

18 Sean C. Keenan, Jorge Sobehart, and David T. Hamilton. Predicting Default Rates: A Forecasting Model For Moody's Issuer-Based Default Rates, *Special Comment, Moody's Investor Service, Global Credit Research*, 1999.

19 Darrell Duffie and David Lando. Term structures of credit spreads with incomplete accounting information, *Econometrica*, 69, no. 3 (2001): 633–664.

20 Ernest Baver. Variance Gamma Option Model, Technical report, Bloomberg Financial Markets Commodities News, March 2003.

21 Edwin J. Elton, Martin J. Gruber, Deepak Agrawal, and Christopher Mann, "Explaining the Rate Spread on Corporate Bonds, *The Journal of Finance*, 66, no. 1 (2001): 247–278.

22 Jing-zhi Huang and Ming Huang. How Much of the Corporate-Treasury Yield Spread is Due to Credit Risk?, *Working paper*, 2003.

23 Georges Dionne, Geneviève Gauthier, Khemais Hammami, Mathieu Maurice, and Jean-Guy Simonato. Default Risk in Corporate Yield Spreads, *Working paper*, 2004.

24 Pierre Collin-Dufresne, Robert S. Goldstein, and J. Spencer Martin. The Determinants of Credit Spread Changes, *The Journal Of Finance*, 56, no. 6 (2001): 2177–2207.

25 Robert C. Merton. On the Pricing of Corporate Debt: The Risk Structure of Interest Rates, *Journal of Finance*, 29 (1974): 449–470.

26 Philipp J. Schönbucher. *Credit derivatives pricing models*, John Wiley & Sons, Chichester, 2003.

27 David X. Li. On Default Correlation: A Copula Function Approach, *The RiskMetrics Group, Working paper*, 99, no. 07 (2000): 1–29.

28 Praveen Varma, Richard Cantor, and David T. Hamilton. Recovery Rated on Defaulted Corporate Bonds and Preferred Stocks, 1982-2003, *Special Comment, Moody's Investor Service, Global Credit Research*, 2003.

29 Norbert J. Jobst and Stavros A. Zenios. Extending credit risk (pricing) models for the simulation of portfolios of interest rate and credit risk sensitive securities, *Working paper*, 2001.
30 Darrell Duffie and Kenneth J. Singleton. Modeling Term Structures of Defaultable Bonds, *The Review of Financial Studies*, 12, no. 4 (1999): 687–720.
31 Fitch Ratings. Recovery Ratings: Exposing the Components of Credit Risk, *Special Report*, 2005.
32 Fitch Ratings. The Role of Recovery Analysis in Ratings – Enhancing Informational Content and Transparency, *Special Report*, 2005.
33 Gregory R. Duffee. Estimating the price of default risk, *Working paper*, 1996.
34 Martijn Cremers, Joost Driessen, Pascal Maenhout, and David Weinbaum, "Individual Stock-Option Prices and Credit Spreads, *Workin paper*, 2004.
35 Fischer Black and Myron Scholes. The Pricing of Options and Corporate Liabilities, *Journal of Political Economy*, 81, no. 4 (1973): 637–654.
36 Didier Cossin and Hugues Pirottes. *Advanced Credit Risk Analysis*, John Wiley & Sons, Chichester, 2001.
37 Kay Giesecke. Credit Risk Modeling and Valuation: An Introduction, *Working paper*, 2002.
38 Darrell Duffie and Kenneth J. Singleton. *Credit Risk: Pricing, Measurement and Management*, Princeton University Press, Princeton, 2003.
39 Robert A. Jarrow and Stuart M. Turnbull. Pricing Derivatives on Financial Securities Subject to Credit Risk, *The Journal of Finance*, 50, no. 1 (1995): 53–85.
40 David Heath, Robert Jarrow, and Andrew Morton. Bond Pricing and the Term Structure of Interest Rates: A Discrete Time Approximation, *Journal of Financial and Quantitative Analysis*, 25, no. 4 (1990): 419–440.
41 David Heath, Robert Jarrow, and Andrew Morton. Bond Pricing and the Term Structure of Interest Rates: A New Methodology for Contingent Claims Valuation, *Econometrica*, 60, no. 1 (1992): 77–105.
42 Thorsten Schmidt. Credit Risk Modeling with Gaussian Random Fields, *Working paper*, 2004.
43 Thorsten Schmidt. An Infinite Factor Model for Credit Risk, *Working paper*, 2004.
44 Philip Gisdakis. Shape Factor Models in Credit Risk, *MSc Thesis, University of Oxford*, 2004.
45 Robert A. Jarrow, David Lando, and Stuart M. Turnbull. A Markov Model of the Term Structure of Credit Spreads, *The Review of Financial Studies*, 10, no. 2 (1997): 481–523.

46. Kenneth A. Froot and Jeremy C. Stein. Risk management, capital budgeting, and capital structure policy for financial institutions: an integrated approach, *Journal of Financial Economics*, 47 (1998): 55–82.
47. Fischer Black and John C. Cox. Valuing corporate securities: Some effects of bond indenture provisions, *Journal of Finance*, 31, no. 2 (1976): 351–367.
48. Stephen Kaelhofer. Managing default risk in portfolios of derivatives, In *Derivative Credit Risk*. Risk Publication, London, 1996.
49. Paul Wilmott. *Derivatives*, John Wiley & Sons, Chichester, 1998.
50. S. R. Das and P. Tufano. Pricing Credit-Sensitive Debt When Interest Rates and Credit Spreads are Stochastic, *Journal of Financial Engineering*, 5 (1996): 161–198.
51. M. Kijima. Monotonicities in a Markov Chain Model for Valuing Corporate Bonds Subject to Credit Risk, *Mathematical Finance*, 8 (1998): 229–247.
52. M. Kijima and K. Komoribayashi. A Markov Chain Model for Valuing Credit Risk Derivatives, *Journal of Derivatives*, 1998: 97–108.
53. Diane Vazza, Devi Aurora, and Ryan Schneck. Quarterly Default Update And Rating Transitions, *Standard & Poor's RatingsDirect*, 2005.
54. David Lando. On Cox Processes and Credit RIsky Securities, *Review of Derivatives Research*, 2 (1998): 99–120.
55. A. Arvanitis, J. K. Gregory, and J.-P. Laurent. Building Models for Credit Spreads, *Working paper*, 1998.
56. D. Nakazato. Gaussian Term Structure Model with Credit Rating Classes, *Working paper*, 1997.
57. John Hull and Alan White. Valuation of a CDO and an nth to Default CDS Without Monte Carlo Simulation, *Working paper*, 2003.
58. Jon Gregory and Jean-Paul Laurent. I will survive, *RISK*, June 2003.
59. Leif Anderson, Jakob Sidenius, and Susante Basu. All your hedges in one basket, *RISK*, November 2003.
60. Oldrich Vasicek. Probability of Loss on Loan Portfolio, *Working paper, KMV Corporation*, 1987.
61. Oldrich Vasicek. Limiting Loan Loss Probability Distribution, *Working paper, KMV Corporation*, 1991.
62. John Hull and Alan White. Valuing Credit Default Swaps I: No Counterparty Default Risk, *Journal of Derivatives*, 8, no. 1 (2000): 29–44.
63. JPMorgan Securities Inc. Par Credit Default Swap Spread Approximation from Default Probabilities, *Special publication*, 2001.
64. Fischer Black. The Pricing of Commodity Contracts, *Journal of Financial Economics*, 3 (1976): 167–179.

65 Mike Harris and Peter Hahn. Credit Option Pricing Model, *JPMorgan research publication*, 2004.
66 John Hull and Alan White. The Valuation of Credit Default Swap Options, *Working paper*, 2002.
67 Farshid Jamshidian. Valuation of Credit Default Swap and Swaptions, *Working paper*, 2002.
68 Damiano Brigo and Aurélien Alfonsi. Credit Default Swaps Calibration and Option Pricing with the SSRD Stochastic Intensity and Interest-Rate Model, *Working paper*, 2003.
69 Jochen Felsenheimer, Philip Gisdakis, and Michael Zaiser. DJ iTraxx: Credit at its best!, *HVB Global Market Research: Credit Derivatives Special*, 2004.
70 John Hull. *Options, Futures, and Other Derivatives*, Prentice Hall, Upper Saddle River, fifth edition edition, 2003.
71 Philippe Jorion. *Value at Risk*, McGraw-Hill, New York, 2nd edition, 2001.
72 Chris Matten. *Managing Bank Capital*, John Wiley & Sons, Chichester, 2000.
73 Matthias Gundlach and Frank Lehrbass. *CrediRisk+ in the Banking Industry*, Springer, Berlin, 2004.
74 Philippe Artzner, Freddy Delbaen, Jean-Marc Eber, and David Heath. Thinking coherently, *RISK*, 10 (1997): 68–71.
75 Philippe Artzner, Freddy Delbaen, Jean-Marc Eber, and David Heath. Coherent Risk Measures, *Mathematical Finance*, 9 (1999): 203–228.
76 R. Tyrrell Rockafellar and Stanislav Uryasev. Conditional Value-at-risk for General Loss distributions, *Working paper*, 2001.
77 Fredrik Andersson and Stanislav Uryasev. Credit Risk Optimization with Conditional Value-at-risk Criterion, *Working paper*, 1999.
78 R. Tyrrell Rockafellar and Stanislav Uryasev. Optimization of Conditional Value-at-Risk, *Working paper*, 1999.
79 Norbert J. Jobst and Stavros A. Zenios. The Tail That Wags the Dog: Integrating Credit Risk in Asset Portfolios, *Journal of Risk Finance*, 3, no. 1 (2001): 31–43.
80 JP Morgan. *CreditMetrics*, JP Morgan, 1997.
81 Credit Suisse. *CreditRisk+: A Credit Risk Management Framework*, Credit Suisse Financial Products, 1997.
82 T. Wilson. Portfolio credit risk I, *RISK*, 10, no. 9 (1997): 111–117.
83 T. Wilson. Portfolio credit risk II, *RISK*, 10, no. 10 (1997): 56–61.
84 Michel Crouhy, Dan Galai, and Robert Mark. A comparative analysis of current credit risk models, *Journal of Banking & Finance*, 24 (2000): 59–117.

85 Jochen Felsenheimer, Philip Gisdakis, and Michael Zaiser. Merton meets Markowitz ... in a CAPM Symphony, *HVB Global Market Research: Credit Derivatives Special*, 2005.

86 Lev Dynkin, Jay Hyman, and Vadim Konstantinovsky. Sufficient Diversification in Credit Portfolios – Number of issues and downgrade risk, *The Journal of Portfolio Management*, 2002: 89–114.

87 Thomas H. Goodwin. The Information Ratio, *Financial Analysts Journal*, 1998: 34–43.

88 Joel Bessis. *Risk Management in Banking*, John Wiley & Sons, Chichester, 1998.

89 Charles W. Smithson. *Credit Portfolio Management*, John Wiley & Sons, Chichester, 2003.

90 Robert A. Jarrow and Donald R. van Deventer. Integrating Interest Rate Risk and Credit Risk in ALM, In *Asset & Liability Management: A Synthesis of New Methodologies*, pages 87–96. Risk Books, The Kamakura Corporation, Honolulu, 1998.

91 Jochen Felsenheimer, Philip Gisdakis, and Michael Zaiser. Welcome the RDAX..., *HVB Global Market Research: Credit Derivatives Special*, 2005.

92 Deutsche Börse Group. Guide to the RDAX Index, *Special publication*, 2005.

93 Edwin J. Elton and Martin J. Gruber. *Modern Portfolio Theory and Investment Analysis*, John Wiley & Sons, New York, 5th edition, 1995.

94 Nadima El-Hassan and Paul Kofman. Tracking Error and Active Portfolio Management, *Australian Journal of Management*, 28, no. 2 (2003): 183–208.

95 William F. Sharpe. Mutual Fund Performance, *Journal of Business*, 1966: 119–138.

96 William F. Sharpe. Adjusting for Risk in Portfolio Performance Measurement, *Journal of Portfolio Management*, 1975: 29–34.

97 William F. Sharpe. Asset allocation: Management style and performance measurement, *Journal of Portfolio Management*, 1992: 7–19.

98 Jochen Felsenheimer, Philip Gisdakis, and Michael Zaiser. It's the economic value, stupid!, *HVB Global Market Research: Credit Derivatives Special*, 2005.

99 Dirk Auerbach and Daniela Klotzbach. Die Bilanzierung von Kreditderivaten nach IFRS, *Kreditderivate – Handbuch für die Bank- und Anlagepraxis*, 2005: 261–276.

100 Basel Committee on Banking Supervision. *International Convergence of Capital Measurement and Capital Standards – A Revised Framework*, Bank for International Settlements (BIS), Basel, Switzerland, June 2004.

Index

a

Accounting 503
– bonds and loans 518
– CDO tranche 527
– credit default swap (CDS) 521
– credit linked note (CLN) 525
– credit spread option 527
– embedded derivative 513, 519
– fair value 505, 508
– fair value option 526
– FTD basket 527
– hedge accounting 515
– iTraxx products 526
– total return swap (TRS) 523
– transaction costs 508
Accrued interest 438
Active management 388–389
Adjustment of ratios 91
Advanced IRB approach 532, 538
Amortized cost 510
Annuity 182
– finite 182
Arbitrage-free pricing 144
Articifial probabilities 188
Artzner, Philippe 367
Asset allocation 379–386
– strategic 381
– tactical 382
Asset backed securities (ABS) 42, 43
Asset swap (ASW) spread 180
Asset–liability management (ALM) 379, 393
ASW spread *see* Asset swap (ASW) spread
At fair value through profit or loss (aFVtPL) 505
Autocorrelation 458
Available for sale (AfS) 506, 519

b

Back-end payment 320
Banks 28
Base correlation 341, 343
Basel I 529, 533

Basel II 529
– advanced IRB approach 538
– CDO tranche 556
– constant maturity credit default swap (CM-CDS) 548
– credit default swap (CDS) 547
– credit derivative 543
– credit linked note (CLN) 551
– credit risk 532
– default basket 553
– digital default swap (DDS) 549
– first-to-default (FTD) basket 553
– iTraxx 555
– market risk 532
– operational risk 532
– pillars 530
– probability of default (PD) 532
– second-to-default (STD) basket 553
– securitization transactions 540
– total return swap (TRS) 550
Basis 481
Basis point 172
Basis risk 451
Beta 47, 470
– estimation 454
– portfolio 459
Binomial distribution 280
Black, Fischer 239, 254, 324
Black-76 model 324
Black-Scholes 239, 254
Bloomberg
– CDSW 449
– YAS 449
Bond
– accounting 518
Bond option 322
Bond optionalities 167
Bootstrapping
– interest rates 158
– survival probability 311
Bootstrapping algorithm 158
Breakeven 47, 470

Active Credit Portfolio Management. J. Felsenheimer, P. Gisdakis, and M. Zaiser
Copyright © 2006 WILEY-VCH Verlag GmbH & Co. KGaA, Weinheim
ISBN: 3-527-50198-3

Brigo, Damiano 323
Brownian motion 134
Bubills 151
Bund spread 175
Bundesanleihe 175
Bundesobligation 175
Business day conventions 147
– following 147
– modified following 147
– modified preceding 147
– preceding 147
Business risk 74
Buy and hold 366, 382, 444

c

Calender mapping 147
Call feature 52
Callable bond 167
– yield spread 177
Capital asset pricing model (CAPM) 187
Capital structure arbitrage (CSA) 124, 237, 252
Carrying amount 511
Cash flow hedge 515, 517
Cash settlement
– Basel II 548
CDO Evaluator 34
CDS index 271
CDS option *see* Credit default swaption
CDS swaption *see* Credit default swaption
Clean P&L 439
Clean price 437
Coefficient of determination 458
Collateral
– Basel II 543
Collateralized debt obligation (CDO) 209
– accounting 527
– Basel II 556
– spread 172
– tranche 172, 271
Commercial paper (CP) 32
Commodities finance (CF) 535
Component value at risk 372
Compound correlation 341, 343
Conditional value at risk (CVaR) 249, 367, 400, 403
Constant maturity credit default swap (CM-CDS) 61, 358–360
– accounting 528
– Basel II 548

– in-advance 359
– in-arrears 359
Constant proportion portfolio insurance (CPPI) 490
Continuous compounding 152
Convexity 164
– convexity risk 451
– effective 166
– negative 167
Convexity risk 451
Copula 283
Core–satellite strategy 477
Correlation 24
– Basel II 535
Correlation derivatives *see* Portfolio derivatives
Correlation matrix 419
Correlation trading 282, 339
Covenant 32, 98
Covered bonds 42
Credit conversion factor (CCF) 539
Credit default swap (CDS) 55, 209, 304
– accounting 521
– Basel II 547
– forward 314
– JPMorgan model 305
– valuation 304–319
Credit default swaption 322–327
– index 326–327
– single-name 323–325
Credit derivative 148
– Basel II 543
– bespoken 172
Credit events
– accounting 521
– Basel II 548
Credit linked note (CLN)
– accounting 525
– Basel II 551
Credit metrics 34
Credit option 322
Credit return 438
Credit risk
– Basel II 532
– default risk 444
– spread risk 444
– valuation 195
Credit risk mitigation (CRM) 543
Credit spread 171
Credit spread option

– accounting 527
Credit triangle 199
Credit value at risk (CrVaR) 365
– Basel II 537
CreditMetrics 285, 373
CreditPortfolioView 373
CreditRisk+ 281, 373
Cross asset hedging 124, 252
Cross-default clause 217
Curve return 438

d

Day count convention (DCC) 147, 148
Default barrier 126
Default basket
– Basel II 553
Default baskets 65
Default correlation *see* Default dependency
Default dependency 282–288
– factor models 284, 286, 292
Default event
– definition 197
Default probability 198
– Basel II 532
– conditional 204–206
– cumulative 206
– forward 206
– marginal 205
– risk-neutral 201
– unconditional 206
Default rate 118
Default risk 196, 444
Deleveraging 23
Deliverable obligation 26
Delta neutrality 473
Delta-normal value at risk 365
Derecognition 512
Digital default swap (DDS) 58, 360–364
– accounting 528
– Basel II 549
Dirty price 437
Discount factor 144
– properties 145
Discount function 145
– slope 157
Discount margin 185
Discrete compounding 151
– quarterly 151
– semiannual 151
– yearly 151

Dollar value of a basis point (DV01) 168
Double-default issue 544
Duration 163
– effective 166
– Macaulay 163
DV01 *see* Dollar value of a basis point (DV01)

e

EBIT interest coverage 85, 91
EBITDA 84
Economic capital 53
Effective convexity 166
Effective duration 165
Effective interest method (EIM) 510
Effective maturity (M) 537
Efficient branch 423
Efficient frontier 420
Embedded derivative 513, 519
– host contract 513
– separation 514
Embedded options 47
Enronitis 138
Enterprise-value models *see* Structural models
Equity default swap (EDS) 58, 258, 357
– accounting 528
Equity markets 123
Euribor 150
Euro credit market 21
Euro medium-term notes (EMTN) 39
Euro-denominated bond 148
Expectations theory 186
Expected default frequency (EDF) 374
Expected shortfall *see* Conditional value at risk (CVaR)
Expected survival amount 233
Exposure at default (EAD)
– Basel II 532

f

Factor models *see* Default dependency
Fair value accounting 505
Fair value hedge 515
Fair value option 526
Fallen angel 23, 40
Federal treasury financing paper 151
Financial guarantee contract 504
Financial instrument 504
Financial risk 82–93
Firm-value models *see* Structural models

First-to-default (FTD) basket 209
– Basel II 553
First-to-trigger baskets 358
Flat correlation 287
Floating rate note
– YTM calculation 177
Forward rate 154
– continuous compounding 155
– instantaneous 157
Forward rate agreement 186
Foundation IRB approach 532, 534
FTD basket
– accounting 527
Funds 30
Funds from operations (FFO) 83
Future spot rate 155

g

Game theory 38
Gearing ratio 86
German government bonds 175
– Bundesanleihe 175
– Bundesobligation 175
GM/Ford turmoil 456
Government support 74
Gundlach, Matthias 365

h

Handelsgesetzbuch (HGB) 503
Hazard rate models *see* Reduced-form models
Hedge accounting 515
– cash flow hedge 515, 517
– cash flow hedge reserve 517
– fair value hedge 515
– hedge effectiveness 515
– hedge of a net investment in a foreign operation 518
– hedged item 515
– hedging instrument 515
Hedge effectiveness 515
Hedge efficiency 458
Hedge funds 30
Hedge ratio 443
Hedged item 515
Hedging
– basis risk 458
– cost of insurance 463
– default risk 445
– efficiency 458

– hedge efficiency 463
– instruments 462
– maturity mismatch 464
– portfolio 452
– similarity of composition 463
– single name 443
– skew risk 458
– spread risk 448
– transaction costs 464
Hedging instrument 515
Held for trading 507
Held to maturity (HtM) 506, 519
– Basel II 551
Heterogeneous portfolio 297
High grade *see* Investment grade
High-volatility commercial real estate (HVCRE) 535
High-yield market 23, 40–41
HLPGC model 283, 292
Homogeneous large portfolio model 272, 281, 292
Homogeneous portfolio 280
Host contract 513
Hull, John 280–282, 292, 323
Hull-White model 280–282, 292, 323
Hybrid bond 220
Hybrids 50

i

I-spread 174
IAS 32 504
IAS 37 505
IAS 39 504
iBoxx 27, 39, 411–413
IFRS 4 505
Impairment 510
Implied correlation 341, 343
Income-producing real estate (IPRE) 535
Incremental value at risk 249, 372
Index 410–418
Industry risk 75
Information ratio 435
Insurance companies 29
Intensity-based models *see* Reduced-form models
Interest deferral feature 52
Interest income 439
Interest rate risk 162
– sensitivity 162
Interest rate swap 158

Interest rates
- forward 206
Internal assessment approach (IAA) 542
Internal rate of return (IRR) 160, 183, 511
Internal ratings-based (IRB) approach 532
International Accounting Standards (IAS) 503
International Financial Reporting Standards (IFRS) 503
Interpolated spread 174
Investment-grade market 39
ISDA 26
Issuer default ratings (IDR) 228
iTraxx 25, 62
- accounting 526
- Basel II 555

j
Jamshidian, Farshid 323
Jorion, Philippe 365, 367

k
KMV 285, 373
Knock-out-on-default 314

l
Leap-put skewness 131
Lehrbass, Frank 365
Leveraged buy-out (LBO) 98, 115
Li, David 283
Libor 150
Linear compounding 150
Liquidity premium 191
Loan 148
- accounting 518
Loans and receivables (LaR) 506, 520
- Basel II 551
Look-through treatment 541
Loss given default (LGD) 195, 198
- Basel II 532

m
Macaulay duration 163
Marginal utility 190
Marginal value at risk 372
Marked-to-market 365
Market discipline 530
Market price risk 196
Market risk
- Basel II 532
Market value at risk 365

Market value component 438
Market-implied recovery rate 227
Marketweight 388
Markov-chain models *see* Transition matrix models
Markowitz, Harry 129, 418
Matten, Chris 365
Maturity adjustment 537
Maturity mismatch 464, 545
Measurement 507
Merton, Robert 123, 129, 250
Merton-type models *see* Structural models
Mid-point approximation 307
Midswap spread 175
Migration-matrix models *see* Transition matrix models
Miller 129
Minimum capital requirements
- Basel II 530
Mixed measurement approach 512
Model competition 300
Modified duration 165, 440
Modigliani 129

n
Negative convexity 167
Net present value (NPV) 160, 175
Netting agreement
- Basel II 543
Normal distribution 280
Notching 201

o
Object finance (OF) 535
Off-balance-sheet adjustments 86
Off-balance-sheet contract 505
One-touch put option (OTP) 258
Operating lease adjustments 86
Operational risk 530
- Basel II 532
Option-adjusted spread (OAS) 177
Ordinary least squares (OLS) approach 455
Overweight 388

p
Par floater 182
Par floating rate note 182
Pari passu 218
Participation rate (PR) 359
Passive management 386–388

Payment-in-kind (PIK) note 49, 97
Physical settlement
– Basel II 548
Poisson distribution 280
Porter model 75
Portfolio
– duration 169
– DV01 169
Portfolio beta 459
Portfolio derivatives 271
Portfolio loss generator 281
Present value 144
Price discovery 300
Price value of a basis point (PVBP) 168
Price-to-book ratio 191
Pricing kernel 189
Pro-cyclicality 29
Probabilities
– artificial 188
– real-world 188
Probability of default *see* Default probability
Project finance (PF) 535
Pull-to-par effect 438
Putable bond
– yield spread 177
PVBP *see* Price value of a basis point (PVBP)

q
Quoted margin 185

r
R-rating 228
Rating agencies 33, 93
Rating-based transition matrix models *see* Transition matrix models
Rating-triggered CDS
– accounting 528
Rating-triggered coupon step-ups 238
Ratings-based approach (RBA) 541
RDAX 413–418
Real-world probabilities 188
Recognition 512
Recovery default swap (RDS)
– accounting 528
Recovery default swaps (RDS) 60
Recovery model
– fixed recovery 224
– recovery of face value 224
– recovery of market value 225
– recovery of par 224

– recovery of treasury 224
– zero recovery 224
Recovery rate 26, 100
– estimation 99
Recovery rating *see* R-rating
Reduced-form models 196, 237–249
Regulatory capital 53
Repurchase agreement (Repo) 500
Return attribution analysis 405, 438–441
Return on capital 85
Rising star 23, 40
Risk aversion 190
Risk budget 381–385, 399
Risk factors 162
Risk neutrality 188
Risk of default *see* default probability
Risk premium 187
Risk-based capital *see* Risk budget
Risk-weight function 534
– Basel II 534
Risk-weighted assets (RWA) 532
Risky annuity 308

s
Savings account 148
Schönbucher, Philipp 245, 249, 295
Schmidt, Thorsten 323
Scholes, Myron 239, 254
Second-to-default (STD) basket
– Basel II 553
Securitization
– Basel II 540
Sensitivity 162, 443
Settlement 57
Sharpe ratio 433
Simple compounding 149
Single-tranche CDO (STCDO) 67, 300
Skew 458, 479
Sovereign risk 74
Spot rate 149, 156
Spread delta 350
Spread measure
– Bund spread 175
Spread measures 171
– asset swap spread 180
– discount margin 185
– for floaters 184
– I-spread 174
– interpolated spread 174
– midswap spread 175

– option-adjusted spread 177
– properties 173
– quoted margin 185
– yield spreads 173
– yield–yield spread 173
– Z-spread 177
– zero discount margin 185
– zero-volatility spread 177
Spread neutrality 473
Spread options *see* credit default swaptions
Spread PV delta 351
Spread risk 196, 444
– idiosyncratic 453
– systematic 453
– unsystematic 453
Spread volatility 47
SpreadDV01 316, 449
Standardized approach 532
– Basel II 533
Standardized iTraxx tranches 338
Step-down feature 48
Step-up feature 48
Straight bonds 45
Structural models 124, 196, 237, 250–260, 284
Sub-sovereigns 41
Supervisory formula (SF) 541
Supervisory review 530
Survival probability 198
– bootstrapping 311
– marginal 205
Swap rates 158
Syndicated loans 136

t

Tail value at risk *see* Conditional value at risk (CVaR)
Tax premium 187
Taylor expansion 164
Technical bid 138
Term structure of interest rates 149
– flat 153
– inverted 153
– normal 153
Term structure of swap rates 158
Theta risk 347
Time value component 438

Total capital ratio 532
Total P&L 437
Total return definition 437–438
Total return swap (TRS)
– accounting 523
– Basel II 550
Tracking error 432
Transaction costs 508
– accounting 508
Transition matrix models 197, 238
Treasury discount paper 151
Treynor ratio 433

u

Underweight 388
Unexpected loss
– Basel II 529
Upfront payment 182, 447
Uryasev, Stanislav 367
US Treasury bills 151

v

Value at risk (VaR) 367, 400, 403
Vasicek, Oldrich 281, 292
VECTOR 36

w

Waterfall principle 220
Weighted-average cost of capital (WACC) 32
Weighted-average rating factor (WARF) 34
White, Alan 280–282, 292, 323

y

Yield spread 173
Yield to best 177
Yield to maturity 159
– yield to best 177
– yield to worst 177
Yield to worst 177

z

Z-score 47, 427, 470
Z-spread 177
Zero coupon bond 144
Zero discount margin 185
Zero-volatility spread 177